# THE FAMILY, MARRIAGE, AND SOCIAL CHANGE

# THE FAMILY, MARRIAGE, AND SOCIAL CHANGE

Second Edition

RICHARD R. CLAYTON

University of Kentucky

D. C. HEATH AND COMPANY
Lexington, Massachusetts   Toronto

COVER CREDITS:

*Young couple:* Ed Lettau from Photo Researchers, Inc.
*Black family:* Joel Gordon © 1978
*Elderly couple:* Frank Siteman

Published simultaneously in Canada.

Printed in the United States of America.

International Standard Book Number: 0–669–01957–7

Library of Congress Catalog Card Number: 78–58070

*This book is dedicated to*
My wife
Nancy
and our children
Reid, Brent, and Charlyn
*with all my love*

# PREFACE

The family, marriage, and social change are phenomena that affect us all. Although it is necessary at birth to cut the umbilical cord, throughout life we symbolically reattach it time and again in the familial context. The familial cord is the pipeline through which we as children gain strength and nourishment, both physical and social-emotional. As we move through infancy and early childhood to adolescence and independence, the types and forms of familial nourishment and influence change to correspond with our individual development. With marriage we sever the tie to our parents, but only in a ritualistic and symbolic sense, so that we can begin to develop our own new lines of transmission. As we become parents we re-create the continuity of the family so that a new generation can go through the same cycle of birth and rebirth.

In this book I have attempted to look at the family, both as an institution of society and as an intimate environment within which we all seek to develop our human potential. Marriage is viewed as the crucial transition between one set of roles and another set that are similar to, yet different from, the first set.

*The Family, Marriage, and Social Change* is essentially organized into five sets of chapters. The first set, Chapters 1 through 3, introduces the student to sociology as a discipline and to sociology of the family as a substantive area of concentration. Chapter 2 presents three conceptual frameworks for family analysis: the structure-functional, the developmental, and the symbolic interactional, which are used as a basis for analysis from time to time throughout the rest of the text.

The second set of chapters, 4 through 8, are organized around the theme of social change and how the family affects it and is affected by it. Chapters 5 and 6 focus on the white family and the black family in the United States and how they operate in reality as opposed to some stereotypical myths that pervade the more popular literature. Chapters 7 and 8 introduce the student to the family in other cultures and societies and to some of the experiments with family structure and functioning.

The third set of chapters, 9 through 13, deal with the phenomena that most occupy the thoughts and time of students—love, premarital sex, and marital selection.

The fourth set of chapters, 14 through 16, deal with the dynamics of married life: marital interaction, power within the family, and marital adjustment and satisfaction. Chapter 15 develops an exchange model of power and expands current interpretations of the concept of power as it applies to family life.

Chapters 17 through 21 deal with the forces that require adaptation on the part of the family as a unit and with adjustments in roles and styles of living by the members of these units. Chapter 17 focuses on parenthood roles, and Chapter 18 analyzes how the family adapts to demands from the work and leisure spheres of activity. Chapter 19 examines the impact of the demographic processes of fertility, migration, and mortality on family decision making; and Chapter 20 discusses marital dissolution.

Chapter 21 discusses the future of marriage and the family, both as a field of study and with regard to what may happen to these institutions in the last 20 years of the twentieth century.

I wrote this book for two audiences; students, and social scientists specializing in the study of the family and marriage. As a teacher I am convinced that the purpose of a textbook is twofold: First, it should provide students with material that is stimulating and useful in their own lives. However, a text should not, in my opinion, be limited to information with some personal application. It should also include information that will free students from the limiting constraints of their own culture and allow them to gain a broader perspective on the world. A second purpose of this text is to encourage students to think through for themselves the complexities of marriage and family life. To do this it is necessary to provide examples of how family specialists go about examining and studying the family and marriage.

I have also used this text as a medium for synthesizing some of my own ideas about the family and marriage and how they are changing. I hope that specialists in the family will find this book a source of ideas for further attempts to clarify and organize studies of marriage and family life. I have tried to develop some models that move beyond a narrow focus on substantive topics to a concern with more abstract phenomena such as attitudes, behavior, power, and adjustment.

### Acknowledgments

No one can write a college textbook in a social vacuum, although I frequently felt like a long-distance runner, alone against the elements and striving for maximum coverage of the ground without breaking stride. The discipline required of an author does not come easily. It comes because of the help he or she receives from students, teachers, family, friends, colleagues, and assistants. I have been particularly fortunate to receive support and encouragement from all these sources.

The earliest source of encouragement came from my mother, Grace Clayton, and my late father, John C. Clayton, who taught me the value of hard work and persistence. My siblings, Cora, Carla, Paul, and Walter, helped me to perceive that each member of a family is different and that the family changes as a unit as each new member adds his or her own personality. My second family of orientation, Robert and Mildred Olson, Connie, and Bob, gave not only encouragement but also an understanding of how marriage can provide a new network of strengthening relationships. My wife, Nancy, and our children, Reid, Brent, and Charlyn, provided the love and warmth, encouragement and inspiration that I needed throughout this period of intense involvement. This book is a tribute to their understanding and sacrifice.

I view writing this text as part of my responsibility as a teacher. I could not have written it without the stimulation provided by some great teachers under whom I have studied. Sarah Frances Anders was the person who awakened my interest in sociology; without her encouragement I would never have entered this field. Meyer Francis Nimkoff, through his enthusiasm and example, convinced me that the family should become my area of concentration. I owe the greatest gratitude to Louis Dotson of the University of Tennessee. He taught me that the family is just one area to which sociology should be applied and that sociology progresses most when we are willing to look beyond our narrow substantive interests. I hope this book justifies, at least to some extent, the efforts these great teachers expended in my behalf.

Much of what we learn is from the informal contacts with colleagues. Although all of my colleagues at the University of Kentucky provided encouragement, Jim Gladden, Bill Kenkel, Jack O'Donnell, Jon Shepard, and Harwin Voss have been particularly helpful. Without the extra effort extended by the staff in the Department of Sociology at the University of Kentucky this text might never have been completed. Sincere appreciation is also due Mary Carpenter, Marlene Pettit, and Teresa Trimble.

No textbook is ever the work of just the author. Countless people at the publishing end of the process offered encouragement and assistance; they provided the maximum degree of help with sensitivity and professionalism.

In the final analysis, this book is a reflection of the numerous exciting and stimulating encounters I have had with students at the University of Kentucky, the University of Tennessee, Stetson University, and Louisiana College. From my students I have learned that teaching is an exciting experience that gains meaning only if the teacher learns from those he or she attempts to teach. I originally wrote this book, and revised it for the second edition, because I felt I owed my students my best effort at a better textbook on *The Family, Marriage, and Social Change.*

R.R.C.

# CONTENTS

# THE FAMILY,
# MARRIAGE, AND
# SOCIAL CHANGE

# PART I

# SOCIOLOGY AS A DISCIPLINE

Bobbi Carey from The Picture Cube

# 1

# THE SOCIOLOGICAL PERSPECTIVE

*What is sociology, and does it provide any real answers to human problems?*

*Can human behavior be predicted?*

*What is unique about the sociological style of thinking and analysis?*

*How can sociology help us to understand the family, marriage, and social change?*

Sociology in the late 1970s is primarily and almost exclusively an academic discipline. But as the baby-boom generation passes on through institutions of higher learning, the prospects of continued growth at the college and university level are fading rather quickly. With the level of college enrollments stabilizing and the number of Ph.D. sociologists increasing, sociology will of necessity move from its warm academic womb into the mainstream and turbulent eddies of society, the political and economic arenas. Sociology as a discipline is now involved, therefore, in a search for a new identity.

Originally sociology was viewed as a discipline that would not only study society but actually direct and change it. In fact, the founder of sociology, Auguste Comte, envisioned sociologists as the eventual high priests of society, an oligarchy of social engineers that would study society, decide where it should go and how, and then lead it to the destination.

As sociology sought academic recognition it adopted the scientific method; in the process, change itself became a subject of study, to be treated as objectively as possible. Emerging with this trend was the idea that social scientists should be value free, engaging in their scientific study of society and human behavior as "pure" investigators, devoid of any personal values and attitudes that might bias their findings.

## HIGH EXPECTATIONS

In recent years, particularly since the 1950s, a number of sociologists have moved back toward the stance of the founding fathers of the discipline, advocating involvement in instituting and directing social change. To sociologists with this orientation the idea of a value-free sociology is a myth. Part of the reason for this partial shift in focus is related to the audiences sociologists must address—primarily college and university students. The current generation of college students has been brought up on a steady diet of civil rights marches, summer riots in urban centers, the war on poverty, political assassinations, protests against the war in Southeast Asia, drug abuse, women's liberation, alternative family styles, a "sexual revolution," and the many other social problems of our society. Thus, in today's college marketplace, it is reasonable to expect students who clamor for relevance to be attracted to the department and discipline that offers courses in such problem-oriented subject areas as race relations, social movements, social problems, juvenile delinquency, and human sexuality. More often than not students expect real answers and prescriptions for action from these courses and from sociologists in general. These expectations of relevance, answers, and action are perhaps naive and are almost invariably too high.

## Action

The critical student will perceive, and correctly, that the university is seldom the locus of action—at least the kind of action that leads to the solution of societal problems. The educational institution in American society is, generally speaking, a highly bureaucratic organization that claims neutrality on almost every controversial issue while it protects the status-quo value system of the nonacademic community. To expect any kind of concerted action to grow out of a course—even a sociology course—is to ignore the realities of the university system.

## Answers

If action is a virtual impossibility, at least within the university system, can students expect any answers to the pressing social problems discussed in their sociology courses? The answer is yes, but a qualified yes, for several reasons: Sociology as an academic discipline was not introduced to American colleges until the twentieth century; hence, its history is brief. Moreover, sociologists are just now reaching the point where they can move beyond explaining why and how certain phenomena occur to predicting the occurrence of such phenomena. In addition, the forces and behaviors that sociologists study are extremely complex, whether the topic is love and premarital sex or the process of modernization occurring in the Third World. Clear-cut answers of the kind found in natural science laboratories are not yet possible. However, if students are intrigued by solutions to complex puzzles, maybe they can find some new answers or at least new ways of asking questions. But earth-shattering breakthroughs from sociology are not available, at least not yet.

## Relevance

Relevance may well be the most ill-defined and sought-after but elusive commodity in the world today. Within the university and particularly within sociology, an expectation of and demand for relevance may be as dangerous as the Big Bad Wolf was to Little Red Riding Hood. Relevance is not absolute but relative—relative to time, socioeconomic status, age, and perhaps even sex. For example, during World War II "winning" against Nazi Germany was extremely relevant to most Americans (we are still fighting that war thirty-five years later) while during the war in Vietnam, "not winning" and actual withdrawal was quite relevant to many Americans. Therefore, what is relevant for one person may not be relevant for someone else, and what is relevant today may be forgotten tomorrow. If sociology is to deal with relevant issues, relevance must be defined very explicitly.

This book is based on the assumption that sociology is a discipline in the liberal arts tradition. A course in the family and marriage should do several things for the student: (1) provide the conceptual tools and theoretical frameworks to adequately define problems or areas to analyze; (2) provide a thorough but selected review of previous attempts to deal with the same problems; (3) provide an opportunity to learn some of the skills and techniques required by the discipline of sociology; and (4) help students understand and cope with their own immediate premarital, marital, and familial experiences.

The relevance of the materials in this book will depend primarily on who reads it. Making sociology relevant at the individual level requires translation of the facts, techniques, and concepts into workable solutions. A reasonable question to ask is, *Why doesn't the family sociologist do the translating? He or she does the studies and is supposedly the expert.* This general question will be addressed in the next three sections of this chapter. The first two sections deal, respectively, with the different sets of issues raised (1) among sociologists studying the family and (2) between those social scientists and the general public whose attitudes and behavior they study.

## FOUR ISSUES THAT DIVIDE SOCIOLOGISTS STUDYING THE FAMILY

When sociologists studying the family address their colleagues, they must face some highly specific problems. These problems are ideological issues that divide social scientists into various camps and perspectives. The four issues are: (1) conceptual versus empirical orientation, (2) pure versus applied orientation, (3) hard versus soft data orientation, and (4) intracultural versus intercultural orientation.

### 1. Conceptual Versus Empirical Orientation

In most social sciences, and particularly in sociology, there is a cleavage between those whose orientation is conceptual, or theoretical, and those whose orientation is empirical or research-oriented. The sociologist studying the family who prefers to analyze problems at a very abstract level, using an ability to manipulate words and ideas as primary tools, is usually considered a theoretical, or conceptual, sociologist. Not many well-known family sociologists have chosen the conceptual orientation as their professional mode of work. Most of them work from an empirical/research perspective, which usually entails drawing a sample of respondents, asking specific questions of these people, coding the responses numerically, and using the computer or calculator to analyze the data statistically. In most instances the sociologist is trying to determine whether people with particular characteristics (for example, upper class, middle class, or lower class) answer questions differently. The empirical sociologist usually has a hypothesis to test—for example, that the higher the social class, the more permissive the childrearing behaviors of the family. If a scientist finds that 75 percent of the upper, 50 percent of the middle, and only 25 percent of the lower class respondents are permissive, he or she might conclude that the hypothesis is correct.

The major distinction in orientation is the approach to asking and answering questions: the conceptual sociologist is like a philosophical observer while the empirical sociologist is like a pollster wearing a sociologist's hat. Sociology is a valid field of study if the conceptual ideas are sound and are thoroughly tested with empirical research. Actually most sociologists are not exclusively conceptually or empirically oriented. The conceptually oriented sociologist usually relies on the empirical studies of others to bolster his or her conclusions, and the empirical sociologist seldom conducts a study that is devoid of conceptual or theoretical underpinnings.

## 2. Pure Versus Applied Orientation

A second issue controversial among family sociologists is that of pure versus applied orientation. Advocates of each stance feel that their view is exclusively correct. The purists generally insist that the paramount role of the social scientist is to study the family objectively, with no obligation to solve real-life problems. These people support the idea that they can and must take into their research a pure mind, free of values, attitudes, beliefs, or general biases that might color or affect their research findings.

On the other end of the continuum are the applied social scientists who feel that their job is to try to solve societal ills or problems. They are usually involved in administering social programs in the health and welfare sector of society. Having a humanistic approach, many applied sociologists feel that the research of sociology should be directed at the real-life problems of real people and that the results of research should be used to solve those problems. Much of the rhetoric of applied sociologists is directed at urging the power elite to use sociological research findings in formulating policies that may ultimately solve social problems. Here again, sociologists seldom have either a totally pure or totally applied approach to their work. Because they cannot divorce their studies from their own experiences, and because most human behaviors can be viewed as somewhat problematic, most sociologists try to be aware of both the impact of their values and attitudes on their studies and the potential applied implications of their research.

### 3. Hard Versus Soft Data Orientation

The third issue concerns the methods of gathering information about marriage and the family. Hard data are those that have been transformed from qualitative answers into numbers and that are ready for statistical analysis. Every effort has usually been made to ensure that the data were objectively gathered and not influenced by the researcher's bias. Soft data are usually the sociologist's observations of specific events over a period of time. The data are called "soft" because there is really no way of systematically determining if the events reported by the researcher really happened that way or if the researcher's biases influenced his or her perception of those events. In other words, a study using hard data can be replicated time and again to check the results. With soft data it is difficult to replicate a study because every observer is different, and each observer sees things from his or her own position or perspective.

### 4. Intracultural Versus Intercultural Orientation

The last issue controversial among sociologists studying the family is the composition of the group studied. Most sociologists would say that they study human behavior and that they hope their results can be generalized to all, or almost all, of the species *Homo sapiens*. Unfortunately, such optimism is more rhetoric than reality. Ideally, sociologists should study marital processes (marital adjustment, decision-making, and so forth) that are not distinctively American, Pakistani, French, or middle-class WASP. Cross-cultural studies are closer to the ideal than intracultural ones. The problem frequently boils down to just how narrowly intracultural a study is. For example, in a study of "marital adjustment among middle-class, urban Americans," everything in the study sounded reasonable until the author reported that 50 percent of the respondents were Jewish. Since less than 3 percent of the United States population is Jewish, the generalizability of the results of this extremely intracultural study became suspect.

The four issues discussed above are of particular relevance to sociologists studying the family in their interactions with professional colleagues. Graduate training for most sociologists emphasizes the empirical, pure, hard-data, and intracultural orientations. With this in mind, the reader of this book should expect that more of the works with these orientations will be cited, primarily because they are so readily available.

## THE UNIQUENESS OF THE SOCIOLOGICAL PERSPECTIVE

What is unique about the sociological perspective? Are there styles of sociological reasoning that pervade the discipline and that characterize a sociologist's approach to the study of human behavior and social institutions? Peter Berger (1963) claims that there are four distinctive features of sociological consciousness, which we will discuss in this section. The central feature of sociology, according to Berger, is that as a way of viewing the world it not only allows but also encourages its adherents to see through the obvious and the facades of human life. The true sociologist supposedly cannot walk down a street without a burning curiosity to know what is happening behind closed doors and drawn shades.

## Debunking

One of the most attractive features of sociology for undergraduates is its seemingly critical stance. The sociologists on most campuses are more likely than their colleagues in other disciplines (physics, chemistry, English) to be highly critical of the "sacred cows" of society—the family, the church, the government, the economic system of society, and particularly the educational system. Berger (1963) says, "The sociologist will be driven time and again, by the very logic of his discipline, to debunk the social system he is studying." This does not necessarily mean that the sociologist as a private person believes his or her own rhetoric. Rather, it is a stance and an action taken because of a commitment to looking behind and through the obvious realities of life. For example, in my role as a teacher I have often lectured on the perilous consequences of the population explosion. To get my audience to react in spite of their apathy, I have occasionally advocated extreme measures, such as reversible sterility universally administered to everyone at puberty. Upon marriage every couple could get its sterility reversed for one child. After a successful birth the mother and father would again be sterilized. A second child would be possible only upon application to the FFA (Federal Fertility Agency). Each month the FFA would randomly select a limited number of couples who would be allowed to have a second child. Two children would be the absolute maximum for any couple.

In the United States, with its set of moral values concerning freedom and choice, this suggestion is one that debunks a number of rights. By adopting an extreme debunking stance, I and my students can examine the basic processes of belief and attitude.

It is actually fun to debunk the institutions to which one's audience gives unquestioning loyalty—fun, that is, for the debunking speaker. I am sure that it is not much fun for the captive audience. But debunking is more than a teaching style or technique. It is a style of thought and work emphasized in sociology. The only way one can be objective about oneself and the world one lives in is to be willing to pick that world apart, piece by piece, to see if there is anything there worth saving. The sociologist, to be effective in the study of society, has to put all of his or her values, attitudes, and beliefs about this world on a shelf—then take them down one by one and analyze them. Perhaps the only way a sociologist can

9

objectively study the organizations to which he or she belongs is to be extra critical. This criticalness should not be misperceived as an exercise in academic demagoguery. Debunking for its own sake is not consistent with the orientation of sociology. The study of society *without* a debunking perspective is *also* not consistent with the best orientations in sociology.

## Unrespectability

A second feature of sociology, particularly in the United States, is a fascination with the seamier side of life. There is no question that the deviant has received much more attention in American sociology than has the conformist—probably more than is proportionately due. There are numerous reasons for this attention: One possible reason is that the deviant is more obvious and easier to spot in a forest of conformists. Second, it is perhaps easier to isolate the *why*—the pervasive sociological question—when it applies to the actions of a few who do not conform, than it is to explain why 90+ percent *do* conform. Sociologists choose these subjects to study so that they can better understand the 90+ percent. The conformists, those who maintain the great degree of social order present in our society, are the real subjects we hope to understand when we study deviants. Our primary goal is to understand the reasons for stability, not those for instability. This unrespectability characteristic is integrally tied to debunking because the sociologist, as a human being rather than as a scientist, has a propensity to identify with the unrespectables he or she studies and to empathize with their plight at being pushed out of society. By studying the unrespectable sector we have access to more ammunition to use in our debunking role.

## Relativization

The third characteristic of the sociological consciousness is relativization, which is based on ethnocentrism and cultural relativity. *Ethnocentrism* is the belief that one's own culture is superior to all others and should be the yardstick by which the others are measured. *Cultural relativity* means that a set of values are relative only to that society. What is valued in one society (in the United States, for example, female beauty is synonymous with a slim and trim figure) may be abhorred in another (some societies view the fattest female as the most beautiful), and who is to say that one is right and the other is wrong? Cultural relativity says that beauty is in the eye of the beholder, or as Flip Wilson says, "What you see is what you get, honey!"

With the proliferation of radios and television in the United States and the advent of satellite relays the American public has been forced to accept cultural relativity. The isolation of Stone Age tribes is difficult for us to imagine; such people have been so sheltered that they cannot project themselves into different lifestyles. But those of us who have daily access to all parts of the world quickly learn to project ourselves into the world of an Israeli agricultural worker, a refugee from Bangladesh, or a Stone Age primitive in the Philippines. Sociology takes pride in strongly advocating an acceptance of cultural relativity as a guiding principle in our lives at a time when many people in the United States are still isolated and sheltered, seemingly as ethnocentric as the premodern tribes mentioned above.

## Cosmopolitanism

Lastly, Berger (1963) characterizes the sociological perspective as "a broad, open, emancipated vista on human life. The sociologist at his best is a man with a taste for other lands, inwardly open to the meaningful richness of human possibilities, eager for new horizons and new worlds of human meaning." Thus the fourth characteristic is that the sociologist and the sociological perspective are urbane, looking for excitement in differences and in new life that is not an endless replication of the past. A cosmopolitan awareness of the endless diversity of human behavior tied together by cross-cultural threads of similarity is the ideal that sociologists have attempted to realize since the inception of the science. As Berger points out, this characteristic is highly valued by our society and should attract even more people to sociology.

The family and marriage are part of the lives of all of us. A reexamination of these institutions from a sociological base can be a valuable and useful educational experience. Although it is true that we can learn from a perspective that debunks everything, we can learn more through a careful, systematic, and positive analysis. We need to see what we have before we decide to reject any or all of it. Therefore, we will examine marriage and the family as they existed in the past, as they exist now in other societies, and how their relationships change or have changed. In this book we will examine the work done by sociologists who have studied phenomena like marital power or marital adjustment, and then we will try to determine what should have been done or should be done to improve upon their work. The message of family sociology is not, *Tear it up and start from scratch*. Rather it is, *Understand why and how it has operated, why and how it is changing, and where it is going*. The next section of this chapter deals with some of the assumptions we will use as a basis for what follows.

## SOME ASSUMPTIONS BY THE AUTHOR

In an era when specialization within all disciplines is increasing, the study of family life is becoming both more specialized and interdisciplinary at the same time. Consequently, we will examine some contributions from

11

psychology, psychiatry, history, economics, theology, and, of course, sociology. Within sociology we will draw from such diverse specialty areas as demography, human ecology, deviance and criminology, social stratification, and social psychology. This can be an exciting experience because there are so many rich materials and resources available from these diverse orientations. It can also make communication between the writer and the reader more difficult. The initial tendency is to be as eclectic as possible; however, the need is for a fusion and synthesis of the best that these disciplines and substantive areas have to offer within a coherent and systematic structure.

## The Family Existing at Different Levels of Reality

After thousands of years of observation scientists view organic life as a series of concentric circles. At the base there are the microorganisms, which are so small they have to be viewed with a microscope. At each succeeding stage of the structure the circle gets larger and concentrically includes all that preceded it. Within the largest circle are macroorganisms and structures that are too large to be observed at one time. In a discipline like sociology a useful dichotomy has developed. Sociologists who study the family as one of the institutions of society focus on macro-level phenomena—those that occur on such a large and abstract scale that they cannot be observed all at once in their entirety. Sociologists who study the interrelationships of a small family group are observing micro-level phenomena—those small enough to be observed in their entirety. Perhaps different concepts are used in each category to explain what is observed. When the family is viewed from a macro perspective, it is possible to say that a certain type of religious climate seems especially conducive to a high birth rate in a society. We know that fertility at the societal level is the result of individual actions from numerous couples, but the macro orientation in essence chooses to de-emphasize this fact in favor of the collective consequences of individual actions. The person with a micro orientation might suggest that being religiously orthodox seems especially conducive to a high birth rate. We know that a high fertility level can have serious consequences for a society, but the micro orientation in essence chooses to focus on the individuals involved in fertility behavior. There are then different levels of sociological reality. Unfortunately, the bridge between macro and micro is seldom crossed. The micro-macro distinction is a useful one only if neither seeks to define the other out of existence. In this book we will treat both as appropriate views of reality, and we will try to fuse the two into a comprehensive overview of family life.

Michael Heron from Monkmeyer Press Photo Service

## Conceptual Orientations and Reality

One of the most exciting yet frustrating periods of life is the high school years, when the individual is physically an adult with adult tastes and appetites, yet socially relatively inexperienced, economically dependent, and politically unenfranchised. The activities that seem to dominate most of the waking and much of the sleeping thoughts are dating, the opposite sex, and sex itself. A sociologist wearing a psychoanalytic hat might explain dating in terms of psychological needs, defense mechanisms, personality traits, and motivation. Another sociologist wearing psychological glasses might view dating as an example of how attitudes, values, personal properties like social class and group memberships, reference group norms, and school climate all operate. A third sociologist, wearing a structure-functionalist uniform, would probably see the dating game as a result of the sex ratio, the opportunity structure, the degree of autonomy in the courtship system, and the amount of differentiation present in the community.

Sociologists studying the family, like everyone else, see what they have been taught to see, and label what they see with the language of their

*Is this a typical modern American family? Scientists in several different sociological subdisciplines are helping us to understand the dynamics of the most basic sociological unit —the family.*

13

perspectives. The same data can thus yield widely divergent interpretations. The reader of this volume should attempt to spot the points of view that have guided the various authors of studies we will discuss. By so doing he or she should find it relatively easy to understand how they reached their conclusions. The reader should then be able to determine how a different approach would have yielded different interpretations.

## Meaning

Sociology is an integrated discipline, and the sociologist should be interested in synthesis—seeing the communality running through phenomena that seem divergent on the surface. This requires some of the "cosmopolitanism" Berger recommended. For example, a myopic sociologist studying the family might get really excited over a finding that fraternity men have premarital intercourse more frequently than nonfraternity men. An equally nearsighted juvenile delinquency instructor might get enthusiastic about a finding that delinquents who are gang members are better adjusted psychologically and more successful in their activities than are "loners."

The sociologist, regardless of his or her special substantive interests, should focus attention on the broader and more abstract phenomena that can facilitate a synthesis of seemingly diverse findings. A number of rather inclusive models of behavior can be used to summarize the findings of a number of discrete studies. In addition, I am convinced that these umbrella-like models are transferable. That is, after studying the models to be presented in this book, the reader should be able to use the same models in other sociology and social science contexts.

## SOME POSSIBLE IMPLICATIONS

*The purposes of a science are to describe, predict, and control the phenomena being studied. In the case of sociology the phenomena are human behaviors. What are the implications of a cadre of social scientists being able to accurately predict human behavior? What will be done about the control of human behavior? Will sociologists and other social scientists of the future become co-opted social engineers?*

*It is not difficult to project our worst fears into the future. The implications of a totally "scientific" society in Orwellian terms are painfully clear: (a) the creation of programed individuals who are designed by society to serve society; (b) the erosion of individual liberties and the loss of control over one's destiny; (c) little or no privacy; (d) the collection and collation of extensive records about each individual; (e) little or no individual autonomy; (f) an abjectly sterile environment controlled by people who consider an expression of human warmth and emotion the ultimate sin.*

*Sociologists are not unaware of these implications, nor is sociology as a discipline in any way closed to debate on the roles sociologists should or will play in an extremely technocratic society. The issues discussed earlier in this chapter about pure versus applied sociology and the use of hard versus soft scientific data are* prima facie *evidence that sociologists recognize the potentialities, positive and negative, and the human responsibilities that go with the role of scientist.*

*A second implication of the sociological perspective concerns the four features of sociological consciousness outlined by Peter Berger. In their initial encounter with sociology, many students are shocked and disturbed by the debunking feature. The values, institutions, and beliefs around which their lives have revolved are attacked and, in many instances, verbally destroyed. Do sociologists have the right to use their position in the university to attack societal institutions and the values that support them? Or is it their responsibility to stir students out of their unthinking and uncritical lethargy by debunking?*

# 2

# CONCEPTUAL FRAMEWORKS FOR ANALYSIS OF THE FAMILY

*How can a knowledge of the conceptual frameworks used in the study of the family and marriage help us to understand these phenomena?*

*Of the three frameworks discussed, is one better than the others?*

*Why and how is a conceptual framework for family analysis different from a sociological theory?*

*How do theory and research operate together to give us a better understanding of the family, marriage, and social change?*

Every discipline has difficulty in its formative years trying to reach a consensus on the labels for the phenomena under study, and on the most appropriate definitions for these labels. The controversy generated by the attempts to label concepts usually arises because the dissenting scholars are looking at the same phenomenon from different points of view. To illustrate this point, let us imagine a situation involving lay people rather than scholars: Suppose you are a journalist assigned the responsibility of conducting a grass-roots poll of the opinions of the common man and woman. The time is the early to middle 1960s during the heyday of the civil rights movement. It is midsummer and you are in a small town in Mississippi or Alabama. You first interview a man, dressed in jeans and a denim work shirt who has just stepped out of his pickup truck. You notice that he has two rifles across the back window of the truck and twelve "Back the Ku Klux Klan" stickers on the rear bumper. You say, "Sir, I'm Elmer Fudd of the *New York Times*. We are interested in what you think about the civil rights movement and its goals." Most of his response would have to be censored, but the gist of it is, "Why, those ———, they are just after our white daughters. If we integrate, before you know it there will be interracial marriage. I think we ought to ship them all back to Africa." You next interview a prim and proper lady, dressed in heels, gloves, and hat, out on a shopping trip. She appears to be in her early sixties. Her response is, "Well, I don't know why they are so upset. They have their own schools and besides, the colored people don't want to go to school with whites any more than whites want to go to school with them." The third person you interview is a young black wearing a FREEDOM NOW! button on his shirt. He says, "Man, we've been treated like slaves long enough. We've had all we're going to take. We want the same rights everyone is guaranteed under the Constitution and we're going to get those rights if we have to burn America down."

Each of these people is viewing the same phenomenon from a different perspective. What they see is determined by their assumptions about the motives behind the movement and its participants. The same kinds of experiences occur in the study of the family and marriage. What sociologists look for, see, and study may be determined primarily by the concepts and definitions they use plus their own experience with the phenomena under study. The answers sociologists get to the questions they ask about marriage and the family depend, then, on their assumptions about them— their conceptual orientation to the phenomena they study.

# CONCEPTUAL FRAMEWORKS

In their study of the family and marriage, sociologists first began to note explicitly the existence of alternative schools of thought in 1960. In that year Reuben Hill and Donald Hansen identified five competing conceptual frameworks for family analysis that had emerged from various disciplines. Although proponents of the various schools studied the same phenomena, Hill and Hansen noted differences between them in the concepts used and their definitions, the assumptions made about what phenomena to study, and the methods deemed most appropriate for examining those phenomena. The frameworks isolated by Hill and Hansen were:

1. interactional
2. situational
3. developmental
4. structure-functional
5. institutional

In 1966 Ivan Nye and Felix Berardo published a book entitled *Emerging Conceptual Frameworks in Family Analysis* in which eleven frameworks were delineated. Except for the psychoanalytic, the eleven represented merely a finer demarcation of the five Hill-Hansen frameworks:

| | |
|---|---|
| 1a. interactional | 4a. institutional |
| 1b. social psychology | 4b. economic |
| 2a. anthropological | 4c. legal |
| 2b. structure-functional | 4d. western Christian |
| 3. situational | 5. developmental |
| | 6. psychoanalytic |

Although it is neither feasible nor desirable to discuss all of these categories, we will examine the central assumptions and features of the three major frameworks: the structure-functional, the developmental, and the symbolic-interactional schools of thought. First, however, we should explain what is meant by the term *conceptual framework*. Basically it refers to three sets of tools that can be used by anyone studying the family: (a) *assumptions* about what in the family is important enough to notice and record; (b) *concepts* that the observer can use to label, describe, and interpret the observations; and (c) *procedures* for determining whether the assumptions are correct or faulty, supported or not supported.

No conceptual framework is all inclusive and covers adequately everything in the family worth studying. Each conceptual framework,

19

because it begins with different assumptions, has something unique to offer in expanding our understanding of family life. All conceptual frameworks provide us with a somewhat biased perspective on the family—each is much like one of the six blind men of Indostan who touched an elephant. In that children's poem each felt adamantly certain that the elephant was like the part he touched—like a rope, a spear, a tree, and so forth.

The family is like an elephant that not-so-blind sociologists see from different angles. The angle used in examining the family and the tools applied (assumptions, concepts, precedures) constitute the conceptual frameworks. Throughout this text we will review studies that used the structure-functional, the symbolic-interactional, or the developmental framework. The sections that follow are designed as an introduction to, and not a fully developed explanation of, those frameworks.

## THE STRUCTURE-FUNCTIONAL FRAMEWORK

Perhaps the most widely accepted yet debated conceptual framework for studying the family is the structure-functional. Part of its attraction is its apparent flexibility. The concepts and assumptions used in a structure-functional analysis of the family as one of the major institutions of society can also be used to study the family as a small group of interacting individuals and roles. What I call flexibility in the structure-functional approach would be labeled ambiguity by its critics. Regardless of the framework's flexibility or ambiguity, it constitutes a major orientation to the analysis of the family. As such it deserves our critical attention.

### Structure

As implied in the label of this framework, structure is a key concept. To understand the term fully we need to clarify some underlying definitions. Structure is really an umbrella construct (see Table 2–1) comprised of the following concepts:

INDIVIDUALS. The simultaneous and reciprocal communication among two or more individuals who share at the least a set of symbols and meanings and a language is known as *interaction*. We assume that society could not exist and function if people did not interact in a meaningful way with one another.

GROUP. If interaction persists long enough that the interacting individuals begin to develop distinctive patterns of relating to each other, and if they begin to think of themselves as a collectivity instead of as individuals, they constitute a group. A *reference group* is one that serves as a guideline for the behavior of other groups or individuals. Three

**TABLE 2–1**
**A Diagram of the Concept of Structure**

STRUCTURE AS A VIABLE CONCEPT AT EACH
LEVEL OF ABSTRACTION

| | | | | |
|---|---|---|---|---|
| 5. CULTURE | | | | family |
| folkways | | position | behaviors | education |
| mores | about | role | relative | economy |
| laws | | norm | to | politics |
| | | | | religion |

4. SOCIETY
    macro-level social system having institutional and geopolitical boundaries

3. INSTITUTIONS
    family
    educational
    economic
    political
    religious

2. GROUP
    micro-level social system
      a. positions
      b. roles
      c. norms

1. INDIVIDUALS
    in interaction

other concepts are needed to give the term *group* a structural meaning:
(1) A *position* is a location in an enduring relationship among two or
more individuals that has significance relative to other locations in the
same pattern of relationships. (2) A *role* is a description of specific types
of behavior that are attached to a position in a group. For example, we
use the term *father* (a role) to refer to a number of types of behavior
that are usually associated with the male's position in the group or family.
(3) A *norm* is an expectation associated with a position role within a
group. The norms are the prescriptions ("do this") and proscriptions
("don't do that") that make our role performances relatively free of anxiety and, relative to the occupants of other positions in the group, predictable. The purpose of positions, roles, and norms is to facilitate smooth
and harmonious interaction within groups.

    Therefore, structure as a concept is applicable at the lowest level
of abstraction if a social group exists. This is particularly true if the
members of that group differentiate the roles they play on the basis of
some criterion, such as age, sex, or intelligence. We could also describe a
group as a social system. By using the term *social system* we can begin
to understand how flexible the structure-functional framework is. If we
think of the single family group as a social system, we also frequently

21

*Our society teaches little boys that a "real" man is "hard as steel."*

describe the family in a society as a social system, although a more common label for family at the societal level is *institution*.

INSTITUTION.   An organized system of social relationships (roles, positions, norms) that is pervasively implemented in the society and that serves certain basic needs of the society is termed an *institution*. There are at least five basic institutions or macro-level social systems: (a) family, (b) education, (c) economics, (d) government, and (e) religion. At times the list is expanded to include the legal, health, military, and artistic institutions. Institutions change over time within societies and differ among societies.

SOCIETY.   A society is a large-scale social system that "survives its original members, replaces them through biological reproduction, and is relatively self-sufficient" (Winch, 1966). Customarily it is limited by geopolitical boundaries, for example, Canadian or Yugoslavian.

CULTURE.   Broad and generalized folkways (customary ways of acting and traditional ways of thinking), mores (prescriptions and proscriptions about thinking and behavior considered essential for group survival), and laws (codified principles of thinking and acting) about position, role, and normative behaviors that occur in one of the institutional spheres of life comprise a culture.

Thus, the term *structure* in the structure-functional approach to the family implies the existence of some organizing skeleton that can be

22

discussed at various levels of abstraction. The real value of the framework becomes apparent with the definition of *function*.

## Function

Marion J. Levy, Jr. (1952) defined function as "(1) a condition, or state of affairs, resultant from the operation (including in the term operation mere persistence) of a structure through time; and (2) the task oriented (and usually cooperative) activity resulting in the state of affairs denoted in (1)."

That all social systems function, whether they are micro-level or macro-level, is a crucial assumption of the structure-functionalists. Two questions or concerns of the proponents of this school are (1) What differences in functioning can be noted where structural differences occur (that is, the operation of mother-headed versus intact two-parent families, or the operation of the family in a polygamous versus monogamous society)?; and (2) What functions are inherent in certain social systems and what functions can be transferred (for example, is the family as we know it necessary for the existence of society)?

Much of this book discusses the first of these concerns. The second is more an academic and perhaps even a moot question and has been discussed as *functional prerequisites,* the "problems which must be solved or the activities which must be performed to insure the survival of a social system on a given level" (McIntyre, 1966). These functional prerequisites, considered universal, correspond essentially to the performance of institutions. Thus, every society must provide at a minimum level the functions indicated in Table 2–2, if it is to survive.

**Table 2–2**
**Institutional Functions**

| INSTITUTIONAL SPHERE | FUNCTIONAL PREREQUISITE |
|---|---|
| Health | Continued biological functioning of individual members (eating, sleeping, living) |
| Family | Replacement of members who die or leave (primarily reproductive behavior) |
| Education | Education into position, role, and norm configurations |
| Economic | Production and distribution of goods and services |
| Political-legal | Maintenance of order both within and among groups |
| Religious | Maintenance of individual, group, and societal motivation for survival |

The concept of function, like that of structure, is also quite flexible because it can be used at both the macro (institutional and societal) and micro (family unit or individual) levels of analysis. For example, among structure-functionalists an extensive debate has raged for years over what is or are the minimal function(s) of the family as an institution in a society. The basic issue is, *Is the family universal?* and if it is, *What is the minimum definition of family from a standpoint of the functions it must perform?*

There is some concensus that the family has existed in all societies known to man. However, there is less consensus as to just how crucial the family is to the existence of society. Some sociologists see the replacement function as the central raison d'être of the family. Ira Reiss (1965a) has suggested, however, that the core function of the family is to provide nurturant socialization to its dependent young. It is this function, according to Reiss, that characterizes all families in all societies.

When the family is viewed as a micro-level unit, the concept of function also proves useful in analysis. Using the functional prerequisites mentioned earlier, many sociologists have studied the different ways in which various races and classes perform replacement, health, socialization, economic, religious, and other functions.

Although the structure-functional framework offers distinct advantages for analyzing the family at both macro and micro levels, its limitations have not escaped the attention of critics. One weakness is that a heavy emphasis on structure and functions depicts the family as a static institution or life environment. There is a great deal more to marital interaction and adjustment, or to love, dating, and courtship than the position-roles occupied and the normative scripts dictated by society and culture. In other words, critics claim that the structure-functional approach misses some of the richness of family life—richness that can be detected only if one looks beyond artificial and stilted structural properties to the real exchange that takes place between real people in a family. Another weakness, say the critics, is the structural-functional assumption that all social systems strive for a rather constant state of equilibrium, homeostasis, or balance. Thus conflict, because it tends to disrupt the family system, is viewed by structure-functionalists as a negative force in family life. The critics claim, and I believe correctly, that conflict is endemic in family and marriage in the modern world. Instead of destroying, it often plays a vital and cohesive role in bringing persons who love each other even closer.

## THE DEVELOPMENTAL FRAMEWORK

Perhaps the most obvious yet remarkable reality of life is change and development. I continue to be amazed that at conception there are only that tiny sperm cell and the egg—combining and dividing, eventually going through a number of stages of development before and after birth, until that being can start the whole process again for another being. That there seem to be distinct stages in the growth process was recognized by Shakespeare:

> All the world's a stage,
> And all the men and women merely players;
> They have their exits and their entrances,
> And one man in his time plays many parts,
> His acts being seven ages. At first the infant,
> Mewling and puking in the nurse's arms.
> And then the whining school-boy, with his satchel
> And shining morning face, creeping like snail
> Unwillingly to school. And then the lover,
> Sighing like furnace, with a woeful ballad
> Made to his mistress' eyebrow. Then a soldier,
> Full of strange oaths, and bearded like the pard,
> Jealous in honour, sudden and quick in quarrel,
> Seeking the bubble reputation
> Even in the cannon's mouth. And then the justice,
> In fair round belly with good capon lin'd,
> With eyes severe and beard of formal cut,
> Full of wise saws and modern instances;
> And so he plays his part. The sixth age shifts
> Into the lean and slipper'd pantaloon,
> With spectacles on nose and pouch on side,
> His youthful hose, well sav'd, a world too wide
> For his shrunk shank; and his big manly voice,
> Turning again toward childish treble, pipes
> And whistles in his sound. Last scene of all,
> That ends this strange eventful history,
> Is second childishness, and mere oblivion,
> Sans teeth, sans eyes, sans taste, sans every thing.
>
> *As You Like It,* Act II, sc. 7, ll. 139–66

It is not surprising that sociologists have adopted the idea of a family developing through a life cycle as a major way of organizing their studies of family life. As might be expected, one of the major concerns with the developmental framework has been the identification of stages. Although most sociologists agree that there are probably four logical stages—formation, expansion, contraction, termination—consensus beyond such abstract categories is lacking.

The first use of developmental stages in family analysis occurred in the 1930s with two groups of sociologists delineating four stages. E. L. Kirkpatrick and his colleagues (1934) chose to focus on the school level of the children in a family. The stages were:

1. The preschool family
2. The grade-school family
3. The high-school family
4. The all-adult family

25

Sorokin and his associates (1931) decided that the important criterion for family development was the configuration of members within the family:

1. Married couples just starting pair living
2. Couples with one or more children
3. Couples with one or more self-supporting (adult) children
4. Couples growing old

It was quickly recognized that the notion of a family life cycle is much more complicated than that of the development of one individual. The number of stages can be influenced by the number of children born (if any), the spacing of children, the ages of both spouses at marriage, when the first and the last child arrive, the permanent or temporary absences of family members, and so on. In essence the crucial problems in delineating stages of the family life cycle are (a) the overlapping of stages and (b) deciding whether to focus on the first or last child or both. For example, a couple who have a second or later child in their middle or late thirties might easily be a family with teenagers and a family with a preschool child at the same time.

Evelyn Duvall (1967) attempted to resolve the problem of overlapping stages by focusing only on the first child. Her assumption was that the family learned to adapt to requirements of each new stage with the oldest child, and the adjustment necessary for subsequent children was thus minimal. The stages proposed by Duvall and the average length of time spent in each stage are seen in Table 2–3.

**TABLE 2–3**
**Family Life Cycle Stages**

| STAGE | FAMILY SITUATION | AVERAGE NUMBER OF YEARS IN STAGE |
|---|---|---|
| I | Couple without children | 2 years |
| II | Oldest child less than 30 months | 2.5 years |
| III | Oldest child from 2½ to 6 | 3.5 years |
| IV | Oldest child from 6 to 13 | 7 years |
| V | Oldest child from 13 to 20 | 7 years |
| VI | When first child leaves till last is gone | 6.5 years |
| VII | Empty nest to retirement | 15 ± years |
| VIII | Retirement to death of one or both spouses | to 16 ± years |

SOURCE: Adapted from Evelyn M. Duvall, *Family Development* (Philadelphia: J. B. Lippincott Company, 3rd ed. 1967), p. 13, Chart 1. Reprinted by permission of the publisher, J. B. Lippincott Company.

Rodgers (1962) is in sharp disagreement with Duvall. He argues, and persuasively, that the family developmental stages are determined by the first and the last children. They set up the outside boundaries of family activity and are primarily responsible for the most drastic mixing of stages. In other words, Rodgers delineates more stages than Duvall, and each stage is more complex than those of Duvall. The stages of the family life cycle according to Rodgers are:

1. Childless couple
2. All children less than 36 months
3. Preschool children with (a) oldest 3–6 and youngest under 3, (b) all children 3–6
4. School-age family with (a) infants, (b) preschoolers, (c) all children 6–13
5. Teenage family with (a) infants, (b) preschoolers, (c) schoolagers, (d) all children 13–20
6. Young adult family with (a) infants, (b) preschoolers, (c) schoolagers, (d) teenagers, (e) all children over 20
7. Launching family with (a) infants, (b) preschoolers, (c) schoolagers, (d) teenagers, (e) youngest child over 20
8. When all children have been launched until retirement
9. Retirement until death of one spouse
10. Death of first spouse to death of the survivor

## Basic Assumptions of the Developmental Framework

Although there is no solid consensus concerning the most appropriate number of stages or the criteria to be used in delineating these stages, there are some basic assumptions underlying the framework on which most sociologists agree:

1. The framework is designed to study the normal, or modal, type of family, the procreative family (a married couple living independent of parents or in-laws, with children either present or anticipated). Little or nothing can be said about the childless couple in terms of either Duvall's or Rodgers's stages, nor is there any way to adequately categorize families of three generations (grandparents, parents, and children). Although the percentage of voluntarily childless couples was at a low ebb in the mid–1970s, there is a distinct possibility that the near future will see an increase in this phenomenon.

2. The central concept of this framework is the *developmental task,* which has been defined by Duvall (1962) as one "which arises at or about a certain period in the life of an individual or family, successful achievement of which leads to his happiness and success with later tasks, while failure leads to unhappiness in the individual, disapproval by

society, and difficulty with later tasks." The definition is very deterministic as applied to individuals. Learning how to eat properly is a good example. It seems to take forever for a child to learn how to find his or her mouth and get a handful of food in it neatly. After that task has been satisfactorily completed, however, comes learning mastery of the spoon, which at first might as well be a huge and complex steam shovel.

When Duvall's definition of a developmental task is applied to a family, it is not as deterministic. The tasks become more like goals to be sought rather than specific jobs. They are not all-or-none affairs. It is possible for a family to move from one stage to another without a completely satisfactory completion of all of the tasks for the earlier stage. For example, Duvall (1967) listed nine ever-changing family developmental tasks that span the family life cycle; these are to establish and maintain:

1. An independent home
2. Satisfactory ways of getting and spending money
3. Mutually acceptable patterns in the division of labor
4. Continuity of mutually satisfying sex relationships
5. Open system of intellectual and emotional communication
6. Workable relationships with relatives
7. Ways of interacting with associates and community organizations
8. Competency in bearing and rearing children
9. A workable philosophy of life

3. A third assumption of the developmental framework is that the success of the family in its tasks is dependent on the complex interactions of family members in meeting their individual developmental tasks. The actions and reactions of each member relative to his or her own life path and those of the other family members is of crucial importance.

4. Although there are some similarities among all families at about the same stage of development, each family is unique in its complex of sex- and age-role structures. In other words, the mix of role expectations, different personalities, and differing situational constraints makes each family unique.

5. A final assumption of the developmental framework is that the family does not exist in a social vacuum. The family—each family—is subject to the influence of other social systems such as the occupational world of the parents who work, the school cultures of the children, and the varying groups to which each of the members belong. Although the family is not completely controlled by these external systems, neither is it unaffected by them.

Most of the research using the developmental framework has been descriptive—cataloguing how developmental tasks differ among the various stages of the family life cycle or explaining why certain phenomena, such as marital adjustment, seem to change from one stage to the next. In fact, some critics have claimed that the framework is nothing but a hueristic device, a mere listing of stages with little or no theoretical, substantive, or predictive value.

A recent article by Harold and Margaret Feldman (1975) may neutralize that criticism. They note the difference between the *lineage family*, the one that lasts over a number of generations, and the *lifetime family*, the one in which we are most directly involved throughout life. The Feldmans (1975:278) differentiate between the lineage and lifetime families on the basis of social positions:

> In any family there are social positions which are filled by persons. In the lifetime family the focus is on the persons who themselves change and fill successive positions as they grow older. In the lineage family the positions remain constant but are filled by successive persons.

The distinction is an important one. Most social scientists who study the family as one of the institutions of society—those who deal with the family from a macro perspective—focus their attention on the lineage family and the cycle of births and deaths that recur from generation to generation. In a sense, this is what Alex Haley did in his epic book *Roots*,

*Little girls are taught to be "sugar and spice and everything nice," and most grow up to be loving and gentle mothers.*

Frank Siteman

in which he traced his heritage all the way back to tribal Africa. Yet Haley, like most of us, became fascinated with the family career of his most distant ancestor, Kunta Kinte. Kunta's career was not cyclical; it occurred in stages. If the focus is on changes in family status and functioning during one person's life, the appropriate term is *career;* if the focus is on several generations of a particular family, the term *cycle* is appropriate. In Chapters 3–8 of this text we will focus our attention mainly on the lineage family. In Chapters 14–20 we will shift our focus to the lifetime family.

The Feldmans postulate that a lifetime family career consists of four separate but interrelated subcareers: (a) sexual experience, (b) marital, (c) parental, and (d) adult-parent.

SEXUAL EXPERIENCE CAREER. Although logically this facet of one's life begins in infancy, the major heterosexual component emerges during adolescence. Essentially, the Feldmans suggest that each partner to a marriage has a sexual experience career. The two careers become legally linked at marriage but may not remain exclusive. With divorce and remarriage sexual experience careers become even more complex.

MARITAL CAREER. This subcareer begins with legal entry into marriage and remains a part of one's life until divorce or death. Because the career is defined by legal status, separation (for example, if a husband is a POW) or desertion does not constitute a "real" end to it.

PARENTAL CAREER. This facet of one's lifetime family career begins with the conception of a child and continues generally until death. As the children go through their various stages of development, so too do the parents.

ADULT-PARENT CAREER. The Feldmans recognize that the parent-child bond of dependency is often reversed when parents get older, hence forming the final subcareer, the intercohort relationship of adults and their elderly parents, which relinks the lifetime careers of individuals with their lineage families.

The thrust of this new and more dynamic developmental framework is based on an assumption that each partner alone and both partners together experience major role transitions—when a cohabitation career becomes a marital career, when a marital career is transformed into a parental career, and so forth. Because of the implications of changes in the lives of the people involved and what these changes portend for the couple or family unit, it is essential that adherents of the developmental perspective be sensitive to critical transition points in lifetime careers. Throughout the text and particularly from Chapter 9 on, we will examine in detail some of these intersecting careers—love, sex, marriage, work and leisure, parenthood, divorce—and their impact on people's lives.

In summary, then, the developmental framework for family analysis suggests that all families evolve through fairly distinct stages. At each stage the individuals within a family, as well as the family itself, must perform certain tasks that are inherent in that stage of the family life cycle. In addition, this framework implies that certain reactions to family living may be affected by the tasks required in different stages of development. For example, suppose that we are interested in studying marital adjustment and satisfaction and how they change over the family life cycle. If we have an adequate number of couples in each of Duvall's eight stages, we would expect to find that perceived marital adjustment and satisfaction would decrease with the onset of children and increase after all the children had left home. Our expectations, derived from the developmental framework, are based on the assumption that the presence of children requires a great expenditure of time and energy which decreases the amount of time and energy available for maintaining good husband-wife rapport.

## THE SYMBOLIC-INTERACTION FRAMEWORK

Perhaps the most widely used conceptual framework for family analysis is based on symbolic interactionism. This school of thought, which emerged in the latter part of the nineteenth and the early part of the twentieth centuries, has also been called *social behaviorism*. As Sheldon Stryker (1972) noted: "In important degree, the theory is peculiarly an American product and its influence remains peculiarly American. In particular, symbolic interactionism has strongly influenced a major segment of American sociologists whose field of concern is the family; and it appears to have made no commensurate impact on any counterpart European cohort."

Two major factors probably provided the impetus for the pragmatist philosophers William James and John Dewey and the father of symbolic interactionism, George Herbert Mead, to establish this conceptual framework. The first was the idea of *instinct*, which was prevalent in American psychology at the time. The symbolic interactionists emphasized the ability and need of humans to be creative, to actively seek to alter and change the environmental conditions in which they live. Mead and others were not so naive as to think that humans were unlimited in the extent to which they could change these living conditions; everybody must operate within certain constraints. But the symbolic interactionists adamantly rejected the idea that human beings act blindly because of instinctual urges. Each human being has a mind and uses it creatively.

31

A second factor that provided an impetus for symbolic interactionism was John Watson's *behavioristic psychology*. Watson contended that human behavior can be essentially and ultimately understood in terms of stimulus and response. It is not necessary to ask what people think—but just to observe what they do relative to the stimuli in their environment. On the other hand, Mead contended that although human behavior is a response to stimuli, the behavior begins at a covert level. The stimulus is recognized, interpreted at the covert level by the unique conceptual and symbolic abilities of human beings, and influenced by their social attitudes and values. The behavior is also influenced by the anticipated reactions of other people in the environment.

## Basic Assumptions of Symbolic Interactionism

1. The possession of a symbolic language system is the most important characteristic distinguishing human beings from lower species of animals. Language enables humans to modify their environment, to preserve their past, and to transport themselves, symbolically at least, into the future.

2. Every person is, at birth, an asocial being. A child becomes human through interaction with others, and humanness develops through the internalization of symbols or language.

3. Every person develops a self, or personality, through this symbolic process by learning to treat his or her self as both a subject and an object. In other words, a person can look at his or her self subjectively as an ego-centered *I* or objectively as a *me*, a view influenced by other people's views of him or her. This process of developing a self occurs in distinct stages.

4. Once an individual has developed a self and has mastered a language system, he or she can begin to classify behaviors into categories rather than simply view them as discrete and unrelated events. In this way a person can define a situation and operate in social interactions that vary from, but are also similar to, other situations previously encountered.

5. The basic unit of study for symbolic interactionism is the *social act*. The social-act concept suggests that every person's actions consist of first defining the situation, then covertly saying to his or her self, "If *I* do A, B, or C, the other person will view *me* in a certain way." On the basis of this internal conversation and viewing one's self as both subject and object, an individual will choose one of the alternative courses of action. Thus behavior exists at an observable and at an unobservable level.

6. Human beings are born into groups and spend all their lives in various groupings of individuals. Humankind, as a species, is also born and lives with some biological properties that influence its behavior. But

human behavior can be understood without reverting to biological causation or relying on macro-level structural characteristics such as culture, society, or nations. This assumption essentially limits the symbolic-interaction approach to the study of relatively small units of individuals. It also implies a need for concepts like position, role, and norm.

## Basic Concepts of Symbolic Interactionism

SOCIALIZATION.   The process in which a person learns the language system, the roles and norms, the attitudes, and the values of the groups to which he or she belongs or desires to belong is called *socialization*. Socialization is most pronounced and apparent in childhood, when a child begins learning to be human, to be a male or female, to be a child and to be a parent. It also occurs throughout life as people change their group memberships and identities.

ROLE-TAKING.   The process of projecting one's self into another's identity in order to better perform one's own role is called *role-taking*. According to Mead, role-taking occurs in three stages: (1) At the earliest stage of development a child belongs to a very small group usually consisting of mother, father, and siblings. These constitute *significant others* in the environment. Being almost totally dependent upon these significant others for sustenance, the small child learns how to use gestures (sounds, movements, and so forth) to elicit responses from the parents. The child soon learns which gestures result in rewards and which in punishments. (2) The child begins to pick up the rudiments of a language system and understands the meaning of a number of words before he or she can verbalize them. In this second phase of self development the child begins to take the role of *particular others*—persons and roles outside the child's immediate social context, such as fireman, policeman, cowboy, mother. (3) The third stage of development marks the inculcation of the child into society and of society into the child. When the child begins to take the role of the *generalized other* (that is, society), he or she has become a full-fledged user of the language system and understands right from wrong as defined by the society and culture.

Human beings are always bound into networks of significant, particular, and generalized others. We constantly take the other's role. During the dating years it is not unusual for a boy or a girl to completely "play out" a date with a significant other before it occurs in reality. The same is true of many of our marital interactions.

POSITION, ROLE, AND NORM.   These concepts, discussed in the section on structure-functionalism, are also central to the symbolic-interaction approach to studying family behavior.

33

Joel Gordon

*Women in our society have proved that sexual equality is a reality in the labor force.*

DEFINITION OF THE SITUATION. This concept entails an understanding of one's position and role and of the norms applicable in a particular encounter. Prominent social scientist Erving Goffman refers to working consensus as a congruent set of definitions of the situation wherein all the members of an interaction agree generally on their positions and roles, and on the norms under which they will operate.

REFERENCE GROUPS. Like position, role, and norm, this term also is common to the structure-functional and symbolic-interaction frameworks.

The person studying family behavior from a symbolic-interaction perspective usually focuses on a small number of individuals, who by occupying certain position-roles behave in certain patterned ways toward one another. Much of the research using this approach has examined parent-child and husband-wife relationships. For example, let us suppose that we are interested in studying how power operates within the family —who has it, and how and when it is used. Using the symbolic-interactionist perspective we might ask husbands and wives each to describe how decisions are reached on a number of different topics such as buying a car, changing residences, going on a vacation, choosing a family doctor. We could ask each how he or she thinks the other would answer the questions. We might also ask the two oldest children in the family to answer the questions from their perspectives, and to say how they think their mother and father would answer them. We would obtain not only a picture of the power structure within the family but also pertinent information on the accuracy of self-other perceptions and on how the marital power-structure situation is defined.

A weakness of the symbolic-interaction approach is that little effort is made by its adherents to relate these behaviors to the broader social and historical context within which these behaviors occur. Thus, the symbolic-interaction approach is usually called social psychology and the structure-functional is labeled sociology. This distinction is, in my opinion, inappropriate; both are sociological but differ in the level of behavior at which each is directed.

## FROM CONCEPTUAL FRAMEWORKS TOWARD THEORY

Conceptual frameworks like those just discussed (structure-functional, developmental, symbolic-interactional) are not theories. They are merely broad and relatively abstract guidelines used by sociologists in their attempts to understand the family. Recently sociologists studying the family have become interested in constructing theoretical models. After a brief historical overview of the problems related to theory in sociology we will further discuss this movement toward models.

In 1959 C. Wright Mills wrote a stinging critique of the state of sociological craftsmanship. He claimed that sociologists were bunched at two polar ends of a continuum. On one end are the "grand theorists," the scholars whose analysis of human behavior is so broad and abstract that their writings are virtually meaningless. Facetiously speaking, the grand theorists are concerned with the "real" problems of life—like the rise and fall of civilizations. At the other end of the continuum Mills placed the "abstract empiricists," those sociologists who attempt to measure everything—even such imponderables as love, desire, passion, adjustment. To the abstract empiricist the most important material substance in life is a computer printout, and human behavior is best seen as a mathematical equation.

For Mills both of these approaches are bankrupt. He claimed, and I think accurately, that the true goal of sociology is to understand human behavior as it occurs and manifests itself in the activity of groups of people and to translate that understanding so that it may be usefully applied to the solution of human and societal problems.

This situation led Robert Merton (1956) to call for "theories of the middle range" that would avoid the absurdity of both the grand-theory and abstract-empirical approaches. As the name implies, a theory of the middle range is one that seeks to cover less ground than a grand theory but that attempts to move away from an extremely narrow and limited examination of some human situation or behavior. A number of theories of the middle range now exist in the marriage and family area and in other substantive areas of sociology. It will be useful to us to

35

**TABLE 2–4**

**A Means-Ends Schema**

| FORMS OF BEHAVIOR | | CULTURAL GOALS | INSTITUTIONALIZED MEANS |
|---|---|:---:|:---:|
| I | Conformity | + | + |
| II | Innovation | + | − |
| III | Ritualism | − | + |
| IV | Retreatism | − | − |
| V | Rebellion | +/− | +/− |

SOURCE: Reprinted with permission of Macmillan Publishing Co., Inc., from *Social Theory and Social Structure*, revised and enlarged edition, by Robert E. Merton. Copyright © 1957 by The Free Press, a corporation.

select one middle-range theory, for example Merton's (1957) means-ends schema (see Table 2–4), which was initially developed to study deviant behavior, and apply it to marriage and the family.

Merton posited that behavior results from the interplay of cultural goals and the means available for obtaining them. By using such a strategy he was able to isolate five forms of behavior that can be applied to substantive interests other than deviant behaviors like delinquency or other criminal and illegal activities. Because of this flexibility, the theory is one of the middle range.

People who accept the goals of society (marriage, children, a home in suburbia) will conform by going through the appropriate and sanctioned steps (engagement, church wedding, invitations). Some, the innovators, will accept the goals (family life and so forth) but come up with their own way of achieving the goals (elopement, living with someone in a "spiritual" marriage). Others will go through the rituals (a wedding and all it traditionally entails) in order to get one facet of the cultural goals (a regular sex partner). The retreatist will reject both the goals and the means by which they should be obtained. In a way, though not entirely, the religious orders are retreatist-oriented regarding marriage and the family for themselves. The rebel periodically accepts and rejects the cultural goals and means, using them as he sees fit for the moment.

Although theories of the middle range like Merton's have proved for the most part to be useful and descriptive of human behavior, they have also been criticized for not achieving a closer union of the conceptual and the research operations of sociology. The theoretical models referred to earlier are a step in the right direction toward solving this problem. Fortunately, the movement toward theoretical models has been accompanied by a continuing commitment to the development of truly reliable and valid research procedures following accepted scientific procedures.

# THEORETICAL MODELS

As mentioned earlier, a conceptual framework is useful because it describes the general features and components of a phenomenon that can be studied. But one cannot study a phenomenon without defining its specific components. The research process in sociology generally requires a large expenditure of time, thought, energy and resources. Most sociologists studying phenomena related to marriage and the family conduct a series of studies, and subsequent research efforts are built upon the successes, shortcomings, and failures of their earlier attempts.

The first step in the research process is to define a research problem. More often than not the problem the researcher chooses to study involves a facet of human behavior that is interesting or perplexing to him or her. A research problem that interested me as an undergraduate and served as a stimulus for several studies can be used to illustrate the research process used to develop and test theoretical models. I was impressed by the seeming inconsistency between an observable religious commitment and premarital sexual behavior. The Christian faith proscribes participation in sex before marriage. Yet, more than a few persons I encountered who claimed a sincere commitment to religious principles were quite active sexually.

To study this inconsistency requires a translation of the components of this phenomenon into variables that can be measured, a process known in sociology as *operationalization*. There are three main types of variables: independent, dependent, and intervening. For example, in the first study I conducted (see Clayton, 1969) on the relationship between religious commitment and premarital intercourse, the independent variable was operationalized as an endorsement of certain orthodox or traditional beliefs of the Christian faith. The dependent variable was whether or not the respondents in the sample reported having intercourse during the school year. A variable that could intervene in and affect the relationship between religious orthodoxy and premarital intercourse was group membership, operationalized as membership or nonmembership in a fraternity.

A conditional statement of the relationship between two or more variables is known as the *hypothesis*. In this study of the relationship between religious orthodoxy and premarital intercourse experience, the hypothesis was *that persons higher in religious commitment would be less likely to report intercourse experience than those who were lower in commitment.* It was also expected that religious orthodoxy would be less of a restraining influence on sexual behavior for persons who belonged to a group that condoned, or at least did not proscribe, premarital intercourse. The purpose of a specific research undertaking is to demonstrate the accuracy of the hypothesis.

Two strategies are possible in social research: those of the *context of discovery* and the *context of justification* (see Phillips, 1972). A study in the context of discovery breaks new ground, investigating phenomena never before studied. In this context one needs to describe the boundaries of activity and the types of activity present. A study in the context of justification adds new clarity and precision to the knowledge of phenomena on which some research has already been performed. Several tactics by which the researcher can implement either strategy are:

(a) participant observation, or direct observation by the researcher;
(b) nonparticipant observation by associates of the researcher;
(c) the use of a laboratory experimental study with an experimental and a control group;
(d) a survey in which the respondents are interviewed; and
(e) a survey in which the persons studied complete a questionnaire.

Each of these research tactics has obvious advantages and disadvantages: Very few research projects can be conducted on an entire segment of the population that might be involved in the behavior under study; there may be too many individuals in the population, they may be too scattered by distance; or not all qualified individuals may respond with the needed data. The social researcher usually works with a *sample,* a designated number of individuals often chosen in advance to conform to specific criteria such as age, social class, or class in school. If the sample is carefully drawn, so that these criteria are met and the sample closely resembles the population from which it was drawn, valid conclusions from this sample may then be extrapolated to the total population under study.

In the 1969 study, the data revealed that about the same percentage of fraternity males with high and low religious commitment reported at least one act of premarital intercourse during that academic year (55 and 62 percent, respectively). Among the nonfraternity men, 39 percent of the less religious—as compared to only 21 percent of the more religious—reported experiencing premarital coitus that school year. In other words, the hypothesis was not fully supported: Religious orthodoxy was apparently a restraining force only for the nonfraternity men. A more important conclusion was that these fraternities might be encouraging coitus, even when religious commitment is high.

After the data are in, analyzed, and interpreted, it is necessary to review the conceptual and methodological operations used, to determine which need improvement and further clarification. In the 1969 study there may be several reasons why the hypothesis was not fully supported: First, the dependent variable was operationalized to include sexual intercourse experienced during the school year. It may be that the most active period of sexual contact was the summer, and the study did not assess that time period. Second, another important feature of the phenomenon of premarital sex—attitudes toward premarital sex—was not measured at all. Third, membership in a group may not be a sufficient index of a group's influence on a member's behavior. Perhaps a perception of the group's norms about sexual behavior would be a more sensitive index of how group membership intervenes between religious commitment and premarital sexual behavior.

In a second and subsequent study, which will be discussed in more detail in Chapter 10 (see Clayton, 1972), the shortcomings of operationalization noted above were incorporated. In addition, in the second study the focus shifted from testing a hypothesis to testing a theoretical model. A *theoretical model* is an attempt to state a general theory in such a way that it may be illustrated by variables that can refer to any kind of phenomenon. In other words, a theoretical model is more abstract and is not

Erika Stone from Peter Arnold

*Sexual equality has permeated society at the conceptual level, but it is experiencing difficulty making its way into the kitchen.*

limited to substantive variables such as religious orthodoxy, premarital intercourse, and fraternity membership. Instead, it can use such terms as attitudes, behavior, and reference group norms. These models are often depicted graphically by means of flowcharts (see the diagram below).

## Contingent Consistency Model

The model tested in my second study (1972) was chosen because it deals with an issue of general theoretical significance in sociology: the degree of consistency between attitudes and behavior. The originators of the model (Warner and DeFleur, 1969) named it *contingent consistency* because it suggests that general attitudes such as religious commitment may be consistently related to behavior only if certain contingent factors are also present. In my study, the two contingent factors selected were attitudes toward premarital sex (a behavior-specific attitude) and perceived reference group norms concerning premarital sex.

After the data for the 1972 study were analyzed I was able to revise the contingent consistency model into what may be an even more realistic and useful theoretical model for sociologists studying the attitude-behavior relationship (see Figure 10–1 and accompanying discussion in Chapter 10). In order to become a theory the model must be refined and tested until it is highly accurate and will work when *other* kinds of attitudes, behaviors, and contingent factors are under study.

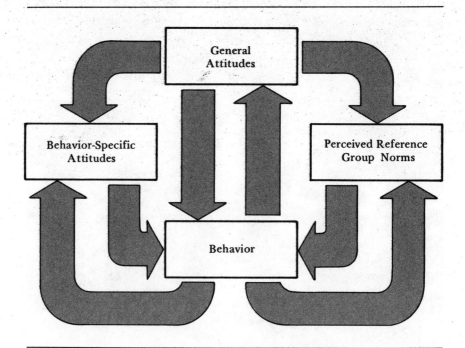

This extended example illustrates the fact that a simple act such as premarital intercourse is not so simple if one attempts to explain why it occurs for some and not for others. The development of prediction capabilities is high on the list of priorities for sociology of the family. In bringing about the achievement of this goal sociologists studying the family have now moved from a conceptual-framework orientation to the testing of theoretical models (see Burr, 1973). The transition has been a difficult one; it has required that we give up narrow interests in family-based activities for the more complex but necessary interest in behavior itself. Some general theoretical models now available in sociology are viable enough to be used in various substantive areas.

The contingent-consistency model is only one example of such models. Throughout this book many other models are discussed and illustrated by figures or tables.

## SOME POSSIBLE IMPLICATIONS

*On the one hand, sociology is moving toward greater scientific sophistication—toward prediction and control—entailing the development and utilization of highly technical methodologies and statistical techniques. The goal of this strategy is the development of testable yet abstract theoretical models leading to theories that are supported by empirical data. On the other hand, sociologists are moving toward more abstract concepts and constructs that can be interrelated at a verbal level. The more technically sophisticated we get, the more abstract our theories become.*

*In a society constantly beset by serious social problems the issue for sociology becomes: Can we afford the luxury of abstract theorizing and the development of a highly technical vocabulary and a repertoire of sophisticated mechanized techniques for gathering and processing data? Put another way, will the usefulness of sociology in helping to solve real human problems be ignored by the movement of the discipline in both these directions? Will the movement of the discipline in these two directions diminish the relevance of sociology for the study of the family? Since most sociologists are actively involved in teaching sociology to undergraduates, does this split mean that sociology will be increasingly less relevant and less interesting to students? Can sociologists maintain a sensitivity to human and social problems and the needs of our prime clientele, the undergraduate students, and simultaneously increase our methodological and theoretical sophistication?*

# 3

# THE STUDY OF KINSHIP

*Why is it important to study and understand the various hypotheses about the origin of the family?*

*Is the incest taboo virtually universal?*

*Why is it important to know all the terms that refer to the kinship system?*

*How can knowledge of the types of marriage, types of families, and rules of marriage, descent, residence, and authority help us to understand how the family and marriage are changing?*

The characteristic that most distinguishes our generation from preceding ones is the necessity to cope with social change—social change that is ubiquitous and pervasive. It has been said that we live at the benchmark of human history, at the great divide that splits the history of mankind into two epochs. Most of the people living now are products of the twentieth century. A roadside historical marker referring to a Civil War event seems to take us back a long way. The two-hundredth anniversary of the United States caused us to conjure up pictures of events that seemed to have occurred a long, long, time ago; in reality, in years, it is only a short time ago. However, in terms of differences in life-styles, the American revolution and its participants could have existed two thousand years ago. As the economist Kenneth Boulding said, "The world of today...is as different from the world in which I was born as that world was from Julius Caesar's. I was born in the middle of human history, to date, roughly. Almost as much has happened since I was born as happened before" (see Toffler, 1970:13).

In his book *Future Shock,* Alvin Toffler divided the last fifty thousand years of human existence into lifetimes of approximately sixty-two years each. There have thus been 800 lifetimes. To illustrate just how "new" rapid social change is, he points out that 650 lifetimes were spent in caves, and not until the 730th lifetime did men and women learn to communicate from one lifetime to another through writing. Only in the last 6 lifetimes have the masses ever seen a printed word. During the last 4 lifetimes human beings developed the ability to measure time with precision. The overwhelming majority of all material goods we use in daily life were developed in this, the 800th lifetime.

Social change is an important, even crucial, phenomenon to consider in a study of the family. Equally apparent is the fact that much of human history is either completely or relatively lost. As Schulz (1972:90) indicated: "A social institution such as the family is poorly reflected in the archeological record. It is not part of the material culture and, therefore, leaves no artifact. Some aspects of family life can be inferred from artifacts, but the inferences are shaky. The historic record gives us a bit more insight, but even so, most aspects of ancient family patterns are unrecorded. They simply were not interesting enough at the time." Therefore, sociologists cannot adequately study the family as it has changed over a long period of time because much of the data are fragmentary and perhaps unreliable. We know very little about early human social institutions. Much of our study of the distant past will have to be based on the construction of possible alternatives with little real evidence available to determine which biography of the family is correct. However, it is important, for several reasons, to review what may have been the origins of the human family. First, an understanding of the beginnings of human history may give us some idea of how much we have evolved. Second, an understanding of how early human beings adapted to a hostile environment may provide some important clues about their creativity and the stability of the family institution. Third, a knowledge of the genesis of the family may help us to understand the development of sex roles, family structures, and functions. That knowledge can be useful to us in our search for a more humane human family context.

## ORIGINS OF THE FAMILY

Human beings are interested in their origins and the origins of their social institutions. Every religion seems to have an answer. The Judaeo-Christian view is monogamous—Adam and Eve were in God's paradise until they sinned and were banished from the Garden of Eden. The Scriptures are incomplete as to how everything else developed except that "they were fruitful and multiplied."

Following publication of Darwin's *Origin of Species,* a number of scholars began to delve into the origins of the family. If Darwin was right, an evolutionary process is also associated with the development of the family. This line of reasoning led these early family historians to look at the structure of the family in antiquity.

### Original Promiscuity

One theory about the original conditions of family life, advocated by leading nineteenth-century scholars like John J. Bachofen and Lewis Morgan, is original promiscuity. While this theory was never freed of ambiguity, essentially it held that no social regulations were placed on sexual relations. No group-sanctioned means established or maintained a relatively permanent man-woman relationship. With extensive and sometimes rather persuasive evidence, the proponents of the original-promiscuity theory argued that little held a man and a woman together. (Love is a relatively new phenomenon in the history of humankind.) Perhaps our spoofs of the caveman hitting a woman on the head with a club and dragging her off to the cave are not too far-fetched. It is almost totally certain that early cavemen were not aware of biological paternity. This is not surprising, in view of the relatively long time that it took human beings to learn to domesticate animals and to use fire for cooking. A woman who got pregnant often and children who got in the way were of little help to a caveman who had to fight huge predators to stay alive and to eat.

45

*The complex family system found among "primitive" groups explicitly designated each person's place in the system and his or her work responsibilities.*

The central arguments used by the proponents of the theory of original promiscuity are as follows:

1. In a number of primitive societies the social rules concerning sexual relationships are relaxed, allowing completely promiscuous behavior.

Societies that allowed and even encouraged early sexual experimentation for both sexes, societies that had a system of segregation of the sexes except for nocturnal visitations for coitus, societies that had late marriages preceded by fairly extensive sexual contacts, and societies with very transitory marital arrangements were all cited by the theory's proponents as evidence that promiscuity was man's original condition. A major criticism is that what to a Western European traveler might appear promiscuous may be very strictly regulated to a primitive. One often wonders what interpretations a "primitive" anthropologist from a "promiscuous" society would have made had he or she visited an "advanced" Western nation in the 1860s or 1870s when Bachofen and Morgan were writing, or in 1931 when Robert Briffault published his book entitled *The Mothers*. The point is that we see what we want to see, and we have been trained to see and interpret these perceptions with a yardstick made in our own culture.

Will the teenagers of today see their children's children as promiscuous? Quite likely.

2. Some practices reported among primitive tribes could be vestiges of an early state of promiscuity.

The proponents of original promiscuity pointed to the practice of wife lending found in peoples living in such diverse climates as the Arctic and Australia. Perhaps if they were around today they would view sexual swingers as another example of man and woman reverting to their old promiscuous selves. Other anthropological evidence cited is the practice of having a bride spend her wedding night with some eminent personage in the village, like the chief or medicine man. The criticism of this line of reasoning is that these practices may serve useful functions for these societies and not be at all indicative of the artificial label of promiscuous— by Western standards.

3. A last argument for original promiscuity is the existence of extremely casual extramarital relationships even where marriage is practiced.

The evidence cited refers to the practice in some societies of a rather casual acceptance of extramarital sexual relations by one's spouse. In some societies discussed by Westermarck extramarital coitus is expected to occur with the husband's friends or guests. The practice of free access across marital ties during certain rituals is also used to support the notion of original promiscuity.

When all of the evidence is examined, two conclusions seem obvious. First, we really do not and cannot know the real answer to the origins of family life among the species *Homo sapiens*. Second, although the original-promiscuity hypothesis seemingly can be supported by a great many data, those same data can also be interpreted as supportive of other, quite different hypotheses.

## Mother-Child Family

Using much of the same evidence that supported the original-promiscuity hypothesis, J. F. McLennan, Robert Briffault, and Edwin S. Hartland suggested that the earliest form of family life and organization consisted of mothers and their offspring. The evidence seems impressive to support their contention. In the first place, there was probably little emphasis given to love, tenderness, and sexual attraction among our distant ancestors. Not only were they without the "essentials" of life like underarm deodorants, colognes, toothpastes, and mouth washes, but most of them were living in cold and damp caves. It is quite likely that there was little to keep a man attracted to a woman, or vice versa, especially on a permanent basis. Second, the biological realities of maternity were principally obvious to the mother who probably gave birth often and under less than ideal conditions. In addition, the child was dependent on the mother for an extended period of time, thus necessitating a rather permanent family-type unit consisting of a mother and her children.

Societies in which this mother-child family unit may have predominated are called Mother-Right. This label is used whenever a society has the following characteristics (Hartland, 1921:32):

1. Descent and kinship are traced exclusively through the mother.
2. The societal rule is predominantly the domain of men but is inherited and passed on through the female side of the family.
3. The marriages that do occur are matrilocal (that is, the husband goes to live in the wife's village or with the wife's mother).

Again the conclusion would have to be that the mother-child family seems plausible enough. Because of the long period of dependency of human children, it seems quite likely that the mother-child unit is the basic building block of human society. Whether the maternal family existed universally is doubtful since in some climates and locales such a system may have been less viable than other types of organization.

## Original-Pair Marriage

The third major hypothesis of the origin of family life suggests that man has always liked sexual exclusiveness and the social security of a woman in the cave. It is fairly obvious that men and women have much to be gained through cooperation in a family-like arrangement, especially in a hostile environment. The woman and children could always use the protection and hunting abilities of a man, and the man could always use the women and children to gather and prepare food and make clothing.

Westermarck and others who advocated the original-pair hypothesis marshaled substantial evidence to support their view. They were able to say that numerous societies practiced premarital chastity. The prevalence of this practice and the fact that some species of apes instinctually sought a lifelong mate were used to bolster the original-pair hypothesis. This is perhaps an unfortunate contention. Instinct is an absolute type of phenomenon. If man has an instinct, then by definition it must be present in all members of the species to roughly the same degree. The great variety in terms of numbers of spouses found in primitive societies suggests that man does not have a monogamous mating instinct.

Therefore, like the other two hypotheses of the origins of the family, the evidence is ambivalent, open to different interpretations, and sketchy at the least. In fact it may be said that the answer to the question of origins is superfluous. What would we do if we had uncontestable evidence that the original-promiscuity, maternal-family, or original-pair hypothesis was the correct one? Since we will never know, we can say only that early human beings probably used whatever best served their needs, and those needs probably varied from locale to locale and for different periods of time.

48

If we examine the impact of social change on the family at the social or institutional level, and vice versa, the focus must be on a period of time for which we have adequate information. In addition, we will have to agree on what it is that is changed. This necessitates a discussion of terms that describe selected aspects of family structure and practices.

## TYPES OF FAMILY SYSTEMS

Two basic types of family systems have been operative in various societies. These types are ideal constructs, that is, they have never existed exclusively in any one society but rather have usually coexisted. However, in most cases one will predominate and can be used to describe the generally accepted practices of most of the population.

The first and more traditional family system is the *consanguine,* which is based on the importance of blood ties. For illustrative purposes we will consider the man as a point of reference, since evidence from so-called primitive societies indicates that families more frequently centered around the male line than the female line. In societies where the consanguine system predominates the most important relationships in a person's life are those between him and his parents. In such a system when a man marries he usually brings his spouse to his parents' home. The son continues to bow to his father's wishes, to work for his father, and to show extreme deference to parental demands. The wife, an outsider who has stolen some of the affection and allegiance of the precious son, is not well received by the mother-in-law. In such a system, when a man's mother and his wife get into an argument, the man is expected by the consanguine norms to side with his mother. The virtual servant status of the wife, however, is ameliorated with the advent of children, especially a son.

The other type of family system is *conjugal,* which emphasizes marital (husband-wife) ties rather than blood (parent-child) relationship ties. The United States has what may be called a conjugal family system, although there are undoubtedly many instances in the conjugal family system in which the strings are never fully cut and where parents interfere with the normal functioning of the marital relationships of their children.

## FAMILY RELATIONSHIPS AND GENERATIONS

One of the more evident characteristics of human beings is their need for anchors that provide an identity, a name, and a distinguishing role position. A person's family unit confers these things upon him or her. A *family of orientation* provides a person with labels that will separate relative from nonrelative, and nonrelatives who are appropriate and inappropriate to consider as friends or as a possible mate. The family of orientation acquaints a person with the world of people with whom to interact.

At marriage, a couple establishes a new unit, a *family of procreation*. This new status likewise provides the spouses with identities and in most cases provides the female with a new name. All of us are affected by our roles within these two types of families, and most of us will belong to a family of orientation and a family of procreation, and provide our children with a family of orientation at some stage in our lives. This implies that there may be at times some propensity for role conflict and conflicting allegiances and obligations.

## MARRIAGE REGULATIONS

A major change occurring on a world-wide scale is the increasing freedom to choose one's mate. This practice has not always been available. In fact, over most of recorded history in most societies, marriages have been arranged by parents with the two participants having little if any input into the decision. There are two general types of marital regulations: (a) endogamy, which refers to rules prescribing that an individual marry someone *within* a certain group, and (b) exogamy, which requires that a person marry someone *outside* of a certain group. These two types can be best viewed as a circle within a circle. The individual must marry someone outside of the smaller inner circle (exogamy) but cannot exceed the societal limitations of the outer circle (endogamy).

Within primitive societies perhaps the most widely practiced form of endogamy is tribal. Less frequently, the outer circle of acceptable mates may include some subdivision of a tribal society such as a clan or village. From anthropological evidence we do know that tribal endogamy is very effective because intermarriage between tribes living in close proximity is infrequent. Some understanding of the intensity of endogamous rule can be gleaned from studying the dicta of the ancient Hebrews in the Old Testament. They suggest that one reason for endogamy is the desire of the group not to lose any of its precious members. An additional reason is to maintain tribal purity—which must not be unduly influenced by the foreigners who must be legitimately adopted by the group. In modern society we see endogamy practiced, with race, religion, and social class forming the bases for defining the acceptable mate. This shift to more diffuse traits is probably a necessary consequence of urbanization, industrialization, and the mobility present in modern societies.

Probably the most interesting occurrence of endogamous rules is the practice of preferential cross-cousin mating, which is either a required or allowed arrangement in a surprising number of societies (see Lowrie, 1940). In the most common situation a male is expected to marry the daughter of his father's brother. Perhaps this type of endogamy arose because it keeps related families bound to one another and thus keeps the family property in the family. Another reason may be that by contributing a daughter to his brother's son, the loss of the donor mother is made up by the introduction of a female back into the male line of the family. A third reason is that in societies where bride-price and dowries are required, the family does not really lose that much when it sends a daughter away. In the next generation it will receive back the goods lost in the dowry, perhaps with some interest added. One wonders if our kissing cousin jokes are a historical residue of preferential cross-cousin marriages. We will discuss endogamy as it operates in the United States in Chapters 12 and 13.

The rules of exogamy, which specify the person-role who cannot be selected as a mate, are unlike those of endogamy. Exogamous rules are primarily kinship based and are usually referred to as incest taboos. However, it would be a mistake to say that incest refers to tabooed intercourse with a close blood relative. As mentioned earlier in this chapter, in most societies biological factors are subordinate in importance to social-kinship factors, which can and do sometimes transcend the biological bonds.

## The Incest Taboo

Perhaps five "facts" about incest taboos are generally accepted by social scientists (see Leslie, 1976) and could provide a starting point for our discussion:

1. Probably no other act elicits such a powerful and emotional response as a violation of the incest taboo, especially within the immediate family.
2. Incest taboos are never confined to the immediate family of parents and children.
3. Although relatives outside the immediate family are always included, no particular relative is in the prohibited category in all societies.
4. The other relatives included in the tabooed group are not necessarily those closest in a biological sense.
5. G. P. Murdock (1949:289–301) contended that child-parent and brother-sister marriages are prohibited in all known societies. His conclusions were based on a study of 250 societies. Kenkel (1977) avoided questioning Murdock's contention by saying, "There is a *partial* exception to this in some societies where *some* of the people have been allowed to practice brother-sister marriage."

Kenkel's partial exceptions to the "universal" rule are the cases of brother-sister marriage among the royal families in Hawaii and Egypt and among the Incas in Peru. Most social scientists have emphasized that this practice was limited to the aristocracy and was not a common occurrence among the masses.

### Incest in Ancient Egypt

Russell Middleton's (1962) study of brother-sister and father-daughter marriages in ancient Egypt questioned not only the universality of the incest taboo but the label "partial exceptions for special groups." He divided early Egyptian history into three periods: (a) the Pharaonic (prior to 332 B.C.), (b) the Ptolemaic (323–30 B.C.), and (c) the Roman (30 B.C. to A.D. 324). In the eighteenth dynasty of the Pharaonic period a majority of the kings probably married their sisters or half-sisters. There is evidence that a nineteenth-dynasty king, Rameses II, married not only two of his sisters but two and perhaps three of his daughters. Another king who reigned from 1397 to 1360 B.C. probably married at least one and perhaps two of his daughters. Very little reliable evidence suggests that brother-sister marriages existed to any extent among commoners during this period. During the Ptolemaic period, Ptolemy II married his full sister Arsinol even though it was prohibited by Greek law. As Middleton indicates, "Of the thirteen Ptolemies who came to the throne, seven contracted such marriages" (that is, brother-sister). Evidently such arrangements were limited to royalty during this period. With a variety of rather indisputable documents available for the Roman period, Middleton concludes that there was a fairly high incidence of brother-sister marriages even among commoners. This would include full as well as half-siblings. The proportion of marriages that were consanguinial reached as high as 15 to 20 percent.

Middleton's study does not negate the existence of an incest taboo in all societies. What it does is question the universal effectiveness of the taboo in restraining all or even the overwhelming majority of incestuous marriages in all societies. The data from ancient Egypt suggest that there

### Explanations of the Incest Taboo

Among the numerous attempts to account for both the existence and the seeming universality of the incest taboo are the four plausible explanations we will discuss briefly.[1]

HARMFUL CONSEQUENCES OF INBREEDING. This explanation focuses on the biological transmission of undesirable traits or characteristics. If a parent marries his or her child, or a brother his sister, then the children of such marriage would, according to this explanation, be more likely to exhibit

[1] This section relies heavily on the excellent coverage of the alternative explanations of the incest taboo found in Leslie (1976) and Murdock (1949:289–301).

*Ptolemy II and His Wife Arsinol. Although the incest taboo may have existed in every society, history indicates some exceptions to the rule being applied, particularly among the aristocracy.*

Culver Pictures, Inc.

may be societies for which we have little or no data on acceptance of brother-sister marriages, even among the commoners, as in the Egyptian Roman period. Murdock's statement is perhaps too final and absolute to be true. It should be apparent from this discussion that no sociological laws are universally supported—only quasi-laws that would probably be questioned if more adequate information were available.

what were formerly recessive characteristics. The fear of the harmful consequences of inbreeding supposedly led to the institutionalization of the incest taboo.

There are several difficulties with this line of reasoning. First, it assumes a level of biological knowledge among primitives that just does not or did not exist. In fact, some anthropologists have reported the existence of tribes that supposedly do not even know about the male's role in conception and that nonetheless have incest taboos. Second, this explanation assumes that our ancient ancestors in diversely located societies were able to observe some debilitating effects of human inbreeding and to develop some incest norms from their observations. This would require transmitting a cultural heritage of detailed observations, many of which would have to be based on a knowledge of biology, or at least

53

a rather certain knowledge of who was father to whom. Both of these conditions seem unlikely.

It is highly improbable that the fear of harmful consequences is responsible for the existence of incest taboos in any society. In addition, the fact that the incest taboos usually transcend purely biological boundaries once moved outside the immediate family reinforces the inadequacy of this explanation.

"INSTINCT" AGAINST INBREEDING. This explanation accounts for the incest taboo at the individual drive level. We supposedly have a built-in horror of breeding with our blood relatives. The term *instinct*—itself under attack in scientific circles for its lack of precision—usually refers to a trait found in all members of a species to the same or virtually the same degree. Thus, cowbirds will deposit their eggs in the nest of some other bird along with the eggs already there. That mother bird will hatch the eggs, including the cowbird egg, even though it is not her own, because of the so-called maternal instinct. Human beings do not have any instincts. If there were an instinctual horror against inbreeding, incest would never occur and we would not really need any socialization to curb an impulse we do not possess. This purported explanation of the incest taboo has been discarded by both biological and social scientists.

FREUDIAN MECHANISM OF REACTION FORMATION. The strong emotional fear of incest has its roots, according to Freud, in the parental restraint of actions of the child who indicates sexual attraction for the parent of the opposite sex. This impulse of sexual attraction is repressed but remains within the unconscious. In reaction formation a continually repressed desire is sometimes neutralized by behavior expressing exactly the opposite desire. In this case, the extreme horror of incest results from a repressed desire for sex within the immediate family. The Freudian theory does not offer any explanations for why the incest taboo is extended beyond the immediate family. Thus, the Freudian theory of the incest taboo is at best weak.

MURDOCK'S COMPOSITE THEORY OF INCEST. Murdock pieced together the best contributions of various disciplines—sociology, cultural anthropology, psychoanalysis, and behavioristic psychology—to construct his theory, which states that the origins of the incest taboo for an individual occur when his or her parents and siblings refuse and quash any sexual attraction expressed toward them. The parents and siblings are more experienced sexually and know the possible consequences for the group if prohibited sexual behavior were to occur.

To the contribution from psychoanalysis is added the idea of cultural sanctioning from sociology and cultural anthropology. The family, being the central unit of production, socialization, and economic cooperation, and being the unit through which the generations are connected, must be protected from external and internal forces that might destroy it. Surely nothing can be as damaging as sexual rivalries within the immediate family. Thus, for the sake of individual family units and for society, the culturally based incest norms are imbued with the strongest sanctions possible.

Kingsley Davis (1960:401) has pointed out that while sexual jealousies within the family might be destructive, the confusion over statuses would be devastating. "The incestuous child of a father-daughter union ... would be a brother of his own mother, that is, the son of his own sister; a stepson of his own grandmother; possibly a brother of his own uncle; and certainly a grandson of his own father."

The third input to Murdock's composite theory of incest is from behavioristic psychology. Murdock reasoned that the answer to why the taboo also refers to some persons not biologically closely related is stimulus generalization, a concept that suggests that if the mother is tabooed, then other women will be tabooed to the degree that they are perceived as similar to the mother. Thus, if the mother's sisters (the aunts) are called by a term similar to mother, they would be tabooed because of the principle of stimulus generalization.

While Murdock's composite theory is a definite improvement over the other "explanations" of the incest taboo, we are still perplexed about the real root causes of the taboo. Much of the information relevant to the incest taboo is lost forever. With the continuous shrinking of the world the number of "primitive" tribes is dwindling. Perhaps we will have to be satisfied with Murdock's theory and variations of it.

## FORMS OF MARRIAGE

Given only two sexes, there are a limited number of possible marriage combinations, which are as follows:

1. *Monogamy*—one man married to one woman at a time.
2. *Polygamy*—multiple spouses of either sex.

    a. *Polygyny*—one male married to more than one female at the same time.

    b. *Polyandry*—one female married to more than one male at the same time.

    c. *Group marriage*—two or more men married to two or more women at the same time.

We will discuss these marital forms in reverse order with the least practiced, group marriage, and continue through to the most widely practiced, monogamy.

55

## Group Marriage

Group marriage usually refers to the marriage of two or more men to two or more women at the same time. Murdock (1949:24) reports that group marriage "appears never to exist as a cultural norm." It should be noted that when anthropologists say that group marriage is exceedingly rare or does not exist, they are referring to the number of societies where it is the preferred marital form, not to the incidence of its actual occurrence either within societies or across societies. We can be certain that Murdock's statement is correct while recognizing that group marriage is possible, has been, and perhaps still is practiced in some areas of our society and other societies as well.

Group marriage occurs among the Marquesans of Polynesia, the Toda of Southern India, and the Kaingang of Brazil. However, what we as Westerners would call group marriage may not be perceived as such by the participants in these societies. This is a problem of semantics. We should look at these societies and decide for ourselves.

The following description by Linton (1936:181–182) of the Marquesans details the existence of a quasi-type of group marriage:

> At the present time group marriage is so rare that its very existence has been questioned. It cannot be denied that certain societies recognize and permit an arrangement by which a group of men and women live together as spouses. Certain writers have claimed that such an arrangement does not constitute group marriage because there is, in all the cases known, a main pair whose marital rights in each other take precedence over those of other members of the group. It seems to this writer that this fact does not invalidate the arrangement as group marriage any more than the existence of a head wife among several wives makes it impossible to call such cases polygyny. Thus [among] the Marquesans the household formerly consisted of a head couple and a series of other men and women who lived with them and had recognized sexual rights both with regard to the heads and with regard to each other. This arrangement differed from the ideal pattern of group marriage only in the fact that the subsidiary partners with the household could be more readily broken than the relationship between the main partners.

Although Linton tries to neutralize critical comments, it is likely that the Marquesans do not have group marriage. As others have pointed out, the men and women added to the chief couple are not married to the group; they merely join. Murdock acknowledges the existence of group marriage if there are economic responsibilities tied to the sexual privileges. As Radcliffe-Brown (1965:5) emphasized, "It is not sexual intercourse that constitutes marriage either in Europe or amongst savage peoples. Marriage is a social arrangement by which a child is given a legitimate position in society, determined by parenthood in the social sense."

The Toda of South India developed an approximation of group marriage out of a practice of polyandry. Because of the practice of female infanticide, polyandry was feasible. Along with the practice of several brothers taking a common wife, the Todas developed strong norms against sexual jealousy. With British rule this practice of polyandry was outlawed. As the sex ratio moved back toward a one-to-one level the Todas adapted by taking an additional wife or more instead of splitting up into marital pairs.

Perhaps the clearest example of group marriage, one that would satisfy the qualifications of Murdock and others, exists among the Kaingang of the jungles of Brazil. Making little or no distinction between appropriate or inappropriate sex partners, avoiding only parent-child, full brother–full sister, and half-sibling marriages, the Kaingang commonly have marriages and love affairs among all other classes of relatives.

The Kaingang have no ideal of love or a single sex interest. Marriage is not economic in the sense that no bride price exists. Being a small society, if someone is without a spouse, that person can always find a welcome at the home of some relative. Thus their society is not fractured by the breaking of a marital relationship. Marriage itself is not a formalized ceremony. It consists primarily of announcing to the group that each belongs to the other. Children are catalysts that make tenuous male-female ties more permanent. After a Kaingang woman has three children a marriage does not break up. This does not mean that the "hunting and gathering instinct" in Kaingang men becomes dormant. On the contrary, the value of diversity learned early in this society is a viable life-style even after marriage. "Adultery" (as we define it) is a way of life for both sexes in Kaingang society. Because marriage and family and kinship are really unimportant in this society, and because there is little or no sexual continence, Western observers have suggested that group marriage exists in this society.

The Kaingang are not numerous. In 1932 the population was reportedly 106. Of these about 36 were adult males and 30 adult females.

Regardless of the fact that group marriage is not widely practiced in any society, the concept continues to persist. Even in our postindustrial world, there are numerous examples of attempts to establish group marriage; its existence as one of many possible forms of marriage must be acknowledged.

## Polyandry

In only a few societies has the practice of one woman married to two or more men ever been widespread. Murdock found only four in his World Ethnographic Sample (1957) of 565 societies. In a much smaller sample William Stephens (1969) classified four societies as "predominantly polyandrous": the Toda, Marquesan, Nayar, and Tibetan.

*Each of this woman's children has three legal fathers. About forty million people in the world still live in polyandrous families.*

Several conditions seem to accompany the practice of polyandry in society. At least these things seem to have occurred in the small sample of polyandrous societies available:

1. The most frequent type of polyandry is fraternal, the sharing of a spouse by brothers. The ritual of marriage is usually between one man and one woman, with the wife becoming simultaneously a wife to all his brothers. Reported instances of father-and-son combinations have been in the minority.

2. Polyandry is easily and frequently changed into polygyny and/ or group marriage. This occurs when the first wife is barren, when the husbands have the economic security to purchase a second wife, or when one of the brothers takes a wife unto himself.

3. Severe economic conditions have accompanied the practice of polyandry—the existence of a subsistence type economy or relatively unfertile soil, and the practice of handing down property intact from one generation to the next. Under such conditions of poverty it probably takes several husbands to care for the needs of one wife.

4. A fourth correlate of polyandry is female infanticide. If one woman can legitimately accommodate several husbands, and if it takes their combined labors to support her, the last thing needed by women is competition. To keep the supply of women at less than a competitive level, societies like the Toda and Tibetan have selectively killed their female infants.

5. A typical Western reaction to polyandry is, "How can those men possibly share the same wife?" Such a response belies not only our occidental focus on sexual coitus, but our latent and sometimes manifest perception of women as sexual property. Because cooperation among males is an absolute necessity for survival, observers of polyandry report that jealousy is repressed to a marked degree. The good of the community is placed above ego-centered desires, and aspirations and close bonds of affection and solidarity develop among men in a polyandrous society.

Biological paternity poses no problem in polyandry. The oldest of the brothers is usually designated as the "legal" father, if such a label is appropriate. He acquires this status by ritualistically "giving the bow," or presenting a symbolic gift to the pregnant wife. After the birth of several children the bow may be given by another of the brothers, and he becomes the father of that child and subsequent children until the bow is passed to a third brother. With only one woman who can be impregnated and several possible donors, plus the practice of a ritual continence after the birth of a child, plus a rather high infant mortality rate (especially for females), the giving of the bow is not a frequent occurrence. Birth control is not a major problem in polyandrous societies—it is built into the whole family system.

The Toda have two other ways of contracting a marriage that are still within the domain of polyandry. The first is wife transfer. As the term implies, a man is permitted to seek a wife from among women who are already married. Once he finds the woman he wants he negotiates for her with the permission of her father, two elders of the tribe, and her husband(s). The second way of contracting a marriage is, in some ways, a legitimate mistress system, occurring when a man and woman come from different groups, both of which are endogamous. Under normal circumstances, neither could marry the other. After the wife and her first husband(s) agree that she can be mistress to the man from the other endogamous group, and after he has paid money and goods to the husband(s) of the bride, the new quasi-husband can "claim marital privileges in scheduled visits or assume what actually amounts to a husband's role and live with the co-husbands" (Queen and Habenstein, 1967:21–25). Because he cannot legitimately and in the fullest sense marry the woman, he is prohibited from giving the bow; other than that formal restriction, he seems to be entitled to husband's rights.

59

Polyandry has been a rather rare occurrence in human societies. Where it has occurred it has been accompanied by severe economic conditions, female infanticide, a tendency toward group marriage, and a marked lack of jealousy among sharing husbands.

## Polygyny

If it were possible to poll all the males in the world and ask them which form of marriage they would prefer if given a choice, the majority would probably opt for polygyny—the marriage of one male to two or more females at the same time. Like polyandry, the most common type of polygyny (Murdock, 1949:31) consists of a man marrying sisters, which is called sororal polygyny. A special form of this type of polygyny is the sororate, which is a cultural rule specifying that the preferred mate for a widower is the sister of his deceased wife. This amounts to a new monogamous relationship, but a rule specifying mate choice limits the classification to sororate polygyny.

Murdock (1949, 1957) has found that polygyny was a fairly widespread occurrence in 193 or 81 percent of his 1949 sample of 250 societies, and in 415 or 75 percent of the 565 societies included in his 1957 World Ethnographic Sample. This does not mean that all eligible males practiced polygyny in those societies. That would be impossible. Most men in polygynous societies practice monogamy out of necessity. There are at least two reasons for this: (1) the cost, or the economic factor, and (2) the number of available mates, or the sex ratio.

It is a truism that two cannot live as cheaply as one. The same is true for three or more. Add to that the possibility that one male, if he timed it right and could persevere, could impregnate at least one female a day, and maybe more. That means extra expenses. Polygyny has seldom occurred in societies where there is widespread affluence. This probably accounts for the privilege of polygyny sometimes being restricted to the aristocracy or wealthy elite of a society. The sex ratio is the number of males per 100 females, and at the time adulthood is reached, it usually stands at about 100 males per 100 females in most societies. Thus, for every male with two or more wives there is a male or more who is without a spouse. Consequently, although many societies allow and prefer polygyny, it is not a commonplace occurrence.

Polygyny is primarily the result of an economic decision. The polygynous male has multiple wives because he can afford them, he needs the extra labor provided by the second or later spouses, and he achieves status in the community from the evidence of prosperity provided by his additional wives. The sexual aspects of polygyny may be seen by many polygynous males as a burden rather than as the liberating and joyful opportunity imagined by their Western counterparts.

Polygyny is on the decline throughout the world. Even in Islamic countries, where the Koran allows up to four wives, polygyny has been outlawed because of various pressures, including that of the Women's Liberation movement. In fact, data from the 1961 census of Karachi, Pakistan, indicate that less than 1 percent of married males had more than one wife, and none had as many as four. Almost all of the polygynous males there had two wives. Furthermore, these multiple marriages were almost evenly distributed among the three major socioeconomic classes. It should also be noted that the United Nations, in its statement on human rights, explicitly frowns on the practice of polygyny.

Perhaps the most celebrated example of polygyny was the biblical King Solomon, who reportedly had seven hundred wives and three hundred concubines.

## Monogamy

Monogamy is now and has always been the most widely practiced form of marriage. It consists of one man married to one woman at a time, and is actually the preferred form of marriage for only 43 (17 percent)

*Is polygyny in Bechuanaland functional adaptation or traditional male dominance?*

N. R. Farbman, *Life Magazine,* © 1946 Time, Inc.

of Murdock's 1949 sample of 250 societies. Nevertheless, it is the only form of marriage that is permitted and recognized in all societies for which we have records. Most men, either by choice or necessity, have been monogamously wed. But this says nothing about the permanency of monogamous marriages. In almost every society mechanisms will release a married pair from their marital contract. In some societies, and in most cases, the male is given greater privileges of terminating the marriage. In fact, marital dissolution and remarriage is so frequent as to suggest that monogamy is an inappropriate label to describe this marital practice. Perhaps serial monogamy is a more accurate descriptive term. However, regardless of the frequency of marital break-ups or the permanency of monogamous relationships, most men and women are contractually bound to only one person at a time. Thus, monogamy is a viable form of marriage that must be studied and understood if we are to discuss the family, marriage, and social change.

## TYPES OF FAMILIES

Having discussed the rules governing the selection of a marital partner (endogamy and exogamy) and the marital forms (group marriage, polyandry, polygyny, and monogamy), we may examine the products of marriage, that is, the types of family formed. We will proceed from the basic building block, the nuclear family, to the composite types of family that fit under the rubric of extended family.

### Nuclear Family

Nimkoff (1965:5) says that "the smallest family unit usually consists of father, mother and offspring. By virtue of its irreducible size, and also because it is the building block of all larger family systems, it is often called the *nuclear* family." The term *nuclear family* carries no connotation of any active and perhaps functional relationships with kin from either of the families of orientation. However, William Goode (1963) believes that nuclear does imply an absence of such ties. Accordingly he used the term *conjugal family* to refer to the same group—the adult couple (mother and father) and their children, if any, plus the connotation of interaction with kin from one or both sides. The British functionalist, A. R. Radcliffe-Brown (1965:4–5), adds a further distinction. He regards the basic unit of kinship as the "elementary family" consisting of a person's parents, siblings, spouse, and children. The most common type of elementary family consists of the "parental family," in which the household includes the parents and their young or unmarried children.

For our purposes we use the term *nuclear* family as defined by Nimkoff and expect the term to imply the possibility but not the necessity of interaction with kin. It also suggests that a nuclear family may consist of a married pair without children or of one of the pair and children.

## Classical Extended Family

The term *extended* family implies that two or more nuclear-type family units are combined. I add the term *classical* to refer to an ideal type of extended family that may not exist to any great extent in reality, though it is a possibility.

In the classical extended family running through the male side, an extended family is one with "three or more generations living in one household, or within one compound, with the grandfather actively serving as the family head, and with married sons and their families, as well as unmarried sons and daughters. This form appears to be the epitome of the patriarchal, patrilocal and patrilineal family, with the family head as the power-center and the major decision maker" (see Korson, 1971). But usually some difficulty is involved in making reality fit with the ideal. For example, as Korson (1971) points out, in 1958 only 17.3 percent of all families living in Karachi, Pakistan, were extended. This is probably a conservative estimate since many nuclear units may be in close proximity to an extended family and may follow the lines of deferences implied in the definition. Even so, the ideal in this Muslim society is for the family to be classically extended.

## Joint Family

The *joint* family is a type of extended family arrangement that has occurred, according to Nimkoff (1965), in the traditional Indian family and in other societies. Korson (1971) says that the joint family "is usually limited to two generations, and consists of two or more brothers, married or unmarried, with their children and unmarried sisters living in one household, or within a compound. The oldest son usually assumes the headship upon the death or disability of the father; married sons, of course, are not required to live with the family head, but, once again, this appears to be the ideal to be achieved." Using the 1958 household survey in Karachi, Pakistan, as a basis, Korson reports that 15.1 percent were of a *joint* family structure. Adding this to the 17.3 percent that were of a classical extended structure, we find that at least 32.4 percent of all families in that city in 1958 were extended—probably an underestimate of the phenomenon and certainly an underestimate of the influence of the extended family in Pakistani society.

63

### Stem Family

The *stem* family, another extended type, reportedly occurred with some frequency in Japan. It was an adaptation of family structure to the problem of limited land holdings and a large family of sons. In this arrangement the extended family would decide which of the married sons would stay on at the family household. Some sons would be selected to start a branch (stem) of the extended family elsewhere, in large cities. Those sons would move their families of procreation to the cities at the expense of the extended family's resources and set up businesses. The stem family member would be required to contribute a portion of his earnings to the extended family's coffers, keeping enough to cover his own expenses and expenses to retain and expand his business enterprise. At the deaths of the father and mother, negotiations would occur to decide if the stem system would remain intact or if the families should break apart and start new extended family units.

### Modified Extended Family

A *modified extended* family is one that may be geographically dispersed but that is united through and by a network of aid and interaction. The conception of the American family as isolated and nuclear was probably an overreaction to the idea that the family exists, almost defenseless, against the pressures to change location and against the pressures of an urbanizing society in which large impersonal bureaucracies govern the lives of their employees. Hard empirical data, discussed at length in Chapter 5, led Eugene Litwak to label this type of family as modified extended.

Integrally tied in with the type of family prevalent in a society are three rules of family life, rules about: (a) ways of tracing lineage; (b) residence location to be selected by a new family of procreation; and (c) types of authority within the family. We will briefly discuss each of these topics in the order given.

## RULES OF DESCENT

Most human societies have developed rather complex rules in determining who a person is (his or her biological and social identity) and how that person is to relate to other persons in the society. The rules of tracing lineage are integrally related to rules about marital selection (endogamy and exogamy) and the prohibition of incest. Of the two levels at which an individual's identity can be said to exist (the individual lineage history and the descent group), the first is certainly the more important.

## Individual Lineage History

Since every person has one biological mother and father, some rather obvious patterns of tracing descent emerge. Although biologically based, descent actually refers to social relationships and family structure. Radcliffe-Brown (1965:39) has succinctly underscored the social salience of descent:

> Every kinship system provides each person in a society with a set of dyadic (person to person) relationships, so that he stands, as it were, at the center of a narrower or wider circle of relatives. During his life the body of his relatives is constantly changing by deaths and births and by marriages—his own marriage and the marriages of his relatives.

## Patrilineal Descent

The most common form of tracing descent focuses on the male lineage only. Thus a male gets his identity from his father and his paternal grandfather and great-grandfather and so on. A woman marries into her husband's family and her male children in particular belong to the father's family. The relationship of a child to his or her mother's biological kin is essentially ignored. In Murdock's (1949) study of 250 primitive societies 105 or 42 percent traced descent patrilineally.

## Bilateral Descent

In Murdock's study, the second most common rule of descent, bilateral descent, was found in 30 percent of his 250 societies. Bilateral descent, as the label implies, refers to the practice of tracing one's heritage through both biological parents. It is the most common practice in the United States. The consequences of this practice are (a) that the size of one's claimed kin group is usually limited to only those relatives that are very close, and (b) that the incest regulations are more limited than in a unilineal society.

## Matrilineal Descent

On the surface at least, matrilineal descent appears to be the mirror opposite of patrilineal descent, that is, descent traced through the female instead of the male line. However, matrilineal descent is more complex than its counterpart. For example, when a couple in a patrilineal society marries, where they will live is an either/or matter. They will live with or near his parents, or they will have the freedom to choose their own residence location. In a matrilineal society a whole gamut of possible alternative residence locations might be found. A second source of complexity in matrilineal societies concerns paternity. Unlike patrilineal societies, it matters little who the father is—the child's status is fixed entirely by the mother. Third, marriage is a minor ritual of little significance in matrilineal societies, whereas it is a crucial transition point in patrilineal societies.

In essence, then, in matrilineal societies the crucial relationships are mother-daughter-brother-sister, with the husband-wife and biological father-child relationships being of little importance. In matrilineal societies a male child is usually more intimately tied to his maternal uncle (a central figure in his mother's household and line) than to his biological father (a visitor in his mother's house).

To put this in perspective, Robin Fox (1967) outlined three basic types of matrilineal organization:

1. That based on the mother-daughter-sister roles and matrilocal residence. Here the burden of control and continuity is to some extent shifted onto the women, and in societies with this basis it is usually the case that women have higher prestige and influence than in other societies.

2. That based on the brother-sister-nephew roles, with avunculocal residence preferred, or, failing this, some means whereby the mother's brother can control his nephews. In this type the status of women is usually lower, as control and continuity are monopolized by the men.

3. That based on the full constellation of consanguine matrilineal roles: mother-daughter, brother-sister, mother's brother-sister's son. Here control and continuity are primarily in the hands of the men, but the status of women need not be low.

Suffice it to say that societies that trace lineage through the female line have more complex and more difficult problems of organization than patrilineal societies. Only 20 percent of Murdock's (1949) sample of 250 societies were matrilineal.

## Double Descent

This last rule of descent occurs in only 7 percent of societies and suggests how complicated lineage systems can be. Double descent means that at birth a person is assigned to two lines of descent: the father's patrilineal group and the mother's matrilineal group. The father's matrilineal relatives and the mother's patrilineal kin are disregarded.

## Descent Groups Versus Individual Lineage

At birth a person can be identified as being the son or daughter of a couple and thus the latest addition to a line of kin, depending on how lineage is traced. In many societies a newborn child is also given a membership in a larger descent group—a clan. The distinction between a clan and a lineage group is that in a lineage group each member can actually, or at least theoretically, trace his or her genealogical connection with any other member by descent from a common ancestor. In a clan, which is a larger body, this is not possible. The term for membership in a father's clan is *patrinymic,* in a mother's clan it is *matrinymic.* Put quite simply, patrinymic and matrinymic mean that a person has adopted and has been adopted into a clan group.

## RULES OF RESIDENCE

As you might expect, rules about where a married couple will live are very closely tied to the rules of descent practiced in a society. To be sure, the possible alternatives for choosing residence are limited since at least one of the pair will have to move at marriage. The various options are presented below:

*Patrilocal.*   The married couple will live with or near the husband's family. It should be noted that the new bride does not live with just her husband but rather with her husband's family.

*Matri-Patrilocal.*   In this rule of residence the husband goes to live with his wife's family for a period of time (for a year or so or until the first child is born) after which they will move to permanent residence either with or near the husband's family.

*Matrilocal.*   The opposite of patrilocal, matrilocal means that the husband will move to live with or near the wife's family.

*Patri-Matrilocal.*   Not a common practice, patri-matrilocal means that a couple will live for a while with the husband's family and then move to a more permanent residence with the wife's family.

*Bilocal.*   The newly married couple can choose which set of parents they will live with or near. The determining factors here will be the strength of personal ties, the relative wealth or status of the sets of parents, and how much aid the couple will need from the parents.

*Avunculocal.*   As Robin Fox (1967) puts it, "The rule of residence whereby a boy has to return to his mother's brother's village (his mother's natal home) either at puberty or on marriage, is known

67

as *avunculocal.*" This is usually found in matrilineal types of societies, where a man is tied to his mother's family and feels an especial closeness to his maternal uncle.

*Neolocal.*   In this type of residence, the kind found most often in the United States, a couple can choose where it will live, and it need not be with or near either of the families of orientation. Although freedom of choice is the ideological base here, the operational practice frequently calls for splitting the distance between the two parental families. The degree of freedom involved may be limited due to severe pressures from both parental families if the family of procreation contemplates a move that will take it far from both sets of parents.

## TYPES OF AUTHORITY

At the ideal level of analysis there are three types of authority patterns possible: matriarchal, patriarchal, and equalitarian. As the prefixes imply, matriarchal refers to control by the mother, patriarchal means father control, and equalitarian implies a division of authority that is relatively equal.

Unfortunately, in a complex society like that of the United States, none of these terms is adequate. Authority over what, where, and how that authority is exercised need consideration. We will discuss more fully these terms and their various meanings in Chapter 15. For the time being, it is important to note that in most less developed societies where the family institution is more central than it is in the United States, authority patterns are more one-sided and thus easier to recognize and discuss.

## SUMMARY

In this chapter terminology that will be used throughout the rest of the book is defined. These terms and the processes and structures they represent are intermeshed in reality. Seldom is it possible confidently to describe a family system in a complex society as conjugal, polygynous, patrilineal, patrilocal, and patriarchal. The terms are merely the goal lines, with most of the actual game plays occurring somewhere in between. The analysis of what happens during the game is what sociologists of the family study. The terms just discussed constitute what in the family can change. Our problem will be to determine how much and in what directions changes have occurred in the United States.

## SOME POSSIBLE IMPLICATIONS

*One of the most engaging attributes of the human race is its diversity. This diversity is seen most clearly in the variety of marital and familial practices found in divergent cultures. As industrialization, urbanization, and modernization advance into all parts of the world a loss of cultural diversity will be an effect. Polygyny is disappearing, and all world family systems are moving toward a conjugal organization. In a very real sense the Western culture, because it is more highly industrialized and modernized, has assumed a totalitarian nature. Its effects have diffused to a world where the advantages and benefits of modernization are seen as a way out of poverty and deprivation. It is not trite to say that the world is getting smaller. The implication is that, in the process, the people of the world and their distinct cultures and practices are losing some of their distinctiveness.*

*Is it morally imperative to preserve these cultural diversities? Should primitive societies be preserved for the benefit of posterity, or is it morally imperative to extend to all peoples and cultures the benefits of modernization? Should certain cultures and societies be relegated to preserves or reservations so that the past will always be with us?*

*These are some of the questions or implications that come to mind about the study of kinship.*

# PART II

# THE FAMILY IN SOCIETY

Jean-Claude Lejeune

# 4

# THE FAMILY AND SOCIAL CHANGE

What is social change, and how can its effect on the family be accurately assessed?

How and to what extent does the family affect social change?

Did industrialization lead to a nuclear family system, or did the nuclear family system facilitate the emergence of industrialization?

How much and how have the family and marriage changed over the years?

There is probably no topic of which we are more acutely aware as individuals, but more ignorant of as social scientists, than social change. This is true even though the explanation, prediction, and control of social change are priority goals for sociology and its specialties like the study of the family. First we shall distinguish between the layman's and the sociologist's perception of the concept of social change.

Many students view social change as something that individuals not only cause but must cause. Social change is frequently equated with efforts like the Peace Corps founded under John F. Kennedy, the civil rights movement of the middle and late 1960s, and the women's liberation movement of the 1970s. The everyday conception of social change is the activist approach—the applied, as opposed to the pure, sociological approach.

The sociological perception of social change is geared toward understanding why change occurs, how it occurs, and what its consequences are for institutions like government and the family. In other words, most sociologists are primarily interested in objectively analyzing events of social change, not in bringing about changes consistent with their subjectively organized and idiosyncratic values, attitudes, and biases.

This chapter focuses on some of the attempts made by sociologists to study the family as a changing system. Before we can begin a study of the changing family, let us review some of the salient facets of the general study of social change.

## THE SOCIOLOGICAL STUDY OF SOCIAL CHANGE

Sociology has been dominantly preoccupied with one major problem since its inception: *What is social change? How can it be conceptualized? How can it be accurately assessed? What causes it?* and *What are its consequences for social systems and individuals?* As sociology developed, different generations of scholars focused on different aspects of these questions. Some of the more important recurring concepts in the study of how society and societies change are discussed below.

One quite early concept that has persisted has been labeled *evolutionism,* or *unilinear change.* The evolutionary approach seems to suggest that all societies move from a simple to a more complex state. The unilinear theme suggests that change in simple societies progresses quite slowly and that as more and more changes occur the rate of change increases exponentially. The eventual consequence is rapid social change that can bring about a massive reorganization of a society in a very short span of time.

A second major concept in the study of social change has been called *developmentalism*. The bases of this approach are outlined in Chapter 2. The developmental social change theorist focuses on stages in social systems: birth, infancy, childhood, adolescence, young adulthood, middle-age, old age, widowhood, and death. Carle Zimmerman (1947, 1949) is a good example of a developmental theorist who studied the family. Zimmerman suggested that the Western family started out at a trustee level, grew to the "best" form, which he labeled domestic, and is moving toward death as the family becomes atomistic. We discuss Zimmerman's theory later in this chapter.

One difference between the unilinear theme and the developmental is that the former does not really allow for a prediction of regression. The unilinear concept projects continued progress and positive change. The developmental concept, on the other hand, not only allows for but actually predicts that the rate of change may diminish. Eventually the negative consequences of change will lead to a regression from progress, perhaps toward the death or at least the stagnation of a society and its institutions.

The third concept in the study of social change, particularly with regard to the family and marriage, can be labeled *functionalism*. Like developmentalism, the functional approach is discussed in Chapter 2, under the heading "The Structure-Functional Framework." The assumption here is that there are certain functions and structures that can change over time. One way to study social change is to determine what a system like the family did for its members in 1860 and then compare it with what it does now. Shifts in functions and changes in structures are indicative of the influence of social change on the family in a culture or society. Perhaps the best example of this approach is the work of William F. Ogburn and M. F. Nimkoff (1965), which is discussed later in this chapter.

A fourth concept in the study of social change can best be labeled *tension management*. The assumption here is that every society is made up of institutions and groups that are in competition for power, influence, and control. Some of the institutions and groups are quite conservative in orientation and seek to restrict or at least restrain both the types of change that occur and the speed with which change occurs. Other groups and institutions are oriented toward the occurrence of change and push for the optimum rate and level of change within the society. The social-change analysts who use the tension-management concept focus their attention on the battle between the prochange and antichange camps and how the ensuing tension is managed.

In their efforts to study the changing family, sociologists have relied on various and diverse sources of data. Some of the most conclusive studies of family change, like Murdock's Human Relations Area Files (1945, 1958, 1961, 1963) and his World Ethnographic Sample (1957), have been based on historical and ethnographic materials. Other students of family change have examined church records, works of literature, content analyses of child-rearing booklets and magazines, and actual census materials. Growing out of all these studies of the changing family has come a consensus, at least of sorts. For example, there is fairly widespread agreement that the family as a unit within a community and as a system within society is more a recipient than an initiator of social change. There is also consensus that four interlocking causal variables in family change are industrialization, urbanization, societal complexity, and modernization. Just how these interlocking variables operate to produce change is still a perplexing problem. As John Edwards (1969:18) noted:

> It seems reasonable to conclude at this point in the study of familial change that industrialization, urbanization, and the family are independent factors which frequently interact. The mode in which they interact is by no means simple; it suggests that the direction of causality may vary from one society to the next and from one time to the next in any given society. Clearly, it can no longer be maintained that the isolated nuclear family invariably emerges under the impetus of industrialization and urbanization.

As Edwards implies, the study of familial change has produced almost as many questions as answers. The research generated to study this problem has been cross-cultural as well as intrasocietal. However, whatever the scope, most of the work is in the quantitative and statistical style characteristic of empirical sociology. Thus, it is appropriate at this juncture to discuss briefly some of the difficulties inherent in measuring social change.

## Difficulties in Measuring Social Change

While our interests in this text are primarily the family and marriage, we should not lose sight of the fact that sociology is a generalizing discipline. When we study changes in the family institution, the primary focus of interest is on the change, not on the family. Therefore, the difficulties of measuring change are applicable to all substantive areas of sociology and other social sciences as well.

DIRECTION OF CAUSALITY. As scientists we are interested in discovering what causes what to occur. When two phenomena have no connection at all, we say that the two are *symmetrical*. For example, the heat of the sidewalk in New York City may be correlated with the birth rate, but it surely does not cause it. When two variables are thought to be possible causes of each other (X $\longleftrightarrow$ Y) we call the relationship *reciprocal*. Reciprocal types of relationships among phenomena abound in sociology, particularly where it is difficult to say which of two phenomena preceded the other in time. Thus, when we claim that industrialization led to (caused) the emergence of the relatively isolated nuclear family, we really should say that both emerged together, reciprocally affecting one another. The third type of relationship, and the one most rewarding to sociologists studying social change, is called *asymmetrical* (X $\longrightarrow$ Y). The assumptions here are that the causal factor precedes the effect factor in time, and that one actually accounts, at least in part, for what happens to the other. For example, the introduction of a family-planning clinic into an isolated village in an underdeveloped society can be said to cause change if the birth rate subsequently changes. However, a follow-up effort must determine if the birth rate dropped specifically because of the family-planning clinic or because of other factors. This difficulty in measuring change is a conceptual or theoretical one, but it is as important as the other difficulties to be discussed below.

TIME DECAY AND IDEALIZATION.   In order to measure change, we have to know what it was like at Time One. Many of the phenomena we study today existed in colonial times—perhaps they existed back to prehistorical times. However, as was amply illustrated in the discussion of the origins of the family, there has been a substantial decay of the data that could be used as a baseline from which to study the changes that have occurred. Even in a record-conscious society like the United States many of the "facts" about family life before 1900 are, at best, unreliable. The reason for this is our tendency to idealize the past. Children in our society grow up with a picture of life on the frontier that is grossly unrealistic. For the sake of developing a spirit of nationalism, historians and others have created myths to take the place of the facts. In the process the facts have been lost or have decayed to the point of nonrecognition. In studying social change it is difficult to know how much something has changed if we do not know what that something was like in the past.

VALIDITY AND RELIABILITY OF INDICATORS OF CHANGE.   The concepts of validity and reliability are of extreme importance to any discipline that seeks to measure certain phenomena. *Validity* is the degree to which an indicator measures what it purports to measure, and *reliability* is the degree of consistency with which an indicator measures a phenomenon from one example to the next. Students are constantly using these terms when they say, "That test didn't really measure what I knew. It wasn't valid! I didn't deserve a D." The instructor looks at the scores for four tests and says, "You made a D on all four tests. If they aren't valid they are certainly reliable." To make the example more relevant to social change let's consider the following:

Assume that you are a sociologist studying the family and that in the fall of 1970 you asked 1,000 freshmen to indicate which of the following types of sexual behavior they had experienced in the year preceding the study—kissing, petting, or coitus. Let us also assume that you asked another sample of 1,000 freshmen the same questions in the fall of 1975. The results you obtain are shown in Table 4–1.

On the basis of your results you might want to classify those engaging in coitus as the most permissive and those who report kissing only as the least permissive. Since the changes for each type of behavior are in the same direction—an increase from 1970 to 1975—you might conclude that your measure of sexual permissiveness is at least reliable. Validity, however, refers to whether you are really measuring sexual permissiveness at the behavioral level. What would you conclude if you found that 90 percent of the respondents who reported coitus in both 1970 and 1975 had had only one partner and had engaged in an average of only two acts of coitus? Would the validity of your assessment of change in sexual behavior suffer if you discover that 80 percent of the respondents who reported petting averaged seven different partners and an average of two petting experiences a week for the past year? The validity of the label "most permissive" would surely have to be reconsidered. As the example implies, reliability of measurement is more easily attained than validity, but both are essential ingredients to the study of changes in human behavior.

AMOUNT OF CHANGE. One major difficulty in measuring the amount of change lies in the selection of information to report. A common tactic in the popular press is to focus on gross numbers or on numbers that do not correspond to a comparable base. For example, in 1968 there were 582,000 divorces, a number that on the surface appears rather large, especially if one considers that there were only 393,000 in 1960. An enterprising journalist would quickly subtract and say that that is a gross increase of

**TABLE 4–1**
**Sexual Behavior Reported by Two Hypothetical Samples**

| | PERCENTAGES REPORTING ACTIVITY | |
|---|---|---|
| ACTIVITY | 1970 | 1975 |
| Kissing | 80 | 84 |
| Petting | 45 | 60 |
| Coitus | 22 | 25 |

189,000 divorces in just eight years! He or she might also report that since there were 2,059,000 marriages in 1968, the divorce rate was 28 percent. The figures are, of course, accurate. It is the interpretation that is faulty, for few of those getting married in 1968 were also candidates for a divorce. A more realistic estimate of the extent of divorce in 1968 would be to compare the number of divorces per 1,000 existing marriages. Since there were about 47 million married couples in the United States in 1968, the rate would be about 12.4 divorces per 1,000 marriages in existence compared to a rate of 9.2 for 1960. That figures out to be a little more than 1 divorce for every 100 marriages in existence in 1968. This figure is less startling and sensational, and consequently less likely to be reported. But the point is that change is usually reported in terms of gross numbers, when accuracy requires a rate and changes in rates over time. These rates are meaningful only when the numerator and denominator are meaningfully connected. Sometimes the perception of great changes occurring is based on faulty information, but more frequently it is based on sloppy work by statisticians or quasi-statisticians.

LEVELS OF ANALYSIS AND CAUSES OF SOCIAL CHANGE. Determining levels of analyses and causes of social change are perhaps the most important difficulties. Sociologists usually divide the world they study into three levels: the cultural, the social, and the personality/individual. Social change is usually viewed as originating at the cultural level and flowing through the social level to the personality/individual level. Thus it is not unusual for many family sociologists to claim that cultural processes such as industrialization, urbanization, and modernization have produced significant changes at the social level in such institutions as the family and religion. In itself, this claim has much evidence and logic behind it. Surely every family unit and the family system in a society must exist within and adapt to the demands of large, well-organized, and wealthy corporations. That the urban family must adapt to the exigencies created by urban centers is obvious.

Nevertheless, what appears to be so clearly an asymmetrical relationship (one-way causality) is, upon closer examination, a reciprocal relationship (joint causality). The progress of a society toward greater industrialization or modernization may be greatly affected by the type of family system present and the types of socialization practices prevalent in the family system. William Goode (1963:22) asks us to consider how the rate of industrialization in the West might have been affected if the family system had included the patriarchate, polygyny, and a strong clan orientation. Talcott Parsons (1965:52) said, "I believe profoundly in the importance of the family system, and I furthermore don't think it always follows, but at times it leads, social change." Meyer Nimkoff (1965:35), whose career was closely tied to that of William Ogburn, also posited a reciprocal relationship: "Even though technological and other economic factors may be the prime movers (accounting for more variation in social systems than do ideological factors), still the family is an independent as well as a dependent variable and may exert significant influence on the social process."

Therefore, evaluating the family system and its relation to social change is not a simple problem. The complexity of the problem is being deciphered, though somewhat more slowly than is desirable. We should all resist the temptation to allow our feelings of individual powerlessness dictate how we view the study of social change and the changing family.

As we move from our general discussion of difficulties inherent in the study of social change toward a focus on the family system, several points should be remembered. First, when we are dealing with macro-level concepts, every effort should be made to "think big." History should be seen as something larger than individuals. We should also resist any proclivity to personalize or individualize the materials covered in this chapter. Second, we should recognize that much of the data needed for a thorough analysis of social change and the family are lost. Some of those lost data have been recreated by persons who idealize the past, and we have been conditioned to accept that idealized picture. Third, change has become a value-laden concept. Most of us tend to view any change as good, and also to overestimate how much change has actually occurred. We should try to get an accurate perception of what something was really like "way back when" before we get too excited about the "revolutionary" changes occurring. Fourth and last, we should try to view the family system as a possible source of change. Family units are made up of human beings, not robots, and human beings are not known for their ready acceptance of change. In fact, hard-core resistance is a much more likely occurrence than ready acceptance of social change. Above all, it should be noted that social change is pervasive in human society—what we need to know is what is changing, how it changes, and what its consequences are at the cultural, social, and individual/personality levels of reality.

## GENERAL THEORIES OF SOCIAL CHANGE

As mentioned at the beginning of this chapter, theories of social change can be usefully grouped into three major categories: (a) those that posit a unilinear or evolutionary process; (b) those that suggest that systems, like individuals, go through a number of developmental stages; and (c) those that focus on the influence of structural changes on the way that functions are performed. Let us examine representative theorists and their views of these three categories of theories.

## Unilinear Evolutionary Social Change

One of the most active orientations to social change focuses on the concepts of modernization, modernity, and modernism. These terms imply a process of becoming—usually that becoming is modern from a point of origin that is traditional. Advocates of this orientation are quick to explicate what they mean by traditional and modern. First, the terms are not used in an evaluative sense but only to designate certain characteristics. Second, a modern society is not necessarily an urban-industrial society. This argument seems more academic than real. However, although it is true that most urban-industrial societies are modern, and vice versa, the proponents of this approach insist that the terms are not interchangeable. Third, the term *modern* is not synonymous with *Western*. The Western societies may be used as models, but they are not viewed as casting dies for the study of social change using the modernization approach.

The most common strategy used by these theorists has been to develop a list of characteristics found in traditional and in modern societies. Individuals are usually classified from traditional to modern on the basis of the characteristics of the society in which they live. Thus a representative listing of societal and individual characteristics would include the items found in Table 4–2.

Everett Rogers (1969) and Alex Inkeles (1969) constructed models of the traditional and the modern man or woman at the individual level.

**TABLE 4–2**
**Selected Societal Characteristics**

| TRADITIONAL SOCIETIES | MODERN SOCIETIES |
| --- | --- |
| Rural | Urban |
| Illiterate | Literate |
| Agricultural | Industrial |
| Designative political structure | Electoral political structure |
| Extended family system | Nuclear family system |
| Low economic participation | High economic participation |
| Low per capita income | High per capita income |
| Low productivity | High productivity |
| Little commerce | Much commerce |
| Poor transportation system | Developed transportation system |
| Oral media system | Mass media system |
| Poor nutrition | Good nutrition |
| High birth and death rates and short life expectancy | Low birth and death rates and extended life expectancy |

SOURCES: Adapted from Everett Rogers, *Modernization Among Peasants* (New York: Holt, 1969), p. 9; Daniel Lerner, *The Passing of Traditional Society* (Glencoe, Ill.: The Free Press of Glencoe, 1958), p. 57; Joseph Kahl, *Measurement of Modernism* (Austin: University of Texas Press, 1968), p. 37.

Drawing upon his study of Colombian peasants, Rogers describes the traditional man or woman as follows:

1. distrusting in interpersonal relations.
2. perceiving a limited good in the world.
3. dependent upon yet hostile to governmental authority.
4. steeped in familism.
5. lacking in innovativeness.
6. fatalistic.
7. limited in aspiration.
8. lacking in the ability to defer gratification.
9. limited in his or her view of the world.
10. demonstrating a low level of empathy.

At the modern end of the continuum, Inkeles (1969:10) describes the traits characteristic of the modern man or woman:

1. An openness to new experiences, both with people and with new ways of doing things such as attempting to control births.
2. The assertion of increasing independence from the authority of traditional figures like parents and priests and a shift of allegiance to leaders of government, public affairs, trade unions, cooperatives, and the like.
3. Knowledge of scientific principles and a general abandonment of passivity and fatalism in the face of life's difficulties.
4. Ambition for oneself and one's children to achieve high educational and occupational goals.
5. A highly developed sense of the value of time, which they do not like to waste.
6. Strong interest and participation in civic and community affairs and local politics.
7. Demands for access to news of national and international import as well as to that dealing with sports, religion, or purely local affairs.

The methods employed by societies or individuals to make the transition from traditional to modern is the most relevant type of information that we can obtain from these theorists. It is here that their hypotheses are unilinear and evolutionary. Regression to an earlier stage of development, while possible, is not ideologically plausible in their point of view. All societies move in the direction of modernism, as do the individuals within these modernizing societies. The key concepts or processes for this school of thought are urbanization, industrialization, literacy, development of mass media systems of communication, economic and political participation and empathy, the ability to comprehend the role of another individual.

For example, Daniel Lerner (1958:69) considers literacy and the development of mass media the most influential factors in creating empathy—and empathy is the moving force behind modernization. Lerner's model would look something like this:

Urbanization ⟶ Literacy → Mass media → Empathy → Economic and
                                                  political
                                                  participation

According to Lerner, empathy is the crucial ingredient for change at the individual level. Increasing urbanization leads to increased literacy and use of the mass media for communication, and empathy leads to more individual participation. According to Rogers (1969), whose theoretical model is probably the most realistic and complex, the end products of modernization are people who are in touch with the new and different society around them. These people are aware of the different options open to them and their children relative to those available for their fathers and grandfathers. Not only are modern people aware of their changing society but also they are willing to participate in it.

A crucial and much debated issue of theories of modernization concerns the end product; is it a homogeneous society? For our purposes in the text, the crucial question is: *Does a unilinear modernization process mean a convergence of all family systems toward a "modern" family system—one especially tailored for a modern society?*

Inkeles appears convinced that there is a convergence at the individual level that is identifiable regardless of the specific culture of origin. "In reviewing the results of our research of modernization, one must be struck by the exceptional stability with which variables such as education, factory experience, and urbanism maintain absolute and relative strength of their impact on individual modernity despite the great variation in culture of the men undergoing the experience and in the levels of development characterizing the cultures in which they live" (Inkeles, 1969:225). Other authors (Feldman and Hurd, 1966; Weinberg, 1969) concerned with the social rather than the individual level offer support of Inkeles's contention of convergence by suggesting that the institutions of society are interdependent yet are led by the economic institution and industrialization toward a uniformity of social structure. In disagreement, Wilbert Moore (1965) contends that diversity is maintained because of cultural forces even where levels of modernization and industrialization are essentially the same. In other words, the influence of the forces of modernization must pass through a powerful cultural filter, with the product being less than uniform across cultures.

What, then, do the modernization theories with unilinear focus suggest about familial change? They suggest (a) a move from the extended toward the nuclear family system; (b) a family unit in which the participation of individual members increasingly occurs outside the family itself; (c) a family system that is primarily a recipient rather than an instigator of change; and (d) a family system that is societally subordinate to the economic, political, and other institutional spheres of activity. A key point to remember is that the modernization theories posit a unilinear development from traditional to modern, regardless of whether the topic of concern is the society, the family, or the individual.

## Devlopmental Social Change

As discussed at length in Chapter 2, the developmental conceptual framework operates under the assumption that systems, whether they be human beings, family units, the institution of the family, or entire societies, go through stages of life that approximate birth, growth through adolescence to maturity, and then decline until death. If one's focus of attention is on individuals, or units that have an identity only through a particular constellation of individuals, the developmental approach will work. When the focus expands to a system that has little difficulty replacing its worn-out components, a zealous advocacy of stages of growth is tactically indefensible.

*What impact will modern technology have on the traditional polygynous Muslim family?*

Perhaps the best example of a developmental theory of familial change appeared in 1949. Carle Zimmerman, then a rural sociologist at the University of Minnesota, was unimpressed by the anthropological

Standard Oil of N.J. Collection, University of Louisville Archives

data available about preliterate tribes as evidence of the development of Western family systems. In fact, he considered such data irrelevant. Besides, according to Zimmerman, primitive peoples are not necessarily representative of the earlier stages of development of the Western family.

The scope of Zimmerman's work is extensive. Zimmerman attempted to study familial change from about 1500 B.C. to the present, organizing his data around centuries and within epochs by types of families and stages of development. The three types of family for Zimmerman were the trustee, the domestic, and the atomistic. For the Greek, Roman, Medieval-Modern, and Future epochs he had the following stages of familial development: primitive trustee, developed trustee, domestic, free atomistic, and anarchial atomistic. One other point should be made here. Zimmerman contended that the family system is in a constant state of competition with the church and the state for the control of its members. As the family goes through various stages of development it alternates with the church and state as to who has the ultimate power over individuals within the society.

THE TRUSTEE FAMILY. For Zimmerman, the trustee family is the most primitive in terms of its appearance in the history of Western civilization. The living members of the trustee family see themselves as one link in a family that is immortal—they are the trustees of the family's bloodline, its property and identity, and they are responsible to both ancestors and posterity for perpetuating the family. The Roman family is used by Zimmerman as an example of the trustee type. The Roman patriarch had extensive powers over the life and death of his wife and children—the power was his to exercise for the benefit of the family whose trust he had inherited.

According to Zimmerman, when the trustee family is dominant, the state is organized around the various trustee family lines. These trustee families combine to make up the state. There is little or no need in this type of situation for laws dealing with familial activities such as divorce or marriage since the family has pervasive and moral authority to operate.

Under the trustee family the civilization moves toward greatness. However, such an imbalance of power and authority, although it leads to wealth because of cheap labor under strict supervision, also produces widespread abuse of the authority and competition/conflict among the various trustee family lines. In such a situation the state and church institutions develop rather autonomous bases of power and authority to check these abuses. At this juncture the domestic type of family emerges.

THE DOMESTIC FAMILY. Because it shares authority over its members with the state and church, encourages individualism within reasonable bounds, and protects the rights of individual family members against authoritarian abuses, the domestic family represents the high point of family

85

development. The domestic family occurs in the stage of maturity for a civilization. However, the movement toward individualism is a force that predestines the destruction of both the family and the society, according to Zimmerman.

THE ATOMISTIC FAMILY.  This third type of family signals the beginning of the end in Zimmerman's theoretical model. With increasing individualism the state becomes powerful while the authority of the family over its members progressively declines. The pursuit of individual aspirations and goals operates at odds with the pursuit of goals of the family as a unit, and the results are low morale and lack of cohesion. Marriage becomes a civil contract with no moral commitments to prevent the widespread use of divorce to terminate an arrangement that fails to satisfy individual goals.

Zimmerman was convinced that the focus on individual rights for children, the emergence of feminist movements demanding equal individualized rights for women, the trend toward fewer children per family, and the independence of the young from the control and influence of their elders constituted the death knell for the family as a crucial carrier of the culture. As the family loses its power, socialization of the young becomes more and more anchored in the public sphere of society, and the society, according to Zimmerman's predictions, disintegrates. In other words, atomism leads to anarchy, and no society can long survive under such a condition.

It is obvious that Zimmerman is less than value free in his analysis. In fact, his three types of family are good examples of ideological axe grinding. His only saving virtue is the far-ranging historical scope of his study. Although it is not explicit in his work, Zimmerman was probably influenced to a great extent by the times in which he lived. He experienced the 1929 depression and two major world wars with the societal upheavals that those events brought. In addition, he observed the rather radical experiments conducted on the family by the Soviet government in Russia. He was closely associated with the Russian sociologist Pitirim Sorokin, who went through the turmoil in the Soviet Union as a result of the overthrow of the Czar by the Menshevik-Bolshevik coalition. Sorokin barely escaped a Bolshevik firing squad and came to the University of Minnesota at the invitation of Zimmerman. All of these contextual influences can be read into his very pessimistic appraisal of the condition of the family in Western civilization and the impending death of Western civilization itself. Needless to say, no one accepts Zimmerman's model as predictive, only as descriptive, and a questionable description at best.

## Functional Social Change

Perhaps the best way to introduce William F. Ogburn's model of social and familial change is to compare his approach to that of Zimmerman. Zimmerman's theoretical notions were applied to the broad expanse of

Photo by Charles Van Schaick, courtesy of the State Historical Society of Wisconsin

*Tied to the soil and frequently extended in form, the premodern American family demanded close cooperation from its members.*

history, but Ogburn limited his views to American society from colonial days to the present. Second, Ogburn was much more interested in measuring the impact of change while Zimmerman was preoccupied with interpreting history. Third and most basic, for Ogburn the family is a recipient of change, almost always the dependent variable, while Zimmerman saw the family system as the locus and instigator of change.

Ogburn's thesis about the changing family is closely tied to his better-known theory of culture lag. The culture-lag theory suggests that culture has two faces—material and nonmaterial. The material culture (technology) tends to change much more rapidly than the nonmaterial culture (ideas, knowledge, values, attitudes, customs, and traditions). Ogburn predicted that over a sustained period of time the material culture would so completely outdistance the nonmaterial culture that society would, in effect, fall apart at the seams. Even as he was writing about the family in 1938, he detected signs of this societal disorganization in the increasing divorce and illegitimacy rates, the increasing proportion of voluntary childless couples, and the rise in youth rebellion, juvenile delinquency, and alienation in general.

Taking the colonial family as a base Ogburn detailed what he felt were the decreasing functions of the American family: (a) providing economic independence, (b) conferring status, (c) educating, socializing,

87

(d) giving protection, (e) providing religious training, (f) providing recreation, and (g) giving affection. Ogburn seemed to think that the colonial family was a tightly knit cohesive unit, self-sustained and contained with little need for or interaction with other agencies or institutions. His writings imply that the prevailing type of colonial family (a) produced most if not all it used or consumed, (b) legitimated individuals in the community by conferring on them a recognizable identity or status, (c) educated its children both formally and informally, (d) protected itself against all threats without outside aid, (e) was God-fearing and quite strict in its practice of religion, (f) provided for the recreational needs of its members with rather frequent social events, and finally (g) was a warm and loving group in which a person could feel secure and protected.

It is quite apparent that Ogburn accepted the idealized view of life in the colonies. Thus his conception of changes that occurred between the 1700s and the 1900s are somewhat contaminated by poor baseline data. If Ogburn thought that the seven functions mentioned earlier were the "ties that bind" in the early American family, his views on the modern family (Ogburn, 1938, as adapted by Winch and Goodman, 1968) indicate that broad changes must have occurred in the intervening period:

> The dilemma of the modern family is caused by the loss of many of these functions in recent times. The economic function has gone to the factory, store, office, and restaurant, leaving little of economic activity to the family of the city apartment. About half of education has been transferred to the schools, where the teacher is a part-time or substitute parent. Recreation is found in moving pictures, parks, city streets, clubs, with bridge and radio at home. Religion doesn't seem to make as much difference in family matters as formerly, grace at meals and family prayers are rare. As to protection, the child is protected at home, but the state helps also with its child labor laws and reform schools. The police and social legislation indicate how the protective function has been transferred to the state, as has the educational function. Family status has been lost in marked degree along with these other functions in an age of mobility and large cities. It is the individual that has become more important and the family less so. On the other hand the family still remains the center of affectional life and is the only recognized place for producing children.

For the moment let us assume that Ogburn's analysis is correct. This means that in less than 200 years the American family has essentially lost to other institutions all seven of its basic functions. Such a fantastic shift in functions obviously did not occur—at least not to the degree suggested by Ogburn. What is probably true is that the seven functions were all performed to some degree by most colonial families, but only by necessity. Information now available supports the idea that few colonial families had a rigorous and active religious, educational, or recreational schedule. In addition, with the expansion of the frontier many people left their families and communities behind, and thus the status-conferring function was not of substantial importance to most early colonists. That leaves the economic, defensive, and affectional functions, all of which were probably less pure in practice than Ogburn suggested.

Certain functions that were thought to be ideally the primary responsibility of the family in colonial days are now being performed by large bureaucracies. How much this represents a real shift in functions or just the performance of functions left by default by the family institution is not known. Whether this apparent shift in functions signals a fatal disease in the American family system is another question.

Of particular relevance to the discussion to follow in this chapter is the presumed cause of the decreasing functions of the family in America. Ogburn's life straddled the years when the automobile, airplane, telephone, radio, and other marvelous technological inventions made the world seem much smaller. They were such radically new means of dealing with problems—particularly those of time, distance, and communication—that a large number of social scientists predicted the worst possible consequences for the family, and for religion in particular. Ogburn was no exception. The crucial point of Ogburn's view, however, was that he interpreted changes in the family's function as resulting from changes in the technology available in society, all of which were possible because of increasing industrialization and urbanization. A diagram of Ogburn's theoretical model would look like this:

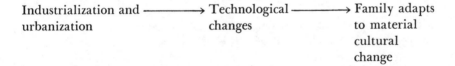

Industrialization and ⟶ Technological ⟶ Family adapts
urbanization                changes           to material
                                              cultural
                                              change

The functional-change theme has been central in attempts of sociologists and other social scientists to understand what changes have occurred in the family, why they occurred, and what the consequences are for individual family members, family units, and society in general.


## THE FAMILY IN TRANSITION

Having reviewed some early attempts to deal with social change in general and its impact on the family, we will examine the three most significant studies of family change conducted to date. The first study, by William J. Goode, was built on some of the ideas suggested by Ogburn. The second study, by Meyer Nimkoff and Russell Middleton, was also influenced by Ogburn in that Ogburn and Nimkoff collaborated on several books, including *Technology and the Changing Family.* The last study to be covered in this section, by Robert F. Winch and Rae Lesser Blumberg, tries to improve on shortcomings in both the Goode and the Nimkoff-Middleton studies.

## William J. Goode (1963)

In his book *World Revolution and Family Patterns*, Goode synthesized the theoretical notions of a number of his predecessors in studying how the family system reacts to societal change. The hypotheses that Goode used as a base are as follows:

### Goode's Conjugal Family Thesis

The term *conjugal family* was developed by Goode as an attempt to avoid the confusion generated by what Parsons called the isolated nuclear family. *Isolated* seems to imply no contact with kinsmen beyond the nuclear family of procreation. Goode recognized that although the respective families of orientation and the families of one's siblings are not an integral part of one's family life, they do constitute a loose network of kin ties. That loose kin network, the conjugal family, does occasionally coordinate its activities and act as if it were an extended family rather than discrete nuclear units. However, this type of activity is usually not regularized and occurs primarily as a result of some crisis. Under ordinary circumstances the conjugal family interacts on an irregular basis with the two families of orientation, selected sibling families, and the families of married children.

Viewing the movement toward the conjugal family system as a rather pervasive ideology, Goode listed several of the main characteristics of a conjugal family system:

1. The extended family pattern becomes rare, and corporate kin structures disappear.
2. A relatively free choice of spouse is possible, based on love, and an independent household is set up (that is, neolocal residence increases).
3. Dowry and bride price disappear (that is, marriage becomes less an economic arrangement between families).
4. Marriages between kin become less common (for example, particularly cross-cousin marriages which served the purposes of keeping wealth within the family).
5. Authority of the parent over the child and of the husband over the wife diminishes.
6. Equality between the sexes is greater; the legal system moves toward equality of inheritance among all children.

1. Louis Wirth (1938). As urbanism as a way of life diffuses, the individual becomes increasingly free of the kinship group that was characteristic of rural America.

2. Carle Zimmerman (1947). As the family becomes more atomistic, the influence of the family over its members decreases.

If Goode's description of the conjugal family system sounds extremely familiar and perfectly logical, it is, especially for a modern and complex society like that of the United States. In fact, one of the major criticisms of Goode's discussion of social change is that he concentrated on societies ranging only from relatively complex traditional to highly complex industrial-urban (see Winch and Blumberg, 1968). A second criticism of Goode's work—one raised by Goode himself—concerns the ambiguity inherent in the term *urbanization*. He says, "The term 'urbanization' covered far too many variables to be usable in quantitative and precise research. Thus, 'urbanization' is not the *cause* of changes; it *is* those changes." A third criticism, again coming from Goode (1964:3) concerns the impact of industrialization on the family and what we are referring to when we say "family":

> Nevertheless, among the various arguments which have been developed to indicate the relationship between industrialism and the family, none of them has been able to show precisely *where* the impact occurs. It can be shown, as I and others have done, that the ideal-typical nuclear or conjugal family is relatively well "fitted" to the open-class industrial system, whether capitalist or not, but precisely how these two *interact* with one another is not at all clear even in theory. Specifically, we do not distinguish three separate sets of family complexes: the ideal, the ideal-typical, and the real. All are important, but how do they interact?

The last point to be made is not a criticism but rather a statement of fact. We conceptualize the processes of industrialization and urbanization as antecedent causal variables in family change when there is ample evidence suggesting that the modal family type prior to the industrial revolution was the conjugal family. This type was evidently more prevalent among the working classes. One would expect, theoretically at least, that the families most successful within the industrial-urban society, the upper classes, would be more prone to exhibit the characteristics of the conjugal family system. Such is not the case. In fact, the working classes, who would be expected to have the most extensive kin networks, were more conjugal than their upper-class counterparts.

91

3. Talcott Parsons (1949, 1955). The isolated nuclear family will increasingly become the dominant form of family life as the society becomes more differentiated through industrialization and urbanization.

4. Ralph Linton (1949). The family system is in a state of virtual collapse as a result of the "extreme degeneration of the extended family, the increasing anonymity of individuals and conjugal family groups, and the decrease of sanctions to prevent marital dissolution."

5. William F. Ogburn and Meyer F. Nimkoff (1955). Change in the American family has resulted from (a) cities, (b) technological inventions in manufacture and transportation, (c) the invention of contraceptives, (d) discoveries in science affecting education and religion, and (e) changing ideologies regarding democracy, the welfare state, humanitarianism, and education not directly traceable to technology.

Goode's synthesis suggests that as societies move toward modernization, industrialization, and urbanization the seemingly diverse family forms in traditional societies (patrilineal, matrilineal, other; polygynous or monogamous, extended or nuclear) all move toward a convergence into what he calls a *conjugal family.*

Although criticisms can be found for any piece of research, particularly a systematic synthesis such as Goode's, it is generally conceded that Goode's study is a very penetrating and useful analysis. It is considered the benchmark against which most studies of familial change at the macro level must be evaluated.

### M. F. Nimkoff and Russell Middleton, "Types of Family and Types of Economy" (1960)

If Goode can be criticized for focusing on only the more complex societies, Nimkoff and Middleton should be scored for focusing their attention on the other end of the continuum, on the simpler societies. Nimkoff and Middleton were interested in the relationship between the predominant economic activities of a society and its type of family system. Their data were from Murdock's World Ethnographic Sample. However, the final sample consisted of only 549 societies, since data as to family type were not available for sixteen societies.

THE DEPENDENT VARIABLE: TYPE OF FAMILY SYSTEM. Of the 549 societies, 301 or 54.8 percent were classified as extended family systems while 248 or 45.2 percent were characterized by the independent family system. A system was labeled independent if (a) most of the familial groups did not include more than one nuclear or polygamous family, and (b) the head of a family of procreation was not subject to the authority or economic control of his relatives. The other family systems were classified as extended. This included the classical extended, joint, and stem families.

**TABLE 4–3**

Economic Subsistence Patterns in Murdock's World Ethnographic Sample

| TYPE OF ECONOMY | DEGREE OF DOMINANCE-IMPORTANCE | | | | |
|---|---|---|---|---|---|
| | DOMI-NANT | CODOMI-NANT | IMPOR-TANT | UNIM-PORTANT | ABSENT |
| 1. Agriculture | a | b | c | d | e |
| 2. Animal hus-bandry | f | g | h | i | j |
| 3. Fishing, shell fishing and marine fish-ing | k | l | m | n | o |
| 4. Hunting and gathering | p | q | r | s | t |

SOURCE: Adapted from M. F. Nimkoff and Russell Middleton, "Types of Family and Types of Economy," *American Journal of Sociology* 66(1960):215–225; by permission of the University of Chicago Press.

THE INDEPENDENT VARIABLE: ECONOMIC SUBSISTENCE PATTERN.    When Murdock coded the economic factor in his World Ethnographic Sample, societies were classified according to the major types of food-getting activities and their dominance and importance. Table 4–3 indicates some of the basic categories that evolved from Murdock's classification. It is quickly obvious that there are a minimum of 16 possible categories of subsistence. When combinations are introduced such as agriculture dominant, animal husbandry important, the number of possible subsistence economies expands geometrically. Nimkoff and Middleton started with 11 basic subsistence patterns and then further narrowed their focus to 6, as shown in Table 4–4.

Nimkoff and Middleton did not say that the type of subsistence pattern directly caused the type of family system found in a society. In fact, they posited that the influence of subsistence patterns on family types is modified and filtered through three intervening economic factors: (a) size of the food supply, (b) degree of spatial mobility involved in subsistence activities, and (c) kind and amount of family property. Their theoretical model appears as follows:

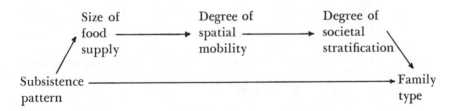

93

What they found essentially was that the independent family system seems to occur whenever families move around a great deal in order to have enough food (hunting and gathering). Because these families frequently must cover great distances to obtain food, the accumulation of property, especially fixed property such as land and houses, is minimal, and the degree of stratification in the society is also quite low. Everybody

**TABLE 4–4**
**Effect of Subsistence Pattern on Family Type**

| SUBSISTENCE PATTERN | FAMILY TYPE | | | |
|---|---|---|---|---|
| | INDEPENDENT | | EXTENDED | |
| | NO. | % | NO. | % |
| *Ungrouped Categories* | | | | |
| 1. Agriculture and animal husbandry codominant | 2 | 11.1 | 16 | 88.9 |
| 2. Agriculture and fishing codominant | 4 | 22.2 | 14 | 77.8 |
| 3. Agriculture and hunting codominant | 1 | 33.3 | 2 | 66.7 |
| 4. Fishing dominant | 15 | 37.5 | 25 | 62.5 |
| 5. Agriculture dominant, animal husbandry important | 72 | 39.8 | 109 | 60.2 |
| 6. Agriculture dominant, animal husbandry unimportant or absent | 73 | 45.6 | 87 | 54.4 |
| 7. Animal husbandry dominant or codominant with fishing | 21 | 48.8 | 22 | 51.2 |
| 8. Fishing and hunting codominant | 7 | 50.0 | 7 | 50.0 |
| 9. Hunting-gathering dominant, agriculture or animal husbandry important | 10 | 55.6 | 8 | 44.4 |
| 10. Hunting-gathering dominant, fishing important, agriculture or animal husbandry absent or unimportant | 22 | 73.3 | 8 | 26.7 |
| 11. Hunting-gathering dominant, agriculture, animal husbandry, and fishing absent or unimportant | 20 | 83.3 | 4 | 16.7 |
| *Grouped Categories* | | | | |
| (a) 1 | 2 | 11 | 16 | 89 |
| (b) 2, 3, 5, 6 | 150 | 41 | 212 | 59 |
| (c) 4, 7, 8 | 43 | 44 | 54 | 56 |
| (d) 9 | 10 | 56 | 8 | 44 |
| (e) 10 | 22 | 73 | 8 | 27 |
| (f) 11 | 20 | 83 | 4 | 17 |

SOURCE: Adapted from M. F. Nimkoff and Russell Middleton, "Types of Family and Types of Economy," *American Journal of Sociology* 66(1960):215–225. Reprinted by permission of the University of Chicago Press.

NOTE: Read percentages across rather than down.

**FIGURE 4–1**
**The Curvilinear Hypothesis**

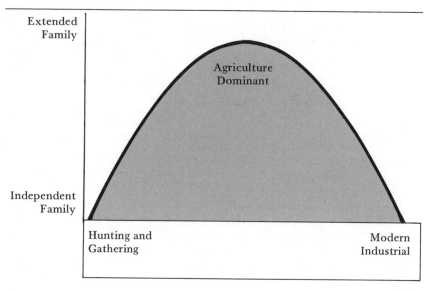

pitches in to help, with little division of labor. On the other hand, the extended family system is associated with the development of agriculture, the limited necessity to move about to gather necessary food items, and a fixed and rather extensive stratification system. Nimkoff and Middleton conclude their study by noting that "the modern industrial society, with its small independent family, is then like the simpler hunting and gathering society and, in part, apparently for some of the same reasons, namely, limited need for family labor and physical mobility. The hunter is mobile because he pursues the game: the industrial worker, the job."

In this observation, Nimkoff and Middleton offered a clue as to how their study of simpler societies could be pieced together with Goode's study of societies at the more complex and modern level. That clue suggests what is called a *curvilinear hypothesis*. Figure 4–1 illustrates the meaning of the curvilinear hypothesis and how it relates to the changing family through time.

### *Robert F. Winch and Rae Lesser Blumberg, "Societal Complexity and Familial Organization" (1968)*

Winch and Blumberg took the implicit curvilinear hypothesis from Nimkoff and Middleton and attempted to test it. In addition, they attempted to modify and extend Goode's contention that family systems

95

throughout the world are converging toward a conjugal family organization and ideology.

SOCIETAL COMPLEXITY VERSUS WORLD REVOLUTION.   Winch and Blumberg recommend that the term *societal complexity* be substituted for Goode's concept of world revolution. Goode's term is considered to be too closely tied to the idea of rapidly increasing industrialization-urbanization-modernization, whereas societal complexity can be viewed as a continuum ranging from least complex to most complex. The obvious value of using the term *societal complexity* is that all societies (those used by Nimkoff and Middleton and those used by Goode) can be considered in the same study.

FAMILY TYPE VERSUS FAMILIAL STRUCTURE.   Both Goode, and Nimkoff and Middleton dealt with rather simple and somewhat limited concepts as their dependent variable. Goode focused almost exclusively on a structural unit—the conjugal family—whereas Nimkoff and Middleton dichotomized family systems into independent and extended. Winch and Blumberg (1968:75–76) contend that familial structure can be expanded to include the following:

> Nuclear family: consists of three possible sets of role-positions (a) husband-father, (b) wife-mother, (c) child-sibling.

By having more than one husband-father the nuclear family can be labeled polyandrous. With more than one wife-mother the nuclear family can be viewed as polygynous. Of course, there can be more than one child in a nuclear family. Whenever there are one or more persons within a family for each role-position, the nuclear family is complete.

> Extended family: exists when there is at least one dyad not considered a part of the nuclear set of role-positions. For example, if it is possible to have a husband-mother-in-law dyad in a household the family is, in essence, extended. Of course, any number of non-nuclear dyads can occur in an extended family.
>
> Incomplete nuclear family: exists when one of the three role-positions is missing, such as married couples without children or mother and children with the husband-father absent.
>
> Domestic family: exists when the occupants of a household are related to each other by blood, marriage, or adoption. An example of this might be when a married man and his wife live with his brother and his unmarried sisters and one or two cousins or uncles.

Winch and Blumberg were attempting to explicate some of the more subtle distinctions that should be made when discussing the family

**TABLE 4–5**
**Familial Functions**

| FUNCTION TYPE | FUNCTIONS PRIMARILY | |
|---|---|---|
| | INSTRUMENTAL | EXPRESSIVE |
| Basic societal | Reproductive | Religious |
| | Economic | |
| | Political | |
| | a Educational | Socializing |
| Derived familial | Position-conferring | Emotional gratification |

SOURCE: Robert F. Winch and Rae Lesser Blumberg, "Societal Complexity and Familial Organization," pp. 70–92 in Robert F. Winch and Louis Wolf Goodman (eds.), *Selected Studies in Marriage and the Family* (New York: Holt, Rinehart and Winston, Inc., 1968), p. 77. By permission of Holt, Rinehart and Winston, Inc.

a Here the socializing-educational function is divided into components proposed to be primarily instrumental and primarily expressive.

type or familial structure. Just describing the family system as independent or extended ignores a wide variety of subtypes under these two general headings.

FAMILIAL STRUCTURE AS AN ADDITIONAL DEPENDENT VARIABLE. Winch and Blumberg, taking a cue from Ogburn's discussion of the functions of the family, suggest that an adequate study of the changing family must not be limited to structure alone. All families, regardless of structure, perform certain functions for the society. In addition, from the performance of these societal functions are derived two more exclusive family functions that are not shared with other institutions.

INTERVENING FILTERS OF THE INFLUENCE OF SOCIETAL COMPLEXITY ON FAMILIAL STRUCTURE AND FAMILIAL FUNCTIONS. Winch and Blumberg used a suburban Chicago sample and a random sample of the state of Wisconsin partially to replicate the Nimkoff and Middleton study in an urban-industrial society. As variables intervening between societal complexity and degree of extended familism they used (a) ethnicity (that is, religious affiliation—Protestant, Catholic, Jewish), (b) migration, and (c) rural-urban residence. The data from their two samples also supported the curvilinear hypothesis implied by Nimkoff and Middleton. The Jewish respondents were more likely to show extended familism than Protestants and Catholics, nonmigrants were more familistic than migrants, and urban dwellers were less familistic than their rural counterparts.

In a more recent study Winch and Blumberg (1972) recoded and reanalyzed the World Ethnographic Sample data used by Nimkoff and Middleton. Their conclusions indicate that they have achieved a synthesis of the linear hypothesis from Goode with the curvilinear hypothesis.

> Our findings agree with those of Nimkoff-Middleton in that the linear or monotonic trend over the simpler societies of the Ethnographic Atlas is for the more complex to have the larger familial systems. Our data also agree with Goode in that there is a tendency for the more developed societies to have smaller family systems. Our data reconcile the two findings by showing that there is a point of inflection, with the maximum proportion of large familial systems occurring among societies with extensive or intensive agriculture without irrigation, in societies whose largest towns are in the range 200–5,000, that have a system of hereditary aristocracy, and one or two levels of political hierarchy beyond the local community.
>
> Accordingly, we believe that we have been able to provide an evidential basis for the curvilinear hypothesis that has been stated more or less as an accepted fact by writers from Lowrie to Marsh. [Winch and Blumberg, 1972: 919]

## ADDITIONAL SOURCES OF CHANGE

The discussion thus far has emphasized macro-level forces like urbanization and industrialization. No one would question their impact on the family system and on society in general. America has been literally transformed from an agrarian-based rural society to one in which most of the populace live in large cities and work in the service sector. It is difficult to relate personally to such impersonal and large-scale forces as urbanization and industrialization. Other forces of social change have a more immediate personal impact upon us.

One such force is the changing role of women in society. For most, if not all, of recorded history women have been subordinated to men, functioning more as appendages to men's life careers than as fully equal individuals in their own right. Fortunately, this is changing, particularly in the developed countries of the world. The evidence is seen everywhere —in the proportion of all women who are working outside the home, in the proportions of women in the labor force who have children under the ages of eighteen and six, in the percentage of women enrolled in graduate and professional schools, and in the percentage of families that can be labelled "dual career." All of these signs attest to the fact that options available to women today are not now markedly different from those available to men. This is, after all, the key to the women's liberation movement—to produce equality in options. The effects on the family and family life of women's changing roles are just now becoming apparent.

Some of these effects are: (a) later ages at first marriage; (b) longer periods of time when both spouses are in the labor force; (c) delayed or permanently postponed entry into parenthood; (d) a greater degree of spouse sharing of tasks formerly and traditionally relegated to the wife/mother; (e) a greater emphasis on the expressive behavior of males; and (f) a greater role of the father in family life. The effects of a major social intervention such as sexual equality are usually slow in coming. Vestiges of the traditional concepts of male and female will remain with us for a long time. Nevertheless, progress is being made, and slowly but surely the changing role of women is transforming practically every facet of life in America—especially life in the family.

Another force of social change is housed in a very unlikely source of social change—the legal institution. The law has always been conservative, imposing restraints on the population and on behavioral trends that seem to challenge traditional customs and practices. However, in recent years the law has been altered and interpreted in ways that reflect a recognition of a new milieu, a new family environment, a new reality.

This is seen most clearly in the passage of no-fault divorce laws. Family law, with its roots deeply embedded in the English common law, has long emphasized the subordinate role of women and the importance

*Age and Sex: These traditional criteria for excluding some people from the labor force are no longer operative.*

Jean-Claude Lejeune

of maintaining adversary proceedings in marital dissolution cases (that is, the charade that one party is guilty, and thus by inference the other is innocent). While legally coherent, such a principle is far from the realities of everyday life. The fact that legal experts have incorporated aspects of reality into the law through no-fault procedures signals a major change in the legal institution, one that may have far-reaching implications for how the family is defined and what the legal responsibilities of husbands and wives are.

Another example of the law acting as a force in social change in family-related matters is seen in recent court decisions giving cohabitants (men and women living together without being legally married) property rights, which may be an important consideration if the relationship is terminated. Tradition-bound family law does not recognize cohabiting partners as a real and legal status. Given the prevalence of this phenomenon (see Chapter 12), it is noteworthy that the legal institution has begun to consider the rights of partners whether the union is legally constituted or not.

A third force of social change that has a daily impact on family life concerns changes in the work experiences of persons in industrial economies. The industrial revolution separated the work place from the home; it also produced tightly scheduled and monitored work experiences and work for pay—wages and salaries. For most of history men and women have had to work extremely long hours in order to meet survival needs (food, clothing, shelter). In this postindustrial age of relative affluence the work week for most of us is short and the income sufficient to justify expenditures for recreation. Further, there are many recreational options available, usually in close proximity and within the price range of the common family.

This new freedom from work has important implications for family life. It has produced on a large scale opportunities for families to become involved in common activities as a unit, not as separate individuals. There is more time and more money to do more things together. This has the potential of being a cohesive force for the American family, pulling together a unit that many have claimed was falling apart because of individuation and the pressures and demands urban life places on individuals, marital partners, and families.


## CONCLUSIONS

The first goal of this chapter was to communicate how difficult it is to assess social change. It is easy to say glibly that we live in a society where change is constant and pervasive; to pinpoint what is changing, how, and what its consequences are, is not so glibly stated. The second goal was to discuss social change from a general sociological perspective. Many of you will perhaps take a course during your undergraduate days entitled Social Change. Since sociology is an integrated discipline, there is no reason why you should not be learning things in this course and text that will carry over into your study of other topics. The third goal was to present the ways that the family has been studied as a changing system, interacting with other systems of society, particularly the economic system.

By now you should be convinced that the family system receives many stimuli from other major systems of society that would lead to an alteration or adaptation in familial structure and functions. What was not emphasized is that the family can also be an active instigator of change —an independent as well as a dependent variable. In effect, we have looked at the family as only a passive receiving system.

To indicate adequately how the family can simultaneously serve as both a recipient and instigator of social change is a difficult task. Perhaps the best way of showing how this can occur is to refer to a very comprehensive and complex model of social change developed by Wendell Bell and James Mau (1971). Unfortunately, with a topic as complex as social change it is not possible to rely on a simplistic model. The Bell and Mau model (Figure 4–2) is called a *cybernetic-decision model* because (1) it recognizes that there are interlocking aspects of the real world that feedback information in a reciprocal (A $\longleftrightarrow$ B) fashion; and (2) it recognizes that all social change is a function of decisions made at the individual, group, social system, or societal-cultural levels. We will use only one example to illustrate how the model works.

PART A OF THE MODEL. The individuals in a society live in different worlds (that is, social systems) and these systems and the roles we play in them are affected by the environment, the available resources, and the technologies for dealing with the environment and resources. If we do not belong to organizations explicitly designed to provide the functions listed under organizational settings, we live in a family setting where these activities do occur with regularity. To make the model more easily understood, the example of a specific decision made by a young couple will serve.

This young couple has two boys, James, who is six, and William, who is two. One of the decisions they as a couple must make concerns fertility and contraception. All the categories listed in Part A of the Bell-Mau model are taken into consideration by them as they plan their family. They have a choice among types of contraceptives to use, or not to use contraceptives "with planning" or "reckless abandon." Their place in the society and the way they view the population, ecosystem, and future resources all affect their thoughts about their family.

PART B. In trying to decide whether to stop at two children or add a third child, they look first to the past. Their beliefs about the past are mostly memories of the joys and difficulties of having a child and being

101

## FIGURE 4–2
## Cybernetic-Decision Model of Social Change

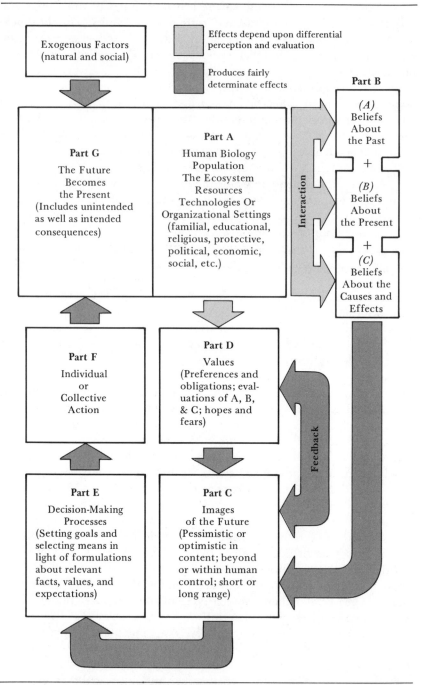

SOURCE: Based on a figure in "Images of the Future: Theory and Research Strategies," by Wendell Bell and James A. Mau, in *The Sociology of the Future: Theory, Cases, and Annotated Bibliography,* edited by Wendell Bell and James A. Mau © 1971 by Russell Sage Foundation, New York.

parents to a newborn baby. Add to this their beliefs about the present, consisting of their evaluation of parenthood and how the addition of a third child would affect their present family (that is, demands on resources, demands on themselves, demands on their two sons). The third contingency, beliefs about causes and effects, is an integration of personal and societal considerations. Their perception of their responsibility in keeping the population explosion under wraps says, Stop at two! Their perception of their own familial goals says, "Although it would be nice to have a girl, it would be unfair to our two boys to add a third child given the possible effect that would have on future resources available to our family and its members."

PART C. Thus, when the three sections of Part B of the model are added, a fairly determinant effect on our image of the future is that they are optimistic—at least at the personal level. They see that their goals and perceptions of life in the future are within their grasp.

PART D. Their images of the future serve to reinforce their values about parenthood and the type of family context they want to provide for their children. They prefer a small conjugal unit and feel obligated to provide such for their sons. The cybernetic feedback is that their preferences and obligations (their values) further refine their image of the future. They find themselves more and more committed to the two-child family.

PART E. As they move back and forth between Part C and Part D, this young couple have made a decision to use the most effective means of contraception available in order to achieve their goals. This is a cognitive process effected through an on-going communication process. Like most couples they frequently say to themselves and to each other, "Wouldn't it be nice to have a little girl?" They then go back through the whole process to further reinforce their commitment to stop at two children.

PART F. As the commitment becomes more and more solidified they practice what they have been preaching—they use the contraceptives to ensure a two-child family. Millions of couples, acting individually, produce a collective action, which leads into Part G of the model.

PART G. The future becomes the present because numerous couples, acting individually as a result of projecting themselves into the future, make the future happen in the present. The intention (manifest function) is to provide a high-quality home life for the family (in their case, James and William). Unintended consequences (latent functions) also accrue from the flow of the cybernetic-decisional model in action. For example, fewer children are available for adoption; increased commitment to verbal communication about sexual behavior is necessary because there are fewer parturition periods; if the pill is related to higher rates of cancer among

103

women, then a greater proportion of the female population is taking the cancer risk; more women are freed sooner from their housewife-mother-chauffeur roles to re-enter the labor market. Of course, as the future becomes the present the categories in Part A of the model are again operative, and the process of becoming begins again.

The real value of the Bell and Mau model of social change is that (1) it allows the possibility that the family is an initiator as well as a receiver of social change (that is, the family is not merely a passive force in society); and (2) it combines macro-level (societal) and micro-level (individual) processes into the same model, thus more closely approximating reality as we all know it.

It should be noted that although the answers are not all in, progress is being made. The amount and quality of the data now becoming available make it more likely that a fuller understanding of how the family changes, why it changes, and what the consequences are of those changes is just around the proverbial corner. However, a relatively complete understanding of the family, marriage, and social change is not so close at hand. We are just now taking the beginning steps; it will be some time before the race is won.

## SOME POSSIBLE IMPLICATIONS

*Not only is social change ubiquitous, but its ubiquity is accelerating at a rate that can and does seem to produce what Toffler (1970) called "future shock." The shock waves of change have affected all the institutions of society, and particularly the family. As we move toward the twenty-first century the world is beset by some of the negative consequences of change—overpopulation caused by excessive fertility; massive environmental pollution; dwindling energy resources; an increase in pathological aggression and diseases, perhaps as a result of overcrowding in decaying and aesthetically ugly urban centers; internal strife and contention within societies and wars among societies; and other indices of disorganization too numerous to mention.*

*Some social critics claim that these negative consequences of social change will be endemic as long as we are committed to continued growth in all sectors of society and facets of life. The solution called for is a state of no growth, a curbing or a stop to change. One possible implication of this proposal is stagnation. If we were able to institute a policy of no growth, it is possible that the creative energies of humans and human societies would attain a state of atrophy, a kind of human paralysis. Can humans and their organizations and societies exist in a state of no growth? Is social change something akin to a basic human need? Can the creative energies of human beings be rechanneled in a society where growth in the industrial and economic sectors of society has slowed down or stopped? What would be the effect of a state of no growth on the human family?*

*Another facet of the study of social change and the family that has implications worth considering concerns what social psychologists call the "experimenter effect"—the change occurring in subjects being studied that results from the bias introduced by the experimenter and by the fact that the subjects know they are being studied. Is it possible or probable that the mere study of social change is a cause of certain social changes occurring? For example, suppose that a demographic unit of the United Nations is interested in studying how the introduction of a birth-control clinic in an Indian village affects the birth rate and attitudes toward fertility and contraception. Perhaps they do find that the birth rate does decrease markedly. It is quite possible that by their study of social change, the experimenters have also caused some real conflicts within the families in that village and some imbalances in the population density that will in future years create some very real problems for the community and its members.*

*The study of social change and the family is a complex process that may have hidden consequences that are unintended to the manifest purposes of the study. What are some of the other implications of the study of social change and the family?*

Ken Heyman

# 5

# THE WHITE FAMILY IN THE UNITED STATES

*Why is it important to know that the white family in the United States is a modified extended one instead of isolated and nuclear?*

*Is the wife the key link between the family of procreation and the families of orientation?*

*Why is it that geographic and occupational mobility do not seem to produce isolated nuclear families?*

*How and how much is the white family in the United States changing?*

The preceding chapter dealt with broad trends in familial change—trends that were and are evident at the macro level of analysis, trends that relate the family as a system to broad societal processes such as industrialization and urbanization. This chapter narrows the focus to the white American family and brings the unit of analysis down in some instances to individual family units and the roles within those units. Most of the chapter centers on the white, middle-class family for several reasons. First and foremost, most of the research to date has dealt with white, middle-class samples, and it would be presumptuous to impose these data on an examination of the family life of the lower class. Second, Chapter 6 details the prevailing patterns of the under class, using the black family in the United States as an example. Third, those of you from middle-class backgrounds can transpose the material to be covered in this chapter into your own biography.

The period from the early 1940s to the middle 1960s was an epoch in which family sociologists attempted to eliminate some of the myths about the American family and to trace empirically the kinds of relationships that existed to tie families of orientation to families of procreation. Coming out of World War II and living in the Cold War era, students of family life were much influenced by Ogburn's ideas about the defunctionalization of the American family. That period also included the exodus of whites to suburban, class-oriented enclaves and the urban migration of blacks and rural whites.

During this societal upheaval the view of the family was pessimistic at best. The sociologist who has exerted perhaps the greatest influence on how the American family was described is Talcott Parsons. A structure-functionalist, Parsons isolated two salient conceptual dimensions for examining the family. One dimension concerns the types of roles existing within the family. The *instrumental* roles are those that seem to correspond to the stereotypical image of the male in Western society: He provides the income on which the family exists, buys the material conveniences that make life in the family comfortable, represents the family in the occupational and community spheres of activity, serves as a final arbitrator in family disputes, determines where the family shall live, and serves as the final authority over the children. The *expressive* roles in the family are those dealing with what Ogburn and Nimkoff call the social-emotional or affective functions of the family. These role behaviors closely resemble the ideal image of the mother-wife—the cohesive role that holds the family together through thick and thin; the dispenser of love, warmth, and Band-Aids of all kinds. See Table 5–1.

**TABLE 5–1**
**The Parsonian Model**

| TYPES OF ROLES | TYPES OF SOCIETAL NORMS | |
| --- | --- | --- |
| | UNIVERSALISTIC | PARTICULARISTIC |
| Instrumental | Ascription ⟶ | |
| | | ↓ |
| Expressive | ⟵————————Achievement | |

SOURCE: Adapted with permission of Macmillan Publishing Co., Inc., from *The Social System* by Talcott Parsons. Copyright © 1951 by Talcott Parsons.

The second dimension of Parsons's schema concerns the breadth of flexibility exhibited by society's institutions. For example, a family system is *universalistic* if the behaviors required of a role or even a family unit remain inflexible for everyone, regardless of extenuating circumstances. A *particularistic* system, on the other hand, is one in which individuals and families are allowed flexibility by society in role playing because every situation is different. However, there are usually specific conditions that require an alteration of how one plays a role.

With the interplay among instrumental and expressive roles and universalistic and particularistic orientations Parsons was able to study what Winch calls the status-conferring function of the family and how it has changed. The status of a family or family member can evolve out of ascription or achievement. In a society where status is ascribed, the individual is born into a position that is primarily determined by the family's status within the community. Thus a Rockefeller has status because of his or her luck or fate at being born into that family. The status is inherited. Quite naturally, a society in which status is allocated on the basis of achievement places the onus on the individual. Accomplishments are the primary factor in determining the status an individual will have.

When Parsons examined societies that were less urbanized and industrialized (less modern), he found that the family was usually dominated by the male (patriarchal). Since in such societies the family was more tied to the land, the extended family was predominant over the nuclear units that made up the larger unit; the female was subordinate to the male and the young to their elders; and status was obtained by ascription. In modern or modernizing societies Parsons observed that the male had lost his dominant power, and the roles within the family were more equitably distributed; that the status an individual obtained was more likely the result of accomplishments than inheritance; and that the extended family no longer was the crucial unit of society.

With these observations Parsons suggested that the family in the United States can be best described as an isolated nuclear family. No one really doubted that the nuclear family was being sheared of its embeddedness within an extended family system that was patrilocal and patriarchal

109

and that was supported by resources obtained from a family business. Most sociologists vehemently objected to the term *isolated*. Isolated implies extreme neolocality due to the requirements of a bureaucratic-corporation job market; alienation from kin because of a fluid stratification system wherein upward social mobility is not only possible but plausible; and a lack of affectional ties that would lead to an estrangement from families of orientation and the families of siblings. The adoption by Parsons of the extreme words "isolated nuclear family" led to a host of research studies designed to disprove the Parsonian terminology and hypothesis.

## THE KIN FAMILY NETWORK

If Parsons's description of the normal American family as isolated was correct, two rather obvious indices of that isolation would be the frequency with which relatives interact, and the existence and amount of aid exchanged between families of orientation and of procreation. A number of studies conducted in the middle 1950s confirmed the finding that nuclear families are rather firmly enmeshed in a functioning and functional kin network of aid and interaction.

In a carefully documented study in Detroit, Axelrod (1956) found that 49 percent of his sample saw relatives at least once a week, and another 25 percent visited with kin at least once a month. Greer (1956) found almost the same frequencies of interaction in his study of two census tracts in Los Angeles. Bell and Boat (1957) confirmed the results

*Three generations, one table, and a love that transcends the years is the cohesive force unifying this family.*

Ken Heyman

**TABLE 5–2**

**Contacts Between Respondents' Families and Related Kin**

| MAJOR FORMS OF HELP AND SERVICE | DIRECTION OF SERVICE NETWORK (IN PERCENTAGES[a]) | | | | |
|---|---|---|---|---|---|
| | BETWEEN RESPON-DENT'S FAMILY AND RELATED KIN | FROM RESPON-DENTS TO PARENTS | FROM RESPON-DENTS TO SIBLINGS | FROM PARENTS TO RESPON-DENTS | FROM SIBLINGS TO RESPON-DENTS |
| Any form of help | 93.3 | 56.3 | 47.6 | 79.6 | 44.8 |
| Help during illness | 76.0 | 47.0 | 42.0 | 46.4 | 39.0 |
| Financial aid | 53.0 | 14.6 | 10.3 | 46.8 | 6.4 |
| Care of children | 46.8 | 4.0 | 29.5 | 20.5 | 10.8 |
| Advice (personal and business) | 31.0 | 2.0 | 3.0 | 26.5 | 4.5 |
| Valuable gifts | 22.0 | 3.4 | 2.3 | 17.6 | 3.4 |

SOURCE: Marvin B. Sussman, "The Isolated Nuclear Family: Fact or Fiction?" *Social Problems,* 6(1959):336, Table 1. Reprinted by permission of The Society for the Study of Social Problems.

[a] Totals do not add up to 100 percent because many families received more than one form of help or service.

of the two preceding studies in their investigation in San Francisco; the results obtained regardless of whether the family status and economic status were low or high. A study by Paul Reiss (1962) in the Boston area found visiting patterns that were less frequent than those found in Detroit, Los Angeles, or San Francisco. This finding was probably due to the fact that fewer of his respondents had relatives in the same metropolitan area. This conclusion was substantiated by Bell and Blumberg's (1959) Philadelphian results, which indicated that of the 56 percent of their sample with relatives living in Philadelphia, 46 percent visited relatives at least once a week.

All of these studies show conclusively that visiting with kin constitutes a major source of recreation and family activity for a substantial proportion of urban families in various urban areas. If these families are isolated nuclear units, they surely are not isolated in the verbal sense.

The second test of the isolation hypothesis focused on the amount of aid exchanged between families of orientation and of procreation. The first major study to examine mutual aid among relatives was done by Marvin Sussman (1953). Sussman studied the relationships that existed between 97 middle-class, white, Protestant, parental couples in New Haven, Connecticut, and their 195 married children living away from home. Rather than estrangement he found a high degree of interlocking involvement. The families were bonded together by rather extensive amounts of aid and interaction (see Table 5–2).

The flow of aid was primarily from parents to married offspring and included (a) direct financial aid to make major purchases (down payments for a house, and in buying cars, gifts of furniture and appliances); (b) indirect financial aid through gifts (savings bonds and clothes

111

## FIGURE 5–1
## Parental Aid to Married Children

### Familial Variables Affecting Economic Support

1. Family Values
   a. Neo-familism
   b. Individualism vs. Organizationalism
   c. Developmental values (Permissiveness)
2. Position of family in the Social Structure
   a. Social class
   b. Residential location
   c. Occupation (Bureaucratic-Entrepreneurial)
   d. Status aspiration
   e. Ethnic group membership
3. Family Economic Position
   a. Wealth relative to class
   b. Security against retirement & catastrophy
   c. Perception of own economic position as relatively risk-free
4. Family Structure
   a. Number of children
   b. Degree of family integration
   c. Patterns of role differentiation
   d. Ordinal position of children
5. Relation to Married Child
   a. Son or daughter
   b. Parent-child harmony
   c. Parental approval of marriage
   d. Age at marriage

### Types of Parent-Child Economic Support

1. Goods
   a. Furnishings at wedding and at later periods during marriage
   b. Hospitality gifts
   c. Use of parent's equipment; automobiles, rent-free house, summer cottage, appliances; food gifts; transfer of property
2. Money
   a. Given at wedding, childbirth, holidays, and anniversaries
   b. Education
   c. Low-interest or interest-free loans
   d. Endowments
   e. Subsidized visits and vacations
3. Services
   a. Emergency and crises: care of family members
   b. Babysitting
   c. Boarding of grandchildren
   d. Shopping
   e. Recreation
   f. Home decorating
   g. Garden and yard work
   h. Home construction

### Intervening Variables

1. Amount of aid
2. Expectation for aid & regularity
3. Stage in family cycle
4. Disguise of aid
5. Parental expectations
6. H. or W.'s parents
7. Parental approval of marriage
8. Emotional attachment to parents
9. Geographical distance
10. Family status
11. Married child's image of in-law
12. Generalized attitudes

### Consequences for Family Patterns

1. H-W relations: friction, power, harmony
2. Intergenerational integration
   Parental power
   a. Occup. choice
   b. Mobility
   c. Mate-choice
3. Higher fertility
4. Support for aged parents
5. Lower divorce (teen marriages)

### Consequence for Individual Personality

1. Dependency
2. Striving & achievement motivation
3. Anxiety & security
4. Freedom to concentrate on arts, politics, family life

### Societal Supports and Constraints on Parental Aid

1. Economic & technological
   a. Productivity and affluence
   b. Inflation
   c. Tax system
2. Group structure
   a. Bureaucratization
   b. Professionalization
   c. Suburbanization
3. Demographic structure
   a. Lengthened education
   b. Early age at marriage
   c. Early child bearing
   d. Lengthened life span
4. Values (as in box above)

### General Societal Consequences

1. Reduction or implementation of geographical and occupational mobility
2. Population growth
3. Economic & occ. striving
4. Cultural development
5. Individualistic vs. other-directed values

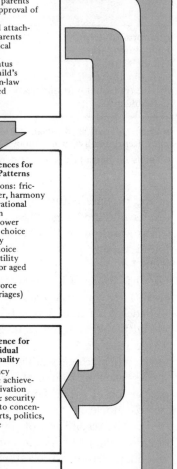

for the grandchildren, provision of vacation resources such as renting a cottage large enough to accommodate both families); and (c) indirect aid through such services as baby sitting, care of married offspring during illness, and countless others. Several pertinent findings answered the almost obvious question, "Weren't there strings attached?" First of all, the parents were adamant that they did not want to interfere in the lives of their married children and did not expect reciprocity or an obligation for repayment. Second, the married children were not offended by the extension of aid—in fact, many welcomed the assistance, financial and otherwise. Third, the parents stated that they would not desire any kind of extended dependence of their married children on their aid.

Sussman found that in 154 of the 195 cases (79 percent) the parents were giving either direct financial support or help and service of some kind. In 120 of these cases Sussman found that parents and children helped out in times of illness, regardless of the distance involved. This was particularly true when a new grandchild was introduced into the kin network.

In another study, in Cleveland, Sussman (1953) found that the kin network was not composed only of unilateral aid from the family of orientation to that of procreation. The aid network also included siblings and other related kin. All in all, these studies by Sussman confirmed the results of Sharp and Axelrod (1956) in Detroit, where almost 70 percent of the couples both gave and received aid from relatives (see Figure 5–1).

The conclusion seems inescapable: the urban white family is not isolated from kin. It is, in fact, part of a functional kin network in which goods and services are freely exchanged on a regular basis. The mutual aid exchanged is not sent C.O.D., nor is there an obligation or expectation of future repayment except that of aid in kind when necessary. Families that would be differentiated and estranged in the Parsonian analysis are, in fact, bonded together with affectional ties that even include a sharing of resources—even when not sharing might enhance the current status of the married offspring.

By 1965 Sussman was able to state: "The evidence on the viability of an existing kinship structure carrying on extensive activities among kin is so convincing that we find it unnecessary to continue further descriptive work in order to establish the existence of the kin network in modern urban society."

Thus, the straw man set up by the use of the extreme (and evidently unintended) term *isolated* by Parsons was quickly and completely destroyed by sociologists studying the family. This era of research was in the *context of discovery* as described by Phillips (1972 and Chapter 2 of this book). The next era, the *context of justification,* began in the early

---

SOURCE (for Figure 5–1): Marvin B. Sussman and Lee Burchinal, "Kin Family Network: Unheralded Structure in Current Conceptualizations of Family Functioning," *Marriage and Family Living* 24(August 1962):233. Used by permission of the National Council on Family Relations.

and middle 1960s with the works of Eugene Litwak, Bert Adams, and others. Their studies begin to offer a theoretical and conceptual specification of how the urban family, primarily of the middle class, adjusts to the demands of life in the rapidly changing society in which we live.

Since Sussman and others showed conclusively that the urban American family is alive with extensive interaction and that mutual aid among kin is a reality for most families, the next step in determining the everyday functioning of the modern American family focused on variables that might specify the degree of interaction and aid. Two major studies, one by Eugene Litwak and the other by Bert Adams, made significant contributions along this line.

## Eugene Litwak: Geographical and Occupational Mobility as Determinants of the Extensity and Intensity of the Kin Network

Litwak (1960a, 1960b) accepted the idea from Parsons that the classical extended family is antithetical to occupational mobility and thus is not congruent with the demands of a modern industrial society. In its stead Litwak (1960a:10) proposed a new terminology, the *modified extended family:*

> [It] differs from the "classical extended" family in that it does not demand geographical propinquity, occupational involvement, or nepotism, nor does it have an hierarchical authority structure. On the other hand, it differs from the isolated nuclear family structure in that it does provide significant and continuing aid to the nuclear family. The modified extended family consists of a series of nuclear families bound together on an equalitarian basis, with a strong emphasis on these extended family bonds as an end value.

In other words, Litwak is deftly accusing Parsons of being simplistic by dichotomizing the family into either classical extended or isolated nuclear. Given such a foundation it is easy to see why Parsons chose the latter as the prototype for a modern industrial society. So Litwak proposed a middle category—the modified extended family—connected by affection not ascription, pervasively neolocal but not isolated. Given our industrially based bureaucratic society, Litwak proposed two variables that might differentially affect the degree of cohesion to be found among a sample of family units and their relatives—occupational mobility and geographical mobility.

Litwak's sample consisted of 920 white married females, all of whom had children nineteen and under and who had moved into new homes in Buffalo, New York, just prior to the study. The variables used in this study were as follows:

I. Occupational Mobility

1. *Stationary upper class*—Respondents whose parents were in the upper class and who themselves are in the upper class.

*This three-genera-tional group exempli-fies the continuing relationships of the modified extended family.*

2. *Upwardly mobile class*—Respondents whose parents came from an occupation lower than the one currently occupied by the husband.

3. *Downwardly mobile class*—Respondent's parents came from higher occupational group than the respondent now occupies.

4. *Stationary manual class*—Respondents, like parents, are manual workers.

II. Commitment to Family

1. *Extended family commitment*—If the respondents strongly agreed with the following two statements: (a) I want a house with enough room for our parents to feel free to move in; (b) I want a location that would make it easy for relatives to get together.

2. *Nuclear family commitment*—If the respondents agreed with either or both of the following two statements: (c) Generally

I like the whole family to spend evenings together; (d) I want a house where family members can spend time together.

3. *Nonfamily orientation*—Those respondents who rejected all four of these statements.

III. Concern for Status

Respondents who agreed with three of the following statements were classified as status oriented, while those who agreed with only one or rejected them all were labeled nonstatus oriented. The statements were: (1) When in public people should be extra careful of their behavior; (2) I'm uncomfortable when I am with people who have bad manners; (3) I want a house that I can be proud to have my friends see; and (4) I think my house has a lot to do with my friends' opinion of me.

The dependent variable, an assessment of family cohesion, was whether the respondents received one or more family visits per week.

The data in Table 5–3, taken from Litwak's study, provide us with an excellent opportunity to test empirically Parsons's ideas about the effects of the isolated nuclear family structure on the interaction between families of orientation and their married offspring. If Parsons's conceptual analysis of American society is correct, the upwardly mobile families that are concerned with status and are either nuclear family or nonfamily oriented should have the lowest proportion of frequent visits from relatives. They are the prototypical organization men climbing the corporate ladders, leaving their parental families behind, and making it on their own in a society where achievement and not ascription is important. As the data labeled with a small *b* indicate, 55 and 40 percent of these respondents reported frequent visits from relatives. These, then, are *not* isolated nuclear families.

In contrast to Parsons, Litwak contends that the families least likely to be part of a functioning network of interaction are those that are nonmobile and at the bottom of the social class ladder, the manual workers, who are nuclear family or nonfamily oriented and who are not status oriented. Clearly the percentages reporting frequent visits from relatives in these groups (labeled with a small *c* in Table 5–3) are much lower, 36 and 27 percent respectively, than the Parsonian groups. In effect, Parsons's hypothesis was not supported and Litwak's was.

Litwak's conclusion is important in that he has shown that occupational mobility does not adversely affect the cohesion of family units as would be predicted by Parsons or, for that matter, common sense. In other words, the "white sheep" of the family are not ostracized because of their occupational success. Rather, they are still accepted by their families.

116

**TABLE 5–3**

Family Interaction
(percentage receiving one or more family visits a week)

| SOCIAL CLASS | EXTENDED-FAMILY ORIENTED | | NUCLEAR-FAMILY ORIENTED | | NONFAMILY ORIENTED | |
|---|---|---|---|---|---|---|
| | HIGH STATUS CONCERN | LOW STATUS CONCERN | HIGH STATUS CONCERN | LOW STATUS CONCERN | HIGH STATUS CONCERN | LOW STATUS CONCERN |
| Stationary upper class | 63(35)[a] | 49(10) | 74(35) | 55(40) | 56( 9) | 47(19) |
| Upwardly mobile class | 61(28) | 75( 8) | 55(49)[b] | 43(51) | 40(15)[b] | 41(32) |
| Downwardly mobile class | 77(13) | 33( 3) | 33(24) | 64(28) | 16(13) | 29(20) |
| Stationary manual class | 73(26) | 60( 5) | 22(41) | 36(67)[c] | 56(23) | 27(52)[c] |

SOURCE: Adapted from Eugene Litwak, "Occupational Mobility and Extended Family Cohesion," *American Sociological Review, 25*(1960):20, Table 8. By permission of The American Sociological Association and the author.

NOTE: Only respondents who have relatives living in the city are considered. This avoids the extraneous consideration of geographical distance.

[a] This cell should be read as follows: 63 percent of the 35 people who had relatives living in the city were extended-family oriented, concerned with status, stationary upper class, and had visits from relatives once a week or more.

[b] According to Parsons's hypothesis, these two groups should have the lowest proportion of frequent family visits.

[c] According to the alternative hypothesis, these two groups should have the lowest proportion of frequent family visits.

In a companion paper from the same data, Litwak (1960b) also found that geographical mobility does not adversely affect the degree of family cohesion as indicated by frequent visits from family members. In fact, "persons separated from their families retained their extended family orientation; those with close family identification were as likely, if not more likely, to leave their family for occupational reasons; those on the upswing of their careers were apt to move away from their families and to receive family support; those on the career plateau were not likely to move or to move toward their family; that considerations of this kind hold only for bureaucratic occupations; and that the modified extended family seems to be uniquely suited to provide succor during periods of movement" (1960b:392).

SUMMARY OF LITWAK'S STUDY.   Litwak's findings are of major importance for two reasons. First, his delineation of the modified extended family is an important conceptual distinction that seems to accurately describe the type of family system operative in our society, at least among whites. Second, with the instant communication and rapid transportation devices

Micha Bar-Am from Magnum Photos, Inc.

*The responsibilities and experiences we share with close friends serve sometimes as a substitute for extended-family encounters.*

available in our society, the geographical mobility and upward occupational mobility that are pervasive in America do not impede or hinder family cohesion. The modified extended family is, then, a functional adaptation to the demands made by the type of occupational system in which we all participate.

Litwak's contribution is the statement and defense of the hypothesis that the type of family system we have in the United States is a functional adaptation or modification of those characteristics of the classical extended family that served to solidify agrarian societies.

## Kin Network Outside the United States

The phenomenon of relatively high family cohesiveness despite separation is not limited to the United States. Shanas (1973:508–509) and her colleagues conducted studies of the kin network and the modified extended family between 1962 and 1969, among large samples, in Denmark

(N = 2446), Great Britain (N = 2500), the United States (N = 2442), Poland (N = 2693), Israel (N = 793 and 349), and Yugoslavia (N = 2645). Two of the conclusions are particularly relevant:

1. From one-half to three-fourths of all old people with children, then, either live with a child or within ten minutes of a child. Neither the long-time industrialization in the three Western countries nor the rapid urbanization of Poland and Yugoslavia has physically removed old people from their children.

2. In every country the proportion of old people living apart who had seen a child within the last week was between 70 and 80 percent.... The evidence is very clear. In industrial Western countries, in the countries of Eastern Europe, and in Israel old people who live apart from their children continue to see at least one of their children regularly.

### Bert N. Adams: Kinship in an Urban Setting

Perhaps the most extensive and thorough study of American kinship was conducted by Bert N. Adams in Greensboro, North Carolina. In the summers of 1963 and 1964 Adams interviewed 467 females and 322 males, all of whom were white, married, and had been married only once and for 20 years or less. It was a relatively young sample in that the median age for husbands was 35 years and for wives 32, with the median length of marriage being 10 years and 10 months. Using the husband's occupation as an index, 62 percent of the sample were white-collar and 38 percent were blue-collar workers. The number and percentage of respondents in each occupational mobility category can be seen in Table 5–4.

**TABLE 5–4**
**Sample Population of Kinship Study**

| OCCUPATIONAL MOBILITY | MALES | | FEMALES | | TOTAL | |
|---|---|---|---|---|---|---|
| | NO. | % | NO. | % | NO. | % |
| Upward mobile | 93 | 30 | 115 | 25 | 208 | 27 |
| Downward mobile | 26 | 8 | 38 | 8 | 64 | 8 |
| Stable white collar | 111 | 36 | 160 | 35 | 271 | 36 |
| Stable blue collar | 80 | 26 | 139 | 31 | 219 | 29 |
| | 310 | 100 | 452 | 99 | 762 | 100 |

SOURCE: Adapted from Bert N. Adams, *Kinship in an Urban Setting* (Chicago: Markham, 1968), p. 21. Courtesy of Professor Bert N. Adams.

SELECTED FINDINGS FROM THE STUDY BY ADAMS.   It is not feasible to report all the findings from this benchmark study. It is by far the most comprehensive study of the kin network to date. We will summarize only the major findings. The serious student of sociology should examine Adams's monograph at first hand to see how the "ideal" sociological study is done:

---

### The Scope of Adams's Study of the Kin Network

Adams attempted to cover some of the areas of kin family functioning that were either ignored or left for future research by Litwak and others. First, he carefully examined the relationships of his subjects with their nearest age sibling. Altogether 697 of his sample reported at least one living sibling, and Adams has data on 170 brother-brother, 324 brother-sister, and 203 sister-sister relationships. Second, Adams recognized that just the existence of a sibling does not imply contact unless there is (a) affectional closeness and/or (b) identification with the sibling. Affectional closeness was measured by the question: "How close would you say you feel to your [sibling]?" Identification or idealization of the sibling was assessed by the question, "Would you like to be the kind of person your [sibling] is?" In addition, he measured the objective frequency of interaction reported. Third, he introduced the idea of value consensus as one of the cementing forces in interaction with kin, whether they be parents or siblings. Fourth, he asked questions about the influence of felt obligation as a factor in continued interaction with parents. This is a good example of what Berger meant by "seeing through and looking behind" the obvious reality of social relationships. Fifth, the Greensboro subjects were questioned about relations with collateral kin—the favorite cousin, an area that has been ignored by other researchers. Sixth, another area of concern in his excellent study was what happens to interaction with kin when the family of orientation is reconstituted. In other words, what occurs with parent-child interaction when widowhood, divorce, or remarriage shapes the parental family? This is an important area primarily because it is such a widespread phenomenon in our society where the divorce rate is relatively high. The obverse problem, divorce and remarriage of the young adult couple, was not covered because all of Adams's sample was in the first marriage. Seventh, the final innovation in Adams's study dealt with the size of the recognized kin network. This information was obtained by asking the respondents how many of the respondent's kin were known. In a society characterized by the bilateral tracing of kin this question is especially important.

1. Using a typology developed by Raymond Firth (1964), Adams investigated the number of kin with whom his respondents were acquainted. Firth distinguished between nominal (you know who they are but don't feel especially related to them) and effective (there is the possibility of a continuing social relationship with them) kin.

With the respondents' own family of procreation (husband, children) and in-laws eliminated, the young females in Adams's sample reported a median of 29.7 kin acquaintances they would recognize at sight, while the median for the males was 26.2.

As the figures in Table 5–5 indicate, females not only have more extensive knowledge of kin but they also are more intensively involved with them.

Somewhat surprisingly, the upward mobile respondents (male and female) know more kin than the other categories of occupational mobility. In terms of both extensiveness of knowledge and the importance attached to kin in the total scheme of things, the downwardly mobile appear to be moving toward isolation. The "black sheep" complex seems to be operating for this group.

Of particular importance to confirming Litwak's findings on geographical mobility and family cohesion, Adams (1968:30) states: "Small numbers of residential distance from the bulk of one's kin do not necessarily result in kin being considered unimportant, since significant rela-

**TABLE 5–5**
**Kin Acquaintances and the Importance of Kin to Young Adults**

| OCCUPATIONAL STRATUM AND MOBILITY | NUMBER OF RESPONDENTS | MEDIAN NUMBER OF KIN | NUMBER OF RESPONDENTS | IMPORTANCE OF KIN (IN PERCENTAGES) | | | |
|---|---|---|---|---|---|---|---|
| | | | | VERY IMPT. | SOMEWHAT IMPT. | RELATIVELY UNIMPT. | TOTAL |
| *Males* | | | | | | | |
| Upward white collar | 93 | 29.7 | 75 | 39 | 52 | 9 | 100 |
| Stable white collar | 111 | 24.7 | 98 | 34 | 52 | 14 | 100 |
| Stable blue collar | 86 | 26.3 | 60 | 45 | 40 | 15 | 100 |
| Downward blue collar | 26 | 18.8 | 22 | 27 | 50 | 23 | 100 |
| *Females* | | | | | | | |
| Upward white collar | 115 | 35.0 | 85 | 52 | 36 | 12 | 100 |
| Stable white collar | 160 | 30.3 | 122 | 64 | 33 | 3 | 100 |
| Stable blue collar | 139 | 24.9 | 94 | 60 | 32 | 8 | 100 |
| Downward blue collar | 38 | 21.8 | 26 | 31 | 54 | 15 | 100 |

SOURCE: Bert N. Adams, *Kinship in an Urban Setting* (Chicago: Markham, 1968), pp. 21, 29. Courtesy of Professor Bert N. Adams.

tives may be considered intimate and a vital part of the individual's life regardless of their location." This is further evidence of the amazing powers of modern systems of communication.

2. A second conclusion reached by Adams is that interaction with parents is frequent and pervasive for his sample of young adults. Again it is clear that females are much more involved with their relatives than are males. This is probably a function of the types of occupations in which wives are involved and the expressivity functions of the female role as discussed by Parsons. While theoretically our society traces lineage bilaterally, it is probably true that the females provide the crucial continuing link, even with the families of their husbands.

Adams found a strong affection for parents that was a mixture both of value consensus and of genuine positive concern for the parents. The young couple was usually responsible for initiating the interaction. A key finding along this line is the degree of felt obligation. As Adams (1968:89) states: "The link between feeling and contact is a strong sense of obligation to keep in constant touch with one's parents." This occurs because the parents are the "only ones I can really count on." The mother-daughter tie is especially strong because the daughter's role has converged with that of her mother. She can now understand and empathize with the sacrifices made by her mother earlier.

Adams (1968:91) sums up his findings on the relationships between young adults and their parents.

> It is not, in the final analysis, isolation from parents which is either desired or accomplished by young adults in our society; it is independence and maturity.... Relations with parents are characterized by age or generational dissimilarity of values. This is the typical, not the ideal or closest, relation with parents. The ideal relationship seems best exemplified in the relations of middle-class daughters and their mothers. This is an involvement based upon diffuseness of activity, or a wide range of patterned contacts, with enjoyment and affection central, and a secondary obligatory component manifested in extremely frequent contact and a willingness to help when needed.

3. In an article based on his Greensboro data, Adams (1967) compared expression of affectional closeness, value consensus, and feelings of obligation toward best friend, parent(s), and the near-age sibling. As the data in Table 5–6 indicate, the respondents see themselves as affectionately closer to their best friends than to their near-age sibling, and higher in value consensus to them than to either their parent(s) or sibling (the matter of choice). However, only 28 percent see obligation as a contact motive with friends compared to 73 percent for parent(s) and 59 percent for siblings.

**TABLE 5–6**
Young Married Adults' Relationships with Others

| SOCIAL CATEGORY | NUMBER OF RESPONDENTS | PERCENTAGES | | |
|---|---|---|---|---|
| | | QUITE OR EXTREMELY CLOSE AFFECTIONATELY | HIGH IN VALUE CONSENSUS | SEEING OBLIGATION AS A CONTACT MOTIVE |
| Best friend | 737 | 61 | 75 | 28 |
| Parent(s) | 724 | 75 | 65 | 73 |
| Near-age sibling | 697 | 48 | 45 | 59 |

SOURCE: Bert N. Adams, "Interaction Theory and the Social Network," *Sociometry*, *30*(1967):72, Table 1. By permission of the American Sociological Association and the author.

The real importance of this finding lies not in the numbers but rather in the conceptual dexterity of Bert Adams. Using the symbolic interactional framework as a basis, Adams suggests that two forces are at work to explain interaction with kin and friend. The primary force that causes family cohesion is interest, perception of need, and affection. Adams grouped these items together under *positive concern*. We choose our friends and maintain contact with them primarily out of a sense of *value consensus*. Another word used quite frequently to mean the same thing is *homogamy*—attraction of similarity. Most writers have tended to treat these forces as independent in their influence on maintaining interaction. Adams suggests that although they may act independently, there is reason to suspect that they also act conjointly.

From the delineation of these two forces Adams (1967) develops five propositions:

1. Consensus is likely to be modal in friendship relations, and concern in kinship relations.
2. In general, interaction is likely to be desired with friends in preference to kin, due to the consensual component of friendship and the absense of strong obligatory feelings toward friends.
3. Positive concern is more likely to lead to relationship persistence than is consensus.
4. The relationship based upon positive concern is more likely than the consensual relationship to have as an element intimate communication.

123

5. The consensual and concern components among social relations demonstrate a substantial overlap among the various structural categories of individuals frequently considered as givens in descriptive interactional studies.

Those propositions are important for the sociology of the family because they signal a recognition that we should look at behavior, as indicated at the close of Chapter 2, rather than family behavior. If we are willing to look for the abstract meaning of what we study, as Adams did, kin interaction and friend interaction are part of what social psychologists call *social attraction*. The same processes account for both types of interaction.

Adams has shown that the sociology of the family can go beyond the parochial boundaries of a substantive interest in the family to an interest in behavior that is pervasive—attraction to and interaction with kin and what might be called *fictive*, or *surrogate*, kin. We constantly catch ourselves saying, "He's like a brother to me" or "I think of her as if she were my sister."

With kin our interpersonal commitments transcend geographical distance and sometimes cross over social class differences because we recognize that our family is part of a larger group—the kin network. Our family of procreation is just one unit in a larger family that we can trace back over time. Our friends are usually found within the community in which we reside, and they are almost always within the same social class. We are bound to our friends because they are like us. When we move we make new friends and label our former associates as old friends. All of us are existential when it comes to friends. We see them occasionally, relive the old days, write Christmas cards, but the current friends are the most salient. You cannot drop relatives like that because we are part of them and they of us. As David Schneider (1968) puts it, a relative is a person. Friends are usually transitory and can be relabeled if the need arises.

Our interactions with kin are likely to transcend generational differences caused by stages in the family life cycle. With friends we are likely to have the closest contact with persons who share common problems that result from being in the same stage of the family life cycle. If a friend happens to be in a different stage of the family life cycle, we can disengage from that friendship in order to develop friends who are more similar. Thus the couple who delays children for an extended period of time is likely to find that they are deserted by friends who have children. It is not that the old friendship means nothing. Rather, it indicates that the basis of similarity between the two couples has somehow lost significance as the couple with children find a need to be with others who are in a similar situation.

Using the terminology of George Herbert Mead, relatives (parents and siblings) are always *significant others* while friends seldom cross the line of intimacy between *particular other* and significant other.

## CONCLUSION

In this chapter we have dealt with some of the central features of the modern American family system. The sociological study of the modern family in the United States has progressed from a descriptive-oriented debate as to how isolated the nuclear family is in an urban and industrial society to a conclusion that the American family system is a modified extended one. With the research of Adams the specifying variables that account for the extended characteristics of the American family have been identified. Adams has taken the study of modern kinship to the point where family behavior is recognized as part of a broader concern with interpersonal attraction between kin and nonkin.

In a society characterized by a fluid stratification system in which social and geographical mobility are not only possible but encouraged; where the pervasive values foster concerted efforts for maximal individual

*A hamburger and a beautiful day are often responsible for bringing the family together for a meaningful experience.*

Richard Kalvar from Magnum Photos, Inc.

achievement; where families and individuals are pressured into expending great amounts of energy and resources in their occupational, recreational, and community spheres of life; where inflation has seriously diminished the money available to most middle-class families—any intergenerational aid and interaction among families can be viewed as prima facie evidence that the family network is viable and crucial as a social system that makes life in these times tolerable. There are certain key links in this functioning modified extended family that are not structural but rather social-psychological, and that are based on a rational and objective perception evaluation of the importance of familial commitments relative to other nonkin related commitments. In particular, aid will be exchanged primarily on the basis of (a) how strong the ties are among families; (b) the feasibility of such aid relative to other commitments in which the giving family is involved; and (c) the seriousness with which the need is felt to exist.

Of course, in some instances the need will be so great that a minimum affectional commitment and an extended overcommitment to nonkin related areas will be overlooked because "they need it." When a parent or sibling experiences a traumatic and demanding crisis, most of us will respond with reserves of love and warmth and generosity that we never knew existed—even at a great sacrifice to our own family and its resources.

We should not forget that the modern American family is part of a broader cultural stream that places great emphasis on concern for others, love of our fellow man, and a recognition that there are times when we must bury past grudges, vault over barriers of social class and geographical and age differences, to bear witness that we are human and have a need to reaffirm that we recognize our past times and past biography.

The fact that such sacrifices occur with great regularity in a society that is frequently characterized as cold, impersonal, fragmented, and alienating is evidence that the family is a vital part of life and an integral part of our society. Such experiences—and most of us have them at some time in our lifespan—are encountered with a positive and self-denying attitude. The data in this chapter speak for a strong family system in the United States, not for a weakened and dying family system. Even with the many signs of weakened commitments to family life, the findings of an extensive, widely functioning, and functional kin family network proclaim the life, not the death, of the family as we know it.

## SOME POSSIBLE IMPLICATIONS

*The United States, historically speaking, is a young society. It is also relatively young in terms of the age structure. In 1900 the median age of the U.S. population was 22.9 years (50 percent of the population was younger and 50 percent older than 22.9). By 1970 this median age had increased to 27.7 years and, given the assumption of constant fertility at the replacement level (an average of 2.1 children per family) from 1970 on, by the year 2000 the median age of the population will be about 35.5 years. So the population is getting older. By the year 2000, close to 30 percent of the population will be over fifty years old. Students in the classroom today, and their parents, will be retiring earlier and living longer than previous generations.*

*What are some of the implications of an increasingly older population, with larger percentages beyond the retirement stage of the family life cycle? What kinds of responsibilities and pressures will emerge for the individual and for the modified extended family in the future?*

*One plausible answer to these questions is that the family in the United States may take on more of the characteristics of the classical extended family. Will the family of the future consist of a common, multi-generational household or a compound of separate residences? Will there be more frequent and closer interaction between families of orientation and of procreation? Will the retired grandparents be responsible for the primary socialization of the children of their married offspring, so that the latter may be productive in the labor force?*

*The family in the United States is adapting its structure and functions to a new environment. Do the implications of fundamental change in this society in the years to the twenty-first century portend a change in the family toward a more extended structure?*

Joel Gordon

# 6

# THE BLACK FAMILY IN THE UNITED STATES

*Did slavery obliterate the African cultural heritage of slaves?*

*Is the black family matriarchal?*

*What might be the effects on black society of its prolonged social, economic, and political eclipse?*

*Can the black family in the United States maintain a distinct pattern, or will it inevitably become more like the white family?*

> Seldom has there been a subject within social science literature about which more value judgments have been allowed to creep in. From the turn of this century until the present, writers (both black and white) have had extreme difficulty in discussing the Afro-American without bias and prejudice, conscious and unconscious. The literature, therefore, must be handled with great caution. [Adams, 1971:115]

This statement by Adams is an especially appropriate point of departure for an examination of the black family in the United States. It is axiomatic to say that blacks have been the subject of much attention by historians, psychologists, sociologists, and students of other disciplines as well. That blacks have been the stimulus for numerous benchmark legal decisions and much political and social change, especially in the decade of the 1960s, is likewise obvious. Unfortunately, many scholarly attempts to study the black family have been based on stereotyped misconceptions, characterized by the selective use of statistical indices, and generated by a desire to solve the "black problem" rather than objectively to delineate the parameters of the black family.

Andrew Billingsley (1968) suggested that, for the most part, the black family has been rather pervasively ignored in American scholarship until recently. He divided the study of the family into about six phases. The first phase, occurring in the late nineteenth century, was predominantly influenced by Social Darwinism. The focus in this first phase was on the earlier more primitive forms of the family (see Chapter 3) and attempted to show the "evolution" of the family from early days to the "ultimate" family form, represented by the European family of the nineteenth century.

The second phase "focused on poverty groups and were almost exclusively concerned with economic conditions affecting family life. No attention was paid to the broader set of relationships between family life and community life, or to the place of family life in the wider society. These studies concentrated on the urban poor and consequently ignored Negro family life, for around the turn of the century Negroes were not an urban industrial force. They were essentially rural peasants located in the deep south" (Billingsley 1968).

The third phase of family studies occurred in the 1920s, when poverty seemed to be under control. Thus the focus at that time was on happiness and adjustment, and research centered on problems faced by middle-class families. Because so few black families were middle class this phase was, in essence, lily white.

The black family did become a focus of concern in American scholarship during the decade of the 1930s (the fourth phase). A massive migration from rural to urban areas and from South to North had made blacks highly visible. This visibility in urban industrial areas, political activity that made blacks an increasingly potent political force, and a recognition that a major restructuring of American society was necessary after the crash of 1929 brought the black family to the attention of scholars. Major studies of the black community and family emerged during this period. In 1932 E. Franklin Frazier published *The Negro Family in Chicago* and in 1939 *The Negro Family in the United States.* In 1945, St. Clair Drake and Horace Cayton published their classic study of the black community, entitled *Black Metropolis,* in which large sections were devoted to the black family.

Between 1940 and 1960 (the fifth phase) the black family again slipped into relative obscurity as American society recuperated from World War II, the Korean conflict, and the Cold War. Of course, the 1960s saw the massive politicization of blacks and the Civil Rights movement. It became painfully obvious to American scholars that blacks were overrepresented in the poverty category; that their income and educational, occupational, and other resources were far below those enjoyed by whites; and that there was a need for massive efforts to rectify the wrong of long-standing discrimination and oppression.

Studies conducted between 1960 and 1974 constitute the sixth and most explosive phase in the examination of the black family. This period was dominated by the Moynihan Report (discussed later in this chapter), with its claim that there are pathological features of the black family that must be changed, and by serious attempts to counter the charges leveled by Moynihan.

We should probably add a seventh phase to those suggested by Billingsley. It began with publication in 1974 of *Time on the Cross,* a quantitative analysis of the impact of slavery and reconstruction on the lives of blacks in America. There has followed an intense interest among family scholars in what is called social history. This interest has sometimes resulted in social scientists adopting historical methodologies and historians adopting social scientific and statistical methodologies. The result has been a quantum leap in what is known about the black and other family systems—particularly the black family during the slavery period and the decades following the Civil War. The "Roots" of the black family have been re-examined, rediscovered, and what is now known requires a complete rewrite of black history. Myths that have long been the "gospel truth" about the black family have been destroyed by facts. In this chapter we will examine both the myths and the facts.

131

## HISTORICAL PERSPECTIVE

The first blacks in America, about twenty in all, landed at Jamestown about two years before the Mayflower landed at Plymouth Rock, 113 years before the birth of George Washington, and 244 years before the Emancipation Proclamation (see Bennett 1969). Philip Curtin (1969) estimated that slightly less than half a million Africans were imported into the United States. Nearly half of these came between 1741 and 1780 and another 25 percent came between 1781 and the abolition of the legal slave trade in 1808. By the first census of the United States in 1790, blacks accounted for 19.3 percent of the total enumerated population. This figure decreased steadily until 1930, when blacks were only 9.7 percent of the total. In 1970 blacks represented about 11.2 percent of the population (22,580,000 persons).

With a spirit and courage perhaps unmatched in human history, blacks in the United States have endured the oppression of slavery, the anarchy created by legal emancipation and reconstruction, and the rootlessness engendered by a massive migration from rural to urban areas and from South to North. These three forces—slavery, reconstruction, and mass urbanization—have all shaped the black family.

### Slavery

One key element in the identity of any people is the ability to locate itself historically and to receive a culture from one generation and deliver it intact to the next. This is obviously a privilege that black slaves never enjoyed. In essence slavery produced what Billingsley (1968) calls a "discontinuity" in the history of the blacks who were captured by slave traders, transported to a new land in less than V.I.P. accommodations, and deprived of their freedom to become the negotiable property of white men.

At least two schools of thought have emerged regarding the discontinuity problem. On one side are those who argue that this involuntary bondage and forced migration effectively obliterated the culture(s) from which the slaves came. Three reasons are usually cited to support the discontinuity-obliteration hypothesis: (1) The slave traders were not at all concerned about the organization of the cultures from which they obtained their property. Thus, in addition to the shock of being abducted from a relatively secure world, blacks from various tribes were thrown together and treated as one people. (2) When a land-based population is forced to travel across the Atlantic in the smelly hold of a slave ship, the constant struggle to survive must have numbed cultural awareness. (3) Once they reached the United States these blacks were forced to learn an entirely new cultural system and language.

In contrast to the idea that slavery effectively erased the cultural heritage of blacks is the discontinuity-acculturation-cultural survival hypothesis. As Herskovits (1941) notes, the proponents of the obliteration hypothesis use their assumptions as data when the facts clearly indicate that those assumptions are based on "the myth of the Negro past." He shows that most slaves were recruited from a rather limited part of Africa, that the cultures represented were not nearly as diverse as originally believed, and that the language and linguistic patterns were similar. In addition, Herskovits goes on to show that the intentional segregation of slaves from similar tribes was not at all successful in suppressing the survival of African culture in the United States.

An even newer hypothesis developed by Rex Nettleford (1972) for Jamaica, but which is of considerable relevance for plantation America, argues that white Americans have been, to some extent, Africanized. In other words, African cultures were not completely erased among blacks, and many cultural elements spread from the Africans to the former Europeans. In some sense there was an emergent culture in colonial America that has since developed characteristics of its own based not only on the European past but to some extent on the African past as well.

Nettleford's hypothesis recently received support from the pioneering social history by Herbert Gutman:[1]

> A period of between eighty and one hundred twenty years separated nearly half of the enslaved Africans brought to the North American mainland from their Afro-American slave descendants at the moment of the general emancipation. Only a few slave generations connect these two moments in time. But a social process of "creolization" (the transformation of the African into the Afro-American) was already well under way by the time the federal Constitution was adopted and before the invention of the cotton gin. Culture formation among the slaves, which began before the War for Independence and well before the plantation system spread from the Upper to the Lower South, blended together African and Anglo-American cultural beliefs and social practices, mediated through the harsh institution of enslavement. Most slaves involved in the spread of the plantation system and of the developing Afro-American culture over the entire South in the six decades prior to the Civil War were the children and grandchildren of that adaptive eighteenth century slave culture, a culture neither African nor American but genuinely Afro-American.

Regardless of the label given the cultural milieu within which they were forced to exist and to adapt, slavery must have been a traumatic experience for those trapped in its bonds.

The impact of slavery on the emergence of a black family system in the United States is probably best viewed from two dimensions: the legal and the sociological. First, since most blacks were considered property or

---

[1] Herbert G. Gutman, *The Black Family in Slavery and Freedom, 1750–1925*, p. 34. Copyright © 1976 by Pantheon Books, a Division of Random House, Inc. Reprinted by permission.

chattel, they possessed no rights before the law. Having no legal recognition (that is, they were nonpersons) they were not able to enter into formal and legally sanctioned relationships. Consequently, the rules or norms governing courtship, marriage, parenthood, premarital and extramarital sex, and marital dissolution were all informal and could vary from plantation to plantation and over time as well. In a society of laws the black family was thus forced to evolve according to the exigencies of men, usually white men.

A second impact of slavery on the type of family that emerged among blacks is integrally related to the problem of legality (that is, legitimacy of relationships) but exists more explicitly as a sociological problem. The United States, more specifically the South during the heyday of slavery, was anything but an open society. The stratification system was quite rigid with the wealth controlled by the white aristocracy in a network of interlocking familial estates. The "poor white trash" constituted one lower-class group, and the black slaves occupied the bottom of the societal barrel.

It has long been considered "fact" that the black family in slavery was matrifocal (mother-centered) and matriarchal. This assumption is reflected most clearly in the following statement by Kenneth Stampp (1959):

> In so far as the family did have significance, it involved responsibilities which traditionally belonged to women. . . . The husband was at most his wife's assistant, her companion, and her sex partner. He was often thought of as her possession ("Mary's Tom"), as was the cabin in which they lived. It was common for a mother and her children to be considered a family without reference to the father.

Gutman (1976:10–11) examined 1865–66 census data that dealt with the composition of black households from three counties in Virginia. His conclusion is pertinent to the claim that the black family was female dominated:

> The fact that more than three-fourths of the households contained either a father or a husband cast doubt on conventional assertions that slavery had shattered the immediate slave family and made the two-parent household uncommon among poor rural blacks fresh to legal freedom.

Although no one would question seriously the assertion that slavery has deeply affected Afro-Americans, the best evidence available suggests that slavery did not destroy or weaken the black family. It certainly did not create a matriarchal family among blacks. The old stereotype perpetrated by Glazer and Moynihan (1963) that "the experience of slavery left as its most serious heritage a steady weakness in the Negro family" is simply *not true*. It is, like so many other stereotypes, *false*.

## Reconstruction

As the popular slogan states, "War is not healthy for children and other living things." The Civil War, the Emancipation Proclamation, and the Reconstruction period effectively destroyed the economic and social structure of the Old South. Although the blacks were not living in the best of all possible worlds under slavery, there was some stability and predictability to their lives. With Emancipation a number of former slaves expected that they would be given land, a mule, and the privilege of a leisurely life supported by the benevolent government that had given them freedom. For a while many blacks were supported by the government, the Freedman's Bureau, and other charitable organizations. However, those

*A four-generational family from a plantation near Beaufort, S.C., pose before their one-room cabin shortly after the 1862 Emancipation Proclamation.*

Library of Congress

sources of sustenance soon dried up. Blacks were left to fend for themselves—illiterate, unskilled, lacking economic resources and the experience of knowing how to save, budget, and exist in a world in which life was governed by laws, not by men.

It has long been held that the black family during the Reconstruction era was almost destroyed. As Donald (1952) noted in his book, *The Negro Freedman*: "Premarital chastity was not prized and illegitimacy, adultery, desertion, and bigamy were widespread. The 250 years of bondage began to take its toll during the Reconstruction period, and the black family, never very stable, almost broke."

More recent examinations of the data reveal that Donald was incorrect. He was not the only writer whose perception of Reconstruction proved to be wrong. E. Franklin Frazier, the noted black sociologist, wrote: "Promiscuous sexual relations and constant changing of partners became the rule among demoralized blacks, and the rest hardly fared better. When the yoke of slavery was lifted the drifting masses were left without any restraint on their vagrant and wild desires."

An examination of data from the census of 1880 led Gutman (1976: 444) to an entirely different conclusion:

> If the slaves had been without a norm that prized the completed immediate family, large numbers of southern blacks in 1880 should have lived in disorganized households. That was not the case. The manuscript pages of the 1880 federal census reveal with unfailing regularity that urban and rural ex-slaves had retained powerful familial connections and that nearly all households had at their core a nuclear family. The typical southern black household, moreover, had at its head a male who was either a farm laborer, a tenant farmer, a sharecropper, an urban service worker, or an urban day laborer.

Gutman also notes that nine out of ten blacks lived in households in which the core relationship encompassed two or more members of a nuclear family. He also states (1976:445) that "the 'three generation' male-absent household (a mother, her daughter, and the daughter's children), considered the archetypal 'matrifocal' family, moreover, hardly existed among southern rural and urban blacks."

The black family was evidently not heavily damaged by the years of bondage and the heady experience of legal emancipation. In fact, the data indicate that the black family was sustained by the remarkable strength of marital and familial ties and commitments that continued throughout the entire period from the beginnings of slavery through Reconstruction.

## Urban Migration

In 1790, of the 757 thousand blacks in the United States, 91 percent lived in the South. This figure had dropped to 89 percent by 1910, the last

**TABLE 6–1**
Net Migration of Blacks Out of the South

| DECADE | NUMBER |
|--------|--------|
| 1910–1920 | 454,300 |
| 1920–1930 | 749,000 |
| 1930–1940 | 347,500 |
| 1940–1950 | 1,244,700 |
| 1950–1960 | 1,457,000 |
| 1960–1970 | 1,380,000 |

SOURCES: United States Department of Commerce, Bureau of the Census, *Historical Statistics of the United States, Colonial Times to 1957* (Washington, D.C.: Government Printing Office, 1963), Series C25–75; ibid., *Current Population Reports*, Series P-25, No. 247, Table 4; ibid., *Current Population Reports*, Series P-25, No. 460, Table 4.

NOTE: The South refers to three census regions: the South Atlantic states (Delaware, Maryland, Washington D.C., Virginia, West Virginia, North Carolina, South Carolina, Georgia, Florida); the East South Central states (Kentucky, Tennessee, Alabama, Mississippi); and the West South Central states (Arkansas, Louisiana, Oklahoma, Texas).

census taken before World War I. Because of certain "pull factors" (need for industrial labor in the North) and "push factors" (diversification and delayed mechanization of agriculture in the South), during World War I, a large-scale migratory flow of blacks from South to North began. This migratory stream slowed up during the depression of the 1930s but accelerated greatly during World War II and its aftermath. Consequently, between 1910 and 1960 the proportion of blacks living in the North and West increased from 11 to 40 percent.

The degree to which blacks viewed the South as "the place not to be in" and the North as a "promised land" can be seen in net migration figures (that is, the number leaving an area minus the number entering that area), as given in Table 6–1.

Six states in the North and West absorbed 72 percent of all black in-migration between 1910 and 1950 (California, Michigan, New York, Illinois, Ohio, and Pennsylvania). These same six states accounted for 68 percent of all black in-migration for the 1950–1960 decade.

The effect of this migration was not only regional but also it transformed blacks from a rural to an urban people. In 1910, 73 percent of blacks as compared with 52 percent of whites lived in rural areas (on farms and in areas with populations of less than 2,500). By 1960, 73 percent of blacks lived in urban areas. This percentage is higher than the 70 percent of whites who were urban. By 1970, 80.7 percent of blacks were urban as compared to only 72.4 percent of whites (see Table 6–2).

The importance of this urban migration is even more dramatic when the destination is examined. In 1910, only 29 percent of blacks lived

**TABLE 6–2**

Percentage Distribution of the United States Population by Race

| YEAR AND AREA | WHITE | NONWHITE | TOTAL |
|---|---|---|---|
| *1950* | | | |
| Urban | 64.3 | 61.7 | 64.0 |
|   Inside urbanized areas | 45.8 | 45.3 | 45.8 |
|     central cities | (31.1) | (39.2) | (32.0) |
|     urban fringe | (14.7) | ( 6.1) | (13.8) |
|   Outside urbanized areas | 18.5 | 16.4 | 18.2 |
| Rural | 35.7 | 38.3 | 36.0 |
| *1960* | | | |
| Urban | 69.5 | 72.4 | 69.9 |
|   Inside urbanized areas | 52.7 | 58.9 | 53.5 |
|     central cities | (30.0) | (50.5) | (32.3) |
|     urban fringe | (22.8) | ( 8.4) | (21.1) |
|   Outside urbanized areas | 16.8 | 13.5 | 16.4 |
| Rural | 30.5 | 27.6 | 30.1 |
| *1970* | | | |
| Urban | 72.4 | 80.7 | 73.5 |
|   Inside urbanized areas | 56.8 | 68.7 | 58.3 |
|     central cities | (27.9) | (56.5) | (31.5) |
|     urban fringe | (28.9) | (12.3) | (26.8) |
|   Outside urbanized areas | 15.7 | 12.0 | 15.2 |
| Rural | 27.6 | 19.3 | (26.5) |

SOURCE: U.S. Department of Commerce, Bureau of the Census, *U.S. Census of Population:* 1950, 1960, and 1970, Volume I.

in Standard Metropolitan Statistical Areas (SMSAs). This percentage had increased to 65 by 1960. The comparable increase figures in SMSAs for blacks and whites between 1920 and 1940 were 65 and 40 percent, respectively. Between 1940 and 1960 blacks more than doubled their percentage in SMSAs (109 percent), while whites increased by 50 percent. Between 1960 and 1970 blacks increased in SMSAs by 20.2 percent while whites increased by only 11.9 percent. This means that 74.3 percent of all blacks lived in SMSAs in 1970.

Blacks not only moved to SMSAs in large numbers but also moved disproportionately to the largest cities (1 million or more) and within large metropolitan areas to the central cities. By 1960, 51 percent of all blacks in the United States lived in the central cities of SMSAs.

What this means essentially is that within a period of fifty years—less than a normal lifetime—the black population of the United States was radically transformed from a rural southern to a highly urbanized population primarily located in the deteriorating high-density slum enclaves of our northern metropolitan areas.

The exact effect of this transformation on the black family is difficult to gauge. In general, the resources of the families undergoing these changes must have been severely strained. Learning to live in a huge city—using the mass transit systems, coping with municipal services (or the lack of them) and with helping agencies, living in high rise apartment buildings—all tax the individuals who must endure such experiences. The failure of large urban area housing projects, which are usually populated primarily by blacks, is well known. Even so, the adaptive strength of the black family can be seen in data from a study of 13,924 black households and subfamilies, most of whom were in the Central Harlem area of New York City in 1925. The central findings are listed below (see Gutman, 1976:xix and Chapter 10):

1. 85 percent of New York City kin-related black households were double-headed.

2. Thirty-two of these 13,924 were father-absent households and subfamilies headed by women under thirty and contained three or more children.

3. Between 7 and 8 percent of females aged twenty-five to forty-four headed male-absent households and subfamilies. Twenty years earlier, the percentage had been higher (10 percent).

4. Three in four males aged forty-five and older were unskilled laborers and service workers, and in that year (1925) three in four of the households headed by males forty-five and older were headed by unskilled laborers and service workers.

5. Five in six children under the age of six lived with both parents.

The black family survived the Great Depression of the 1930s, the modernization of Southern agriculture, the exodus to the North and to urban centers, World War II, recessions and riots, prejudice and discrimination, dehumanizing urban ghettos and massive poverty—just as it had survived slavery and Reconstruction. All of these forces of social change have had their effects, to be sure, but none has destroyed a family system whose roots reach beyond American history to societies and cultures that flourished when this country was unknown to the white man.

Descriptions of the black family in the 1960s and early 1970s tended to reflect the political orientation of the times—if a social problem exists, define it and then develop a social program to solve it. The whites who controlled the political forces at the time tended to focus on what they viewed as "pathological" features of the black family—female-headed households, illegitimacy rates, and unemployment. They saw the black family as a social problem in need of a program. Perhaps the best-known and most controversial of the attempts to define the black family as a "problem" is the Moynihan Report. We now turn to this report and its critics.

## THE MOYNIHAN REPORT

The Moynihan Report, *The Negro Family: The Case for National Action* was authored by Daniel Patrick Moynihan in 1965, when he was Assistant Secretary of Labor in the Johnson administration. Moynihan, an urban sociologist, was academically well qualified to analyze the data on the black family. He was not and is not an untrained ideologue, although there have been serious questions raised as to how he treated the data he did use in his report and more specifically as to the "corrective" steps he advocated to solve the "problem" of the black family in the United States.

Moynihan's report used census data and information from several special studies. The Report documents (a) the higher unemployment rates and lower wage rates among blacks as compared to whites; (b) the larger family size and differentially high fertility rate among the poor—particularly blacks; (c) the higher illegitimacy rates among blacks; and (d) the higher percentage of black families that are female headed as compared to whites. We will examine some of the relevant data relating to the findings of the Moynihan Report in the hope of shedding some new light on whether the black family is a pathological problem for American society or a victim of statistical mythology.

### Matriarchal Structure

Perhaps one of the most controversial conclusions of the Moynihan report deals with whether female-headed families constitute a problem for the black family. Moynihan states (1965:29):

> In essence, the Negro community has been forced into a matriarchal structure which, because it is so out of line with the rest of American society, seriously retards the progress of the group as a whole, and imposes a crushing burden on the Negro male and, in consequence, on a great many Negro women as well.

A conceptual distinction should be made here. The term *matriarchal* refers to the distribution of power within the family—information not available directly to Moynihan. Just because a family is female headed (that is, no male head is present according to the census definition of head of household) does not necessarily mean that it is matriarchal. So there are two questions that need to be discussed: (1) To what extent are black families differentially headed by females? and (2) What is the actual distribution of power within black families?

The proportion of all white families headed by a woman has increased only slightly since 1950, from 8.8 to 10 percent, leaving almost nine out of ten white families still headed by a husband-wife team. The situation is different among nonwhites, the overwhelming majority of whom are black. The proportion of those headed by a woman has increased from 18.8 percent in 1950 to 33 percent in 1973. Herein lies part of the difficulty with the Moynihan report. He emphasized the "facts"

140

that (1) almost one-fourth of all nonwhite families were female headed and (2) this was considerably higher than the figure for whites (9 percent). A careful and nonpoliticized evaluation of these data should have led Moynihan to the conclusion that, in 1965, three out of four nonwhite families were headed by a husband-wife team. He should also have noted that this was probably an underestimate since the census does not account for families in which the black male is regularly present, acting in a quasi–husband-father role but not legally married to the resident female head of the family. Unfortunately, Moynihan chose to ignore these obvious caveats, or conditional factors, affecting his data.

This does not mean that Moynihan's claims should be ignored or dismissed outright as rank prejudice. As the data in Table 6–3 show, a significantly larger proportion of nonwhite families are headed by women. In 1973, 33 percent of all nonwhite families had a female head (up from 22 percent in 1960). The respective figures for low-income families were 63

**TABLE 6–3**
**Selected Measures of Family Stability**

| VARIABLES | WHITE | NONWHITE |
| --- | --- | --- |
| | (IN PERCENTAGES) | |
| Proportion of all Families with a Female Head | | |
| 1960 | 9 | 22 |
| 1973 | 10 | 33 |
| Proportion of Low-Income Families with a Female Head | | |
| 1960 | 20 | 33 |
| 1973 | 33 | 63 |
| Proportion of Low-Income Families with Children under 18 with a Female Head | | |
| 1960 | 25 | 35 |
| 1973 | 48 | 71 |
| Proportion of Children under 18 Living with both Parents | | |
| 1960 | 92 | 75 |
| 1973 | 87 | 52 |
| Proportion of Children under 18 Living with both Parents in Low-Income Families | | |
| 1960 | N.A. | N.A. |
| 1973 | 61 | 34 |
| Proportion of Births that Were Illegitimate | | |
| 1960 | 2 | 22 |
| 1973 | 6 | 42 |

SOURCE: Heather L. Ross and Isabel V. Sawhill, *Time of Transition: The Growth of Families Headed by Women*. Washington: The Urban Institute, 1975, p. 68. Courtesy of The Urban Institute.

percent in 1973 compared to 33 percent in 1960. The interrelationship of low income, female-headedness, and the presence of dependent children is painfully clear. Ross and Sawhill (1975:72–73) say that most of the non-white-white differences in family stability are due to a greater degree of marital disruption among black families with children and to higher illegitimacy within the black community. Additional factors accounting for the recent higher rate of increase in the percentage of nonwhite families headed by females include: (a) the continuing urbanization of the black population; (b) increased sexual activity and improved health, combined with a low level of effective contraception among teenagers; (c) bleak employment prospects for black men with little education; and (d) the greater availability of income outside of marriage for the poorest group of black women (Ross and Sawhill, 1975:88).

Now what about the matriarchal structure—the power distribution

### The Ten Houten Study

Another way of finding out who has the power in black families and consequently whether it is matriarchal is to ask observers—perhaps children. Warren Ten Houten (1970) did just that for a small but painstakingly drawn and representative sample of black and white, lower and higher socioeconomic status, intact families in the Los Angeles area.

Ten Houten cogently suggests that an important question to ask is: *In which roles—conjugal and/or parental—is the black man subordinate to the black wife?* Using a scale designed to measure adherence to a

**TABLE 6–4**
**Socioeconomic Status (SES) and Family Type**
**(in percentages)**

| CONJUGAL TYPE | LOWER SES | | HIGHER SES | |
|---|---|---|---|---|
| | BLACK (N = 96) | WHITE (N = 46) | BLACK (N = 50) | WHITE (N = 66) |
| Autonomic | 67 | 30 | 64 | 61 |
| Conflict | 12 | 9 | 20 | 12 |
| Husband-dominant | 19 | 56 | 12 | 24 |
| Wife-dominant | 2 | 4 | 4 | 3 |

SOURCE: Warren D. Ten Houten, "The Black Family: Myth and Reality," *Psychiatry* 27(May,1970):164. By permission of *Psychiatry: A Publication.*

NOTE: Responses were taken only from the two oldest children in the families studied.

question? The evidence here is inconsistent. Blood and Wolfe (1960), in their study of a sample of families in the Detroit area, note: "Negro husbands have unusually low power"; and while this is a characteristic of all low-income families, the pattern is pervasive in the black social structure because of "the cumulative result of discrimination in jobs, . . . the segregated housing, and the poor schooling of Negro men." "Whereas the majority of white families are equalitarian, the largest percentage of Negro families are dominated by the wife." The Blood and Wolfe conclusions should be treated as tenuous at best, since only wives were interviewed, and only 103 black wives at that. In their study the criterion of power was decision making. Some 44 percent of the black families were wife-dominant, 19 percent were husband dominated, and in 38 percent of the families, black wives said they shared familial power equally with their husbands.

male-dominant ideology he found that lower-class black husbands were higher than middle-class black and lower-class and middle-class white husbands. In addition, Ten Houten asked the two oldest children in these families to characterize the conjugal power configuration operative between their mother and father with regard to certain decision-making situations. The results found in Table 6–4 indicate that the Moynihan thesis is not supported.

The Moynihan thesis would predict that a large percentage of black families, especially lower-class, would be wife dominated. In fact, only 2 percent were matriarchal as perceived by the two oldest children. The modal category for lower-class blacks was autonomic (neither husband nor wife clearly has the power, and they seem to negotiate their differences). The atypical group consists of lower-class white families with the husband dominant. Ten Houten (1970) concludes that:

> In general, the data from the empirical study do not show lower-class black husbands to be powerless in either their conjugal or their parental roles. Black wives do appear to be powerful in their parental roles, but there is no indication that this emasculates the black husband-father.

Additional support for these tentative and discrepant conclusions by Ten Houten comes from Hyman and Reed (1969), who reported that the woman's influence execeeds that of the man in a number of instances. What they found in a reanalysis of data from three existing surveys was that the disproportionate female influence was almost identical for whites and blacks.

143

CONCLUSIONS. In concluding our study of the structure of the black family, we must ask a rhetorical question: *How can we possibly continue to characterize the black family in the United States as matriarchal?* The available evidence, outlined below, suggests just the opposite:

1. Over two-thirds of all black families in the United States are headed by a husband-wife team, and this is probably an underestimate, given the moralistic and legalistic definition of female-headed families used by the Census Bureau and the scholars who have used census data. In effect, the black boyfriend who fulfills the husband's roles in a de facto sense (see Liebow, 1967; Schulz, 1972) is rather pervasively ignored by governmental enumerators who apply white, middle-class legal and moral definitions of the terms, *husband* and *father*.

2. As Ten Houten (1970) (see the accompanying box) and Hyman and Reed (1969) have shown, the conjugal and/or parental roles in black families are not female dominated relative to white females. In fact, from an economic standpoint, only a small minority of black families in which both parents are present are dependent on the mother for their maintenance.

3. It is also curious, again from an economic standpoint, that black females who had a median income of $2,084 in 1970 would have an economic advantage over black males whose median income in 1970 was $4,240.

4. As Staples (1970) made quite clear, the black woman is actually in a poor position to be matriarchal.

> Making decisions that black men cannot, or will not, make is a poor measure of the power a black woman has in the family. The chances are good that no decisions are made that he actively opposes. The power of black women is much like American democracy—it is more apparent than real. Power alignments are frequently based on the alternatives an individual has in a situation where there is a conflict of interests. It is here where the black male achieves the upper level of the power dimension.

The black matriarchy, therefore, is myth, not reality. That myth has been perpetrated and perpetuated by a misuse of available data, perhaps unintentionally. Regardless of the intentions, the myth is a cruel hoax.

## Illegitimacy

Another factor that looms large in the Moynihan report is the extent of illegitimacy among blacks. Although there is no direct charge that blacks are sexually depraved or morally corrupt, there is the implicit hypothesis. Ryan (1965) stated:

> The values of Negro culture (produced by centuries of slavery and mistreatment, to be sure) are such that there is little commitment to the

main components of family organization—legitimacy, material stability, etc. The implicit point is that Negroes tolerate promiscuity, illegitimacy, one-parent families, welfare dependency, and everything else that is supposed to follow.

What is the evidence of illegitimacy? How does illegitimacy relate to family stability? The second question is fairly simple to answer. If a woman becomes pregnant premaritally, her chances for a stable marriage are, at best, less than they would be if she were not pregnant premaritally. In addition, if a child is born to an unmarried mother, his or her chances to grow up in a home with both parents present are not good (Vincent, 1961; Bowerman et al., 1963).

The sources of data on illegitimacy are limited. At present only 34 states make any judgment as to legitimacy status. This is a decline from the 45 states that recorded and reported births by legitimacy in 1940. Consequently, the national illegitimacy numbers and rates are estimates compiled by the National Center for Health Statistics using as a base the data from the 34 reporting states.

Since 1940, the proportion of all illegitimate births has risen steadily, accounting in 1976 for 14.8 percent of the total. There is a substantial difference by race, as the data in Table 6–5 show. In 1976, 7.7 percent of all live births to white mothers were illegitimate compared to 45 percent

**TABLE 6–5**
**Illegitimate Births**

| YEAR | NONWHITE | | | WHITE | | |
|------|----------|---|---|-------|---|---|
| | NUMBER OF ILLEGITIMATE BIRTHS | PERCENTAGE OF ILLEGITIMATE LIVE BIRTHS | ILLEGITIMACY RATE [a] | NUMBER OF ILLEGITIMATE BIRTHS | PERCENTAGE OF ILLEGITIMATE LIVE BIRTHS | ILLEGITIMACY RATE |
| 1940 | 49,000 | 13.6 | 35.6 | 40,000 | 1.8 | 3.6 |
| 1950 | 88,000 | 16.8 | 71.2 | 54,000 | 1.7 | 6.1 |
| 1960 | 142,000 | 21.6 | 98.3 | 83,000 | 2.3 | 9.2 |
| 1970 | 224,000 | 35.0 | 89.9 | 175,000 | 5.7 | 13.8 |
| 1971 | 238,000 | 37.4 | 90.6 | 164,000 | 5.6 | 12.5 |
| 1972 | 243,000 | 40.3 | 86.9 | 161,000 | 6.1 | 12.0 |
| 1973 | 244,000 | 41.6 | 84.2 | 163,000 | 6.4 | 11.9 |
| 1974 | 249,600 | 42.7 | 81.5 | 168,500 | 6.5 | 11.8 |
| 1975 | 261,600 | 44.2 | 80.4 | 186,400 | 7.3 | 12.6 |
| 1976 | 271,000 | 45.2 | 78.1 | 197,100 | 7.7 | 12.7 |

SOURCE: National Center for Health Statistics, Monthly Vital Statistics Report, Final Natality Statistics, 1976, Vol. 26, No. 12, March 29, 1978, and previous years.

[a] Illegitimacy rate is the number of illegitimate births per 1,000 unmarried women aged 15–44.

for nonwhite mothers (see Table 6–5). When one examines illegitimacy rates, the racial differences are clear although the trend is definitely downward for nonwhites. Among whites the rate peaked in 1970 at 13.8, moved downward through 1974, and has begun to inch upward again. As Farley and Hermalin (1971:9) indicated: "Since the mid-1960s nonwhite and white illegitimate birth rates have apparently moved in opposite directions. Among nonwhites, there have been decreases in the rate of illegitimate childbearing, but among whites, these rates have continued their climb. The rate at which unmarried nonwhite women bore children seemingly peaked during the early 1960s and has declined slightly since then."

Several factors account for these figures: First, the proportion of all illegitimate births is affected by the number of legitimate births. For example, if the number of illegitimate births remained stable from one year to the next and legitimate fertility declined markedly, the proportion of all births that would be classified as illegitimate would go up. Second, the illegitimacy rate is especially sensitive to the number of unmarried women "at risk" to have illegitimate births. Given the passage of the baby boom generation through their late teens and early twenties, an increased age at first marriage, a generally greater amount of sexual activity, and poor utilization of contraceptives—it is not surprising that the illegitimacy rate is considered high. However, the factors listed above would suggest that the high figures do not represent degenerating morals as much as the operation of macro-level demographic factors.

Differences by race in the rates of illegitimate births seem to remain rather constant over time—about seven to one. How does one explain these differences? Was Moynihan correct in his assessment that the extent of illegitimacy signals an inherent weakness in the black family system? These are socially important and politically sensitive questions. They demand a factual and controlled analysis.

Ross and Sawhill (1975:80) used data from a nationwide study of sexuality among fifteen-to-nineteen-year-old females (see discussion of the Zelnik and Kantner study in Chapter 10) to answer the question of why there are race differences in illegitimacy. Their answer is built around five explanatory factors, all of which contribute:

1. higher rates of premarital intercourse among black females
2. less effective use of contraceptives, which leads to a higher rate of pregnancy among the sexually active
3. less legitimation of pregnancy through a rushed marriage
4. fewer abortions, which leads to a higher proportion of full-term births
5. less adoption, which leads to a higher proportion of single mothers living with their children.

The findings of Ross and Sawhill are quite consistent with the conclusion of Cutright (1973) that about 45 percent of the race differential in illegitimacy is due to the greater prevalance of poverty in the nonwhite population.

Illegitimacy, at least as illustrated in public statistics, is more endemic among nonwhites: 42 of every 100 live nonwhite births were illegitimate in 1973 compared to 6 of 100 among whites. It is at this point that the interpretations Ryan says are implicit in the Moynihan report—the toleration of promiscuity, one-parent families, welfare dependency, and a lack of commitment to family stability—crop up. What other factors could account for a 7-to-1 ratio (black-to-white) in the percentage of illegitimate births?

REPORTING. Besides the fact that national illegitimacy statistics are estimates from only thirty-four states, illegitimate births are significantly underreported. In addition, the nonwhite, unmarried female is more likely than her white sister to give birth in a public rather than a private hospital; more likely to have a physician who is not a personal and private doctor; more likely to have a white doctor who may be less than sympathetic to her plight; and less likely to have the cooperative services of various social agencies. In other words, the white mother of an illegitimate child is protected and perhaps concealed by the white power structure—especially if she has socioeconomic resources. No one protects an economically disadvantaged black mother of an illegitimate child. If the reporting of illegitimate births were not biased, it is quite possible that the ratio would be substantially lower than 7 to 1.

FORCED WEDDINGS. A second reason the black illegitimacy rate is reported so much higher than the white rate has to do with voluntary legitimization of status. Farley and Hermalin (1971) calculated an estimate of the percentage of births that were not illegitimate because of forced marriages. This was done by finding the percentage of births that occurred among first married women during the first seven months of marriage. The figures are probably a conservative estimate of premarital conceptions, but it should be a relatively solid index of the extent of forced marriage. See Table 6–6.

Farley and Hermalin's interpretation of these data (1971:13) support the view being proposed here that the racial differences in the illegitimacy rates may be more artificial than real:

> These figures demonstrate one important reason why nonwhite illegitimacy rates exceed those of whites: premarital pregnancies are less likely to lead to marriage among nonwhites. In 1960–64, apparently fewer than one in five nonwhite women who became premaritally pregnant married within seven months but three in five white women married. This implies that racial differences in premarital conception rates are smaller than racial differences in illegitimate birth rates.

147

**TABLE 6–6**
**Estimates of Forced Marriages**

| DATES | PERCENTAGE OF PREMARITAL PREGNANCIES RESULTING IN RAPID MARRIAGES: 1940–64 | |
| --- | --- | --- |
| | NONWHITES | WHITES |
| 1940–49 | 23 | 55 |
| 1950–59 | 19 | 63 |
| 1960–64 | 18 | 60 |

SOURCE: Reynolds Farley and Albert I. Hermalin, "Family Stability: A Comparison of Trends Between Blacks and Whites," *American Sociological Review, 36* (February 1971): 13. By permission of the American Sociological Association and the authors.

Goode (1961) concluded that blacks have a lower commitment to legitimacy than whites and this accounts for the smaller percentage of rapid marriages. His argument is that blacks were deprived of their original cultural heritage, prohibited from being accepted into the Western European cultural heritage, and hindered in establishing their own cultural systems. The result is a low commitment to legitimacy. In addition, it costs money to get married. Add to that the fact that the black child who is illegitimate is not stigmatized in the black community and neither is the mother. In the legalistic and moralistic white community illegitimacy is about as bad as leprosy.

The difference in illegitimate birth rates, then, may be artificially inflated because of fewer forced weddings among nonwhites. When this is added to the biases inherent in the reporting of illegitimacy, the Moynihan report seems even less plausible.

DIFFERENTIAL USE OF ABORTION. The third factor that may partially account for the race differential in illegitimacy rates is the fact that abortion has been primarily a white phenomenon. An estimated one-fourth to one-half of all abortions in the United States are performed on unmarried women. Thus, the white illegitimacy rate is an understatement of white commitment to legitimacy since abortion is one way of not having an illegitimate child—evidently a way used much more frequently by whites than by nonwhites.

## SUMMARY AND CONCLUSIONS

White and black scholars alike have reinforced stereotypical views of the black family that are more myth than reality. The available evidence suggests that the black family in the United States is not matriarchal; it

Joel Gordon

is matrifocal, but it is not matriarchal. If matrifocality is a pathological condition indicative of a breakdown in the black family, then the white suburban family is also quite sick. The fact is that the mother is the central family figure in American society. That role is more visible and central in the black community because socioeconomic forces detract from the vitality of the husband-father role.

We also saw that there is an unwarranted emphasis given to illegitimacy rates as an index of family disorganization among blacks. The differential illegitimacy rates are quite possibly the result of biased reporting, a greater percentage of forced marriages among whites, and a greater

149

reliance on abortion by premaritally pregnant white women. This doesn't mean that illegitimacy is not a problem for blacks. There is a much higher number of multiple illegitimate births among blacks, and it is here that illegitimacy constitutes a social problem for the black family.

Warren Ten Houten (1970) best summarizes the point:

> The weight of existing evidence, however, suggests that the stereotype of lower-class black families as matriarchal, pathological, and "approaching a state of complete breakdown," may in reality constitute social mythology. The reality is that such a view is not supported by a convincing body of social research.

What, then, can we say about the black family in the United States? I prefer to be optimistic, to look on it positively. Blacks constitute about 12 percent of our population—the largest minority group. They are the most urbanized ethnic minority in our society; 81 percent were urban dwellers in 1970. Because of historical and primarily economic forces, 57 percent of blacks in urban areas live in the deteriorating central cities of our largest metropolitan areas. Blacks are disproportionately found in the unskilled levels of our occupational force, are generally paid lower wages than whites, and are much more likely to be jobless.

All these contextual factors work against the black family achieving greater stability. The resilience of the black family against such overwhelming odds is amazing. A reason for that resilience is found partially in the social structure of the slum, which has been described thoroughly by Gerald Suttles (1968). Suttles has shown, through an extensive participant observation study of an urban slum area, that what appears to an outsider to be disorder is, in fact, an orderly community.

One problem affecting the study of the black family in the United States has been the ethnocentric application of white terminology (kinship based on blood ties) to the study of a conjugal family system where the distinctions between kin and nonkin are less salient. It is here that the term *soul brother* is quite appropriate, but the real significance of that term has been virtually ignored by white sociologists. We cannot seem to contemplate the concept of *community* as a substitute for *family*. Perhaps a kibbutz-raised sociologist would see a community-family if he or she were to do a participant observation study in the black community.

## SOME POSSIBLE IMPLICATIONS

*Today the black population constitutes about 12 percent of the total population and is over 80 percent urban. A disproportionate number of blacks live in our largest cities, and there they are predominantly clustered in the poorer and decaying central-city areas. Blacks are also disproportionately clustered in the lower income, occupational, and educational categories. The unemployment rate among blacks is much higher than for whites.*

*Possibly as a consequence of the civil rights movement of the 1950s and 1960s, many governmental agencies at the federal, state, and local levels have directed their primary energies at the black population and black families. All too often the whites who generally administer these programs view the black family as pathological, in need of remedial services.*

*One consequence of this approach has been an attempt to intrude in and manipulate the black community—a kind of intrasociety foreign aid program. This leads to some serious implications. What are the effects of this labeling process that makes the black population clients for the welfare arm of government? Is the government attempting, even unconsciously, to make blacks more like the prevailing middle-class white? Are our laws, particularly the Aid to Dependent Children statutes, designed to keep the black male out of the black family? Do our statutes and norms about the dispersion of contraceptive information and techniques encourage unwed pregnancy among blacks? Is it possible that a consequence of making blacks the target for family planning programs will be eventual racial genocide?*

*If you are white, try to put yourself into the shoes of a black person. How would you view the white community and the governmental services that are directed at the black population?*

*As Pinkney notes: "The black family is a complex social institution, and its members must not be blamed for the problems imposed by the larger society."*

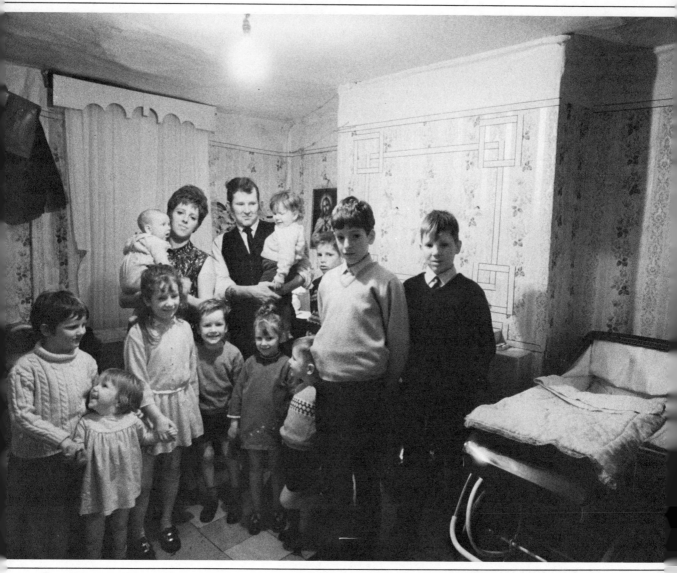

# 7

# THE FAMILY
# IN IRELAND AND THE
# ISLAMIC COUNTRIES

*What are the essential components of a stem family system?*

*What are the major characteristics of the family under Islam and how are those characteristics changing?*

*Why are some societies committed to a "traditional" type of family?*

*How do population, organization, environment, and technology account for a commitment to a traditional family orientation?*

In preceding chapters we alternated between looking at the family in the broadest terms and at the two types of families, white and black, that are indigenous to the United States. Perhaps the best way to understand both the cultural richness and the points of cultural deprivation in our family system is to look at the family in other cultures. In this comparative approach we should learn something about others at the same time we learn more about ourselves.

We will examine the family system of a Western European country that is predominantly Roman Catholic, the Republic of Ireland, and the family system that is found among the adherents of Islam, one of the major world religions but that is geographically indigenous to North Africa and Asia Minor. Different family practices in these two cultures may be tied to the same kinds of causal processes. But this kind of interpretation can be decided only after examination.

## THE FAMILY IN IRELAND

We turn first to a unique and interesting country in Western Europe, Ireland. The uniqueness of Ireland is found in several dimensions. First, during the last 120 years it is the only country in Western Europe whose population has declined. Between 1841 and 1951 the population declined by 54 percent. Of that decline, 47 percent occurred because of emigration in the years 1841–91. Second, Ireland is still predominantly an agrarian society with a large percentage of the labor force classified as agricultural. In addition, the Irish farm is usually rather small and can generally be labeled a subsistence type of operation. Third, since the country is almost completely Roman Catholic, not only divorce is prohibited but the inroads of secularization have been effectively blocked by an extremely conservative morality fostered by the Church. Fourth, the Irish have a stem type family system in which traditionally only one male is allowed to inherit the family homestead and the other male children are forced to migrate or emigrate.

Against this background of traditionalism and conservatism Ireland has experienced remarkable and extensive changes since World War II. Rampant industrial development has been accompanied by a large-scale rural-to-urban shift in population. These two forces have produced dramatic changes in the whole fabric of Irish society, including marriage and family patterns. Perhaps the best place to start is with a discussion of the importance of land in Irish society.

154

## Symbiotic Land-Family Tie

It is difficult for people with a frontier history like Americans to understand the reverence the Irish have for their land. Although the United States has existed for 200 years, many Irish can trace their families back 400 years or more on the same farm or within the same village. This "sense of history" and tie with the past play important roles in how the Irish view their property.

In the 1600s Ireland was colonized by the British, and much of its land was confiscated and given to loyal subjects of the crown for plantations. It was not until the late nineteenth and early twentieth centuries, after a series of land acts, that most landlords were replaced with small landholders who finally became proprietors of their own farms. As this

*Irish children, especially boys, are taught early the importance of the land, which in many cases has been in the family for generations.*

Dan Budnik from Woodfin Camp & Associates

was occurring, the present, dominant Irish farm pattern emerged—dispersed family farmsteads, small in size, depending heavily on livestock production and the making of hay, with a secondary emphasis on the growing of crops.

This long historical battle to gain control of the land led Gallaher (1973) to suggest an Irish syndrome of uncertainty of tenure. Consequently, a farm is seen as having the "family name on it" and has become a symbol of the unity and viability of the family, no matter how widely dispersed the members of that family may be. This qualification that geographical mobility is nonconsequential is an important one, since the Irish have experienced massive internal migration as well as emigration. This dispersal does not constitute a dissolution of the family; it is merely a hindrance to communication and visiting. In a way, it can be said that the land with the "family name on it" is like a totem pole—it is the family in symbolic form, and that farm is the center of the family, no matter where the members happen to be. We will come back to this idea of the salience of land, but first let us examine some of the dramatic changes occurring in Irish marriage and family customs.

## Heterosexual Contacts Prior to Marriage

One of the more striking characteristics of rural Ireland is the traditional separation of the sexes across a wide range of activities. Prior to 1945 females in the country were expected to spend almost all of their time on the isolated farmstead, coming to the village only for Mass at 6:00 P.M. on Sunday. Even then there were no mechanisms whereby boys and girls could get together socially. On the other hand, males were expected to frequent their favorite pubs regularly to "raise a pint," throw some darts, and participate in the very cohesive male-group camaraderie. However, no comparable outlet existed for the Irish female.

About the only provision for male-female socializing prior to 1945 were infrequent dances held at various farmsteads, by invitation only. In spite of the social conservatism of these affairs, the Roman Catholic Church was apprehensive about the morals of its youth. Through Church influence the government passed the dance-hall bill banning farm dances and authorizing dances to be held only in parochial halls adjacent to the churches. This not only allowed the church to closely observe the social lives of its young members but also provided the church with additional revenue. According to many critics, the latter was a primary goal of the dance-hall bill. The church dances were not unlike the typical junior high school dance in the United States, with the males clustered at one end and the females at the other. After they met in the center for a dance they retreated to the same-sex enclaves for moral support. Seldom did the dancers arrive together and only occasionally did they leave together.

However, postwar Ireland is drastically different from the old prewar days. With the introduction of the automobile a kind of dating has emerged. The mobility provides the opportunity to attend dances in other nearby communities, where parental screening is less likely and where males and females can more easily pair off after the dance. Gallaher (1973) says that "the automobile has intervened to strike the greatest innovative blow yet for liberalizing courtship patterns." A second liberalizing force is the addition of lounges in many rural pubs so that female customers may be served. Now that there is a place to meet, a way to get around, and a place to go after the dance or movie, rural Irish youth are beginning to gain control of the courtship system. It would not be surprising if the courtship patterns, even in rural Ireland, follow the same or similar lines found in the United States after the automobile became a way of life.

## Traditional Marriage Patterns

Traditionally, the marriage of the son who will inherit the farmstead has been the key event in the rural Irish family. Since the family is a stem system, this event signaled the exodus of the unmarried sons. In prewar Ireland the traditional marriage was between cousins, with the match arranged by the parents of the couple.

In his study of a rural parish called Corofin, Gallaher (1973) found that from two to three in five of the 120 marriages among the farmer class between 1925 and 1945 were matches arranged by the parents. Of the 90 marriages occurring between 1946 and 1965, one in five were considered arranged matches. Interviews by Gallaher on the match concept show agreement in all sectors of the community that "it is no longer the preferred, nor is it the typical, normative pattern. It is an alternative available, but it is the one least valued, and there are some people, in fact, who consider it downright stigmatic."

What this means is significant for the Irish family system. Evidently rural Irish youth are seriously challenging the traditional authority of the family to determine who may marry whom, when, and under what conditions. The resulting patterns of marriage are thus more likely to be based on personal choice with love rather than on economic considerations as the deciding factor.

Gallaher (1973) found that the girls he interviewed were committed to the ideal of a nuclear family household in which the stem family influence was minimal. In fact, 55 percent of the girls of thirteen to nineteen years of age flatly rejected the notion of marrying a small farmer because it might mean marrying into an extended household. He felt that most of the 34 percent who were undecided would in the long run reject the small-farm housewife role (living in a stem household with the husband's parents). These rural girls wanted husbands with similar interests, of roughly the same age, who would allow them to hold jobs outside the house, and who would not require them to do the usual onerous tasks associated with farm life.

The young men Gallaher interviewed were well aware of these marital goals and seemed generally willing to play the game by the girls' rules. The major concern voiced by the rural males was for wives who would not nag them and complain excessively about their lot—an indication that young Irish males still want the prerogative of visiting the pub with the boys without interference from their wives.

## Age at Marriage

One of the most frequently mentioned characteristics of the Irish family system is the traditional practice of late marriage for both sexes. Although there are numerous explanations offered to account for this tradition, the chief ones are (a) economics and (b) family obligations. Since the family of orientation loses its prerogative of authority and power at the marriage of the son designated as heir to the family farm, rural Irish parents have traditionally postponed the transferral process as long as possible. Thus, in prewar Ireland it was not unusual for a man to wait until his forties to get married. A second factor in late marriages is the tremendous camaraderie found among the men. A male's peer group could give him a great deal more social satisfaction and certainly less responsibility and hardship than marriage and a wife. To ease the prolonged dependency of rural males, the father usually refers to his sons (some 35 to 50 years old) as boys. This terminology, coupled with the smothering affection of the Irish mother for her sons and the warm womb of the peer group, made the bachelor status a rather comfortable one.

However, the age at marriage has dropped significantly from the higher level that prevailed in 1946. As the data in Table 7–1 indicate, the median age at first marriage fell six years for males (32 to 26) and three years for females (from 27 to 24) between 1946 and 1969. These changes not only reflect the decreasing importance of the rural population and the concomitant impact of the urban but also represent an emergent perception of marriage among all sectors of the Irish population. As Walsh (1972) states: ". . . but the phenomenon of first marriage at a fairly advanced age persists. . . . The proportion of marriages, in which there was less than five years gap between the ages of the bride and groom rose from 49 percent in 1946 to 71 percent in 1969. The percentage of marriages in which the groom was ten or more years older than the bride has fallen from 22 to seven percent."

Even with the decreasing ages at first marriage, the desires for greater similarity between spouses, the demise of the match system, and the rejection of the small-farm housewife role, marriages in the countryside are still homogamous. Gallaher (1973) found that 50 percent of all the marriages occurring between 1925 and 1965 were of couples from the same parish (Corofin). About 42 percent were of couples from adjacent parishes. Thus, while the free-choice ideology of marital selection with the major emphasis on love has diffused, the wings of love seem especially weak for rural Irish youth. In addition, Gallaher found a strong commitment to marriage within the same social class. Seldom did he observe a willingness to consider marrying down or up the class ladder.

While Irish youth have seemingly adopted the ideology of love marriages, they still conform quite readily to the traditional endogamous norms about age and social class differences. The Irish young people Gallaher interviewed indicated somewhat idealistic conditions for their marriages—conditions that probably will be compromised when they face the realities of choice.

What I have described, while fictitious, is probably not too far removed from the reality of the prewar Irish farm family. The symbolic-

**TABLE 7–1**
**Median Age of Irish First Marriages**

| YEARS AND AREA OF RESIDENCE | MEDIAN AGE | | DIFFERENCE |
|---|---|---|---|
| | BRIDES | GROOMS | |
| 1946[a] | | | |
| Urban | 25.8 | 29.2 | 3.4 |
| Rural | 28.0 | 33.6 | 5.6 |
| Total | 27.0 | 31.8 | 4.8 |
| 1957 | 25.9 | 29.4 | 3.5 |
| 1958 | 25.7 | 29.2 | 3.5 |
| 1959 | 25.4 | 28.9 | 3.5 |
| 1960 | 25.3 | 28.6 | 3.3 |
| 1961 | 25.1 | 28.3 | 3.2 |
| 1962 | 24.9 | 27.9 | 3.0 |
| 1963 | 24.6 | 27.7 | 3.1 |
| 1964 | 24.5 | 27.4 | 2.9 |
| 1965 | 24.2 | 27.0 | 2.8 |
| 1966 | 24.0 | 26.9 | 2.9 |
| 1967 | 24.0 | 26.6 | 2.6 |
| 1968 | 23.9 | 26.3 | 2.4 |
| 1969 | 23.8 | 26.0 | 2.2 |

SOURCE: Adapted from Brendan M. Walsh, "Trends in Age at Marriage in Postwar Ireland," *Demography, 9* (1972):188. Copyright © Population Association of America, used by permission.

[a] All marriages, including remarriages. Based on the 14,338 usable returns from the 1946 census. The total number of marriages in the preceding twelve months was 17,859.

interactional framework (see Chapter 2) offers us the best basis for a discussion of the dynamics of role relationships within the traditional Irish family.

### Role Relationships

HUSBAND-WIFE RELATIONS.  Whenever marriage partners are bound together because of economic considerations in a match arranged through institutional mechanisms, it is not unusual for husband-and-wife relations to be formal. If there is to be love between husband and wife, it has to grow from nothing because there is no way for love to develop prior to marriage. After marriage there are a host of factors that make the develop-

### From Institution to Companionship

The traditional rural Irish family is a remarkable institution now undergoing dramatic changes. It exists in a society in which the most basic customs and traditions are being challenged for the first time, and the results are fascinating to watch. We have discussed some of these changes without providing an adequate picture of family life itself. Therefore, let us reconstruct the family life of the traditional rural Irish family by creating a fictitious man, Peter O'Callahan, and his intended, Alice McGee. The example is, admittedly, an exaggerated one for illustrative purposes. Although things were probably never this severe in most rural Irish families, there is more than one grain of truth to the story.

The chances are good that Peter and Alice know each other but not well. They are probably second cousins and have grown up in the same parish. Peter is thirty-five years of age, and Alice, thirty. His father and mother are getting on in years, both in their sixties, and are well worn from years of trying to scratch out a life from their rocky farm. Peter feels especially close to his mother, for she has given him a great deal of affection, understanding, and protection from his father. In fact, Peter's mother has waited on him hand and foot since birth. On the other hand, Mr. O'Callahan has been an autocratic and dictatorial father to his "boy," for he still calls Peter "boy," although Peter has been doing a man's work since he was a teenager. Peter still has to ask his father's permission to go to the village, and he gets a pittance of an allowance from the old man, and only occasionally at that. Peter knows that his father has consented to his marriage only grudgingly, and that he was extremely difficult to deal with when arranging his match to Alice.

ment of love problematic. First, there is an absolute division of labor and a traditional separation of the sexes in all areas of life. The wife-role demands that she be submissive in all affairs and that she work long hard hours for no pay and for little or no other kind of reward. The traditional husband-role prescribes that he make all decisions about the family; that all the money in the family is his to use as he sees fit; that he is to maintain all of his old habits, particularly those relating to his continued participation in the male-only peer group.

This absolute separation of the male and female roles leads to a considerable amount of role-strain. There are obviously two marriages involved in the traditional Irish family—the husband's and the wife's. Whenever the wife tries to communicate disagreement with a family

In his thirty-five years Peter has seen little affection expressed between his mother and father. In fact, Mr. O'Callahan has never complimented his wife on anything—just growled and demanded that this or that be done, and quickly. For as long as he can remember his parents have slept in separate beds and have sometimes gone for weeks without speaking to one another.

Now the time has come for the farmstead to be passed on to one of the sons. Peter's two older brothers have already left the family farm. One works in a factory in Dublin, and the other left years ago for America. Peter has stuck it out primarily because of his mother. And now that he cannot keep up with all the chores and responsibilities, Mr. O'Callahan has decided that Peter should marry Alice. Peter's three younger brothers will now have to leave, since the farm cannot support them. They will probably go to Dublin and get factory jobs.

So Peter and Alice O'Callahan start married life, living in the same house with Peter's grouchy old father and his supersensitive and protective old mother. Alice will step in immediately to take over Mrs. O'Callahan's workload. She will take care of the cows and young pigs, clean house, cook the meals, wait on the elder O'Callahans, and sew for the entire family. Alice will become a tired old woman quickly. She will have little affection from Peter, and little or no help from anyone. Peter will spend a great deal of his time in the village, lifting a pint with his friends and throwing darts, and generally he will come home late, less than sober. Whenever he gets the urge, and it will not be very often, Alice will submit herself to him sexually, and when he is finished he will turn over and go to sleep.

Courtesy, The Irish Tourist Board

decision, the wife loses and the husband feels that he has been unjustly saddled with a nagging wife. The obvious solution to the strain is for the husband to leave home for awhile, that is, go to the pub and his understanding male friends, where the cycle of role-strain is further fueled. The lot of the Irish farm wife was not a happy one, to say the very least.

FATHER-CHILD RELATIONS. Once children arrive, especially males, the chances for a husband-wife love relationship to develop are further diminished. The father traditionally has little or nothing to do with child-rearing, which is the woman's bailiwick. As the children get older, it is the father's responsibility to direct the free labor that they provide him. This requires the father to be authoritarian in his orientation. The father, as mentioned previously, usually refers to his sons as boys throughout their life. The analogous role in American society is the marine drill instructor with his loud and constant hassling with no show of emotional softness, no show of appreciation, and no indication that any task performed is well done. In other words, ever-present fear and constant strain characterizes the typical father-son relationship. For the man who has had to endure such a relationship with his own father, who had to wait almost forever for the chance to exercise power and authority over the farm, giving up that power is to be prolonged as long as possible. Eventually, under the stem family system, the father must designate his heir and pass on the family farmstead. An Irish son might respect and even fear his father; to love him is virtually impossible.

MOTHER-SON RELATIONS. The traditional Irish mother is at the very least a paradox. On the one hand she accepts an onerous role-position, is beset by back-breaking work and isolation, is essentially exploited by her middle-aged adolescent-husband—and yet she is the centerfold of the Irish family system, the cementing pillar of stability in a patriarchal, patrilineal, male-oriented society. On the other hand, she is seemingly so starved for emotional gratification that her male children are smothered into an acquiescent dependency that not infrequently lasts until they are forty or older. She frequently exercises a firm veto on any possible spouse for her boys. She is an important buffer of defense for her children, especially the males, in their relationships with their father. She is usually in alliance with her children against the husband-father, and she may be the major factor in containing a potentially explosive intrafamily conflict situation.

The mother-son relationship in rural Ireland is extremely close. That closeness has its positive aspects (provision of security for male sons who fear their fathers, provision of a close and warm socialization experience for her children, provision of a central figure around which family life revolves) as well as some negative ones, in particular, the emotional smothering of male children to the point of extended dependency.

## Summary: The Family in Ireland

The Irish family life in the Republic of Ireland is experiencing a rapid demographic, industrial, and urban transformation. As in any society whose history is one of struggle and whose institutions are extremely conservative, the old customs and traditions are difficult to change, but change they do. The traditional stem family in Ireland, tied to the land and a subsistence type of farming, is changing to a more conjugal configuration with farms increasing in size, families moving to the city, young people revamping their values and attitudes and behaviors, and Irish folk in every sector of society recognizing that to be modern means a commitment to many options, not just those of the past. Rural Ireland is an ideal laboratory for the social scientists interested in observing change and its consequences.

## THE TRADITIONAL ISLAMIC FAMILY

Now that we have examined a patriarchal family in which the mother emerges as the central figure, even though she has no legitimately recognized power—the family in rural Ireland—we will center our attention on a male-dominant culture—the family under Islam. However, before discussing the particulars of Muslim family life, a brief overview of the Islamic religion might be informative.

163

## Introduction to Islam

Islam, the youngest of man's great universal religions, is in many ways the simplest and most explicit. It venerates a single, all-powerful God. Its founder, Muhammad, was neither savior nor messiah, but one through whom God chose to speak. Its faith concerns itself as much with man's behavior in this world as with his fate in the hereafter. Islam did not evolve slowly like most of the other world religions, but developed rapidly and with overwhelming speed enveloped a large part of the world. Within a few years after Muhammad's death in A.D. 632 it had conquered the entire Middle East; within another century it had extended its influence as far east as India and as far north as Spain. Today, Islam has over 550 million adherents (about as many as Roman Catholicism) in the northern half of Africa, the Mediterranean basin, the Middle East, south central Asia, Southern Asia, Indonesia, and the Philippines. However, the overwhelming majority of Muslims live in the Middle East.

Islam has neither an organized priesthood nor sacraments. Every man is his own priest and must adhere to a number of ritualistic observances, known as the Five Pillars of Islam, which are (a) the proclamation of the unity of God and belief therein, as expressed in the creed, "There is no God but Allah; Muhammad is the Messenger of Allah"; (b) prayer, performed five times daily, facing Mecca, wherever one might be; and on Fridays in the mosque; (c) almsgiving, as an offering to Allah and an act of piety; (d) the fast of Ramadan; and (e) a pilgrimage to Mecca. In addition to these major directives of religious duty, the Koran, the sacred book, also contains certain moral and legal ordinances. It forbids believers to eat pork, to gamble, or to practice usury, and it lays down rules for marriage and divorce, for penalties for crimes, and for other matters (Potter 1954).

Islam is an all-pervasive religion. Every possible relationship among human beings is of significance to the institution of religion. Thus, Islam is very explicit about familial relationships and customs leading to the establishment of a family. It should also be noted that Muhammad constructed a system of religion that would meet the needs of a people who were mainly agrarian and frequently nomadic.

Schacht (1964) in his book on Islamic law says that "the family is the only group based on consanguinity or affinity which Islam recognizes. Islam is opposed to tribal feeling, because the solidarity of believers should supersede the solidarity of the tribe." In other words, the family is the basic unit in the Islamic religion. As mentioned previously, it is quite difficult to separate the family from religion and vice versa.

## Six Structural Properties of the Islamic Family

Six basic structural properties characterize the Islamic family system. These properties deal with what Merton (1957) calls "the patterned arrangements of role-sets, status-sets, and status-sequences." The properties to be discussed are extended family structure; patrilineal descent; patri-local residence; patriarchal authority; polygynous marriage; and endogamous group structure.

EXTENDED FAMILY STRUCTURE.    Raphael Patai (1958) said that the Muslim family is definitely extended. That is, under traditional circumstances prevailing in the majority of cases, the family constituting one household consists of an elderly man, his wife or wives, his unmarried daughters, his unmarried as well as married sons, and the wives and children of the latter.

Goode (1963) dismissed this description as ideal rather than real, and said that the principle of the extended family under one roof was rarely practiced. Certainly the custom was not pervasive, primarily because the facts of fertility, mortality, and finances prevented all but a few from attaining the ideal. However, Goode believed that it is likely that many Arabs have at some time lived in an extended family either as adolescents, as adults who continued to live at home after marriage, or as married adults keeping their married sons at home.

Some of the characteristics usually associated with an extended family system are easy to recognize and document among the nomadic Arab groups that roam the desert areas of the Middle East. For example, Peters (1965) provided a detailed description of one Bedouin camp that contained six tents. All the residents of the camp were related to each other through their ties to a famous patriarch who died leaving his family under the care of his number one son. The tents were arranged so that those closest to the chief of the camp lived in closest proximity to his tent. The major characteristic of this extended family was its functioning as an economic unit of production and consumption. All property was owned by the group, and the work was allocated along strict age and sex lines. The men performed all tasks related to earning a living, and the women were in charge of the maintenance of the tents, the care of the children, and the preparation of the food. The work of the males was explicitly divided according to age and ability.

PATRILINEAL DESCENT.    The Muslim family is patrilineal, which means that each man is regarded as belonging to the family to which his father belongs. Each man traces his identity through the father and his paternal relatives. For a long time, however, there has been some controversy about the actual familial structure of the Arab society. There are four basic levels of family structure: (a) the *Qbila,* or tribe; (b) the *ashirah,* or subtribe; (c) the *hamula,* or clan, kindred, or lineage; and (d) the *'ahel, bet,* which means family, house, or extended family.

Inasmuch as social groupings larger than the extended family are almost always composed of extended families and not of individuals, every person automatically becomes a member of that larger group (clan, subtribe, tribe, and even political party) to which his father's extended

165

family belongs. Actually, there are three larger social structures that deal with kinship, two of which are sufficiently unambiguous to be mentioned. The first is the *khamseh*, which includes all people within five degrees of patrilineal relationship. These people form the core and perhaps the origin of the *hamula* (tribe) grouping, and comprise all those who can be counted on when blood vengeance is called for. Of course, the *khamseh* no longer functions in the city and probably is a thing of the past even in the most isolated regions. Regardless, an individual counts from himself five kinship steps beyond, upward, or any other direction and finds his *khamseh*, which, thus, is different for each person. The second of the larger kinship structures is the *bani'am*, which is usually viewed as a relationship of brotherhood requiring certain reciprocal duties. This form of structure has no chief and does not seem to be an organization of families of a higher order or even a political unity. In fact, it may include several subtribes or sections of a tribe—its components are ill defined. Outside of tribal areas, this form of social structure has lost its meaning.

PATRILOCAL RESIDENCE. A third basic property of the Islamic family is patrilocality. This means that generally upon marriage the young couple takes up residence in or near the home of the bridegroom's father. As a result of this custom brothers usually live together and continue to form part of the extended family even after they have married. Sisters, how-

*Courtesy of Professor Raymond F. Betts*

*A boy's first feast of Ramadan, traditionally shared with his father, is a family occasion of great importance.*

ever, live separately from one another and from their family of orientation. An interesting aspect of this arrangement is that a woman's family of orientation remains responsible for her moral conduct even after she has married and lives with her husband's family.

PATRIARCHAL AUTHORITY.    A significant property of the Islamic family is that it is patriarchal. The father is master of his own conjugal family, and the eldest male is the head of the entire extended family grouping. In olden times the patriarch had the power of life and death over those under his leadership, besides the other rights and responsibilities afforded him. The prevalent moral code in Islam requires complete obedience and respect for anyone older. With a premium value placed on masculinity, patriarchy is an appropriate form of authority.

Not unlike other male-dominated cultures, the mother in Islam is a central figure. Since her sons provide her with a sense of status, it is not surprising that she is an extremely proud and passionate mother—almost overprotective. The mother-son relationship provides relief for some social and emotional needs not normally met by the Islamic husband. On the whole, however, Islamic women have suffered from disenfranchisement, a generally low status, and an exceedingly rough life.

POLYGYNOUS MARRIAGE.    One of the most widely publicized characteristics of the Islamic family is its polygyny. Westerners can easily conjure up a picture straight out of *1001 Arabian Nights,* but reality for the average Arab was never quite like that picture. The reason is simple—most men probably could not afford multiple wives.

The Koran does explicitly advocate polygyny for it says: "marry of the women who seem good to you, two or three or four, and if ye four that ye cannot do justice, then one." Some critics have argued that monogamy was the real ideal of the Islamic family and that polygyny was practiced only to meet the needs of a situation contemporary to the Prophet. However, these critics have little more to stand on than speculation. In the Traditions (purported sayings of the Prophet), Paradise is pictured with men having a phenomenal number of wives. This hardly suggests a monogamous ideal. Additional evidence that polygyny was probably the ideal is the fact that the Prophet, whose life is considered a model for all to follow, left nine wives before passing on to Paradise.

Two rather important questions have been raised with regard to the practice of polygyny. First, why did the Muslims adopt this marriage form? Among several plausible reasons the economic one seems most realistic. The Muslims were, for the most part, a nomadic and/or agricultural people. It stands to reason that the more wives a man has the greater the amount of work performed. An additional woman was an economic asset because she freed the male from menial tasks, normally in the domain of women, for more important work. A second factor in the emergence of

167

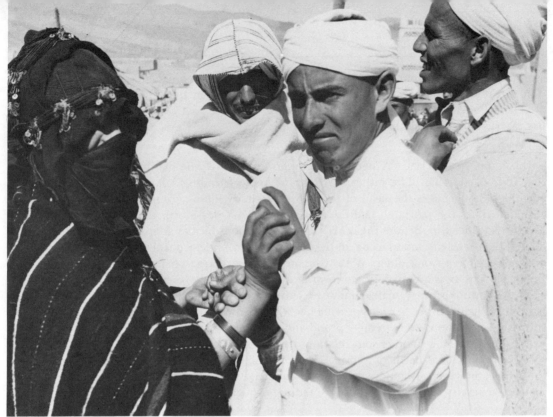

*Courtship and marriage among Muslims in remote areas has remained essentially unchanged for hundreds of years.*

polygyny is status. A man who could afford multiple wives received extra deference from his less fortunate brothers. In addition, multiple wives could produce more sons, a supplementary source of status and future workers.

The second question is, How widespread was the practice of polygyny among Muslims and what are the trends today? The extensiveness of polygyny is not wide. In the first place an extra wife is a luxury. In addition, for every adult male with two or more wives some male is necessarily a bachelor. It is not likely that polygyny was allowed at any time by the Muslims to seriously interfere in the right of every male to take a wife.

It is safe to say that polygyny is a dying practice among Muslims. Increasing urbanization and industrialization make an additional wife more of an economic burden than a necessity, and the increasing educational levels of Muslim women has led to a rather strong protest against the "inhuman" aspects of the practice. It is also true that most Muslim states have declared polygyny illegal. This is a major social change since it significantly altered a Koranic prescription and is contrary to the Prophet's example.

Goode's contention that most family systems are moving toward the conjugal family and are accepting a conjugal ideology is obvious among Muslims, especially with regard to polygyny.

ENDOGAMOUS GROUP STRUCTURE.   Patai (1955) described the Islamic family as "extended, patrilineal, patrilocal, patriarchal, occasionally polygynous, and emphatically endogamous." The distinctive endogamous rule among Muslims is called *bint'amm*, parallel cross-cousin marriage. There is an unwritten law that a man has the right to marry his father's brother's daughter (*bint'amm*), and that nobody else is allowed to marry her until and unless he (her father's brother's son) gives his consent.

Although no adequate cross-cultural explanation has been given of why this pattern became so firmly entrenched in Arab family life, some of its consequences are clear:

1. Since in such a marrage brother (father of the groom) would be giving money to brother (father of the bride), the bride price was usually much lower than it would be otherwise.
2. Since both sides would be interested in maintaining the honor of the same lineage, the husband could be sure that his wife's chastity had been guarded adequately before the marriage.
3. Land and any other property would remain in the same agnatic (paternal) lineage.
4. Children of brothers would have about the same social rank, and the Koran enjoined the marriage of equals.

*Family life in Middle Eastern urban areas is often an incongruous mixture of the traditional and the modern.*

Florita Botts from Nancy Palmer Photo Agency

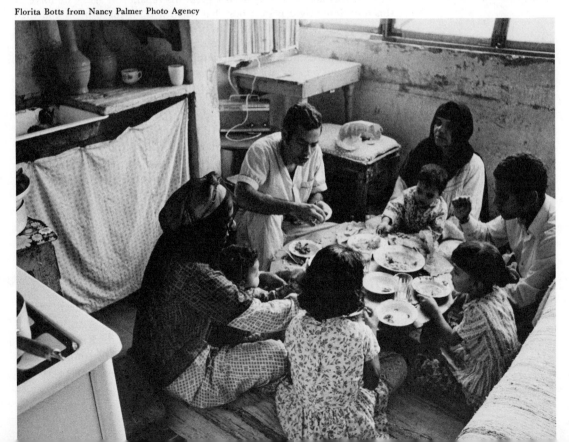

These statements, it must be remembered, are not reasons for the creation or the maintenance of the custom. They are the consequences of the practice of the custom of parallel cross-cousin marriage. However, the same sought-for consequences can be found in many other cultures in which this mating pattern is not found (see Goode, 1963).

An important point to mention is the strength of this custom of cross-cousin marriage and its power over the woman. A man had an absolute right to marry his cousin—in fact, first-cousin marriage was the law in most areas, backed by religious and social sanctions.

Patai (1955) says that in Iraq, as well as in northeastern Arabia, first-cousin marriage is the invariable rule. A girl belongs, of right, to the son of her father's brother (*ibn'amm*) unless he expressly renounces his right to marry her. Even in this case she may not marry without his permission. If the girl breaks this rule, or her parents prevail on her to marry someone else, her rightful lord (her first cousin) will murder her if he can. According to Patai (1955:371), this is the cause of most of the tribal killings of women, especially in Iraq and northeastern Arabia. Patai continues:

> In all parts of the Arabian peninsula (with very few exceptions, of which more later), a man's right to his father's brother's daughter is upheld. This right is not voided by even a great discrepancy in age. The force of this traditional right is so strong that when it is infringed upon and then avenged by the offended male cousin by bloodshed, this meets public approbation. In the reports on the cousin's right, no difference in emphasis can be discovered between the accounts of travellers and explorers of the 19th and 20th century, which seems to indicate no relaxation of this traditional right has taken place in the first 100 or 150 years.

Reports on the extent of patrilateral cross-cousin marriage have differed considerably. The major similarity in the studies is that they all note a trend toward more freedom of choice in mate selection. In other words, the trend is toward a decline in the exercise of the custom of cousin-right marriage.

Perhaps the best available study of the extensiveness of cross-cousin marriage was conducted in 1965 by Henry Korson using a sample of 765 unmarried graduate students in West Pakistan. Korson (1971) asked his respondents to indicate whether their parents and married brothers and sisters had themselves married relatives. As the data in Table 7–2 indicate, 25.8 percent of the brothers of his respondents had married a relative. The corresponding percentages for married sisters and parents were 19.6 and 41.2. As the data also show, a central source of marital partners in West Pakistan is still first cousins. In a previous study Korson (1965) noted that the average age differential between husband and wife for middle-class and upper-class Pakistanis was 7.3 and 6.2 years, respectively.

TABLE 7–2

Cross-Cousin Marriages in the Families of Pakistani Graduate Students

| RELATIONSHIP TO RESPONDENTS | RELATIONSHIP OF MARRIAGE PARTNER (IN PERCENTAGE) | | | |
|---|---|---|---|---|
| | FIRST COUSINS | SECOND COUSINS | OTHER RELATIVES | TOTAL |
| Brothers | 12.7 | 1.4 | 11.7 | 25.8 |
| Sisters | 8.3 | 2.0 | 9.3 | 19.6 |
| Parents | 18.7 | 6.1 | 16.4 | 41.2 |

SOURCE: J. Henry Korson, "Endogamous Marriage in a Traditional Muslim Society: West Pakistan." *Journal of Comparative Family Studies,* 2(1971):148, Table I. By permission of the *Journal of Comparative Family Studies.*

While Korson (1971:153)[1] sees some changes occurring in the practice of parents arranging marriages and in the cross-cousin preference, he does not foresee rapid and drastic change in the future.

> In any case, social change in the family will not come rapidly in West Pakistan. Should a young couple be attracted to each other, an arrangement would have to be made for a member of the boy's family to approach the girl's family with a proposal that the two families consider the possibility and desirability of union by the marriage of the principals. A marriage arranged by the families continues as a *sine qua non,* even among educated families. There may be a trend toward democratization in mate selection in West Pakistani families by permitting greater participation of the principals in making the final choice, but it is more likely that the statement that "the criteria for a successful marriage are not necessarily companionship and love, but fertility, permanence and the alliance of two family groups" (Shah, 1960) still holds. There is no question but that cultural intrusion from the West will continue to influence both the younger generation as well as their parents, but for the foreseeable future it is unlikely that rapid social change in the process of mate selection can be predicted.

The major criticism of the studies on cousin-right marriage is the lack of explicit definitions. None of the authors say exactly what determines who is a cross cousin and who is not. If a man has a son and several brothers with marriageable daughters, which one will his son have the right to marry? None of the authors specifies the procedure or criteria used to effect this decision. None of the authors discusses the problem of "claimed kin" as opposed to actual agnatic kin. Because of these gaps in

---

1 Excerpt in Chapter 7, p. 153, from J. Henry Korson, "Endogamous Marriage in a Traditional Society: West Pakistan," *Journal of Comparative Family Studies* 2(1971):145–55. Used by permission of *JCFS.*

information, a valid assessment of cousin-right marriage at this time is somewhat difficult.

Marriage is an especially salient part of the Islamic culture. According to an expert on Islamic law (Schacht, 1964:160; see also Korson 1968, 1969, 1970):

> Marriage is a contract of civil law, and it shows traces of having developed out of the purchase of the bride. The bridegroom concludes the marriage contract with the legal guardian of the bride, and he undertakes to pay the nuptial gift or "dower," not to the legal guardian of the bride as was customary in the pre-Islamic period, but to the wife herself. The contract must be concluded in the presence of three witnesses, two men or one man and two women. This has the double aim of providing proof of marriage and disproving unchastity.... This contract is the only legally relevant act in concluding marriage; privacy between husband and wife, and consummation are facts which may have legal effects when the marriage is dissolved, but are not essential for its conclusion.

Marriage and family life are of great importance to the Muslim people. This is probably due to two major facts related to their religion. First, the Prophet's life is used by the Muslims as a guide to the right life. His manner of life has become normative in the Muslim world. The Prophet is purported to have said: "Marriage is my custom, he who dislikes it does not belong to me." "When a servant of Allah marries he thereby perfects half his religion." "Marry and multiply so that I may be glorified in my community over other communities." Therefore, since Muhammad emphasized the family and marriage as a religious duty it has held a major place in the value system of Islam over the years. Second, in Islam there is no distinction between religion and law. When someone accepts Islam as his religion, he also accepts the law of Islam and its dictates. In a theocratic way Islam is all pervasive, and the family plays an important role in it.

In his advocacy of the importance of marriage and family life the Prophet was but following the values of his milieu. It is true that the celibate ideal had been introduced into the Near East, and even into Arabia, but it had met with little favor. Tradition was against it. The patriarchs were family men. The prophets were family men. The Prophet Muhammad was a family man. Jesus was exceptional in this aspect—the Muslims accepted him even though he was not married. However, it is interesting that Muslim tradition regarding the return of Jesus at the end of the age is unanimous in asserting that he will then marry and have children (Jeffrey, 1959).

## Summary: The Family Under Islam

Things under Islam are changing. The Islamic culture, once nurtured in isolation, is now front and center with its crucial geopolitical location in the Middle East and its vast wealth in oil. Nowhere has the incursion of Western attitudes and values been more apparent than in marriage practices. As coeducation has increased, the power traditionally held by the family over courtship has diminished. What was once a fairly rigid social caste system has given way to a class system with upward mobility possible via education. As a consequence marriages are more and more often based on the choice of the principals with the family being forced, in essence, to accept the marriage. This new freedom-of-choice ideology also spells the beginning of the end of dower, parentally arranged marriages, and obligatory submission of women to men for whom they feel little or no love. Islamic society is becoming Westernized and "modern," and the marriage and family practices of the past are being covered by the shifting trends of change. Polygyny has been shorn of its legality, and the example of the Prophet quickly ignored or labeled irrelevant in modern times.

The extended family tradition of being a single-dwelling household has been difficult to maintain in a new Arab world in which modern cliff dwellings have replaced the tents of the desert. However, the Muslim family system is very adaptable. In many cases the patriarchal head will live in one apartment in the same building with his married sons, or in very close proximity so that he can continue to exert his authority in major decisions. Even so, such forced changes have a slowly but steadily eroding effect on traditional practices that emerged originally to meet the needs of a nomadic society.

Other old traditions and customs that are less functional for the society and that seem especially anachronistic in the jumbo-jet days of the

*The liberation of Arab women through education will have far-reaching effects on marital and family life.*

Alain Nogues from Sygma

1970s are being rather quickly and easily discarded. Take for example *purdah,* the practice of an unmarried female not allowing a male to see any part of her body except the eyes. Seasoned travelers in the Middle East are still taken aback when Yemeni women, who normally live in a sixteenth-century context, show such an amazing acceptance of the modern. One reported seeing a Yemeni woman boarding a plane wrapped in her full-length veil without an inch of skin showing. Soon after take-off this veiled mystery disappeared into the toilet. A few moments later she emerged dressed in Western clothes; her face was uncovered and she was smiling, reveling in the taste of "liberation."

Throughout the Islamic world traditional roles are changing as a theocratic culture finds itself buffeted by industrial, urban, and secular forces. The Islamic family is becoming a conjugal system, much like the Western prototype.

## The POET Model

We will use the POET scheme developed by Duncan (1959) for Human Ecology to discern the underlying threads of similarity present in these two societies. The acronym refers to Population, Organization, Environment, and Technology.

POPULATION. A society's population dynamics can influence its family practices in a number of ways, and vice versa. Our interest is primarily in the influence of the population variable on the family. The following hypothesis would seem to be supported in both Ireland and the Islamic world:

Commitment to traditional family organization, authority, and practices decreases as (a) the population becomes more urban, (b) the population becomes younger, (c) the population becomes more physically mobile, and (d) the population becomes more aware of the differences between their life-style and that of other cultures.

ORGANIZATION. Both the Irish society and those societies predominantly Muslim are heavily influenced by an extremely conservative and orthodox set of religious values. In Ireland and Islamic societies there is an extreme division of labor by age and sex, and both societies give a high priority to family as the center of life. The following hypothesis would seem supported by both systems:

Commitment to traditional family organization, authority, and practices decreases as (a) secularization erodes the influence of religion; (b) equalitarian values replace a ritualistic adherence to age and sex

# CONCLUSIONS

Having examined the changing family in Ireland and among Muslims discretely, let us put the two seemingly diverse systems together by focusing on their similarities. All family systems change in response to structural or societal processes. To understand how change is perceived by individuals we must first understand the broader context within which they operate.

CONCLUSIONS FROM THE POET MODEL. Although there are several ways that Population, Organization, Environment, and Technology can be arranged relative to a society's commitment to a traditional family orientation, perhaps the best-fitting model would appear as depicted in Figure 7–1. In this POET model, Organization, particularly the institutional

distinctions; and (c) other societal institutions replace the family as the main occupier of the time, energy, and attention of the population.

ENVIRONMENT. This term usually refers to physical features such as topography, climate, fecundity of the soil, and the diversity of crops possible. It could also refer to the sociocultural environment within which the society is historically rooted. Using the "physical" meaning of the term *environment,* the following hypothesis seems plausible:

Commitment to the traditional family organization, authority, and practices is strongest where (a) the physical environment is sufficiently hostile or unpredictable, and therefore agricultural or other innovations will not increase yield from the family's holdings; and (b) it normally takes more than one nuclear unit to maintain economic subsistence.

TECHNOLOGY. Technological innovations are blamed for both the good and the bad that befalls any modernizing society, and Ireland and the Islamic countries fit into that category. The diffusion of innovations that can effect some control over the physical aspects of the environment is partially a function of the sociocultural environment mentioned above. The following hypothesis, then, refers both to technology and to a particular meaning of the term *environment:*

Commitment to traditional family organization, authority, and practices decreases as (a) the society and its people become less isolated (that is, mass media introduce the population to the outside world), and (b) the technologies from more modern countries are introduced into the receiving traditional countries.

**FIGURE 7-1**
**A POET model of Commitment to Traditional Family Patterns in Ireland and the Islamic Countries**

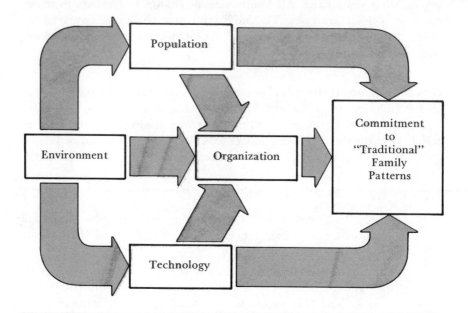

SOURCE: Model adapted from material in O. D. Duncan, "Human Ecology and Population Studies," in P. Hauser and O. D. Duncan (eds.), *The Study of Population* (Chicago: University of Chicago Press, 1959), pp. 678–716.

forces and set of values associated with the Roman Catholic Church in Ireland and with the Islamic ethos, would serve as the final filter of influences on a commitment to traditional family patterns from Population, Technology, and the Environment.

The environment is a given that must be dealt with by the entire population. It influences the population dynamics (that is, one way to cope is to emigrate from a hostile to a better environment or migrate to a better locale) and technological innovations that are accepted by the indigenous population to make life more pleasant. In addition, the environment is probably, to some extent, responsible for the basic values espoused by the predominant social organizational institutions (in the case of Ireland and the Muslim countries, religion). The religious organization in both these systems is a reflection of the environmental context within which the family must operate.

Population factors and technological changes have a direct influence on the degree of traditionalism found in family practices; they also influence the family indirectly through the organizational adaptations to a changing world. Perhaps the best example of this is the overreaction of the Catholic Church to farm dances. That organizational response led to the establishment of dance halls near church buildings in rural Ireland. However, the automobile has intervened to give rural Irish youth greater mobility and some ability to escape the traditional tight control of the Church and the family over heterosexual relationships. Finally, the predominant organization in these two societies, the religious institution, has adapted to a modernizing and less isolated situation by modifying the rigor with which it advocates certain practices (the endorsement of polygyny by the Islamic faith); consequently, commitment to traditional family practices changes.

This is a rather simplistic analysis. However, the purpose has been to examine seemingly diverse situations in order to show that sociology is a generalizing discipline. We are interested in making diversity manageable by pooling communalities and deemphasizing specifics. The POET model is a more abstract theoretical model that allows us, as social scientists, to understand order where deviation is the first thing seen. We should train ourselves as critical thinkers to sort and sift what our everyday senses tell us is different into piles of phenomena that our critical senses tell us is common.

## SOME POSSIBLE IMPLICATIONS

*In this chapter two family systems from other cultures were examined. Both the Irish and the Islamic families are located in societies that are beginning to feel the effects of modernization that was experienced by other, more industrialized societies thirty to forty years ago. In both of these family systems the religious system has exerted an almost dictatorial control over marital and familial practices. The inroads of secularization and modernization are loosening the hold of the Roman Catholic Church over the Irish population, while the Islamic religion is taking a less prominent position of influence because of a rise in nationalism among various Muslim peoples.*

*Serious students of social change in the West have extensive data on the effects that industrialization, urbanization, modernization, and nationalism have wrought on Western societies. Should the Irish and Muslim societies be treated as natural laboratories for the study of social change? Do Western social scientists have a moral obligation to study social change in these societies and to offer their assistance in facilitating the transition? Or would the interference by outside "experts" be an inappropriate and irresponsible action with possible negative consequences for Ireland and the Islamic countries?*

177

Marvin E. Newman from Woodfin Camp & Associates

# 8

# EXPERIMENTS WITH THE FAMILY

*What are the similarities and differences among the Soviet, Israeli,*
    *and Oneida Community experiments with the family?*

*Is the family universal?*

*What are the minimum functions of the family in a society or group?*

*What factors are conducive to a commitment to a nontraditional*
    *type of family?*

In Chapter 7 we saw how the Irish and Muslim peoples are committed to a traditional type of family. In this chapter we turn to the opposite end of the continuum to see how, and perhaps why, the traditional family was replaced in the Israeli kibbutzim, in Russia after the overthrow of the Czar, and in the nineteenth-century Oneida Community. These three experiments with alternative family forms were chosen for several reasons. First, they represent contrasts in size: The Russian experiment was societal in scope; the Israeli kibbutzim represents a large-scale and rather diffuse movement; the Oneida Community was rather isolated and was organized around a charismatic leader. Second, each of the three family experiments were or are somewhat successful in rearranging the traditional family structure and roles and the functions usually provided by the family. Third, adequate information is available from all three experiments to provide a basis for generating new hypotheses about the ingredients essential for successful attempts at innovations in family life. This is particularly salient since a great deal of interest has been shown recently in the communal movement in the United States. Since most communal groups in the United States today have not been in existence for very long, and new ones seem to crop up regularly, perhaps we can learn how to study them by looking to the better-established experiments in Russia and Israel, and to the nineteenth-century experiment in upstate New York. We hope to specify the POET model by examining what happens when the commitment is to break with tradition in familial practices.

Since we discussed the Islamic family at the end of Chapter 7, perhaps it would be best to look first at the family system of the Israeli kibbutzim—another Middle Eastern cultural phenomenon.

## THE FAMILY IN THE ISRAELI KIBBUTZ

There are probably numerous reasons why the Israeli kibbutz constitutes an ideal place to study the family. Yonina Talmon (1972) isolated the three most important reasons: First, the kibbutz provides an invaluable test case for studying family organization in terms of structure, functions, and revolutionary and collectivist movements. Second, within a single kibbutz community and within the kibbutzim seen as a social movement, it is possible to chart changes in ideology, the interaction of systems both within the communities and between the kibbutzim and the larger Jewish society, and the meaning of changes to the individuals involved in life in the kibbutzim. Third, because the kibbutz ideology was extremely anti-familistic initially, it is possible to examine the minimum definition of the family and to isolate the root functions of the family. However, before we get involved in a close examination of the family in the Israeli kibbutz let us examine the development of the kibbutz movement in order to gain some perspective.

## The Kibbutz in Historical Perspective

Like the Irish, the Jews have a long and disjointed history of attempting to gain control over a land they can call their own.[1] This goal has permeated Jewish thought for centuries. The active movement to establish a "publicly recognized and legally assured home in Palestine" was the cornerstone of the Zionist movement, which held its first meeting in 1897. Fifteen years before the inaugural Zionist Congress, the first Jewish farming community had been established in Palestine. Since most of these early settlers were not proficient in farming, these early communities were run by professional farm managers. By 1909 the dissatisfaction with working for someone else, fueled by the increasingly salient conclusion that socialism was the best means of achieving the Zionist goal of a Jewish nation in Palestine, led to the establishment of the first *kvutza* (Hebrew word for group), designed to be a communal-socialistic farming community.

The early kvutzot (plural for kvutza) served as the pattern or prototype for the later kibbutzim and were distinguishable from the kibbutzim by their smaller size, their vehement distrust of the use of industrial techniques, and their disinterest in developing a political point of view. Underlying the whole movement toward a communal living style were six basic values or ideological positions.

The first and central value revered by the early settlers was manual labor, considered part of the pioneering spirit or *chalutziut*. Work, the harder the better, was viewed as a measure of the commitment of a person to the kibbutz and its goals. Hard work, besides being necessary to carve out a home in a hostile environment, was approached almost compulsively by these early pioneers in Palestine.

The second value component of the kibbutz ideology was *shevayon*, or equality in all matters. As Diamond (1957:82)[2] states:

> to live in shevayon meant to consider even trivial prerogatives of personal taste sinful expressions of "egoism." It meant that the individuality of one person vis-à-vis another was irrelevant, since we were voluntarily subordi-

---

[1] This section of the chapter relies considerably on the excellent article by Stanley Diamond, "Kibbutz and Shtetl: The History of an Idea," *Social Problems* 5(1957):71–99. Used by permission of the Society for the Study of Social Problems.

[2] Used by permission of the author.

181

nated to the chalutzic idea. This emotional charge of shevayon was evident, also, in the reluctance to recognize important distinctions between the sexes, its militantly feminist component. Finally, shevayon was a radically antimanagerial attitude. Ideally, no individual was to wield more power or influence than any other. And it was considered a cultural good for individuals to circulate from job to job, since the specialist would tend to become lord of his particular domain.

The third central value of the early kibbutz was asceticism, or a disdain for the accumulation of material goods of any kind. There were few possessions that any resident could call his or her own. All living quarters were distinctly bare of any ornamentation, and the clothing style was the same for both sexes—drab and without any shape.

The fourth value of central importance to life in the early kibbutz was the salience of communality in all matters. All meals were eaten in the communal dining or *heder ochel,* which served not only as a place to eat but also as a social center, a ceremonial center in which most community affairs were held, and a place where everyone met to conduct the business of the kibbutz. In effect, it was the symbol of the collectivistic orientation to life in which all participated and to which all were committed.

The fifth component of the ideology of the kibbutz has particular relevance for the place of the family in the total scheme of things. Some authors have claimed that the kibbutz was antifamilistic (see Spiro, 1954). Yonina Talmon (1972:13) takes a slightly different view:

> It should be noted that although Kibbutzim limited the functions of the family drastically, they did not abolish it altogether. Nor was the antifamilistic policy adopted in the Kibbutz based on a preconceived or fully worked out ideology. Most early formulations of ideological position did not propose to do away with the family. The imposition of restrictive norms was justified as a means of liberating the family, not of eliminating it. The family was expected to come into its own, purged yet renewed and strengthened by its liberation from extraneous duties and cramping legal prohibitions. Pronouncements of strong antifamilistic views were quite rare. Ambivalence was much more prevalent than outright hostility.

The last central component or value found in the ideology of the Kibbutz was also related to a set of behaviors usually allocated to the traditional family, child rearing. Early on, the kibbutzim opted for a collectivistic strategy for rearing children. Because all adults were expected to work full time—in fact were needed for work purposes in order to survive—the care of children was accomplished by placing them in communal nurseries organized around age groups. From a pragmatic position, then, collective child rearing was a necessary consequence of the commitment to hard work, to equality, and to the community over individualistic desires or preferences.

But there was also the commitment to a style of child rearing that was virtually independent of the other demands on members of the kibbutzim. Diamond (1957:89)[3] isolated the essence of the child-rearing logic:

> Put another way, the concrete relationships between the generations were abstracted, an *institution* was interposed between parent and child. The family no longer served as mediator between society and the child, diffusing, individualizing and synthesizing social imperatives, and affording the possibility of idiosyncratic response. This function of the family, which may well emerge as its indispensable *raison d'être,* as the pressures of public life increase, was, in the Kibbutz, abandoned. Society had become the *direct* socializing agency, the collective *idea* had triumphed over the concrete *person*.

In consequence, the *sabra* is called a "child of the kibbutz" (though technically the term includes all natives of Israel or Palestine) for two reasons: First, he or she has been relatively sheltered and isolated from the adult generation. Second, and in conjunction with the first, most of the socialization is accomplished by peers, with coordination of activities the function of the nurse, and formal education that of the teacher. In a traditional sense and particularly for the first generation of children of the kibbutz, the possibility of a close affective and identificative bond to parents was rechanneled toward the establishment of a more impersonal and formalistic bond to the community. Diamond (1957), among others, has suggested that this resulted in a uniform and mechanical personality for the early sabra, thus creating a type of marginal person, unlike his or her parents and unlike any kind of child anywhere else.

## The Motives Behind the Kvutza/Kibbutz Arrangements

To the family specialist the kibbutz poses some interesting and curious paradoxes. Historically and traditionally the Jewish culture has been widely acknowledged as productive of cohesive families and a family lifestyle that is remarkably free of signs of strain or pathology. Why and how did such innovativeness with traditional family functions develop among Jews? Perhaps the most plausible answer lies in the family and community biographies of the early kvutza and kibbutz settlers.

Most of the early pioneers came from Eastern Europe. Diamond (1957) offers an interesting hypothesis and contends that the patterns of organization in the kibbutz constitute an over-reaction to the shtetl, the dominant pattern in Eastern European Jewish culture: Diamond's view is that the shtetl was essentially a caste-community encircled by the larger class-oriented Gentile community, separated from the outside by distinctly visible modes of dress and conduct. Within the shtetl, prestige and

---

[3] Used by permission of the author.

rank were determined by evidence of scholarship and money. The competition for status and deference was intense, and the goal of having material goods was paramount. Perhaps this overemphasis on the materialistic produced the rejection of such values in the kibbutz.

Diamond states that the central organizing feature of a person's life within the shtetl was the family, in which the father, regardless of his status within the Jewish community, was the Jew, the husband, the male. Like the Muslim male, the Jewish male probably was grateful that he was not born a woman. The rigid difference between male and female could have been the motive behind the kibbutz emphasis on the value of equality. Within the shtetl family, the mother oriented herself toward the children, especially the sons. She gave them much love and affection, frequently in an attempt to compensate for the lack of support and warmth from her husband. According to Diamond, a reaction to this practice could have been the basis for the child-rearing practices adopted by the kibbutzim.

Within the shtetl, religion and the rituals associated with it were rigid, with little or no allowance for individual religious expression. The changes accompanying the Industrial Revolution filtered into the shtetl culture during the latter half of the nineteenth century and raised, for the first time, the possibility that options besides the old and traditional styles of life were available. In other words, the Zionist movement back to Palestine and back to the land occurred at a "historically appropriate moment" when all of the shortcomings of the shtetl culture were being recognized. Herein lies at least part of the motivation for designing new styles of thought and action in the kibbutz. The collectivistic orientation of the kibbutz is an over-reactive effort to negate and obliterate the weaknesses of the shtetl existence from which most of the early settlers had come.

## The Changing Society in which Kibbutzim Must Operate

Before we get into a description of some of the changes that have occurred in the family as the kibbutz movement has evolved in Israel, it may be pertinent to discuss just how many persons are involved in the kibbutzim today. It is exceedingly easy for a Westerner to view Israel as predominantly rural, and to think that there are numerous kibbutz communities in Israel. As the figures in Table 8–1 show, both assumptions are incorrect. In 1971, 82.5 percent of the population of Israel was considered urban, living in 29 towns and cities. There were 806 villages, including kibbutzim and moshavim, another type of village to be discussed later.

A kibbutz is defined as a communal or collective village governed by the general assembly of all members. All property is collectively owned, and work is organized on a collective basis. Members give their labors and talents, and in return they receive housing, food, clothing, and social services. There are central dining rooms, kitchens, and stores, communal kindergartens and children's quarters, and social and cultural centers. Individual living quarters are available to ensure some personal privacy.

**TABLE 8–1**
**Living Environments in Israel**

| TYPE OF HABITATION | POPULATION (IN THOUSANDS) | PERCENTAGE | NUMBER OF LOCATIONS |
|---|---|---|---|
| TOTAL | 3,001.4 | 100.0 | 884 |
| *Urban* | 2,477.0 | 82.5 | 78 |
| Towns | 2,039.4 | 67.9 | 29 |
| Urban areas | 437.6 | 14.6 | 49 |
| *Rural* | 523.5 | 17.5 | 806 |
| Large villages | 181.6 | 6.1 | 48 |
| Small villages | 73.0 | 2.4 | 106 |
| Moshavim | 122.7 | 4.2 | 347 |
| Collective moshavim | 5.6 | 0.2 | 26 |
| Kibbutzim | 85.1 | 2.8 | 229 |
| Bedouin tribes | 38.4 | 1.3 | (45) |
| Institutions, farms, etc. | 13.3 | 0.4 | 50 |
| Living outside villages | 3.9 | 0.1 | — |
| JEWS | 2,561.4 | 100.0 | 781a |
| *Urban* | 2,288.6 | 89.3 | 74 |
| Towns | 1,878.2 | 73.3 | 27 |
| Urban areas | 410.4 | 16.0 | 47 |
| *Rural* | 271.9 | 10.7 | 707 |
| Large villages | 16.7 | 0.7 | 6 |
| Small villages | 27.2 | 1.1 | 50 |
| Moshavim | 122.3 | 4.8 | 347 |
| Collective moshavim | 5.5 | 0.2 | 26 |
| Kibbutzim | 84.9 | 3.3 | 229 |
| Institutions, farms, etc. | 13.2 | 0.5 | 49 |
| Living outside villages | 2.2 | 0.1 | — |
| NON-JEWS | 440.0 | 100.0 | 110a |
| *Urban* | 188.4 | 42.8 | 11 |
| Towns | 161.2 | 36.6 | 8 |
| Urban areas | 27.2 | 6.2 | 3 |
| *Rural* | 251.6 | 57.2 | 99 |
| Large villages | 165.0 | 37.6 | 42 |
| Small villages | 45.8 | 10.4 | 56 |
| Moshavim and kibbutzim | 0.6 | 0.1 | — |
| Bedouin tribes | 38.4 | 8.7 | (45) |
| Institutions, farms, etc. | 0.1 | 0.0 | 1 |
| Living outside villages | 1.7 | 0.4 | — |

SOURCE: "Facts about Israel, 1972." Tel Aviv: Israeli Ministry for Foreign Affairs, Information Division.

a Six mixed towns and one mixed urban area appear in both Jewish and non-Jewish totals.

185

*Kibbutz workers must be both productive and ever vigilant.*

David Rubinger for Black Star

The kibbutzim, originally predominantly agricultural in orientation, are turning more and more toward sizable industrial-type enterprises. In 1971 there were 229 kibbutzim with populations ranging from 60 to 2,000. As Table 8–1 indicates, only 2.8 percent of the total Israeli population live in kibbutzim, a rather small percentage to be sure. As Schlesinger (1977:772) indicates, "It is not the number of members that is significant, but rather the uniqueness of this social organization and communal life style which has endured 60 years and has seen more than three generations."

There are two other types of collective communities in Israel: (1) A *moshav* is a cooperative village in which each family maintains its own household and works its own plot of land for private profit. Marketing and supply are handled cooperatively, and to a varying degree, capital and means of production are jointly owned. The average moshav has a population of 60 to 100 families. In 1971 there were 347 moshavim, comprising 4.2 percent of the population of Israel. (2) A *moshav shitufi* is based on collective ownership and economy, as is the kibbutz, with land

and equipment owned collectively, but each family is responsible for running its own household. Work, pay, and profits are adjusted to individual circumstances. There were in 1971 a total of 26 *shitufiyim* (plural) with a total population of nearly 6,000.

A primary purpose for presenting these data is to suggest that they may contain some clues as to the future of the kibbutz as a social institution in Israel, and the family therein as a system with which experimental arrangements can be conducted. Several things are seemingly apparent and certainly plausible from the data contained in Table 8–1:

1. Israel is no longer a rural society that will need to keep its workers on the kibbutz. In fact, if Israel follows the pattern of most industrialized countries, the agricultural sector of society can expand with a decreased demand for agricultural workers. This means that many if not most kibbutzim will have to diversify toward other more industrialized activities. The impact of this development will have ramifications throughout the community and will touch all facets of life in the kibbutz. As Schlesinger (1977:777) pointed out, "Whereas industrialization created new jobs outside of the home for both men and women in the Israeli society at large, decreasing the differences between sex roles, in the kibbutzim it appears to have increased the differences between sex roles."

2. Because Israel has so rapidly expanded the scope of its urban boundaries, kibbutzim that were on the frontier not too many years ago are now either suburban enclaves or "downtown communes." It will become increasingly difficult to convince the members of urban-annexed kibbutzim that they should continue a commitment to the land, manual labor, and other rural ideals. The hardest task will be to sell asceticism to the younger members of the more urban kibbutzim.

3. The years from the establishment of the first kvutza in 1909 to Israeli independence in 1948 exacted a tremendous commitment from the members of kibbutzim, who were literally fighting for their economic, social, and particularly political survival and identity—the establishment of the long-sought-after state of Israel. The promised land has not overflowed with milk and honey, but in the twenty-two years from 1948 to 1970 the population increased from only 879,000 to 3,001,400. Not surprisingly, the percentages of the population living in kibbutzim has declined drastically and the degree of political influence exerted by the various kibbutzim has also been declining.

4. The increasing influence of the mass media in Israel, particularly television, will likely be contradictory to the values that served as the foundation for the kibbutz movement.

Thus, the kibbutz movement was a truly remarkable institution, ideally suited to the historical context for which it was invented. That context has changed more drastically than anyone would ever have imagined. The institution called the kibbutz is involved in changes that will lead it far from what its founders meant it to be. Certain of the basic

187

Marvin E. Newman from Woodfin Camp & Associates

*Work in the kibbutz, once primarily an agricultural experience, now mirrors the effects of industrialization in Israeli society.*

features of the kibbutz will remain unaltered, some will be only slightly altered, while other features now central may be modified greatly or even completely destroyed. The next section of this chapter will focus entirely on the changing family patterns in the Israeli kibbutz.

### The Kibbutz Family in Transition

As previously indicated, the kibbutzim, the family within the kibbutzim, and the entire Israeli society are in a state of dramatic and rapid social change. Talmon (1972:2) suggests that the kibbutzim are moving from a "bund" stage to a communal stage of development. (The Bund was a socialist labor organization in eastern Europe, which was active during the 1880s and 1890s, when early Zionist groups were forming. As such, it had an important influence on early collectivist kibbutz ideology.) The five primary characteristics of the bund stage are (a) dedication to an all-pervasive revolutionary mission, (b) intensive collective identification, (c) spontaneous and direct primary relations among all members, (d) informal social controls, and (e) homogeneity. Translated with regard to the family system this shift means that the relatively antifamilistic ideology has changed so that the family increasingly resembles the traditional model found in most urban and industrialized societies. The specifics of the new kibbutz family are outlined below:

1. Whereas formerly the family members took all of their meals at the community center, frequently separated from one another, it is now appropriate for the family members to eat their afternoon snack and even the main meal as a unit in the family's apartment.

2. The care of clothes, once the explicit prerogative of the kibbutz laundry, is now a family chore conducted at home, particularly for the best articles of clothing.

3. Housing that was once austere in a barracks sense increasingly consists of separate dwellings, which the family may feel free to decorate in its own individualistic style.

4. There is an increasing trend toward a more explicit division of labor by sex, with the women moving toward the traditional work roles performed by women in other societies as opposed to work being allocated without much if any regard to sex. This is seen most clearly in a Labor Force Survey conducted by the Bureau of Statistics and published by the Israeli government. Some 52 percent of the workers classified in the personal and other services category were women. In the kibbutzim, 84 percent of workers in this category were female (Schlesinger, 1977:776).

Ken Heyman

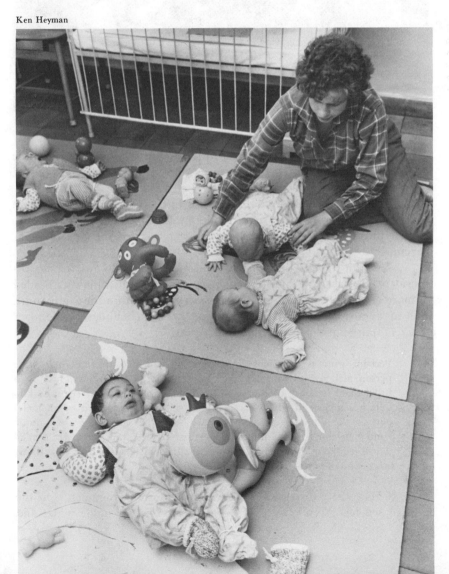

*Taking care of kibbutz children, a communal responsibility, has increasingly become the exclusive bailiwick of women.*

189

*The ritual of lighting Sabbath candles and blessing children signifies the mutual salience of religion and the family in Judaism.*

Ted Spiegel for Black Star

5. In contrast to the early constraints on fertility, demographic data indicate an increasing birth rate in kibbutzim, and a longer period of free time is now allowed for women after childbirth.

6. Although the parental functions in the kibbutz still emphasize equality, there is an increasing trend toward differentiation, with the mother providing child care and the father serving as the chief disciplinarian.

7. Even though the concept of communal child rearing is still prevalent, the fact that families now have a more explicit identity has led to more of the socialization experiences occurring within the family unit, and to a greater sense of identification between siblings. Schlesinger (1977:773) has put this dynamic into perspective:

> Perhaps what is of utmost importance is not that the *metapelet* (the person assigned to care for the children in the children's house) is a full-fledged member of the same *gemeinschaft* society, but that the kibbutz is a society in which each child is called and regarded by all members as the kibbutz son/daughter, while at the same time the unique bond between parent and child persists. Indeed, the parent-child relationship in the kibbutz has its own quality which sets it apart from any other kind of relationship in the kibbutz.

8. The early disregard for allocating housing assignments on the basis of sex has given way to the practice of keeping single males and

190

females apart. Concomitantly there has been a movement away from the concept of a permissive premarital sexual ideology toward an ideology that proscribes premarital sexual encounters.

9. There has also been a shift toward a more restrictive informal code against divorce or separation. The family and its continued intactness is now considered a matter of primary concern.

All these trends, and more we could mention, suggest that the kibbutzim are becoming familistic in orientation, and the familistic ideology prescribes traditional instead of nontraditional roles and functions. Perhaps the simplest and most adequate model to explain these trends is the POET scheme developed in Chapter 7.

As the population in Israel has (a) expanded, (b) stabilized, and (c) become urban; as the environment has become less and less an all-pervasive obstacle to overcome; as the society has changed its locus from the agricultural to the technological; and as the entire organizational structure of society has become less revolutionary and more bureaucratic, the family has changed status from an obstacle to stability to a necessary structure for stability within the kibbutzim. It is not suggested that the family system in the kibbutzim will ever completely adapt to the point of being synonymous with the nonkibbutz Israeli family. The experiments conducted on various aspects of family structure and functioning produced some very positive results that will no doubt be continued. However, the differentiating characteristics of the kibbutz family will not be as apparent as Israel moves toward greater industrialization, urbanization, modernization, and general overall stability.

## THE RUSSIAN FAMILY

The experiments with the family that were conducted in the Soviet Union were the result of a set of contingencies different from those affecting the Israeli population. The POET model will again serve as a guideline in tracing some of the changes that the Soviet government sought to institute.

### The Family Prior to the Revolution: A Historical Perspective

The country many of us call Russia is more formally known as the Union of Soviet Socialist Republics.[4] Its fifteen constituent republics cover a huge area. The Soviet Union is three times the size of the United States, larger than all of North America, and covers fully one-sixth of the land area of the earth. The 3,000-mile expanse of the United States is small in comparison to the 6,000 miles that stretch from the Soviet Union's border with

---

[4] This section on the history of the pre-Soviet family relies heavily on the excellent chapter on the Russian family in Kenkel (1977).

Europe to the Pacific Ocean. The Soviet Union is not only geographically large but is also the home of many peoples, with contrasting cultural histories and life-styles and a multitude of linguistic variations.

Because of a long history of geopolitical fragmentation and extreme cultural diversity, there is no unified history of the Russian family. Much of the history was never recorded. However, enough information is available to allow a partial reconstruction of the past.

Some evidence, albeit fragmentary, suggests that at a very early point in time a matriarchal-matrilineal family was common, particularly among the Slavic population (see Elnett, 1926). As the Slavs became a truly agricultural people the family changed toward the patriarchal and extended form found in most agricultural societies (see the discussion of hypothesis of Nimkoff and Middleton in Chapter 4).

In the tenth century religion became a potent force in Russia when Christianity and the Greek Orthodox Church were embraced by the ruling princes. As the Church gained wealth and authority the influence of religion filtered down and influenced the daily lives of ordinary people. One major consequence of the entry of religion into the lives of the masses was an absolute reduction in the status of women, who were not allowed to participate in religious functions and who were generally regarded as the cause of all things evil, being, as they were, like "sinful Eve."

When the oriental invasion of what is now the Soviet Union occurred in the thirteenth century, and for about 200 years after that, tremendous cultural changes occurred, particularly as a result of intermarriage of the Mongols with the indigenous populations. The most relevant point regarding family life during this period was the solidification of the patriarchal family system as a cultural imperative and operative norm. It seems that the oriental view of women was even harsher than the Christian. From a political perspective it is also important to note that authority at this time became centralized under one prince in Moscow. After the Mongols were driven out, it was not long before an even more autocratic centralization of power occurred under Ivan the Terrible. Gradually the entire social structure evolved into two dichotomous strata: the hereditary landowners and the peasants or serfs.

In the seventeenth and eighteenth centuries the conditions under which the peasants lived progressed from bad to worse. The serfs were little more than slaves—disposable cogs in an oppressive machine. Even the family, frequently a refuge and source of sustaining identity in times of crises and duress, was cruelly oppressed. Families were grouped together into communes or cooperatives because neither individuals nor families could own land. The father (or *bolshak*), as head of an extended household, wielded great power as the person who was responsible to the commune for providing the labor necessary for survival against the devastating pressures of the environment. He was also responsible to the landlords, who were constantly asking for more from the peasants. The father's authority was legitimated by the Russian Church and its "all males are like unto God" ideology. Unfortunately for all females and children, that ideology viewed God as a tyrant whose words or actions were not to be questioned, only emulated or obeyed.

Consequently, the Church strongly advocated heavy corporal punishment for children, particularly males, and not much less for wives and daughters. There was little time or inclination for the expression of warmth and love with which to make the family hovel a decent place to live in. However, some relief came in 1861, when Czar Alexander II officially abolished serfdom. On the farms in Czarist Russia this meant little change in the family, for families were still organized under the communal system.

By the 1870s industrialization was firmly established, and it had brought with it the migration of many families from their oppressive rural surroundings to equally oppressive urban conditions. In the years following, a number of unorganized strikes and uprisings occurred, none of which was successful. However, within this context the Social Democratic Party was formed in 1898, its platforms based on the writings and doctrines of Karl Marx. Five years later, in 1903, the party split into two opposing camps consisting primarily of the Menshevik and Bolshevik factions. A rather strong feminist movement that had developed primarily among the bourgeois women in the latter part of the nineteenth century joined forces with the male revolutionaries in the party. This, then, was the state of affairs that provided the impetus for the overthrow of the Czar in February 1917, a precursor to the October Revolution in 1917 in which the Bolsheviks came to power.

It is important to note that the masses were innocent bystanders in the revolution and the intraparty struggles that followed. Most were illiterate—probably close to 70 percent—and most were living at the barest levels of subsistence. However, anything was an improvement over the past, and the possibilities of freedom proposed by the Communist party must have sounded like heaven for people who had been captives of the devil and living in hell for years.

## Ideological Bases for Changing the Russian Family

The predominantly young, tough, and extremely idealistic revolutionaries who took over the reins of a huge and disjointed country were in an ideal position to change the family. And, in fact, an overriding goal of the party was to reconstruct totally the society that became the Union of Soviet Socialist Republics, including all its institutions, its legal superstructure, and to a large extent its cultural values and norms. Nothing was to be ignored, for here was a unique opportunity to put into practice the doctrines and beliefs of Marx and Engels and to institute the reforms deemed necessary by the charismatic Lenin.

193

With specific reference to the family, the writings of Marx and Engels were clear—certain features of the family were cancerous and must be surgically removed before a "superior" socialist family system could emerge. For example, Engels (1884) states:

> The first class antagonism appearing in history coincides with the development of the antagonism of man and wife in monogamy, and the first class oppression with that of the female by the male sex. Monogamy was a great historical progress. But by the side of slavery and private property it marks at the same time that epoch which, reaching down to our days, takes with all progress also a step backwards, relatively speaking, and develops the welfare and advancement of one by the woe and submission of the other.

Thus, the ideology to which the new leaders of the Soviet Union adhered advocated a form of family life in which equalitarianism pervades—an ideal diametrically opposite the common behavioral norm that had its origins back in the tenth century. Engels likened the wife as a prostitute who sold her body for life instead of for one night. The rich imagery embodied in the terms *subjugation, oppression,* and *inequality* were well understood by Russian women, whose familial experiences were far from free or happy.

In their zeal, a small but very vocal minority of revolutionaries added to the ideology their own interpretations of other needed alterations in family practices. One such change was the advocation of "free love" or intercourse for the satisfaction of bodily needs, not for bourgeois emotionalism. Another change loudly advocated concerned the abolition of such capitalistically based terms as *my* husband, *our* home, and *our* children. These indicated a sense of possessiveness, an indication that others were viewed like property, something anathema to the committed Communist.

## Legal Reforms Designed to Create the Socialist Family

*There has been no hesitancy on the part of Soviet leaders to change policies regarding the family.* In fact, in more than one instance earlier policies have been either rescinded or reversed by later family codes. Perhaps the best way to examine changes in the Soviet family is to trace them chronologically from 1917.

THE FAMILY CODE OF 1918.   This first family code contained a number of provisions that were designed to correct the inequalities and other "sinful" (from a thoroughly secular and socialist perspective) aspects of the family system prevalent at that time. The following list contains the primary features of the earliest Soviet family code:

1. Marriage was fully the prerogative of the principals, with no one and no institution encroaching on the personal liberties of individuals.

2. Only civil marriages were recognized. In other words, only a secular marriage was legally acceptable. Marriages were in effect once they were registered; in fact, it was not even necessary that the partners be present at a ceremony. Marriage was seen as a completely private arrangement between a man and a woman.

3. Community property rights at marriage were abolished. However, should either party be out of work, the spouse was "required" to provide support.

4. A name change per se was not necessary. However, it was necessary to inform the government of the names each of the married pair would use.

5. The husband no longer had the right to insist that his wife live where he chose to live. The choice of residence was an individual matter negotiated by the couple.

6. Inheritance, because it entailed the transfer of property (no longer jointly owned by the spouses) and because it usually stayed in the male line, was abolished. Property that formerly would have been inherited reverted to the state.

7. Divorce was easily obtained, particularly if both partners were in consent. They needed only to go to a registry office with identification and proof of marriage, state their intentions and the names each would adopt, and sign the divorce decree. If only one person were seeking the divorce, the other party had to be informed of the impending split. Consequently, a notice appeared in the newspaper that the application for divorce had been filed; in addition, the other person was sent a postcard informing him or her of the application.

8. As would be expected, the children of divorced parents were amply protected by the family code. An agreement as to who would keep them was duly recorded at the time of the divorce. However, even after the divorce both parents were equally responsible for the maintenance of children. If the child would be better off in an institution, both parents were required to help defray the expenses.

9. Finally, the Code of 1918 provided that "birth itself shall be the basis of the family. No differentiation whatsoever shall be made between relationships by birth, whether in or out of wedlock" (see Gsovski, 1947). Thus illegitimacy was abolished by legal principle.

195

The Family Code of 1918 represented a concerted effort by the Soviet government to restructure the family system and to bring familial practices more in line with the ideological tenets of Marx and Engels and the radical feminist branch of the Communist party. By 1920 the feminists had achieved a major victory when the government allowed abortions. This does not mean that abortion was encouraged—there was little need for encouragement. Besides the humane side effect of lowering the death rates wrought by the clumsy hands of abortionists, women also gained some control over the sexual side of life—a necessity if full equality of sexes is to occur.

It is interesting to note that the Soviet criminal code had no provisions for the punishment of incest, bigamy, adultery, or homosexuality. This was probably, at least to some extent, a function of the intense commitment to the freedom of the individual. It could also have been the result of a rather vocal minority that insisted on the obligations of true comrades to share their bodies with needy comrades of the opposite sex.

COMMON-LAW MARRIAGE IN 1926.  In 1926 the Soviet legal system recognized the legal existence of de facto or common-law marriages. Although the preference was for a marriage to be registered, two people were considered legally married if they were cohabitants in a common houshold, if they admitted their "married" status to a third party, and if they practiced mutual support and the joint raising of children. This constituted at the time a major departure not only from existing Soviet law but also from the family laws in the West. Most societies require some effort beyond a mere common-law existence before a marriage or family is recognized, but not the Soviets, who were bound and determined to experiment with family life.

THE REVISED FAMILY CODE OF 1936.  The Revised Family Code of 1936 brought with it some reversals of the earlier more permissive stance regarding family life. For example, abortion was prohibited except for serious medical considerations. In addition, the 1936 statutes provided broader aid for mothers and children, adding an annual bonus that would be paid for large families. Provision was also made for an expansion of the facilities that would take care of children of working mothers. Regarding divorce, it became necessary for both parties to appear before a family court, and a fee was added. In other words, the 1936 family code was designed to encourage fertility and in general to strengthen the Soviet family system.

Gsovski (1947) quotes a 1936 article from *Pravda* that seems to depict the new view of family life: "So-called free love and loose sexual life are altogether bourgeois and have nothing in common with Socialist principles and ethics or with the rules of behavior of a Soviet citizen. Marriage is the most serious affair of life. . . . Fatherhood and motherhood become virtues in the Soviet land." Gsovski also quotes a Soviet professor of law named Boshko: "Marriage, basically, and in the spirit of Soviet law, is in principle essentially a lifelong union. . . . Moreover, marriage receives its full life-blood and value for the Soviet state only if there is birth of children, proper upbringing, and if the spouses experience the highest happiness of motherhood and fatherhood."

The young and idealistic revolutionaries who were in their early twenties in 1917 were nearing forty in 1936, and Soviet law was moving toward a more realistic and pragmatic stance with regard to the role of the family in the achievement of a truly Socialist society.

By 1944 the Soviet system was reacting to the tremendous costs of World War II. As Kenkel (1977) noted,

> An estimated 20 million Russians lost their lives, more than half of them civilians. In the Ukraine alone, half of the means of production was destroyed. It is obviously no small matter for a society to lose half of all its factories and ships, half of its machinery and tools, half of its farm equipment, port facilities and railroad stock. In addition, 82,000

*The decoration of mothers as "heroines" indicates the continuing importance of the family in Soviet society.*

John Launois from Black Star

schools in which 15 million children had previously been enrolled, were destroyed, to say nothing of the homes and personal possessions of Russian citizens.

1944 FAMILY CODE. The 1944 Family Code was explicitly designed to strengthen the Soviet family in whatever way possible. Some of the provisions of the 1944 code were as follows:

1. Only registered marriages were considered fully legal. The allowance of de facto marriages was rescinded in order to increase family stability.
2. Divorce was made extremely difficult to obtain by charging a heavy fee and by instituting an involved process for filing for divorce.
3. Child bearing was strongly encouraged with the provision of payments for the third child and every additional child beyond the third. In addition, mothers with large numbers of children were awarded medals and an honorific status by the state.

The Soviet government was responding to the serious consequences of the disaster of World War II. The family was seen as the vehicle through which the society was to be rebuilt. Parenthetically, it should be noted that an easing of divorce regulations was introduced in 1955, and by 1966 divorce procedures were almost back to the situation that prevailed in postrevolutionary days. This almost full-circle movement regarding divorce from extreme permissiveness through severe restrictions and back to permissiveness is a reflection of the negative reaction of the Soviet masses to the restrictions, and a recognition by the Soviet government that stability was being achieved at a societal level, both economically and politically.

## Women in Soviet Society

A key to understanding the Soviet family and its place in Soviet society lies in the woman. More than in any other societies, the Soviet woman's impact is felt. For example, women make up more than half the country's population—132.5 million or 53.8 percent. They constitute about 51 percent of the Soviet labor force, the same percentage as in 1926. One-third of the deputies to the USSR Supreme Soviet and 46 percent of the deputies to the local Soviets are women.

More than 80 percent of the able-bodied women in the USSR work or study. As Sacks (1977) notes: "There is no other modern industrial nation in which women's employment has played as crucial or as extensive a role." Because of this fact, women in the Soviet Union have the lowest retirement age in the world—fifty-five. Women who have borne five or

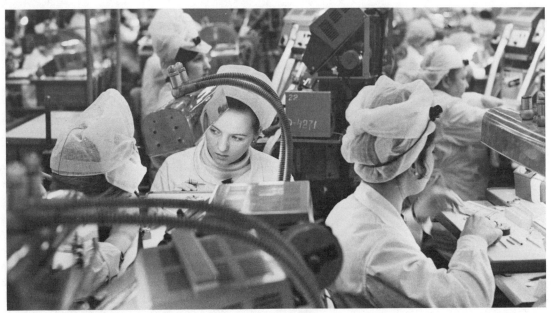

Henri Cartier-Bresson, Magnum Photos, Inc.

*Women are a vital cog in the Soviet labor machine, a key to the development of the USSR as an industrialized nation.*

more children and raised them to the age of eight are entitled to a pension at age fifty, after having worked for fifteen years. In 1972 some 72 percent of the doctors in the Soviet Union (528,000) were women. There were 1.7 million women teachers, 71 percent of the total.

As central as they are to the Soviet economy, women have not escaped the traditional tasks associated with being housewives. The occupational structure is open—it is the work they do after work that is not. This is seen most clearly in time-budget studies conducted shortly after the revolution and again in the 1960s. "Overall, between the 1920s and the 1960s there have been no startling changes in the general pattern of time usage by workers. There is clear evidence of a continuity in women's crushing 'double burden,' that is, full-time employment combined with housework consuming the equivalent of two-thirds of the total time associated with formal work. Males continue to have as much free time as females have housework." The search for sexual equality in the Soviet Union is not unlike that in the Israeli kibbutzim—well-intentioned ideals have some difficulty being translated into reality when those ideals must do battle with centuries of tradition and male chauvinism.

## Living Conditions of the Soviet Family

The modern Soviet family is relatively stable. The lopsided sex ratio produced by World War II is moving back toward normality, and the marriage and divorce rates are in line with the prevailing rates in the West. The crucial problems faced by the modern Soviet family are, according to Geiger (1965), shortages of time and space and consumer goods. The

199

average Soviet family has an extremely limited housing area even though the Soviet government is involved in a crash program of constructing prefabricated apartment houses. These apartments are rented for an amazingly low rate per month; the difficulty is that the demand for them far exceeds the supply. Besides the space problem, the average Soviet worker spends long hours on the job with equally long hours spent working on committees. The result is that little time is available for family interaction. In addition, severe shortages of food products and other consumer goods require that large amounts of time be spent waiting in lines at the state-run food stores.

### Summary: The Soviet Family Experiment

Although this review of the Soviet experiment with the family has been sketchy and short, some conclusions can be drawn about how and why the experiments occurred. Once again the POET model seems applicable.

The commitment to a nontraditional family system evolved from the interacting influences of (a) a population that had to be harnessed and guided from a patriarchal and rural orientation to one consistent with an ideology of equalitarianism and the necessity of becoming an urban and industrial world power; (b) a technology that had to become more industrial in focus while increasing productivity, which required a massive movement of women into the labor force and away from the home; (c) a physical environment in which agricultural production is limited to a relatively short growing season and a sociopolitical environment in which the losses of a devastating world war had to be regained very quickly. The organizational forces were the crucial mechanisms through which a commitment to an experimental family orientation was achieved. It is doubtful that the Soviet Union could have achieved its fantastic progress on all fronts if the regimes in power had been more democratic. Because of the complete centralization of power in a small group of people who controlled the mass media and the legal system, it was possible to institute and make operative marked changes in the ways that families were formed and allowed to function. These same four factors—population, technology, environment, and organization—are now interacting to produce a commitment to a more traditional and conservative, yet distinctively Soviet, family system. If circumstances should arise that would require more experimentation, the Soviet government would probably not hesitate to embark on a course of further experimentation with the Soviet family, of how it is structured, and how it functions.

## THE ONEIDA COMMUNITY

The third utopian experiment with the family, the Oneida Community, is unique. It differs from the Israeli kibbutzim and Russian experiments in a number of ways. First, the size and scope of the experiment was much smaller. The Oneida Community probably never contained more than 300 members at any one time. With regard to scope, Oneida did not encompass even a small proportion of the population; it did not require a massive migration to a "foreign land"; although it existed in "hostile" territory there were no pitched battles per se and no revolution; and Oneida was almost entirely apolitical—the prevailing world view of the residents was based exclusively on a religious ideology.

A second characteristic that distinguishes Oneida from the Russian and Israeli experiments is the degree to which one charismatic leader was deemed responsible for its success, and perhaps for its failure as well. The Soviet Union looked to Lenin and Israel to David Ben Gurion, but these two men were symbolic leaders who designated many of the leadership tasks to others. Oneida was dominated by only one man, and his leadership was not symbolic or in the abstract—it was daily and thoroughly real and personal. Because of the small size of the Oneida Community John Humphrey Noyes literally touched the inner lives of each of the members.

A third difference, and a very important one, is the fact that the Oneida Community was the most radical of the three utopian experiments discussed in this chapter. Its religious ideology, the practice of economic and sexual communism, the thoroughly successful practice of contraception for the first twenty years of its existence, the experiments with eugenics, and the almost total lack of serious intracommunity strife puts the Oneida experiment into a class by itself. It is the "ultimate" utopian experiment with the family and familial practices, and it failed. We will abstract the salient features of this unique community, again, using the POET model as a guideline.

### John Humphrey Noyes

It is not possible to understand the Oneida experiment without an explicit examination of the personality and career of its founder, John Humphrey Noyes. Noyes was the son of a well-to-do and conservative Vermont businessman who served two years in the U.S. House of Representatives. John Humphrey Noyes graduated with high honors from Dartmouth, and after a one-year attempt to practice law, he was converted to Christianity and entered the ministry. His theological training, one year at Andover and one at Yale, culminated in being licensed to preach as a Congregational minister in 1833.

On February 20, 1834, Noyes announced from the pulpit an electrifying message, one that would quickly lead to his being forced from the

## A Radical View of Marriage

In 1837 Noyes created another furor with the publication of a paper entitled *"The Battle Axe and Weapons of War."* The title is rather misleading, for the paper proposed a rather radical view of marriage. "When the will of God is done on earth as it is in Heaven there will be no marriage. Exclusiveness, jealousy, quarrelling have no place in the marriage supper of the Lamb. In a holy community, there is no more reason why sexual intercourse should be restrained by law, than why eating and drinking should be—and there is as little occasion for shame in the one case as in the other."

In 1836 John H. Noyes had returned to his family home in Putney, Vermont, and began to teach Bible classes. He converted his family to his views and in 1838 he married another convert, Harriett Holton. In 1840 he established the forerunner of the Oneida Community then known as the Putney Association. By 1846 the small group had begun to practice his ideas of sexual communism called complex marriage and the contraceptive technique of male continence known as coitus reservatus. This was just too much for his orthodox neighbors in Putney, and John Humphrey Noyes was indicted for adultery. Rather than face trial Noyes left the state, and in 1848 he moved the entire group to a tract of land in the Oneida reserve in upstate New York. By January 1, 1849, the Oneida commune consisted of fifty-eight adults and twenty-nine children.

What kind of man was John Humphrey Noyes? Carden's (1969:34–35) description is probably the best available.

> The community members held Noyes in awe. Because no one really knew him, each could imagine that the leader satisfied his personal conception of the ideal man. In addition to his being away for long periods at a stretch, he spent much time alone when at Oneida. He was aloof and serious. Except for making an occasional pun he had no sense of humor. He demanded complete obedience, yet he refused to assume full responsibility for others. . . . He fascinated his followers by making them feel that they were almost, but not quite, accepted. They thought that if they continued to obey and to follow his principles, he would eventually accept them.
>
> Noyes' doctrines were too radical for most, but the few persons who were seriously attracted by perfectionism were taught by a man capable of inspiring the utmost devotion.

Suffice it to say that John Humphrey Noyes was a charismatic leader, a complex and sometimes contradictory and contrary man, a man committed to very unorthodox orthodoxies who initiated and successfully led one of the most radical experiments with the family ever attempted.

formal ministry and cut off from his college, his church, his family, and his friends. That message was that Christ has already returned to earth and that it is not only possible but also paramount that people live perfect and sinless lives. This was not in line with the religious beliefs of the day. In fact, John H. Noyes was labeled a heretic and a crazy man. The germ of this message was to become the basis for his religious views called "perfectionism."

## The Central Components of the Oneida Experiment

The Oneida Community was self-contained and self-sustaining. Since the communal land and living quarters were in the countryside and given the fact that transportation and communication facilities were not well developed in the middle 1800s, frequent interaction with the outside world was virtually nonexistent. This location had two basic effects. First, the intrusion of outside values and attitudes into Oneida was minimal. Second, because of this isolation it was not possible for the Oneida residents to feel deprived in any sense since there were few if any points of comparison. In a colloquial way, the Oneida Community residents could be cohesive because they could not see the forest for the trees.

Perhaps this was one major reason why the community was able to continue its radical experiments. Another was its phenomenal economic success as a result of the invention and marketing of a steel trap that was used worldwide and of the development of the Oneida silverware industry.

With regard to the experiments with family life, several practices need to be discussed: (a) the stratification principles utilized within the community, (b) the principle of complex marriage, (c) the contraceptive and eugenics practices and child-rearing techniques, and (d) the technique of mutual criticism.

THE PRINCIPLE OF ASCENDANCY. Noyes believed quite simply that the community should be stratified from those who were least to those who were most nearly perfect. Thus, those members who wished to achieve greater spiritual perfection should seek to associate as much as possible with those who were ascendant to them in the community.

COMPLEX MARRIAGE. Complex marriage was the community's name for their social system, in which each person was married to all persons instead of to one as in the decadent monogamous practices of the outside world. Since sexual intimacy is an integral part of marriage, it was necessary to develop a mechanism whereby sexual intercourse could be arranged. This was done through a coordinating committee. If a person desired intercourse with someone, he or she would make this desire known to the

203

committee and a committee member then contacted the second party. In this way it was possible for the target person to refuse. It is not known just how often the committee facilitated a negative or positive response to the requests. If the answer was affirmative, the couple would meet for an hour or two in the room of one of the members, and afterward each would retire to his or her separate room. The committee was thus able to ensure that these liaisons did not become habitual and evidence of "sinful exclusiveness" between any two members.

It would be easy, given the values and attitudes concerning sex that are prevalent in modern American society, or for that matter those prevalent in mid-nineteeth century America, to think that the community was continually involved in a "free for all" sexual orgy. Such is not the case; William Kephart (1972) put complex marriage in its proper perspective:

> John Humphrey Noyes was a devout man, and the Oneida community was a deeply religious group and any assessment of their sexual practices must take these factors into consideration. Insofar as the records indicate, the Colony abided by the doctrine of Complex Marriage not for reasons of lust as was sometimes charged, but because of the conviction that they were following God's word.

CONTRACEPTIVE AND EUGENICS PRACTICES AND CHILD-RAISING TECHNIQUES. One of the most impressive features of the Oneida Community and its ideologies is the way everything seemed to fit with everything else. A good example of this is the practice of male continence, coitus reservatus, which meshed well with complex marriage and the principle of ascendancy.

The feasibility of male continence as a contraceptive technique evolved quite naturally for Noyes. His wife, Harriett, had borne five children in succession, all but one of whom had been stillborn. Noyes reasoned that the responsibility was his and his alone not to put his wife through such a cycle of recurring anguish. So he practiced coitus reservatus for two years without his wife becoming pregnant. Soon thereafter he introduced the technique in the Putney community.

The technique was woven into the principle of ascendancy through behavioral socialization. The reasoning was that since younger members are less perfect than older members, younger men should develop their skills of continence with the older, more experienced women (that is, those past menopause). The obverse is that older, more perfect, and experienced men should train the younger women. The younger women would grow spiritually through encounters with their superiors and, of course, would not get pregnant. The system was completely logical at the ideological level and not seen as parasitic by the members of Oneida. A positive side effect is that it ensured continued sexual partners for the older, more perfect women who might not fare so well in a competitive market dominated by younger, less perfect, but more attractive female members.

204

Many outsiders were openly cynical about this technique, claiming that it was not only impossible to practice but may actually be adverse to the health of the men involved. However, it seems that the Oneida men were more resolutely committed than the average man. As Carden (1969: 51) notes: "Between 1849 and 1869, forty-four children were born in the Community. Eight of these had been conceived before their parents joined Oneida, and at least five more conceptions were sanctioned by the Community. Consequently, at most, thirty-one children were accidentally conceived over a period of twenty-one years." Such an accomplishment is, by any standards or criteria, a truly remarkable fact. It is just one index of the commitment felt by the members of this organization.

By 1869 Noyes felt that the community was at a crucial transition point that made it plausible to propagate the second generation of community members. He had been very impressed by the writings of Darwin on evolution and Galton's ideas on the means by which the human species could be improved. He therefore introduced what he called "stirpi-culture"—in actuality, a program of eugenically planned parenthood. Noyes himself headed the committee that made final decisions on who would mate with whom. Probably no more than one-fourth of the matings

*John Humphrey Noyes (standing near the front) was leader and spiritual "father" to the entire Oneida Community.*

Oneida Community Historical Committee

were suggested by the committee and the others were suggested by willing volunteer couples. "During the 1869–1879 decade, fifty-eight live children were born at Oneida, to a total of forty-four women. Although all were classified as stirpiculture children, thirteen were the result of accidental conceptions" (Carden, 1969:63). Noyes was father of ten of the fifty-eight stirpiculture children, and his son, Theodore, born before Oneida was established, accounted for three more.

All of the community's children lived in the children's house and were raised in a fashion similar to the kibbutzim sabras. The children were taught that they were to share everything with their brothers and sisters. They received close but not harsh supervision, plus a solid education. They were also constantly socialized to think in terms that precluded selfishness or exclusiveness. The only evidence by which this aspect of the Oneida experiment can be evaluated—and such evidence is fragmentary—suggests that there were no adverse side effects to the practice of stirpiculture and the concomitant communal child-rearing practices used.

THE TECHNIQUE OF MUTUAL CRITICISM.  Mutual criticism was a technique initially practiced at Putney whereby a member would periodically submit to a searching examination of his or her good and bad points. Evidently the perfectionists were not able to purge themselves of all human foibles. This type of therapy was conducted in a clinical spirit and constituted quite an ordeal for the person undergoing it. However, in a fashion not unlike the self-criticism approach utilized in the Peoples Republic of China after the Red Guard movement of the 1960s, retrospectively the persons criticized reported the experience as spiritually cathartic—the experience of a lifetime and a chance to map out the paths that must be followed before perfection became a spiritual reality. As actually conducted, mutual criticism closely resembles modern-day sensitivity training sessions with a religious connotation applied to the context in which it occurred.

## Summary: The Oneida Community Experiment

The Oneida experiment, then, consisted of rather radical experiments with economic communism, with the meaning and practice of marriage, with sexual communism, control of conception, and planned parenthood eugenically based, and with communal child rearing. All of this occurred during a period of history that was not conducive to experimentation with the family institution and familial-parental-marital behaviors. And it was successful, at least for a while.

The POET model can be readily applied to the Oneida Community to account for, at least partially, its commitment to a nontraditional family system. The following specific hypothesis seems plausible.

A commitment to a nontraditional family ideology was possible because (a) the population size was quite limited and strict recruitment procedures and an extended probationary period ensured a loyal membership; (b) the development of a series of profitable economic enterprises based on an industrial technology allowed the community to be financially independent; (c) the natural environment in which the community was located allowed it to be self-sustaining agriculturally and to be isolated from a social environment that might have made continuing commitment to unorthodox practices more problematic; and (d) the organization ideology was such that the informal norms controlled all interpersonal relationships, ensuring total conformity and seriously proscribing any deviant behavior or even overt expressions of dissatisfaction.

The Oneida Community was a highly successful experiment with the family for about thirty years, but then it broke apart. Complex marriage was abandoned for the worldly and decadent practice of monogamy, and the economic enterprise was dissolved into a joint stock company—the perfectionists proved to be anything but perfect and sinless. Perhaps the most thorough and penetrating exposition that seeks to account for the multiple factors that led to the dissolution of Oneida was written by Constance Noyes Robertson (1972), the daughter of Pierrepont B. Noyes and granddaughter of John Humphrey Noyes. She says (1972:14): "In so common a happening as a divorce, the breakup of a single marriage, the odds must be a hundred to one against a single simple cause for the parting. In the case of the dissolution of the Oneida Community, where there was not a single but a complex marriage, where there was not the usual small family unit but a family unit of nearly three hundred persons, the odds against a single, simple cause of its breakup must be astronomical. And add to the incredibly complicated web of human relations existing there the almost equally complicated structure of its business organization and you have a riddle to daunt a modern Oedipus."

Robertson (1972) outlines several reasons for the community's failure:

1. The enigmatic personality of John H. Noyes—charismatic in his earlier years but much less effective in the years just before he left Oneida—was one major factor. Noyes's decreasing effectiveness led to divisions within the flock.

2. There were increasing demands for new freedoms and rules for the practice of complex marriage during the latter years in the community. This was an early example of the youth revolting against their elders. The locus of the opposition centered around the sexual constraints engendered by the principle of ascendancy.

3. The practice of stirpiculture, although central to the perfectionist plan, evidently led to a kind of labeling that those left out felt was prejudicial.

207

4. The continued insistence by John Humphrey Noyes, while he was still at Oneida, that his only son by Harriett be designated as the heir apparently led to considerable dissension. This was a particularly sore spot since Theodore Noyes never publicly admitted to a belief in the principles of the Oneida Community.

5. Another strand in the process of dissolution was the active campaign waged by the outside clergy against Oneida. They were unrelenting in their attacks against the cancer of Oneida.

6. The last factor was the enormous complexity of the business enterprises run by the community. In a sense, success spoiled the community.

Regardless of the differing degrees of influence of each of these factors, the fact remains that the Oneida Community was a radical experiment that succeeded against overwhelming odds, and for a considerable period of time.

## CONCLUSIONS

This chapter outlines the salient features of three similar, yet distinct, experiments with the family institution and familial, marital, and parental roles. In each of these experiments the family system was altered to meet the demographic, environmental, technological, and organizational contingencies facing the persons and groups involved. Although none of the experiments has been wholly and undeniably successful, all provide evidence of the inherent adaptability of men and women and of the social inventions of marriage, parenthood, and the family. These experiments do not prove the indispensability of the family, particularly the nuclear family. They do provide evidence that the family, however it is defined and structured, can and does serve useful functions even under conditions that are highly problematic. These experiments also provide evidence that men and women can and do question their underlying assumptions about the family system in which they were raised.

Experiments with the family, its structure, its functions, its roles and the norms applied to these roles are and will always be with us. Such experiments are not only useful but also necessary if we are to continue a search for the most meaningful and practical ways to live in a world that grows more complex each day.

### SOME POSSIBLE IMPLICATIONS

*Experiments with the family and marriage are not a new phenomenon. The Oneida Community was able to significantly alter traditional marriage and family practices in the nineteenth century. It was eminently successful for at least thirty years. The immigrants to Israel who estab-*

*lished the kibbutzim were able not only to forsake an orthodox Jewish family ideology but to substitute in its place a rather radical and experimental set of marital and familial practices. The Communist government in the Soviet Union was able markedly to transform the family life of diverse cultural groups by radically altering the legal system to accomplish their goals.*

*These experiments and others have led some social scientists to question whether the family is or must be universal in human society. Others have questioned what familial functions are minimal for there to be a family system in a society. In addition, a number of writers interested in the future of marriage and the family speculate that experimentation with marriage and family practices will become almost endemic in our society.*

*A number of questions arise regarding experimentation with what some have called the basic unit of society—the family. Is the family a kind of "sacred" institution, essential for the survival of our cultures, or is the family, as we know it, expendable? How much experimentation with marital and family practices can and will be tolerated by our society? To what extent are all of us obligated to encourage experimentation with marital and family practices? What about experimentation in our own intimate environments—should we seek opportunities to experiment with our own marriage and family?*

# PART III

# THE PROCESS OF MARITAL-PARTNER SELECTION

# LOVE: A SOCIOLOGICAL PERSPECTIVE

*What are the "crucial" ingredients of romantic love?*
*How does romantic love usually develop?*
*What is the crucial final question to ask before marriage?*
*Is romantic love a positive or negative force in society relative to the*
     *family system?*

There is probably no term more widely used and abused in the English language than *love*. We love our parents and our dogs, our brothers and sisters and our cars, our sweethearts and our alma mater, our country and flag; we love animate and inanimate objects, vegetables and fruit, attitudes and behavior. Love is the overwhelming topic of concern for songwriters, novelists, journalists, teenage boys and girls, and their parents.

We get married because we love our future spouse, and we get divorced perhaps because we love our children and do not want to see them get hurt; some Americans kill other men because they love their country and freedom whereas other young men abandon their country—because they love their country and freedom. Some Christians love their fellow men so much that they spend huge sums of money to carry "the gospel" to Africa, but love their church so much that they would like to refuse admittance to people with an African heritage who live down the street. Love is a perplexing, complex force that all of us experience in many different ways. It varies in intensity from time to time and, depending on the object, can be consistent and inconsistent at the same time.

## DEFINITIONS AND CHARACTERISTICS

What is love? Can you define it, conceptualize it, sort out its essential components? Is the love you feel for your sweetheart, friend, parent, child the same emotion? How are these loves different? Quite obviously, each social scientist who asks these questions has a stake in the answers—he or she must rely on past and present experiences and projections for the future. To ease the problem of discussion somewhat, let us limit ourselves to heterosexual romantic love—the kind that usually is claimed between male and female, the kind that each will probably use to justify a commitment to marriage and "living happily ever after."

Reiss (1971) calls this "courtship love," and defines it as a "type of intense emotional feeling developing from a primary relationship involving a single male and female and consisting of rights and duties similar to those of husband and wife." Kephart (1972) puts together three characteristics shared by most definitions of love. They are: "(1) a strong emotional attachment toward a person of the opposite sex; (2) the tendency to think of this person in an idealized manner; and (3) a marked physical attraction, the fulfillment of which is reckoned in terms of

Charles Gatewood

touch." The psychologist Harry Stack Sullivan (1947:292) says that a state of love exists "when the satisfaction or the security of another person becomes as significant to one as is one's own security."

If these three characteristics of love can be taken as representative of the social-scientific approach, it should be apparent that romantic love signifies an intense emotional experience that probably varies from person to person and within one person over time. Understandably, some authors have balked at defining such a fleeting and complex term. Their strategy has usually been to check off the characteristic components of love. Perhaps the best example of an early attempt to outline what love (charity) is is found in the Bible, I Corinthians 13:

> Though I speak with the tongues of men and of angels, and have not charity,
> I am become as sounding brass, or a tinkling cymbal.
> And though I have *the gift of* prophecy, and understand all mysteries, and all knowledge; and though I have all faith, so that I could remove mountains, and have not charity, I am nothing.
> And though I bestow all my goods to feed *the poor,* and though I give my body to be burned, and have not charity, it profiteth me nothing.
> Charity suffereth long, *and* is kind; charity envieth not; charity vaunteth not itself, is not puffed up,
> Doth not behave itself unseemly, seeketh not her own, is not easily provoked, thinketh no evil;

215

Rejoiceth not in iniquity, but rejoiceth in the truth;

Beareth all things, believeth all things, hopeth all things, endureth all things.

Charity never faileth: but whether *there be* prophecies, they shall fail; whether *there be* tongues, they shall cease; whether *there be* knowledge, it shall vanish away.

For we know in part, and we prophesy in part.

But when that which is perfect is come, then that which is in part shall be done away.

When I was a child, I spake as a child, I understood as a child, I thought as a child: but when I became a man, I put away childish things.

For now we see through a glass, darkly; but then face to face: now I know in part; but then shall I know even as also I am known.

And now abideth faith, hope, charity, these three, but the greatest of these is charity.

Ralph Turner (1970), a sociologist, developed a list of "distinctive characteristics of an attraction that lead us to regard it as love" that is not vastly different from the first-century views. He said that love is

1. relatively enduring
2. pervasive rather than segmental
3. intimate in that conventional interpersonal boundaries can be violated
4. trusting
5. altruistic and self sacrificing
6. compassionate
7. consensual in that both parties seek to agree
8. responsive to the needs, wishes, desires of the other
9. built on mutual admiration
10. spontaneous when the lovers are together
11. consists of mutual obligations that are morally binding.

Turner does not bother to say if love is all of these things—at the same time or with what degree of intensity.

A somewhat different tack, one that is an expansion of Sullivan's notions of care and concern for the satisfaction and security of the other, is offered by Erich Fromm. Fromm (1956) discusses various types of love, including brotherly love, motherly love, erotic love, and love of God. Central to all of these types are care, responsibility, respect, and knowledge:[1]

Mature love is union under the condition of preserving one's integrity, one's individuality. Love is an active power in man; a power which breaks through the walls which separate man from his fellow men, which unites him with others; love makes him overcome the sense of isolation

[1] Erich Fromm, *The Art of Loving*, New York: Harper and Row, Publishers, Inc., 1956, pp. 21–24. Used by permission of the publisher.

and separateness, yet it permits him to be himself, to retain his integrity. In love the paradox occurs that two beings become one and yet remain two. . . .

Love is an activity, not a passive affect; it is a "standing in," not a "falling for." In the most general way, the active character of love can be described by stating that love is primarily giving, not receiving. . . .

What does one person give to another? He gives of himself, of the most precious he has, he gives of his life. This does not necessarily mean that he sacrifices his life for the other—but that he gives him of that which is alive in him; he gives of his joy, of his interest, of his understanding, of his knowledge, of his humor, of his sadness—of all expressions and manifestations of that which is alive in him. In thus giving of his life, he enriches the other person, he enhances the other's sense of aliveness by enhancing his own sense of aliveness. He does not give in order to receive; giving is in itself exquisite joy. But in giving he cannot help bringing something to life in the other person, and this which is brought to life reflects back on him; in truly giving, he cannot help receiving that which is given back to him. Giving implies to make the other person a giver also and they both share in the joy of what they have brought to life. In the act of giving something is born, and both persons involved are grateful for the life that is born for both of them.

Fromm has elegantly described love—the kind of love a husband experiences with his wife and children, a fulfilling paradoxical exchange in which one encounters previously unknown reservoirs of care and concern, respect and knowledge, a love that grows when one expends it and contracts when one keeps it to oneself. But Fromm, Turner, and the others so far cited have not detailed how romantic love develops—where it comes from in a sociological sense. Definitions, lists of ingredients, and elegant phraseology are important but not adequate. As social scientists we need to know how persons of opposite sexes get to the point of selfless mutual concern and giving. To make an analysis of love seems almost profane. To ignore or refuse to analyze such an important process would be, however, immoral. Therefore, let us examine the most adequate available theory of the development of love relationships.

## REISS'S WHEEL THEORY OF LOVE

In 1960 Ira Reiss presented a "wheel theory" of love—a circular and developmental process starting at rapport, moving then through self-revelation or self-disclosure to a stage of mutual dependency and finally to the zenith of the process—personality need fulfillment (Figure 9–1). According to Reiss, the circularity of the wheel is reversible—put in the vernacular, one can "fall into" and "out of" love. Let us look at the basic components of Reiss's theory and test it against reality. The first stage is rapport. Two people are attracted to one another, and after an initial contact, they start building up a foundation for further communication.

217

**FIGURE 9–1**
Ira Reiss's Wheel Theory of Love

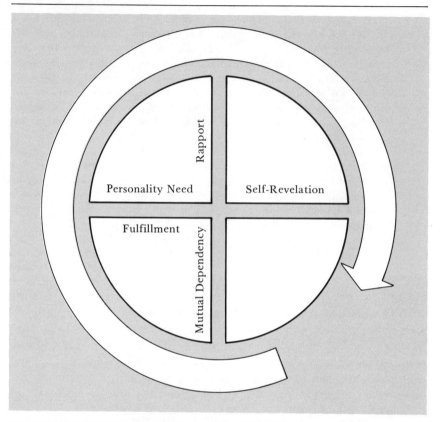

SOURCE: Ira L. Reiss, "Toward a Sociology of the Heterosexual Love Relationship," *Marriage and Family Living* 22(May 1960):143, Figure 1. Used by permission of the National Council on Family Relations.

This is the small-talk, game stage in which each is at his or her best behavior. If this basic sense of rapport develops, the chances are good that the relationship will move to stage 2.

At the second stage of the wheel theory, things get a little more serious. Some trust has developed and each begins to talk of his or her attitudes, values, goals, aspirations, fears, and anxieties. There is not a wholesale baring of soul at this stage, but rather a patterned and deliberately staged opening up of one's life to the other. As reciprocity emerges there is a back-and-forth give and take of revelation and disclosure.

Reiss labeled the third stage "mutual dependency." The more ostensible commitment of each to the other becomes apparent here, both to the "lovers" and to those around them. Companionship is constant, and a message is beamed to everyone who will see—we are a pair, two in the process of becoming one. Each of the two begins to sense the warm security he or she feels when with the other and the vacuum that exists when they are separated.

This mutual dependency leads quite naturally to the fourth stage of personality need fulfillment. Only when a couple "moving toward love" can shift their focus from the more conscious, socially oriented needs to the more basic personality or gut-level needs are they finally committed, in love for sure. It is here that Reiss says they recognize not only their similar needs but also their divergent needs and those qualities of the other that can best fulfill these basic needs of the personality.

Reiss does not say it explicitly, but hypothetically the wheel continues to turn around and around like a spinning top, with rapport, self-disclosure, mutual dependency, and personality need fulfillment blurring into each other as the love becomes more intense and mature—a kind of spiraling, cumulative, and interlocking circle of love experiences.

## The Wheel Theory Expanded

Reiss's wheel theory is impressive for several reasons. First and foremost, it is elegant in its simplicity. Second, the four parts to the theory not only seem to develop logically one from the other, but the components seem to represent the developmental sequence that all of us who have ever been in love went through. Third, the theory seems general enough to apply to almost any kind of interpersonal attraction, from the platonic love we have for friends to the erotically tinged love that precedes and continues through marriage. Even with these compliments, the theory is incomplete. Let us build upon each of the four sections of Reiss's wheel theory to see if an already adequate theory can become more adequate.

WHAT LEADS TO THE ESTABLISHMENT OF RAPPORT?  From a sociological and very practical standpoint, this question is crucial. Most of us come into daily contact with dozens if not hundreds of persons of the opposite sex, many of whom we consider physically attractive. Yet, most of us focus our attention and energies toward establishing rapport with only one or a very small number of potential love objects. Propinquity or closeness is just one of the factors that affect our choice. Initially, we are attracted by the physical characteristics—relative height and weight, hair-skin-eye color, the way a person dresses or walks, the way he or she talks or what is said, a smile or a glance. There is considerable evidence to suggest that persons with relatively *equal* amounts of social attractiveness are drawn to one another. It is no accident that people who end up married to one another often resemble each other in a number of ways (Figure 9–2).

However, rapport can never develop between two persons who are mutually attracted if both are too shy to seize the opportunity for interaction. All of us have regretted at some time not striking up a conversation with an especially attractive person of the opposite sex.

219

**FIGURE 9–2**
**The Determinants of Rapport**

Propinquity
Physical-social attractiveness (mutual)
Perceived opportunity for interaction (seized)
Perceived basis for developing rapport

Rapport

HOW DOES RAPPORT LEAD TO SELF-DISCLOSURE? Rapport does not happen all at once. It is usually a slow and evolving process that requires a mutual expenditure of time, energy, and the exchange of resources. In the process of building rapport, two people begin to disclose their attitudes and values, first at a general level. During this first stage they talk about things like political beliefs, religious ideas, social values; they exchange their knowledge about various topics of mutual interest. As time goes on and they perceive similarities their focus shifts to style of thought, styles of expression, statements of goals for their lives, disclosures of per-

Clemens Kalischer

*Sometimes a long evening's talk will lead to serious mutual disclosure, and suddenly the girl-boy game is over and an important emotional relationship has begun.*

sonal preferences and attitudes. There is a movement toward exposing more of their real selves—their fears and anxieties, their disappointments and successes, their dreams and aspirations (Figure 9–3). Aspects of playing the boy-girl game are discarded, and they begin to open up to someone who is now a trusted confidant. When they discover that their secrets will not be betrayed, that each can trust the other, the self-disclosure process becomes an enjoyable episode, something they look forward to.

In other words, rapport must filter through an ideological-cognitive (similar intellectual styles and attitudes-values-beliefs) component before self-disclosure becomes a *personal* experience. If similarities are not sufficient at the general ideological-cognitive level, commitment to each other will not develop. The basis of any kind of permanent male-female relationship is usually similar interests, congruent values and

---

**FIGURE 9–3**
**Moving from Rapport to Self-Disclosure**

---

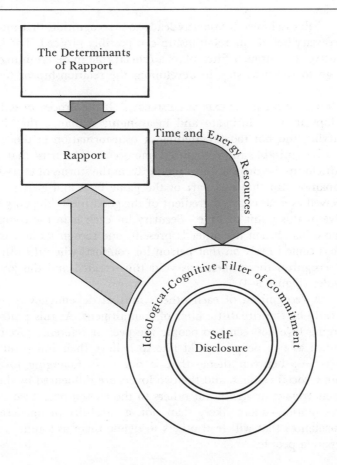

attitudes, styles of life and goals that mesh, and a mutual feeling of trust that the other will listen and understand the self that is revealed.

There is a broken line flowing from self-disclosure back to rapport. This feedback loop is a recognition that all of us have difficulty opening up our private worlds to people we do not really know. Also, we seldom find another person with whom we agree on every issue. Thus a mediation process is part of every emerging male-female relationship. The couple tries to decide what degree of dissimilarity on which issues they are willing to tolerate. For example, perhaps a boy and girl are both liberal on all social issues; from the same social class, and religious and ethnic status; but one is a staunch Republican and the other an equally staunch Democrat. By going back through a negotiating round of rapport and self-disclosure perhaps they can effect a settlement that will allow them to proceed with the relationship. Or, perhaps there is agreement on everything except the disclosure that the male expects his future spouse to play the traditional housewife role, and the female has always wanted a career in law. Each has to decide if the potential relationship is worth the conflict or if there may be some way of converting the other to his or her view.

Self-disclosure frequently leads to a recognition that more rapport is necessary before the relationship can possibly proceed. The ideological-cognitive commitment filter plays a crucial role in determining if the two will go to the next step in developing the relationship or terminate it.

WHEN DOES MUTUAL DEPENDENCY EMERGE? If the process of self-disclosure develops into an intimate and meaningful exchange that is mutually gratifying and not too threatening, a transformation of the two persons into a recognizable and recognized one occurs. The trust that emerges in self-disclosure becomes a warm shelter from the storms of everyday battles. Companionship that was part of the game boys and girls play becomes perceived as a necessary ingredient of the good life—"the only life I want to live at this point in time." Security for each is in the companionship of the other. When the other is present, one recognizes how much he or she has come to rely on that person for comfort; when the other is away, one recognizes the tremendous void thus created and the joy the other provides (Figure 9–4).

A recognition of each other's mutual dependency is shaped dramatically by the ritualistic filter of commitment. At this juncture in the emerging love between two people the peer or reference group intrudes. As much as two people would like to believe their independence—that love is just between them—that is not true. Emerging love develops within a social context, and the two lovers are influenced by the reactions of their friends or significant others to the chosen one. Two lovers stage a presentation—more likely than not, a carefully planned sequence of performances that will lead others to define them as a unity rather than as separate people.

**FIGURE 9–4**
**Moving from Self-Disclosure to Mutual Dependency**

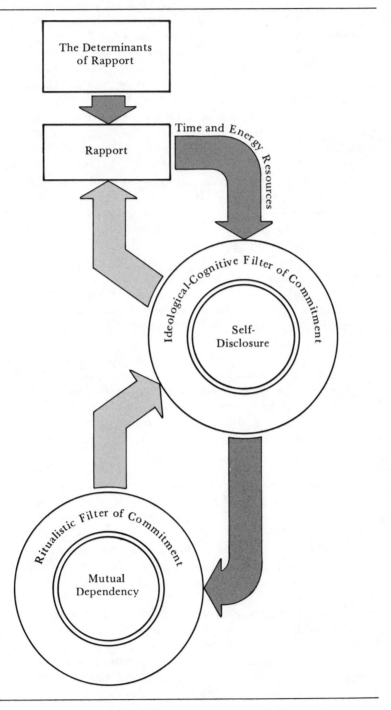

The lovers begin to develop a routine, a ritualized presentation of themselves as a couple to various audiences. They eat together at the same table or in the same restaurant. They are seen at the same table in the library on Monday, Wednesday, and Friday from ten to twelve. This behavior has two effects. One, it announces to the world, particularly to significant others, that "unless you have strong objections, we are getting serious!" The second effect is that it allows each of the lovers to play the role of a visible and normal partner—to see how it feels to be thought of as part of a committed pair.

Usually, at this stage of the development of romantic love "I love you" is verbalized—over and over again. Anniversaries are also part of the ritual and further add to the commitment of each to the other. However, the broken line from mutual dependency back to self-disclosure is included to suggest that the mutual dependency stage has a great potential for conflict. At this stage of development the words "You take me for granted" are heard most often. All of us are aware that it is easy to hurt those who are dependent on us for emotional support—not necessarily in an intentional way, but by being blasé and insensitive to things the other does not verbalize yet expects us to hear. For example, two college students have been dating each other for one year this Friday. Every Friday night they study for a couple of hours and then go out for a pizza. They have discussed this anniversary, and the girl has insisted that they will not do anything different and no gifts will be exchanged. So they go to the library as usual, study, get a pizza, go out and park for awhile as usual, and go back to the dormitory. As the boy is about to leave, the girl practically throws a neatly wrapped package at him and dashes up the stairs in tears. Sometimes "yes" means "no," and "I don't want anything" means "You had better not forget to get me something." All of us seek the patterned regularity and security of a ritualized relationship but frequently get lulled into a state of insensitivity by it.

HOW DOES THE LOVE THAT GROWS OUT OF A RECOGNITION OF MUTUAL DE-
PENDENCY DEVELOP INTO THE MATURE LOVE OF MUTUALLY SATISFYING PER-
SONALITY NEEDS?   The verbal expression of a love commitment, like any other repetitive sound, can fade into the background unless the commitment matures and finds other avenues of expression. Love is mature when each recognizes the meshing of his or her personality with the other's. This recognition is not something that is exclusively cognitive. It occurs at the gut level of experience, deep in the center of one's being. It is here that the fusion process that started back at rapport becomes complete. This is the reason for including an experiential filter of commitment. Each of the lovers is so much a part of the other's life that neither can fathom an existence apart. At this point many people say that they are "spiritually married," that the ties are at the soul level of being and are so satisfying and fulfilling that heaven could not be better (Figure 9–5).

**FIGURE 9–5**
**Moving from Mutual Dependency to Personality Need Fulfillment and Beyond**

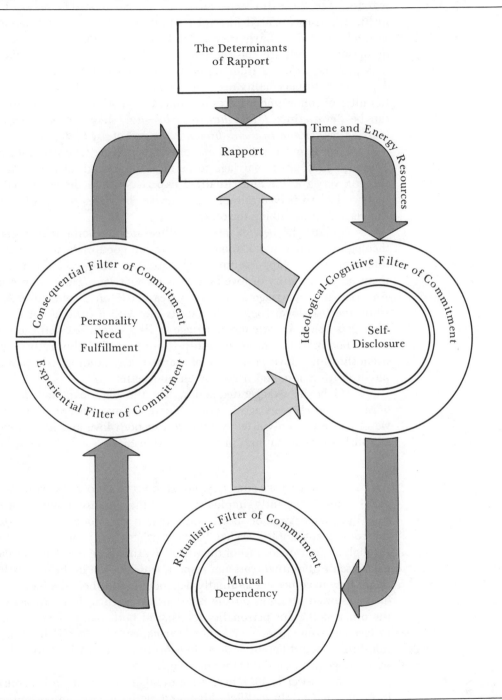

IF LOVE IS "HEAVENLY," WHAT ELSE IS NEEDED FOR THE MODEL TO BE COMPLETE? A large proportion of the couples who claim to be spiritually married take the extra step and make it legal. For that reason I have included a consequential filter of commitment. Because the word *love* is so freely used, it is fairly easy to "fall in love." Sometimes, especially if he or she or both are "on the rebound," lonely, "chomping at the bit," it is possible to move from rapport through self-disclosure and mutual dependency to personality need fulfillment very quickly. The consequential filter of commitment forces one to ask a question the answer to which can be devastating: *I* love *him/her, but do I* like *him/her enough to marry him/her and live with him/her the rest of my life?*

Love is not a sufficient reason for marriage. One has sincerely to *like* one's lover for a marriage to be meaningful and satisfying. Married life is a very routine and ritualized experience, and the emotional high that we feel with *love* cannot long survive the rigors of everyday living. Marriage requires liking the other.

Perhaps the best example to illustrate the point is this story: A theological student was kissing his girl friend good night when they were interrupted by a Japanese ministerial student, who proceeded to lecture them on the fragility of love as a basis for marriage. He said, in essence: An occidental marriage is like a hot tea kettle on a cold stove. After a while the tea (love) cools. What starts out with a fusillade of fireworks soon gets cold. An oriental marriage is like a cold tea kettle on a hot stove. The basis for the relationship is not blind love but rather a warm friendship—the love grows out of warm understanding, not passionate physical attraction, and it gets better and better.

Maybe he exaggerated a bit, but the logic expounded on that dormitory porch years ago is sound. There are many people in this world we can love but only a few whom we can both love and like enough to establish a permanent and intimate relationship.


LOVE AFTER MARRIAGE: DOES THE WHEEL CONTINUE TO TURN OR DOES IT GO FLAT? Reiss's elegantly simple model and the expansion of it are still not fully adequate. A major shortcoming is that the model seems to stop at the consequential filter. What happens when two people have made it through all four quadrants of the wheel? By that time they have developed a deep sense of mutual trust and respect, which began in the self-disclosure stage; they have become mutually dependent, and their significant others have bestowed blessings on the relationship; each feels an attraction for the other at the gut personality levels; and both like each other enough to face the consequences of a more permanent and legally binding relationship. Stated differently, does the wheel of love continue to roll along in marriage just as it did before marriage?

The answer is *no!* There are a number of ways in which courtship love and marital love differ. First and perhaps most importantly, the

*The mementos of a lifetime are visible reminders of the invisible connection between two who, over the years, have become one.*

Clemens Kalischer

projected *lifetime* of the relationship is extended—" 'til death do us part." Prior to marriage both must recognize, though seldom are they willing to admit to it, the possibility that something may destroy the relationship. Terminating a courtship love relationship, although painful, is not nearly as difficult nor intrapersonally as stigmatizing as terminating a marital partnership. This means for most unmarried couples in love that the future is *now*—an existential reality that results in everything being crammed into unbelievably tight schedules. After marriage both realize that the relationship could last a lifetime—twenty-five, thirty, forty, fifty or more years. The love that both partners give, receive, and share does not have to be rushed. There is less need to be frantic about the relationship; more time can be devoted to nurturing the strong forces that brought the two together in the first place. Thus, love in marriage usually benefits from the more open-ended time the partners know exists for their relationship.

A second way marital love differs from courtship love is seen by some as a disadvantage—I see it as a sign of strength. Usually marital partners voluntarily choose to forego certain symbols of freedom and individualism. Practically everyone who has ever written of love emphasizes sacrifice, that "it's better to give than to receive." The essence of the commitment in marriage is willingness to let what seems best for the couple to take precedence over the needs of each individual in the relationship. This is not to say that each partner loses his or her identity and must sublimate personal goal attainment for the good of the other partner. Rather, in marital love the couple dimension is dominant—each learns to

227

give a little in order to get a little. In the courtship stage of love development, neither partner is linked legally or inextricably to the opportunities afforded the other. More than a few really deep and loving relationships have shattered because there was no firm commitment to a couple dimension vis-à-vis personal ambition and opportunities. Had these people been married, the marital love relationship would have dictated a joint search for, and negotiation of, a future that would yield the best for both partners.

A third way that marital love differs from courtship love is in the way it is presented to the world. It is anchored usually in a family system. The families of orientation—for better or worse—are to enjoy or endure. The nuclear unit—the new husband and wife, who have selected each other from among the masses and who together have traveled the often rough and rocky road from rapport through self-disclosure and mutual dependency to arrive at personality need fulfillment and an answer that each is willing consequentially to be married to the other—they are the *new* link in a history whose roots can run deep. Recognition of this fact can be an important and impressive experience. This cannot and does not happen prior to marriage, regardless of how intensely the love is felt. It does not occur among persons who are living together. Cementing the love relationship in this manner is restricted to marital partners.

Marital love differs considerably from courtship love in a number of ways, all of which reflect the fact that both partners occupy roles deemed important by society. As Orlinsky (1972) notes:

> Love experiences occur in socially patterned relationships, and can be understood adequately only in terms of the person's participation in such relationships . . . each stage in the life cycle is marked by the onset or emergence of a new form of love experience, and the form of love which is closest to a person's "growing edge" at any given time in his life is the form that is most absorbing and exciting to him.

Orlinsky underscores the fact that love is a dynamic process, ever changing over the entire life cycle. Marriage provides the roles, norms, and social contact within which a couple can explore in detail—together—the unique but very common experience of two seeking to become *one* while retaining and encouraging personal and individual growth.

For most married couples the love process continues to evolve, but not always in a single and positive direction. Rapport is not etched from stone; it must be established again and again. The trust that emerged through self-disclosure needs to be nurtured and stroked; occasionally, it must be completely rediscovered. The dependency that was mutually established in courtship often needs to be redirected from a state of unilateral dependency, especially if the wife adopts a housewife/mother role. Finally, it takes effort and ingenuity to keep the fire lit in a marriage buffeted by the strains and stresses so prevalent in the modern world.

228

There are times in the healthiest of marriages when one or both wonder if the sparks have gone forever. Virtually every married partner has wondered if it is possible to survive one more day of the marital life.

Most married couples take the good with the bad and heartily endorse the benefits and challenges of love after courtship.

### Additional Thoughts About Love and Reiss's Wheel Theory

1. Love and its development is dynamic, not static. We should not think of the wheel theory as if it were a steel-belted radial tire. Actually, the model should be viewed as if each of the four components were fastened by thumbtacks and connected by rubber bands. If two painfully shy people were attracted to one another, the self-disclosure point might have to be stretched considerably. This allows for the varying amounts of time it takes two people to make interpersonal progress. For some people who have been in love before, perhaps many times, other connections might be extended and stretched (see Figure 9–6). The rubber-band idea also allows for the criticism frequently heard from more idealistic students, "Love is different for everybody. You can't draw love on the chalkboard."

2. The most glaring omission from Reiss's wheel theory of love is sex. If the theory represents how romantic love develops, then sex is

**FIGURE 9–6**
**A Flexible Rubber-Band Model of Romantic Love**

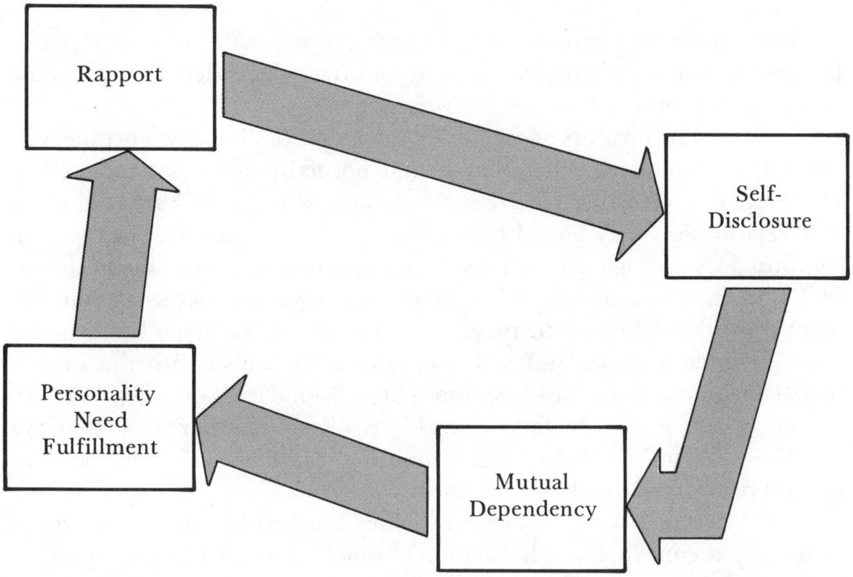

*Love involves closeness, touching, affection; and it produces a mutual sense of identity, security, and warmth.*

Richard L. Good from Black Star

obviously intimacy concomitantly emerging along with building rapport, increasing self-disclosure, recognizing mutual dependency, and being aware of each other's basic personality needs.

Sexual intimacy is an explosive force that can blast two people well beyond the boundaries that they would normally define for themselves. However, it is probably true that two people who are seeking to build a love relationship play sexual games that progress in intimacy as the relationship goes through the various stages and their respective commitment filters. In the expanded model, four sexual stages of progressing commitment coincide with the four quadrants of Reiss's wheel hypothesis. In the space between rapport and self-disclosure each probes into the other's sexual attitudes, likes, dislikes, and stated boundaries of acceptable behavior. These probes include expressions of a physical nature that are usually quite mild—kissing, light fondling, holding each other and in general being gentle with one another.

The second stage of sexual intimacy can best be labeled as testing. It usually occurs in the self-disclosure–mutual-dependency love quarter. The couple is actively involved in being with one another, talking and talking some more, exploring all aspects of the other's personality and person. There is during this stage of development a hoped-for rush toward a love commitment. Each is testing the other to determine if and how good a physical (sexual) adjustment they can attain. The physical expressions of love usually include heavier petting and kissing, exploration of each other's body. Research has shown that females generally require a verbal expression of love with some chance of a more permanent commitment. Therefore, full intercourse may not be found at this stage of development.

The verbal expression of a love commitment usually occurs after a recognition of mutual dependency. Both recognize that the probability of a more permanent commitment has increased. There may even be a mutual conclusion, occurring between the mutual dependency and personality need fulfillment stages, that the couple is spiritually married. This stage of sexual intimacy involves exploring boundaries. Each knows there is a good chance of marriage and wants not only to express his or her love but also to determine the outside boundaries of mutual sexual satisfaction. It is not an unusual occurrence for the couple to engage in an unplanned sexual encounter, retreat back into petting, and move slowly back toward a greater physical commitment.

Of course, sex is just one of the needs that must be fulfilled in order for the love relationship to be satisfying and meaningful. The last stage of sexual intimacy occurs in the fourth quarter of the wheel theory and can be called solidifying strengths. The sexual expressions here are not limited to just a physical exchange—sex at this stage of the love relationship includes all of the things that the lovers do. This is when the couple begins asking how much each *likes* the other, and love is now something that transcends the physical. The relationship is totally symmetrical, well rounded, and totally fulfilling.

## FACTORS THAT COMPLICATE LOVE

Love is an extremely complex, frequently confusing, and occasionally painful experience. Because it is impossible for us to love in a vacuum, loving is complicated by cultural values and the social contexts within which it occurs. A series of factors complicate and sometimes impede the development of a love relationship between two otherwise consenting adults.

### Age Differences

Even in a society like the United States, that ostensibly has a system of free choice in mate selection, extremely powerful cultural norms specify who may love whom. One very explicit proscription is: *Don't fall in love with someone who is old enough to be your father/mother or young enough to be your son/daughter.* The obverse and less explicit prescription is: *Love someone who is close to your age.*

231

A year is measured differently by males and females and means different things for different-aged people. An eighteen-year-old freshman woman thinks nothing of dating junior and senior men. In fact, it is an axiom of college life that upperclass males feel obligated to make freshmen women welcome. It is generally taboo, however, for a freshman male to date an upperclass female and heresy for an upperclass woman to date anyone who, by the accident of birth, entered college after she did.

The importance attached to relative differences in ages diminishes somewhat after males and females pass the age of 21. Even then, though, there is a tendency for women to seek out older men, and for men to seek out younger women. During postcollege years there is still an aversion to women falling in love with younger men. Somehow our culture considers an older woman–younger man love relationship a case of robbing the cradle, as in the case of a 31-year-old woman and a 24-year-old man. The sanctions and complicating pressures are especially harsh when a young girl falls in love with someone 10, 20, 30 years her senior. The robbery in this case is defined as, "He's stealing her youthful days and she will have to care for him in his old age."

Society does not usually tolerate the emergence of a love relationship between two adults of diverse ages, although there are some cases in which this occurs. Age, rather relative age, is just one complicating factor in love.

## Status Differences

A second complicating factor in the development of love is relative status. As more and more women enter the labor force it is not an unusual occurrence for a man and a woman of different status levels to fall in love. One example is the wealthy socialite who does volunteer work in a drug rehabilitation program and falls in love with a lower-class addict. They come from different social worlds that are miles apart. Love that emerges across status lines, although it does occur with some frequency, is problematic from its inception.

This is a complicating factor for love because the basis for similarity in such cases seldom transcends the situation. If the love is pursued and marriage occurs, both will soon discover that love has difficulty transcending certain social boundaries.

## Racial Differences

Regardless of how much parents love and trust their children of marriageable age, they cannot help but feel very concerned to hear, "Guess who is coming to dinner!" Love in the United States may be generally depicted as blind—but not color-blind. Whenever love develops between two people of different racial backgrounds, or merely different ethnic back-

Clemens Kalischer

*The prospect of a child's interracial marriage may bring to light the inherent conflict between idealism and realism—the difference between how things should be and how they really are.*

grounds or religions or social classes, complications are bound to arise. Regardless of the rhetoric of tolerance, brotherhood, freedom, love, few observers of a cross-something (racial, social class, ethnic, religious) love relationship are able to remain objective. They are usually so persistent that they are able to force the loving couple to consider potential complications to the relationship. Differences, particularly racial, are a complicating factor in love in this society and many others as well. Although racial intolerance does not represent human beings at their best, it is a fact of social life to consider when one is becoming a lover. If one does not consider it, someone will remind him or her of it very quickly.

## Different Experiences in the Expression of Love

Love is something that involves the expression—verbal and nonverbal—of the feeling one has for another person. In many families communication of any kind is not only problematic but, practically speaking, nonexistent. On the other hand in some families love and the expression of it is a way of life—families in which everyone is very demonstrable about his or her feelings.

Love can be complicated by the involvement of one person from a family that is trapped in an emotional "poverty cycle" in which love is just not expressed with a person from a family in which love is openly expressed. More likely than not the partner from the love-deprived setting

233

will want to learn how to express himself or herself. The partner from the love-satiated background should not expect miracles—it is hard to escape a cycle of emotional poverty. Even after the escape is seemingly complete, it is not unusual for temporary lapses, a reversion to the old nonexpressive self.

A similar situation can occur with a male from an expressive family playing the traditional male role, the big and tough he-man. Such males usually put off their partners by saying, "I'm a man. I just don't think about such things as birthdays, and saying thoughtful things, and sissy stuff like that." Love is something that transcends the cultural norms about sex roles. Love is a force that should be liberating, not complicated by the crutches all of us use so frequently. The excuse that "I never learned how to express affection and love" should never be used and certainly should not be accepted as a valid reason for not expressing one's feelings for one's lover.

## The Historical Evolution of Love as a Cultural Ideology

There are probably four phases through which the concept or idea of love has evolved historically.[2] The first occurred in the fifth century B.C. in the Greek culture of Plato and in the first century A.D. in the Roman culture of Ovid.

Plato, writing about upper-class Athenians, felt that love would inspire virtue. He divided love into two types: common and heavenly. For Plato a common love could be either homosexual or heterosexual in focus and concern itself with physical satisfaction. A higher type of love, heavenly love, was primarily spiritual in nature and existed between two men. This is the origin of the term *platonic love*.

Ovid's conception of love was sensual and heterosexual in focus, what Plato called common love. Ovid did not view love as a force that existed inside marriage. Rather, it was the experience a man had with a married woman in an adulterous affair. Ovid offers suggestions that might be made by a lover to the married woman he loves as to how she can project her love to him in the presence of her husband when all three are at a party. He also offers advice to the Roman woman who wants to be attractive. In essence, Ovid saw love as a game to be played in the social arenas of Roman life.

The second phase in the evolution of love as a cultural ideology occurred in the twelfth century in the courts of Europe. This kind of love

2 This section of the chapter relies rather heavily on the excellent discussion in Reiss (1971:74–89).

## LOVE: A MACRO PERSPECTIVE

Somehow it seems almost profane to deal with love at a level where the dynamics of interpersonal interaction are essentially ignored. Yet, a discussion of romantic love that is limited to the micro perspective is inadequate. Love is also a macro-level societal phenomenon and should be examined as such.

### Effects of Present-Day Love Ideology

Biegel (1951) suggests that the integration of sex and love in marriage resulted from the need for social and emotional security in a culture in which the family had lost functions, the father and male had lost authority, and urbanization and industrialization had created a sense of isolation and alienation.

is known as *courtly love*. It refers to an abstract and distant love as man would have for a woman other than his wife. The sexual drive was sublimated and the expression of courtly love took the form of an unselfish loyalty and devotion of the knight to the noble lady.

As Biegel (1951) notes:

> The cultural significance of this concept (courtly love, RRC) lies in the fact that the idealization of the female initiated her social elevation and that it introduced voluntary fidelity, restraint, and the magnanimous gentleness of the male consciously into the relation between the sexes, qualities that were not considered essential or even possible in a marriage based on the semi-patriarchal concept of the Middle Ages.

The third phase through which love evolved began in the fourteenth century and continued into the seventeenth and eighteenth centuries. In other words, the courtly love ideology filtered down out of the castles into the villages and cities rather slowly at best.

The court society of the seventeenth and eighteenth centuries redefined the distant and nonsexual orientation of courtly love to include sexual favors outside of marriage. By the seventeenth century it became acceptable for love to be an experience encountered by a woman and a man who were engaged to be married. Finally, in the nineteenth century, the concept of love moved into the fourth phase when the Romantic Movement in art and literature—with its emphasis on the primacy of feeling and of the tragic elements of human existence—further intensified the Western ideal of romantic love as the be-all and end-all of life.

235

The Bettman Archive, Inc.

*Love, from rapport through personality need fulfillment to marriage, a dynamic inter-personal force in times past and as contemporary as today.*

Shulamith Stein, © Catherine Noren

The love ideology has evolved to a point where it is considered both an essential prerequisite to marriage and the cementing force that holds a married couple together. But love, like most other cultural phenomena, has come under criticism. The romanticists see love as the salve that miraculously cures all pains; the cynics see pain and disorganization as a result of relying on love, an emotional experience, instead of on rational and systematic thought. Biegel (1951) sees love as a positive force. He states:

> Seen in its proper perspective, it has not only done no harm as a prerequisite to marriage, but it has mitigated the impact that a too-fast-moving and unorganized conversion to new socio-economic constellations has had upon our whole culture and it has saved monogamous marriage from complete disorganization.

On the other side of the argument is William Goode (1959), who noted that the introduction of a love ideology in some cultures can be very disruptive. He refers to societies in which marriage is essentially an arrangement between families tending to support the existing social stratification system. To allow love to be a basis for mate selection is antithetical to the prevailing patterns of interaction and exchange in such societies.

## SUMMARY

The first of two goals in this chapter is a realistic and thorough picture of how romantic love develops, at least in most situations in the United States. Taking Reiss's elegant wheel theory, we added some aspects of love that were missing from his model. The second goal was to express the idea that there is always room for improvement, for disagreement, for constructive criticism.

Love is something we all need to understand if our lives are to be more meaningful. Love is most complete when it is being given. Love is the very essence of life. The poetry, musical lyrics, and art forms in practically every culture proclaim softly but firmly that the world needs love, now, and for everyone. Only the cynical would disagree.

## *SOME POSSIBLE IMPLICATIONS*

*Love is something all or most of us vigorously seek and hold onto with extraordinary strength when we get it. It is something we enjoy giving as well as receiving. Love is the* sine qua non *that we are committed to a person, perhaps for life. Few if any of us would consider marrying someone we do not love, and most of us would add the extending phrase, "with all my heart."*

*Yet love in these terms is not an integral part of the courtship process, the ideology of marriage, or the goal that necessarily is to be pursued in marriage in many parts of the non-Western world. In fact, in more than a few modernizing societies love is considered dysfunctional to the man-woman relationship, particularly in marriage. Love is viewed as a serpent that can maim and destroy a family in which one or more of the members become "deviant" and apply the emotion of love to their familial and marital relationships.*

*Is love really all that important in a human relationship at the adult level, especially the emotional type of love? Is a reliance on love as the "final filter" between a commitment to marry or a decision not to marry evidence of an abdication of rationality? Are there not more realistic reasons for a commitment between human beings of opposite sex, such as economic stability and potential; sociability, responsibility and maturity; similarity or homogamy in such areas as social class, religion, attitudes-beliefs, and values? Why is love so important to us?*

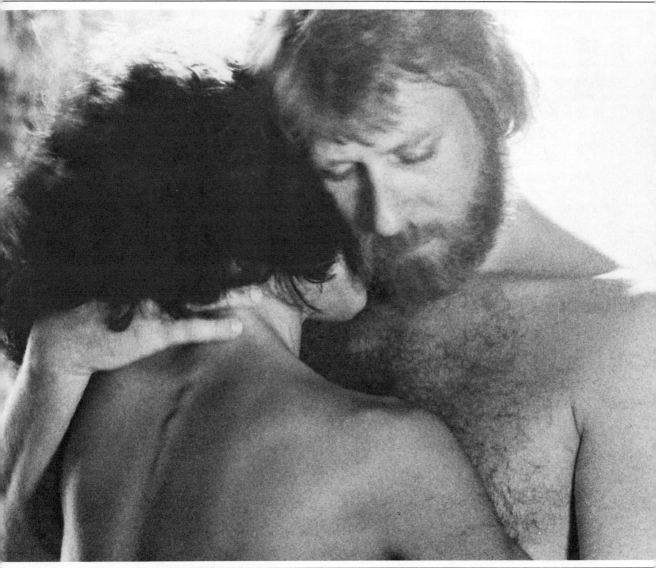

Frank Siteman

# 10

# PREMARITAL SEXUAL BEHAVIOR

*Is it possible to be twenty-one, single, and a virgin?*

*Is there a sexual revolution occurring in the United States today?*

*What distinguishes those who do from those who do not engage in premarital intercourse?*

*Is premarital intercourse a behavior that sociologists can predict, or is it too much of a private dynamic experience to be put under a sociological microscope?*

The preceding chapter on love was written from a very informal perspective to serve as an introduction and basis for the more formal research and ideas in this chapter on premarital sex behavior, the one that follows it on premarital sexual attitudes and standards, and the two subsequent chapters on marital selection. Premarital sexual behavior is a topic that is discussed extensively and is one that has or has had direct personal relevance for almost everybody. Whether one is for or against it, has or has not tried it, and should or should not engage in premarital sexual behaviors is strictly a personal matter. The aim in this chapter is to present the questions that sociologists have asked about premarital sexual behaviors and the answers that their research has uncovered. Some of the questions that will be examined are:

1. When does petting and premarital coitus usually first occur, and how prevalent is petting and premarital intercourse?
2. What is the average number of petting and coital partners for those who do engage in premarital sexual activity?
3. How extensively have petting and premarital coital behavior changed over the years?
4. What are the factors that differentiate those who do from those who do not choose to engage in premarital intercourse?
5. At the conceptual/theoretical level, how can we account for premarital intercourse behavior?

## THE STUDY OF SEXUAL BEHAVIOR

According to Ehrmann (1964), scientific writings on human sexual behavior have fallen into three major categories. The first category consists of anthropological studies conducted primarily among preliterate peoples. These reports usually have attempted to describe the role of sexual behavior in holding society together. In addition, the anthropological studies have usually been complete in recording such information as the frequency of coitus and the appropriate partners by age and kinship status. The following quote by Fortes (1936:591) illustrates the emphasis of anthropological studies on the bonding nature of intercourse behavior:

There is, in most societies, a tendency to condemn sexual intercourse between persons who are forbidden to marry. But there are many instances in which a man and woman who may not marry may carry on a temporary affair without this being considered the grave offence to which we give the name of incest, and without being subjected to any legal or religious sanction. Amongst the Tallensi of West Africa there are women whom a man is prohibited from marrying but with whom intercourse is not regarded as incestuous; the Tallensi themselves say "copulation and marriage are not the same thing." Similarly, amongst the Nkundo of the Belgian Congo there is a special term (lonkana) for sexual intercourse with women whom a man may not marry but with whom such connection does not constitute incest; they are women of a clan (or linkage?) which is related to his own and into which he may not marry for this reason.

The second category of writings on sexual behavior was labeled clinical studies by Ehrmann. These clinical approaches to sexual behavior usually focused on physiological changes that occur during or immediately after coitus. Perhaps the most widely cited clinical study in recent years was conducted by William H. Masters and Virginia Johnson (1966). These researchers at Washington University actually filmed and physiologically charted the stages that occur in female orgasm:

> With the introduction of artificial coital techniques, the reactions of the vagina during coition became available to direct observation and repeatedly have been recorded through the medium of cinematography. These vaginal reactions first had been observed during sexual response cycles stimulated by manipulation of the mons area and clitoral body. During artificial coition the reactions of the vaginal barrel initiated under direct stimulation conformed in exact detail to the vaginal response patterns which developed subsequent to the indirect stimulation of the mons area or clitoral-body manipulation.

Both of these categories of writing on sexual behavior tend to ignore some very relevant questions: (1) What are the distinguishing characteristics of those who do and those who do not engage in sexual liaisons normatively defined by society as deviant (that is, premarital and extramarital sexual intercourse)? (2) Why, in a causal sense, do sexual behavioral patterns differ both within and between sexes? (3) What are the social and situational contexts within which one might be willing to violate societal, reference group, and perhaps his or her own standards of appropriate conduct? The answers to questions such as these have been the focus of the third category mentioned by Ehrmann: sociological survey studies. The selected literature review that follows focuses on the sociological studies.

Prior to 1940 there were probably six major studies of human sexual behavior. These studies utilized samples of various sizes, none of which was truly random or representative of any particular group or categories of persons. The primary focus of these studies was to describe the "normal" sexual activities of the respondents. The studies served the

243

social purpose of showing, in a journalistic sense, that the stated attitudes of aversion to sex were not in correspondence with the actual reported behavior of a sizable proportion of the population. Little attempt was made in these studies to explain in a causal way the relationships between certain types of social variables (that is, social class, religious commitment) and the reported sexual behavior. Listed below are the authors of these early studies and the size and type of their samples.

| | |
|---|---|
| 1. Exner (1915) | 948 college men |
| 2. Davis (1929) | 2,200 women |
| 3. Hamilton (1929) | 100 married couples |
| 4. Terman (1938) | 792 married couples |
| 5. Bromley and Britten (1938) | 1,300 college students |
| 6. Carney Landis (1940) | 153 "normal" and 142 "psychiatric" patients |

Most of the significant sociological research in human sexual behavior has been conducted since 1940. These studies have been sociological in the sense that attempts have been made to relate key social variables to the reported sexual behavior. In other words, these researchers have tried to isolate characteristics that seem to differentiate those who do from those who do not engage in coitus, especially premarital and extramarital coitus. In lieu of reviewing all of the studies that have been conducted since 1940, we will review a few major works, starting with the Kinsey studies.

### Kinsey Studies (1948, 1953)

Alfred Kinsey, a zoologist, Wardell Pomeroy, a psychologist, and Clyde Martin, a statistician, were responsible for the very important studies that have served as a comparison model for most if not all studies of sexual behavior since they appeared in 1948 and 1953. Several key methodological factors should be discussed before any references are made to the sociologically relevant findings of the Kinsey studies.

1. Kinsey, Pomeroy, and Martin personally conducted the interviews with nearly 12,000 respondents, divided roughly between the sexes. These were exhaustive interviews usually lasting several hours. The researchers spent over a year training themselves and memorizing detailed codes before any interviews were conducted. The key point here is that these interviewers were professionals who were probably the best trained interviewers in any sociological research project. In addition, their interview strategy was bluntness—if they thought that someone was not telling the truth, they said so. Their intensive training plus their bluntness probably cut the degree of lying and/or conventionalized responses to a bare

minimum. Perhaps the best indication of their skill as interviewers is the fact that few interviews were terminated before completion.

2. Although few criticisms have been leveled at the interviewing phase of the study, the sampling procedures have been repeatedly singled out as a probable source of error. The Kinsey group, because of a fear of refusals given the nature of the study, used a group sampling procedure. The Kinsey group would make contact with the leader of an organization and solicit the leader's endorsement in order to get the members to cooperate. The range of cooperation was 26 to 100 percent with about one-fourth of the groups having total participation. A wide variety of groups were utilized, such as college classes, fraternities and sororities, mothers' clubs, PTA groups, women's clubs, church congregations, prisoners, and prison staffs. As you might expect, the total sample was less than representative of the adult population of the United States. About 75 percent of the women had gone to college, although in 1950 the median years of education of all adults in the United States was 9.9 years, or approximately the second year of high school. In addition, about 58 percent of the females in the Kinsey study were single, as compared to a national percentage of only 20 percent of women, fourteen years old or older. A sizable proportion of the lower-class male sample was composed of convicts and ex-convicts, hardly representative of the lower-class male in American society. As Reiss (1971:130) points out: "The groups that Kinsey's sample most closely represented were white, urban, Protestant, college-educated people from the Northeastern quarter of the country."

3. A third methodological consideration concerned the focus of interest of the researchers. Reflecting Kinsey's background in zoology, most of the research questions dealt with phenomena that were primarily physiological or psychological in nature, the latter perhaps indicative of Pomeroy's influence. For example, Kinsey attempted to show that males and females differ in their sensitivity to sexual stimuli. He found that males were more arousable by erotic stories, observing the opposite sex, observing portrayals of nude figures, observing burlesque shows, observing sexual action, observing their own and the genitalia of the opposite sex, and observing animal coitus, whereas females were more responsive to romantic activities. A clear physiological focus was evident in the Kinsey studies, with much emphasis placed on the frequency of coitus, duration of coitus, and the quality of orgasm.

## What Did the Kinsey Studies Reveal?

Kinsey and his associates were thorough, to say the least. They included questions on solitary behavior like masturbation, relatively rare events like sex with animals, and the extensive variety of nonmarital and marital sexual experiences that human beings have with each other. For our purposes here we will deal with masturbation, petting, and premarital coitus.

245

MASTURBATION.   This is, of course, a solitary and conscious form of sexual behavior that does not require two persons. It is not a sexual behavior that elicits a strong negative societal response, although young people "caught in the act" by their parents may be severely admonished either to quit or at least to curtail their activity.

By the time of marriage, 41 percent of Kinsey's sample of females and 94 percent of the males had engaged in masturbation to the point of orgasm. It should be fairly obvious that masturbation provides not only a logical but also a rather common outlet of sexual expression for the unmarried. It is likewise used after marriage, probably to a larger extent than most of us realize. There seems to be a rather clear association of masturbation with educational attainment, with the act a more salient part of the sexual activities of those with higher education.

Masturbation is usually accompanied by a fantasy of sexual activity that is mutual in focus instead of solitary. In this sense it allows the person involved to project himself or herself into an interpersonal situation where kissing, petting, and/or coitus are possible items on the agenda. The function thus served by masturbation is akin to "taking the role of the other" in a symbolic interaction perspective and also to anticipatory socialization.

PETTING.   To put it in the vernacular, petting is "different strokes for different folks." It can include such seemingly mild forms of sexual stimulation as fondling each other outside the clothes to nibbling the other's ear to a highly sensual and orgasm-producing event in which both participants are completely naked.

For some people petting is merely the prelude to full-fledged coitus, whereas for others petting is the sexual end of the encounter. In this sense petting can and does serve the function of providing an intense sexual experience while potentially preserving the virginity of the participants. Degrees of petting experience are easily recognized. Most petting starts out above the waist and outside the clothes, with the male the initiator. The next step is usually to go inside the clothes above the waist. Unless he is an unusual male, petting above the waist seldom includes the male as a recipient. Petting above the waist can also include oral contact. The same dimensions of intensity exist below the waist—inside or outside the clothes, unilateral or mutual, orgasm or not, and oral contact unilateral or mutual.

Among the females Kinsey studied who were virgins at marriage and who were born after 1910, with thirteen to sixteen years of education, 100 percent had been kissed, 70 percent had experienced manual stimulation of the breasts, 30 percent oral stimulation, 33 percent had received manual stimulation in the genital area, and 22 percent had manually stimulated the male sex organs. In fact, between one-fourth and one-third of the female virgins at marriage in the Kinsey sample could be considered virgins in a technical sense only, since most were highly experienced sexually.

The evidence that petting is endemic to the dating and courtship process can be found by looking at the number of partners with whom petting occurred. Only 10 percent of the Kinsey sample of females who were already married had limited themselves to only one partner. Nearly one-third had had from two to five petting partners, 23 percent had from six to ten partners, and 35 percent had ten or more petting partners. In a purely relative sense, it may be appropriate to say that American males and females are promiscuous with regard to petting.

Kinsey found, as would be expected, that petting experience increases with education and later ages at first marriage. In any comparison of males and females, males are more active and promiscuous in petting. It was also found that although religious identification (Catholic, Protestant, and so forth) did not differentiate females who were active in petting from those who were not, the degree of devoutness within each group was a good predictor of petting experience.

PREMARITAL INTERCOURSE.   The best predictor of premarital coitus experience for males in the Kinsey study was educational attainment or its potential. Among the males who stopped at a grade-school level, 98 percent reported premarital coitus. The percentage of high-school males was 84 percent, and the figure for college-level males was only 67 percent.

In the total sample of females Kinsey studied, about 50 percent reported having intercourse prior to marriage. This is not exceedingly dissimilar from the 38 percent figure obtained by Terman in his 1938 study of 777 college and high-school level females, and the 47 percent obtained by Burgess and Wallin (1953) in their study of 604 females with a college and high-school level education.

The most significant predictor of premarital coitus for females in the Kinsey study was religious devoutness. For example, among women who had not married by the age of thirty-five years, 30 percent of the devout Protestants and 24 percent of the devout Catholics had had coitus, while the respective percentages for religiously inactive Protestant and Catholic females were 60 and 55.

## PREMARITAL SEXUAL BEHAVIOR IN THE 1970S

There have been three major studies conducted in the 1970s that are important additions to the knowledge available about premarital sexual behavior. Two of the studies consisted of interviews with nation-wide samples of white and black females fifteen through nineteen years old. The samples were drawn so as to be representative of the American female population in these ages. Interviews were conducted for the first study in

247

Jean-Claude Lejeune from The Stock-Market

*Sex and the Single Woman: A narrowing of the double-standard gap is one product of the Women's Liberation Movement.*

1971 and for the second study in 1976 (see Zelnik and Kantner, 1972, 1977). The data used by Zelnik and Kantner were from the approximately 90 percent of the samples who were not married.

The third study was sponsored by the Playboy Foundation and reported by Morton Hunt (1973a and b). It included 982 men and 1,044 women drawn from twenty-four cities in the United States. About 90 percent were white; 71 percent were married, 25 percent were never married, and 4 percent were previously married but not remarried. Hunt claims that the Playboy sample is representative of the urban and suburban population over seventeen years of age.

### The Playboy Survey (1973)

The validity of the Playboy sample is questionable for the following reasons: (1) Only percentage figures are presented, and thus it is not possible to know the base number of respondents referred to by any percentage. (2) A questionnaire was used and no mention is made as to whether the respondents were aware that the study was being sponsored by the Playboy Foundation. Of those completing the questionnaire, if they were aware that Playboy was footing the bill, one may suspect, perhaps wrongly, that some of their answers may have been somewhat embellished to coincide with the Playboy philosophy. Even with these reservations, however, the Playboy survey is important because Morton Hunt chose to

248

**TABLE 10–1**
**Survey on Premarital Coitus**

| AGE | PERCENTAGES REPORTING PREMARITAL COITUS | |
| --- | --- | --- |
| | MALES | FEMALES |
| Under 25 | 95 | 81 |
| 25–34 | 92 | 65 |
| 35–44 | 86 | 41 |
| 45–54 | 89 | 36 |
| 55 and Up | 84 | 31 |

SOURCE: Morton Hunt, "Sexual Behavior in the 1970s, Part II: Premarital Sex," *Playboy*, November 1973, p. 74.

contrast the findings with those of Kinsey. The following findings emerged from the Playboy survey (see Morton Hunt, 1973a, 1973b:74):[1]

> Only a little more than a quarter of Kinsey's males had ever petted to orgasm by the age of 25, while more than two-thirds of ours have done so in just the past year.... Only about a quarter of Kinsey's younger women had ever experienced orgasm through petting by the age of 20 and about two-fifths by the age of 25; of our single women between 18 and 24, substantially more than half—and possibly many more—did so in just the past year.
>
> A little more than two-thirds of Kinsey's noncollege males had had coitus by the time they were 17; today the figure is closer to three-quarters. For men who go to college, the increase is more dramatic: In Kinsey's sample, fewer than one out of four had had any coitus by the age of 17, while in our sample, half had done so. At 20 and 25, Kinsey's figures are higher—and ours higher yet.
>
> Fewer than a tenth of Kinsey's females had had any premarital coitus by 17, and only a third by 25; in our sample, more than twice as many have done so by 17 and by 25, nearly half of the married women and three-quarters of the single ones have had premarital coitus.

Hunt examined the married respondents (71 percent of the 2,026 males and females studied) who had ever had premarital coitus by their age at the time of the survey and obtained the results given in Table 10–1.

As the data in Table 10–1 show, there is a rather steady progression upward as the ages of the respondents get younger; 81 percent of the

[1] Morton Hunt, *Sexual Behavior in the 1970s*, New York: Playboy Press, 1974, copyright © 1974 by Morton Hunt. (Originally published in "Sexual Behavior in the 1970s, Part II: Premarital Sex," *Playboy* (November, 1973):74.) Used by permission of Playboy Press.

**TABLE 10–2**

**Premarital Coital Partners for Females: The Kinsey Study and the Playboy Survey**

| PARTNERS | KINSEY STUDY (1953) | | PLAYBOY SURVEY (1973) | |
|---|---|---|---|---|
| | BORN BEFORE 1900 | BORN 1910–1919 | BORN 1938–1947 | BORN 1948–1955 |
| Fiancé only | 40% | 42% | 49% | 54% |
| Others only | 20 | 12 | 8 | 3 |
| Fiancé and others | 40 | 46 | 43 | 43 |

SOURCE: Morton Hunt, "Sexual Behavior in the 1970s, Part II: Premarital Sex," *Playboy*, November 1973, p. 75.

females and 95 percent of the males under 25 report having had premarital coitus. Unfortunately, Hunt does not differentiate among racial, educational, and social levels, and he does not indicate how extensive the premarital coitus was. His conclusion relative to the data in Table 10–1 (1973b:74) does, however, shed some light on these questions.

> Remarkable as these figures are, they by no means imply a total break with the cultural values of the past. Today's unmarried young, by and large, are not indiscriminate, they do not practice kinky sex, and while they want sex to be physically intense, they also want it to be emotionally meaningful.

Hunt also compared the Playboy data with Kinsey's data on the source of premarital coital partners. The data in Table 10–2 rather clearly indicate that "while many more single girls are having coitus, they do so with men they love and hope to marry—as did girls a generation and more ago." "Among singles under twenty-five, only one male out of six and one female out of twenty have ever experienced such impersonal forms of sexual conduct as partner swapping and sex with more than one partner simultaneously, and most of these have done so only once." With regard to first coitus, Hunt's findings are especially interesting: "More than a third of our young males and close to two-thirds of our young females experienced regret and worry afterward; and even after many experiences, a fair number continue to worry about pregnancy and V.D. and to be troubled by emotional and moral conflicts."

In summary, Morton Hunt's (1973a, 1973b) reporting of the results from the Playboy survey indicate that premarital sex is more an integral part of the dating and courtship process now than it was formerly. The college-level males and females are closer to the sexual norms of the non-college population than were the Kinsey college-level respondents. However, the Playboy data seem to indicate that the same kinds of restraining influences in operation a generation or so ago are still influential today.

## The Zelnik-Kantner Surveys (1972, 1977)

The surveys conducted by Zelnik and Kantner deal only with unmarried females between the ages of fifteen and nineteen. The findings are particularly relevant since they are representative of the total United States population in this age-sex range.

The data in Table 10–3 indicate that

> 35 percent of the unmarried teenagers interviewed in 1976 had experienced sexual intercourse, as compared to 27 percent of a comparable group in 1971—an increase in prevalence of 30 percent.... The increase in premarital sexual experience occurred between 1971 and 1976 for both blacks and whites at each year of age. The proportionate change is about the same for both races at age 15, but is two times greater overall for whites than for blacks. As a result, although blacks continue to show higher rates of prevalence than whites, the relative differences are smaller in 1976 than in 1971. In total, 63 percent of unmarried black teenagers interviewed in 1976 report having had sexual intercourse, as compared to 31 percent of comparable whites. By age, the proportion sexually experienced rises in 1976 from 18 percent at age 15 to 55 percent at age 19 (Zelnik and Kantner, 1977:56).

**TABLE 10–3**
**Never-Married Females Who Have Had Intercourse**

| | PERCENTAGES [a] | | | | | |
| | 1971 | | | 1976 | | |
| AGE | TOTAL | WHITE | BLACK | TOTAL | WHITE | BLACK |
|---|---|---|---|---|---|---|
| 15 | 13.8 | 10.9 | 30.5 | 18.0 | 13.8 | 38.4 |
| 16 | 21.2 | 16.9 | 46.2 | 25.4 | 22.6 | 52.6 |
| 17 | 26.6 | 21.8 | 58.8 | 40.9 | 36.1 | 68.4 |
| 18 | 36.8 | 32.3 | 62.7 | 45.2 | 43.6 | 74.1 |
| 19 | 46.8 | 39.4 | 76.2 | 55.2 | 48.7 | 83.6 |
| 15–19 | 26.8 | 21.4 | 51.2 | 34.9 | 30.8 | 62.7 |

SOURCE: Melvin Zelnik and John F. Kantner, "Sexual and Contraceptive Experience of Young Unmarried Women in the United States, 1976 and 1971," *Family Planning Perspectives* 9(March/April, 1977):56. Table adapted from Table 1.

[a] Base excludes those for whom no information was obtained on intercourse; this amounted in 1971 to 1.2 percent of the never-married blacks and 1.3 percent of the whites; and, in 1976, to 0.9 percent of the blacks and 0.7 percent of the whites.

One question of considerable import in the study of nonmarital sexual behavior concerns the number of partners. That is an important question because the answer to it determines whether we label our society as permissive or promiscuous. In both the Kinsey and Playboy surveys it was found that most females limit themselves to only one partner whereas males are more likely to have had more than one partner. Zelnik and Kantner's data (1977:61) show a change toward less exclusivity:

> Most sexually experienced unmarried women in the 1971 survey tended to confine themselves to one partner. Whites and blacks were quite similar except that whites were considerably more likely than blacks to have had six or more partners. By 1976, both whites and blacks at each age show less exclusivity in the choice of sexual partners. The change in general is greater among blacks than among whites. Thus, whereas in 1971 more than 61 percent of sexually experienced whites and blacks had had only one partner, in 1976 this was true of only 53 percent of comparable whites and 40 percent of blacks.

Another question of importance answered by the Zelnik-Kantner (1972) study concerns one of the possible consequences of nonmarital coitus—pregnancy. All unmarried females, and most if not all of their partners, think about the risk of pregnancy immediately prior to the act or during, and certainly after, the indulgence. If the thought or fear of pregnancy does not enter into the sexual act, the reality of this consequence of premarital coitus is definitely considered several months later by a rather sizable percentage of young females. As the data (Table 10–4) from the first survey indicate: "One-fifth of all never-married black females (the sexually active as well as the virgins) between the ages of 15 and 19 have experienced a pregnancy, a figure almost 10 times the proportion of whites who have ever been pregnant" (Zelnik and Kantner, 1972:371). While teenage pregnancy has reached epidemic proportions in this country, the second Zelnik-Kantner survey did find a significant improvement in contraceptive practice between 1971 and 1976, with more effective methods being used and more regular use of all methods. Even so, the 1976 survey found that a substantial proportion of teenagers initiate intercourse before beginning to use contraceptives and that many wait until after they have experienced a pregnancy to start using contraceptives.

In summary, Zelnik and Kantner's studies provide very important baseline data on national probability samples of females fifteen to nineteen. What they found was a rather pervasive sexuality, with blacks more involved and earlier than whites. In 1976, they found that 34.9 percent of the unmarried females had engaged in intercourse at least once. It should be noted, however, that their study did not include higher ages. Had the study included unmarried women up to say age twenty-five, this overall

**TABLE 10–4**

Percentage of Teenagers Who Have Ever Been Pregnant

| CURRENT AGE | BLACK | | WHITE | |
|---|---|---|---|---|
| | SEXUALLY ACTIVE | ALL FEMALES | SEXUALLY ACTIVE | ALL FEMALES |
| 15 | 19.0 | 6.1 | 7.3 | 0.8 |
| 16 | 34.0 | 15.7 | 2.4 | 0.4 |
| 17 | 41.3 | 23.5 | 13.7 | 3.0 |
| 18 | 48.9 | 29.6 | 12.1 | 4.0 |
| 19 | 50.9 | 41.2 | 11.0 | 4.5 |
| Total | 40.8 | 21.9 | 10.0 | 2.3 |

SOURCE: Melvin Zelnik and John F. Kantner, "Sexuality, Contraception and Pregnancy Among Young Unwed Females in the United States." In Charles F. Westoff and Robert Parke, Jr. (eds.), Commission on Population Growth and the American Future, Research Reports, Volume I, *Demographic and Social Aspects of Population Growth* (Washington, D.C.: Government Printing Office), pp. 355–374; see especially Table 17, page 371.

"experienced" rate would have certainly been higher. The females they studied were, like those in the Kinsey and Playboy surveys, definitely not promiscuous, with the modal number of partners being one, although about 50 percent of all the females studied, blacks and whites combined, had had more than one partner. However—and this is of considerable interest—the whites were somewhat more likely to have had multiple partners than the blacks, and to have had intercourse more frequently.

Altogether, the Playboy and Zelnik-Kantner studies provide a highly interesting and provocative update of the Kinsey data. Unfortunately, they, like the Kinsey studies, are more descriptive than explanatory. A second limitation of these studies is their failure to place American non-marital sexual behavior in any kind of cross-cultural perspective.

The next section of this chapter will focus on four studies that have bridged the change over time limitation: Christensen and Gregg (1970), Bell and Chaskes (1970), Vener and Stewart (1974), and King, Balswick, and Robinson (1977). In addition, the Christensen and Gregg study reports on data gathered cross-culturally.

## OTHER STUDIES OF CHANGE

As noted in Chapter 4, the study of social change is not simple and easy. Numerous difficulties are inherent in any attempt to assess how a phenomenon changes over time—and premarital sexual behavior is no exception.

## Bell and Chaskes (1970)

One approach is to study the population of a certain community at two points in time. Robert Bell and Jay Chaskes (1970) did just that in studying coeds at a large urban university in 1958 (sample size of 250) and ten years later (sample of 205). Their major interest was to see if the commitment status (dating, going steady, or engaged) and the occurrence of premarital coitus were related in the same way in 1958 as compared to 1968. Their data indicate some rather significant changes:

> The number of girls having premarital coitus while in a dating relationship went from 10 percent in 1958 to 23 percent in 1968, and the coitus rates while going steady went from 15 percent in 1958 to 28 percent in 1968. While there was some increase in the rates of premarital coitus during engagement, from 31 percent in 1958 to 39 percent in 1968, the change was not as striking as for the dating and going steady stages. . . . Therefore, the data suggests that the decision to have intercourse in 1968 was much less dependent on the commitment of engagement and more a question of individual decision regardless of the level of the relationship. To put it another way, if, in 1958 the coed had premarital coitus, it most often occurred while she was engaged. But in 1968, girls were more apt to have their first sexual experience while dating or going steady.

Thus, Bell and Chaskes are suggesting that the major change that occurred between 1958 and 1968 for their samples was the increased likelihood that a female would engage in premarital coitus without the relative security of an engagement commitment.

## Christensen and Gregg (1970)

Christensen and Gregg used basically the same tactic as Bell and Chaskes in assessing change in premarital sexual attitudes and behavior. In 1958 Christensen conducted a very important cross-cultural study. Two assumptions were implicit in his initial study: (1) Attitudes and behavior are consistently related to each other. Thus, they expected to find a low degree of sexual involvement in a society in which the attitudes toward sex were restrictive, and a high degree of sexual involvement in a permissive society. (2) Societies differ in their degrees of acceptable sexual permissiveness with regard to both attitudes and behavior.

In 1958 Christensen chose samples of students from three modern cultures that seemed to fit somewhere on his continuum from restrictive to permissive with regard to premarital sexual matters. The societies and the sizes of the 1958 samples are shown in Table 10–5.

The findings for the 1958 study were almost textbook perfect: (1) The Danish group, as predicted, were the most permissive attitudinally

**TABLE 10–5**

**Christensen's Samples**

| SAMPLE DESIGNATION AND DEGREE OF SEXUAL RESTRICTIVENESS | SOURCES AND SIZES OF 1958 SAMPLES |
| --- | --- |
| *Intermountain* "Restrictive" | 94 male and 74 female university students from Utah, primarily Mormons |
| *Midwestern* "Moderately restrictive" | 213 male and 142 female university students from the Midwestern United States |
| *Danish* "Permissive" | 149 male and 86 female university students from Denmark |

and behaviorally, with the Utah students at the other extreme and the Midwestern students in between. (2) The Danish group showed the lowest amount of guilt for sexual behavior and the Utah group the most. (3) There was less haste involved in completing the marriage when pregnancy occurred for the Danish than for the Midwestern and Utah groups. (4) The greatest discrepancies between attitudes as to what is appropriate and actual sexual behavior occurred for the groups at the ends of the continuum. The Danish group did less than they considered sexually appropriate, while the Utah students were more likely to allow their behavior to exceed their conservative attitudinal standards.

The 1968 samples were from the same universities and included slightly larger numbers of both male and female students at each place. The comparisons of students in the three cultures and in 1958 and 1968 who had premarital coital experience are shown in Table 10–6.

**TABLE 10–6**

**Premarital Coital Experience Compared in Three Cultures**

| YEAR | INTERMOUNTAIN | | MIDWESTERN | | DANISH | |
| --- | --- | --- | --- | --- | --- | --- |
| | MALES | FEMALES | MALES | FEMALES | MALES | FEMALES |
| | | | (IN PERCENTAGES) | | | |
| 1968 | 37 | 32 | 50 | 34 | 95 | 97 |
| 1958 | 39 | 10 | 51 | 21 | 64 | 60 |
| Difference | −2 | 22 | −1 | 13 | 31 | 37 |

SOURCE: Adapted from Harold T. Christensen and Christina F. Gregg, "Changing Sex Norms in America and Scandinavia," *Journal of Marriage and the Family 32*(1970):616–627. Copyrighted 1970 by the National Council on Family Relations. Reprinted by permission.

The data for Intermountain and Midwestern males indicative virtually no change in the percentage with coital experience in 1958 as compared to 1968. However, in 1968, it was still true that 13 percent more Midwestern than Intermountain males were reportedly nonvirgins (50 to 37). The Danish males were approaching maximum levels of nonvirginity by 1968 with 95 percent experienced in coitus, a jump of 31 percentage points since 1958. Danish females experienced the same relative increase as their male Danish counterparts, reaching 97 percent experienced by 1968. The most dramatic changes in sexual behavior in the 1958–68 decade was for females, at least according to the Christensen-Gregg (1970) study. Unlike the American males, the premarital coital experience rate increased substantially from 21 to 34 percent in the Midwestern sample and from 10 to 32 percent in the Utah sample of women. Perhaps more important is the fact that the gap between the Midwestern and Utah females that existed in 1958 was closed by 1968, and the experience levels for Utah males and females were nearly equal in 1968 as compared to 1958.

### Vener and Stewart (1974)

Vener and Stewart (1974) examined the prevalence of a variety of sexual behaviors among adolescents in a west-shore Michigan community in 1970 and again in 1973. Though the study is not national in scope, Vener and Stewart did question youths in *about* the same age range (thirteen to seventeen) used by Zelnik and Kantner (fifteen to nineteen). Of perhaps more importance, eight different types of sexual activity were studied, among males as well as females, and at two points in time (that is, longitudinally).

As the data in Table 10–7 indicate, between 1970 and 1973, there were no substantial or dramatic increases in the percentage of boys or girls who had *ever* participated in the eight sexual behaviors. It is also apparent that for Levels I–V the differences between the sexes are not marked, in either year. The only evidence of a double-standard of behavior appears in what Vener and Stewart call "heavy petting," and in whether the student had "gone all the way" with one or with two or more partners. This double-standard sex difference apparently vanishes as the youth get older. The authors (1974:735) report that: "The 1973 findings show that by the age of 17, the impact of the double-standard seems to have become attenuated." In 1970 there was a difference of eleven percentage points (38 to 27 percent for boys and girls respectively) in coital experience. In 1973, 34 percent of the girls had experienced coitus at least once.

Vener and Stewart also noticed very slight increases from 1970–73 in the percentage of coital-experienced students, boys as well as girls, who had had intercourse with more than one partner. Altogether, in the 1973 study 27 percent of the boys and 12 percent of the girls who had ever

**TABLE 10–7**

Adolescent Sexual Behavior, 1970 and 1973

| LEVELS OF SEXUAL ACTIVITY | PERCENTAGES OF STUDENTS WHO HAVE PARTICIPATED IN AN ACTIVITY AT LEAST ONCE | | | |
| --- | --- | --- | --- | --- |
| | MALES | | FEMALES | |
| | 1970 (989) | 1973 (937) | 1970 (924) | 1973 (1035) |
| I. Held Hands | 87.6 | 88.5 | 89.2 | 89.4 |
| II. Held Arm Around or Been Held | 80.5 | 81.7 | 84.6 | 86.5 |
| III. Kissed or Been Kissed | 76.6 | 79.7 | 81.6 | 81.2 |
| IV. Necked (Prolonged Hugging and Kissing) | 63.3 | 63.7 | 67.8 | 64.1 |
| V. Light Petting (Feeling Above the Waist) | 57.3 | 59.0 | 49.7 | 51.4 |
| VI. Heavy Petting (Feeling Below the Waist) | 45.1 | 49.3 | 33.6 | 37.5 |
| VII. Gone All the Way (Coitus) | 27.8 | 33.4 | 16.1 | 22.4 |
| VIII. Coitus With Two or More Partners | 14.2 | 19.4 | 5.7 | 8.9 |

SOURCE: Arthur M. Vener and Cyrus S. Stewart, "Adolescent Sexual Behavior in Middle America Revisited: 1970–1973." *Journal of Marriage and the Family* 36(1974):731. Copyrighted 1974 by the National Council on Family Relations. Reprinted by permission.

NOTE: Numbers in parentheses above columns are the sizes of the groups interviewed.

experienced premarital intercourse had done so with four or more partners.

In addition to the fact that no significant increases in sexual activity occurred from 1970 to 1973, the most important finding from the Vener and Stewart study is the convergence of boys and girls by age seventeen vis-à-vis the percentage who had ever engaged in premarital intercourse. This further underscores the importance of the sex-role revolution that this society has experienced in the last decade. The long-standing tradition of a double standard of sexual behavior is becoming, or has become, obsolete.

## King, Balswick, and Robinson (1977)

The finding by Vener and Stewart that the gender gap in sexual experience seems to vanish by age seventeen is supported by data from studies conducted by King, Balswick, and Robinson in 1965, 1970, and 1975 at a Southern university. The samples were nonrandom and consisted of 129 males and 115 females in 1965. The respective numbers involved were

257

**Table 10–8**
**Student Participation in Premarital Sexual Activities**

| | PERCENTAGES | |
| --- | --- | --- |
| | MALES | FEMALES |
| *Premarital Intercourse* | | |
| 1965 | 65 | 29 |
| 1970 | 65 | 37 |
| 1975 | 74 | 57 |
| *Heavy Petting* [a] | | |
| 1965 | 71 | 34 |
| 1970 | 79 | 60 |
| 1975 | 80 | 73 |

SOURCE: Karl King, Jack O. Balswick, and Ira E. Robinson, "The Continuing Premarital Sexual Revolution Among College Females." *Journal of Marriage and the Family* 39 (1977):456. Adapted from Tables 1 and 2. Copyrighted 1977 by the National Council on Family Relations. Reprinted by Permission.

[a] Manual and oral stimulation of genitals

137 and 158 in 1970, and 138 and 298 in 1975. The convergence of the sexes in terms of self-reported behavior can be seen quite clearly in Table 10–8. As the authors note: "In 1965, nearly three out of every four males engaged in heavy petting while only approximately one out of three females did so; by 1975 the difference between male and female petting behavior had become almost indistinguishable suggesting that the double behavioral standard is diminishing."

## SUMMARY

Having covered the best available evidence on the incidence and prevalence of premarital sexual behavior and the changes that have probably occurred since Kinsey's studies, a logical question arises: To what extent has a sexual revolution occurred in the United States?

The question is stated in such a way that any answer offered is appropriate, and virtually every answer is at least partially correct. The reasons are that the answers to the question are complex and depend, to some extent, on which part of the forest one chooses to describe.

Several leading scholars in the study of sex (Reiss, 1967; Bell, 1966; Gagnon and Simon, 1970) have claimed that the revolution (the sexual revolution that occurred between World War II and the near present) has been primarily in the area of attitudes about sex rather than in actual behavior. They point out that numerous studies of premarital sex among

Kenneth Murray from Nancy Palmer Photo Agency, Inc.

college students in the 1950s and 1960s yielded little change in reported behavior but wholesale shifts in attitudes toward various sexual behavior. The demise of the double standard and the widespread acceptance of its replacement, the permissiveness-with-affection standard, has been thoroughly documented (see Reiss, 1960, 1967, and Chapter 11 of this text).

It is not difficult to endorse the position that the sexual revolution has been primarily attitudinal and not behavioral. The 1960s and 1970s produced the Free Speech movement at Berkeley and elsewhere, paperback books by the thousands that were explicitly sexual in content, movies with nudity and sexual acts in living color, simulated and not-so-simulated sex on the stage—all with little more than a few "naughty-naughty" comments from the established powers that be. Whether this is what Marshall McLuhan meant when he said "the medium is the message, or the massage" is debatable—but that this society has witnessed a revolution in attitudes about sex is not debatable.

There is little doubt that the prevailing sexual attitudes and standards in America today allow males and females to engage in coitus if they are engaged, in love with, or feel strong affection toward their

259

partners. Few could argue with the impressive array of data garnered by those who believe the sexual revolution has been primarily attitudinal in nature. Somehow, though, it would seem that these changed attitudes and standards would find expression in changed patterns of behavior.

Some students of sexual behavior believe that the second behavioral revolution of this century is now occurring. Robert Bell, in his article with Chaskes (1970), and the Christensen and Gregg (1970) study point to the locus of the behavioral sexual revolution as a narrowing of the gap between the sexual activity of males and females. Even Ira Reiss (1972) predicts that the percent of nonvirgins will reach 70 to 75 percent in the 1970s. The Zelnik and Kantner (1972) study also indicates that females in this society are active sexually, regardless of race, with 40 percent of white females between fifteen and nineteen and 80 percent of blacks nonvirginal.

But a behavioral sexual revolution is not limited to the incidence and prevalence of premarital coitus. For example, there is little doubt that petting is now an endemic part of the dating-courtship process and that this sexual activity is seldom limited to just one or two partners. In addition, Hunt's (1973b) discussion of the Playboy survey findings indicates that oral-genital sexual activity is a widespread phenomenon premaritally, whereas it was in the Kinsey data primarily limited to the marital realm (see also King, Balswick, and Robinson, 1977).

A reasonable question to ask is, When will the sexual revolution taper off, or will it? Will close to 100 percent of the children of today's classroom students, who will be in their dating years around the turn of the twenty-first century, be engaging in premarital coitus, like the 1968 Danish sample of Christensen and Gregg (1970)? The answer to these questions will have to be speculative for awhile. My best guess is that the percentage of nonvirginal will level off at about 80 to 85.

## EXPLAINING PREMARITAL SEXUAL BEHAVIOR

The studies already cited have been descriptive of premarital sexual behavior. A prevailing theme in this text is that the study of marriage and the family is moving and must move toward the two other goals of any science: explanation and prediction.

The way to achieve these two goals is to move away from specific substantive concepts (for example, premarital sexual intercourse, marriage adjustment, marital power) toward more abstract and inclusive concepts like attitudes, norms, and behavior. In the final sections of this chapter an attempt will be made to treat behavior and not premarital coitus as a key concept. The adoption of this strategy is aimed at developing a more general theoretical model that could apply to the study of premarital coitus as well as to other types of behavior (such as drug usage, friendship selection, juvenile delinquency) that are not usually discussed in classes dealing with the family and marriage. In other words, if the model developed in this chapter is viable in explaining behavior, it should be possible to take the model into other courses in sociology and to utilize it in understanding other types of human behavior. To achieve this goal I will rely on some of my own research, not because it is the best available—it is probably not—but because it illustrates a model that I feel has some promise for sociology.

Much of the research attempting to explain why some persons do and others do not engage in premarital coitus has focused on causal variables that are essentially attitudinal in nature, such as religious commitment and premarital sexual permissiveness (attitudinal). In other words, an overriding theoretical issue is: What is the relationship between attitudes and behavior? Ehrlich (1969) was a little more specific when he asked: "Under what conditions, and to what degrees are attitudes of a given type related to behaviors of a given type?"

In 1969 Lyle Warner and Melvin DeFleur suggested that there are three approaches to answering these questions about the attitude-behavior relationship. The first, the "postulate of consistency," indicates that attitudes, if they are accurately measured, should be predictive of behavior. Thus, persons who would adopt a conservative and moralistic attitude toward sex, based in a traditional religious commitment, would be much less likely to engage in coitus than a less religious and less moralistic person. This is the assumption used by Christensen in his 1958 study (see Christensen, 1960). The second approach, labeled by Warner and DeFleur the "postulate of independent variation," is based on the assumptions that (1) attitudes are difficult to measure with any degree of accuracy, (2) human beings are not necessarily consistent in what they either say or do, and (3) to posit any kind of causal relationship between attitudes and behavior is, at best, futile.

The third approach, and the one expanded on here, is called the "postulate of contingent consistency" (see Chapter 2). The assumptions underlying the contingent-consistency model are that: (1) different sets of attitudes are interrelated and perhaps mutually supportive (that is, a person high on religious commitment will likely be low on attitudes toward sexual permissiveness and these factors will work together to restrain sexual behavior); (2) behaviors are not isolated events, but are mutually reinforcing (that is, a person who regularly attends church may center his or her dating behaviors around church-related events); and (3) if attitudes and behavior are related, it is only through the mediating influence of some intervening conditional factors (that is, a person high on religious commitment will be low on premarital coitus if the intervening norms of the group he or she belongs to are likewise restrictive regarding sex).

261

## A TEST OF THE CONTINGENT-CONSISTENCY MODEL

In 1970 I conducted a study of the sexual behavior of the students at a small and private liberal arts university in Florida, the same school I studied in 1967 (Clayton, 1969). The primary purpose of this study was to test the Warner and DeFleur (1969) contingent-consistency model of the relationship among attitudes, intervening contingent factors, and behavior. The sample consisted of 287 males and 369 females. These 656 respondents represented about 70 percent of the students enrolled in the school's winter term session and was rather heavily made up of freshmen men and women. The contingent-consistency model required an assessment of attitudes, the intervening contingent factors, and behavior. Consequently, all respondents were assigned a score on the following variables.

### General Attitudes

RELIGIOUS COMMITMENTS.   Three different religious attitude scales were used, each of which was designed to represent a separate dimension of religious commitment at the attitudinal level. The three dimensions were (a) the ideological or belief commitment, (b) the ritualistic or overt religious behavior, and (c) the experiential or covert religious experiences. I will utilize only the ideological dimension scores to compare the results with my earlier study.

### Behavior-Specific Attitudes

PERSONAL ATTITUDINAL PERMISSIVENESS (PAP).   One of the more obvious limitations of my 1967 study was a failure to obtain an estimate of what the respondents felt was appropriate sexual behavior for persons of their sex. Therefore, to assess this type of attitude, which could function both as an attitude and as a contingent factor, I used five items from Reiss's (1967) premarital sexual permissiveness scales.

1. I believe that kissing is acceptable for the male (female) before marriage if he (she) is not particularly affectionate toward his (her) partner.
2. I believe that petting is acceptable for the male (female) before marriage if he (she) is engaged to be married.
3. I believe that petting is acceptable for the male (female) before marriage if he (she) is not particularly affectionate toward his (her) partner.
4. I believe that full sexual relations is acceptable for the male (female) before marriage if he (she) is engaged to be married.

5. I believe that full sexual relations is acceptable for the male (female) before marriage if he (she) is strongly affectionate toward his (her) partner.

## Contingent Factor

NORMATIVE REFERENCE GROUP NORMS OF SEXUAL PERMISSIVENESS (NRG). The 1967 study at the same school had indicated that membership in a fraternity or sorority might be less important than the norms of sexual behavior perceived to be operative in a person's most important reference group. To assess these norms I first asked the respondents to name their most important reference group (like fraternity, sorority, music school crowd, girls on my floor of the dorm, the "freaks," and so forth). I then adapted the items from the Reiss scales so that each person was telling me how most of the people in the group felt about the various sexual behaviors under those conditions. Each statement began with the phrase: "They believe that . . . ."

## Behavior

REPORTED PREMARITAL INTERCOURSE. The behavior I was trying to explain was coitus reported to have occurred during the preceding twelve months. My hypothesis was that religious commitment and reported premarital intercourse would be consistently related only if the person's personal attitudinal permissiveness (PAP) and the norms perceived to be prevalent in his or her reference group were consistent with his or her religious attitudes. Table 10–9 shows the logic behind the contingent-consistency approach.

**TABLE 10–9**
**The Contingent-Consistency Model**

| RELIGIOUS COMMITMENT | PAP | NRG | REPORTED PREMARITAL INTERCOURSE |
|---|---|---|---|
| (a) High | Low | Low | No |
| (b) High | Low | High | |
| (c) High | High | Low | |
| (d) High | High | High | |
| (e) Low | Low | Low | |
| (f) Low | Low | High | |
| (g) Low | High | Low | |
| (h) Low | High | High | Yes |

The persons in categories (a) and (h) are perfectly consistent. In (a) the persons are highly religious, low in terms of personal attitudinal permissiveness, and perceive their most important reference group to be endorsing a "don't do it" standard. The persons in category (h) are on the opposite end of the continuum. Categories (b) through (g) provide inconsistent cues as to what one's sexual behavior should be.

As the data in Table 10–10 indicate, the predictions of the contingent-consistency model held for both sexes in categories (a) and (h), where all three variables involved were consistent. However, the model's overall effectiveness in explanation is not good. This can be seen most clearly in category (d), where the respondents are high on religious commitment but also high on personal permissiveness and belong to groups they perceive to be permissive. For both males and females, the influence of religion is neutralized by behavior-specific attitudes and reference-group norms. Another finding that is also readily apparent in this table and in the entire study is that reference-group norms are of little influence on female coital behavior, but are of much importance for the males.

**TABLE 10–10**

**A Test of the Contingent-Consistency Model**

| RELIGIOUS COMMITMENT IDEOLOGICAL DIMENSION ONLY | PAP | NRG | REPORTED PREMARITAL INTERCOURSE | | | |
|---|---|---|---|---|---|---|
| | | | MALES | | FEMALES | |
| | | | % YES | N | % YES | N |
| (a) High | Low | Low | 14% | 6/43 | 11% | 19/176 |
| (b) High | Low | High | 31% | 8/26 | 20% | 4/20 |
| (c) High | High | Low | 30% | 3/10 | 32% | 9/28 |
| (d) High | High | High | 70% | 42/60 | 43% | 16/37 |
| (e) Low | Low | Low | 50% | 7/14 | 27% | 9/34 |
| (f) Low | Low | High | 44% | 8/18 | 14% | 1/7 |
| (g) Low | High | Low | 40% | 2/5 | 54% | 14/26 |
| (h) Low | High | High | 69% | 61/88 | 57% | 13/23 |

SOURCE: Adapted from Richard R. Clayton, "Premarital Sexual Intercourse: A Substantive Test of the Contingent Consistency Model," *Journal of Marriage and the Family 34*(1972):277–278, Tables 3 and 4. Copyrighted 1972 by The Natural Council on Family Relations. Reprinted by permission.

NOTE: 137 out of 264, or 52 percent, of the males reported premarital coitus during the preceding year as compared to 85 out of 351, or 24 percent, of the females.

PAP refers to personal attitudinal permissiveness.

NRG refers to norms of premarital sexual permissiveness perceived to be prevalent in one's most important reference group.

# A MODIFIED CONTINGENT-CONSISTENCY MODEL

What happens when one tests a theoretical model and finds that it is not supported by one's data? If there is absolutely no support, besides considering a number of unmentionable things, one begins to re-examine the entire logic behind the model and one's predictions. When the data offer some but not uniform support, one begins by conducting a post-mortem on the model, the variables involved, how one measured them, and everything else related to the model.

The major weakness of my original view of the contingent-consistency model is that it was sterile—sterile in two ways. First, I treated reported premarital intercourse as the same for everyone. Did you engage in coitus during the past twelve months—Yes or No? This means that the male or female who had intercourse one time, with a stranger during spring vacation, is treated as part of the same group as the swinger whose goal in life is sexual variety and satisfaction as well as the person who is engaged to be married and "preping" for the honeymoon. The same is true for the No category. It includes those persons who report no coitus because they had absolutely no male-female contacts during the past year (the nones), those who have petted to orgasm an average of once or more a day for the past year, plus those who were very active last year or the year before last, but who have not had intercourse this year for some reason. Thus, from a methodological viewpoint, my assessment of intercourse behavior is less than adequate.

Second, my original conception of the model assumed, at least implicitly, that every act of premarital intercourse is the same. That is not true. For the virgin, the first act of coitus is a milestone never to be passed again. For the second-timer, the territory, norms, actions, and reactions are understood—and viewed in the light of experience.

With these and other recognized limitations in mind I reworked the logic of the relationships among attitudes, contingent factors, and behavior. My goal was to develop a more realistic picture of how these three concepts relate to one another in real life (Figure 10–1). To discuss this modified contingent-consistency model I created a character and a situation that, although exaggerated and simplistic, is close to reality. This model is untested—the product of my interpretation of existing data and the clues provided by my two studies of premarital sex. The reader should keep his critical and debunking eyes open for flaws in the modified model.

## Conclusion

The illustration is quite consistent with what actually happens to most people who engage in premarital intercourse. Premarital coitus probably is seldom an impulsive experience since all of us grow up with sex seen as a part of the process by which love and strong affection can be expressed.

*Winston P. Bear, 1962*

Our hero is a virgin; for illustrative purposes let us call him Winston P. Bear. His friends call him Pooh. Pooh is a sophomore at a large university and is a finance major. He is a large, rather handsome guy, very gegarious and, to hear him talk in the fraternity house, quite a swinger with the opposite sex.

PROPERTY VARIABLES.   Pooh comes from an upper middle-class family. His father is a business executive, and his mother is very active in community and church affairs. Pooh has an extensive wardrobe and a neat sports car. In terms of status on campus, he is in one of the more prestigious fraternities and is active in student government.

GENERAL ATTITUDES-VALUES.   Because of his background Pooh is generally conservative in his religious and political beliefs and rather conservative also in his economic and moral standards. His aspirations are to follow in the footsteps of his father by obtaining a good job, salary, a house in the suburbs, and all that goes with that style of life. Not unexpectedly, he wants to marry a virgin.

REFERENCE GROUP NORMS.   As in most all-male social groups, there is a great deal of talk about sex and making it with women. In fact, it would be a supreme sin for anyone to admit to being a virgin, although there are undoubtedly more than a few in the group who are, like Pooh, virgins. The norms, at least at the verbal level, encourage a rather blasé and permissive attitude toward premarital intercourse. Everyone knows that the group expects its members to be sexually active.

BEHAVIOR-SPECIFIC ATTITUDES.   Pooh's attitudes toward the appropriateness of premarital intercourse allow males to engage under almost any condition, but emphasizes the value of feeling some affection, especially love, for the partner. But what a person will allow for others of his or her own sex is quite different from what a person will allow for himself or herself. Pooh's attitudes toward sex are, understandably, quite diffuse since he has never personally participated in intercourse. It is now March, and Pooh has fallen in love with a very attractive female who is also a virgin. They see each other quite regularly and have gone through all of the preliminaries—they are at the stage of heavy petting and are verbally expressing how much they love each other. It is the time of their fraternity weekend, which is being held at a vacation resort.

PERCEIVED OPTIMAL OPPORTUNITY.    Pooh and his partner for the weekend are no longer strangers in any sense of the term. Both are primed for the chance to go the last step in the process of sexual intercourse. Both have a mutual commitment to the relationship—there is the optimal opportunity to lose their technical virginity.

BEHAVIOR.    Following the almost natural course of events Pooh and his partner find themselves alone and both proceed beyond the heavy petting stage quite easily into premarital coitus, one time on the last night of the weekend.

NEUTRALIZATION OF GUILT.    Pooh is now experienced, but in reflecting on the weekend he needs to go through a reorganization of his attitudes and values. He has violated some of his moral standards. He says to himself, "It was fun! and no one was hurt" (denial of injury). "Both of us really wanted to do this and besides, we *love* each other" (denial of a victim). "My parents would probably be quite upset if they knew; they wanted me to save myself for marriage. Hell, I bet they weren't virgins when they got married" (condemnation of the condemners). "Besides, I think I may ask her to marry me next week" (appeal to higher loyalties). Any guilt Pooh may have felt about his actions has, by now, been neutralized.

Pooh now sees his reference-group norms as totally consistent with his own behavior. His attitudes about intercourse are no longer diffuse and applicable to males; they now apply to him personally. The chances are pretty good that he will be looking for another optimal opportunity setting and looking forward to another sexual encounter with his non-virgin partner.

Since all of the facts of his life are now consistent with his previous behavior, that behavior will now be an influence, along with his general attitudes, reference-group norms, and behavior-specific attitudes on his subsequent intercourse behavior. In fact, then, after the virgin goes through the whole agenda one time, behavior becomes an independent or causal variable in the process.

**FIGURE 10–1**
**A Modified Contingent-Consistency Model**

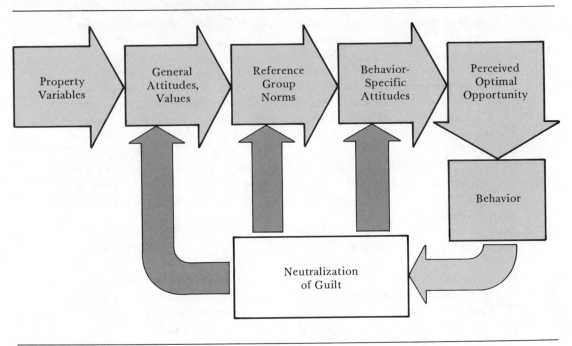

The modified contingent-consistency model just presented could apply equally well to behaviors like drinking or the use of marijuana and other drugs. It is a general model that could apply to almost any kind of behavior that is defined by society as "somewhat deviant." For that matter, the same model might be equally applicable for explaining how and why extramarital coitus is approached.

## SOME POSSIBLE IMPLICATIONS

*To be very technical about it, sexual intercourse entails a violation of "private" property. It is an encroachment on or into one's body space, that most intimate of personal environments. That most societies view sexual organs as truly private domains can be seen in the development of covering garments that, although they may not be used prior to puberty, are almost always used by those who have attained puberty. What is there about sexual intercourse and the sexual organs that lead human beings to attach a special significance to them? Is it the idea that this is the only means thus far discovered by which reproduction can take place? If there ever is a society in which conception takes place only through artificial insemination, would copulation become extinct?*

*Why is it that we describe sexual intercourse between two consenting adults as "making love"? Is it because love means for us a sharing of our most intimate private spaces—our thoughts and feelings, hopes and aspirations, not to mention our bodies? Is it because love is commonly defined as the giving of the best that one possesses?*

*What are the implications for a society in which virtually all persons will engage in premarital coitus at some time, with perhaps a majority doing so with more than one person? Will sexual intercourse lose some of its mystery, its concomitant meaning with love under such conditions?*

*Do adults and adult-run institutions have a responsibility for encouraging young people not to engage in premarital intercourse, or are they abdicating their responsibility by not providing adequate sexual and contraceptive socialization?*

*Premarital sex is a topic that can cause vociferous debate, pro and con. Pervasive experience with premarital sex is not only a reality in modern society but also a very real and personal and sometimes troubling experience for the participants. Most of us go through our premarital years debating within ourselves what to do or not do regarding sexual activity, both in anticipation of the first coital experience or in reflection on previous sexual encounters. In the final analysis, premarital intercourse is an existential personal experience based on a decision usually reached by application of situational ethics.*

Richard Good, Black Star

# 11

# PREMARITAL SEXUAL ATTITUDES AND STANDARDS

*What are the standards of sexual conduct in America, and how are these standards changing?*

*Are attitudes about sex and actual premarital sexual behavior related?*

*What is the difference between what someone will allow for others and what he or she will allow for himself or herself regarding premarital sex?*

*How permissive is our society relative to premarital sex?*

Now that we have extensively covered the study of premarital intercourse, let us examine another equally vast topic—attitudes toward or standards about premarital sex, or what Reiss (1967) calls "premarital sexual permissiveness." Not unlike other topics of interest to family specialists, this area has been dominated by the ideas and research of one man, Ira L. Reiss, Professor of Sociology and Director of the Family Study Center at the University of Minnesota.

Professor Reiss's contributions to the study of the family have been far ranging: a major article on the issue of the universality of the family (1965b, see Chapter 8 of this text); the wheel theory of love (1960, see Chapter 9); an attempt to integrate the study of premarital sex with the study of other types of deviant behavior (1970); and a major textbook in family sociology (1971) entitled *The Family System in America*. However, his most notable contributions have consisted of an excellent monograph on *Premarital Sexual Standards in America* (1960), the development of attitude scales to measure individual premarital sexual permissiveness (1964), and a book based on a national survey of the American population entitled *The Social Context of Premarital Sexual Permissiveness* (1967). Most of what we know about premarital sexual permissiveness comes from the seminal works of Ira Reiss. Consequently, much of this chapter is devoted to a review and a critique of those works.

## A HISTORICAL PERSPECTIVE

Perhaps the best way to begin a discussion of premarital sexual attitudes and standards is to look at the historical record. As pointed out in Chapters 3 and 4, such a search is sometimes less than productive because of the time decay of records and the idealization of the past that sometimes clouds the major secondary sources of information. In effect, we must be careful to sift myth from reality—a difficult job, but let us try.

With regard to sexual practices, what best depicts the idealized version of our history? Reiss (1972:167) has put it well: "One of our most prevalent myths is that in past centuries the typical form of courtship was that of two virgins meeting, falling in love, and doing very little with each other sexually. They then married, learned about sex together in the marital bed, and remained faithful to each other until death separated them." Reiss goes on to say that although this may have and may still happen, "it was never the common pattern for most Americans." Is Reiss

272

correct in his rebuttal of the myth? What is the evidence? Could it be that the ethic of Puritarianism was primarily verbal, and the mouth did not know what was happening to the rest of the body? Although the evidence is somewhat slender at times, there is enough to question seriously the prevailing myth.

### Factors That Influenced Changes in Premarital Sexual Behavior

With regard to other indications of the extent of premarital sexual behavior in the American population, perhaps the best source is the Kinsey studies (1948, 1953). As Reiss (1972:169) indicates: "According to our best information the majority of American women have been entering marriage non-virginal for over fifty years. Kinsey's findings indicated that about half the women born in the 1900–1910 decade were non-virginal at marriage. This proportion rose only slightly until the late 1960s but since then it seems to have risen rapidly. Sometime around the first world war the proportion of non-virginal women almost doubled from about 25 to 50 percent and during the late 1960s the proportion probably has risen from about 50 to 70 or 75 percent."

Probably a number of factors have accounted for these changes. Certainly industrialization with its effect of getting women out of the home and into the labor force contributed some impetus. The diffusion of coeducational instruction was also an important force. The growth of urban areas, where the informal norms of restrictiveness found in small towns were impossible to develop, also exerted an influence toward greater permissiveness. The rapid development of various forms of mass media— radio, television, movies, and slick magazines—surely added fuel to the permissiveness trend. In addition, various advances in contraceptive technology that greatly reduced the risk of premarital pregnancy and venereal disease certainly made premarital intercourse less risky.

These and other forces have had an influence in expanding premarital sexual experience in the American population. However, the greatest changes that occurred from 1920 to the present were probably in attitudes toward sex rather than in the behavior itself. As women gained control of the ability to control conception, they also gained a heightened opportunity to explore and expand their own sexuality. As this was occurring men were moving toward a greater emphasis on person-centered sex as opposed to sex that is focused only on physiological release. There has been, thus, a general convergence in American society between sexual attitudes and behavior so that, unlike the situation that prevailed in the nineteenth century, twentieth-century Americans are more likely to express sexual beliefs verbally that are consistent with what they are doing sexually. If for no other reason, this general openness about all matters sexual is probably conducive to a more stable coping with sexual problems and a general state of mental health regarding sexuality.

## America's Sexual Past

Among the facts cited by Reiss (1972) and others are:

1. Records from a well-known church in Massachusetts indicate that in one year alone about one-third of the married women in the congregation confessed to having had premarital intercourse. The purpose of the confession was to ensure that the child, premaritally conceived, could be baptized. Undoubtedly there were others who were not pregnant at marriage and thus were not in "need" of confession. Nathaniel Hawthorne had some insight into the inconsistencies between behavior and stated attitudes and standards, which are seen in *The Scarlet Letter*.

2. The evidence available from the frontier days likewise contradicts the glorified "sugar and spice" (and everything "nice") portrait found on television and in movies. Probably few heroes on white horses and even fewer cowboys were more attached to their horses than to the dance-hall girls. Without doubt these dance-hall professionals were not in any way analogous to college girls working as waitresses in McDonald's or at Howard Johnson's. In fact, the red light district terminology originated in the frontier of America, where "men were men" practically any chance they could get.

3. In the 1870s, an incident, usually reported as evidence that the myth is not factual, occurred concerning two early radical feminists, Victoria and Tennessee Chaflin. Victoria openly advocated the principle of free love in her weekly newspaper—a love-them-and-leave-them approach if love diminished. There was considerable animosity between the Chaflins and the Beecher sisters, Harriet and Catherine, whose feminist ideology was much more conservative. The Beecher sisters were probably influenced by the fiery preaching of their famous minister brother, the Reverend Henry Ward Beecher.

Evidently, Victoria Chaflin was fed up with attacks by the Beecher sisters. Victoria was having an affair with a Mr. Tilton, whose wife was having an affair with the Reverend Beecher. Victoria threatened Henry Ward with public exposure if he did not intervene in the dispute with his sisters. No one knows for sure how much effort he made to stop them, but we do know that Victoria Chaflin was a woman true to her word. She printed a story about the adulterous Reverend Beecher and Mrs. Tilton on November 2, 1872. Since adultery was illegal, a trial followed. Reverend Beecher was acquitted by a hung jury, and Mrs. Tilton was charged by a church committee with "indefensible conduct."

4. In 1884 Grover Cleveland was running for president on the Democratic ticket. The Republicans claimed that he had fathered an

*The Rev. Beecher, on trial for adultery before a jury and courtroom of his peers: Let him who is without sin cast the first stone.*

illegitimate child in 1874. This claim was true, and even though we tend to think of this as an era in which sexual indiscretions were unusual and severely frowned upon, he was elected.

Although these are isolated events, in most instances related to people in high places, we have little reason to believe they were highly unusual or not commonplace occurrences throughout the society. In fact, it is probably true that the more restrictive societal norms are about sex, the higher the curiosity level and, perhaps, the greater the desire to examine the mysterious and proscribed behaviors. Regardless, there is ample evidence that human beings are quite sexually oriented and that sexual behavior, premarital and extramarital, have been relatively prevalent throughout America's history.

## TYPOLOGIES OF PREMARITAL SEXUAL STANDARDS

In 1960 Ira Reiss published a mongraph entitled *Premarital Sexual Standards in America.* In this book he developed a typology of the various standards that individuals could adopt regarding premarital sex. This typology is as follows (Reiss 1960:251):[1]

1. Abstinence (premarital intercourse is considered wrong for both sexes)
   a. Petting Without Affection (petting is acceptable even when affection is negligible)
   b. Petting With Affection (petting is acceptable only in a stable, affectionate relationship)
   c. Kissing Without Affection (only kissing is acceptable, but no affection is required)
   d. Kissing With Affection (only kissing is acceptable, and only in a stable, affectionate relationship)
2. Double Standard (males are considered to have greater rights to premarital intercourse)
   a. Orthodox (males may have intercourse, but females who do so are condemned)
   b. Transitional (males have greater access to coitus, but females who are in love or engaged are allowed to have intercourse)
3. Permissiveness With Affection (premarital intercourse is acceptable for both sexes if part of a stable, affectionate relationship)
   a. Love (love or engagement is a prerequisite for coitus)
   b. Strong Affection (strong affection is a sufficient prerequisite for coitus)
4. Permissiveness Without Affection (premarital intercourse is right for both sexes regardless of the amount of affection present)
   a. Orgiastic (pleasure is of such importance that precautions are not stressed)
   b. Sophisticated (pleasure is stressed, but precautions to avoid VD and pregnancy are of first importance)

Reiss assumed that there were three types of sexual behavior about which persons would have a belief: kissing, petting and premarital intercourse. The first standard, abstinence, prohibits intercourse for both sexes.

---

[1] Adapted with permission of Macmillan Publishing Co., Inc., from *Premarital Sexual Standards in America* by Ira L. Reiss. Copyright © 1960 by The Free Press, a corporation.

However, kissing and petting may be considered appropriate depending on whether affection and/or a stable relationship exists between the partners. It is obvious that most people probably adhere to the abstinence standard at some time in their lives, probably during early adolescence before they are into the heavy dating scene. The likelihood of maintaining such a standard probably decreases steadily with age and experience and opportunities for advancement.

The other three standards discussed by Reiss deal with the conditions under which premarital intercourse is appropriate. The standard that has been in existence the longest is the double standard. Under this standard males are generally accorded greater sexual privilege than females. The orthodox double standard prohibits females from any right to engage in coitus prior to marriage. The transitional double standard will allow females to be coequal sexually with males, but only if they are engaged or in love with the partner. It should be obvious to females who have older brothers that many parents today still subscribe to the transitional double standard, and with a great deal of tenacity.

The sexual standard that is probably most prevalent in America today, especially among college and high school students, is permissiveness with affection. It allows premarital intercourse for both sexes with the qualification that love or strong affection *must* be present.

The last standard is probably most prevalent among those in the sexual avant garde, and in certain subcultures consisting primarily of persons who have finished their education but are not yet married. It emphasizes a bodily-centered focus and is labeled by Reiss as permissiveness without affection.

Reiss's typology of standards was designed as a paradigm for his research into premarital sexual permissiveness. Other authors have examined sexual standards from different perspectives with different subsequent purposes in mind. Rubin's typology was built around the idea that sex standards are in a state of transition and that this situation has certain implications for the education of young people:[2]

1. Traditional Repressive Asceticism. This standard is most rigidly and vocally supported by those who view sexual behavior in absolute and moral terms. Sex, for these persons, is linked to procreation and is to be definitely avoided outside of marriage. The adherents of this standard might also insist that coitus within marriage should be primarily for procreation only.

---

[2] Isadore Rubin, "Transition in Sex Values—Implications for the Education of Adolescents," *Journal of Marriage and the Family* 27 (1965):185–89. Reprinted by permission of the National Council on Family Relations.

2. Enlightened Asceticism. The proponents of this standard view control in the sexual and other areas as necessary for the maintenance of social order in this culture. These persons are not rigidly antisex, they are merely for a rational safeguarding against sexual overindulgence, which they consider a likely outcome if the sexual standards are "diluted."

3. Humanistic Liberalism. The proponents for this standard are most concerned with the interpersonal relationship and not necessarily with social order at the societal level. They see the institutions that have traditionally set the sexual standards losing their power and influence. The assumption is that standards will increasingly become a matter of individual decisions growing out of interpersonal situations. This is quite close to Reiss's "permissiveness with affection" and also Smigel and Seiden's (1968) "sex with affection" standards.

4. Humanistic Radicalism. This standard suggests that our society has been saddled for too long with an ethic of sex that is too moralistic, and its consequence is needless guilt. Sex for these persons is a natural act that has been misdefined as moral. The proponents of this standard advocate the adoption of a social action program which would exorcise the Puritan ethic of sex and replace it with genuine sexual freedom.

5. Fun Morality. The basic assumption of this standard is that sex is both physically pleasurable and psychologically stabilizing. The more fun an individual has, the better his chances for psychological stability. The persons who take this stand would advocate that any well-informed and adjusted person should not only be allowed to engage in coitus without fear of sanction but should be encouraged to engage in premarital intercourse.

6. Sexual Anarchy. This standard advocates the abolishment of all sexual taboos and controls. Everything is considered acceptable. It is analogous to the idea that if we declared everything appropriate there would be no crime or deviant behavior.

Rubin's typology is much less analytical than Reiss's and the terminology he used does not seem very effective in covering up his own perspective toward permarital sexual behavior. While some of Rubin's types overlap with those presented by Reiss (Humanistic Liberalism with Permissiveness with Affection, and Fun Morality with Permissiveness Without Affection), others such as Sexual Anarchy are not considered plausible or even relevant by Reiss.

Since we are examining attitudinal permissiveness from a sociological perspective, it seems most appropriate to continue to center our discussion around the sexual standards outlined by Reiss. There should be little question that Reiss did, in fact, cover the area adequately.

# THE MEASUREMENT OF PREMARITAL SEXUAL ATTITUDES

From Reiss's delineation of sexual standards in America came the mechanism by which an individual's premarital sexual permissiveness at an attitudinal level could be assessed. Reiss assumed that most persons would view kissing as more acceptable than petting, and petting more acceptable than full sexual relations. The conditions under which the three behaviors would be differently acceptable are related to the degree of intimacy or affection present between the partners. Thus Reiss delineated four intimacy states: (1) engaged, (2) in love, (3) strong affection, and (4) not particularly affectionate. Put another way, Reiss assumed that attitudes toward premarital sexual behavior exist along a single dimension and that, if one knows the maximum acceptable sexual behavior for a person, one can predict what other sexual behaviors that other person will accept as appropriate. This approach to developing an attitudinal index is called Guttman scaling after its designer, Louis Guttman. Guttman's assumption was that if one endorses (agrees with) a more difficult item (for example, item 12, full sexual relations, not particularly affectionate toward the partner) then one would endorse all other items that are less difficult to endorse. As one can see in Table 11–1, Reiss's definition of the continuum seems to fit quite well into the basic framework of Guttman scaling.

The premarital sexual permissiveness scales Reiss developed consisted of twelve items each for each sex (male, female), broken down into three behaviors (kissing, petting, full sexual relations) and the affectional conditions under which the behaviors could occur (engaged, in love, strong affection, not particularly affectionate). Thus, the questions he asked in order to measure premarital sexual permissiveness at the attitudinal level were as follows:

I believe that kissing
       petting               } is acceptable
       full sexual relations }
       for the male   } before marriage
            female }
       when he/she is engaged to be married
       when he/she is in love
       when he/she feels strong affection toward his/her partner
       even if he/she does not feel particularly affectionate toward his/her partner

Since all of Reiss's respondents answered the questions in a same-sex and an opposite-set context, it is possible to get an estimate not only of how much permissiveness a person will allow for either sex but also, by examining both sets of responses, of how equalitarian one is. If,

279

**TABLE 11–1**

Reiss's Premarital Sexual Permissiveness Scale

| SCALE TYPES | FULL SEXUAL RELATIONS | | | |
|---|---|---|---|---|
| | NOT PART. AFFEC. | STRONG AFFEC. | IN LOVE | ENGAGED |
| 12 | + | + | + | + |
| 11 | − | + | + | + |
| 10 | − | − | + | + |
| 9 | − | − | − | + |
| 8 | − | − | − | − |
| 7 | − | − | − | − |
| 6 | − | − | − | − |
| 5 | − | − | − | − |
| 4 | − | − | − | − |
| 2 | − | − | − | − |
| 1 | − | − | − | − |
| 0 | − | − | − | − |

SOURCE: Adapted from Ira L. Reiss, *The Social Context of Premarital Sexual Permissiveness* (New York: Holt, Rinehart, and Winston, 1967). Used by permission of the author.

therefore, a person endorsed one or more of the "affectionate coitus" items for females and item 12 for males, he or she would be classed as a "transitional double standard." The "permissiveness without affection" standard requires that a person endorse all 12 items for both sexes.

Reiss's assumption that his twelve items are unidimensional has been thoroughly verified. In fact, by just knowing the most difficult item a person endorsed on the male and female scales, Reiss was able to predict accurately (about 95 percent of the time) how these persons would endorse the less difficult items.

The Reiss permissiveness scales are probably the most widely used and consistently verified Guttman-type scales in existence today. This does not mean, of course, that they are perfect. In fact, it would be useful to examine them critically before continuing our investigation of premarital sexual attitudes.

## CRITICISM OF PREMARITAL SEXUAL PERMISSIVENESS SCALES

Probably several possible sources of potential bias should concern us with regard to Reiss's definition and measurement of premarital sexual permissiveness. First, the responses given by persons answering the scales tell

| | PETTING | | | | KISSING | | |
|---|---|---|---|---|---|---|---|
| NOT PART. AFFEC. | STRONG AFFEC. | IN LOVE | ENGAGED | NOT PART. AFFEC. | STRONG AFFEC. | IN LOVE | ENGAGED |
| + | + | + | + | + | + | + | + |
| + | + | + | + | + | + | + | + |
| + | + | + | + | + | + | + | + |
| + | + | + | + | + | + | + | + |
| + | + | + | + | + | + | + | + |
| − | + | + | + | + | + | + | + |
| − | − | + | + | + | + | + | + |
| − | − | − | + | + | + | + | + |
| − | − | − | − | + | + | + | + |
| − | − | − | − | − | + | + | + |
| − | − | − | − | − | − | + | + |
| − | − | − | − | − | − | − | + |
| − | − | − | − | − | − | − | − |

us only what they consider appropriate for males and females, not what they consider appropriate for themselves. To get at this datum Reiss would need to phrase the statements as follows: I believe that full sexual relations is acceptable for *me* before marriage even if *I* don't feel particularly affectionate toward my partner. It is probably safe to assume that what one will allow as acceptable for others, one may consider totally inappropriate at a personal level.

Second, it should be noted that all the statements are presented in a positive tone, and all twelve items are included in one short section of the interview schedule. It is hard for me to believe that college students, many of whom are constantly being asked to complete questionnaires, are not able to see what Reiss was attempting to measure, and consequently, that the remarkable amount of consistency obtained with these scales may be, at least to some extent, a result of the transparency of the items. It might help if some of the items were worded negatively and if the items were not bundled together.

The third and fourth criticisms that might be leveled at Reiss's scales concern the basic definition of premarital sexual permissiveness and the differentiation between the four affectional conditions specifying the sexual behaviors studied. Let us look at the definition of sexual behavior first. Perhaps Reiss has not been specific enough regarding sexual behavior—petting, especially. A more complete list of sexual behavior might include the following types:

281

1. Kissing
2. Light petting
   a. Above the waist outside the clothes
      (female passive, male active)
   b. Below the waist outside the clothes
      (female passive-active, male passive-active)
3. Heavy petting
   a. Above the waist inside the clothes
      (female passive, male active)
   b. Below the waist inside the clothes
      (female passive-active, male passive-active)
4. Oral contact above the waist
   (Female passive, male active)
5. Extra heavy petting (one or both partners completely naked) but
   no intercourse.
6. Full sexual intercourse
7. Oral-Genital contact
   (female passive-active, male passive-active)

Thus, some persons answering the Reiss items may be thinking about *light* petting, others may be thinking about *heavy* petting, and still others may have an oral fixation. In other words, an endorsement of the petting items may not mean the same thing for different respondents.

The four conditions of intimacy used by Reiss are also inadequate. How can we separate engaged, in love, and strong affection? Surely two people who are engaged have vowed their love and affection for one another, and two people who have declared their love for one another must feel a strong mutual affection. Perhaps the scales would be more valid if there was less overlap among the conditions of intimacy.

A more differentiating set of conditions for sexual behavior might include the following:

1. Engaged to be married
2. In love but are not committed to marrying each other
3. Express a mutual affection but are not in love
4. Regular dating partners but are definitely not in love
5. Just good friends
6. Just casual dating partners
7. Do not feel particularly affectionate toward partner

These seven affectional conditions probably contain somewhat less overlap than the four used by Reiss. But one's reaction might be, "Yes, but that would require a minimum of sixty-three attitude items for males and at least as many for females!" Indeed, parsimony is not the strongest

Steve Hansen, Stock, Boston

*Should I go or stay? How do sociologists measure the components of such a decision?*

aspect of these alternatives. Reiss's scales are, therefore, the best we have to date. Perhaps they do not represent the best we can do to define the phenomena that constitute premarital sexual permissiveness. Just because the scales are so consistent in producing a reliable measurement of permissiveness as Reiss has defined it, does not mean that Reiss's definition of permissiveness is adequate or that the scales are necessarily valid. The development of any discipline, including sociology, requires that all theories and methodological techniques be constantly criticized in the hope that something more adequate may emerge, only to be replaced a short time later.

## REISS'S STUDY OF PERMISSIVENESS

Unlike many social scientists, Reiss has chosen to focus on the same basic research problem throughout most of his professional career to date. Besides phenomenal productivity, the result has been especially beneficial to the sociology of the family for several reasons. First, he has gathered

283

together a mass of data that has been thoroughly analyzed. Second, his singular concentration on one major research problem has allowed Reiss to touch all of the bases in reaching his national study. Third, not only has the number of interpretations expanded, but also the quality of the interpretations has been refined. Last, he has moved toward an integration of the macro with the micro sociological aspects of permissiveness —a major contribution in and of itself.

## The Samples

Reiss's 1967 monograph is based on (a) a five-school student sample in which the sample from each school was randomly selected (a white Virginia college, $N = 274$; a black Virginia college, $N = 202$; a white Virginia high school, $N = 151$; a black Virginia high school, $N = 65$; a white New York college, $N = 211$); (b) a national adult sample ($N = 1,515$) which was interviewed in June, 1963, and which was representative of the adult population of the United States; and (c) a nonrandom white Iowa college sample ($N = 316$). It is particularly significant that Reiss is the first and only person to study permissiveness with a nationwide representative sample of the American adult population.

The seven specific and one general propositions that Reiss included in his theory of premarital sexual permissiveness are presented here. In particular, focus is on the first two propositions, since they have generated a substantial number of critical research articles and a rather sizable debate among family specialists. The propositions are as follows:[3]

1. The lower the traditional level of sexual permissiveness in a group, the greater the likelihood that social forces will alter individual levels of sexual permissiveness.

2. The stronger the amount of general liberality in a group, the greater the likelihood that social forces will maintain high levels of sexual permissiveness.

3. To the extent that individual ties to the marital and family institutions differ, individuals will tend to display a different type of sensitivity to social forces.

4. The higher the general level of permissiveness in a group, the greater the extent of equalitarianism within the abstinence and double-standard classifications.

5. Differences in the potential for permissiveness in one's basic set of parentally derived values is a key determinant of the number, rate, and direction of changes in one's premarital sexual standards and behavior.

---

[3] Ira L. Reiss, *The Social Context of Premarital Sexual Permissiveness*, New York: Holt, Rinehart, and Winston, 1967, pp. 51, 73, 89, 103, 122, 139, 156, and 167, respectively.

6. There is a general tendency for the individual to perceive of his parents' permissiveness as a low on a permissive continuum and his peers' permissiveness as a high point, and to place himself somewhat closer to his peers, particularly to those he regards as his close friends.

7. The greater the responsibility for other family members and/or the less the courtship participation, the greater the likelihood that the individual will be low on permissiveness.

A General Proposition

The degree of acceptable premarital sexual permissiveness in a courtship group varies directly with the autonomy of the courtship group and with the degree of acceptable premarital sexual permissiveness in the social and cultural setting outside the group.

## The Debate Over Proposition 1

PROPOSITION 1: The lower the traditional level of sexual permissiveness in a group, the greater the likelihood that social forces will alter individual levels of sexual permissiveness (Reiss, 1967:51).

Initially, we should briefly discuss the variables that Reiss used to measure the concepts contained in this proposition. He isolates one group that is traditionally low on permissiveness (whites and females) and a group traditionally high (blacks and males). "Individual levels of permissiveness" refers, of course, to the response given on the permissiveness scales discussed earlier. Thus, he expected that the attitudes of permissiveness for whites and females would be more influenced by social forces than they are for blacks and males.

Reiss's indices of the concept "social forces" are (a) religious commitment as measured by the frequency of church attendance, (b) romantic love beliefs, an eight-item Guttman-type scale, and (c) the number of times a respondent said he or she had been in love. The term *social forces* is a problem. It implies factors that are not individual properties or characteristics, but rather broad-scale forces operative at the macro-societal level, forces like industrialization, urbanization, and secularization. The frequency of an individual's church attendance or their individual beliefs about romantic love are not really social forces. With this criticism in mind, let us see what Reiss (1967:52–53) found:

Thus, within traditionally less-permissive groups—women and whites—individual permissiveness is more likely to be affected by such social forces as church attendance, belief in romantic love and falling in love. In the traditionally more-permissive groups—men and Negroes—individuals find support and justification for liberal sexual attitudes in the groups' traditions, and their permissiveness is therefore less subject to

285

control by social forces. Highly permissive individuals in tradition-ally low-permissive social groups are permissive not because they have long standing traditions to support them, but because they are located in the social structure in such a way as to avoid inhibitory forces (church attendance and the idealistic version of romantic love for example) and to maximize experiences that promote permissiveness (like falling in love).

Put another way, Reiss found strong support for his traditionalism proposition. Other studies attempting to test this proposition have not been so fortunate. For example, Heltsley and Broderick (1969) found that the traditionalism proposition held only for the racial dichotomy (blacks and whites). Ruppel (1970) used the following four groups and found no real support for the proposition:

a. Rural and urban
b. Freshmen and seniors
c. Blue collar and white collar
d. Religious type based on religious affiliation: liberal-moderate-conservative

Using the data gathered in 1970 I used a different tactic in examin-ing the adequacy of the traditional proposition (see Clayton 1971). My assumption was that the crucial social force is religious commitment and the most important differentiating characteristic may not be group (males and females) but rather as follows:

a. Reported premarital coitus during the year
b. A person's propensity for lying as measured by the lie scale from the Minnesota Multi-Phasic Inventory
c. Perceived reference group norms of permissiveness

As the data in Table 11–2 show, as a social force, religious com-mitment (measured along three dimensions of religiosity, the ritualistic, experiential, and ideological plus a composite index of religious commit-ment at the attitudinal level) was more likely to be influential on a tra-ditionally high-permissive group, males, than on the traditionally low-permissive group, females. This, of course, is inconsistent with Reiss's finding.

The first assumption was that the religious commitment-to-permis-siveness relationship might be influenced by the respondents' reports of premarital intercourse during the preceding year (an indication of behav-ioral permissiveness). For males, who are supposed to be traditionally high on permissiveness, religious commitment was an especially important pre-dictor of attitudinal permissiveness, particularly for those who reported no coitus during the year. For the traditionally low-permissive females,

**TABLE 11–2**

**Correlations Between Religious Commitment and Premarital Sexual Permissiveness**

| BASIC CORRELATION FACTOR | | REPORTED COITUS | | LIE PROPENSITY | | REFERENCE GROUP NORMS | |
|---|---|---|---|---|---|---|---|
| | | YES | NO | LOW LIE | HIGH LIE | LOW NRG | HIGH NRG |
| MALES | | | | | | | |
| Ritualistic | −.67 | −.45 | −.65 | −.74 | −.69 | −.60 | −.56 |
| Experiential | −.56 | −.49 | −.46 | −.55 | −.58 | −.54 | −.52 |
| Ideological | −.52 | −.14 | −.64 | −.45 | −.71 | −.21 | −.36 |
| Composite | −.58 | −.27 | −.69 | −.53 | −.78 | −.56 | −.57 |
| FEMALES | | | | | | | |
| Ritualistic | −.48 | −.36 | −.45 | −.58 | −.35 | −.47 | −.58 |
| Experiential | −.55 | −.39 | −.51 | −.67 | −.42 | −.59 | −.52 |
| Ideological | −.51 | −.33 | −.46 | −.55 | −.47 | −.66 | −.28 |
| Composite | −.46 | −.54 | −.36 | −.54 | −.38 | −.59 | −.40 |

although religious commitment was an important social force, it was less salient as a predictor of attitudinal permissiveness for those who reported no coitus that year than it was for males. Perhaps Reiss would have been well advised to have used reported behavioral permissiveness as an index of group within the sex and racial categories, instead of just sex and race.

The second assumption made was that there may be some consistent fudging on the variables used to evaluate the traditionalism proposition. Some very interesting findings emerged. For the supposedly high-permissive males, the religious commitment-permissiveness relationship was much stronger for those who had a higher propensity for lying. Just the opposite occurred for the low-permissive females. Those with a lower propensity for lying consistently had a stronger religious commitment-to-permissiveness relationship. These findings relate to one criticism of Reiss's permissiveness scales—the giving of conventional or expected responses to the items, particularly since it would not be difficult for most college students to psych out what the scales are designed to measure.

The third assumption was that the religious commitment-to-permissiveness relationship might be affected by the level of permissiveness perceived to be prevalent in one's most important reference group. As the data in Table 11–2 clearly indicate, for males, perceived reference group norms is an intervening variable. For females, except for the ritualistic index, the religious commitment-permissiveness relationship is

287

strongest for those who perceive their most important reference group as low-permissive. However, in all four cases the original relationship for females was specified, thus indicating some support for Reiss's proposition.

The consequence of all of this discussion is simple. The research of Heltsley and Broderick (1969), Ruppel (1975) and my own research (Clayton, 1971) suggest that Reiss's so-called traditionalism proposition, Proposition 1, would be better labeled a hypothesis—tentatively stated and begging for further testing. This does not negate in any way the solid support Reiss obtained, from a better set of samples at that, it merely questions the confidence we can have in the proposition.

## The Debate Over Proposition 2

PROPOSITION 2: The stronger the amount of general liberality in a group, the greater the likelihood that social forces will maintain high levels of sexual permissiveness (Reiss, 1967:73).

Reiss, like most American sociologists since Kinsey, had assumed that individuals in the higher socioeconomic status categories are relatively low in premarital sexual permissiveness, and that persons low on SES (socioeconomic status) are rather high on sexual permissiveness. Such an assumption seemed justified since the Kinsey data were so unequivocal. For example, for the males in his sample, Kinsey found the following percentages were virgins at age twenty-five (Kinsey, 1948:550):

| | |
|---|---|
| Some college education | 36% |
| High school education | 16% |
| Eighth grade education | 10% |

For females between the ages of sixteen and twenty, Kinsey found that 82 percent of those entering college had not engaged in coitus as compared to 62 percent of the females who did not enter high school (Kinsey, 1953:337).

Reiss, however, found no pronounced relationship between social class and premarital sexual permissiveness. This result was unanticipated. The zero-order correlation between social class and permissiveness for his student sample was only .01 (gamma) and .13 for the adult sample.

In order to check the relationship, Reiss controlled for church attendance, his measure of religious commitment and a "social force." "Among those higher on church attendance, the *negative* relationship postulated by Kinsey and others did appear, that is, the lower status groups were more permissive. Those who were low on church attendance displayed a somewhat weaker but *positive* relation between social class and sexual permissiveness" (Reiss, 1967:60–61). The value of gamma for those high on church attendance was −.35 and low on church attendance +.14.

Reiss then reasoned that high and low church attendance were indices of "conservative" and "liberal" styles of life or general orientations. He felt that liberal individuals would favor change rather than tradition, particularly changes that involved use of the intellect. He also felt that liberals would emphasize individual expression and a universally applicable ethic of sex. A conservative, according to Reiss, would be likely to support the traditional social standards and would place less value on individualized expression and a universally applicable ethic. "In this connection, it was hypothesized that among generally conservative people those of higher status would be less permissive than those of lower status, whereas among generally liberal individuals the reaction would be in the opposite direction" (Reiss, 1967:62).

Reiss then developed thirteen matched indices of liberal versus conservative setting and tested the relationship of social class to permissiveness by controlling these settings (Table 11–3). Of the thirty-three possible checks, the hypothesized relationship of class to permissiveness was supported thirty times. This seemed to be rather consistent evidence that the liberal-conservative settings specified the class to permissiveness relationship and supported Proposition 2.

MARANELL, DODDER, AND MITCHELL CRITIQUE. In a critique of Reiss's second proposition, Maranell, Dodder, and Mitchell (1970:85) suggested that "being a liberal or conservative person and being in a liberal or conservative setting are somewhat independent characteristics." They then tested the proposition using more direct measures of liberalism and conservatism. To measure religious attitudes they used a religious fundamentalism scale. To measure liberalism they used three scales: (a) an idealism index to assess a dedication to lofty principles and ideas such that compromise on causes important to the individual were considered wrong; (b) an authoritarianism scale to identify the person who believes in, advocates, practices, and enforces obedience; and (c) a scale of academic orientation-identified attitudes that support scholarly endeavors, learning, academic freedom, and respect for academic life and academicians. The father's occupation was used as the index for social class. Maranell, Dodder, and Mitchell (1970:87–88) concluded:

> This study attempted to test the hypothesis that among conservative individuals, those of higher status would be less sexually permissive than those of lower status, while among more liberal persons the relation would be reversed. Unlike earlier research, this study used direct measures of personal liberalism and conservatism. It was not possible, however, to detect the hypothesized relationships.

The more direct measurements of the key variables found in the Maranell study seem to offset some of the problems introduced by their rather limited sample. Although Reiss's data offer some support for his

289

**TABLE 11–3**
**Social Class and Permissiveness**

| CHARACTERISTIC | DIRECTION OF OBSERVED RELATIONSHIP | |
|---|---|---|
| | STUDENT SAMPLE | ADULT SAMPLE |
| *Liberal Setting: Positive Relationship Predicted* | | |
| Divorced | + | + |
| No religious affiliation | + | + |
| Jewish | + | + |
| Lives in town of 100,000 or more | + | − |
| Lives in New England or Middle Atlantic Region | + | |
| Low church attendance | + | |
| Low on romantic-love beliefs | + | |
| In love twice or more | + | |
| Believes his standard does not apply to others | + | |
| Believes sex is not dirty or nasty | + | |
| Age 21–35 | | − |
| Favors integrated schools [a] | | + |
| Would take part in civil rights march [b] | | − |
| *Conservative Setting: Negative Relationship Predicted* | | |
| Widowed | − | − |
| Protestant | − | − |
| Lives in town of 10,000 or less | − | − |
| Lives in South Atlantic region | − | |
| High church attendance | − | |
| High on romantic-love beliefs | − | |
| Believes his standard applies to others | − | |
| Believes sex is dirty and nasty | − | |
| Lives in southern region | | − |
| Age 50 or over | | − |
| Has only teenage children | | − |
| Favors segregated schools [a] | | − |
| Would not take part in civil rights march [b] | | − |

SOURCE: Ira L. Reiss, *The Social Context of Premarital Sexual Permissiveness* (New York: Holt, 1967), p. 63. By permission of Holt, Rinehart and Winston, Inc.

NOTE: Only the first four "liberal" and the first three "conservative" items were asked of both samples.

[a] Asked of white respondents only (used by courtesy of Herbert Hyman and Paul Sheatsley).

[b] Asked of black respondents only (used by courtesy of Norman Miller).

Proposition 2, the fact that he used liberal and conservative settings instead of more direct measures seems to detract from the overall strength of the support. In general, the lack of consistency of support for this proposition leads to the conclusion that hypothesis 2 is, at best, tentative.

## Summary

One should not be misled into thinking that these few pails of cold water dropped on Reiss's permissiveness scale and his 1967 theory of premarital sexual permissiveness are capable of drowning Reiss's works or his findings. The contributions of this man are truly remarkable. Time and further study will be the true tests of his theory. No doubt Ira Reiss will be expanding and refining his theoretical notions very soon. In addition, the significant number of students who have studied under Reiss will also be making some very significant extensions, deletions, and modifications

*For males especially, there is strong pressure to conform with peer-group expectations that one be sexually active.*

Peter Vandermark

of the theory in the next several years. All in all, Ira Reiss has provided those interested in the study of premarital sexual permissiveness with a foundation from which to develop new theories and new analytical devices in the best tradition of American scholarship.

## FACTORS INFLUENCING PREMARITAL SEXUAL PERMISSIVENESS

Reiss's concepts and variables seem to fit into the modified contingent-consistency model discussed at the end of Chapter 10 and illustrated by Figure 10–1.

### Properties

What Reiss has labeled groups are in essence personal characteristics of individuals that seem to predispose them to scale either high or low in permissiveness. The traditional part of his designation merely reflects the fact that our socialization process is basically double-standard in orientation (males are allowed to be more sexual than females) and whites generally live in social contexts in which overt sexuality is more often sanctioned than is true for blacks. Another personal property that differentiates the content and intensity of socialization about sex and that determines to a large degree the kind of social context for whites and blacks is social class. Thus, sex, race, and social class can be viewed as properties.

### General Attitudes

What Reiss has designated as social forces—a label with which disagreement was indicated—can be easily viewed as general attitudes or behaviors reflecting a general attitude. Religious commitment as assessed by church attendance, beliefs about the importance of romantic love, and equalitarianism are really reflections of generalized attitudes and values, a set of general guidelines for behavior that are closely tied to the way a person determines what is morally appropriate or morally reprehensible. As one would expect, these general attitudes are rather closely related to Reiss's dependent variable, attitudes toward premarital sexual permissiveness, and are probably the result of the person's personal properties.

### Contingent Factors

Reiss isolated a number of variables that should intervene in and specify the relationship of the personal properties and general attitudes and premarital sexual permissiveness. In the contingent-consistency model these would be called contingent factors. Listed below are the variables from Reiss's study that could be contingent factors:

1. Liberal versus conservative setting
2. Dating background
   a. Age at first date
   b. Exclusiveness of dating (that is, only one dating partner versus a variety)
   c. Number of steadies
   d. Number of times in love
3. Reference group identification
   a. Similarity of sexual standards to parents
   b. Similarity of sexual standards to peers
   c. Similarity of sexual standards to close friends
4. Marital role responsibilities

Each of these contingent variables should specify the degree of consistency among one's personal properties (tradition of low or high permissiveness), general attitudes (the degree to which one would tend to view sexual activities from a moral or restrictive stance), and one's attitudes toward premarital sexual behaviors and the appropriateness of those behaviors under varying conditions of affection.

## Behavior-Specific Attitudes

This category of the model fits perfectly the variable Reiss tries to explain: premarital sexual permissiveness at the attitudinal level.

The contingent-consistency model implies that to the degree that personal properties, general attitudes, the contingent factors, and the behavior-specific attitudes are consistent about permissiveness, an opportunity to enact one's sexual standards at a behavioral level will be sought.

With regard to the necessity of utilizing the techniques of neutralization when one has violated one's sexual standards, Reiss says: "To summarize the findings concerning changes in sexual standards, behavior and guilt feelings in adolescents—females exhibit greater changes than males and greater feelings of guilt, and they show the general tendency to continue guilty behavior until it becomes accepted" (Reiss, 1971:121). In other words, because females usually start out with less permissive standards, they go through more and greater changes in their personal attitudes toward sex than males. Consequently, they encounter greater guilt from their sexual behaviors and, in order to reduce the guilt from inconsistencies between attitudes and behavior, they usually end up changing their attitudes so that these will be consistent with their sexual practices.

293

This reintroduces the crucial point raised in the contingent-consistency model—a person's behavior influences his or her attitudes toward that behavior. Because it is not possible to erase the fact of a behavior after it has occurred, the logical way to obtain the consistency all of us seem to need is to change our attitudes so that they are consistent with what we are doing.

## SUMMARY

Sex is a very important part of everybody's life, especially during adolescence, when we are seeking autonomy and our identity as adults. An understanding of how we learn to be sexual creatures and how we learn to cope with sex is a topic of concern for all social scientists. This chapter has tried to sort out the process that young people have encountered. Perhaps the most important aspect of the process of human sexuality has not been discussed, primarily because it is virtually impossible to study—the dynamic nature of sexual decision making that occurs when one is with someone of the opposite sex and must develop, on the spot, the modes of interaction that will determine just how far to go sexually. As social scientists we have focused on rather diffuse variables and have missed the dynamics of sexual decision making. Perhaps that is all to the good. Probably some things should not be hamstrung with excessive rationality—some things that are too dynamically human to be placed in a model of human behavior.

## SOME POSSIBLE IMPLICATIONS

*In the preceding chapter it was noted that premarital intercourse is not a rare event, either in terms of the proportion of the population who experience it or how often it occurs for individuals. Yet, in terms of the number of premarital partners, ours is not a permissive society. In this chapter it was noted that the prevailing sexual standard in the United States today is permissiveness with affection—the belief that premarital coitus is appropriate for both sexes if love or strong affection is present. There is little evidence that our society will endorse a permissiveness-without-affection standard.*

*What are some of the implications of the prevailing attitudes about premarital sex? Some of the answers to this question are readily apparent. First, sexual experience prior to marriage is likely to be an integral part of the courtship process for most, if not almost all, young Americans as we move toward the twenty-first century. Second, the courtship system will continue to operate rather autonomously, with little input allowed from adults. Third, it may become imperative that the schools and churches institute sex and contraceptive education programs. Fourth, a new set of moral ethics regarding premarital sex may emerge in the last quarter of this century in order to reduce the gap between a restrictive sexual ideology and a permissive set of behavioral norms. All of these are plausible implications that could emerge to coincide with what seems to have been happening in our society with regard to premarital sexual attitudes and behavior.*

# 12

# MATE SELECTION: A MACRO PERSPECTIVE

*To what extent is our choice of a marital partner determined by societal-level endogamous norms?*

*How likely is it that one will marry someone who is similar to oneself in age, religious orientation, and social class?*

*How widespread is interracial marriage in the United States?*

*Why is it that a sizable proportion of married couples grew up in the same community? Is not ours a highly mobile society?*

The preceding three chapters examined love and premarital sexual behavior and attitudes, phenomena that are integrally tied to the process of marital selection—at least as that process operates in the United States. Not unlike other topics of concern to specialists who study the family and marriage, marital selection can be usefully divided into two sections, the macro and the micro. In Chapter 12 we focus on the macro-societal level facets of the mate selection process, and in Chapter 13 the major emphasis will be on the more dynamic features of how we choose a marital partner at the micro-social psychological level. We begin by discussing a rather rare occurrence, intermarriage, and close Chapter 12 with a discussion of the common pattern, marital selection of a quite similar chosen one.

## INTERMARRIAGE AS A GENERAL CONCEPT

A problem that has been the focus of much study is intergroup marriage or more simply, intermarriage. This refers to the problem of the linkages of two societies or groups that may occupy essentially the same territory, that may utilize the same environmental and social-institutional resources, but that are organized around distinct, different, and perhaps mutually hostile values, goals, and behavior patterns. Each of the groups may desire to constrain their youth from contacts with the youth from the other group. To do so the powers that be may set certain restrictions on where a young person may go, when, and with whom. This can usually be achieved with some degree of efficiency without explicit rules and can be done at the parent-child level of interaction. However, in order to maintain the cohesiveness of the total group and an undisturbed group identity, many groups have very explicit rules about who may marry whom. These group constraints on intermarriage may be based on religious, political, cultural, social class, and/or racial-ethnic differences.

The basic question that must always be answered in studying intermarriage rules is: What determines the acceptable boundaries of eligible from ineligible marital partners? Yinger (1968 a and b) suggests that intermarriage is any marital contract across a socially significant line of distinction. Just what constitutes a socially significant line of distinction varies (a) with the groups involved, (b) with the society in which the situation occurs, and (c) with the historical period in which the situation exists. In some societies the crucial line of distinction is social class regardless of any other factors. In Brazil, for example, the population is about as racially mixed as any modern society because the socially significant line

of distinction is social class. In the Peoples Republic of China the crucial boundary is ideological devotion to the sociopolitical ideas of Mao regardless of social class, education, and other distinctions (see Huang, 1962 *a* and *b*). Ruth Cavan (1970) clarified matters a great deal by developing a workable definition of social significance:

> Social significance refers to basic values widely accepted in a given society, to which members are deeply committed, and to which an observer distinguishes this society from others. Religious intermarriage, thus, might be defined as marriage of members of two religions whose values are sufficiently different that one or both religions perceives its values to be threatened.

There is the possibility that socially significant lines of distinction may be additive. For example, intermarriage may be threatening when the two members are of different religions and also are from different races and socioeconomic classes. In such a case the violation of multiple boundaries of social significance plausibly suggests that the degree of threat to the groups involved is heightened.

As discussed in Chapter 3, social scientists have coined terms that specifically refer to the problem of intermarriage between groups. The terms, *endogamy* and *exogamy,* which serve to delineate the eligible marital partners from those that are considered ineligible, are defined as follows:

> *Endogamy:* The rule restricting marriage to members of the same tribe, village, caste, or other social group (Fairchild, 1964).
>
> *Exogamy:* This term refers to the rule requiring a member of a certain group to marry outside of certain socially defined and prescribed webs of relationship. For example, it is usually considered inappropriate in the United States to marry a parent, sibling, step-parent, in-law, or first cousin.

Thus, endogamous and exogamous rules serve the function of isolating those characteristics of persons or group identifications that are inappropriate for marriage purposes. Heuristically, these two terms would appear as two circles (see Figure 12–1).

The group thus requires that its members go outside the smaller circle (exogamous rules) for a mate but cannot, without specific approval or fear of sanction, go outside the larger circle (endogamous rules) of eligible partners. Exogamous rules are frequently limited to kinship relations and are also usually codified into laws. The sanctions applied for the violation of exogamous rules are frequently highly structured and are tied to the legal system in most societies. The sanctions applicable in violations of endogamous rules are usually informal and consist of public disowning, banishment from the group and some or all of its rituals, and other more subtle forms of punishment.

299

**FIGURE 12–1**
**The Marriage Universe**

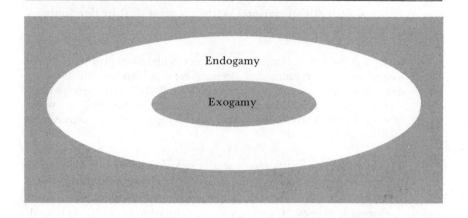

Cavan (1970) offered two ways of viewing endogamous rules. The first concerns the relationships among various types of in-groups. These in-groups may be hostile, indifferent, or friendly to each other. They may also be strongly endogamous, have preferential endogamy, or be rather permissive with regard to endogamy, as shown in Table 12–1. The second way of viewing endogamous rules concerns the degree of independence of the group from the larger society of which it is a part. Cavan (1970) uses religious groups to illustrate this phenomenon.

## Total Society

In a religious group that supplies all or most of the needs of its members within a physically bound community, such as the Hutterites of the Western plains, some Orthodox Jewish communities, and the Mormons of a century ago, endogamy is inclusive. The member who marries outside the group essentially severs all ties with that group and, as far as the group is concerned, he or she is a nonentity.

## Subsociety

Some religious groups provide some social functions, such as religious and secular education, that are also available from other sources, but still retain many contacts with the larger society. Cavan cites the Roman Catholic Church and the conservative branch of Judaism as examples of the subsociety type. In such groups endogamy is highly valued and is definitely preferred, but it is not always absolutely possible. In extenuating circumstances a violation of endogamous rules might be allowed, but the

**TABLE 12–1**

**Probable Intermarriages Among Various In-Groups**

| | IN-GROUP A<br><br>HOSTILE TO OTHER IN-GROUPS AND STRONGLY ENDOGAMOUS | IN-GROUP B<br>INDIFFERENT TO OTHER IN-GROUPS AND HAS PREFERENTIAL ENDOGAMY | IN-GROUP C<br>FRIENDLY TO OTHER IN-GROUPS AND HAS PERMISSIVE ENDOGAMY |
|---|---|---|---|
| *In-Group D*<br>Hostile to Other In-Groups and Strongly Endogamous | No Intermarriages | Almost No Intermarriages | Few Intermarriages |
| *In-Group E*<br>Indifferent to Other In-Groups and has Preferential Endogamy | Almost No Intermarriages | Many Intermarriages | Many Intermarriages |
| *In-Group F*<br>Friendly to Other In-Groups and has Permissive Endogamy | Few Intermarriages | Many Intermarriages | Almost No Restrictions on Intermarriage |

SOURCE: Adapted from Ruth Shonle Cavan, "Concepts and Terminology in Interreligious Marriage," *Journal for the Scientific Study of Religion,* 9(1970):314. By permission of The Society for the Scientific Study of Religion, Inc., and the author.

participant would still lose some status within his or her group, and the nonmember partner would not be fully accepted, at least until conversion occurs.

## Institutions

Often religious groups are even more interdependent with the larger society and resemble institutions instead of subsocieties. Cavan uses the reform branch of Judaism and most Protestant denominations as examples. In these groups endogamy is preferred, but the general attitude toward intermarriage is rather permissive.

## RELIGIOUS INTERMARRIAGE IN THE UNITED STATES

What sociologists know about religious intermarriage in the United States is very tentative for the following reasons. (1) Only two states ask persons seeking a marriage license for information about religious affiliation, and in these states the question is optional. Iowa began this procedure in 1953

301

and Indiana in 1959. These states are probably not very representative since they are both in the Midwest and both have been predominantly agricultural and rural in their demographic make-up. (2) Only the Roman Catholic Church through its American Catholic Directory regularly reports data on mixed marriages. These, of course, concern only mixed Catholic marriages. (3) The only available data from a nationwide sample dealing with religious affiliation and marriage was collected in 1957 by the U.S. Census Bureau's Current Population Survey for March, 1957. Thus Monahan (1971) states:

> As a consequence of the lack of national data on religious preference, our knowledge of interreligious marriage in the United States is based on special studies and surveys, which may or may not have national validity, or upon limited record keeping by local church or governmental agencies.

Table 12–2 shows that the Jewish group is the most endogamous with only 8 percent intermarried while the percentage for Protestants was

**TABLE 12–2**

**Religious Homogamy and Heterogamy Among White Married Couples in the United States, 1957**

| RELIGION | PERCENTAGES | |
|---|---|---|
| | SPOUSES WITH THE SAME RELIGION | SPOUSES WITH DIFFERENT RELIGIONS |
| Total (All Protestant denominations considered the same religion) | 90.4 | 9.6 |
| Total (All Protestant denominations considered different religions) | 82.5 | 17.5 |
| Protestant (Denominations considered the same religion) | 87.8 | 12.2 |
| Protestant (Denominations considered different religions) | 76.6 | 23.4 |
|     Baptist | 79.4 | 20.6 |
|     Lutheran | 73.9 | 26.1 |
|     Methodist | 75.9 | 24.1 |
|     Presbyterian | 76.0 | 24.0 |
|     Other | 76.3 | 23.7 |
| Roman Catholic | 76.7 | 23.3 |
| Jewish | 91.7 | 8.3 |
| Other | 55.8 | 44.2 |
| No religion | 29.3 | 70.7 |

SOURCE: Adapted from Thomas P. Monahan, "The Extent of Interdenominational Marriage in the United States," *Journal for the Scientific Study of Religion*, 10(1971):88. By permission of the Society for the Scientific Study of Religion, Inc., and the author.

NOTE: Data are from previously unpublished tables from United States Department of Commerce, Bureau of the Census, *March 1957 Current Population Survey* (Washington, D.C.).

Charles Gatewood

*An interreligious (Christian-Jewish) and inter-ethnic (Spanish-American–Jewish-American) wedding in New York City. Is the first step necessarily the hardest?*

12 and for Catholics, 23 percent were intermarried. These data, however, treat all Protestants as if they were homogeneous. A number of writers (Bealer, 1963; Willits, 1963; Bouma, 1963; Bossard and Letts, 1956; Yinger, 1968 a and b) have suggested that interdenominational marriages of Protestants may be more culturally disparate than marriages of Catholics to some Protestant denominations. What is needed, then, is a breakdown of the Protestant category into at least the major denominations.

The data indicate that the intermarriage rates for the separate major Protestant denominations produce some interesting changes in the interpretation of intermarriage rates by religious affiliation. It should be noted, for instance, that Catholics and the Protestant groups are in the same range of "mixed" scores, between 20.6 and 26.1 percent. Also of some importance is the fact that the total mixed-marriage percentage rose from 9.6 percent (Table 12–2) when the Protestants were all lumped together to 17.5 percent when the Protestants were subdivided into major denominations.

Another way of looking at mixed religious marriages is to compare the actual number of marriages in which both were of the same affiliation to the number of same-affiliation marriages that would occur if marriages were contracted without any regard to religious affiliation, that is, at random. The groups in Table 12–3 are listed in order from highest to lowest endogamy. For example, the ratio of actual Jewish-Jewish marriages to what would be expected if random mating occurred was twenty-six. That is, Jewish-Jewish marriages occurred twenty-six times more than would be expected by chance alone. Monahan (1971) reacted to these

303

**TABLE 12–3**
**Religious Homogamy for White Couples in the United States, 1957**

| AFFILIATIONS | RATIO OF ACTUAL TO EXPECTED RANDOM MATINGS | DEGREE OF ENDOGAMY |
|---|---|---|
| Other non-Protestant | 60.40 | High |
| Jewish | 26.21 | ↑ |
| No religion reported | 24.06 | |
| Presbyterian | 12.57 | |
| Lutheran | 9.92 | |
| Methodist | 5.64 | |
| Baptist | 5.20 | |
| Other Protestant | 3.80 | ↓ |
| Roman Catholic | 3.25 | Low |

SOURCE: Thomas P. Monahan, "The Extent of Interdenominational Marriage in the United States," *Journal for the Scientific Study of Religion*, *10*(1971):89. By permission of the Society for the Scientific Study of Religion, Inc., and the author.

NOTE: Data are from previously unpublished tables from United States Department of Commerce, Bureau of the Census, *March 1957 Current Population Survey* (Washington, D.C.).

figures by stating: "If these data can be accepted as at all indicative, and we have none other, as yet, then American Catholics are the least religiously endogamous of all the major denominations here displayed."

The question the sociologist asks is, Why? Why are the Catholics the least endogamous? Why are the other non-Protestants (probably consisting primarily of Russian and Greek Orthodox), who grew out of essentially the same religiocultural context, the most endogamous? If we are to be able to answer the question why, we must solve the three basic problems of any science: (a) conceptualization, (b) operationalization, and (c) theoretical integration. First, it is necessary to carve out of the real world some phenomena that can be clearly described and labeled. Second, a science must design means of measuring the empirical referents of the concepts. A third problem is to describe and explain with precision the ways the concepts and their empirical referents are related to each other—at both a concrete and an abstract level. Cavan (1970) has neatly summarized the condition of sociology with reference to these problems of science and the topic of religious intermarriage:

Research of any kind rests on conceptualization and precision of terminology; theories may follow later. Research on interreligious marriage has scarcely gone beyond limited surveys of rates of intermarriage; discussions tend to be partisan in nature by proponents of one religion or another. These approaches are more or less at a standstill; little that is new is being uncovered. The time is at hand for placing interreligious marriage in a conceptual framework and for developing greater precision in terminology, both for the sake of clarity and to break away from some of the inadequacies of present research.

# A TYPOLOGY OF MIXED RELIGIOUS MARRIAGES

Cavan (1970) developed and defined a three-part typology of types of mixed religious marriages. At least three other types of combinations of mixed religious marriage are needed for the typology to be complete.

1. *Interreligious Marriage:* A marriage in which the members are from two religious groups.
   Example: Judaism and Christianity

2. *Interfaith Marriage:* A marriage in which the members come from major divisions of a religious system.
   Example: Roman Catholic and Major Protestant

3. *Interdenominational Marriage:* A marriage between members of separate factions of the same faith.
   Example: Judaism—Orthodox and Conservative
   Orthodox and Reform
   Conservative and Reform
   Example: Major Protestant Groups— Baptists (American and Southern Conventions)
   Congregationalists
   Disciples of Christ
   Episcopalians
   Lutherans (American and Missouri Synods)
   Methodists
   Presbyterians
   Note: An interdenominational marriage would consist of the combination of any two of these major groups.

4. *Denomination-Sect Marriage:* The marriage of a member of one of the major Protestant denominations to a member of one of the sect groups.
   Example: One of the major Protestant groups with a member of an Adventist, small Baptist sect, Pentecostal, or Church of God group

5. *Intersect Marriage:* A marriage consisting of members of different religious sects.
   Example: Jehovah's Witness and Pentecostal Holiness

6. *Mixed* (One with Religious Affiliation and One with None): A marriage between one person who is religiously affiliated and one who has no religion.
   Example: Baptist and Religious None

There are, of course, other possible combinations, but these seem to constitute the six major varieties of mixed religious marriages that exist.

## INTERRACIAL MARRIAGE IN THE UNITED STATES

A second type of intermarriage, which has been studied primarily as a societal phenomenon and which has strong endogamous values associated with it, is interracial marriage. History is replete with stories of how various societies have attempted to maintain strict endogamy with regard to interracial marriage, or what certain peoples believed to be interracial marriage. In the United States interracial marriage became a very prevalent topic of conversation shortly after the 1954 desegregation decision of the Supreme Court. In the 1960s the Supreme Court declared that laws banning interracial marriages were unconstitutional. So, legally at least, the barriers to interracial marriage are no longer operative.

Like all topics that are socially sensitive, the first question that usually arises concerns incidence. To what extent does interracial marriage exist in the United States today? Like the data on interreligious, interfaith, and interdenominational marriages, the data on interracial marriages are scanty and incomplete. However, using the available data, I will make an attempt to answer this question.

Charles Gatewood

*Does society have the right to intervene in individual decisions, such as whether to date and marry interracially?*

*Interracial Marriage: 1970 Census Data*[1]

In the 1960 census, for the first time, national data on the race of the husband were classified by race of wife for all married couples in the United States. The 1970 census continued this system and used a seven-category classification of race that, although it is inadequate for precise differentiations, is the best available.

The seven racial categories used were:

1. White
2. Negro
3. American Indian
4. Japanese
5. Chinese
6. Filipino
7. All other nonwhite not listed in 2 through 6 above

Rather than presenting these data in a large table I have broken them down into more manageable sections, with a comment on each. These data were compiled from the 1970 census volume on marital status.

WHITE INTERRACIAL MARRIAGE.    Table 12–4 shows that the total number of married couples who are racially mixed is only 328,690, seven-tenths of 1 percent of all married couples in the United States in 1970. All but 9.4 percent of the racially mixed couples included a white spouse, either a husband or a wife. The three largest categories of interracial marriage were: white husband and American Indian wife (13.7 percent), white husband and Japanese wife (13.4 percent), and white wife and black husband (12.5 percent). It should be noted that most of the white men married to Japanese wives imported their wives from Japan. American women of Japanese descent seldom marry across racial lines. The most important point to be made about these data is that less than 1 percent of all married couples in the United States in 1970 were interracially married. This had increased only slightly since 1960, when four-tenths of 1 percent of all married couples (163,800 out of 40,491,000) were married across racial lines.

---

[1] The data used in this section are from U.S. Department of Commerce, Bureau of the Census, *Subject Reports, Marital Status*, PC (2)-4C, 1970, Table 12, p. 262. For an excellent discussion of interracial marriage data for 1960 see Carter and Glick (1970).

**TABLE 12–4**
**White Interracial Marriages**

| | NO. % |
|---|---|
| Total number of married couples, United States, 1970 | 44,597,574 |
| Total number of racially mixed couples, United States, 1970 | 328,690 (0.7%) |

| | NO. | % |
|---|---|---|
| White husband and | | |
| a. Negro wife | 23,566 | (7.2) |
| b. American Indian wife | 44,903 | (13.7) |
| c. Japanese wife | 44,138 | (13.4) |
| d. Chinese wife | 6,941 | (2.1) |
| e. Filipino wife | 12,238 | (3.7) |
| f. Other race wife | 30,434 | (9.3) |
| TOTALS | 162,220 | (49.4) |
| White wife and | | |
| a. Negro husband | 41,223 | (12.5) |
| b. American Indian husband | 40,039 | (12.2) |
| c. Japanese husband | 9,872 | (3.0) |
| d. Chinese husband | 7,188 | (2.2) |
| e. Filipino husband | 15,674 | (4.8) |
| f. Other race husband | 21,706 | (6.6) |
| TOTALS | 135,702 | (41.3) |
| TOTAL, all other racially mixed couples, United States, 1970 | 30,778 | (9.4) |

BLACK INTERRACIAL MARRIAGE. As the data in Table 12–5 show, about 23.3 percent of all racially mixed couples in the United States in 1970 include a black spouse. The most likely combination is a black husband and a white wife (53.9 percent). When the black-white combinations are added they constitute 84.7 percent of the 76,431 interracial marriages that include a black spouse. Blacks, then, are quite selective in their choice of a partner across racial lines, restricting themselves primarily to whites.

ADHERENCE TO RACIAL MARRIAGE NORMS. The most outstanding feature of these data is that most couples honor the endogamous racial norms that pervade our society. This is particularly true for whites and blacks, with the endogamous percentage figure for each race close to 99 percent. One reason for the lower figures for races other than white or black is that these groups constitute such a small percentage of the overall population that it is difficult to find eligible mates within them (see Table 12–6).

**TABLE 12–5**
**Black Interracial Marriages**

| | |
|---|---|
| Total number of racially mixed couples, United States, 1970 | 328,690 |
| Total number of racially mixed couples involving a Negro spouse, United States, 1970 | 76,431 (23.3%) |

| | NO. | % |
|---|---|---|
| Negro husband and | | |
| a. White wife | 41,223 | (53.9) |
| b. American Indian wife | 2,835 | (3.7) |
| c. Japanese wife | 1,793 | (2.3) |
| d. Chinese wife | 316 | (0.4) |
| e. Filipino wife | 1,187 | (1.6) |
| f. Other race wife | 1,907 | (2.5) |
| TOTALS | 49,261 | (64.4) |
| Negro wife and | | |
| a. White husband | 23,566 | (30.8) |
| b. American Indian husband | 1,527 | (2.0) |
| c. Japanese husband | 137 | (0.2) |
| d. Chinese husband | 324 | (0.4) |
| e. Filipino husband | 712 | (0.9) |
| f. Other race husband | 904 | (1.2) |
| TOTALS | 27,170 | (35.5) |

**Table 12–6**
**Racial Endogamy in the United States, 1970**

| RACE | PERCENTAGES BY SEX | |
|---|---|---|
| | HUSBAND | WIFE |
| White | 99.7 | 99.6 |
| Negro | 99.2 | 98.5 |
| American Indian | 61.0 | 64.2 |
| Japanese | 66.8 | 88.6 |
| Chinese | 87.8 | 86.5 |
| Filipino | 72.8 | 66.5 |
| Other race | 54.9 | 62.7 |

### Heer's "Negro-White Marriage in the United States"

A second major question, usually asked immediately after, if not before, the one dealing with the extent of interracial marriage, is, How rapidly is the interracial marriage rate in the United States increasing? To answer this question we need data on rates over time—data that are virtually nonexistent. The only black-white intermarriage figures available are those for California (1955–59), Hawaii (1956–64), Michigan (1953–63), Nebraska (1961–64), New York State excluding New York City (1921–24) and Boston (1900–04). Therefore, because of these scanty data we can offer no really valid answer to the question of how rapidly the rate of interracial marriage is increasing. However, certain trends seem evident:

1. Heer (1966) stated: "It is apparent that the rate of Negro-white marriages for Negroes in New York State in the early 1920s was higher than the recent rates for either Michigan or California. On the other hand, the intermarriage rate for whites is higher in California and Michigan in the recent period than in New York State 40 years ago." Heer's explanation for these results was that there are higher proportions of blacks in the current populations of California and Michigan than in New York State some 40 years ago.

2. "The Negro–white intermarriage rate for Negroes in Hawaii during 1959–1964 was higher than any previously recorded in any part of the United States during any time period. The closest competitor to Hawaii in this respect is the city of Boston in the period 1900–1904. For Boston during this period the proportion of Negro grooms marrying white brides was 13.7 percent as compared to 20.3 percent in Hawaii in 1964. The proportion of Negro brides marrying white grooms was 1.1 percent as compared with 8.6 percent in Hawaii in 1964" (Heer, 1966). Heer suggests that while these figures for Boston in that period seem relatively high, they declined rather continuously, reaching lows of less than 5 percent for black males and declining to 0.7 percent for black females (see Wirth and Goldhamer, 1944). Using the data from Hawaii, Michigan, and Boston, Heer predicts that the black male–white female rates are the ones to observe. The black female–white male intermarriage rates seem to remain very stable.

3. Overall, Heer suggests that the rate of black-white intermarriage is increasing, but not enough to achieve any kind of substantial racial intermixture. Heer does not foresee any large intermingling within the next hundred years.

The most crucial question the sociologists can ask concerning the data on racial intermarriage is, Why are the rates changing the way they are? With the only data that exist on any kind of time dimension, Heer found increasing rates of black-white intermarriage. He offers two hypotheses that were supported by his data, and a third that is speculative at this point:

**TABLE 12–7**

**Married Couples of the Same Race**

| RACE | PERCENTAGES BY SEX | | | |
|------|---------|------|---------|------|
| | 1960 | | 1970 | |
| | HUSBAND | WIFE | HUSBAND | WIFE |
| *Total* | 99.6 | 99.6 | 99.7 | 99.7 |
| White | 99.8 | 99.8 | 99.7 | 99.6 |
| Negro | 99.0 | 99.1 | 99.2 | 98.5 |
| Other races (total) | 82.1 | 75.8 | 70.2 | 77.9 |
| American Indian | 82.5 | 75.8 | 61.0 | 64.2 |
| Japanese | 93.9 | 76.3 | 66.8 | 88.6 |
| Chinese | 85.9 | 89.2 | 87.8 | 86.5 |
| Filipino | 53.1 | 73.8 | 72.8 | 66.5 |
| All other | 69.4 | 56.6 | 54.9 | 62.7 |

SOURCES: U.S. Department of Commerce, Bureau of the Census, *U.S. Census of Population: 1960, Subject Reports, Marital Status,* Final Report PC(2) (Washington, D.C.: Government Printing Office, 1960), Table 10; ibid., *U.S. Census of Population: 1970, Subject Reports, Marital Status,* Final Report PC(2)-4C (Washington, D.C.: Government Printing Office, 1970), Table 12.

> *Hypothesis 1:* The greater the racial segregation within an area, the lower the ratio of actual interracial marriages to expected interracial marriages.
>
> *Hypothesis 2:* The higher the black status, the higher the ratio of actual to expected intermarriage rates.
>
> *Hypothesis 3:* (tentative) The higher the tolerance of the white community to interracial marriages, the higher will be the ratio of actual interracial marriages to expected interracial marriages.

It is quite easy to overestimate the percentage and number of mixed racial marriages in the United States. The actual volume is more meaningful when the percent of all husbands and wives of a given race who have married a spouse of the same race is examined. This constitutes a more refined index of racial endogamy. The data in Table 12–7 from the 1960 census and brief comment about them taken from Carter and Glick (1970) illustrate the overwhelming degree of racial endogamy currently found in this country. The 1970 data indicate that little change has occurred in racial endogamy in the 1960–70 decade. Carter and Glick summarized their findings as follows:

> By contrast with white spouses, who had nearly complete racial endogamy (99.8 percent), and Negro spouses, who had nearly as high a value

311

Eric Kroll from Taurus Photos

*The overwhelming majority choose dating and marriage partners of the same race.*

(99.0 percent), "other races" as a whole had a rate of only 79 percent. Wide variations existed in the figures for specific minor races, notably the quite high proportion of Japanese husbands married to Japanese wives (94 percent) and relatively high endogamy figures for both Chinese husbands and Chinese wives (86 and 89 percent, respectively); the intermediate values (around 75 percent) for wives who were American Indians, Japanese, and Filipinos; and the quite low values for Filipino husbands (53 percent) and wives of "all other" races (57 percent).

Wives had slightly higher racial endogamy rates than husbands among the white, Negro, and Chinese groups, and Filipino wives had a much higher endogamous rate than Filipino husbands. Husbands had substantially higher racial-endogamy rates than wives among the remaining groups—American Indian, Japanese, and "all other."

## SOME HOMOGAMOUS FACTORS AFFECTING CHOICE OF MARITAL PARTNER

Sociologists have traditionally made a conceptual distinction between factors that are of significant import in restricting marital choice (endogamous factors) and those that are less significantly important (homogamous factors). Homogamy refers to a similarity among the partners to a marriage with regard to age, residence location, previous marital status,

312

and social class. There are societal norms regarding the marriage of persons whose ages differ substantially. However, society is usually more willing to accept age difference than racial difference. The same is true when a divorcée marries someone who is single or widowed or when spouses come from different social-class backgrounds. In other words, the sanction applied by society for the violation of a homogamy norm is usually not as severe as when an endogamy norm is violated. In the sections that follow, pertinent data on homogamous factors that affect marital choice will be discussed.

## Age

Age has been and still is a prominent factor to consider in studying the marital selection process. Besides its obvious physiological meaning, every society attaches to age some psychological and sociological meanings that are related to the levels of industrialization, urbanization, and modernization in that society. In other words, how age is treated as a factor in marital selection is related to the society and its levels of development. In the United States several trends in the age and marital selection relationship should be noted.

1. The median age at first marriage has dropped over the last century. As the data presented in Table 12–8 indicate, the median age at first marriage in the United States (1890–1976) has dropped from 26.1 to 23.8 for males and from 22 to 21.3 for females. However, the modal year of first marriage for females is 18 (that is, more girls get married at the age of 18 than any other year of age). This should be expected since most states have laws requiring school attendance until a certain age and since a high-school diploma is now considered the very minimum education. In addition, the proportion of women going to college has been increasing, thus leading both to more married college students and to a slight increase in the age at first marriage.

2. The difference in age between bride and groom at first marriage has narrowed. One of the norms that seems to operate in most if not all societies is that the female should be younger than her husband. In the United States this norm is still in operation, but the available evidence indicates that the difference in ages has been decreasing.

Parke and Glick (1967) compared men and women who were 45–49 years old in 1966 to men and women who were 25–29 years old with regard to their age at first marriage. They found that the differences in ages at first marriage had declined considerably and that the trend was continuing.

3. The trend in teenage marriages was upward until the late 1950s, but during the 1960s was downward for women and may have been downward for men. Carter and Glick (1970) state: "For the men in their late forties in 1966, 9 percent had married under 20 years of age, and those in

313

**Table 12–8**
**Median Age at First Marriage in the United States**

| YEAR | MALE a | FEMALE | YEAR | MALE a | FEMALE |
|------|--------|--------|------|--------|--------|
| 1976 | 23.8 | 21.3 | 1958 | 22.6 | 20.2 |
| 1975 | 23.5 | 21.1 | 1957 | 22.6 | 20.3 |
| 1974 | 23.1 | 21.1 | 1956 | 22.5 | 20.1 |
| 1973 | 23.2 | 21.0 | 1955 | 22.6 | 20.2 |
| 1972 | 23.3 | 20.9 | 1954 | 23.0 | 20.3 |
| 1971 | 23.1 | 20.9 | 1953 | 22.8 | 20.2 |
| 1970 | 23.2 | 20.8 | 1952 | 23.0 | 20.2 |
| 1969 | 23.2 | 20.8 | 1951 | 22.9 | 20.4 |
| 1968 | 23.1 | 20.8 | 1950 | 22.8 | 20.3 |
| 1967 | 23.1 | 20.6 | 1949 | 22.7 | 20.3 |
| 1966 | 22.8 | 20.5 | 1948 | 23.3 | 20.4 |
| 1965 | 22.8 | 20.6 | 1947 | 23.7 | 20.5 |
| 1964 | 23.1 | 20.5 | 1940 | 24.3 | 21.5 |
| 1963 | 22.8 | 20.5 | 1930 | 24.3 | 21.3 |
| 1962 | 22.7 | 20.3 | 1920 | 24.6 | 21.2 |
| 1961 | 22.8 | 20.3 | 1910 | 25.1 | 21.6 |
| 1960 | 22.8 | 20.3 | 1900 | 25.9 | 21.9 |
| 1959 | 22.5 | 20.2 | 1890 | 26.1 | 22.0 |

SOURCE: U.S. Department of Commerce, Bureau of the Census, "Marital Status and Living Arrangements: March 1976," Series P-20, No. 306, January, 1977.

NOTE: Figures for 1960 to 1976 are for the United States and figures for 1890 to 1959 are for conterminous United States.

a Figures for 1947 to 1976 are based on Current Population Survey data supplemented by data from the Department of Defense on marital status by age for men in the Armed Forces. Figures for earlier dates are from decennial censuses.

their late twenties twice as many, or 18 percent, married under 20. The corresponding figures for women increased from 28 to 49 percent."

4. There has been a recent decline in very early marriages (under 18 years of age). Actually few men marry before they are 18 and few women before they are 16. Parke and Glick's (1967) survey found that only 2.9 percent of those males in their study who were 18 or 19 had married before they were 18. For women 30 to 34 years old in the 1966 survey, 23 percent had married under the age of 18 while only 15 percent of the females 18 or 19 had married under the age of 18.

There are several plausible reasons for the reduction in very early marriages: (1) There is a great emphasis on the critical importance of obtaining at least a high-school diploma. (2) Coupled with this is the further emphasis on going on to college or to a technical school if possible. (3) The continuing and prevailing norm that a woman should marry someone at least two years her senior has led to a shortage of potential spouses. The following statement by Akers (1967:908) indicates how the marriage squeeze is a function of the sex ratio, which itself was strongly influenced by the baby boom of the 1940s:

Consider, for example, girls born at the height of the postwar baby boom. There were 1.9 million born between July, 1946, and June, 1947. In recent years, girls have married boys who were two years older than they on the average. Yet there were only 1.5 million boys born between July, 1944 and June, 1945. Thus 400,000 women (21 percent of all girls in the baby boom cohort) would find it difficult to find husbands. Since these women may delay marriage in hopes of finding someone of a suitable age, eventually, they must marry a man of less appropriate age, or not marry at all. The dilemma faced by girls now (1966) reaching the age of marriage has been referred to as "the marriage squeeze."

An attractive female who is not hampered by physical or mental disabilities or who does not belong to a racial or ethnic minority or who is in a low or extremely high socioeconomic class would not have to consider the sex ratio problem. Some females who realize the problem generated by the sex ratio make application to predominantly male schools in the hope of increasing their chances for a good mate.

## Propinquity

One of the findings of family sociologists that is most difficult for students to accept is the idea that propinquity (physical nearness, usually referring to place of residence) is perhaps the most significant limiting factor in marital selection (see Catton and Smircich, 1964). College students see that many of their classmates come from different cities and even different states. Most of us are myopic enough to think that most people are like us, in college. This is not true, and the findings on propinquity as a factor in marital selection are a good example of how common sense is often not congruent with social facts.

Clarke (1952) for example found that over one-half of those persons who married in Columbus, Ohio, lived within sixteen city blocks of each other at the time of their first date. William Kephart (1972) neatly summarized the importance of propinquity in marital selection by stating: "Cherished notions about romantic love not withstanding, it appears that when all is said and done, the 'one and only' may have a better than 50-50 chance of living within walking distance!"

Katz and Hill (1958) developed a norm-interaction hypothesis to explain the propinquity findings. The assumptions of their theory are:

1. Marriage is normative, that is, cultural and group norms define for us the appropriate characteristics of a spouse.
2. Within normative fields of eligibles, the probability of marriage varies directly with the probability of interaction. It follows naturally that we marry those individuals with whom we have a chance not only to interact, but to interact at the least cost in terms of time, energy, and money.

315

3. The probability of interaction is proportional to the ratio of opportunities at a given distance over intervening opportunities. It also follows naturally that, other things being equal, one will not spend hours commuting to and from a person's house when there is, in much closer distance, an intervening opportunity for heterosexual interaction that is just as attractive.

## Social Class

Social class is a composite concept having at least three major components: education, occupation, and income. Centers (1949) and Hollingshead (1950) found that both men and women tend to marry within their social class; if they cross lines, it is between contiguous categories of social class. With regard to interclass marriages, Hollingshead found that men more often select a mate from a lower class than their own than do women. For some time in family sociology this was considered a general truism. However, Rubin (1968), in a study based on a national representative sample, found that only for the marriages between the professional managerial and white collar classes do women marry up more frequently than down.

The incidence of interclass marriages has been used in the past as an index of the rigidity or fluidity of American society. Observers of the American scene have felt that if interclass marriages did occur with some frequency, this was an indication that achieved status and upward mobility were still viable goals. A decline in interclass marriage was considered indicative of a static class system having ascribed status and little chance of upward mobility as by-products. However, what seems to be happening is a homogenization of society. That is, sharply distinctive class lines are blurring, and there is a convergence toward the middle-class style of life for everyone. In this situation small differences are overlooked, such as the marriage between the daughter of a college professor and the son of a plumber. The college professor has status because of education whereas the plumber has status because of his income. The two create a life-style that might be similar, and thus little conflict in what would have been a significant class difference twenty to thirty years ago. There is still a novelty to interclass marriages in which the partners come from class backgrounds that are vastly different. When the son of a Rockefeller marries a domestic servant, this difference is viewed as a significant interclass marriage.

## Previous Marital Status

Another homogamous factor concerns the previous marital status of the partners to a marriage. As Figure 12–2 indicates, single men tend to marry single women, widowers tend to marry widows, and divorced men tend to marry divorcées. There are no well-defined answers for the phenomena represented in Figure 12–2 other than the idea that people tend to marry

**FIGURE 12–2**
**Previous Marital Status of Brides and Grooms**

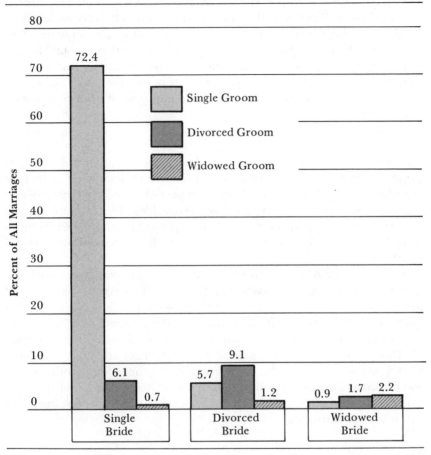

SOURCE: U.S. Department of Health, Education, and Welfare, *Remarriages: United States*, Series 21, No. 25 (Washington, D.C.: Government Printing Office, December 1973), p. 12.

those who are most similar to them in every possible way. Previous marital status is just another personal attribute that goes into the marital choice formula.

## COHABITATION

In 1972 (see Macklin, 1972) social scientists first took note of a mate/marital selection phenomenon, cohabitation, that has since generated a considerable amount of attention and speculation. The intense interest in cohabitation by family specialists was fueled by a general fascination with alternative life-styles and the possibility that cohabitation might be a "new" invention, a "new" stage in the tradition-bound courtship process.

A number of studies were conducted, almost all limited to small, nonrandomly drawn samples of white college students. The general conclusion in these studies (see Henze and Hudson, 1974; Peterman, Ridley, and Anderson, 1974) was that cohabitation was relatively widespread, involving perhaps as much as 20–25 percent of all college students. This led to fearful speculation by many parents and other self-proclaimed conservators of the American way that the American family and marriage were on the skids, almost ready for the grave or antique shop. The eulogy may have been premature; certainly it was pronounced prior to any solid research evidence.

CLAYTON AND VOSS STUDY (1977). The first and only nationwide study of cohabitation to date was based on personal interviews with 2,510 men born between 1944 and 1954. They were part of a study of drug use and were randomly drawn from Selective Service files. The response rate of 84 percent suggests that the data may be representative of the experiences of men who were twenty to thirty years old when they were interviewed in 1974–75.

Two questions were asked: (1) At present are you (a) married and living with your wife, (b) living as a partner with a woman you are not married to, or (c) are you not now living with a wife or partner? This question provided information on the *current prevalence* of cohabitation. The *lifetime prevalence* of cohabitation was obtained by the question: (2) How many times have you lived as a partner for six months or more with a woman you were not married to at the time? Six months period was chosen as the minimum duration to ensure that reported cohabitation experiences were more serious than short-term liaisons. The findings from this study are listed below:

1. Only 120, or 5 percent, of these men were currently living with a woman to whom they were not married. This is considerably below the figures suggested by the college studies mentioned above.

2. Some 444, or 18 percent, of the men in the sample had lived as a partner for six months or more with a woman to whom they were not married at the time. Thus, the lifetime prevalence of cohabitation approaches one in five. Of these, two-thirds had cohabited only once.

3. Only 14 percent of the 1,370 men who had been married once had *ever* cohabited, compared with 35 percent of the 107 men who had been married more than once. If cohabitation becomes an integral part of the courtship process, these data indicate it may be more prevalent for second marriages than for first marriages.

4. A substantial proportion of the 2,510 men interviewed were "at risk" of cohabitation—821 had never married or cohabited. Of the 2,066 men who had never cohabited, 1,152, or 56 percent, were currently married; 273, or 13 percent, were still living with their parents; and 627, or 30 percent, were living independently of both parents and members of the opposite sex. We can thus assume that eventually more than 18 percent of these men will have cohabited, given the divorce rate and the fact that some may cohabit prior to entering their first marriage.

5. Cohabitation was much more likely to have occurred for blacks (29 percent) than for whites (16 percent). This race differential suggests that cohabitation is not a new phenomenon. It is merely newly discovered among whites. It has evidently been a part of the marital milieu among blacks for some time.

6. Some 23 percent of the 394 men with less than a high-school education had cohabited compared to 17 percent of the 1,183 men who had attended college. This finding underscores the kind of tilted perspective one gets when one's observations are limited to white, middle-class college students.

7. Men who have cohabited are considerably more likely than those who have not to have used drugs, and to have used drugs more extensively than other men. This is true regardless of the drug class—alcohol, tobacco, marihuana, psychedelics, stimulants, sedatives, heroin, opiates, or cocaine. Further, those who have cohabited are more likely than those who have not to have been involved in other forms of deviance as well.

CONCLUSIONS ON COHABITATION. Overall, these nationwide data suggest that cohabitation (a) is not yet normative (that is, it is still considered somewhat deviant); (b) is more prevalent among blacks than whites and among noncollege than college-trained people; and (c) has not reached a peak in terms of prevalence.

It is too early to know whether cohabitation will become a new stage in the courtship process—a transitional stage that eventually will be experienced by most people on the way to the marital state. The emergence of cohabitation as a new stage would certainly be consistent with trends in sexual permissiveness and in later ages at first marriage. However, as the population gets older and as the proportion of the population under thirty gets smaller, it is possible that orientations toward important statuses, like marriage, will get more conservative. The fact is, we simply do not know what to expect.

Nevertheless, it's a good bet that cohabitation will become more prevalent, touching perhaps close to 50 percent of those under forty years of age by 1990. Also, cohabitation is much more likely to be an integral

319

part of mate selection for those with previous marital experience than for first marriages. If the median age at first marriage goes past twenty-five for both sexes, cohabitation will then likely become a rather common part of the marital selection process for more than half of the population.

## SUMMARY

This chapter has dealt with norms that affect marital choice, not with individual traits or characteristics or social perceptions or anything that could be construed as a social psychological phenomenon. These group norms exist at two levels. The first level is relevant to a large collectivity of persons. These are endogamous and exogamous norms; rules that determine the eligible from the ineligible marital partners as defined by groups. Any violation of endogamous or exogamous marital norms is considered a serious problem by the groups involved. On the second level are homogamous norms, which are more easily tailored to the historical and situational contexts in which marriageable persons are found. The homogamous norms are oriented toward the social demographic characteristics of potential marital partners. Any incongruence in socially significant sociodemographic traits between potential partners can lead to the operation of these norms. However, persistence on the part of the couple involved in such a situation can lead to the neutralization of these normative sanctions and an acceptance of the couple as an exceptional case.

At present, no general hypothesis incorporates both the endogamous and homogamous types of norms to explain marital selection as a macro-level phenomenon. In addition and quite unfortunately, the data that could be used as an empirical base for the development of such a theory are virtually nonexistent. Until more inclusive and better data are available, macro-level explanations of marital choice will be tentative and at a low level of abstraction.

The chapter that follows focuses on dating and marital selection from a social-psychological perspective. The quality of the data and the number of testable and tested theoretical propositions at the micro level are much better. At the end of the next chapter we can integrate the macro and micro approaches into a general theoretical model to explain marital selection in the United States.

## SOME POSSIBLE IMPLICATIONS

*Every society imposes structural constraints on who may marry whom. These are usually expressed through endogamous norms about mate selection that specify the most appropriate partner for a person as one who is of the same race, religion, and social class, and nearly equal in age. As our society undergoes change, what are some of the implications for mate selection from a macro perspective?*

*First, the average age at first marriage is likely to go up. Teenage marriages, so prevalent in the 1950s, will become a relatively rare occurrence. Second, as the birthrate continues to decline or remain stable at the replacement level, the number of males per 100 females (the sex ratio) in the marriageable ages may, for the first time in recorded history, go above 100. If this occurs, the long-standing trend of males marrying females who are younger than they are may reverse. In other words, by the year 2000, on the average, women may be marrying men who are younger than they are.*

*Third, as the visible differences among social classes diminish, social class may cease to be a viable endogamous norm in mate selection. Fourth, as institutionalized religion becomes a less potent force and as major Protestant groups continue to merge, endogamous norms tied to religious differences will be less viable constraints.*

*Macro-level endogamous norms will diminish in importance as our society moves toward greater homogenization.*

Frank Siteman

# 13

# DATING AND MARITAL-PARTNER SELECTION

*What functions does dating serve in modern society?*

*When and how are marital selection norms applied in the United States?*

*How can we account for this statement made frequently to husbands and wives: "You look enough alike to be brother and sister!"?*

*What are the forces that lead a man and a woman mutually to commit themselves to marriage?*

In the preceding chapter we focused on two types of macro-level norms governing mate selection—endogamous and homogamous norms. Both types of norms are used to determine whether potential marital partners are eligible or ineligible. We saw that endogamous norms, particularly with regard to race, are seldom violated (that is, less than 1 percent of all couples are married across racial lines). Although endogamous norms governing religious identification are not as rigorously applied, it is apparent that they still operate, though more effectively for some groups than for others.

Notwithstanding the persistent and idealistic rhetoric about how people have the freedom to choose whom they will marry, the data presented in Chapter 12 indicate rather clearly that homogamous norms are quite effective. Most people choose marital partners from the same social class, the same general age range, the same community, and the same previous marital status.

In this chapter we will focus on the dynamics of marital-partner selection—how people choose partners and why they choose one specific person from the field of eligible partners, given the endogamous and homogamous norms operative in our society. To outline some assumptions about the whole process, a combination of the developmental and symbolic interactional frameworks discussed in Chapter 2 are used as a base.

## ASSUMPTIONS ABOUT THE PROCESS

1. Marital-partner selection is not something that becomes salient at the onset of puberty or right after the first "real" date. The actual beginnings of marital selection occur during the first few years of life and continue consistently until a person marries.

2. Partner selection is unavoidably tied to the physiological maturation process and to the prevailing cultural definitions of age and adult in a society. Thus, in a society where the definition of adult for the male is age fourteen and for the female is the onset of puberty, marital selection is appropriate during the period other societies call childhood.

3. Marital-partner selection is, whether we in the United States like to admit it or not, very much tied to the prevailing kinship system in our society. In the United States, when a couple marries, the two members become a separate unit, conceptually a family of procreation, and they are usually a separate household physically. But they are also the crucial link between two families of orientation that were previously unconnected.

4. Since marriage involves, in most cases, the linkage of two families of orientation through a new family of procreation, parents are important others to consider at every stage of the partner-selection process. It is too easy to focus attention wholly on the two selectors and to ignore the fact that the standards and techniques they use to select each other are probably influenced, to a significant degree, by the entire socialization process going back to childhood.

5. All potential marital partners have group affiliations and are thus under the influence of reference-group norms that affect their selection of each other from the field of eligibles. These reference groups are extremely powerful in making or breaking a potential alliance for the individual members of the group.

6. Marital-partner selection has traditionally been an integral part of the life of any community. In a way a marriage reaffirms the future of the community and its various organizations and agencies. Extracommunity forces such as cultural norms and the government have had a major influence on partner selection in the United States by shaping the residential patterns of the population. These residential enclaves have tended to reinforce endogamous and homogamous norms by the isolation principle.

7. Last, marital-partner selection is something that happens between two persons, who as individuals go through various stages of experience until they become committed to each other in such a way that they marry. Although it is quite possible that this commitment process is never fully identical for any two couples, there are certain uniformities that can and will be discussed.

## A GENERAL CONCEPTUAL MODEL

### Major Concepts

A. The baseline of the model shown in Table 13–1 is chronological age, or years. The rationale is that marital-partner selection is not an experience or activity sprung on a young person at adolescence. It is a process extending from earliest childhood until marriage. The baseline has been divided into five major stages, more or less distinct and nonoverlapping. The stages are:

| | |
|---|---|
| I. Early childhood | Birth to six years of age |
| II. Predating | Six to junior high |
| III. Dating | Junior high to senior high |
| IV. Premarital | Usually eighteen to engagement |
| V. Engagement | Onset of engagement to marriage |

325

**Table 13-1**

**A Model of the Marital-Partner Selection Process in the United States**

| CONCEPTS AND FACTORS | STAGES OF DEVELOPMENT | |
| --- | --- | --- |
| | I. EARLY CHILDHOOD | II. PREDATING |
| A. Time period | Birth to 6 years | First grade to junior high |
| B. Socializers | Parents, older siblings | Parents, older siblings, other adults in particular institutions, reference group peers |
| C. Content of marital selection norms | Exogamous | Endogamous and exogamous |
| D. Sanctions for violating norms | Verbal | Verbal chastisement and withdrawal of affection or privilege |
| E. Processes Operative at the group level | Sex ratio, industrialization and urbanization, rigidity of class structure, type of family system in society | Rigidity of class structure and consequent residential segregation |
| F. Factors operative in the family situation | Size and quality of parent-child relationship | Available father model, younger siblings, mother working |
| G. Individual-level factors | Birth order, birth defects | Shyness, breadth of heterosexual interaction, need affiliation |

B. Since this model implies following a cohort of individuals from birth to marriage, it suggests that a key process is socialization. Thus the model must delineate the most salient socialization agents or *socializers* at each stage in the process.

C. The model suggests that the marital selection process operates smoothly because the socialization agents are able to inculcate certain types of norms in the population. By focusing on the varying *contents of marital-partner selection norms* for each stage in the marital selection process, one should be able to see (a) how an integrated and conforming

| III. DATING | IV. PREMARITAL | V. ENGAGEMENT |
|---|---|---|
| Junior high to end of participation in school culture | End of participation in school culture to engagement | Engagement to marriage or termination of engagement |
| Peers and reference groups, parents | Significant others, reference groups, parents | Close friends and acquaintances, parents, specialists |
| General homogamous, endogamous, and exogamous | Individual-centered homogamous, general homogamous, and endogamous | Highly individualized and specific for each couple |
| Withdrawal of affection and/or financial supports, forced expulsion from family or group | Personal pressure to conform to family or group desires | Subtle hints, strong pleas, threat-filled demands, removal from situation |
| Sociometric socialization into clique hierarchy in school culture | Propinquity and intervening opportunities | Rate of unemployment, cost of living, availability of housing |
| Age of parents, father work involvement, spread in ages of children, work of mother | Separation from family and degree of communication | Health, wealth, and intactness of family of orientation |
| Factors related to self concept | Physical attractiveness and loneliness | Psychological needs and drives, personality factors, attitudes and values |

view of the appropriate type of spouse is achieved and (b) what may account for dysfunctional choices of spouses.

D. A crucial feature of the study of norms is the type of sanctions and intensity of their application for following or deviating from the norms. The norms are, to some extent, only as effective as the value placed on the positive sanction as against the fear of receiving a negative sanction. This model suggests that the applicable sanctions, especially *sanctions for violating norms,* are different at each stage of the process, in correspondence with the norms operative at that stage.

E. The fifth set of variables in the model suggest that marital-partner selection always occurs within the context of a society and/or non-familial group or community. Processes operative at the group level, such as population density, urbanization and industrialization, and racial, ethnic, or socioeconomic segregation, are also relevant factors to consider.

F. The most influential social context over an extended span of years is a person's family. Certain *factors operative in the family situation* could have a decided bearing on partner selection. These might include family size, degree of authoritarianism present from adult figures, amount of time the father spends in the household during the formative years, and so on.

G. The last variable present in this model focuses on the *individual-level factors* involved in the selection process. These take into consideration such factors as size, birth defects, and/or personality traits.

## STAGES OF THE PROCESS

### Stage I: The Preschool Years

A. TIME PERIOD.   In the United States this is from birth to age six, or entrance to the first grade.

B. SOCIALIZERS.   The primary socializing agents during this period are the parents, older siblings if present, and other adults who though transitory in the life of a child, can and do significantly influence his or her social development.

C. CONTENT OF NORMS.   The marital-partner selection norms during this period are quite diffuse. However, the family does focus on exogamous norms such as the incest taboo. In addition, certain rudimentary marital roles are learned through role modeling, explicit teaching of the "proper" sex-related behavior (for example, "nice little girls don't do that"), and the incidental socialization that takes place through observation and "playing house."

D. SANCTIONS FOR VIOLATING NORMS.   Sanctions are used, not to punish actual violations of the norms, but to prevent possible future violations. During this stage of development the children are taught such things as which restrooms are for men and which are for women, and they are *verbally sanctioned* for behavior not appropriate for their sex.

E. PROCESSES OPERATIVE AT THE GROUP LEVEL.   The partner-selection process pervades the entire life of the individual up to marriage; there are also certain societal-level processes that will and do influence as a group the children who will later choose each other as marital partners. Among these are (a) the sex ratio; (b) the society's level of industrialization; (c) the degree of urbanization; (d) the rigidity of the class structure and the class into which the child was born; and (e) the type of family system.

F. FACTORS OPERATIVE IN THE FAMILY SITUATION.   Factors such as the size of the household, number of parents or parental substitutes present, degree of warmth present in the parent-child relationship, and the amount of contact between parents and child are operative in the family situation.

G. INDIVIDUAL-LEVEL FACTORS.   Factors such as the birth order, presence or absence of birth defects, physiological and mental capabilities at the "normal" level, and distinguishing birthmarks are individual-level factors considered.

## Stage II: The Predating Years

A. TIME PERIOD.   In the United States the period normally covers from entrance into the school system to somewhere in the junior high school years. The cut-off point for this stage is the introduction of dating by the cohort as a normative practice (that is, strong peer group pressures to date or be labeled a deviant).

B. SOCIALIZERS.   The primary socialization agents at this point of development are numerous. (1) The parents still control such essential resources as time available for leisure activities, freedom of physical movement, and money. The parents at this stage of the process use restrictions on resources as the primary tool of socialization. (2) In addition, older siblings can be of significant influence as role models for younger siblings since the older children may be actively involved in the dating process. (3) During the predating stage the conjugal family transfers the more formalistic socialization functions to particular others in other institutions of society such as the church, the school, and the mass media. (4) During the predating stage of development the peer-level reference group begins to exert a significant influence on most of an individual's actions.

C. CONTENT OF NORMS.   The marital-partner-selection norms at this stage of development are becoming particularistic rather than remaining diffuse. These norms are geared to the endogamous level and delineate the kinds of persons who would be appropriate or inappropriate as friends and associates (the latent meaning would be relative to marriage).

D. SANCTIONS FOR VIOLATING NORMS.   The sanctions for violating endogamous norms, with the manifest reference to playmates or friends, are usually verbal chastisement, the withdrawal of affection, and/or restrictions on movement and free time.

329

*By age thirteen or fourteen, young people may be taking their first painful steps in the process of marital-partner selection.*

E. PROCESSES OPERATIVE AT THE GROUP LEVEL.   In the predating stage the most significant extrafamily collectivities are the neighborhood and the school. Both of these collectivities are, in essence, segregated and thus restrict the field of eligible playmates and friends. Within both neighborhoods and schools strong endogamous norms and loyalty to the members of one's collectivity usually develop. The major group-level factor from stage I that is clearly operative at stage II is the degree of rigidity in the class structure. If the class structure is fairly static, then the endogamous norms are likely to be quite evident in both the residential patterns of segregation and the school system.

F. FACTORS OPERATIVE IN THE FAMILY SITUATION.   The primary familial variables operative in stage II are (a) whether the father is generally available or not for communication with his children and as a role model, (b) whether younger siblings make the mother somewhat inaccessible to her other children, and (c) whether the mother works and what degree of supervision is available after school. In addition, a young person's social class and the material objects associated with social class become extremely important factors in delineating, endogamously speaking, the "good" guys and girls from the "bad" guys and girls.

G. INDIVIDUAL-LEVEL FACTORS.   In the predating stage individual-level factors might be shyness, breadth of interpersonal and particularly heterosexual interaction, and such psychological factors as need affiliation and the need for achievement.

## Stage III: The Dating Stage

A. TIME PERIOD. In the United States the dating stage usually begins in the junior high school years, when heterosexual dating becomes a normative practice, and continues, for most young men and women, through to graduation from high school. It is quite possible in this stage for the marital selection process to terminate. For example, the dating couple could get married, the girl could get pregnant, and/or one or both could drop out of the school dating culture and marry. However, although substantial numbers of persons marry during or immediately upon graduation from high school, some time lag exists between the end of high school and marriage for the larger group.

B. SOCIALIZERS. Although parents still have a great deal of control over such things as the amount of leisure time available, money for recreation, and physical mobility, the primary socialization agents are peers and reference groups. The socialization that does occur is less structured; more frequently than not it is quite implicit and sometimes even accidental. Part of the strength of peer-group influence over behavior at this time is couched in the fact that the peer group itself can seldom be explicitly identified, nor can its rules be explicitly codified. The peer group socializes effectively even though the peer group is, at best, a frequently changing abstraction having few empirical referents.

*Dating, which first became established in the 1930s, has become an integral part of the marital-partner selection process in North America.*

Ken Heyman

C. CONTENT OF NORMS.  Although the particularistic-level endogamous norms are still operative, primarily discussed and enforced by parents and representatives of other institutions, the general homogamous norms are most important here. They become more salient than endogamous ones at this stage of development because of the following "facts of life": (1) Children are no longer children, but fledgling adults with adult appetites, desires, needs, drives, sizes, and many other visible as well as invisible characteristics. (2) Many of these emerging adults are at the decision-making point maritally, and homogamous norms are more pragmatically focused than endogamous norms. In other words, the principals involved in a potential marriage (that is, both individuals and their families) have to get down to "brass tacks." For example, an Italian family can accept a Polish girl (give up ethnic endogamous preference) because she is Catholic (a more important endogamous preference) and, more importantly, because she is from the same social class, is attractive and not pushy, and comes from a good family and neighborhood.

D. SANCTIONS FOR VIOLATING NORMS.  The adult-level others in a person's environment will be more upset by the violation of a particularly salient endogamous norm (that is, religious affiliation) than by the violation of several less salient homogamous norms (age and social class where the differences are not significant). However, the peer group will be more concerned with violations of the homogamous norms, since they are the ones responsible for setting the limits on these norms. The sanctions used by the adults are (a) threat to withdraw or actual withdrawal of affection and/or financial support, (b) forced expulsion from parental home, and (c) banishment from the conjugal and/or extended family. The sanctions used by the peer group are similar to these in some ways, but in other ways they are more subtle. The first tactic is embarrassment, then attempts to rationally talk a guy or girl out of it, and finally, threats of banishment.

E. PROCESSES OPERATIVE AT THE GROUP LEVEL.  The most important group-level process operative at the dating stage is what I would call sociometric socialization. The high-school social system is usually divided into cliques that are hierarchically graded according to prestige, which is dependent upon prevalence of certain valued homogamous characteristics. In other words, each clique defines the boundaries of the field of eligibles on the basis of the general homogamous norms of the community as reflected in the school subculture and also as a function of a clique prestige hierarchy indigenous to that particular school. The clique has a stake in which clique lines of distinction are crossed in dating situations.

F. FACTORS OPERATIVE IN THE FAMILY SITUATION.  Numerous factors inherent in the family situation could influence the partner-selection process at the dating stage: (1) The ages of the mother and the father are particularly relevant—for example, if the mother is going through menopause and is having a difficult time. (2) In upwardly mobile middle-class homes the father reaches a peak of involvement in his career when his children are getting most active in their dating. (3) If there is a substantial spread in the ages of the children in a household, the parents frequently unconsciously focus their attention on the simpler and less sensitive problems of the younger children. (4) Mothers past the age of child-bearing may start or continue a career interrupted by children.

G. FACTORS OPERATIVE AT THE INDIVIDUAL LEVEL. The individual factors of substantial influence at this stage of the process are primarily related to the self concept. These factors include physical and social attractiveness, shyness, a feeling of or lack of heterosexual experience, and/or a general and relative lack of self-confidence. Clearly associated with the individual self-perception factors are the needs for conformity and acceptance relative to peer reference groups.

## Stage IV: The Premarital Stage

A. TIME PERIOD. In the United States the premarital period normally runs from high school graduation, or whenever a person leaves the school dating culture, to the time when he or she becomes engaged. This stage can be left and returned to many times if engagements or their equivalent are broken.

B. SOCIALIZERS. The primary socialization agents in the premarital stage are partially determined by his or her residence. Parents can still exert a day-to-day influence on the life-style of their children. The peer group and certain normative reference groups are usually the crucial socializers. This is true whether the person lives at home or away from home, in the same community or in a separate area, is working, or is a student. Although the most important reference group is a crucial source of norms, perhaps even more important are significant others such as roommates, girl or boy friends, and similar models.

C. CONTENT OF NORMS. The norms in the premarital stage are still primarily homogamous. However, the content of these norms is somewhat more individual-centered than those operative at the dating stage. This is especially true if the persons involved are not part of a school culture. In other words, the marital-selection norms are centered in small normative reference groups or among significant others and are focused on the personality and/or physical characteristics of the potential spouses. The reference groups and significant others will apply specific homogamous norms rather than general ones. They are not concerned necessarily with the potential spouse's social class but with how well he or she will fit in with the group and with their member's life-style.

333

D. SANCTIONS FOR VIOLATING NORMS.   The sanctions applied for actual or expected violation of the marital selection norms are more personal and less formal at this stage of development. If a person chooses to date someone who is considered a bad choice, it is quite likely that the peer group or significant other will say it. In many cases they will try to separate the pair—"for their own good," of course. They will talk about the date's bad traits, ferret out insidious information from the past, and threaten banishment from the group if the norms are violated by marriage.

E. PROCESSES OPERATIVE AT THE GROUP LEVEL.   The primary forces operative at the group level are (a) propinquity and (b) intervening opportunities. The evidence is impressive that marital selection is strongly influenced by the opportunity for interaction, which is itself a function of physical proximity. Since marriage is considered a serious contract, it is seldom entered into quickly or without due consideration. Propinquity is virtually a necessary condition for marital selection. Intervening opportunities are what Erving Goffman would call an everyday fact. These are best illustrated by the lines from a recent popular song "If you can't love the one you want, love the one you're with." In effect, then, one is forced to choose a spouse from among those persons with whom one has the greatest opportunity to interact (propinquity), and, if there are equally attractive intervening opportunities for marital selection, one should or will choose the closer of the two potential spouses.

F. FACTORS OPERATIVE AT THE FAMILY LEVEL.   The family unit may exert a rather constant influence on mate selection at this stage of development if the person lives at home or in the same community (that is, if it is rather small). However, when the person is separated from the close scrutiny of his family of orientation, the familial influence on marital selection is operative through reminders of endogamous-homogamous norms in letters and phone calls. When a person chooses a potential spouse, he or she frequently brings the chosen one home to meet the family. At this time the family can give or withdraw approval. In most cases in which disapproval might be a definite option, the family will relent and accept the prospective in-law in order not to lose the son or daughter. This is the "grin-and-bear-it" rationalization.

G. FACTORS OPERATIVE AT THE INDIVIDUAL LEVEL.   This stage of development is dominated by two factors: (a) physical attractiveness and (b) loneliness or the need for companionship. The first is always operative since, if a young person is living away from home and perhaps away from normative reference groups, the initial pull factor is attraction. The second factor fits in quite well with the first. The distinguishing feature of the premarital stage is the separation of the person from a warm environment to one in which he or she has to fend for himself or herself, usually with few social anchors. Beauty is in the eye of the beholder, and loneliness and deprivation have been known to distort perception considerably.

## Stage V: The Engagement Stage

A. TIME PERIOD. The engagement stage varies considerably in the United States because of differential marriage ages by social class and because of the differing definitions of engagement. For some, engagement occurs during high school with marriage occurring either before graduation or immediately thereafter. For a considerable proportion of both sexes, engagement occurs after a period of "shopping" for the right spouse in the premarital stage. Engagement is defined as the publicly announced intention of becoming married at some future date. This stage covers the period from the announcement to the marriage. In some instances there is never a formal announcement of the engagement, but its existence is recognized by the potential spouses and their acquaintances. Should the engagement be terminated, as are about one-half of all first engagements, both partners return to the premarital stage.

B. SOCIALIZERS. There are many socialization agents available who are willing to give specialized information and guidance to the prospective marriage partners. Which ones are the primary agents depend to some extent on the ages of the prospective couple, their proximity and emotional closeness to parents, their ability to fend for themselves socially and financially, and the circumstances under which the marriage is contracted (voluntary versus less than voluntary incentives). If the parents are not available (particularly the bride's parents) or sought after for advice, the primary task of socialization falls upon close friends and occasionally upon specialists in the marriage trade. The socialization content here is pragmatic, instrumental, and in many cases decidedly nonromantic. The insurance agent wants to talk about making sure the new bride is not left a lonely and poor widow if her bridegroom dies on the honeymoon. The mother of the bride wants to make sure the bride did not forget anything important in packing her suitcase. Ministers, the nonfriend or relative agents likely to be participating in the socialization at this stage, are frequently more concerned with whether the marriage is "God's will" and that each knows what to do in the ceremony than with whether each seriously and rationally knows what he or she is about to do.

C. CONTENT OF NORMS. The norms operative in the engagement stage are illustrative of the concept of anticipatory socialization. The engaged couple is expected to display in its manner and demeanor the type of special relationship only young and idealistic lovers have. The norms are no longer universalistic. They are highly individualized and relevant for specific couples, not for all or even most engaged couples. The relatives,

335

friends, and acquaintances of the couple are observing the prospective husband/wife pair for their performances as a unique team. In other words, the norms for each prospective couple are tailored to their personalities and life-styles. They will be evaluated on the basis of their joint performance.

D. SANCTIONS FOR VIOLATING NORMS. The norms at this stage are centered on the ability of the prospective pair to convince their relatives and associates of the viability and compatibility of the relationship. Persons such as relatives and close friends and associates usually feel that they have a big stake in the relationship and a responsibility to help make, or perhaps break, the relationship. The performances required of engaged couples are closely watched and are almost always up front and at center stage. A faux pas or two are usually ignored or overlooked unless they are perceived by the audience (interested "helping" parties) as indicative of a poor marital choice. The norms then applied range from subtle hints to strong pleas, to threat-filled demands that the engagement be stopped or else, to virtual kidnapping. To paraphrase a little, hell hath no fury like prospective in-laws when they feel that their son or daughter has made a mistake.

E. PROCESSES OPERATIVE AT THE GROUP LEVEL. Since the engagement stage is usually terminated with a marriage ceremony, the most salient group-level processes seem to exist at the societal level. These processes affect the life chances of the couple should they marry and include such things as the rate of unemployment, the cost of living, availability of housing, and/ or wars and the draft. Although these factors seem far removed from a loving couple, they do affect the chances that an engagement will make it to the contract stage.

F. FACTORS OPERATIVE IN THE FAMILY SITUATION. The health, wealth, and conjugal intactness of the families of orientation of a prospective bride and groom are, in many cases, crucial factors to consider. Regardless of how things appear, and in connection with the materials presented on the extended kin network, the degree of potential support resources (both financial and otherwise) present in the families of orientation can and do affect decisions to marry or not to marry.

G. INDIVIDUAL-LEVEL FACTORS. In the final analysis, getting married is something that happens to two individuals—not to families of orientation or reference groups or communities. This being true, these factors would include such things as psychological needs and drives; personality traits; physical and personal-interpersonal strengths and weaknesses and tolerances; values, beliefs, opinions, and attitudes; role perceptions, expectations, and abilities to enact and perform certain role-tasks. All of these and many more individualized characteristics are crucial forces operative in the marital-selection process. They are most manifestly salient in the engagement stage because it is here that a man or a woman may preserve a unique status—never married. Once a person has crossed the engagement threshold to marriage, he or she loses a status that can never be completely regained.

## DATING IN THE UNITED STATES

Dating is probably one of the first major contributions that American society made to the repertoire of marriage and courtship practices currently available in the world today. Dating emerged shortly after World War I, primarily among college students. Although direct causal relationships cannot be plotted, some of the possible causes of the emergence of dating are (a) the extension of coeducation, (b) the continuing emancipation of women, (c) the general emancipation of youth from parental control, (d) rising standard of living, (e) increased amounts of leisure time, and (f) the increased mobility of our population, which is both a condition for and an effect of industrialization and urbanization. By the early 1930s dating was beginning to filter into the high schools, and it was firmly established there before World War II. By the early 1940s dating was becoming a rather common phenomenon at the junior high school level.

### Functions of Dating for the Individual

According to Winch (1962), dating in the United States serves the following functions for the individuals involved.

1. *Recreation.* Dating can be an end, in and of itself. It is an effective outlet for the use of leisure time and can be completely unrelated to the process of selecting a marital partner.
2. *Status-Grading.* Because of rather pervasive legal requirements, most young people are in school until age sixteen. It is in the school that they first begin to move from a reliance on ascribed status (derived from parents) toward achieved status (derived from their accomplishments in the school environment). The stratification network operative in each school has ascribed (freshman, sophomore) as well as achieved (yearbook editor, football captain) components. The dating patterns that emerge in a school are usually a reflection of the status network—a network that is time and place specific—but that can and sometimes does

337

follow a particular cohort of individuals throughout their lives in that community.

3. *Socialization.* Dating provides the members of both sexes an opportunity to learn the proper as well as the most efficient means of intersex and intrasex interaction within the boundaries of a rather complex stratification system.

4. *Personality Testing.* The dating process provides structured opportunities for an individual to discover his or her stimulus and attractiveness value to members of the opposite sex. In addition, dating provides the individual with an experimental situation in which he or she can test, modify, and expand his or her interpersonal communication techniques.

5. *Narrowing the Field of Possible Marital Partners.* Dating provides an individual with the opportunity for determining what type of person, in terms of personality and values, he or she would find most desirable as a spouse. The individual also discovers which of his traits and characteristics will be of most salience in attracting members of the opposite sex with the intention of marriage.

6. *Anticipatory Socialization.* Since, in our culture, dating is prerequisite to marriage, much time in dating is spent playing marital- and familial-type roles. The more serious the commitment between two individuals, the greater the intensity of the anticipatory socialization experiences.

As Winch pointed out, the dating relationship is not really an accurate rehearsal for married life, even though some anticipatory socialization does occur. Although dating is fun and recreation centered with the couple frequently engaging in a ritual of erotic teasing, much of the content of marital and familial roles involves instrumental and task-oriented activities such as making purchases, cleaning house, and taking care of children. Thus, the anticipatory socialization that does occur in dating is usually only partial and perhaps somewhat deceptive.

Besides serving the needs of the individuals participating in the courtship process, we should not ignore the functions dating serves for parents and for society. For example, because of dating parental responsibility is minimal for (a) providing structured and supervised recreation activities, (b) socializing the offspring in all types of marital and familial roles, (c) protecting the virginity of their offspring, (d) screening and choosing a marital partner for their children, (e) providing a dowry in the case of female children, and (f) having close contact and negotiations with the potential son- or daughter-in-law's parents. In other words, dating provides the parents and adult society in general with an easy way out of the responsibility for establishing new families of procreation.

338

## Waller's (1937) Rating and Dating Complex

In every specialty area of every science is some pioneer whose ideas and work serve as the base from which other researchers start their work. Willard Waller was one of the first sociologists to study systematically the dating phenomenon in the United States, and his ideas are still discussed as the baseline.

Waller's ideas were developed at Penn State, and his research, although at an appropriate level of sophistication for the 1930s, would probably be inadequate by today's standards. Perhaps because of this problem, Waller's original formulation of the "Rating and Dating Complex" has found little support in subsequent tests and has led to some controversy. Waller made a conceptual distinction between dating and courtship. Dating, he said, allows for a period of dalliance and experimentation between the sexes, and is an end in itself. Fun is the manifest or intended outcome. One component of dating that was important to Waller's ideas was what he called "thrills" or physiological stimulation and the release of tension. He felt that such things as dancing, drinking, attending the movies, using the automobile, petting, and necking were circumstances conducive to thrill-seeking. The thrills sought in dating were thought by Waller to vary, with males inclined to seek sexual gratification while the women were inclined to seek status by getting the more desirable man. Waller's assumption was that the dating relationship is a bargaining one. The man provides the satisfactions the woman wants from the date (that is, status derived through appearances at the right events and the appropriate expenditure of money for the occasion) while the woman is expected to reciprocate with relatively equal amounts of affection.

According to Waller the bargaining works out equitably in many if not most cases and does, in fact, become the basis of commitment between those involved that may eventually lead to marriage. However, when individuals bargain from unequal positions (that is, different resources), the basis exists for exploitation. Waller formalized his analysis of this competitive-exploitative dating pattern into the Rating and Dating Complex.

The Rating and Dating Complex purports to describe the classification of students according to their desirability as dating partners, who will pair off with whom, and the resulting patterns of interaction that occur on dates. The desirable dating traits of men, according to Waller, are fraternity membership, the possession of a car, adequate spending money, being a good dancer, dressing well, and being "smooth" in manners and appearance. There was a hierarchy of fraternities on the campus based on prestige, and according to Waller, dating centered around the fraternities. The general conclusion was that the more the appearance and manner of the man approximated the campus ideal, the higher his status, and the more money available to him, the more successfully he could

339

compete. The traits salient to a girl's desirability as a dating partner were (a) sorority membership, which was also ranked on the campus, (b) appearance and physical attractiveness, (c) being a sharp dresser and dancer, and (d) perhaps most important, the girl's popularity as a date. Waller felt that men competed for the privilege of dating the most popular girls. This was probably a function of the fact that there were six men to every woman at Penn State then. Also included in the desirable traits was what Waller called "the line," an idealization that was an essential attribute to being popular as a date.

The rating on campus was not limited to individual traits. Waller felt that there existed a status hierarchy on campus similar to the social-class system in society, and that every person was well aware of his or her place in that system. One's position was a composite of his resources of traits considered generally desirable. If he had money, a car, high fraternity status, and was good looking to boot, he was in a higher class than a male who was not good looking but possessed the other traits. The same structure was true for females.

Waller found a tendency for individuals with equal campus dating status to pair off—the homogamy principle in operation. These couples would have approximately equal bargaining positions, and each commitment by one essentially demanded a reciprocal commitment from the partner. Such relationships frequently progressed rather rapidly to courtship and marriage. This is an example of what happens when the rating and dating complex functions smoothly.

The system has some dysfunctional aspects of operation also. Not all persons date at the same level, and interlevel dating does occur. For example, when high-status males date down they are in a better bargaining position for sexual favors. This type of exploitation was called by Waller the "principle of least interest." Ehrmann's (1959) study at the University of Florida and Clayton's (1969) study indicate that this type of exploitation continued to operate in the 1950s and 1960s. Females with higher status dating down were in a position to bargain for less overt affection toward the lower status partner while they were searching for other, more desirable dating partners. This cross-class dating at Penn State was especially conducive for lower status females (with a six to one ratio in their favor) who could gain upward mobility and could bargain for lower levels of physical accessibility simply because there were so few females immediately available.

The courtship stage occurs quite naturally in the dating process, according to Waller. Courtship, he said, grows out of dating as one or both partners succumb to the temptation of emotional involvement. The principle of least interest continues to operate in the courtship stage since he or she who is least involved in continuing the relationship tends to control it. Waller felt that the process of involvement and commitment was irreversible; that is, once the reciprocal give and take had progressed to the point at which each has indicated to the other an emotional involvement, it was not possible to go back to a lower level of involvement.

Central to Waller's view of courtship is the concept of idealization. He believed that each partner, under the influence of mutual "lines," tended to create an idealized image of the other based on the presentation of the best self instead of the real self. Since the couple is "blind," outsiders see the couple more objectively and, assuming the relationship is a socially acceptable one, help to push the couple through the courtship stage to marriage.

## Empirical Attempts to Replicate Waller's Hypothesis

At least four studies have directly attempted to test Waller's hypothesis— Christensen (1958) at Purdue University, Smith (1952) at Penn State, Blood (1955) at the University of Michigan, and Reiss (1965a) at William and Mary College. All four studies used the questionnaire approach and forced-choice lists of dating traits and characteristics. Waller's original formulation was not supported by any of these tests. Three of these attempts at replication will be discussed briefly below.

SMITH (1952). Smith's study reported that many of the materialistically oriented values that Waller found prevalent and that afforded prestige at Penn State in the 1930s were no longer effective or used at the same school in the 1950s. However, he did find some evidence of an awareness of a rating-dating complex. He also found less exploitation, perhaps as a function of the drop in the sex ratio. In addition, Smith reported that dating was no longer distinguished from courtship. If the rating-dating complex was operative at all it was before serious involvement occurred.

BLOOD (1955). Blood used random samples of the male and female students at the University of Michigan to retest the dating and personality characteristics found to be operative in Wallers's study at Penn State. Blood's (1955:47) conclusion is a sufficient summary:

> In short, Waller's 1929–30 picture of a competitive-materialistic rating complex which governs casual dating but is dysfunctional in relation to mate selection seems to be questionable at every point so far as its applicability to 1953 Michigan undergraduates as a whole is concerned.... However valid Waller's picture may have been in 1929–30, it seems doubtful that it should any longer be assumed to be typical of rating and dating on American campuses.

From the same study Blood (1955) also found that the gap between desirable characteristics for a popular date and an eligible potential spouse had narrowed considerably from the 1930s, when Waller did his

341

study. He found that premarital dating and marital preferences were largely identical for both sexes. These characteristics were: (a) pleasantness and cheerfulness, (b) a sense of humor, (c) to be a good sport, (d) naturalness, (e) to be considerate, and (f) neatness in appearance. He did find, however, that although students were aware of a free floating set of campus values, only a small proportion of students subscribed to them in their own dating behavior. The values that are similar to Waller's list were most adhered to by fraternity and sorority members on the Michigan campus. In other words, he found significant variations in the dating values held by fraternity and nonfraternity students.

REISS (1965a). Reiss studied the serious dating relationships of 112 fraternity men and 133 sorority women at William and Mary College in Virginia. He got a prestige ranking of the fraternities and sororities on campus by using a random sample of all single students on campus. He proposed two hypotheses: "(1) serious as well as casual dating will be in line with a campus (class) system; (2) the campus class system and the related dating will reflect parental class background" (Reiss, 1971).

By examining who seriously dates whom among high-ranked "Greeks," low-ranked "Greeks," off-campus persons, and independents, Reiss concluded that there was a four-tiered campus class system consisting of (a) high-ranked "Greeks," (b) low-ranked "Greeks," (c) independent females, and (d) independent males. In order to see whether the campus class system was analogous to the societal class system, Reiss checked the occupational levels of the respondents' fathers. The data in Table 13–2 indicate the ranking of members of the campus groups by their parents' social class. Reiss concluded that the campus social system is in many ways merely a reflection of the societal social class system.

Reiss also made some attempt to relate his study to Waller's theory by explaining the reason some "Greek" organizations were rated high

**TABLE 13–2**

**Members of Campus Groups with Fathers in High-Status Occupations**

| GROUP | PERCENTAGE | N |
|---|---|---|
| High sorority | 80 | 25 |
| High fraternity | 69 | 13 |
| Low sorority | 60 | 10 |
| Low fraternity | 54 | 13 |
| Independent female | 42 | 31 |
| Independent male | 41 | 22 |

SOURCES: Ira L. Reiss, "Social Class and Campus Dating," *Social Problems, 13*(1965):198. Reprinted by permission of the Society for the Study of Social Problems and the author.

in prestige and others lower. The most frequently mentioned factors were the members' sociability, intelligence and maturity, and campus activities. The minor factors mentioned were quite similar to those major factors outlined by Waller: good looks, good manners, dress, and dancing ability.

## Summary

Thirty to forty years ago the United States was far less industrialized and urbanized, between world wars, on the verge of a depression, and less mature as a society, especially with regard to its moral standards and the allowable relationships between male and female. Women were nominally treated as second-class citizens, and the double standard was operative though probably disliked by many men and women.

Waller's theory was developed for a privileged class of persons who were in college in the 1929–30 school year, and the overall number of females afforded such an opportunity was quite small. Dating was distinctly separate from courtship then—a fact that is obvious from the topics of songs of that era. The dating and courtship values uncovered by Waller were also quite limited to fraternity and sorority females—and they were seemingly materialistic and exploitative by today's standards. It is not at all surprising that things have changed, given the increasing proportion of females in college, the increasing urbanization and geographical mobility made available through the availability of cars, the civil rights movement and its impact on the women's liberation movement. Now mate selection tends to be structured in terms of stages in the dating process—casual dating, steady dating, being dropped, being pinned, and engagement (DeLora, 1963).

## Early Dating and Early Marriage

BAYER (1968). As Bayer notes, there is no overwhelming consensus on whether early dating is conducive or detrimental to sound mate selection and heterosexual maturity. Most of the evidence has been on the negative side, but these data have usually been based on small samples drawn from relatively homogeneous populations. In addition, most of these studies have asked the respondents to reconstruct their dating experiences from memory. Bayer utilized data from 32,833 persons who were tested as twelfth-grade students and retested five years later. Thus, the data were longitudinal and were from an original stratified national sample of 73,000 high-school seniors. Bayer's data are not only longitudinal but also representative of the United States at large.

Bayer substantiated Lowrie's (1965) finding that early dating is more prevalent in the higher socioeconomic groups. For Bayer's sample, substantially over one-half of the boys and girls from the lower socioeconomic classes had not begun to date by the age of fifteen, whereas only about 30 percent of the boys and one-fourth of the girls from the higher socioeconomic classes had not started dating by age fifteen. Regarding the relationships between socioeconomic status and marriage age, two-fifths of both sexes in the lower socioeconomic status categories married early compared to only one-fourth of the boys and one-fifth of the girls from the highest socioeconomic-status levels marrying early. In his conclusion, Bayer[1] notes:

> One of the most consistently demonstrated findings in family research has been that of a strong relationship between early marriage and poor adjustment in marriage. Those who have experienced early marriage are considerably more likely to experience greater marital discord, including less marital satisfaction and more marital dissolution, than are those who marry at a later age (see Inselberg, 1961; Udry, 1966; Glick, 1957; Bauman, 1967). It is also those in the lower socio-economic strata who experience the greatest marital disruption (see Hollingshead, 1953, 1966; Bernard, 1966; Udry, 1966, 1967)....
>
> In light of these findings, the results of this present study yield questionable conclusions with regard to the ultimate relationship between early dating and marital outcomes. Early dating is related to early marriage, which implies greater marital instability; but early dating is also more prevalent among those from higher socio-economic backgrounds, where subsequent marital instability is generally less frequent....
>
> A more compelling conclusion from the current data is that the age of commencement of dating is largely *unrelated* to any particular future marital outcome. Rather it is the *length* of the dating experience prior to marriage which may have a crucial impact on subsequent outcome. Such a hypothesis is consistent with the fact that those in the lower socio-economic strata begin dating later, but have a shorter hiatus from commencement of dating to marriage and experience greater marital instability than do those from higher socio-economic groups. This hypothesis is also consistent with the prevalent theory of dating, viz., dating is an educational experience through which the skills required for valid marital selection and personal growth necessary for sufficient "marriage readiness" are cumulatively acquired over time.

## HYPOTHESES AND THEORIES

There have been more attempts at theory development in the marital-partner-selection area than in any other topic of concern for sociologists studying the family. Almost all of these attempts have been at the individual or social psychological level of analysis with some but not much emphasis on group or societal factors. The theories discussed in this section are representative but not inclusive of all such attempts. As yet, there

---

[1] Alan E. Bayer, "Early Dating and Early Marriage," *Journal of Marriage and the Family 30*(1968):628–32. Reprinted by permission of the National Council on Family Relations.

is no consensus among sociologists as to the most adequate approach, although there does seem to be some emerging consensus on what are the major concepts and factors to consider.

## Parental-Image Hypothesis

The parental-image hypothesis grew out of psychoanalytic literature and probably American folklore. With its base in the Oedipus and Electra complexes of Freud, the basic assumption of this hypothesis is that men and women seek marital partners who are substitutes for their parents of the opposite sex in physical appearance and temperament. Occasionally, some striking resemblance is noted between a man's wife and his mother or a girl's husband and her father—but the resemblance is probably as explicable in other terms as in parental-image substitution. As one author states, "While it admittedly would seem reasonable to expect parent images to either encourage or discourage a person marrying someone like his parent, no clear evidence has been produced to support the hypothesis" (Eckland, 1968).

## Value Hypothesis

The basic assumption of the value approach is that marital partners are chosen on the basis of similarity of values and/or beliefs. The major proponent of the value hypothesis also believes that endogamous or homogamous factors such as race, religion, and social class operate largely as a function of values. For example, a person may wish to marry someone with the same religious affiliation because intrafaith marriage may be a very important value in and of itself. The value theory is not without empirical support, at least general support. Numerous studies do show that married and engaged couples generally have far more consensus on various matters than do randomly matched couples. This seems to be true on highly specific as well as highly generalized (such as economic and aesthetic) values and beliefs. However, it is not convincing that values are equally salient at all stages in the courtship process, or why and where this salience of value homogamy changes. It is too easy to take married or engaged couples (groups in which selection has already occurred) and compare them on middle-class oriented paper-and-pencil tests and then to note the degree of consensus. Unfortunately, these are the types of data used most readily as support for the value theory.

## Complementary-Needs Theory

No other social-psychological theory of marital selection has generated as much controversy as the complementary-needs theory of Robert Winch (1958), which begins with the observation that marital selection has been shown to be predominantly homogamous with regard to age, race, religion, social class, education, residence, and previous marital status. According to Winch, these variables merely specify the field of eligible spouses—they do not account for the actual selection within the field of eligibles.

The basic hypothesis of the complementary-needs theory is: "In mate selection each individual seeks within his or her field of eligibles for that person who gives the greatest promise of providing him or her with maximum need gratification" (Winch, 1967).

Since most of the criticisms of the complementary-needs theory have focused on the methodology used by Winch, it might be beneficial to review his research in some detail:

SAMPLE: Winch selected twenty-five married undergraduate couples at Northwestern University in 1950. None of these couples had children, and all had been married less than two years, 50 percent less than one year.

RESEARCH PROCEDURE. The first research encounter was a "need interview" which was based on fifty open-ended questions. Each question was designed to assess the intensity of the needs or traits (that is, the strength of each need) and to find out how the respondent went about obtaining gratification for a need or expressing a trait. The needs utilized by Winch (1958:90)[2] were derived from the work of Henry A. Murray (1938:123–124). The second interview focused on the respondent's perceptions of his or her relationships with parents, siblings, and peer groups throughout his life. The interest was in how the subject saw these relationships as being related to his psychic and social development. The third procedure involved the use of the Thematic Apperception Test, which asks a person to tell a story about an ambiguous picture. For each respondent, these three sets of information were examined and rated by two or more trained analysts.

Winch hypothesized two types of complementariness: type I, in which the same need is gratified in both spouses, A and B, but at different levels of intensity. If A is high on need X, then B will be low on that need. Thus, the interspouse needs would be negatively correlated; and type II, in which different needs are gratified in the spouses A and B. For example, if one spouse is high on nurturance (giving), the other spouse will be high on succorance (dependent or receiving). The interspouse correlation here could be either positive or negative.

From the thirteen needs listed by Winch, two dimensions seemed to emerge: (a) nurturance receptivity, or a psychological disposition to give and to receive; and (b) dominance-submissiveness. The statistical tests of the hypothesis by Winch indicated that the hypothesized direc-

2 Robert Winch, *Mate Selection: A Study of Complementary Needs,* New York: Harper and Row Publishers, Inc., 1958, p. 90. Used by permission of the author.

| NEED | DEFINITION |
|---|---|
| Abasement | To accept or invite blame, criticism, or punishment; to blame or harm the self. |
| Achievement | To work diligently to create something and/or to emulate others. |
| Approach | To draw near and enjoy interaction with another person or persons. |
| Autonomy | To get rid of the constraint of other persons; to avoid or escape from domination; to be unattached and independent. |
| Deference | To admire and praise another person. |
| Dominance | To influence and control the behavior of others. |
| Hostility | To fight, injure, or kill others. |
| Nurturance | To give sympathy and aid to a weak, helpless, ill, or dejected person or animal. |
| Recognition | To excite the admiration and approval of others. |
| Sex | To develop an erotic relationship and engage in sexual relations. |
| Status Aspiration | To desire a socioeconomic status considerably higher than one has. (A special case of achievement) |
| Status Striving | To work diligently to alter one's socioeconomic status. (A special case of achievement) |
| Succorance | To be helped by a sympathetic person; to be nursed, loved, protected, indulged. |

| GENERALIZED TRAIT | DEFINITION |
|---|---|
| Anxiety | Fear, conscious or unconscious, of harm or misfortune arising from the hostility of others and/or social reaction to one's own behavior. |
| Emotionality | The show of affect in behavior. |
| Vicariousness | The gratification of a need derived from the perception that another person is deriving gratification. |

tions were supported and that the data were adequate to support the theory but not overwhelming.

Among the number of attempts to criticize, expand, or eliminate Winch's complementary-needs theory is a most thorough attempt by Rosow (1957), whose four criticisms were: (1) It is not clear whether the needs were operative at the overt behavioral level or at the covert or even subconscious levels. (2) Winch's theory does not take into account the possibility that these needs are gratified outside of the marital dyad. (3) The theory does not explicitly provide criteria for deciding which needs are complementary and when. (4) In many cases similarity of need and intensity of the same need may be as functional to the marriage as complementarity.

347

## Kerckhoff-Davis (1962) Filter Theory

Kerckhoff and Davis were interested in testing both the value consensus and the complementary needs theories with the assumption that they might operate at different stages in the courtship process. The researchers chose a sample of student couples who were engaged, pinned, or seriously attached in October. These same couples (ninety-four in all) were again tested in May. The dependent variable was the degree of progress toward a more permanent union. In May the couples were asked if, since October, they were closer to, farther from, or about the same with regard to a more permanent type of commitment. The degree of value consensus was assessed by asking each respondent to rank ten standards by which marital success could be measured. The degree to which the ranks given these standards were similar was an index of value consensus. Need complementarity was assessed by William Schutz's (1958) Firo-B Scales. These are six scales with 9 items each, and each scale is concerned with what Schutz calls "inclusion," "control," and "affection." Each respondent is asked to complete the scales as he or she would desire to have others act

*The wedding marks the official end of the marital-partner selection process and the beginning of the marital-adjustment process.*

Cary Wolinsky, Stock, Boston

toward him or her or how he or she would like to act toward others. These two directions are called "wanted" and "expressed." A control variable was the total length of association of the couples, long term (eighteen months or more) and short term (less than eighteen months).

The Kerckhoff-Davis hypotheses were: (1) A degree of consensus is positively related to progress toward a permanent union; and (2) A degree of need complementarity is positively related to progress toward a permanent union.

Kerckhoff and Davis found that the couples in their study had already limited their field of eligibles by using such attributes as age, religion, and social class, but they were far from having limited it with respect to value consensus. The two researchers concluded that there are various "filtering" factors operating during the mate-selection process. The social attributes presumably operate at an early stage, but values and needs are more clearly operative later on. Kerckhoff and Davis are explicit in stating that this is not a continuum going from attribute similarity through value consensus to need complementarity. What they do say is that for those couples who survive despite lack of value consensus, need complementarity seems to be the cohesive that holds them together.

Kerckhoff and Davis indicated three ways that their research added to the study of the mate selection process: (1) The research added support to both the homogamy and complementary needs theories and tentatively posited the relationship between these two theories during the courtship process. (2) By using a longitudinal study design (that is, studying the same individuals over time) Kerckhoff and Davis were able to show that need complementarity does make a difference in the actual selection process. (3) This study was the first in which paper-and-pencil measures pointed to a significant contribution of need complementarity in the selection process. Overall, it might be said that the filter theory approach of Kerckhoff and Davis is a major study of mate selection, one that will be seen historically as an important transition between a groping stage and a refinement stage in the study of the process of mate selection.

## Murstein (1970) S-V-R Theory

Murstein's basic assumption is that marital-partner choice in the United States is relatively "free." It is the individual's decision to marry or not to marry. Like Kerckhoff and Davis, Murstein (1970) constructed a processual stage theory that he labeled stimulus-value-role or S-V-R to explain marital choice. Rather than quoting all nineteen hypotheses, I have summarized the core ideas of the theory as follows:

1. STIMULUS STAGE. Murstein assumes that persons who choose each other as marital partners must be initially attracted at a physical level. In a

349

"taking the role of the other" sense, each assesses his or her qualities and how they measure up to those of the other. Then, in what he calls pre-marital bargaining, Murstein suggests that the assets and liabilities of each partner are tallied in a cost versus reward ledger to determine if the relationship should be continued. This, according to Murstein's first hypothesis, accounts for the better than chance similarity of couples with respect to physical attractiveness.

2. VALUE STAGE.    The second stage of the S-V-R theory is not dissimilar to the key link in Kerckhoff and Davis's (1962) filter theory. Murstein suggests in hypothesis 2 that individuals considering marriage will be quite similar in their ranking of the following six values: (a) conventionality, (b) conservatism, (c) importance of physical attractiveness in others, (d) moralistic, (e) concern with philosophical problems, and (f) commitment to intellectual activities.

3. ROLE STAGE.    The complexity of the third stage of Murstein's theory is seen in the fact that it covers hypotheses 3 through 19. There are five subsections of the role stage and each will be discussed separately.

a. ROLE FIT.    Three central concepts are utilized in the three hypotheses that fall under the heading of role fit. The first of these is self-acceptance or self-esteem. Murstein suggests that couples with high self-acceptance are more likely to view their partner as similar to them than are couples wherein one or both have low self-acceptance. The second concept introduced here by Murstein is courtship progress or movement toward marriage. The third concept, perceptions of partner's self and ideal self and conceptions of ideal-spouse, is directly related to the idea of courtship progress. Murstein hypothesizes that couples who make the most satisfactory progress in courtship are those who are able accurately to perceive the partner's self and ideal-self even during the earlier stages of relationship. In addition, the greater the congruence between an individual's conception of an ideal-spouse and his or her perception of the partner, the greater the likelihood of positive courtship progress.

b. PERSONAL ADEQUACY.    There is some overlap between this section of the role stage and the section on role fit discussed above. Here Murstein is suggesting that individuals choose partners who are similar to them in self-acceptance and whose level of neuroticism is also similar. He points out that couples with dissimilar levels of neuroticism will make less satisfactory courtship progress than couples who are of comparable neuroticism. The fourth hypothesis in this section on personal adequacy posits that "high self-acceptance individuals are more likely to perceive their partners as approaching their concept of ideal-spouse than are low self-acceptance individuals" (Murstein, 1970:474).

c. SEX DRIVE. Murstein suggests that men with a high sex drive are generally less accurate than men with a low sex drive in their estimate of the partner's self-conception and in how the partner views them. In addition, he posits that couples wherein the man has a high sex drive will show less courtship progress and role compatibility than couples wherein the man's sex drive is low. However, according to Murstein, women making courtship progress will manifest a higher propensity for orgasm than will women making poor courtship progress.

d. THE GREATER IMPORTANCE OF THE MAN IN COURTSHIP. The key point made by Murstein in hypotheses 14 through 17 is that good courtship progress is more dependent on the woman's confirmation of the man's self and ideal-self concept than of the man's confirmation of the woman's self and ideal-self concept. In other words, women making good courtship progress will be more accurate in predicting their partner's selves and ideal-selves than women making poor courtship progress.

e. CHRONOLOGICAL SEQUENCE OF STAGES. In the last two hypotheses of the S-V-R theory, Murstein suggests that the stimulus and value-consensus factors should not differentiate between couples making good and poor courtship progress when progress is assessed during the role stage of the relationship. He sees three stages as essentially different phases of the march to marriage, linked only because they are part of the same relationship. Thus, the stimulus and value stages provide little input into the decision to marry or not marry at the role stage of courtship.

## Criticisms of Murstein's S-V-R Theory

All nineteen hypotheses of Murstein's theory received at least moderate support from extensive data from ninety-nine couples who were engaged or going steady. These subjects were paid to take a series of tests and answer questionnaires including the Edwards Personal Preference Schedule and Murstein's Marital Expectations Test, and nineteen of the couples were given the Baughman modification of the Rorschach and Thematic Apperception tests at one point in time and six months later.

Several criticisms of Murstein's theory and the test of it are as follows: (1) The sample was certainly atypical in that it consisted primarily of college students in New England. (2) No indication was given of the homogeneity of the couples by such social attributes as religion, age, socio-economic status, or race. (3) If the terminology of the hypothesis is indicative of anything, some of the hypotheses were formulated post hoc (that is, after the data were gathered). (4) The time for courtship progress was six months. No indication is given as to how long these couples had known each other, and perhaps six months is an inadequate period of time to measure courtship progress. (5) There is an indication by Murstein that

351

these are three distinct and nonoverlapping stages. It is difficult to fathom physical attractiveness declining in importance as the relationship develops to the "role" stage since the physical-sexual role in marriage is a crucial one. (6) It is difficult to say that better courtship progress is made by females with a higher average orgasm rate because the sample is small, perhaps homogeneous, and nonrepresentative. The same kind of criticism applies to sex drive. What is it, and how was it measured?

In other words, Murstein's theory, although impressive in its complexity and thoroughness, is conceptually quite similar to the filter stages theory of Kerckhoff and Davis. The idea that couples are mutually attracted to each other physically, through interaction they then determine value consensus, and then through role playing they achieve some degree of role compatibility is logical. But no data are presented on couples as they are meeting each other at stage I. No data are available on dropouts—couples whose engagements are broken at the various stage levels. Such data are crucial to a better evaluation of the S-V-R theory of marital choice.

## CONCLUSIONS

In Chapters 12 and 13 we dealt with the complex phenomenon of marital selection. Chapter 12 reviewed the influence that society has on the process of choosing a mate through endogamous and homogamous norms. Everyone, even in a society like ours, in which the freedom to choose is rather pervasive and permissive, is constrained by norms that say you must select someone from the same race and religion, the same social class and age range, and a similar previous marital status. The consequence of endogamous and homogamous norms is that the field of eligible partners is actually much smaller than infinity.

In Chapter 13 a number of other homogamous norms and theories of marital selection that focus on the rather specific and individualized characteristics we use to determine who will be our marital partner were covered. Figure 13–1 suggests that numerous pressures work toward making marital selection a rational instead of an emotional experience.

Because love is considered an integral part of the formula used in determining the choice of a marital partner, Reiss's (1960a) wheel theory was adopted to depict the mate selection process. Mate selection is seen as a process by which two people with numerous opportunities for choosing mates move from a point of no commitment to a state where both are mutually committed. Essentially agreement can be made with Murstein's (1970) S-V-R model, in which stimulus leads to a recognition of attitudes-value similarity subsequently leading to a commitment to marry that is anchored in role compatibility. An important part of this sequence is the increasing degree of involvement in expressing a commitment to the other physically (Figure 13–1).

**FIGURE 13–1**
**A Commitment-Wheel Model of Marital-Partner Selection**

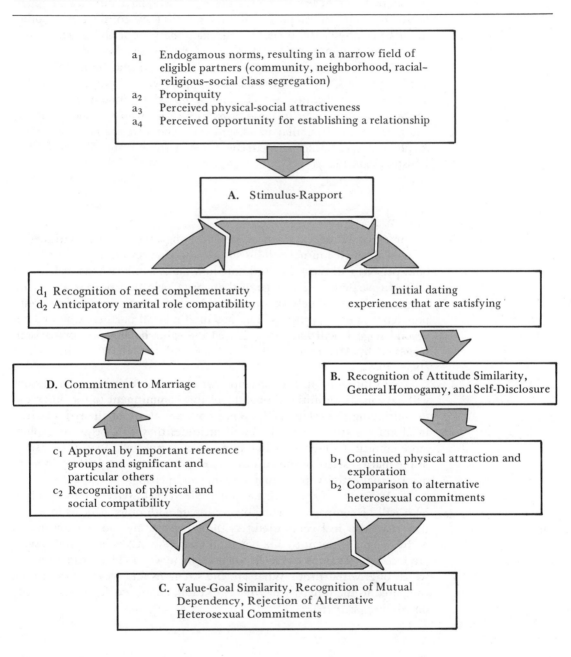

## Part A

It is axiomatic that few if any couples marry who have not had an opportunity to establish rapport and find out if they consider each other stimulating physically, socially, and emotionally. But this essential first step in the commitment wheel model of marital selection is determined by each of the constraining factors ($a_1$ through $a_4$) that limit the field of eligible partners. We tend to establish rapport with stimulating potential mates primarily because we are almost forced to choose from among persons who are living in close proximity to us, who are endogamously and homogamously similar to us, and with whom we are relatively equal in physical and social attractiveness (see Berschild and Walster, 1969; Walster et al., 1969).

## Part B

If our early dating experiences are satisfying and rapport continues to develop through mutual self-disclosure, the chances are fairly good that both persons will recognize and note how many similarities exist between them. In particular, this stage of the marital selection process will facilitate an exchange of beliefs, attitude and value orientations, and interests, preferences, and aspirations. The potential marital partners who make it beyond stage B will have experienced the value homogamy comparisons suggested by Murstein (1970), Kerckhoff and Davis (1962), and Winch (1958, 1967).

By this time in the development of the relationship both persons will have made an initial though revokable commitment to the other and to continuing the relationship. Since both are aware of their similarities in abstract matters like values and attitudes they will begin to explore more empirical similarities like physical attractiveness. It is at this stage of the marital selection process that most potential mates will begin more overt sexual activity, particularly kissing and petting.

In many cases the pair has not attained exclusivity in dating. Thus, both will be comparing their potential mate with other persons to whom they may also feel committed. As these persons are moving toward an exclusive commitment to one potential mate (Part C) some hard decisions are faced (for example, Which potential mate will I choose to retain and which ones will I drop? What are the strengths and weaknesses of each compared to the others? Am I ready to think about settling down to only one dating partner?).

## Part C

By this stage in the marital selection process the two persons recognize a feeling of mutual dependency and are willing to reject alternative heterosexual commitments. This is the engaged-to-be-engaged stage of the courtship. At this juncture both partners begin to delve more deeply into the extent to which they are mutually similar in values and goals.

As discussed in Chapter 9, an important facet of this part of marital selection is the integration of the potential mates into each other's reference groups. Each partner usually seeks approval of the budding relationship by their close friends and, in most cases, by their parents. In addition, the mutual dependency commitment heightens the physical and sexual interaction of the pair. They explore more fully their social and physical compatibility.

## Part D

By now the couple has enough data gathered to make the commitment public and an announcement of their intentions to get married (that is, engagement). A mutual recognition is that each is capable of satisfying the other's needs, and the couple begins the process of anticipatory marital role playing. They may start looking for furniture for a honeymoon apartment; and all of the other aspects of marital role playing, including sexual intercourse, may occupy their time and energies.

## Lewis (1973): Formation of a Premarital Dyad

The model and process depicted in Figure 13–1 are not markedly different from a model developed by Robert Lewis of Arizona State University. Lewis listed the following six ways of enhancing the interpersonal developmental process, leading to formation of a premarital dyad:

1. Perceiving *similarities* in each other's:
   a. sociocultural background
   b. values
   c. interests
   d. personality
2. Achieving *pair rapport,* as evidenced by a pair's:
   a. ease of communication
   b. positive evaluations of each other
   c. satisfaction with the pair relationship
   d. validation of each person by the other
3. Achieving openness between partners through *mutual self-disclosure.*
4. Achieving *role-taking accuracy.*
5. Achieving *interpersonal role fit,* as evidenced by a pair's:
   a. similar personalities
   b. complementary role
   c. complementary need

355

6. Achieving *dyadic crystallization,* as evidenced by a pair's:
   a. progressive involvement
   b. functioning as a dyad
   c. boundary establishment
   d. commitment to each other
   e. identity as a couple

## *Summary*

Lewis's approach is primarily social psychological and reifies the wheel theory of love developed by Reiss (1960, see Chapter 9) and the Stimulus-Value-Role model of marital selection developed by Murstein (1970). Along with the model in Figure 13–1, all these attempts to understand mate/marital selection suggest: (a) that the process goes through recognizable stages of development; (b) that important hurdles must be cleanly cleared, one-by-one (for example, rapport, self-disclosure, and so forth); (c) that the marital selection process can get bogged down at any step or stage and often is terminated completely; and (d) that if one doesn't succeed the first time, he or she will try again and again until the marital selection process is completed and translated into the marital interaction process.

Suffice it to say that participation in the marital selection process is a meaningful, fulfilling, and exciting stage in the life cycle. A decision to marry is one of the most important and significant events all of us ever encounter. The dynamics of the process are so complex that perhaps social scientists will never be able to capture in a theoretical model all or even most of the concepts and variables that go into the marital selection equation. But, like the process itself, such an exercise is a very rewarding endeavor.

## *SOME POSSIBLE IMPLICATIONS*

*What can be anticipated about dating and marital selection from a social-psychological perspective in the last quarter of the twentieth century? What are the changes that may occur in the courtship process? What will the process of marital selection be like for our children—how will it differ from the process we have used to select our marital partners?*

*Will love become a less important precursor and determinant of marital selection as a larger proportion of couples begin to live together as a part of the marital selection process? Or will love gain an even greater significance as couples in the future are able to determine prior to marriage their sexual and marital role compatibility? Will an increase in knowledge about personality matching lead to a situation where almost all couples will make a final choice on the basis of computer analysis?*

*Will those of you who test marital compatibility by cohabitation prior to marriage be willing to tolerate or encourage your children to do the same when they are ready to get married?*

*Dating, courtship, and marital selection processes are undergoing major changes in the postindustrial world. What may the marital selection criteria and process be like in the year 2000?*

# PART IV

# THE DYNAMICS OF MARRIAGE

Richard Kalvar, Magnum Photos, Inc.

# 14

# MARITAL INTERACTION

*What are some of the forces that shape the interaction of a man and a woman?*

*How does a "skeleton in the closet," when found, affect marital interaction?*

*What, if anything, is unique about marital interaction?*

*How do culture and society affect marital interaction?*

Marriage in the United States is pre-eminently an announcement of a social commitment. It is a public happening—the establishment of a legally and socially sanctioned sexual relationship that can legitimately produce children. But, it is more than that. It is the rite of passage between one status and role and another—the culmination of the courtship process we examined in Chapters 9–13. Few if any American young people go into marriage without a declaration of love. This love leads to marriage only after the couple has gone through a complex mating ritual that includes the establishment of rapport, mutual self-disclosure that leads through mutual dependency to a recognition of the need each has for the other for his or her personality to be fulfilled.

But marriages are not based only on love. They represent a mutual selection that is affected by macro-level endogamous rules concerning the relative ages of the partners, and their racial, religious, ethnic, and social class characteristics as well. Once the macro hurdle had been cleared the selection process probably became, in most cases, a complicated maze of interpersonal and homogamous barriers that also must be navigated.

This chapter is the first in a series of five chapters that deal with various facets of married living. Chapter 15 examines power within the family, and Chapter 16 focuses on the processes and problems of marital adjustment and satisfaction. Chapters 17 and 18 center around parenthood, childhood, and the adjustments required and how the family mixes the worlds of work and leisure. The aim is to weave all five chapters into a congruent and understandable overview of what married living entails. To accomplish this goal the strategy of writing about marital interaction in a very informal style has been adopted. Marital interaction will be treated initially from a descriptive, instead of a strictly scientific, approach. The portrait drawn of marital interaction in this chapter is slightly satirical and cynical. Idealistic pictures of the joyous side of married life are abundant. A hard-nosed picture painted from a realistic perspective will serve to call forth a rational analysis of this aspect of life.

## REASONS FOR MARRIAGE

Although it is no doubt true that the motives for entering married life vary from couple to couple, probably some motives are prevalent enough to merit discussion. These are organized into "push" and "pull" factors.

The push motives are those that pressure a couple to move more rapidly toward the married state. The pull motives serve as a kind of magnet. They seem to neutralize the fears that many single persons have about married life, such as losing their freedom and being tied down.

## Push Factors

CONFORMITY.   In the final analysis, at least as our society now operates, there are not many viable or highly desirable alternatives to married life. Over 90 percent of all persons reaching adulthood in the United States get married at some time in their lives. Most of us were brought up in homes where our parents were legally married. The whole socialization experience, from early childhood on, emphasizes preparation for the husband-wife-father-mother roles that we are expected to enter. From high school days on we are pushed toward pairing off with someone who might be a good mate. In fact, our friends and associates often get rather nervous if we show less than a "normal" interest in getting married. If a man is not married by the time he is twenty-six, and a woman by the time she is twenty-three, they are frequently subject to rather extensive manipulations by their more conforming friends who want to "set them up."

Somehow, a single person seems to represent a failure of the societal norms to produce a conformist. A nonconformist evidently makes all the conformists feel extremely uncomfortable. The American culture is so thoroughly structured to produce married couples that conformity is a primary, though not necessarily a manifest and readily recognized, reason for marriage in the United States.

MANIFEST STATED REASON: LOVE.   If we were to hire all the hotel and motel desk clerks to interview honeymooning couples as to why they got married, the overwhelming response would be, "Because we love each other!" We have come to expect marriage to be the normal way of translating our emotional commitments into a more permanent and visible type of social commitment.

LEGITIMATION OF SEX.   Traditionally, our society sanctions sexual intercourse only among persons who have publicly and legally declared a commitment to each other. Although there is ample evidence, discussed in Chapter 10, that a large proportion of both males and females engage in premarital coitus, it is likely that a regular sexual encounter will, in a large percentage of cases, lead toward a decision to legitimize the sexual acts via marriage. Even couples who vehemently disavow any acceptance of societal norms about marriage will usually make some effort to declare their mutual commitment publicly so that their associates will not regard the relationship as totally hedonistic or exploitative.

363

LEGITIMATION OF CHILDREN.   A primary reason for marriage in our society is to give any children born of the relationship a legitimate identity. Without parents who are married the children are considered illegitimate—a stigma that is not easily ignored. With the increasing occurrence of premarital coitus in our society, a logical reason for marriage is to ensure that the first child is legitimate. As the data in Table 14–1 indicate, the number of first births per 1,000 women has been increasing in recent years. It seems that whites are considerably more likely to rush into marriage in order to legitimate children than are blacks. It is also apparent that this motive for marriage has become increasingly important for each successive cohort of women, black and white, since 1900.

**TABLE 14–1**
**Premaritally Conceived First Births per 1,000 Women**

| | ALL RACES | WHITE | BLACK | SPANISH ORIGIN [a] |
|---|---|---|---|---|
| Total premaritally conceived first births | | | | |
| 1965–69 | 244 | 210 | 517 | 305 |
| 1960–64 | 225 | 194 | 477 | 266 |
| 1955–59 | 195 | 165 | 434 | 237 |
| 1950–54 | 137 | 114 | 331 | 182 |
| Child born before mother's marriage | | | | |
| 1965–69 | 85 | 59 | 293 | 127 |
| 1960–64 | 76 | 51 | 271 | 109 |
| 1955–59 | 68 | 47 | 236 | 96 |
| 1950–54 | 46 | 33 | 153 | 68 |
| Child born after mother's marriage | | | | |
| 1965–69 | 159 | 151 | 224 | 178 |
| 1960–64 | 149 | 143 | 206 | 157 |
| 1955–59 | 127 | 118 | 198 | 141 |
| 1950–54 | 91 | 81 | 178 | 114 |
| Percentage born after marriage | | | | |
| 1965–69 | 65.2 | 71.9 | 43.3 | 58.4 |
| 1960–64 | 66.2 | 73.7 | 43.2 | 59.0 |
| 1955–59 | 65.1 | 71.5 | 45.6 | 59.5 |
| 1950–54 | 66.4 | 71.1 | 53.8 | 62.6 |

SOURCE:   U.S. Department of Commerce, Bureau of the Census, *Current Population Reports,* "Premarital Fertility," Series P-23, No. 63, August, 1976, Table 18.

a People of Spanish origin may be of any race.

## THE REQUIREMENTS OF MARRIED LIFE

If the primary push factors for entering married life are conformity, love, the legitimation of sex, and a desire to legitimize children, what are the pull factors? Surely there must be something about the married state that is virtually irresistible. What is there about married life that makes it so attractive? Are these prior expectations realistic, or are they smoke dreams that somehow lose some of their appeal once the cloud has lifted? What does married living require of its participants?

### Pull Factors

COMPANIONSHIP. Perhaps the most salient pull into married life is the prospect of a regular companion, an available sex partner that will eliminate the necessity of searching for sexual satisfaction on a hit and run basis. The expectations prior to marriage of the advantages of regularized sex are probably oversold. Married life also introduces the obligation of sex on a fairly regular basis with the same partner. But, the obligation goes far beyond just sex. Married life requires extreme intimacy. For young married couples this intimacy is frequently accentuated by a small apartment, limited resources for outside entertainment, and heavy demands on each partner's time (job responsibilities, especially if both are working or if one is working and the other is in school).

SHARING. A second pull factor is the desire to share ideas and money, a house or apartment, time and one's whole life. Prior to marriage this sounds very appealing. However, married sharing is usually more rationalistic and less exciting in the real world than it was when both were dreaming on the backs of their eyelids. Sharing includes washing dishes, typing papers, housecleaning, washing the car, and all the other things that make married life routine.

COMMUNICATION. The desire for real communication is a third pulling force for entering married life. It is not unusual for couples anticipating married life to say, "I want to really get to know her/him—to communicate fully and openly—I don't want to play any more games." The rhetoric seems to describe an exciting prospect. But communication is a two-way exchange. It entails giving communication, but also taking criticism. The intimacy with which married couples must contend, coupled with demands made on limited resources, is fertile ground for misunderstanding, for bargaining, for gamesmanship, for broken and frequently strained communications.

Our society has developed a rather pervasive description of the beauty of married living that sometimes hides the reality that togetherness is *not* always to be preferred to singleness, that the emotional and legal

365

commitment is also an economic one. Expectations about married life are frequently so inflated by the media that couples are occasionally dismayed by the reality that married life is often routine. Married life is a day-to-day existence that is peppered with some very exciting peak periods, but for the most part, it consists of predictable and regularized encounters at the plateau level on which most of us live.

### Summary

The marriage ceremony in our society is, in reality, merely a symbolic representation of the transformation of two single persons into a joint entity—a legal, social, and personal process that leads to a recognition that each is responsible to and for the other. The transformation represented by the ceremony has usually occurred over a period of time in which extensive and intensive communication between the two involved has led to a mutual desire to live together as man and wife, "for better, for worse."

## THE DRAMATURGICAL FRAMEWORK

The marriage ceremony itself does not change the two involved, but being married and engaging in marital interaction does bring about change. This chapter examines some of the many facets of marital interaction: where it occurs, how it occurs, and some of the interpersonal forces that impinge on the dynamic interaction between married people.

The next five sections of this chapter will rely heavily on the dramaturgical approach of the anthropologist Erving Goffman (1959, 1967). This approach, which is a branch of symbolic interactionism (see Chapter 2), views interaction as a performance staged by the actors in the marital play and uses the terminology of the theater to label what we, as detached observers in the audience, see. It should be re-emphasized that some of this chapter has been written from a somewhat satirical and cynical perspective.

### The Location of Marital Interaction

FRONT AND BACK REGIONS.   In the everyday world of married life, as in the theater, some of our joint performances occur in the public arena, on stage in front of an audience. Of course, marital interaction also occurs backstage, in the wings and the dressing rooms or where the performances are rehearsed before the audience is allowed to see the marital play. Quite naturally, a married couple acts at times as individuals and at other times as a team. And, sometimes the cues are missed, and the performance does not go as smoothly as planned.

George Gardner

*At a quarter to seven in the morning, a cup of coffee is a necessary prerequisite to any kind of interaction.*

The marital interaction that occurs on front stage usually entails a more formal presentation. The couple is at a restaurant, at a party, or entertaining friends, the boss, the in-laws. The couple is usually expected by the audience in these cases to present a cohesive and consistent image, one that is free of open conflict, one that does not lead the audience to be critical of either the husband or the wife or the married pair. The couple attempts to convey the message that everything is all right between them. Quite often such a performance can be so smooth that the audience never knows that immediately prior to the play (that is, before they arrived for dinner), there was a tremendous fight that continues every time the couple retires to the kitchen to get more food or drink.

This brings up backstage behavior. The marital interaction that occurs behind closed doors is informal and is usually free of acting. The roles in the backstage region are more relaxed, and the masks are removed so that the selves that each defines as more real can interact.

Marital interaction is not just something that happens between a husband and wife. It is usually a phenomenon that must be fitted into the conflicting demands of public versus private regions. Since, in an evening, the performance may consist of a succession of front and back region encounters, the chances for dissension and conflict are tremendous. Nothing can be more disruptive to a marital relationship than the necessity of living constantly in the front region without adequate opportunities to review the play in the back region of a marriage. When the marital interactions are frequently before live audiences, another source of conflict is upstaging of the spouse. This occurs when one spouse dominates the performance and does not give the other a chance to play his or her role.

367

Each married couple consciously plans how they will relate to one another in public and in private. The joint performance in public is determined by how well the audience knows each of the performers, and how many of the secrets of the married pair are shared with the audience. When the audience consists of good friends or parents, the performance in the front region can closely approximate that of the back region. When the audience consists primarily of strangers, the marital interaction is usually much more formal.

## Identities in Marital Interaction

A central assumption of symbolic interactionism is that each spouse has, at any one time, a self-concept that influences how he or she acts and reacts to the other. That self-concept actually consists of a number of selves that can be pulled out of the actor's repertoire of roles he or she has played. Goffman calls these multiple roles *identity documents.*

The *dominant identity* is the self that one normally and regularly plays when with the spouse. If we were to interview married couples and ask them to describe their spouses, they would probably list a number of personality characteristics and acting styles such as he/she is quiet, has a quick wit, laughs a lot, always sees the bright side of everything, is calm in crises, makes everyone feel at ease, is affectionate and sensitive to my needs, listens well. The dominant identity is the predictable part of being married and characterizes the usual everyday interactions that occur in married life.

The *reserve identity* is the self that comes out of hiding only in special situations or during times of stress. For example, the calm and quiet spouse who throws a temper tantrum occasionally is showing his reserve identity. All of us have these reserve identities that are not part of our normal repertoire of roles. Another example is the person who usually projects an image in public of self-confidence and constant happiness but who, in the privacy of his or her marital interaction, may indicate feelings of inadequacy and depression.

The *relic identity* is the self that represents the past—perhaps repressed or completely hidden from the spouse. The relic identity is one that occasionally and inadvertently comes out of hiding, as when a person's parents or old friends start talking about the past. For example, the teetotaler who never talked about drinking heavily and often back in high school or college. Another example is the spouse who has effectively obscured his past sexual activities (relic identity). When an old friend drops in, however, and they are reliving the past, the old friend talks about the girl the spouse used to see regularly. Needless to say, the relic identities that suddenly are unearthed can have serious impacts on current and future marital interactions.

Marital interaction is a dynamic interchange of each spouse playing roles—roles that reveal various facets of a person's self, past and present. Most marital interaction is regularized and routine; it is the communication that takes place when each is playing his or her dominant identity, occasionally spiced by the use of a reserve identity. In the process of living together as a married pair, most of us reveal selected aspects of our relic identities. A knowledge of all of the identities of the spouse is necessary if the marital interaction is to be relatively free of conflict. Nothing can damage a good marriage as badly as unpredictability—the use of identities previously unknown to the spouse.

## The Interactional Setting

As in any interactional encounter the husband and wife attempt to maintain poise relative to the other. When they are performing for an audience, they operate to maintain the poise of their team, making sure that nothing happens that will be embarrassing. Gross and Stone (1964) identified five elements of the self and situation that may give rise to embarrassment and that may seriously affect both the husband-wife interaction and their interaction with an audience. Most of these elements, however, apply explicitly to a husband-wife-team presentation to an audience in the front region.

*Spaces.* Spaces include the boundaries within which interaction must occur. In most instances these spaces are rather clearly marked, and appropriate interactions are normative for different areas. When a couple gives a cocktail party and leaves the bedroom door shut, this signals that the only appropriate place for social exchange is in the area that is not shut off. The couple may be using the bedroom as a place to retire to (the back region) in case they must consult about something that is not public business. Interaction is adversely affected if someone enters a space where he has no business being. The hostess who enters her bathroom during a party only to find it occupied is likely to be embarrassed because her identity as hostess does not extend, even in her own house, to an area that is off limits. Perhaps a better example is embodied in a song that was popular in the early 1960s:[1]

> Splish splash I was taking a bath,
> Along about a Saturday night,
> Rub dub just relaxing in the tub,
> Thinking everything was all right—
> Well I stepped out of the tub,
> Put my feet on the floor,

---

[1] © Copyright 1958 Travis Music Company, New York, New York.

369

Wrapped the towel around me
and I opened the door—
Then splish splash, I jumped back in the bath,
How was I to know there was a party going on!

PROPS.    The term *props,* taken from the terminology of the theater, refers to objects that fit within the spaces where interaction occurs and that remain fairly stationary during an encounter. Props are especially relevant to reserve and relic identities. For example, the husband and wife are spending a quiet evening at home talking about the times before they were married. In reminiscing they decide to pull out their old yearbooks from high school. As they are going through the husband's yearbook, they come upon an extremely explicit love note written by an old flame. This relic prop, a skeleton from the past, may seriously affect the continued interaction of the husband and wife, especially during that evening.

EQUIPMENT.    Although props are relatively stationary, Gross and Stone (1964) say that equipment is very movable and can refer to words as well as to physical equipment. For example, it can be highly embarrassing if, when the husband and wife are engaged in an intimate encounter, he inadvertently calls her by the name of his old girlfriend. The loss of control over equipment can lead not only to embarrassment but also to seriously impeding the flow of communication for days and weeks to come.

CLOTHING.    Clothing is the fourth element of the self and situation that may affect both the husband-wife communication and their performance as a team before an audience. The effect occurs most frequently when a husband and wife are invited to a social event and miss the cues as to proper dress. They may show up at the supervisor's house dressed for a dinner they thought was to be formal, and their hosts are in casual clothes for a cookout. The husband-wife are embarrassed before their hosts and angry at each other for not checking—consequently the whole evening may be a very unhappy one.

BODY.    The last element that Gross and Stone delineate is the body. Control over the body, a readiness to act in the appropriate way, is necessary to maintain poise and facilitate mutual interaction. The remembrance of an incident of lack of this control may affect marital interaction for a long time. For example, let us say a young married couple has been invited to a formal dinner at the home of the husband's supervisor. During dinner the husband passes a dish to his wife and it slips, covering the front of the wife's dress with food. The rest of the evening is thus adversely affected.

Marital interaction is a mixture of one-to-one exchanges in private, one-to-one exchanges occurring in front of an audience, and performances staged by the couple as a team for an audience. All of these can be influenced by elements that are parts of the two selves involved and by the situational factors that provide the setting within which the interactional exchanges occur. Although it would be desirable for all of these exchanges to be conducted with poise, occasionally the control over spaces, props, equipment, clothes, and body may produce embarrassment that will affect the interaction of husband and wife.

## Interactional Cues

In any interactional encounter, even within marriage, there is often a spontaneity and existential quality to the communications exchanged between spouses. Although marital interaction does occur on the basis of thematized views each has of the other (that is, the idea of reacting to the dominant role as opposed to the individual person), in many situations the husband and wife act and react to one another according to their interpretations of cues. These interactional cues may be as obvious as a spoken command, request, threat, or entreaty, or as subtle as the way one's legs are crossed, how the hands and eyes are used to communicate a point, or the inflection of one's voice.

Goffman (1959) suggests two terms that include the obvious and subtle cues mentioned above. *Appearance* refers to how a person is dressed. For example, let us assume that a husband walks into the bedroom and his wife is there in her most alluring nightgown, the lights are toned down, and soft music is on the stereo. It would seem, at least initially, that she is trying to say something meaningful to her spouse. The husband has just come in from a week-long business trip. After taking off his tie and coat he says, "Hi honey, have you fed the dog yet?" Wheeling around, he heads for the basement to get the dog food. Fifteen minutes later, when he returns, the music is still on and the lights are still low, but the wife is sound asleep with the cover pulled up over her neck. Goffman suggests that appearance is coupled with the *manner* in which a person gives off the interactional cues that are used by the other person in deciding how to react. In some cases what we say verbally is completely superfluous, since our appearance and manner are communicating a different meaning. In other cases our appearance is obscured by the distinct clarity of our style or manner.

All of us learn to relate to our spouses in a routinized way. Our verbal communications are usually predictable because they are merely a replay of what has happened to us during the day. We react to each other as role occupants most of the time. However, if a marriage is to be exciting, there must be times when the partners intensely communicate, spontaneously in the here and now, not as two roles but as two persons— interaction that is meaningful and personal. This type of interaction requires each spouse to read the silent language of the other's manner and appearance. Words are less important here than action and activity, expressions and impressions.

371

## EXCUSES AND JUSTIFICATIONS USED IN INTERACTION

In the interactive marital encounter, as in other interactive situations regardless of the relationship, verbal acts can be classified under certain categories. One scheme, developed by Robert Bales (1950), suggests that a group (for example, husband and wife) with a common task faces problems in six areas: (a) communication, or arriving at a common definition of the problem, (b) evaluation, or ascertaining if the two are approaching the problem from a common value system, (c) control, or the mediation of the attempts of each to control the other, (d) decision,

**TABLE 14–2**
**Interactions Within Relationships**

| GENERAL CATEGORY | TYPE OF ACT | PROBLEM [a] |
|---|---|---|
| Positive reactions | 1. *Shows solidarity,* raises other's status, gives help, reward. | |
| | 2. *Shows tension release,* shows satisfaction, laughs, jokes. | |
| | 3. *Agrees,* shows passive acceptance, understands, concurs, complies. | |
| Problem-solving attempts | 4. *Gives suggestion,* direction, implying autonomy for other. | |
| | 5. *Gives opinion,* evaluation, analysis, expresses feeling, wish. | |
| | 6. *Gives orientation,* information, repetition, confirmation. | a b c d e f |
| Questions | 7. *Asks for orientation,* information, repetition, confirmation. | |
| | 8. *Asks for opinion,* evaluation, analysis, expression of feeling. | |
| | 9. *Asks for suggestion,* direction, possible ways of action. | |
| Negative reactions | 10. *Disagrees,* shows passive rejection, formality, withholds help. | |
| | 11. *Shows tension,* asks for help, withdraws out of field. | |
| | 12. *Shows antagonism,* deflates other's status, defends or asserts self. | |

SOURCE: Robert F. Bales, *Interaction Process Analysis* (Boston: Addison-Wesley, 1950), p. 9, Chart 1. By permission of the author.

[a] Problem:
   a. Communication—Gives orientation and asks for orientation.
   b. Evaluation—Gives opinion and asks for opinion.
   c. Control—Gives suggestion and asks for suggestion.
   d. Decision—Agrees and disagrees.
   e. Tension Reduction—Shows tension release and shows tension.
   f. Reintegration—Shows solidarity and shows antagonism.

or negotiating a final decision on the problem that is satisfactory to both, (e) tension reduction, or attempting to deal with any tensions that may arise in the process of reaching a decision, (f) reintegration, or work aimed at solidifying the cohesiveness of the marriage. As you can see in Table 14–2, the problems of communication, evaluation, control, and decision include giving and asking for orientation, opinion, and suggestions, and disagreeing or agreeing. The twelve categories defined by Bales are fairly exclusive and have been used in a multitude of studies dealing with small-group interaction.

A second scheme, by Scott and Lyman (1968), examines interaction in terms of accounts. An account is "a statement made by a social actor to explain unanticipated or untoward behavior—whether that behavior is his own or that of others, and whether the proximate cause for the statement arises from the actor himself or from someone else."

There are two general types of accounts delineated by Scott and Lyman (1968:47): "*Justifications* are accounts in which one accepts responsibility for the act in question, but denies the pejorative quality associated with it." "*Excuses* are accounts in which one admits that the act in question is bad, wrong, or inappropriate but denies full responsibility."

Both excuses and justifications are socially acceptable verbal techniques for relieving a person of his or her responsibility for acting in a certain untoward or unappropriate fashion. However, justifications (originally called techniques of neutralization by Sykes and Matza, 1957) assert the positive value of an act. In other words, when a justification account is used in interaction, the person is saying, "I know what happened appears bad to you, but it's not as bad as it seems—there is a valid reason for the action."

Table 14–3 indicates the three types of excuse accounts isolated by Scott and Lyman (1968) and four of the five justification (neutralization) accounts originally discussed by Sykes and Matza (1957).

**TABLE 14–3**

**Accounts: Excuses and Justifications**

| ACCOUNTS THAT ARE EXCUSES | ACCOUNTS THAT ARE JUSTIFICATIONS [a] |
| --- | --- |
| Appeal to accidents | Denial of injury |
| Appeal to defensibility | Denial of victim |
| Appeal to biological drives | Condemnation of condemners |
| | Appeal to higher loyalties |

SOURCES: Adapted from Marvin B. Scott and Stanford Lyman, "Accounts," *American Sociological Review*, *33*(February, 1968):46–62; Gresham M. Sykes and David Matza, "Techniques of Neutralization: A Theory of Delinquency." *American Sociological Review*, *22*(December, 1957):664–670. By permission of the American Sociological Association and the authors.

[a] A fifth justification or neutralization account initially discussed by Sykes and Matza, denial of responsibility, was ignored by Scott and Lyman.

### Mr. Y Pleads His Case

The husband, Mr. Y, has just been confronted by his wife with a charge that he committed adultery while on a business trip three years earlier. The wife identifies her source of information as the wife of the husband's business partner. She is demanding an account of his untoward behavior. He will probably start off with some excuses. "When Mr. X, my client, arrived at the hotel for dinner, he had two of his secretaries with him. He said he owed them a dinner, and besides, they knew more of the facts about our deal than he did." Thus the husband is claiming that he was with another woman by accident—it was not his idea and he certainly did not want to offend or embarrass his client and risk losing the contract. The husband continues, "After dinner we went to several bars and night clubs and all of us got looped. Mr. X is divorced, you know. Well, as we got back to the hotel Mr. X suggested that we should go up to my room for one last drink to seal the contract. I just couldn't say no." Here the husband is claiming defensibility—he was drunk, could not think very rationally, and did not want to lose the business at that point.

By now the husband is hoping that he has the wife empathizing at least a little. He continues the tale. "Well, one of the girls said she was so sleepy she had to go to bed for a short nap. Mr. X and I had a couple of more drinks with the other girl and signed the contract. We tried to get the other girl to wake up but she wouldn't so Mr. X suggested I let her sleep it off until morning. After they left I went to sleep on the other bed. I don't know when it was, but when I woke up the girl was in

The purpose of an account in an interactive encounter is to solicit the other persons acceptance, understanding, and/or forgiveness for one's inappropriate behavior. Let us take an example that might occur between a husband and wife and try to see how accounts are offered and accepted.

## ADDITIONAL COMPONENTS

While Goffman's dramaturgical approach to the study of interaction is provocative and seems readily applicable to the study of communication between spouses, it seems to leave out much that is valuable. Nevertheless, our understanding of marital interaction is enhanced if we are aware of differential performance requirements in the front and back regions; if we bed with me, and we were making love." The excuse now is biological drive or instinct.

If the wife has gone along with the story up to this point, the husband might switch tactics and try to find some positive value in his action—the justification for his inappropriate behavior. The account is being given and, he hopes, being taken in by his wife. Now Mr. Y might say, "This is the only time this has ever happened." Thus the claim is that there is really no injury in just one transgression. The denial of injury is closely followed with the implication that the wife is not really a victim since "I was drunk and I don't even remember the girl's name or what she looked like." The third justification is designed to make the wife feel that the husband is really not as bad as he seems. He says, "That loud mouth Charley (his partner), why he sleeps with someone everytime he goes out of town." Condemnation of the condemner is a justification that implies that his action is minor compared to actions of other men in his position or situation. The final justification account offered by the husband is an appeal to higher loyalties. He says, "Sweetheart, it will never happen again—I promise you. We have a good marriage and you're the only person I have ever really loved. Can you forgive me?"

This example entails a rather extreme type of untoward behavior but illustrates how excuse and justification accounts are given and received in marital interaction. Less extreme inappropriate behaviors are accounted for by the same kind of interaction strategies—the reliance on excuses and justifications for behavior.

recognize the impact of dominant, reserve, and relic identities on continuing interaction and communication; if we know when poise is lost and how the spouses regain composure after failing to control such things as spaces, props, equipment, clothes, and body; and if we know how accounts for untoward behaviors are called for and honored. However, there is certainly more to marital interaction than just a review of the marital play or performances. In married life the script is constantly being revised and rewritten, frequently on short notice. There is no stand-in even when the stars of the show do not feel up to a performance. The actors not only work together at the theater but also share the same dressing rooms and auxiliary material that constitute part of the play. Also, rather strong traditions prohibit or at least restrain the actors in the marital play from quitting and seeking employment elsewhere. The show must go on!

## Marital Role Expectations

One component of marital interaction is the expectations each has of his or her own role performance and the role performance of the other. Udry (1971) outlines three sources of marital role expectations that we will examine briefly: (a) the concepts of husband and wife roles that are inherent in the culture and present in the mass media portrayals of married life, (b) the view of husband-wife roles derived from observing one's parents, (c) prior interactions between the husband and wife (that is, their repertoire of marital-role performances as a team).

Lynn (1961) and Winch (1962) demonstrated in their studies of the process of identification with parents (see Chapter 17) that girls seem to get a rather cohesive set of expectations about the wife role from their mothers. However, boys do not seem to internalize an equally coherent view of either husband role or wife role from their fathers. This fact may partially explain why males consistently show a preference for a traditional and male-dominant conception of the wife role (see Dunn, 1960; Lovejoy, 1961). Males are probably much more reliant on the cultural definitions of appropriate sex roles—the types of definitions espoused with some regularity in the mass media.

Even with these rather divergent early experiences in the formation of marital role expectations, as the materials in Chapters 12 and 13 show rather clearly, the end result of the filtering process during courtship is a couple with somewhat similar conceptions of the husband-wife roles and some consensus in expectations (see Kirkpatrick and Hobart, 1954; Motz, 1950).

The third source of marital role expectations outlined by Udry, the dynamic revisions that almost automatically emerge from an everyday involvement in interaction with the spouse, has not been systematically explored by family sociologists. We know that marital role expectations are almost constantly under review in most marriages and can undergo changes resulting from a continuing process of give and take in marital interaction. But how does this work?

## Thematized Versus Dynamic Marital Interaction

What are the expectations we have for marital role performance—for ourselves and our spouse? Where do they really come from? Are they essentially predetermined by the internalized images we obtained from our parents and the images of husband-wife roles as defined by our culture and the mass media? Surely not!

In responding to these questions let us look at two points. First, it is easy to miss some of the realities of what marital interaction entails while searching for sociologically relevant variables. One of these realities is that the occupants of marital roles are not categories but people—live human beings with feelings and emotions, attitudes and values, preferences and needs, reservoirs of pride and anger—people who like to be praised and appreciated, who generally avoid open conflict but like and enjoy an occasional confrontation and disagreement, who find it hard to say, "I'm sorry, it was my fault." Social scientists sometimes act as if the roles interact instead of the people who play the roles.

A second reality that we sometimes fail to recognize is that marital interaction occurs between persons with a long history of interactional experiences with each other. We tend to think of marital interaction as a series of discrete and almost unconnected experiences, when in fact all the interactional encounters from the first attempts at establishing rapport to the present add up to a sum total. As noted in Chapter 13 (see Winch, 1958; Kerckhoff and Davis, 1962; Murstein, 1970), during the courtship process two individuals who are attracted to one another expend tremendous amounts of time and energy finding out if they are similar enough in attitudes, values, and interests, and complementary enough in needs and role conceptions to get married.

In other words, the consequence of all this premarital interaction is the building of an image of the other, of how the self relates to the other, and of the two as a pair. This emergent thematized image of the relationship is useful in that it is economical. We begin to develop routines and styles of interaction that require less and less immediate involvement on the part of the other spouse. An example is the cartoon of the husband eating his breakfast, his head buried in the newspaper. The wife says, "George, I am having an affair with Reverend Milktoast." He responds, the way he always has, "Oh, great, honey. I think that is fine!"

Not only is there a tendency for couples to become so patterned in their schedules and rhythms of life that their interactions become stagnant but also there is a propensity to rely on thematized views of the spouse that are outmoded. This is particularly true in families in which the wife, once a highly trained professional, has been out of the labor force and preoccupied with child rearing for an extended period of time. On reentering the outside world she begins to exert the newly found freedom and power she has been repressing for years. The husband may be totally unable to see the "new woman" because he has come to rely so heavily on his thematized image of her.

It is hardly possible or feasible to be totally engrossed in a dynamic marital interaction encounter day in and day out. Most of us need economical and generally reliable social devices like thematization to operate in a world filled with countervailing demands for our attention. This is not to suggest that it is next to impossible for us to revise our thematized conceptions of our spouse. But change comes hard for most people, as does breaking a habit. The old habit serves a useful purpose. It lends order to life and its social exchanges.

377

Marital role expectations are a rather fluid phenomenon. They change as each of us changes. They are affected by the everyday experiences each spouse brings to the marriage. We tend to thematize our marital relationship in order to solidify our place relative to the spouse. It is also possible for outside observers, as well as the partners directly involved, to thematize marital relationships by examining the prevailing style of interaction and the degree of sharing and warmth.

## A GENERAL MODEL

Up to this point in the chapter the orientation has been predominantly informal, subjective, impressionistic, and social psychological in focus, and for a good reason. We were infiltrating the lines of the marital play to expose some of the more subtle and microscopic facets of how husbands and wives may relate to one another. By now you should have gained an appreciation for some of the dramaturgical dynamics of marital interaction. It is now time to take a more objective and sociological view. We need a broader picture of just what marital interaction entails. To facilitate gaining an overview, a general model has been developed that contains the central components of marital interaction (Figure 14–1). This model will serve as a foundation for an examination of power in the family in Chapter 15 and the discussion of marital adjustment and satisfaction in Chapter 16.

### Assumptions About Marital Interaction

FORMS OF MARITAL INTERACTION. The first assumption is that certain forms of marital interaction exist in all marriages, and in any marriage over time. The six forms of interaction listed in the table are problems faced by almost any group and were initially outlined by Robert Bales (1950). They were also discussed earlier in the chapter and outlined in Table 14–2. They are called "forms" of interaction because they do not change, regardless of the topic of interaction. No matter how heated or calm the husband's or wife's remarks may be, each and every communicative act and response may be classified into one of these six forms. For example, as power within the family is discussed in Chapter 15, we may find that persons who are more dominating in a relationship use certain forms of interaction more often than those who are less dominating.

CONTENT OF MARITAL INTERACTION. If all marital interactions take one or more of these six forms, what do married people talk about? The second assumption of the model is that the contents of marital interaction are determined, to a rather large extent, by the stage the family life cycle is in. For example, two couples marry at about the same time. After nine years, one couple has two children while the other remained childless. The contents of the interactions between the first couple reflect the fact that they have moved from stage I to stage IV of the family life cycle. Many of their conversations concern how to perform their roles as parents and the parental roles shift as their children go through their own various stages of development. Their friends are still in stage I of the family life cycle. The composition of their family has not changed. The primary roles they were playing in the early months of marriage, the marriage and work roles, have remained essentially the same. The point is that the stage in the family life cycle is responsible for defining the boundaries of marital interaction, at least to a large extent. The presence of children and the changes they undergo provide a focus of mutual concern for a married couple and a continuous topic of conversation, communication, and interaction.

**FIGURE 14–1**
**A General Model of Marital-Partner Interaction**

| Forms of Marital Interaction | Styles and Climate of Marital Interaction | | |
|---|---|---|---|
| | Conflict Habituated<br>Devitalized<br>Passive-Congenial | The Vital<br>The Total | |
| | **Marital Adjustment Tasks** | | |
| 1. Communication<br>2. Evaluation<br>3. Control<br>4. Decision<br>5. Tension reduction<br>6. Reintegration | A. Marriage Sociability<br>B. Marriage Companionship<br>C. Economic Affairs<br>D. Marital Power | E. Extrafamily Relationships<br>F. Ideological Congruence<br>G. Marital Intimacy<br>H. Role Expectations | |
| | **Stages of the Family Life Cycle** | | |
| | No Child   Infant   Preschool   Elementary School   Teenage   Oldest Child Lives Away From Home   Empty Nest   Retirement to Death | | |
| | I    II    III    IV    V    VI    VII    VIII | | |

Judy Gelles

MARITAL-ADJUSTMENT TASKS. A third assumption of the model is that there are certain marital-adjustment tasks faced by each couple at every stage of the family life cycle that must be discussed by them. How important each of these tasks is, and their relative priority in married life, may change somewhat from stage to stage, yet each requires continuing attention by the spouses. For example, although the frequency and quality of sexual intimacy seems most salient before children join the family, sexual intimacy is a recurrent source of interest and interaction in each stage of development. The most important point is that these tasks are recurring sources of strain in a marriage and require—force may be a better word—the spouses to interact in order to achieve a maximal degree of satisfaction and happiness. Although there might be some disagreement on the number of categories, most family sociologists would probably endorse the following classification of marital adjustment tasks (see Chapter 16 for a more detailed account):

1. *Marriage sociability*—Interaction here would deal with the degree and types of social life the couple will have.
2. *Marriage companionship*—Couples must continually talk with each other about their needs for companionship and how they can be best satisfied.
3. *Economic affairs*—A significant number of the interactions among spouses concern how to spend the family income.
4. *Marital power*—Most married people spend much time and energy in negotiation about who will make certain decisions, how and when the decision will be made, and in arguing for their individual positions on these matters.

5. *Extrafamily relationships*—Every married couple must deal with how to relate to and cope with the demands made on the family by the husband's and/or wife's job responsibilities, the in-laws, and school and other sources of outside demands on the family's resources.

6. *Ideological congruence*—Virtually every couple is faced, from time to time, with issues of philosophical and ethical concern, whether it is about child-rearing tactics, how to deal with political, religious, or moral matters, or what to do about certain questions that require a stand from one or more of the family members in support of or reaction against an ideological system.

7. *Sexual intimacy*—Every couple must work out how they will deal with sex and expressions of affection in their marriage.

8. *Role expectations*—As noted earlier in this chapter, role expectations and the division of labor in the family are generally somewhat negotiable, and married couples must and usually do spend a fair amount of time interacting about role expectations and role performances and the divergences between them.

STYLE OF MARITAL INTERACTION. A fourth and final assumption of the model is that each couple develops a "style," or "climate," of interaction that seems to pervade the relationship. The style of interaction is determined to some extent by the personalities of the husband and wife. If both are rather dogmatic and argumentative, the chances are fairly good that their interactions will be occasionally, if not frequently, conflict oriented. If both are rather calm and passive, then the interactions will be characterized by an easy give and take with little overt conflict.

## Styles and Climates of Marital Interaction

John Cuber and Peggy B. Harroff (1965) developed a typology of interactional styles and climates based on their interviews with 107 men and 104 women from the upper-middle class who had been married more than ten years to the same spouse and who had not considered divorce. The five types follow, with a brief description of each.

SUMMARY. Cuber and Harroff (1965) developed a typology of marital relationships that depicts the modal kinds and quality of interaction that may be present in marriage. These types are not indicative of marital adjustment since even those couples who are conflict habituated are adjusted to such a style and climate of interaction. Conflict habituated, devitalized, passive-congenial, vital, and total are merely labels that are probably representative of styles and climates of interaction that may pervade any marriage.

381

## Types of Marital Interaction:
### Cuber and Harroff

CONFLICT HABITUATED. In this type of marriage there is a great deal of conflict and tension, both in the front and back regions, although there are usually attempts to conceal the true intensity of conflict from friends, relatives, and children. Even so, attempts at concealment are seldom totally successful. Cuber and Harroff found that conflict-habituated couples acknowledge that "incompatibility is pervasive, that conflict is ever potential, and that an atmosphere of tension pervades the togetherness." In this type of relationship, participating in yet attempting to control the level of tension and conflict become dominant activities of the husband and wife. Cuber and Harroff suggest that these couples may need the conflict at a psychological level, and that the tension and conflict are the cohesive forces that hold the couple together, even for a lifetime.

DEVITALIZED. This second type of relationship is described by Cuber and Harroff as "exceedingly common." As the term implies, what was an exciting marriage in earlier years has lost its vitality. For devitalized couples sex has become a minor part of married life, little time is spent together because each has different and separate commitments, and the time spent together is viewed by each as his or her duty. As Cuber and Harroff (1965:49) describe it: "On the subjective, emotional dimension, the relationship has become a void. The original zest is gone. There is typically little overt tension or conflict, but the interplay between the pair has become apathetic, lifeless. No serious threat to the continuity of the marriage is generally acknowledged, however. It is intended, usually by both, that it continue indefinitely, despite its numbness."

PASSIVE-CONGENIAL. The passive-congenial style or climate of marital interaction, although similar to the devitalized, is divergent in one important respect. That is, "The passivity which pervades the association has been there from the start." Cuber and Harroff (1965:52–53) suggest that there are two routes by which people make their way into the passive-congenial mode of interaction—by default and by intention. "Perhaps in most instances they arrive at this way of living and feeling by drift. There is so little which they have cared about deeply in each other that a passive relationship is sufficient to express it all. In other instances the passive-congenial model is a deliberately intended arrangement for two people whose interests and creative energies are directed elsewhere than toward the pairing—into careers, or in the case of women, into children or community activities. They say they know this and want it this way. These people simply do not wish to invest their total emotional involvement and creative effort in the male-female relationship."

Abigail Heyman, Magnum Photos, Inc.

*The Empty-Nest Syndrome: Often, if a marriage has been built around the children, it is left devitalized after they are grown and have left home.*

THE VITAL.   The type of marital relationship in which the mode of interaction is vital is found in only a minority of marriages. The vital couple is like most other couples; they argue, disagree, occasionally engage in conflict, but in all negative confrontations there is a willingness and a commitment to forgive and forget. The essence of the vital relationship is that "the mates are intensely bound together psychologically in important life matters. Their sharing and their togetherness is genuine. It provides the life essence for both man and woman." This does not mean that they agree on or share in everything. Rather the vital marital relationship is one in which the spouses have reached a virtually total consensus on what is mutually important. They then have reached a mutual agreement to attack these areas with vigor and together.

THE TOTAL.   The total marriage relationship is a vital relationship and more. Couples in this last type of marital interaction are totally meshed in interests, tastes, needs, role performances. They spend all of their time together, revelling in each other's company. The two have become in essence one—separate yet together, individuals yet deindividualized. It goes without saying that although many may have a total relationship as an ideal goal, most couples never attain and maintain such a state of marital perfection. For those who do, the bliss is obvious.

## SEX IN MARRIAGE

One of the most important components of marital interaction involves the intimate sexual exchanges that take place backstage in a relationship. Prior to marriage all of us look forward with great anticipation to having a regular sex partner, a partner with whom we are "in love," a partner with whom we can explore the depths of physical and emotional love. After marriage sex usually assumes a central position in the relationship and is one form of recreation that seems to continue, even when conflict, strain, and stress characterize other regions of the marital relationship.

One would think that such a vital part of the marital relationship, an activity that seems to consume so much of our time-in-thought, an activity of overriding interest and concern to both males and females, would have been the subject of extensive study and research. As we saw in Chapters 10 and 11, extensive research has been conducted on premarital sex—surely the same must be true for marital sex. Almost 90 percent of the population spends possibly 90 percent of its sexually adult years in marriage and in marital sexual activity. Furthermore, marital relationships are more enduring than either premarital or extramarital relationships. In addition, marital sexual relationships are the only ones that are sanctioned in our society. The fact is, however, we know very little about marital sexuality. What we do know is generally from non-random samples, which are often of persons seeking help for sexual problems.

### The Redbook Survey

One study that attempted to focus on "normal" women was conducted by Robert and Amy Levin (1975) for *Redbook* magazine. Their questionnaire was answered by more than 100,000 women. Although not "statistically representative" of all American women, it is difficult to ignore what these women have to say about the quality of their sexual encounters in marriage. Listed below are some of the more important findings from the *Redbook* survey:[2]

1. No matter how many years they have been married, 7 out of 10 women report that the sexual aspect of marriage is good or very good, and 2 out of 10 describe it as fair.
2. The percentage of once-married and remarried women who rate sex as good or very good is identical: 68 percent.
3. Women with children are just as likely to be satisfied with sex as married women without children, and women with two or more children are as satisfied as women with just one child. In

---

[2] Robert J. and Amy Levin, "Sexual Pleasure: The Surprising Preferences of 100,000 Women," *Redbook* (September, 1975). Reprinted by permission.

other words, when it comes to sexual satisfaction in marriage, *children make no appreciable difference.*

4. The younger women in Kinsey's sample were just slightly more likely to have experimented with oral-genital sex; it was practiced by 57 percent. Today, as *Redbook*'s survey indicates, *the comparable figure for all respondents between 20 and 39 years of age is 91 percent.* Ninety-one out of 100 of these women have experienced oral-genital sex, both giving and receiving it. Of those 91, 40 engage in it often and another 45 occasionally, 5 tried it just once, and 1 did not mention frequency.

5. *Thirty out of every 100 women who answered the questionnaire acknowledge having had sex after smoking marihuana.* Most of them were under 30. The percentages who have ever combined use of marihuana and sex declines regularly with age: under 20 years old, 63 percent; 20–24 years old, 48 percent; 25–29 years old, 28 percent; 30–34 years old, 17 percent; 35–39 years old, 10 percent; 40 years old and older, 5 percent.

6. The sexually passive female was, in 1975, an extremely rare individual—not even 1 out of 100. Women who say they have very good sex lives are more likely to be active participants during intercourse than women who say that their sex lives are no better than fair.

## The Numbers Game

One of the things that characterizes our approach to evaluating marital sex is numbers—we seem to equate frequency, either of intercourse or orgasm, with success-happiness, satisfaction. The data in Table 14–4 show

**TABLE 14–4**

**Frequency of Intercourse and Satisfaction with Marital Sex: The *Redbook* Survey**

| ESTIMATED MONTHLY FREQUENCY OF INTERCOURSE | DEGREE OF SATISFACTION (PERCENTAGES) | | |
|---|---|---|---|
| | VERY GOOD OR GOOD | FAIR | POOR OR VERY POOR |
| None | 9 | 8 | 83 |
| 1–5 times | 35 | 34 | 31 |
| 6–10 times | 72 | 23 | 5 |
| 11–15 times | 86 | 11 | 3 |
| 16–20 times | 91 | 7 | 2 |
| More than 20 times | 93 | 5 | 2 |

SOURCE: Adapted from Robert J. and Amy Levin, "Sexual Pleasure: The Surprising Preferences of 100,000 Women," *Redbook,* p. 55. Reprinted by permission.

that this is, to some extent, true. For those couples who engage in intercourse six or more times a month, a substantial majority rate their satisfaction with marital sex as very good or good. Frequency of orgasm is also directly related to satisfaction with marital sex. However, failure to achieve orgasm or achieving it only occasionally does not guarantee that marital sex is unsatisfactory. As Levin and Levin (1975:58) note: "For a considerable number of women, other pleasures experienced during intercourse are enough to create a sense of sexual satisfaction."

### Effects of Communication on Sexual Satisfaction

A final "fact" to emerge from the *Redbook* survey fits well into the content of this chapter—marital interaction. Of every 100 women who always discuss intimate feelings with their husbands, 88 say they have good sex lives; 70 out of 100 women who never discuss these feelings with their husbands say they have fair or poor sex lives (Levin and Levin, 1975:58).

This linkage between sex as a physical form of interaction and the communication by the wife of her sexual needs, desires, and feelings is very important. The key to a satisfactory sexual adjustment does not lie in technical competence or technique; neither does it lie in soft music, perfume, and sexy garments; rather, the key lies in an open and honest exchange in which each partner shares his or her needs. To the extent that the partners listen to each other and make adjustments to satisfy the other, sexual satisfaction will result. As Levin and Levin (1975:58) conclude: "Sex is a physical expression of emotional unity that, perhaps better than words, permits a man and woman to tell each other that the bond between them is still present and strong."

## THE POSSIBLE UNIQUENESS
## OF MARITAL INTERACTION

The interactive encounter of a married couple is, in some ways, like that which might occur between any two people, regardless of their sex or status, or the degree of intimacy that characterizes the relationship. Almost all interactive situations involve an attempt to communicate ideas and information, beliefs and feelings, preferences and desires; to replay the past and forecast the future. An important question for us to consider is: Can and how can marital interaction be different from other types of interaction? The answers offered below are necessarily a reflection of my own marital experiences, what I have observed among married couples, and my values and attitudes concerning marriage and married life.

Marital interaction is unique in that it is based on a voluntary commitment to fuse two lives, two personalities, two selves into a relationship that is culturally sanctioned and legally endowed with privileges, rights, and responsibilities not found in any other type of relationship.

This is not meant to negate the possibility that two people who are living together in what has been termed a spiritual marriage can achieve a total and meaningful fusion of personalities. Undoubtedly this occurs, and with some frequency. However, such relationships do not have the benefit of the cement provided by cultural sanction, at least not yet. Such interactive relationships can be severed with much greater ease than one involving marital interaction. Somehow the legal status of the commitment seems to provide a stimulus to maintain the lines of communication even when there are serious pressures to quit. This kind of stimulus is unique to marital interaction.

Marital interaction may be unique, at least in a culture with equalitarian ideals, in that it usually involves a commitment to maximizing actualization of the self and the other. As discussed in Chapters 12 and 13, on mate selection, our culture socializes us to seek out that person from the field of eligibles with whom we can achieve a maximum amount of self-fulfillment. The model operative in the selection process emphasizes that self-actualization is most likely to occur as an exchange of the opportunity to help the other achieve his or her maximum potential. If my expansion of Reiss's (1960) wheel hypothesis of love is accurate, then most couples are rather constantly seeking to increase their rapport, self-disclosure, mutual dependency, and personality need fulfillment through the marital interaction process. Love and the last stage of the wheel, personality need fulfillment, are not experiences that once achieved are maintained forever. They must be constantly improved upon. I believe that marital interaction is unique as a vehicle for recycling the attempts at actualization and self-actualization.

*A young married couple—together, happy, ready for the journey through life as partners.*

Rose Skytta, Jeroboam Inc.

Marital interaction is unique in its facilitation of a commitment to constructive openness. Because of the legal and social nature of the marriage arrangement, married couples are almost forced to seek full and frank openness with one another. Unlike most other affectional relationships, married couples have the opportunity to develop, and the culture encourages the development of, the closest possible cooperation. In a society in which competition permeates almost all relationships, marriage is sanctioned as a noncompetitive retreat from the so-called rat race. Husbands and wives are expected, almost required, by the norms to be sympathetic and empathetic helpmates—the one person with whom the other can divulge his or her fears and anxieties, goals and desires, without the threat of being negatively sanctioned. Marriage, then, is unique in providing a context wherein openness and honesty are expected, and there is an obligation to help.

## A MACRO PERSPECTIVE ON MARITAL INTERACTION

It is obvious that not all marriages are productive of the kinds of marital interaction just described. In fact, it is probably safe to say that most interaction in marriage is routine—an attempt to deal with the pragmatic and day-to-day tasks that consume so much of our attention and time. In the preceding sections focus has been on the micro aspects of the interactive experience in marriage—the positive and negative facets of living together as husband and wife. But marital interaction, at least in terms of its perceived and real consequences, can also be viewed from the macro perspective. In other words, perhaps the proportion of persons who enter marriage is some indication of the pull toward the potentialities of marital interaction. Those whose first marriage ends in divorce or widowhood and who remarry may be confirming the real value attached to the marital situation in our society. With this in mind let us examine the marrying behavior of the American population.

Information on marriages in the United States is usually available from at least two sources, the marriage registration of states and the special surveys of the Census Bureau. The data presented here were obtained from the latter source and represent the marital histories of persons born between 1900 and 1959 who were between the ages of 16 and 75 years of age at the time of the survey, 1975.

The figures in Table 14–5 confirm the contention that nearly all persons get married at some time during their lives. For those males born between 1935 and 1939 (thirty-six to forty years old in 1975) only 6.5 percent were still single while 77.8 percent were in their first marriage and 15.6 percent were in their second or subsequent marriage. For the females born in those years a smaller percentage (4.5 percent) had remained single,

**TABLE 14–5**

Percentage Distribution by Number of Times Married as of 1975

| RACE, SPANISH ORIGIN, AND YEAR OF BIRTH | MEN | | | | WOMEN | | | |
|---|---|---|---|---|---|---|---|---|
| | SINGLE IN 1975 | ONCE | TWICE | 3 OR MORE | SINGLE IN 1975 | ONCE | TWICE | 3 OR MORE |
| Total born 1900–59. | 26.1 | 62.5 | 9.8 | 1.5 | 20.6 | 67.0 | 10.8 | 1.7 |
| White | 25.2 | 63.7 | 9.7 | 1.5 | 19.5 | 68.1 | 10.7 | 1.7 |
| Black | 33.3 | 53.2 | 11.7 | 1.8 | 29.0 | 57.7 | 11.8 | 1.5 |
| Other races | 35.3 | 58.3 | 6.1 | 0.3 | 23.3 | 69.4 | 6.6 | 0.8 |
| Spanish origin[a] | 29.9 | 61.1 | 8.2 | 0.8 | 23.5 | 66.2 | 9.3 | 1.0 |
| Born: | | | | | | | | |
| 1955–59 | 93.9 | 6.0 | 0.1 | — | 83.9 | 15.9 | 0.2 | — |
| 1950–54 | 54.7 | 43.5 | 1.7 | 0.1 | 37.6 | 58.9 | 3.3 | 0.2 |
| 1945–49 | 20.0 | 73.2 | 6.3 | 0.5 | 12.8 | 77.8 | 8.8 | 0.6 |
| 1940–44 | 9.7 | 78.6 | 10.6 | 1.1 | 6.9 | 80.0 | 11.7 | 1.4 |
| 1935–39 | 6.5 | 77.8 | 13.9 | 1.7 | 4.5 | 79.6 | 13.8 | 2.1 |
| 1930–34 | 5.0 | 80.4 | 12.6 | 2.0 | 4.2 | 79.4 | 13.9 | 2.5 |
| 1925–29 | 5.1 | 78.9 | 13.6 | 2.4 | 4.1 | 78.2 | 15.4 | 2.3 |
| 1920–24 | 5.2 | 77.5 | 14.6 | 2.7 | 4.2 | 78.1 | 15.2 | 2.5 |
| 1915–19 | 5.4 | 77.4 | 14.5 | 2.7 | 4.8 | 77.0 | 15.1 | 3.1 |
| 1910–14 | 4.7 | 75.0 | 17.8 | 2.6 | 6.1 | 74.2 | 20.7 | 2.9 |
| 1905–09 | 5.2 | 74.3 | 16.9 | 3.6 | 5.9 | 73.7 | 17.4 | 3.0 |
| 1900–04 | 4.7 | 71.5 | 20.5 | 3.2 | 7.3 | 73.8 | 15.2 | 3.7 |

SOURCE: U.S. Department of Commerce, Bureau of the Census, *Current Population Reports,* Series P-20, No. 297 (October, 1976). Washington: Government Printing Office, p. 1.

[a] People of Spanish origin may be of any race.

a somewhat larger percentage had been married only once (79.6) and 15.9 percent had been married two or more times.

Although it is not appropriate to generalize from these figures down to individual couples, it is plausible to suggest that there must be something about the marital context that attracts large numbers of volunteers. The fact that 74 or 75 percent of the males and females between the ages of 61 and 65 in 1975 were still married to their first and only spouse should indicate that their marital interaction experiences were at least positive enough to continue. Certainly some positive needs are being fulfilled in these marriages since the options for severing the relationship are rather easy to initiate.

The permanence of the first marriage is affected by the family income and the educational levels of the husband and wife (Current Population Reports, Series P-20, No. 239, September, 1972, p. 2):

In 71.7 percent of the households where the husband was 35 to 54 years old and the family income was less than $5,000, both the husband and

389

the wife had been married only once. However, both had been married only once in 77.2 percent of the households where the family income was $5,000 to $9,999, 80.8 percent of those with an income of $10,000 to $14,999, and 83.0 percent of those with incomes of $15,000 or more. Both partners had been married only once in 75 percent of the households where neither the husband nor the wife was a high school graduate. But, in 83.1 percent of the households where the husband and the wife had graduated from high school and 90.4 percent of those where both partners were college graduates, the husband and wife had been married only once.

The cynic might claim that these data are an index of the complacency of most married people. I prefer to read the data as indicative of the potential for self-fulfillment in marriage. If the interactive experiences in marriage were primarily negative, a smaller proportion of persons would enter marriage, would stay married to the same spouse for a shorter period of time, and an even smaller proportion would remarry. The facts suggest that marital interaction is not only functional for most people, but evidently the source of overall satisfaction that is considered more desirable than living without a spouse.

In Chapters 15 and 16 we examine some of the dynamics related to the distribution of power within marriage and the degree of perceived satisfaction, success, and adjustment of married couples. Most of the focus will be at the social-psychological level.

## SOME POSSIBLE IMPLICATIONS

*In a world in which social change is ubiquitous, the interactions that occur between married spouses are necessarily affected. The premarital biography of a married couple in the last quarter of the twentieth century may be quite different from the premarital biography of a couple who went through the marital selection process in the period from 1900 to 1960. Will the marital interactions of the coming generation be different because of changes in the marital selection process, dating, and premarital sexual behaviors? What are the implications of marital interaction for couples who are likely to have not only enjoyed premarital sex together but also lived together prior to marriage?*

*One positive possibility is that marital interactions may be more open, with less frustration, anxiety, and conflict about sexual matters and marital role playing. In other words, married couples in the future may be better able to communicate with each other than their counterparts of earlier days. Another positive possibility is that couples having difficulty with marital interactions may have access to more outside help in solving their differences. The proliferation of marriage counseling agencies and personnel may mean that marital-interaction difficulties can be more often solved before they lead to the dissolution of the marriage.*

    *A possible negative consequence of changes in the courtship and marital selection processes and the prevalence of premarital sexual experience may be an increase in the prevalence of extramarital sexual affairs. If such occurs, then it is almost certain that the phenomenon will have a negative impact on the quality of marital interaction for these couples.*

# 15

# POWER WITHIN THE FAMILY

*What is power, and what are its essential components?*

*What are the different ways that power manifests itself in the family?*

*Does an equalitarian orientation to the family necessarily imply equal power?*

*Is it better to give or to receive power in the family?*

Power is a concept used in almost every field of study from engineering and physics to religion and sociology. It is a term that has a plethora of meanings and that can elicit a tremendous variety of images, some very positive and some equally negative. Perhaps the most common analogues to the concept of power are control, strength, and that something that goes with position. For example, it is rather commonly accepted that a parent (position) has almost absolute power over a child, at least up to a certain age, because the parent is stronger and, in an economic, legal, and traditional sense, has control over the child. This holds true whether the parent is warm and loving or cruel and insensitive. In a similar fashion, the patriarch of the traditional Muslim family (see Chapter 7) could exercise an almost dictatorial power over his wife or wives because the culture ascribed to the male (position) the right, privilege, and obligation to control her life opportunities and if she did not obey his wishes, to beat her into submission (strength).

Both of these examples fit well into a very traditional view of power as something inherent in a position that is reckoned in terms like *strength* and *control*. Although such a traditional approach to power is still valid, it must be modified to be applicable to male-female and parent-child relationships in a society that places such a high premium on full equality, individuality, and nonexploitation. Few would disagree that there has been a substantial diminution of power associated with positions that have been traditionally imbued with many options for control and the use of strength or force, where and when necessary, to bring about compliance and deference. It was just such a situation that led many conservative students of social change to decry the declining power of husbands and fathers in American society (see Chapter 4 and Sorokin, 1937; Zimmerman, 1949; Ogburn and Nimkoff, 1965). They predicted, and accurately, that increasing urbanization, widespread affluence, the development of equal educational opportunities for women, a growing industrial economy that pulls more and more women into the labor force, and pervasive mobility due to the automobile would create a new order among men and women and parents and children.

In this chapter the goal is to examine power within the family in two ways. First, we will review some research that has used the more traditional conception of power as inherent in certain positions and as manifested in control and strength. The limitations and criticisms of this approach will be outlined. Second, we will develop an exchange model of power that may be more consistent with the new order emerging in our society relative to male-female and parent-child relationships.

# A TRADITIONAL STUDY OF FAMILIAL POWER

Of all the topics that have been researched by sociologists studying the family, the family power structure has received more than its fair share of attention. From all the studies on material power conducted during the 1960–70 decade, Safilios-Rothschild (1970) has pointed to at least ten major studies and numerous other studies that have been either replications of or attempts to further specify earlier findings.

Not unlike other areas of concern for specialists of the family, there is one study against which all others are usually compared. This classic study was conducted by Robert Blood and Donald Wolfe in 1960 and involved 731 urban and 178 farm wives living in the greater Detroit area.

The two assumptions that formed the nucleus of Blood and Wolfe's conceptualization of power seem to recognize the new order. First, they point out that historically the husband's economic and social role gave to him the prerogative to be dominant, if not completely autocratic. This, they say, has now changed to the point where husbands and wives are potential if not actual equals. Man, because of his sex, is no longer sanctioned by culture or social tradition to be the boss. They state (1960:30), "The role of culture has shifted from sanctioning a competent sex over an incompetent sex to sanctioning a competent marriage partner over the incompetent one, regardless of sex." In other words, they treat the current marital system as if it were permeated by equalitarian norms.

Their second assumption follows quite naturally from a view that the equalitarian marriage is now the norm. Blood and Wolfe subscribe to what is called a "resources" theory of power. They reason that if equality is present at the beginnings of married life, then any tipping of the marital power scale toward one partner (usually the husband) occurs because that partner has more resources (education, occupational experience, higher status background, and so forth) than his spouse.

With these two seemingly nontraditional assumptions serving as a foundation, Blood and Wolfe developed a rather traditional scale to measure family or marital power. Power for them consisted of who makes the final decision in each of the eight areas listed in Table 15–1. (In every family somebody has to decide such things as where the family will live and so on. Many couples talk such things over first, but the *final* decision often has to be made by the husband or wife.)

Two types of scores are obtained from the Blood and Wolfe scale. The first, the shared authority score, can range from zero through eight and is computed by adding the number of times the "Husband and Wife Exactly the Same" category is checked. Since the entire scale is designed to assess the power-authority situation in a family, the higher the shared authority score, the more equalitarian is the family decision-making or power process.

The second type of scoring produces a four-fold classification of the power distribution within a family. Wolfe (1959) had developed this

395

**TABLE 15–1**

**Decision-Making Scale of Marital Power**

| | HUSBAND ALWAYS | HUSBAND MORE THAN WIFE | HUSBAND AND WIFE EXACTLY THE SAME | WIFE MORE THAN HUSBAND | WIFE ALWAYS |
|---|---|---|---|---|---|
| A. Who usually makes the *final* decision about what car to get? | [5] | [4] | [3] | [2] | [1] |
| B. Who usually makes the *final* decision about whether or not to buy some life insurance? | [5] | [4] | [3] | [2] | [1] |
| C. Who usually makes the *final* decision about what house or apartment to take? | [5] | [4] | [3] | [2] | [1] |
| D. Who usually makes the *final* decision about what job the husband should take? | [5] | [4] | [3] | [2] | [1] |
| E. Who usually makes the *final* decision about whether or not the wife should go to work or quit work? | [5] | [4] | [3] | [2] | [1] |
| F. Who usually makes the *final* decision about how much money your family can afford to spend per week on food? | [5] | [4] | [3] | [2] | [1] |
| G. Who usually makes the *final* decision about what doctor to have when someone is sick? | [5] | [4] | [3] | [2] | [1] |
| H. Who usually makes the *final* decision about where to go on a vacation? | [5] | [4] | [3] | [2] | [1] |

SOURCE: Reprinted with permission of Macmillan Publishing Co., Inc., from *Husbands and Wives*, by Robert O. Blood and Donald Wolfe. Copyright © 1960 by The Free Press, a corporation.

typology, which was labeled "relative authority" in a paper that appeared before *Hubands and Wives*. He argued that each spouse has a range of authority, part of which is exclusively one spouse's domain; the residual range is shared between them. There may also be certain regions where neither has authority over the other—a kind of stand-down area.

Thus, the second score is obtained by considering both the Shared Authority and Relative Authority scores. The Relative Authority figure is obtained by adding the scores obtained on the eight decision items, and it can range from 8 to 40. Wolfe's classification of power distribution in the family is as follows:

1. *Wife Dominant* (a relative authority score of 19 or less). This occurs when the wife's range of authority, at least on these eight items, is considerably larger than the husband's. For example, let

us assume that the answer was "Wife Always" on every item but A (what car to get) and D (what job the husband should take). The Shared Authority score would be 2. To obtain the Relative Authority score we would add the scores of all eight items (A = 3, D = 3, B, C, E, F, G, and H = 1), resulting in a total Relative Authority score of 12.

2. *Syncratic* (a relative authority score of 20–28 and a shared authority score of 4 to 8). This type of authority/power arrangement consists of couples for whom there is nearly a balance of relative authority, and the shared range is equal to or greater than the combined ranges of husband and wife.

3. *Autonomic* (a relative authority score of 20–28 and a shared authority score of 3 or less). The relative authority is nearly equal, but the hubsand and wife's ranges together are greater than the shared range.

4. *Husband Dominant* (a relative authority score of 29 or more). In this type of situation the husband's range of authority is considerably broader than the wife's.

### Selected Findings from the Blood and Wolfe Study

The largest percentage of families were Autonomic (41 percent), which indicates a division of labor in decision making with shared authority rather low. About 31 percent of their sample was labeled syncratic, with the shared authority range equal to or greater than the husband and wife ranges of discrete authority. Not surprisingly, Blood and Wolfe found that 25 percent of the families were husband dominant, and only 3 percent were wife dominant.

The resources hypothesis posited by Blood and Wolfe was supported in that the higher the husband's occupational prestige, income, and general status (based on occupation, income, education, and ethnic background), the more power he had to make family decisions. They found, however, that middle-class, white-collar husbands generally had more power than blue-collar husbands; but when blue-collar marriages were considered separately, the lower blue-collar husbands had more power than higher blue-collar husbands.

The relative resources of husbands and wives was also found to be important. The wife with small dependent children had less power than the wife without children or with children who were no longer dependent. The wife who was gainfully employed had more power than the housewife.

A rather large amount of space has been devoted to the Blood and Wolfe study for several reasons. First, as previously mentioned, it is the benchmark against which most subsequent studies have been evaluated. Second, the Detroit study has been replicated a number of times, both

397

within the United States and abroad, with less than uniform support for the resources hypothesis. Third, and perhaps most important, the Blood and Wolfe study has been severely criticized on a number of points. We will look first at criticisms that deal with the methods used by Blood and Wolfe and then at criticisms of their concepts of power and their findings.

## Methodological Criticisms

WIVES' SOCIOLOGY. Initially the most telling criticism of Blood and Wolfe's study is the type of sample they used, 731 urban wives and 178 rural wives from the greater Detroit area. Explicitly stated, it takes two to have a marital power arrangement, and they limited their data to the perceptions wives have of power within the family. Safilios-Rothschild (1969b) has called this "wives' family sociology." Unfortunately, this criticism also applies equally to studies dealing with topics other than marital power.

DISCREPANCIES IN HUSBAND-WIFE PERCEPTIONS OF POWER. What Safilios-Rothschild is suggesting is that Blood and Wolfe might have reached different conclusions if they had bothered to ask husbands the same questions. There is considerable evidence that spouses disagree as to who has the power. Heer (1962) found that husbands and wives reported having less power than their spouses attributed to them. Kenkel (1957) suggested that wives tend to overestimate their husbands' power and that there is a considerable discrepancy in husbands' and wives' reports of their respective roles in decision making (see Kenkel and Hoffman, 1956).

In her study of Detroit residents, Safilios-Rothschild (1969b) found discrepancies in answers ranging from 55 to 76 percent. It could be that both husbands and wives are giving the conventional and expected responses in these cases rather than the truth. Another, and more plausible, answer is that each person within a family views the same phenomena from different perspectives. This was shown most clearly in a study conducted in Oregon. Larson (1974) found that agreement on a general measure of power existed in only 56 percent of the family units (father-mother-child). Agreement on problem-solving processes (*who* is responsible for determining *how* disagreements are settled in the family) was found in only 24 percent of the families studied. Regardless of the reason for these discrepancies in the study of power, this methodological shortcoming is an important one to consider.

DECISIONS TO BE INCLUDED. As discussed earlier, Blood and Wolfe asked about decision making in only eight areas. The criteria they used in selecting these eight were that: (a) they are all relatively important decisions that nearly all families make at some time or another; (b) they should constitute a representative listing of decisions that are either traditionally male or female decision areas; and (c) they should be decisions that affect the entire family.

Centers et al. (1971) disagree that the eight decisions are representative and suggest that the cards are stacked in favor of male dominance. To neutralize this bias they added the following decision-making problems: (a) what people you will invite to the house or go out with, (b) how to decorate or furnish the house, (c) which TV or radio program to tune in, (d) what the family will have for dinner, (e) what clothes you will buy, and (f) what type of clothes your husband (or wife) will buy.

The results obtained for their Los Angeles sample of husbands and wives were predictable—the power shift was toward the wife but constituted only a 10 percent loss in the husbands' average power score. In addition, Centers and his associates found almost no discrepancy in the perceived decision-making power between spouses.

ALL DECISIONS TREATED AS EQUAL. This last methodological criticism is concerned with the problem of the importance of the decision to the person who always makes it. Thus, it might be possible for a family to be considered husband dominant because none of the decisions listed are considered important by his spouse or wife dominant because the husband does not regard the decisions listed as important. For example, a decision on which job the husband will take may not be important for the wife whose husband was a fireman when she married him and has never been anything else. The problem just does not occur with enough frequency to be important.

Quite obviously it is significant to consider the frequency with which the decisions occur or must occur if we are going to equate one decision with another. Merely to add the answers without assessing how important they are is poor math and even worse logic.

*In an equalitarian marriage, sharing extends to all domains of life.*

Richard Kalvar, Magnum Photos, Inc.

## MEASURING POWER IN FAMILIES

The criticisms leveled at the methods used by Blood and Wolfe and others to measure marital power may seem a little harsh, although they are clearly appropriate. Perhaps other approaches or measurement methods are not any better. In any case the assumption was tested in a study conducted among 842 individuals in 211 families in Toronto (see Turk and Bell, 1972).

Power relations within these families were examined using nine different measures that had been used in previous studies. In addition to questionnaire items like those used by Blood and Wolfe (1960), the Heer (1958, 1962) questions on who usually wins when there is a disagreement, and the Hess and Torney (1962) question on who is the "real boss," Turk and Bell actually observed the families solving tasks and, in the process, derived power scores from observation of family interaction patterns.

Of the thirty-six possible intercorrelations among these measures of power within families, fifteen were below .10, and fourteen were between .10 and .19. If these various measures were tapping the same phenomenon of power, the correlations would have been much higher, somewhere above .70. The conclusion is quite clear—the various measures of family or marital power devised by sociologists are not comparable. Further, Turk and Bell (1972:221) found that a researcher's "findings depend on which family member is used or treated as the key informant. . . . Respondents in different positions in the family group respond with their own particular perceptions."

The overall conclusion drawn by Turk and Bell is consistent with that reached by Safilios-Rothschild (1970) in her review of all articles published on the family power structure between 1960 and 1969: "Continued use of these measures is not justified without further specification of what aspect of the general phenomenon is being measured by any given index. The possibility also exists that there is no one meaning to power, or, if there is, that such measures as these are not measuring the phenomenon with enough precision to be useful. Clearly a reanalysis of the concept of power is a requirement for the resolution of the issues being posed."

## SOME CONCEPTUAL CONSIDERATIONS
## ABOUT MARITAL POWER

The criticisms leveled at the methods used to measure marital power by Blood and Wolfe and others are only the major ones. Numerous other criticisms are just off stage and could be listed if only we had space. The important point to consider is that even the classic studies have shortcomings. This does not detract from the contributions of these studies or the authors. Sociology is a cumulative science and the future breakthroughs will be founded on the myopic errors of today's researchers and theorists.

The reason that so many criticisms are obvious is not methodological but conceptual. Starting with Blood and Wolfe and extending even until today, marital power has been narrowly equated with making the final decision on a small number of family tasks or problems. Surely the exercise of marital power is more complex than just decision making. Other facets of the exercise of marital and familial power should be considered before family sociologists can feel satisfied with this area of concern. Perhaps the best place to start would be an attempt to describe the assumptions I make about marital/familial power:

EMERGENCE. Power can emerge in a marital situation quite subtly because of the influence one spouse has over the other, or less subtly because one spouse has more authority than the other. For example, in most states a husband has the legal authority (that is, power) to require his wife to move with him to a new area. If she refuses he can charge her with desertion and file for divorce on these grounds. The opposite does not apply. This is only one example of why the Blood-Wolfe assumption of equalitarianism being prevalent is faulty. Legalistically speaking, we still give the husband the power (authority) over the wife in many facets of marital life (see Gillespie, 1971).

All married couples vie for power in the marital relationship through the exercise of influence. The stereotype of the little woman who sweet-talks her man into doing whatever she wants is a good example of the exercise of power that is not based on cultural or normative authority. In fact, of course, married life is a constant exchange of attempts to influence the other to agree or to do something one wants done. For some couples, particularly those that Cuber and Harroff (1965) would describe as conflict habituated, the everyday attempts at influence are probably seen as serious moves in a battle that only one person can win. In such a situation, any influence, strategy, or tactic is appropriate—no tricks are "dirty." For other couples, like those who have a vital or total type of relationship, neither partner is seriously threatened by attempts to influence or by the struggle for marital power. In fact, it is probably a "we-both-win affair" since the lively banter of influence attempts adds spice to the marriage.

Marital power, then, is a combination of acts that acquire their legitimacy because of the authority vested in one partner and the acts based on skills of influence regardless of one's authority. Part of power is what one gives up rather than controls. On almost any grounds the cultural norms in the United States require that the woman give up more than the male (her name, freedom of choice of residence, perhaps her career, and so forth). Consequently, most women start from a weakened position in the marital power game, and the struggle is uphill most of the way.

401

A DYNAMIC PROCESS. Marital power is a dynamic process that makes the past of the present, and the present a basis for the future. Decision making is obviously one of the more observable, if not important, indicators of who has the power in a marital relationship. "Dynamic," then, can refer either to the stages through which a decision goes before it gets made, or to the fact that most decisions have been made before. However, the history of decisions on a certain problem can also be a dynamic part of the exercise of power in a family. Take, for example, the decision to move from one apartment or house to another. If a couple has lived in nine different apartments in their first nine years of marriage, the process of selecting that tenth residence is clearly affected by the previous nine decisions. Let us assume that the couple is equalitarian in terms of decision-making power, and that neither would unilaterally commit the pair to an apartment without consensus.

As the couple moves through the searching and elimination process, each attempts to influence the other by describing his or her preferences ("I like a fireplace, an electric stove, and a separate dining room" countered by "But this is on the wrong side of town, and I don't like the size of the bedrooms"). In addition, the couple engages in a "plea to history exercise." One will say, "This reminds me of our little apartment on East Sixth Avenue. Remember that one? You liked it, but it was entirely too small!" The other will respond by saying, "Yes, but the townhouse you want to get is just like John and Jane's. When we stayed with them last year, you vowed we would never live in a townhouse—remember?"

The point is that marital power and the decision-making process is dynamic. No one decision is made in isolation from preceding decisions about that matter or similar matters. In addition, the marital power process is dynamic in that most decisions are made over time and in stages so that each partner can engage in a number of counteracting influence attempts until the couple reaches a consensus.

THE WIFE'S IMPORTANCE. Marital power is not and cannot be adequately viewed as the sum of who makes the final decisions on numerous problems or, for that matter, as a reflection of traditional male and traditional female roles. Sociologists have, in my opinion, too easily accepted the idea that males make most of the instrumental decisions in families and females take care of the expressive side of the house. Even a cursory examination of the everyday activities of American couples indicates just how instrumental the wife's role really is, especially if the wife is not employed for pay and the husband is away at work most of the time. The average American housewife has to have the patience of Job, the confidence of Patton, the skills of an Indianapolis 500 racer and a C.P.A., not to mention a strong back, stomach, and the ability to withstand the strains of a monotonous, sometimes alienating and definitely underpaid job.

If marital power is defined in terms of the total number of decisions made that affect the family or the importance of these decisions for the family, practically all American families are probably wife dominant. (I am firmly convinced that most males would fall apart at the seams if they had to endure the pressures their wives face on a daily basis.) But marital power, if it is to be adequately conceptualized, must not focus on who makes the final decisions in a limited number of areas or be based solely on an instrumental-expressive definition of marital tasks.

PARTICIPATION OF CHILDREN.  The marital power struggle is not limited to just the husband and wife. When children are present, especially older children who are beginning to establish or have already established themselves in a network of friends outside the family, the exercise of power by either the husband or the wife, or by both as parents, is sometimes sabotaged by the wishes (that is, influence) of the children. It is not unusual for a father-husband to exert his authority by saying, "This year we are going to take our vacation in the mountains from June 12 to June 24 and that is final!" The wife-mother may not really object since she has subtly influenced her spouse to go somewhere besides his mother's place. All of a sudden one of the children says, "I'm not going—I have to be here for Little League." After some arguments, threats, crying, and so forth, everyone gets ready for bed. Thirty minutes after everyone is in bed for the night a voice, just loud enough to be heard, says, "I *never* get to do what I want to do." The child has made the final decision, and the father confirms it at breakfast. "Okay, you win! We'll take a quick trip to the beach instead."

Children exercise a great deal of power in American families even though they generally have no actual authority to do so. This is one aspect of familial power that has been virtually ignored by sociologists who study the power dynamics in the family.

Another aspect of marital power that has also been ignored is the coalition. Whenever there are more than two people involved in a struggle for power, one ploy consists of the theme Divide and Conquer. More often than not the coalition is composed of Mom and the kids against Dad. The father comes home ready to announce his decision to the family; little does he know that the audience is about to upstage him. He is the victim of a well-laid plot hatched while he was at the office. The wife is ready for him with a kiss, his favorite dinner, the newspaper, and a story of how she has just saved the family a sizable sum of money by not buying items X, Y, and Z. The children are happy to have old Dad home and put on a great show of love, respect, and deference. Needless to say, he is off guard. In a scene not unlike Caesar's encounter with Brutus, the team beats Dad to the punch and gently lets him know that they have decided to do something entirely different from what he has planned. And, because he is such a great guy they will let him go along for the ride.

I realize that this example is rather stereotypical and that although coalitions often exist, they are usually less planned and manipulated than suggested. Even so, the old axiom that "there is strength in numbers" is

403

part of the marital power game. Unfortunately, few studies have examined this facet of the exercise of power within the family.

INFLUENCE OF OUTSIDE FORCES.    Marital power and the exercise of it may be predetermined or, at the least, severely limited by forces outside the family. It is all too simple to limit a discussion or examination of family power dynamics to what happens inside the family. It is also unrealistic. Families exist in a web of entanglements that is the sum of all the demands made on the members plus the limitations of time and money (discretionary income) available for putting decisions into operation.

Let us take as an example a couple with two small children and a limited income. The wife is very close to her parents, but they live a considerable distance away. It has been two years since the two families have been together. The wife occasionally, no more than once a day, says, "We just have to visit my parents soon; they're missing the children in their cutest years." The husband, sensitive to this and his wife's feelings, says, "Okay, as soon as school is out we'll take some vacation time and visit your parents." He has exercised authority in response to the wife's influence attempts.

It all sounds simple—power has been exerted in the family. Yet, the couple does not have the money for such a trip and cannot afford to borrow it. There is a gasoline shortage, the old family car is already on its last leg, it may not be feasible to plan such a trip, and serious medical expenses have depleted the family's savings. In other words, the exercise of authority, influence, power—call it what you will—is of no avail. Outside pressures and entanglements will prohibit the successful completion of family decisions and the exercise of power within the family.

## A RECONCEPTUALIZATION OF FAMILIAL POWER

To this point in our discussion of the operation of power within the family I have been very critical of the existing studies, particularly those that have used the Blood and Wolfe orientation. But debunking should not be indulged in just for the sake of exercise. It should serve as the foundation for a new and improved conceptualization of the process of family power dynamics. In the remaining pages of this chapter the major facets of power within the family as I view them will be specified.

THE THREE REALMS OF POWER.    Power within the family is exercised in three different realms, which, although they may overlap somewhat, should be considered as separate since different roles (requirements, expectations, and enactments) and role relationships are involved. The three realms are the marital, the parental, and the familial.

The first realm, the *marital,* involves only the husband and wife. The major exchanges here begin in the premarital stage and extend

Jean Boughton, Stock, Boston

*Conflict is an ever-present potential in marriage.*

throughout the entire life span of the marriage. Put another way, each married couple has a biography, a history of the shifting balance between husband and/or wife dominant and of the situations in which some kind of negotiated settlement of the operation of power within the marriage is made. It is quite possible that if each spouse were to write an auto-biography of the power exchanges during their life together, there would be some inconsistencies—even some direct contradictions.

The second realm, the *parental,* begins with the introduction of children. Most of the power exercised in this realm is unilateral from parents to children. During the early stages of the family life cycle the major tone of parental power is based on authority. As the children get older the parents increasingly are required to use influence tempered with the threat to use more autocratic techniques if the influence techniques fail. Depending on how close the family of orientation is to the family of procreation, the parents could be a filter for the exercise of influence attempts by the grandparents. For example, a teenage boy was quite short for his age and very sensitive about his height. His parents tried to influence him to try out for basketball, but were unwilling to exercise authority to get him to comply. A meddling grandmother was quite upset that her grandson did not want to play basketball so she offered him $50. When he refused she upped the ante to $100. Parents can and do also serve as the accomplices in efforts made by teachers and other extrafamily members to exercise quasi-parental power.

In the third, the *familial* realm, the power that is exercised is usually by family members for the family. All members may not vie for the chance to make decisions or to control the activities of the others. In some families the familial realm may be as traditionally organized as the marital and parental realms. However, especially in those families with children old enough to be articulate and relatively independent in thought, there may be a rather constant struggle for power and control —sometimes for fun and sometimes with great intensity and seriousness. Power struggles between husband and wife in the marital domain may occasionally if not frequently spill over into the familial as each spouse attempts to co-opt familial support, either overtly or in terms of psychological reinforcement.

Thus, although power within the family may take many forms, it may be useful initially to identify in which realm or domain the power attempts occur, knowing that we will be better able to identify the actors involved and to know something about the tactics or strategies that may also be involved. I am firmly convinced that most acts that may entail the exercise of power in the modern family, regardless of which stage of development is involved, fall within the marital, parental, or familial realm.

TYPES OF POWER. If there are three major realms within which power may be exercised in the family, what is power and what are its components? To reiterate, the study of power within the family is not and cannot be adequately examined by focusing only on decision making, especially if that means who makes the final decision. Every family has a biography that affects its continuing day-to-day activities and its plans for the future. In addition, decisions are made over time and in phases. For example, when a husband and wife walk into a car showroom and the husband says, "We'll take this model," and the wife says, "We want a green one with bucket seats, air conditioning, and an AM-FM radio," we are seeing the end product of much discussion and many negotiated influence attempts. The truly important power plays probably occurred at numerous points in the process, and the actual decisions are routine and anticlimactic, perhaps even irrelevant to the study of power within that family.

Hallenbeck (1966) borrowed some terms from French and Raven (1959) to describe the types of power that may be exercised in a familial situation. The two most important types she discussed are reward power and coercive power. *Reward power* occurs when one person has the resources and the concomitant ability and position to offer inducements for compliance or the threat of withholding desired rewards if compliance does not occur. Reward power is most likely to occur in the marital and parental realms. *Coercive power* is, as the term implies, the option one person has to demand obedience under threat of a negative sanction. We usually think of coercive power in terms of brute force, particularly when small children are concerned. However, as already stated, it is possible under current judicial rules for a husband to coerce his wife to comply with his wishes. Besides a legal sanction to force his spouse to reside with him, the husband has the prerogative to coerce his spouse to submit to his sexual advances since rape is not legally possible in marriage, at least according to current legal definitions. No doubt that coercive power is used more often in the marital realm than we realize.

The other types of power discussed by Hallenbeck are *legitimate power* (the legally or culturally sanctioned ability to control another's behavior), *referent power* (the ability to control another's behavior because of one's position or status within a group) and *expert power* (the recognition of one's ability to perform certain tasks because of training or skills in an area of competence).

DEFINITION OF POWER. The most adequate overall discussion of power was developed by Peter Blau (1964) and emphasizes the idea that it entails an exchange that occurs among members of groups like a family. For Blau (1964:117–118), *power* is "the ability of persons or groups to impose their will on others, despite resistance, through deterrence, either in the forms of withholding regularly supplied rewards or in the form of punishment, inasmuch as the former as well as the latter constitute, in effect, a negative sanction."

Blau lists three implications of his definition: First, power refers not to a single instance of influencing a decision, but rather to *recurrently occurring attempts* of one person to impose his or her will on another. Second, "the punishment threatened for resistance, provided it is severe, makes power a compelling force, yet there is an *element of voluntarism* in power—the punishment could be chosen in preference to compliance, and it sometimes is—which distinguishes it from the limiting case of direct physical coercion." Third, power is essentially *asymmetrical*—that is, it implies a one-sided affair. Power, then, must rest on "the net ability of a person to withhold rewards from and apply punishments to others—the ability that remains after the restraints they can impose on him have been taken into account. Its source is one-sided dependence. Interdependence and mutual influence of equal strength indicate lack of power."

Put another way, power is exercised only in situations in which one person has some services that are deemed desirable or necessary by others. If these services cannot be obtained anywhere else, then dependence occurs and the receivers are obligated to comply with that person's requests. Power can, however, be neutralized.

Richard Emerson (1962) suggested four such power-neutralization tactics that could free dependent persons of their obligations: First, dependent persons could reciprocally supply the powerful person with a needed service. If this can be accomplished, the person who would be dependent, were it not for the reciprocity, can escape the obligation to be compliant and show deference. Thus, the housewife of a rising young executive, who is dependent on her spouse for economic support, can neutralize her obligation and his power by providing him with services he must have if he is to maintain his position in the business world.

Second, the dependent person could obtain the needed services from some other supplier. For example, it is not unusual for the college-

407

educated wife who has left the labor force to care for the children to feel trapped, a slave to her husband and his career. If he begins to lord over her the fact that her status in life is tied to his accomplishments, the obligations for compliance to his demands and for deference could be neutralized by her re-entry into the labor force and the status derived from her accomplishments.

A third technique for neutralizing a power-dependence relationship is to beat the other person at his or her own game. This implies a coercive tactic on the part of the dependent person (that is, forcing him or her to provide the service without the concomitant feeling that the dependent person should be thankful for what he or she got). In the marital realm this exchange, more likely than not, is tied to the marital bed. It is probably not an unusual occurrence for dependent housewives to neutralize obligations in other areas by sexual domination (that is, the extension of or withholding of rewards deemed important by the husband).

A fourth reaction to a power-dependence relationship does not neutralize the power entirely. It involves resigning oneself to do without the service, perhaps finding some substitute for it. For example, suppose an insensitive husband seeking deference from his wife threatens to withhold his attention and affection. She can neutralize his power play by saying, "Okay, have it your way. I don't need your affection and support. I get all I need from the children."

## STRUCTURAL LIMITATIONS ON THE EXERCISE OF MARITAL POWER

Before depicting the usual ways that power is exercised in the marital realm, I shall outline several factors that seem to limit or constrain power within the white, middle-class American family. First, in a very precise sense, marriage seldom involves two fully equal partners. Our society, like many others, has norms that prescribe that deference should be given to those who are older, better educated, have more prestigious jobs, and who are paid more. As indicated in Chapters 12 and 13, males usually marry younger women. In many cases this means that the female spouse will be less educated. There is also abundant evidence that women are paid less than men in the same job and that men are more likely to obtain more rapid advancement in the most prestigious jobs in our society. Thus, using characteristics that are what Blood and Wolfe call resources, women in our society have a better than 50–50 chance of starting married life as less equal than their husbands.

Second, even though child-care services are proliferating and the birthrate and size of families are decreasing, the prevailing ideological preferences are for women to choose motherhood as a full-time profession, at least until the children are in school. If the husband is in an occupation in which advancement is possible through productivity, precisely when he is getting most involved in his work and obtaining rewards for success, the wife is tied to her work with little or no possibility for advancement and even less control over valued services or rewards.

Third, in a society in which the knowledge explosion makes some skills obsolescent almost before they are mastered, the professional mother is asked, almost forced, by society to limit drastically her chances to obtain services valued by society.

Although other limitations on potential husband-wife equality could be listed, the point should be clear that from a structural point of view the white, American, middle-class housewife has an unequal chance to exercise power as it is defined by Blau—especially in the marital realm. She is forced by a large array of pressures to be the copilot, navigator, or perhaps the tail-gunner in marriage. If this is true for the white, middle-class, college-educated housewife, it is even more true for her counterpart in the lower class, who has even less of a chance for equality than her better-educated sister.

## APPLICATION OF BLAU'S EXCHANGE MODEL

If power is defined as the ability to impose one's will on others because one person has control over valued services and rewards, and the recipient(s) incurs an obligation to comply, then how does power operate in the marital, parental, and familial realms in the white, middle-class, American family? It should be noted that the following discussion excludes blacks and is probably best limited to middle-class whites. Blacks are not included because they constitute a somewhat distinct subculture; the social class restriction on whites is also invoked because of subcultural considerations and because of the different meanings of the terms *services* and *rewards* in the upper and lower strata of society.

### Four Conditions That Affect the Processes of Social Exchange and Power (Blau)

STAGE OF FAMILY DEVELOPMENT. The stage in the development of the relationship between the exchange participants is an important condition. Thus, the marital power configuration for a newly married couple should be different from that which exists for a pair in the empty-nest stage of development, and both should be different from situations in which the family consists of parents plus children. In the parental realm the expression of power probably changes in focus and tone as the children get older and as they obtain the ability and resources to counteract parental power through one of Emerson's (1962) techniques. The same comment applies for the exercise of power in the familial realm.

409

CHARACTER OF THE RELATIONSHIP. A second critical condition affecting the exchange processes is the character of the relationship between the exchange participants. Although it is possible that this could refer to short-term events, more likely the term *character* refers to the overall pattern of how, in the marital, parental, and familial realms, the exchange participants relate to one another. This is touched on briefly in Chapter 14 in suggesting that there is a tendency to thematize relationships.

For example, when a couple goes through the entire courtship process and the first twelve years of marriage with each playing the traditional (husband-dominant and wife-passive) roles sans complaints, the chances are quite good that each will thematize the other and the relationship around the traditional roles. In the thirteenth year of their marriage the wife, whose children are all in school and who has recently returned to work, gets involved in the women's rights movement. Needless to say, a strong likelihood is that the old thematized actions and reactions will become inappropriate because the basic character of the relationships (husband-wife, mother-child, father-child) among the exchange participants is changing.

REWARDS STRUCTURE. A third condition that affects the processes of exchange is the nature of the benefits (that is, rewards) that enter into the transactions and the costs incurred in providing them. You will recall, Blau (1964) suggests that control over the reward structure in a relationship is the key to the power and dependence configuration. The value attached to a reward by either the recipient or the giver is related to how much it will cost each of the exchange participants. In some cases the recipient of a reward may consider the cost of accepting too great in terms of future obligations to the giver. For example, in the parental realm of power, a teenage son or daughter may refuse the offer of a car from his or her parents on the grounds that acceptance will obligate the child to be dependent and compliant in other areas, and these other areas of independence may be more important to the son or daughter than the status derived from having one's own means of transportation. On the other hand, in the marital realm of power, the husband may consider that the costs outweigh the benefits in giving the wife what she has always wanted and would be willing to incur an extensive obligation for it (for example, a fur coat or a diamond ring).

Blau (1964:100) devised a typology of rewards (see Table 15–2) that is directly applicable to the three realms of power within the family that we have been discussing. Within the Blau model four different types of rewards allow for reciprocity. That is, the dependence or obligation that might occur if one person gives and the other receives may be easily neutralized by reciprocation. One category of rewards is intrinsic and involves personal attraction and social acceptance being mutually exchanged. The second category is more extrinsic and involves social approval and the

**TABLE 15–2**
A Typology of Rewards

| | MUTUAL RECIPROCITY POSSIBLE | | UNILATERAL |
| | INTRINSIC | EXTRINSIC | |
| --- | --- | --- | --- |
| Spontaneous evaluations | A. Personal attraction | B. Social approval | E. Respect-prestige |
| Calculated actions | C. Social acceptance | D. Instrumental services | F. Compliance-power |

SOURCE: Peter Blau, *Exchange and Power in Social Life* (New York: Wiley, 1964), p. 100. By permission of John Wiley and Sons, Inc.

exchange of instrumental services. An example of the latter in the marital or familial realms would be based on the division of labor (for example, if you do this for me, I will do that for you) . I believe that the great bulk of familial activities in the marital and familial realms of power occur as either the exchange of intrinsic or extrinsic rewards.

A structure-functionalist would say that if reciprocity of intrinsic and extrinsic rewards is in either the marital or familial realms, the system or group is in a state of equilibrium or balance. Blau would say that the attempts to exercise power have been neutralized, and thus power is not operative at all in these instances.

Power within the family, then, consists primarily of the unilateral provision of services or rewards when there is little chance for the recipient to reciprocate. When the exchange involves the evaluation one person has of the other(s), the result is deference (or what Blau calls respect-prestige). This might correspond to what Hallenbeck (1966) calls legitimate, referent, or expert power. I suspect that most exchanges in the marital realm of power are actually situations in which one spouse defers to the other because he or she has more expertise or more resources with which to make a decision.

The most obvious exercise of power, particularly in the marital and parental realms, consists of calculated actions in which one person has almost absolute control over rewards or services, which he or she dispenses with the understanding that compliance and obligation are conditions for those rewards or services being provided. For example, the father might say to a son or daughter, "If you want to go to the party next week and take the car, then you must agree to do the following things." In the marital realm, the wife might say, "If you want to take this new job with all its attendant responsibilities and you expect me to cooperate, I must have (a) a new wardrobe, (b) a full-time maid, (c) an increased household budget, and (d) preferably a new house." The key term in this latter example is the control of cooperation. Without it the husband cannot possibly expect to perform adequately in the new job.

411

Doug Wilson from Black Star

SOCIAL CONTEXT. The last condition that affects the exchange processes and power is the social context in which the exchanges take place. Blau (1964:104–105) identified four facets of this condition. First, the exchange is certainly constrained by the role-set of the participants. This is quite similar to the idea that spouses relate to each other primarily as roles and dominant identities. Therefore, the usual role of the spouses and the resources (referent and expert power) each has relative to the other define a social context for decision making and the exercise of power. This corresponds to the spontaneous evaluations-unilateral focus of Blau's model, and results in respect-prestige interactional exchanges.

Second, according to Blau, the situational and rather spontaneous exercise of power is limited by a prevailing rate of exchange in a marriage or family. No spouse or family will allow one member to make a huge power play since it would violate the understood boundaries of normal exchanges.

A third facet of the social context that affects exchanges and power is the potential for coalitions. As was rather clearly shown in the chapter on the Irish family, a powerful and patriarchal father is restrained from fully exploiting his culturally supported position by the very real possibility of contending with a mother-son coalition.

The fourth and last aspect of the social context affecting exchange and power in the family concerns the interrelationship of all acts. Whenever one person in a family attempts to be all powerful, in numerous, more subtle areas of power he or she may have to moderate power or even take a loss in order to have the others comply in public. Perhaps the best way to illustrate this point is to refer to the male (father-husband) who

412

insists on playing the patriarch in public. The other family members may allow this type of behavior with the power-figure's understanding that such public compliance will cost him dearly in the back regions of family life.

## SUMMARY AND CONCLUSIONS

We have critically reviewed the predominant orientation of family sociologists in the study of power within the family. On a number of points, both methodological and conceptual, the Blood and Wolfe focus on final decisions is inadequate. To build on these weaknesses some assumptions about power were delineated, and usage of an exchange paradigm for the study of power in the marital, parental, and familial realms of family life was advocated.

If previous studies of family power have fallen short of perfection, the reason may be the complexity of the problem rather than the inadequacies of the researchers. The exercise of power within the family is, to a large extent, governed by the tremendous number of interactions that occur during a day, week, or year of a family's life. In addition, all kinds of forces and pressures from outside the family affect its individual members and heavily influence power in a family context.

The chapter that follows deals with marital adjustment and satisfaction that may be influenced by the interactions and power exchanges occurring within families.

## *SOME POSSIBLE IMPLICATIONS*

*One of the most significant phenomena of the late 1960s and early 1970s relative to the family in the United States was the resurgence of the feminist movement. Injustices of the past were brought to the forefront of the public's consciousness. Most of these dealt with power and its exercise. What are some of the implications of the women's liberation movement for the American family?*

*Will this and future generations of children be taught that men and women are equal in all matters? Will the traditional division of labor in the family along sex lines become a historical artifact? Will equality between husband and wife and father and mother finally become a reality in the American family? Will the women's liberation movement create a gap between men and women that will make the generation gap of the 1960s look minor in comparison? Will the push for equality of the sexes in marriage create a pervasive battleground in the family near the close of the twentieth century? Is it possible that the most functional power configuration within the family is one in which the division of labor exists along traditional sex lines?*

413

Kosti Ruohomaa from Black Star

# 16

# MARITAL ADJUSTMENT AND SATISFACTION

*Is it possible to be married and satisfied?*

*What is the effect of children on marital adjustment and satisfaction?*

*What do you marry when your spouse is committed to a career—the person or the job?*

*What is marital adjustment, and what are its essential components?*

The third chapter in the trilogy on married life treats a topic that is as diffuse and slippery as marital power or interaction, yet as thoroughly researched as the problem of power in marriage. This chapter deals with the results and consequences of marital interaction and power—the marital happiness, marital satisfaction, and marital adjustment of couples involved in the everyday theatrical performance of family life, in which cues are constantly given, accepted, or ignored, and in which power is exchanged with great frequency. The research in this area has been extensive, but unintegrated, occasionally inspired, but generally routine and uninspiring, yet amazingly consistent in debunking the common-sense assumptions and beliefs found so often in popular literature and in the mythology about married life.

## MYTH AND REALITY

What are some of the more pervasive beliefs about marital interaction, adjustment, and satisfaction that have not been supported by research? To answer this question, let us create a true-false test:

|  | TRUE | FALSE |
|---|---|---|
| 1. The longer a pair has been married: |  |  |
| a) the more they will agree with one another. | ( ) | ( ) |
| b) the more they will understand one another. | ( ) | ( ) |
| c) the more accurately each will perceive how the other thinks and feels. | ( ) | ( ) |
| 2. The more frequent the interaction between the spouses: |  |  |
| a) the greater the agreement with each other. | ( ) | ( ) |
| b) the more they will understand one another. | ( ) | ( ) |
| 3. The greater the agreement between the spouses, the greater their understanding of each other. | ( ) | ( ) |
| 4. The more democratic the relationship: |  |  |
| a) the greater the amount of agreement between the spouses. | ( ) | ( ) |
| b) the greater the understanding of each other. | ( ) | ( ) |
| 5. The greater the involvement of the husband in his occupation and in the community, the greater the marital satisfaction of both spouses. | ( ) | ( ) |

6. The "happiest" marriages are those in which the personalities of the husband and wife change very little, or if the personalities do change, it is in the same direction and to the same degree.    ( )    ( )

7. For optimal marital satisfaction and adjustment it is highly important that both husband and wife accurately perceive the other's role.    ( )    ( )

8. Husband-wife consensus on such matters as religion, recreation, finances, philosophy of life, ways of dealing with in-laws, friends, and demonstrations of affection will not decrease with length of marriage.    ( )    ( )

9. The longer a pair has been married the greater the amount of marital adjustment.    ( )    ( )

10. The longer a pair has been married the greater the amount of marital satisfaction.    ( )    ( )

The correct answer to each statement is FALSE. What this means is that many of our "common-sense" and idealized notions about married life have not been supported by research.

ITEMS 1–4.   The first four items on the test (actually eight items counting the a, b, and c subparts) were used by Udry, Nelson, and Nelson (1961) in an explicit attempt to see if these widely held assumptions about marital interaction were true. Their sample consisted of 34 student couples who had been married for an average of three years. Not one of the hypotheses was supported.

ITEM 5.   Jan Dizard (1968) analyzed some data on couples who had been studied when they were engaged, three to five years after marriage, and again about twenty years after marriage. These data were from the Burgess-Wallin (1953) study, which will be discussed later. A central finding uncovered by Dizard was that the marriage is more likely to be satisfying to both partners if the husband is willing to limit and curtail his occupational and community commitments.

ITEM 6.   According to Uhr (1957), who used data on personality changes in husbands and wives originally gathered by Kelley (1955), the "happy marriages" are those in which the husband's personality changes very little and the wife's personality changes to adapt to the various contingencies of the family life cycle. Unhappy wives are those who change very little in personality over the life span of the marriage.

ITEM 7.   Another rather prevalent common-sense assumption about marital satisfaction and adjustment is that both spouses should accurately perceive and understand the other's role. Stuckert (1963) and Luckey (1960) both concluded that it is highly important for the wife to accurately perceive her husband, but not important, in and of itself, for the husband to understand his wife and her role.

ITEM 8.    Another commonly held assumption about married life that has not been supported by research concerns consensus. Pineo (1961), in analyzing the twenty-year follow-up of the Burgess-Wallin sample, found a substantial loss of consensus on such factors as religious matters, recreation, finances, philosophy of life, ways of dealing with in-laws and friends, and demonstrations of affection. The rather uniform decrease in consensus led Pineo to label this process "disenchantment with marriage."

Udry (1971:253) concludes that "married couples do not agree more, nor do they create a shared way of looking at life, in spite of their abundance of interaction; if anything, *couples have less consensus after many years of marriage than they did in the beginning.*"

How can we account for these findings that challenge our "common-sense" expectations for marital adjustment and satisfaction? Are these results a true picture of the state of married life in the United States, or are they produced by some shortcomings of the research techniques used to study marital satisfaction and adjustment? Clear-cut answers to these questions are difficult to determine, to say the very least.

Here, as elsewhere in this text, one should keep in mind that the viability of sociological interpretations is affected by the assumptions leading to the research, the type of sample selected, and the questions asked. Most of the studies that have dealt with marital happiness, satisfaction, and adjustment have used questionnaires, given to a sample (not always representatively selected) at one point in time with the questions reflecting a white, middle-class conception of what married life should be like. In other words, the dynamic situational flavor of marital life is usually missed because happiness, satisfaction, and adjustment are assessed at only one point in time.

ITEMS 9–10.    Two excellent studies in which attempts were made to tap the dynamics of married life over the family life cycle provide evidence of what happens to marital satisfaction and adjustment, and when the changes occur. They also provide clues as to why the amount of satisfaction/adjustment does not generally increase the longer a pair has been married.

## THE FAMILY LIFE CYCLE

If there is one commonality among the incurable optimist, the realist, and the dour cynic, it is probably their projections on their wedding nights of years of married bliss. Although all of us would probably allow the possibility that marriage is not a bed of roses, few enter marriage looking for thorns. All of us are curious about the future prospects for marital satisfaction and happiness, and few if any of us are willing to enter what seems like a losing proposition. What, then, does happen to marital satisfaction and adjustment as the length of marriage increases? Of the two excellent studies available, the older and better known was published by Ernest Burgess and Paul Wallin in 1953.

### The Burgess-Wallin Study (1953)

This study was begun in 1936 with 1,000 engaged couples for whom marital (success) prediction scores were obtained. A total of 666 of the couples who were still together after 3–5 years were again studied to see if their satisfaction with and adjustment to married life could have been predicted from their scores during engagement. A smaller sample (400) of these couples (see Pineo 1961) were studied 18–20 years after marriage for the same purpose.

A major strength of the Burgess-Wallin study is that it was longitudinal in design (that is, the same couples were followed and tested over time). Longitudinal studies are especially valuable for sociology for two reasons. One, they allow the researcher to make predictions at an earlier date that can later be checked for accuracy. Second, it is possible to determine which factors assessed by the earlier data (personality, role expectations, homogamous characteristics, and so forth) are most predictive of later satisfaction and adjustment. A weakness of the Burgess-Wallin study, and one that is generally unavoidable in longitudinal research, concerns attrition. For example, the twenty-year follow-up included only 400 couples—those who had stayed together. No comparable data were available for the 600 couples whose marriages had been dissolved. Our knowledge of the process of marital adjustment and satisfaction would be greatly enhanced if we were able to pinpoint exactly why these couples had decided to call it quits so that they could be compared more directly with the "successful" couples.

The most dramatic finding is that there was a rather consistent and significant decline in marital adjustment from the early years of marriage (3–5 years) to the later years (18–20 years). A rather marked decline was also noted in companionship, demonstrations of affection, common interests, and consensus. However, there was no significant change in the degree of reported marital happiness, sexual adjustment, and the idealization and rating of the mate's personality.

### The Rollins-Feldman Study (1970)

A second and more recent study providing a view of marital satisfaction over the family life cycle was conducted by Boyd C. Rollins and Harold Feldman in 1970. Unlike the longitudinal design of Burgess and Wallin, the design used by Rollins and Feldman was cross-sectional, which

419

entailed having couples at various stages in the family life cycle report on their happiness and satisfaction. The major weakness of the cross-sectional study is that it is difficult to draw inferences about the "real" effect of time and the family life cycle on adjustment and satisfaction. Rollins and Feldman used the eight stages of family development that were proposed by Duvall (1971):

Stage I.  Beginning Families (couples married 0 to 5 years without children).

Stage II.  Child-bearing Families (oldest child, birth to 2 years 11 months).

**FIGURE 16–1**

**Marriage Adjustment and Companionship Experiences**

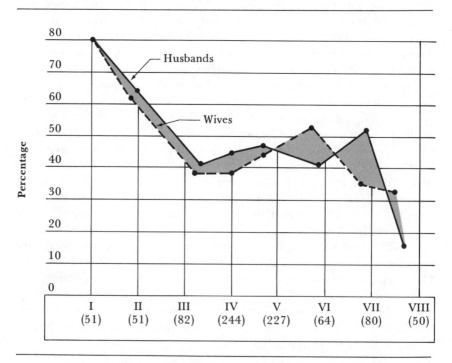

SOURCE: Boyd C. Rollins and Harold Feldman, "Marital Satisfaction over the Family Life Cycle," *Journal of Marriage and the Family* 32(1970):26. Used by permission of the National Council on Family Relations.

NOTE: This graph shows the percentages of individuals in each stage of the family life cycle (from Stage I, "beginning marriage" to Stage VIII, "retirement") reporting positive companionship experiences with their spouse at least "once a day" or more often. (Figures in parentheses indicate the number of husbands and the number of wives in each stage. There was a total of 1,598 cases.)

Stage III.  Families with Preschool Children (oldest child, 3 years to 5 years 11 months).

Stage IV.  Families with School Age Children (oldest child, 6 years to 12 years 11 months).

Stage V.  Families with Teenagers (oldest child 13 years to 20 years 11 months).

Stage VI.  Families as Launching Centers (first child gone to last child's leaving home).

Stage VII.  Families in the Middle Years (empty nest to retirement).

Stage VIII.  Aging Families (retirement to death of first spouse).

Perhaps the most sensitive index of married life is the day-to-day companionship experiences reported by a couple. The balance between positive and negative daily encounters probably tells us more about the dynamic quality of marital interaction than marital adjustment scores at widely separated points in time. As Figure 16–1 indicates, the early positive

Joel Gordon © 1978

*Love can last a lifetime if it is nurtured by a hug.*

421

companionship declines rather rapidly to a low ebb in the preschool stage and never fully regains its strength.

When Rollins and Feldman asked the couples at various stages of the family cycle how satisfying their married life was, the relationship was clearly curvilinear (See Figure 16–2). A rather high percentage were willing to say "very satisfactory" at stages I, II, and VIII. The lowest proportion willing to call marriage "very satisfying" was in stage VI, when the family was serving as a launching center. Thus, both husbands and wives show a rather marked decline in their willingness to consider their present stage very satisfying from stage I through the low point, stage VI. There is, then, a short jump higher for stage VII and an extremely high increase for stage VIII.

**FIGURE 16–2**
**Marriage Adjustment and Satisfaction**

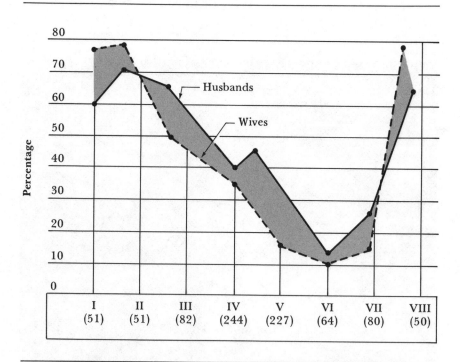

SOURCE: Boyd C. Rollins and Harold Feldman, "Marital Satisfaction over the Family Life Cycle," *Journal of Marriage and the Family* 32(1970):26. Used by permission of the National Council on Family Relations.

NOTE: This graph shows the percentages of individuals in each stage of the family life cycle (from Stage I, "beginning marriage" to Stage VIII, "retirement") reporting that their present stage of the family life cycle is very satisfying. (Figures in parentheses indicate the number of husbands and the number of wives in each stage. There was a total of 1,598 cases.)

## Summary

The question that needs to be answered is, Why?: Why is it that couples seem to have less consensus the longer they are married? Why does not understanding increase with the length of marriage? Why does marital adjustment decline drastically over the life span of a marriage? Why is there such a consistent decline in companionship from stage II of the family life cycle on? Why do couples view their marriges as less satisfying at stages III through VI of the family life cycle than at stage I, II, VII, and VIII? These are the proverbial $64,000 questions for which there are no easy answers, only speculative and plausible ones.

For example, consensus, understanding, and vibrant interaction may decline because they are crucial ingredients only in the courtship process. Once married and secure in the knowledge that they no longer have to score in the game of searching for a mate, perhaps many couples rather quickly lose their incentive for empathy and deep and serious communication. In other words, perhaps marriage dulls the appetite for understanding, whereas habit and ritualized interactions work against regular testing to see if consensus persists.

*There is something very special about that first child.*

Jim Harrison

Marital satisfaction is rather closely tied to the level of companionship achieved and the continuous successful completion of marital adjustment tasks. Both companionship and satisfaction may diminish as a result of the pressures for adjustment brought on by children in stages III–VI of the family life cycle. Marriage may be generally satisfying to both spouses before children arrive and in the infancy stage when the parental role still has its novelty. Perhaps the excitement of being together again, finally, in stages VII and VIII, accounts for the rise of marital satisfaction at the end of the life cycle. Put another way, the stresses produced because of the demands for adjustment in child rearing are sufficient to cause a decline in companionship and a reduction in marital satisfaction.

Suffice it to say that marital happiness, satisfaction, and adjustment are difficult to attain and maintain at a high level. For most couples a process of disenchantment with married life corresponds closely to stages of the family life cycle—the disenchantment is greatest during the child-rearing stages.

At least three other plausible explanations for the research findings run counter to our common-sense expectations for marital adjustment and satisfaction. All three concern the methodology family sociologists use to assess adjustment and satisfaction. First, maybe the techniques or scales used in measuring marital adjustment are inadequate. Second, what we have measured may not be marital adjustment, but rather a reflection of the conventionality of subjects answering marital-adjustment inventories. Third, perhaps the dimensions of marital adjustment have not been adequately understood or measured.

## THE MEASUREMENT OF MARITAL ADJUSTMENT

It would be a gross overstatement to say that scholars studying the family agree on the conceptual definition, the number of components or dimensions that constitute marital adjustment, or the best and most adequate way of measuring marital adjustment, happiness, satisfaction, success, or whatever else one may want to call it. Therefore, included below is a representative marital-adjustment scale illustrating how some family sociologists view marital adjustment. The weighted score for each response is given, and the total marital-adjustment score for an individual is obtained by adding all of the responses. The maximum score is 148; the higher the score, the higher the level of marital adjustment on the Locke-Wallace (1959) Short Form of Marital Adjustment (see p. 426).

Several features of the scale and its underlying assumptions deserve special mention. First, the scale is multifaceted in that it assesses marital happiness (item 1), marital adjustment (items 2A–2H), marital satisfaction (items 6 and 7), and marital companionship (items 3–5 and 8). In and of itself this is not a liability. However, these four facets of married life are not always perfectly correlated one with the other. For example, a conflict-habituated couple (see Chapter 14) might be rather high on happiness yet low on adjustment, satisfaction, and companionship. A passive-congenial couple might come out low on happiness, high on adjustment and satisfaction, yet low on companionship. Thus, one criticism of the scale and its assumptions is that much more than adjustment is being measured.

Second, marital satisfaction and companionship are rather narrowly conceived and indirectly assessed. For example, the answers to items 6 and 7 may tell us virtually nothing about satisfaction, only about daydreams of opportunities missed. Items 5A and 5B, dealing with leisure time, give the lowest weight to one spouse liking to stay at home and the other liking to be on the go, a situation that may in fact be a sign of adjustment to the marital situation.

Third, two rather important facets of marital adjustment are left out of the scale. No mention is made of children and how to deal with them and the adjustments they require of the parents. In addition, the intrusion of the occupational lives of the husband and wife into marriage and the consequent adjustments required is completely ignored.

Fourth and last, the scale is designed for individuals, not couples. Consequently, many studies of marital adjustment fall into the wife's or husband's sociology category when in fact it takes two to have an adjusted or maladjusted marriage. It may be that the most important data obtained from a study of marital adjustment would be the discrepancies in how the items are answered, not in the individual responses to each item by only one partner.

## CONVENTIONALITY AND IDEALIZATION

Perhaps the most serious challenge to the studies of marital adjustment has come from the work of Vernon Edmonds (1967, 1972), who questioned the validity of marital adjustment tests. The term *validity* refers to whether a scale like the Locke-Wallace Short Form really measures what it purports to measure. Edmonds was convinced that married individuals answered the questions in a conventional fashion (that is, they give the answer they think is expected of them—the answer a married person should give). To test his hypothesis, Edmonds constructed a Marital Conventionalization Scale, which consisted of statements to be labeled true or false. The answers were either honest or conventional. With a sample of 100 married students at Florida State University, Edmonds obtained the responses found in Table 16–1 (p. 428).

Now, even considering the possibility that most of these individuals were probably in the earliest stages of the family life cycle, it is hard to believe that 57 percent would answer true to the statement: "If every person in the world of the opposite sex had been available and willing to marry me I could not have made a better choice." In addition, Edmonds found that his conventionalization scale correlated highly with the Locke-Wallace adjustment scale (.63 for the married student sample). The correlation between marital adjustment and marital conventionalization was .53 for a randomly selected sample of 152 married persons in Winchester, Virginia, in 1967 and .70 for a randomly selected sample of forty Williamsburg, Virginia, women with children in grade school who were studied in

## The Locke-Wallace (1959) Short Form of Marriage Adjustment

1. Check the dot on the scale line below which best describes the degree of happiness, everything considered, of your present marriage. The middle point, "happy," represents the degree of happiness which most people get from marriage; and the scale gradually ranges on one side to those few who are very unhappy in marriage, and on the other, to those few who experience extreme joy in marriage.

| • | • | • | • | • | • | • |
|---|---|---|---|---|---|---|
| 00 | 02 | 07 | 15 | 20 | 25 | 35 |
| Very Unhappy | | | Happy | | | Perfectly Happy |

State the approximate extent of agreement or disagreement between you and your (husband/wife) on the following items. Please check one block opposite each item.

| | ALWAYS AGREE | ALMOST ALWAYS AGREE | OCCA- SION- ALLY DIS- AGREE | FRE- QUENTLY DIS- AGREE | ALMOST ALWAYS DIS- AGREE | ALWAYS DIS- AGREE |
|---|---|---|---|---|---|---|
| 2A. Handling family finances | [ 5] | [ 4] | [3] | [2] | [1] | [0] |
| 2B. Matters of recreation | [ 5] | [ 4] | [3] | [2] | [1] | [0] |
| 2C. Demonstrations of affection | [ 8] | [ 6] | [4] | [2] | [1] | [0] |
| 2D. Friends | [ 5] | [ 4] | [3] | [2] | [1] | [0] |
| 2E. Sex relations | [15] | [12] | [9] | [4] | [1] | [0] |
| 2F. Conventionality (right, good, or proper conduct) | [ 5] | [ 4] | [3] | [2] | [1] | [0] |
| 2G. Philosophy of life | [ 5] | [ 4] | [3] | [2] | [1] | [0] |
| 2H. Ways of dealing with in-laws | [ 5] | [ 4] | [3] | [2] | [1] | [0] |

1970 (see Edmonds et al., 1972). This means that the persons who would be considered the "best adjusted" are quite likely to be the persons giving the most conventional answers. Edmonds also discovered that his marital conventionalization scale correlated rather highly with the Lie scale from the Minnesota Multiphasic Personality Inventory.

Basically, Edmonds (1967, 1972) suggested that the scores obtained from marital adjustment scales are contaminated by conventionalization—

3.  When disagreements arise, they usually result in:
    [ 0] husband giving in
    [ 2] wife giving in
    [10] agreement by mutual give and take

4.  Do you and your (husband/wife) engage in outside interests together?
    [10] all of them
    [ 8] some of them
    [ 3] very few of them
    [ 0] none of them

5A. In leisure time do you generally prefer:
    [  ] one who prefers to stay at home and the other to be on the go
    [  ] to be "on the go"
    [  ] to stay at home

    10 = Both at home
    3 = Both on go
    2 = One on go and one at home

5B. Does your (husband/wife) generally prefer:
    [  ] to be "on the go"
    [  ] to stay at home

6.  Do you ever wish you had not married?
    [ 0] frequently
    [ 3] occasionally
    [ 8] rarely
    [15] never

7.  If you had your life to live over, do you think you would:
    [ 5] marry the same person
    [ 0] marry a different person
    [ 0] not marry at all

8.  Do you confide in your (husband/wife):
    [ 0] almost never
    [ 2] rarely
    [10] in most things
    [10] in everything

SOURCE: Harvey J. Locke and Karl M. Wallace, "Short Marital Adjustment and Prediction Tests: Their Reliability and Validity," *Marriage and Family Living*, 21(1959):252–54. By permission of The National Council on Family Relations.

the tendency of test-takers to answer questions in the way they think they should rather than truthfully. One way of testing this hypothesis is to examine the statistical correlation between marital adjustment (the dependent or effect variable) and some variables that precede marital adjustment in time and that may be predictive of it (the causal variables). One of the predictor variables used by Edmonds was religious activity (for example, frequency of church attendance for both spouses before and after marriage, attendance at the same church after marriage, and so forth). The correlation between religious activity and marital adjustment was .41. When Edmonds examined the religious activity–marital adjustment relationship by statistically controlling the intervening variable, marital conventionalization, the size of the correlation dropped to .02. This means that all of the alleged impact of religious activity on marital adjustment can be attributed to the intervening influence of conventionalization.

**TABLE 16–1**

**A Short Form of Edmonds's Marital Conventionalization Scale**

| CONVENTIONAL RESPONSE AND PERCENT IN THAT CATEGORY | | ITEMS |
|---|---|---|
| False | 43 | There are times when my mate does things that make me unhappy. |
| True | 47 | My marriage is a perfect success. |
| True | 51 | My mate has all of the qualities I've always wanted in a mate. |
| True | 46 | If my mate has any faults I am not aware of them. |
| True | 63 | My mate and I understand each other completely. |
| True | 42 | We are as well adjusted as any two persons in this world can be. |
| False | 58 | I have some needs that are not being met by my marriage. |
| True | 36 | Every new thing I have learned about my mate has pleased me. |
| True | 43 | I have never regretted my marriage, not even for a moment. |
| True | 57 | If every person in the world of the opposite sex had been available and willing to marry me I could not have made a better choice. |

SOURCE: Adapted from Vernon Edmonds, "Marital Conventionalization: Definition and Measurement," *Journal of Marriage and the Family*, 29(1967):686. By permission of the National Council on Family Relations.

If Edmonds's contention is correct, then the implication is that all studies of marital adjustment may be partially to completely invalid, depending on the levels of conventionality among the respondents. However, it is all too easy to accept such a devastating criticism of all studies without applying the same standards to the critic's work. There are several factors that may render Edmonds's study less than perfectly valid.

In the first place, Edmonds's (1967) sample consisted of only 100 persons, supposed to be representative of married students at Florida State University. Edmonds failed to report a breakdown of his sample by sex, classification in school, length of marriage, or by any other discriminating characteristic. If by chance most of these 100 persons happened to be older students, with children, then the loss of consensus, the disenchantment process, may have already occurred. The other two samples were likewise small, even though they were selected randomly. The Williamsburg sample dealt only with women, and the sex and other distinguishing characteristics of the Winchester sample were not reported.

A second limitation of Edmonds's study concerns the real meaning of conventionality as it relates to marital adjustment. For younger married couples, especially those without children, what Edmonds calls conventionality may in fact be idealization of the spouse and of the marriage situation. For most married couples the honeymoon experience continues for awhile after the return to normalcy has taken place in the more routine aspects of living. Thus, although Edmonds implies that conventionality is pathological, for his sample it may merely be an uncovering of "love blindness."

A third aspect of Edmonds's study that needs comment is the fact that only one spouse's responses are recorded. As noted in Chapter 15, the results may be criticized as the wife's sociology or, as is likely in his initial study at Florida State, the husband's sociology.

The last criticism of Edmonds's study is conceptual in focus. Edmonds assumes that the correlation between conventionality and marital adjustment indicates a lack of validity for the marital-adjustment scale. I disagree. In a very real sense, some conventionality may be important to the whole process of marital adjustment and satisfaction. All or at least most married couples, although they may be conventional when telling their spouses, "I love you more than I could ever love anyone else" or "I couldn't live without you," are also involved in strengthening their mutual commitments. Such efforts at facilitating marital satisfaction may be a crucial element in making a tolerable marriage situation even more productive of satisfaction. In fact, it may be that researchers should include marital conventionalization as one of the several components of marital adjustment, assuming that some degree of it is a lubricant that makes the relationship run smoothly whereas too little or too much conventionalization either aggravates or clogs it up.

## DIMENSIONS OF MARITAL ADJUSTMENT

The research findings on marital satisfaction and adjustment that contradict common-sense expectations may result not from conventionality or the invalidity of the adjustment scales, but rather from an inadequate understanding of the dimensions and components of marital adjustment. Marital satisfaction and adjustment may consist of several dimensions or components, each of which is only slightly if at all related to the others. In his excellent review of the literature on marital adjustment, Udry (1971) states: "Every scholar who has conducted these studies would admit that marital adjustment has never been shown by anyone to be a single general factor—that is, that all these separate areas of the composite are, in fact, systematically related on one dimension." On the other side of the coin, Udry is suggesting that it is inappropriate to ask all of the separate questions included in the Locke-Wallace Short Form, or any other index, and just add them up. To do so implies that marital adjustment consists of only one dimension and all the adjustment areas covered in the adjustment scale fall somewhere on that one line.

The question that quickly becomes central is: If marital satisfaction and adjustment are composed of several dimensions, what are these dimensions and how are they related to one another? There are at least two studies that may offer some clues to an appropriate answer to these questions.

### Orden and Bradburn (1968)

In this nationwide study of 781 husbands and 957 wives, a total of 1,738 persons not married to each other, the authors used eighteen items to assess the marital relationship. The eighteen items clustered into three

*Married life carries with it responsibilities that two can share.*

Rose Skytta, Jeroboam Inc.

meaningful dimensions of marital adjustment: (a) marriage sociability ("good laugh" through "did something other appreciated"); (b) marriage companionship ("visited friends" through "ate out in restaurant"); and (c) marriage tensions (the remaining items in Table 16–2).

As you can readily see, most of the respondents reported experiencing companionship and sociable activities with their spouses during

**TABLE 16–2**
**Responses to Marriage Relationship Items**

| ITEMS | PERCENTAGE ANSWERING YES | | |
| --- | --- | --- | --- |
| | MEN (N = 772) | WOMEN (N = 944) | TOTAL (N = 1,716) |
| I'm going to read you some things that married couples often do together. Tell me which ones you and your (husband/wife) have done together in the past few weeks: | | | |
| Had a good laugh together or shared a joke | 96 | 94 | 95 |
| Been affectionate toward each other | 96 | 94 | 95 |
| Spent an evening just chatting with each other | 85 | 84 | 84 |
| Did something the other particularly appreciated | 81 | 77 | 79 |
| Visited friends together | 75 | 74 | 74 |
| Entertained friends in your home | 71 | 69 | 70 |
| Taken a drive or walk for pleasure | 68 | 60 | 64 |
| Gone out together—movie, bowling, sporting, or other entertainment | 54 | 54 | 54 |
| Ate out in a restaurant together | 52 | 49 | 50 |
| Now I'm going to read you some things about which husbands and wives sometimes agree and sometimes disagree; would you tell me which ones caused differences of opinions or were problems in your marriage during the past few weeks? | | | |
| Being tired | 25 | 28 | 27 |
| Irritating personal habits | 20 | 29 | 25 |
| Household expenses | 20 | 19 | 19 |
| Being away from home | 20 | 18 | 19 |
| How to spend leisure | 18 | 12 | 15 |
| Time spent with friends | 12 | 11 | 12 |
| Your (husband's job) | 10 | 9 | 10 |
| In-laws | 8 | 11 | 10 |
| Not showing love | 9 | 8 | 9 |

SOURCE: Susan R. Orden and Norman Bradburn, "Dimensions of Marriage Happiness," *American Journal of Sociology*, 73(1968):719, Table 3. By permission of the University of Chicago Press.

**TABLE 16–3**

**Coefficients of Association Among Measures of Marriage Adjustment**

| MEASURES | COMPANIONSHIP | SOCIABILITY | TENSIONS | HAPPINESS |
|---|---|---|---|---|
| Companionship | 1.00 | .34 | −.08 | .44 |
| Sociability | .37 | 1.00 | −.01 | .20 |
| Tensions | −.15 | .02 | 1.00 | −.36 |
| Happiness | .40 | .26 | −.41 | 1.00 |

SOURCE: Adapted from Susan R. Orden and Norman Bradburn, "Dimensions of Marriage Happiness," *American Journal of Sociology*, 73(1968):723, Table 6. By permission of the University of Chicago Press. © 1968 by the University of Chicago. All rights reserved.

NOTE: Responses above diagonal for men (N = 781); responses below diagonal for women (N = 957).

the "past few weeks." By the same token, almost 20 to 25 percent also reported tensions arising from being tired, irritating personal habits, household expenses or one spouse being away from home. So, marital satisfaction/adjustment is both positive (being together) and negative (the presence or relative absence of tensions).

To test the idea that marital satisfaction/adjustment does in fact consist of separate and unrelated dimensions, Orden and Bradburn (1968: 723) added the Yes scores on the three dimensions and correlated the resulting scales with each other and with a self-perception of one's overall happiness in marriage (see Table 16–3).

For both men and women the highest correlation with perceived marital happiness is companionship (.44 and .40, respectively). It should be noted that a perfect correlation would produce a coefficient of 1.00. None of the correlations, then, could be considered high. The lowest correlation for both sexes occurs between tensions and sociability (−.01 and .02, respectively).

The Orden and Bradburn study suggests, then, that marital adjustment is not unidimensional. Rather, it consists of at least three dimensions that are at best weakly related to one another and to one's overall perception of marriage happiness.

## Spanier (1976)

Without question, Graham Spanier at Penn State is responsible for the most comprehensive and sophisticated attempt (a) to understand conceptually what is involved in marital adjustment and (b) to isolate statistically the dimensions of adjustment.

An exhaustive review of all articles written on marital adjustment produced 300 separate questionnaire items. Eliminating duplications and some items that independent raters felt would not tap marital or dyadic adjustment, a questionnaire was developed that included 200 items. These were answered by a sample of 218 married (109 of each sex) and 90 recently divorced persons (41 males and 49 females). The married and divorced samples were then compared on every item. Any item on which there was not a statistically significant difference in response between the two samples was eliminated. This left 40 questions. A more sophisticated procedure called factor analysis was then employed. Factor analysis essentially looks at all of the correlations among the 40 items and tells the researcher which of them seem to hang or cluster together into conceptually meaningful factors. Eight more items were eliminated using this procedure because they did not cluster into any of the factors.

Spanier discovered that there were four factors represented by the thirty-two items isolated in the factor analysis procedure. Listed below are the factor labels and the types of items used to measure them.

FACTOR 1—DYADIC CONSENSUS. Factor 1 concerns the extent of agreement-disagreement reported on such matters as:

1. handling family finances
2. matters of recreation
3. religious matters
4. friends
5. conventionality or good and proper conduct
6. philosophy of life
7. ways of dealing with in-laws
8. aims-goals-things believed important
9. amount of time spent together
10. making major decisions
11. household tasks
12. leisure time interests and activities
13. career decisions

Stated differently, the dyadic consensus factor taps how well the spouses get along with each other on the things that are part of the daily routine of married life—the events and activities that determine what will take place backstage. Dyadic consensus involved negotiated agreements/disagreements that provide the contents of marital interaction—what husbands and wives talk about—money and free time and how both will be spent; who will be responsible for what around the house; what as individuals and as a family unit the couple will be doing in the near and distant future.

433

FACTOR 2—DYADIC SATISFACTION. The items in this factor deal with a perception of how often certain things either occur or are considered by the spouses. For example, how often:

a. one confides in his/her mate.
b. the partners quarrel.
c. the partners get on each other's nerves.
d. each or both leave the house after a fight.
e. one regrets that he or she ever got married.
f. the partners have discussed or considered divorce, separation, or terminating the relationship.
g. the partners think things are going well in the relationship.
h. the partners kiss.

Two other items fell into the dyadic satisfaction factor. One is worded almost exactly the same as the first item in the Locke-Wallace scale and deals with the perceived degree of happiness in the relationship. The other asks the respondent to say which of the following statements best describes how he or she feels about the future of the relationship:

I want desperately for my relationship to succeed and
(a) *will go to almost any length* to see that it does.

I want very much for my relationship to succeed and
(b) *will do all I can* to see that it does.
(c) *will do my fair share* to see that it does.

It would be nice if my relationship succeeded, but
(d) *I can't do much more than I am doing now* to help it.
(e) *I refuse to do any more than I am doing now* to keep the relationship going.

My relationship can never succeed, and
(f) *there is no more that I can do* to keep the relationship going.

Thus, the dyadic satisfaction factor assessed by Spanier is similar to the marriage tensions dimension suggested by Orden and Bradburn. The primary difference is the labeling. Spanier emphasizes a relative lack of conflict/tension to mean satisfaction. It should also be noted that this factor elicits reports of behavior (that is, how often events occur) rather than attitudes about or agreements on issues.

FACTOR 3—DYADIC COHESION. The third factor in Spanier's schema deals with what Orden and Bradburn call marriage sociability. It includes items that determine on a scale of from never to more than once a day how often the partners (a) have a stimulating exchange of ideas, (b) laugh together, (c) calmly discuss something, and (d) work together on a project. In addition, the partners are asked what proportion of outside interests are engaged in as a couple.

FACTOR 4—AFFECTIONAL EXPRESSION. This last factor in Spanier's study of dyadic adjustment is unique. It is measured by four items, two of which deal with the extent to which the partners agree on (a) demonstrations of affection and (b) sex relations. The other two items ask whether (c) being too tired for sex or (d) not showing love has caused differences of opinion or were problems in the relationship during recent weeks.

Affectional expression, the exchange of intimacy between spouses, is clearly one of the most important facets of married life. It usually occurs only in the most guarded and private inner spaces of the relationship. It is an experience most of us look forward to and enjoy, yet it constitutes a set of behaviors deeply affected by psychological states many of us do not understand. It is thus significant that Spanier's scales give special attention to the expression of affection.

In summary, the dyadic adjustment scales developed by Spanier represent a solid and significant contribution to our knowledge of the marital relationship—to its major dimensions and how they should be measured. Four additional pieces of information about the scales deserve mention. First, when all of the items from the four subscales (dimensions or factors) were summed into an overall index of adjustment, the overall index proved to be valid; it distinguished clearly between the married and the divorced groups—average scores of 115 and 71 respectively. Second, the average correlation among the four subscales/dimensions was .68, substantially higher than that mentioned earlier from the Orden and Bradburn study. This simply means that dyadic consensus, cohesion, satisfaction, and affectional expression overlap and are interrelated. Third, the reliability of each of the subscales is high—for the overall index it was .96 out of a possible 1.00. This means that the scales would yield essentially the same distributions if used repeatedly on similar samples. Finally, the correlation between Spanier's overall index and the Locke-Wallace Short Form of Adjustment was .86—rather high. Although this may be due in part to the fact that many of the items in both instruments are identical or similar, it could also reflect a failure on Spanier's part to consider conventionalization.

## Conclusions of the Orden-Bradburn and Spanier Studies

These studies show rather conclusively that marital adjustment consists of several separate dimensions that are at best weakly related to one another. This suggests that the lack of support for our common-sense expectations may be a function of the way marital-adjustment scores

435

have been obtained. It is seemingly inappropriate merely to add the answers on various questions like those included in the Locke-Wallace Short Form. Marriage adjustment is not adequately assessed by a composite of responses to a series of questions—the questions themselves may be a reflection of different facets of the marital experience, and married couples seem to compartmentalize their experiences.

## UNDERSTANDING THE MARITAL RELATIONSHIP

It should be quite clear that the marital experience is an extremely complex phenomenon—one that is difficult to measure and even harder to conceptualize. In the remainder of this chapter we will more adequately examine the complex and confusing facets of marital relationship.

### Clarification of the Terminology

One source of confusion that permeates this area of study is the free substitution of terms. There are four terms that have been used interchangeably time and again: (1) marital success, (2) marital happiness, (3) marital satisfaction, and (4) marital adjustment. Although there is some justification for thinking that these terms overlap one with another, perhaps we should attempt to untangle them:

1. *Marital success* has traditionally been assessed by the permanence of the marriage, the presence of children who seem well adjusted and who are relatively successful in school, and the continued companionship and overt affection shown between the spouses. I view marital success—perhaps marital adequacy is a better term—as a result of the performance of a married pair in the other three categories discussed below: marital happiness, satisfaction, and adjustment.

2. *Marital happiness* refers to a reading of one's overall marital situation at a given point in time. Obviously it is possible that the perception of happiness can vary a great deal over time for any one person or couple. Spontaneous reactions to various pressures, the unexpected emergence of a reserve or relic identity, frustration at not being able to pursue a desired course of action, irritating personal habits of the spouse—all these and other forces not mentioned can cause one's perception of his or her marital happiness to drop considerably. Orden and Bradburn (1968:717) compiled the results of several studies that asked respondents to rate the degree of happiness present in their marriages. As these data reveal, most subjects in studies of marital happiness are unwilling to rate theirs as a marriage that is not too happy. In the thirty years between the publication of Terman's study (1938) and the Orden-Bradburn study (1968), a rather stable percentage of persons view their marriage as very happy (Table 16–4).

Marital happiness, then, refers to a spot check on one's overall marital situation and is heavily influenced by transitory events, some of which are cognate to the marital relationship and some of which may be only peripheral.

3. *Marital satisfaction* occurs in relation to categories of marital events, not to highly specific areas of interaction and negotiation. It should be possible, then, to be satisfied with one major aspect of married life and either unsatisfied or dissatisfied with another. For example, in a reflective moment a person might decide that he or she is very satisfied with the parental, division of labor, and companionship facets of his or her marriage; unsatisfied with the affectional-emotional aspect (perhaps he or she feels that it could stand some improvement); and dissatisfied with the way family life mixes with the demands made by a job. On the basis of this review, that person could easily consider his or her marriage as very happy if he or she focused on the first three areas mentioned above; pretty happy if the focus was on the second aspect; and not too happy if the focus was on the third facet of the marriage.

Marital satisfaction, then, refers to an examination of general categories of marital events. Although the term may overlap somewhat with

**TABLE 16–4**
**Marriage Happiness Ratings**

| SELECTED STUDY | PERCENTAGES | | | TOTAL | |
|---|---|---|---|---|---|
| | VERY HAPPY | HAPPY | NOT TOO HAPPY | % | N |
| Present study | 60 | 36 | 3 | 99 | 1,738 |
| Bradburn and Caplovitz [a] | 76 | 23 | 1 | 100 | 363 |
| Gurin, Veroff, and Feld [b] | 68 | 29 | 3 | 100 | 1,875 |
| Landis [c] | 83 | 16 | 1 | 100 | 409 |
| Terman [c] | 85 | 9 | 5 | 99 | 792 |
| Burgess and Cottrell [c] | 63 | 14 | 22 | 99 | 526 |

SOURCE: Susan R. Orden and Norman Bradburn, "Dimensions of Marriage Happiness," *American Journal of Sociology*, 73(1968):717, Table 1. By permission of the University of Chicago Press. © 1968 by the University of Chicago. All rights reserved.

[a] N. M. Bradburn and D. Caplovitz, *Reports on Happiness* (Chicago: Aldine, 1965), p. 40. The authors used a four-point scale: "very happy," "little happier than average," "just about average," "not too happy." We combined "very happy" and "little happier than average" into the "very happy" category.

[b] G. Gurin, J. Veroff, and S. Feld, *Americans View Their Mental Health* (New York: Basic Books, 1960), p. 92. The authors used a four-point scale: "very happy," "above average," "average," and "not too happy." We continued the "very happy" and the "above average."

[c] J. T. Landis and M. G. Landis, *Building a Successful Marriage* (New York: Prentice-Hall, 1953), p. 678. The authors converted the Terman ratings (seven-point scale) and the Burgess and Cottrell ratings (five-point scale) to a three-point scale, which they labeled "very happy or happy," "average," and "unhappy or very unhappy."

George Gardner

marital happiness, marital satisfaction is tied to a more specific and more reflective evaluation of married life than is marital happiness.

4. *Marital adjustment,* the most specific term of the four, is based on an evaluation of each partner's adjustment plus the pair's joint adjustment. In a true sense, marital adjustment is the only term that explicitly entails a perception of how both spouses are performing on a number of discrete tasks related to the marital situation. Adjustment, then, takes place in marriage with regard to sexual interaction, the use of leisure time and money, relating to in-laws, reducing or negotiating conflicts, and other highly detailed types of tasks.

If this conceptualization of marital adjustment is accurate, then it is apparent that most couples are actively involved in achieving individual and pair adjustment on a number of tasks throughout married life. It is also true that once adjustment has been achieved at a level that both agree is adequate, that adjustment may be lost if the focus of attention is shifted to other tasks. Adjustment is not something that can easily, if at all, be summed up, because some tasks are viewed as more salient to one spouse than to the other.

Even when a task is viewed by each as important or salient, there may be a difference in perception of the adjustment's adequacy if different aspects of the task are important to each spouse. For example, a married male may be willing to claim that he and his wife are sexually adjusted so long as they have coitus three times a week. Sex is important to him. The wife may feel that the sexual side of marriage is just as important. However, she views the sexual adjustment as adequate only if there is extensive foreplay and afterplay coupled with a great deal of affection, verbal and otherwise.

Marital adjustment, then, refers to a dynamic process whereby each spouse and the two as a couple achieve what they consider to be an adequate performance on a number of specific tasks in their mar-

438

riage. The adjusting that occurs must include the following adjustment conditions or techniques: (a) agreement on the salience of each of the tasks and on the priorities of each task relative to the others, as seen by each spouse; (b) agreement on how intensely each of the spouses will attempt to adjust to the various tasks they mutually must perform; and (c) agreement on the amount of flexibility each spouse is allowed in playing his or her role in the adjustment process.

## Clarification of the Total Marriage Relationship

Bearing in mind the three conditions or techniques of adjusting (agreement on salience and priorities, intensity, and flexibility), we can relate the four terms just discussed (marital success, happiness, satisfaction, and adjustment) to each other in a more systematic discussion of the total marriage relationship. My assumption is that marital success or adequacy is the goal being sought in most marriages. It is achieved by an adequate adjustment in the tasks listed under marital adjustment, an evaluation of satisfaction with the major facets of the marital experience, and a continuing perception that the marriage situation is happy. It should be noted that no a priori ordering of the adjustment tasks is implied by Figure 16–3. Neither is it suggested that each task is solidly attached to the category under which it occurs. For example, Orden and Bradburn (1968) include expressions of affection under the marriage companionship category whereas Spanier would assign it to the affectional expression dimension.

Each spouse and each couple must continually engage in negotiated efforts to achieve adjustment in each of the tasks listed in the first part of the diagram. An adequate adjustment is achieved through agreements on what is important or not, the priorities of tasks to be addressed, and the flexibility each allows the other in the playing of his or her marital role. Quite naturally, certain marital adjustment tasks are more salient at one point in the family life cycle than at others. Over time, the possibility always exists that some tasks will be relegated to a status that says, in effect, "We just can't seem to reach an adequate adjustment here; therefore, we will let this task ride and spend our energies on something else." An adequate adjustment in the early stages of married life regarding philosophy of life may be reclassified as maladjustment if one of the spouses adopts a different ideological commitment. Each of these adjustment tasks may be the source of tension if the achievement of an adequate adjustment is not forthcoming.

Marital satisfaction is evaluated in terms of the performance in broad areas, not by one performance in one specific task area. Thus, a married couple can classify their marriage as satisfying in one or more areas, relatively unsatisfying in another area or so, and completely devoid of satisfaction in another area. The evaluation of marital satisfaction is limited to various categories, but does not imply an evaluation of the overall arrangement.

439

**FIGURE 16–3**
**A Model of the Total Marital Relationship**

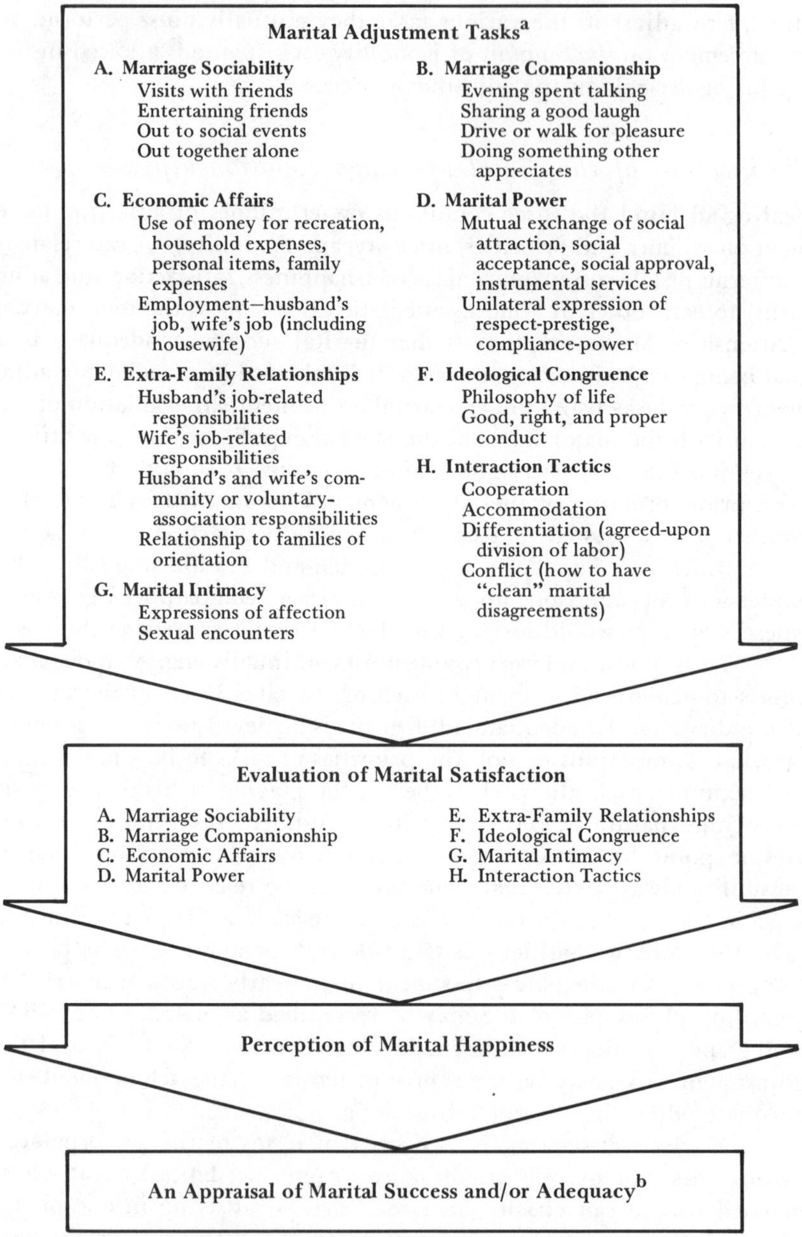

---

**Marital Adjustment Tasks[a]**

**A. Marriage Sociability**
Visits with friends
Entertaining friends
Out to social events
Out together alone

**B. Marriage Companionship**
Evening spent talking
Sharing a good laugh
Drive or walk for pleasure
Doing something other
appreciates

**C. Economic Affairs**
Use of money for recreation,
household expenses,
personal items, family
expenses
Employment—husband's
job, wife's job (including
housewife)

**D. Marital Power**
Mutual exchange of social
attraction, social
acceptance, social approval,
instrumental services
Unilateral expression of
respect-prestige,
compliance-power

**E. Extra-Family Relationships**
Husband's job-related
responsibilities
Wife's job-related
responsibilities
Husband's and wife's com-
munity or voluntary-
association responsibilities
Relationship to families of
orientation

**F. Ideological Congruence**
Philosophy of life
Good, right, and proper
conduct

**H. Interaction Tactics**
Cooperation
Accommodation
Differentiation (agreed-upon
division of labor)
Conflict (how to have
"clean" marital
disagreements)

**G. Marital Intimacy**
Expressions of affection
Sexual encounters

---

**Evaluation of Marital Satisfaction**

A. Marriage Sociability
B. Marriage Companionship
C. Economic Affairs
D. Marital Power

E. Extra-Family Relationships
F. Ideological Congruence
G. Marital Intimacy
H. Interaction Tactics

---

**Perception of Marital Happiness**

---

**An Appraisal of Marital Success and/or Adequacy[b]**

---

[a] Mediated through agreement on salience and priorities, intensity, and flexibility.

[b] An appraisal of marital success or adequacy is primarily conducted by the community
or associates of the marital couple, not by the couple themselves.

Ellis Herwig, Stock, Boston

When the overall or total relationship is examined by the couple, their perception is of happiness and the degree of it that is present at that point in time. However, Orden and Bradburn (1968) found a very high correlation between the perceptions of marital happiness for their respondents at time 1, time 2, time 3, and time 4. The degree of correlation by sex was at least .82 and reached as high as .94 for women between the second time and third time they were asked to evaluate the degree of their marital happiness.

The appraisal of marital success or adequacy is, for all intents and purposes, out of the hands of the married couple. This appraisal is conducted on a regular basis by the community, teachers, neighbors, the police, and the associates of the pair. By looking at how the couple conduct themselves and how they treat their property, how their children behave and are evaluated by their peers, the community agencies and the members of the community attribute to the family a "well-done"

441

or a "tsk, tsk." So, the end product, the goal of much adjustment, many evaluations of satisfaction and a constant effort to look at the positive side of life—the label of "successfully married"—is either extended or withheld by persons outside the family, the audience, as it were.

## SUMMARY AND CONCLUSIONS

This chapter constitutes not only a review of the major results of research on marital satisfaction and adjustment but also an attempt to account for the findings that challenge our common-sense expectations for married life. As in many other areas studied by sociologists, there is always the possibility that someone will say, "I don't believe it! These results don't correspond with my experience!" Sociologists, although they use the responses from individuals to conduct their studies, usually aggregate the responses so that they can talk about this, that, or some other behavior as it occurs differentially for persons from different social-class levels. A sociologist will seldom if ever say that some characteristic or behavior is found in all or even most persons or families that are in the upper class—only that that behavior is more likely to occur in the upper class than in the middle class or under class. Therefore, the finding that marital satisfaction, consensus, understanding, or any other facet of the marital experience seems to decline with length of marriage does not mean such will or must happen to a specific couple.

Marital adjustment, satisfaction, happiness, and success are things that occur to human beings who have consciously and, in most cases, voluntarily chosen each other as marital partners. Because much is expected of this bond between two complex human beings who may have different backgrounds, different orientations to life, and different socialization experiences, the chances for failure are rather high. Perhaps the expectations are too high. On the other hand, perhaps most couples who are married need the high expectations as an incentive for working out the adjustments that must be made in any marriage.

I believe that marriage is a commitment that should be entered rationally and critically. However, such admirable traits should not be allowed to interfere unduly with mutual affection or the mutual expression of love. Although a systematic immersion in various manuals for marital adjustment, satisfaction, happiness, and explicit socialization may help—such preparation is no guarantee. Neither is deep love, or a mutual commitment to God, country, or anything else.

An invisible and amazing transformation takes place in marriage that is like, but different from, the experience in any other relationship. Perhaps it is the legal nature of the arrangement, the love bond, the sanction of culture and the community—whatever it is, the marital experience is tried by almost all persons, at least in the United States, and there is some evidence that more than a few find it a richly rewarding experience.

## SOME POSSIBLE IMPLICATIONS

*In this chapter it was noted that research has failed to support many of our common-sense notions about marital adjustment and satisfaction. In particular, it is apparent from available research that marital satisfaction seems to drop with the onset of children and remains fairly low until the children leave home to establish their own families. One particular change that is occurring in our society, the drop in the fertility rate to near the replacement level (an average of 2.1 children per family), may have very positive implications for the level of marital adjustment and satisfaction in most marriages.*

*Married couples will be having fewer children on the average, and most of these will be born before the woman is thirty years old. This means that, in most families, the children will be reaching an age of relative independence when the average couple is still in their thirties. Is it possible that the marital satisfaction of the average couple in the future will be less affected by children? Will the quality of married life in the future be higher because of social changes in the area of fertility?*

# PART V

# THE SUBSTANCE OF MARRIAGE

Charles Gatewood

# 17

# PARENTHOOD AND MARITAL ADJUSTMENT

*What is distinctive about the parental role?*

*How does a child learn?*

*How important is the parent as a model for his or her children?*

*How do we grow up to be functional citizens and reasonably intelligent adults?*

Marital adjustment and satisfaction take a sharp dip with the onset of children and do not seem to recover fully until the children have left home. This finding is not surprising. In fact, given the tremendous physical, mental, and emotional costs of being a parent, it is no wonder that the husband-wife relationship seems to suffer somewhat from the demands of parenthood. Yet most couples readily and enthusiastically adopt, voluntarily at that, the parental role-set. It would probably be safe to predict that a substantial majority of the volunteers will somehow forget the voluntary aspects of their decision to become parents and will later feel that somehow parenthood was thrust upon them, that they were unprepared and unsuspecting of the rigors required of the role, and, although they would not pass up the joys provided by their children, they surely would not be as easily persuaded to volunteer so soon if they had it to do all over again. Thus, one major focus of this chapter will be on the parental role in general and on the differing demands of the mother and father roles.

A second major axis of concern in this chapter will be on the developmental task of socialization. Some of the questions we will ask and seek to answer are, What is socialization? What are its components? How do children learn? How important is early childhood? How does socialization change as the children grow older? What are the differences in socialization by social class?

## THE PARENTAL ROLE

One of the most enlightening articles ever written on the parental role (see Rossi, 1968) suggests that it has four unique features.

CULTURAL PRESSURE TO ASSUME THE ROLE. Our society prescribes that every married couple should seek to have children. The couple that announces their intent to remain childless is likely to face extreme pressure to recant from their "un-American views." The couple that remains childless for some years after marriage will continually receive subtle and not-so-subtle hints that they had better "get with it" and have a child while they can. Somehow the values prevalent in our society proscribe childlessness, and this proscription is seemingly very successful. For example, in 1971 only 7.3 percent of the women aged 30–34 had never borne a child. Only 6.3 percent of those aged 35–39 were childless.

The effectiveness of the dictum "be fruitful and multiply" may, however, be losing some of its former power. In 1971, about 15 percent of the women aged 25–29 had not borne a child. As Kenkel (1973:217–218) notes: "Whether they will remain childless or are merely postponing childbearing cannot yet be determined. The recent increase in childlessness warrants close and continual scrutiny for it can have effects on the average size of completed families. Possibly, too, it indicates that the young married women are responding to the persuasive mass media articles dealing with the need to limit family size and control population growth."

Regardless of the recent trends in childlessness, there are still strong cultural pressures to join the ranks of parenthood.

INCEPTION OF THE PARENTAL ROLE. Rossi (1968) makes several salient points about the importance of when the parental role is adopted. First, she points to the differences between the completely voluntary nature of the decision to marry and the not infrequent involuntary conception, "the unintended consequence of a sexual act that was recreative in intent rather than procreative." Second, she points out that with the contraceptive technologies available today, the inception of parenthood frequently occurs after the couple has had the opportunity to establish a workable marital relationship. In most cases the husband and wife have both been working, giving the couple a better chance to work out a more equalitarian division of responsibilities that could have an impact on the roles each will assume after the first child has arrived. Rossi's major point is that parenthood is a crucial transition today, usually distinct from the transition to marriage. Before the widespread availability of effective contraceptives, parenthood more closely coincided with marriage, and adoption of the marital role usually meant an almost immediate transition to parenthood as well.

IRREVOCABILITY. This third unique feature of the parental role focuses on the obvious but important power of involuntary commitments. As Rossi (1968) notes, "We can have ex-spouses and ex-jobs but not ex-children." Once that little sperm cell has pierced the egg cell in the fallopian tube the die is usually cast—not only biologically but socially as well. Although abortion is more readily available today than it ever was, there is still a sense of irrevocability attached to the state of pregnancy, and the cultural pressures to carry a child full term are still quite strong.

PREPARATION FOR PARENTHOOD. The most critical aspects of the critical transition to parenthood result from an almost complete absence of training for the role. First, there is what Rossi (1968) calls a paucity of preparation. Our society trains women to be workers but not mothers. Most women facing the birth of their first child have had almost no experience

449

with the role and no formal training in it. Second, because most women bearing their first child continue to work during pregnancy, there is little or no time to spend getting prepared. Third, the transition is abrupt, to say the least. After birth the new mother usually stays in the hospital three to five days and then she is released—thrown into a 24-hour-a-day job of caring for a tiny and mysterious object that is completely dependent on her for all its needs. Last, there are no guidelines available for successful parenthood beyond the advice of friends and parents. About the only training available is "on the job," and every new parent probably feels partially or completely helpless whenever he or she pauses to think about the tremendous responsibilities of parenthood.

QUALIFICATION OF ROSSI'S VIEWS. Although it is difficult to argue with Rossi's contentions, especially her concern for the lack of preparation for the parental role that most new parents experience, her concern is too negative in outlook. Most new parents, although uneasy with the transition, probably go through a great deal of anticipatory practice, at least at the talking level of interaction. To be sure, they have approximately nine months to get ready for their new responsibilities. After the initial anxieties over caring for the new youngster, they soon learn that it will not break, diapers can be changed, and eventually the child will quit crying, especially if it is fed. Fortunately, most new babies spend a great deal of time sleeping. If the new father can overcome a condition of being all thumbs, most couples find that a new baby is like a new toy—fun to watch and play with. It does not take long before new parents begin to take pride in their accomplishments, like changing diapers, feeding the baby, and rocking it to sleep. These can be and usually are joyful experiences, experiences that quickly neutralize any fears that may result from a perceived lack of preparation. However, those fears may later crop up as the child gains mobility, a facility for talking and for saying "no" in many forms. It does not take long for new parents to realize that a baby will eat when it is hungry and will let the parents know when that time has come.

Therefore, a lack of explicit training and guidelines for parental behavior does not necessarily spell catastrophe for the new parent. In fact, I would be willing to argue that just such an ambiguous set of conditions is beneficial for the new parent. The ambiguity allows new parents to develop their own style of parental behavior, tailor made to suit individualistic and idiosyncratic couple needs and preferences. The lack of training and guidelines offers an opportunity, perhaps even a mandate, for enthusiasm and joyful happiness for most couples, without the self-imposed expectation that one should feel guilty at such displays of spontaneous pride. Because each child is entirely different from all others, the lack of explicit norms and guidelines provides a justification for making parental role enactments something that varies to some extent

Clemens Kalischer

*The christening ritual symbolizes the dreams of the parents for the future of a son or daughter.*

with each child. It encourages a craftsman's approach to the parental role as opposed to the impersonal and monotonous track that emerges with the efficient industrial approach to life. I, for one, hope that we never get so self-assured that we think parental behavior can be programmed. Just as no two children are ever born into the same family, so no two parents can ever fully relate to two children in exactly the same fashion. Each child is a distinct, unique human being and should be seen for that uniqueness.

This reaction to Rossi's (1968) article should not be seen as an encouragement to enter parenthood, but merely as an attempt to see a different and less negative view of the options facing new parents.

## THE FIRST CHILD

Just how extensive or intensive is the impact of parenthood on the marital relationship? Does it constitute a crisis or is it merely a brief transition stage between one stage in the family career and another? These are important questions that have been researched rather thoroughly since

451

the late 1950s and early 1960s. Although the results have not been uniformly consistent, a consensus does seem to be emerging.

LeMasters (1957) found that 83 percent of forty-six white, middle-class couples experienced what was jointly agreed to be an extensive or severe crisis at childbirth. LeMasters felt that the reason for this reaction was a tendency to romanticize parenthood and a lack of preparation for the parental role. Dyer (1963) found that 53 percent of the couples in his study were in the extensive or severe crisis category, and that this was particularly likely if the child was unplanned.

Evidence contrary to that found by LeMasters and Dyer is more extensive and methodologically more impressive. The first such study (see Hobbs, 1965) involved fifty-three couples chosen randomly from public birth records. Some 87 percent of the couples were classified in the slight crisis category and none in the extensive or severe crisis categories. Other studies (see Meyerowitz and Feldman, 1966; Hobbs, 1968; Beauchamp, 1966; Uhlenberg, 1970) seem to confirm the relatively positive or at least neutral findings of Hobbs versus the negative, even pathological, findings of LeMasters and Dyer. Perhaps the strongest confirmation of the findings of Hobbs of a transition rather than a crisis is found in a study by Russell (1974). With data from a random sample of 271 couples in Minneapolis, she discovered only 5 percent of the males and 3 percent of the females were in the extensive and severe crisis categories combined—over 95 percent of both sexes experienced no more than moderate difficulty adjusting to the first child. Further, 42 percent reported that the marital relationship had improved while 43 percent said it had remained the same.

The conclusion reached by Hobbs and Cole (1976:730) seems appropriate: "It is more accurate to think of beginning parenthood as a transition, accompanied by some difficulty, than a crisis of severe proportions." This does not mean that the transition into parenthood is not stressful. The mere presence of a dependent infant creates demands on parents that cannot be delayed or postponed. A new child can markedly alter a couple's schedule, priorities in life, and free time. Perhaps this is what is happening when the marital adjustment (see Chapter 16) declines considerably, on the average, in stage II of the family life cycle. Perhaps more is made of this decline than is justified. The marital adjustment scales measure marital, or conjugal, factors. None of the major scales tap the amount of satisfaction/happiness that accrues from a person's/couple's parental experiences. Perhaps that decline in marital adjustment is compensated for by the challenge and rewards of parenthood. Such is certainly the case for me and my wife.

## THE MOTHER ROLE

If there is one proposition with which most if not all sociologists would agree, it is: As society becomes more complex, social systems and the roles within them will become more differentiated (that is, a division of labor will occur at the role level). The role of mother within the family system is an exception, a deviant case to which the proposition seemingly does not apply. Let us examine more closely some of the forces that pull and tear at the American, middle-class mother, producing countervailing strains that require great strength to endure.

THE EXPANDED WIFE ROLE.    Most mothers are wives. One's first reaction may be, "Sure, so what?" But let us think for a minute about the changes that have been occurring in our society since 1900. Then, a wife was virtually a prisoner in her husband's home, subject to his demands and

Jean-Claude Lejeune from The Stock-Market

*It's not the quantity of parent-child interaction that counts—it's the quality.*

453

sometimes autocratic whims. She was first and foremost a helpmate to her husband, having little or no identity of her own. Her chances for equal educational and occupational opportunities were close to zero. She was forced by a male-dominated culture to do what her mother and her mother's mother had done. Her role was restricted to the home, and her tasks kept her there from daylight to long after dusk. As a wife she had little flexibility.

Today's mother is quite likely to have achieved some if not equal success relative to her husband in the educational arena. She has almost constant reminders that her life is not just limited to the home and to her husband's life path. She can be and is expected to be an individual with her own aspirations, which may be divergent from her husband's. She is not by cultural imperative submissive to his demands, his wishes, or his whims. She is expected to be an equal companion outside the home while still being primarily responsible for all of the tasks and more than her mother and grandmother had to perform within the home. To put it another way, the modern woman, unlike her counterpart at the beginning of this century, is expected to play two very demanding roles, mother and wife, equally well. To say the least, this is very difficult. The push for sexual equality in our society has placed additional strains on the American woman in that the wife role has been greatly expanded in the area of companionship. The modern wife is expected to share in and understand the husband's work world and, with increasing opportunities for joint leisure activities, to be an active participant in the recreational life of the husband.

THE EXPANDED WIFE/MOTHER ROLE.    Mothers today are more than mothers and wives. In 1900, because the means of transportation were primitive and many more families lived in rural areas, the mother was forced to spend much of her time as a full-time mother to her children. Today, this is not true. She has to be a full-time chauffeur to her children; the middle person between a whole host of service personnel and the home, which is a depository for complex machines that seem to be constantly in need of repair; the source of volunteer efforts to better the community; the liaison between the family and educational and community agencies; the person responsible for purchasing hundreds of consumer items from countless stores; a stalwart supporter of various recreational endeavors in which her children participate. The mother role in today's world requires that she make many more instrumental decisions under greater pressures than did her mother and grandmother—perhaps even more instrumental decisions than her husband. In other words, while her mother role has become differentiated to a fantastic degree, she is responsible for all of these additional tasks plus all of the same expressive tasks that she has always been required to perform.

OVERCOMMITMENT OF THE WIFE/MOTHER.    Mothers today are also breadwinners. As we will detail more specifically in the next chapter, women today are involved extensively in the occupational arena for pay. Many

454

of these women must simultaneously perform the traditional role of mother plus the other less traditional tasks mentioned in the two preceding sections. The fact that working mothers are out of the home and on the job for forty to fifty hours a week supplementing the family income does not markedly diminish their home management or mothering responsibilities after they finish their work.

As a result of all this, most American mothers are overcommitted (see LeMasters, 1970). Too much is required of the occupant of the role primarily because the role itself has expanded to include tasks made necessary by the changes that have taken place in our society. The fact that the overwhelming proportion of women in our society can adequately perform all their roles plus the traditional wife-mother role is, in my opinion, prima facie evidence of the strengths of the female sex.

CRITICISMS OF MOTHERHOOD.   One would think, given the tremendous pressures with which mothers in today's complex society must contend, that the mother role would be the most revered of all roles. Such has not been the case. In 1946 Edward Strecher, a psychiatrist, suggested that the United States almost lost World War II because American mothers had emasculated their sons. Philip Wylie (1942) accused American mothers of castrating their sons and labeled them as *A Generation of Vipers*. Betty Friedan (1963) in *The Feminine Mystique* charged that the retreat of American mothers to the relatively safe confines of the home had had deleterious effects on everyone—sons, daughters, husbands, and on the mothers themselves.

An even more stinging claim was made by Betty Rollin:[1]

Motherhood is in trouble, and it ought to be. A rude question is long overdue: Who needs it? The answer used to be (1) society and (2) women. But now, with the impending horrors of overpopulation society desperately doesn't need it. And women don't need it either. Thanks to the Motherhood Myth—the idea that having babies is something that all normal women instinctively want and need and will enjoy doing—they just *think* they do.

When motherhood is no longer culturally compulsory, there will, certainly, be less of it. Women are now beginning to think and do more about development of self, of their individual resources. Far from being selfish, such development is probably our only hope. That means more alternatives for women. And more alternatives mean more selective, better, happier, motherhood—and childhood and husbandhood (or manhood) and peoplehood. It is not a question of whether or not children are sweet and marvelous to have and rear; the question is, even if that's so, whether or not one wants to pay the price for it. It doesn't make any sense any more to pretend that women need babies, when what they really need is themselves. If God were still speaking to us in a voice we could hear, even He would probably say, "Be fruitful. Don't multiply."

This motherhood myth, as Rollin has presented it, is long overdue for burial. Just because most women have the biological capacity for childbirth does not mean that all have the psychological and sociological wherewithal to be mothers in the truly complex, modern meaning of the role. Fortunately it is now possible, given the ideological milieu prevalent today and the obvious reality of the population problem, for women to legitimately (as defined by society) opt for another alternative. The consequence of such a state of affairs should be that motherhood will be a role truly voluntarily adopted, and the quality of the performance of the mother role should increase markedly. This should ensure a better and happier childhood, motherhood, personhood, and fatherhood for all involved.

## THE FATHER ROLE

If the mother role has been castigated, what have the critics been saying about fathers? The sad but truthful answer is, Nothing. LeMasters (1970: 138–143) thoroughly documents the extent to which social scientists have ignored the father role in studies of family life. He points to the following major research efforts as clear-cut examples of what Safilios-Rothschild (1969) called "wives' sociology": (1) Clark Vincent's (1961) study of unmarried mothers reports that the ratio of studies on girls as compared to boys was 25 to 1. This study, of course, dealt only with the premaritally pregnant mothers—the fathers were ignored altogether. (2) A classic study by Robert Sears (1957), entitled *Patterns of Child Rearing,* is actually based on interview data with 379 mothers. No attempt was made to interview any father. (3) The classic study by Miller and Swanson (1958) on *The Changing American Parent* reports the results of interviews with 582 mothers and no fathers. (4) William Goode's (1956) study of divorce and its effects is focused on 425 divorced mothers in Detroit—no divorced fathers were interviewed. (5) LeMasters also notes that there are only five specific references to fathers in 1,140 pages of the encyclopedic work edited by David Goslin (1969) and entitled *Handbook of Socialization Theory and Research.*

What LeMasters (1970) reports is surely no accident. I would be thoroughly amazed if Sears (1957) and Miller and Swanson (1958) left the father out of their studies by anything but conscious design. The obvious question is, Why? Is not the father role important in childhood socialization? Is the father in American society just there for the purpose of bringing home the bread? How can someone study *Patterns of Child Rearing* and *The Changing American Parent* and ask their questions only of mothers? Perhaps the best place to start is with an examination of the salient characteristics of the father role.

456

THE SECONDARY STATUS OF THE FATHER ROLE. The father role is secondary or tertiary for most American males, and certainly less than central for the American family system and society. As we shall examine more fully in the next chapter, the paramount role in the lives of most males is occupational. This is particularly true for those men who are in professional and managerial positions, but it is also true for men who occupy lower status occupations yet have a high need for achievement. To put it quite bluntly, most males identify themselves by the work they do for a living, not the living they do when away from work. Likely as not most males are thinking about their work while enacting the father role with the kids, talking with the wife, and perhaps even while making love.

Not only is the father role secondary for most males, it is likewise considered secondary for the family system. The mother is the primary parent—the crux of the family system, the spring of strength and hope for the future. It is the mother who provides the biological prenatal shelter; it is the mother to whom the child is umbilically connected; it is the mother who is equipped to nourish the child after birth.

If we were to believe American folklore, the father is merely the vehicle through which sperm is provided for conception, the source of economic support during pregnancy and thereafter, a sort of detached and bureaucratically sterile arbiter of family disputes, the hit man who carries out the punishment orders that have accumulated during his daily absence from home. As such, there is little the father can contribute that could not be found in an alternative form. He is less than indispensable—that is, if we accept the folk beliefs.

SECONDARY STATUS OF FATHERHOOD. A secondary characteristic of the father role that may account for its being generally ignored in American scholarship is best put by Leonard Benson (1968): "Womanliness is still often equated with motherliness and succorance; manliness is hardly ever identified with fatherhood, especially in modern industrial societies. Even the emergence of industrialism has not deprived women of their maternal claims, although it has permitted them to stake out some new ones."

As discussed earlier, Rossi (1968) has clearly delineated the extreme cultural pressures for women to become mothers. If anything, men are encouraged *not* to become fathers. Put another way, there is a close congruence between the sex-role term *female* or *woman* and the familial role term *mother*. Male and father are two terms that do not cluster together in the cognitive worlds of most Americans, perhaps because fatherhood is not a significant status for most males and also because most families could exist fairly easily without the father role being present.

SOCIETAL EXPECTATIONS OF THE FATHER ROLE. The guidelines for successful fatherhood are much more diffuse and ambiguous than those for

457

motherhood, and failure to reach the minimum level of competence is less likely to bring sanctions. Somehow American folklore has developed an image of the father as a sort of bumpkin—someone who can be molded and manipulated quite easily by his wife and children, someone who is out to obtain the truly simple pleasures of life and to escape complications of any sort—the Dagwood Bumstead image. Society has devised different normative patterns that allow a male-father to leave his family, usually without much sanction, if the pressures get too intense; such behavior for a mother is treated as if it were a capital crime.

Fathers can generally escape the blame for a child who gets into trouble. If the father is away from home a great deal, "he had to because of his job." If he is home on a regular basis, the child became delinquent "because of the crowd he or she runs with." If neither of these accounts will be accepted, there is always the mother to blame since "she is the primary parent, you know!"

SUMMARY OF THE FATHER ROLE.   In summary, the central characteristics of the father role in American society have been these: (1) The father role is generally much less salient than the male's occupational role and, at a more abstract level, the father role is less salient in the family system than is the mother role. (2) There is not nearly as much correspondence between the male-father role expectations as there is for the female-mother configuration. (3) Society has rather explicit standards for mothering, but almost no consensual standards for fathering.

I believe all of this is changing and rather rapidly at that because of several factors. First, at least partially and perhaps mostly, as a result of the women's liberation movement, the American male is getting out from under a repressive set of cultural expectations that are not relevant for the modern world. The traditional and stereotypical male sex-role behaviors emphasize survival techniques that may have been appropriate in frontier days but are now antisocial at best, and outrageously obnoxious at worst, today. The new American male is being socialized to be sensitive, cultured, gentle, and less pugnacious. A second sign of change in the father role is the increasing recognition, at least in popular literature, that fathers can and should participate in the child-rearing facets of family life. If they do not, they miss out on a chance for self-development, an opportunity for what Maslow (1970) called self-actualization.

A force that facilitates this movement toward a redefinition of the male-father role is the increasing amount of leisure time available to the American male. Leisure is also being redefined as a commodity that should be spent with family instead of the same-sex peer group. This movement cuts across social class levels primarily because the lines of distinctions among classes have blurred in an economy where it is no longer axiomatic that the blue-collar worker has either less education or a lower income than the white-collar worker.

George W. Gardner

*Enlargement of the father role beyond the traditional areas of economic support and discipline may be one result of changes in women's status.*

Now, rather than devoting a whole section of the chapter to the child role, we will move into the area of parent-child interaction. This discussion should resolve the issue of what the child's role in our society is and can be.

## SOCIALIZATION

The primary function of the parent is to socialize the child—to teach the child all the social skills he or she needs to become a functional and functioning member of the family, the community, and society. A great deal of time, energy, effort, and considerable financial cost is involved. Just how substantial the cost is can be seen in the following quotation ab-

*The Parental Role*

The last twenty years of this century will likely produce a more uni-sexual definition of the parental role. Fathers and mothers will be performing more and more of the same parental tasks either side by side or as a result of a negotiated division of labor that essentially ignores the traditional sex-role split of the past. If this does occur—and many social scientists think it will—the result will be a better quality of family life. Perhaps such a movement will also signal a convergence of the cultural definitions of manhood and womanhood.

To date the achievement of manhood and womanhood status has meant distinctly different achievements and characteristics. The traditional conception of a "man" has included sexual proclivity and success in the occupational sphere. The man in our society has been defined as someone who is rational and calculating, someone who is calm under stress and who does not openly express emotions and affection. The traditional evidence of achievement of womanhood has been marriage, an adequate performance of the wife role, and becoming a mother, once, twice, three, or four times. The "woman" in our society is someone who is warm and affectionate, someone who openly expresses her emotions, sometimes in a direction opposite to rationality.

Perhaps a movement toward a greater mutual and shared involvement in a unitary parental role as opposed to the traditional and separate father and mother roles will produce a complementarity of behaviors and characteristics that are similar instead of opposite. Perhaps it will produce at least a partial reversal of the findings that marital adjustment and satisfaction suffer because of the onset of children.

stracted from a report made by Reed and McIntosh (1972) for the President's Commission on Population Growth and the American Future (*see Family Planning Digest,* Vol. 1, No. 5, September, 1972). These costs were computed with figures current in 1969:

> An average U.S. family must spend about $40,000 in direct costs—from hospital delivery through college education—to raise its first child, and more than $98,000 if the mother's lost earnings (opportunity costs) due to her withdrawal from the work force for childbearing and rearing are taken in account. For each additional child, costs average about $48,000 in direct and opportunity costs combined.

Socialization is usually defined as an interactional process whereby a person's behavior is modified to conform to expectations held by the members of the group to which he or she belongs. Socialization occurs throughout life as a person changes positions within a group or changes groups. Within the family the socialization agents (parents primarily but also older siblings) change their tactics or forms of socialization and the content of the socialization as the child reaches new levels of maturity and evidences changing needs for knowledge and skills.

## The Content of Socialization

Just what it is that the parents as socializing agents seek to instill in their children naturally changes as the child gets older. In keeping with Duvall's (1971) definition of a developmental task (see Chapter 2), the content of subsequent socialization efforts is based on the achievement by the child of an adequate performance at earlier stages of development. Thus, socialization designed to polish mate-selection skills in adolescence and young adulthood is based on an adequate performance of heterosexual skills in a peer group in childhood and on an adequate inculcation of proper sex-role identification in infancy and early childhood. Listed below are some of the major content areas of socialization focused upon by parents during their children's infancy, childhood, and adolescence:

*Infancy*

1. Adequate motor development
2. Adequate control of body functions
3. Adequate sex-role identification
4. Adequate language facility
5. Adequate social interactional skills
6. Adequate preparation for school

*Childhood*

1. Continued sex-role identification
2. Adequate internalization of moral values

461

3. Adequate social skills

4. Adequate involvement with peer group

5. Adequate degree of independence

6. Adequate control of aggressive impulses

7. Adequate performance of intellectual skills

*Adolescence*

1. Continued development of independence

2. Greater facility with social skills

3. Skills in selecting and reacting to peer group norms

4. Determination of occupational-educational goals

5. Success in the courtship and mate-selection system

6. A general preparation for launching the child

Although this list is not exhaustive, the items included probably cover the primary foci of attention of parents during these three broad stages of development. Obviously, other socialization agents are working on the child in each stage, helping the parents in molding the child into a functional member of society. In some cases a conflict exists between the goals of the adult agents of socialization and the contents of socialization coming from the peer groups. Such conflict, although inevitable, is usually a reflection of differences in perceptions existing between generations—a condition resulting from change, which is ubiquitous. In addition, occasional conflicts occur between the adult agents of socialization, such as between father and mother, or between either or both of them and other adults (that is, teachers, coaches, group leaders, and so forth). The conflict is usually over what the child will be taught, how he or she will utilize time, and who will be the teacher. The child is more often than not caught in the crossfire of these conflicting goals, aspirations, and socialization efforts of these adults. A culture can never be passed from one generation to the next totally intact. Progress can occur only as one generation dispenses with orthodoxies of the past that do not fit with the new contingencies of today's modern world.

## Socialization: How Does Learning Take Place?

Socialization should not be viewed as a totalitarian process in which the defenseless children in a society, or even a family, are filled with a repertoire of values, attitudes, expectations, and aspirations as if they were merely empty molds waiting for a filling substance. Individuals are subjected to different socialization contents presented in different formats with varying degrees of pressure to accept or acquiesce. The recipient children can also have differing reactions to these socialization attempts that are a function of maturation, intelligence, and metabolic processes. In essence, then, the same socialization process (form and content) can produce distinct differences among children just as different socialization processes can lead to amazing similarities among children.

Of course, although most socialization is asymmetrical (that is, from parent to child), we should not ignore the fact that children also socialize their parents—both directly and indirectly, consciously and incidentally. For example, a new baby or young infant can very definitely socialize the parents into the adoption of new schedules of activity and different styles of life. How many parents would consider routinely getting up at 2:00 A.M. if they did not have an infant to feed? How many would keep their bedroom doors closed when making love if there were no children at home? As the children get older, parents are constantly being socialized into new language and fashion styles, and they learn directly from their children about the changing norms of attitudes and behavior, sometimes painfully. Our concern in this chapter is with the parents-to-child flow of socialization.

Socialization includes such a complex set of components that a division of labor has developed even among those who specialize in the study of childhood development. One set of specialists has been concerned with the forms of learning, that is, How does learning occur in childhood? From a parental perspective the question becomes, How do I get my child to learn those things I deem essential? There are probably at least five ways that learning occurs in small children. Four of these will be briefly discussed here; a separate section will be devoted to the fifth, which is identification with models.

OPERANT LEARNING.  The first form of learning is most closely associated with the work of psychologist B. F. Skinner (1953, 1957). An *operant* is a response emitted by the child with reference to a certain stimulus. The central and guiding principle of the operant learning approach is that when an operant (response) is followed by reinforcement, the probability of the later occurrence of the response is increased. Reinforcement may take one or both of the following forms: (a) positive, the operant leading to a rewarding stimulus and/or (b) negative, the response preventing or removing a punishing stimulus.

For example, a two-year-old child must learn to use the toilet instead of wetting or messing in his or her pants. When the appropriate response is made, he gets a positive reinforcement stimulus—massive applause, smiles, encouraging "good boy!" remarks, and whatever else his parents can muster.

Negative reinforcement is a more difficult concept to illustrate. Suppose that a child has been exceedingly difficult all day, into everything he or she should not be into, and the mother is at her wits' end. She threatens with a negative stimulus. "You just wait—when your father gets home, you're going to get a spanking you'll never forget." The child goes

Peter Vandermark

into his or her room, which looks as though a cyclone has hit it, at least twice. When the father gets home, he is dispatched immediately to the child's room, which, to the mother's amazement, is meticulously clean. The child is sitting at a table or desk reading a book, looking like a little angel. The operant (response) may have prevented a very negative stimulus. If the parents then congratulate the child for doing such a good job on cleaning the room, the negative reinforcement may be sufficient to make this activity, cleaning up the room, a recurring response.

Operant learning is probably the most widely used child-rearing socialization technique. It is used almost unconsciously and is usually quite effective if the parents persist.

DIRECT TUITION. The second form of socialization differs from operant learning in that it involves the intentional guidance of behavior and the purposive manipulation of reinforcement. This, in layman's terminology, is the old child-psychology tactic. A rather common example is: "If you will do this, this, and this while our company is here, your reward will be thus-and-so. And, if you don't do what I want, your punishment will be something else." Children quickly learn to assess and behave according to what the probabilities of reward are versus how fearful they are of the potential punishment.

After the child has mastered the problem of language development, this technique becomes a rather prevalent tactic of childhood socialization.

INCIDENTAL LEARNING. The third form of learning that embellishes the whole experience of childhood socialization occurs when the child observes something for which someone is reinforced and then imitates the behavior. At a party, a little boy wandered into the party room, awakened from his sleep by the loud noises but very drowsy. As his mother picked him up a friend dropped something in the kitchen and uttered an audible "damn!" His parents had been very careful not to teach him such expressions. The next day he dropped something, and you guessed it—a very appropriate "damn!" Children are astute observers of everything they encounter. Incidental learning provides them with a vast repertoire of language and behavioral skills. Such learning is especially salient in their development, particularly as they move out into the peer-group play world, and especially if they play with older children.

PUNISHMENT. The fourth socialization technique is generally viewed by parents more as a control device than as a mechanism for learning purposes. It is certainly true that the decisions parents must make about punishment, how much, when, and how to use it, probably cause almost as much anxiety, frustration, ambivalence, and anticipatory guilt as occurs from the actual application of the punishment itself. Even though some uncertainty exists for most parents concerning the specifics of punishment, Americans in general seem to have a rather strong commitment to the idea that punishment works. Our criminal justice system is handcuffed to the assumption that incarcerated isolation not only prevents crime but also rehabilitates the prisoner. American business seems to have generally adopted the assumption that their workers' productivity will reach expected levels if they are punished for low productivity by docking their salaries, placing them on probation, or temporarily suspending them.

The assumption that the effects of punishment will be positive, at least as defined by the person or group administering the punishment, certainly permeates the child-rearing practices and, to some extent, the ideology of childhood socialization in the United States. The ideology, of course, labels severe punishments as detrimental to the goals of socialization, while the law proscribes such activities as a violation of the child's

465

civil liberties. Nevertheless, punishment is widely used as a technique for eliminating undesirable behavior.

As a number of researchers have indicated, punishment can be dramatically effective in eliminating an undesirable behavior, particularly if it is judiciously combined with a reward for some alternative behavior that is analogous to the behavior to be suppressed. In such cases the punishment must be tied to something that is highly valued by the child, and the reward must be at least as desirable as the privilege or object lost due to the punishment.

But, punishment is like a two-headed monster with severe punishment on one and extreme permissiveness on the other head. David Heise (1972:29–30) has put the monster into some perspective.

> A great deal of research on parent-child relationships has been carried out, but all too often results have seemed to conflict. While nearly all researchers have found that loving parents produce more adjusted children than hostile parents, studies disagree concerning the kind of personality that loving parents produce or the kind of personality that hostile parents produce. Studies also have conflicted in defining the consequences of strict versus permissive discipline; for example, sometimes strict discipline has been seen to produce neurotic children and at other times obedient, well-behaved children have been identified as a consequence. . . . The degree of love and the degree of control exercised in a parent-child relationship are seen to interact, and the different combinations have qualitatively different outcomes. . . . It would seem that when conservatives call for more obedience and liberals call for more permissiveness, they both assume the existence of loving parent-child relationships; and when obedience or permissiveness is condemned, it is condemned because of the kind of person it produces when parent-child relationships are hostile.

## Guidelines for Effective Teaching and Learning

Several guidelines that seem to aid any type of learning are:

1. Love for children is not something that can be expressed only in verbal terms or through the buying of affection. Younger children are particularly responsive when affection is sincerely expressed through touch.

2. Punishment must be administered almost immediately after the undesirable act. Delayed punishment is seldom perceived by the child as connected to the undesirable act. More likely than not, delayed punishment is seen by the child as undeserved parental aggression.

3. Punishment is most likely to produce the effects desired by the parents if an explanation is offered, if the alternative behavior that would be desired is outlined, if the punishment is not

rescinded (that is, spank the child and then apologize for doing so), and if the punishment is consistently applied (it does little good to punish a child for an action in the morning if the same action is ignored in the afternoon).

4. Children are generally more responsive to parents if there are rules for virtually everything. Children want to know where they stand with the parents. They feel extremely uncomfortable and confused if they do not know the boundaries between acceptable and unacceptable, or if the boundaries are constantly shifting. Most adults react the same way to ambiguity.

5. Finally, parents should be acutely sensitive to the fact that a child's behavior is tied to his or her body changes (growth spurts affect metabolic processes) and to the social roles children are playing. For example, a child experiences a rather strong set of social pressures when he or she is in a state of transition from a preschool to a school status (onset of first grade), and from an elementary to a junior high status (this usually coincides with the transition to the teenager status). The latter transition is particularly important because it also signals the onset of puberty with the changes usually associated with that process. Clausen's (1968) statement succinctly summarizes this point: "Maturational readiness is certainly a requisite to effective training; no amount of parental pushing can overcome this stubborn fact."

## Becker's Model of Parental Behavior

Perhaps the most thorough model of parental behavior with regard to discipline was developed by Wesley Becker (1964). Becker views parental behavior as existing along three dimensions: (a) warmth versus hostility, (b) restrictiveness versus permissiveness, and (c) calm detachment versus anxious emotional involvement. Eight different types of parents are depicted by Becker's model: (a) democratic, (b) indulgent, (c) organized-effective, (d) overprotective, (e) rigid-controlling, (f) authoritarian (hostile-neurotic), (g) neglecting, and (h) anxious-neurotic (Figure 17–1).

Becker (1964:176) says: "Both the democratic parent and the indulgent parent (by definition) are high on the dimensions of warmth and permissiveness, but the indulgent parent is high on emotional involvement while the democratic parent tends to be low on this dimension (calm detached). Both the organized-effective parent and the overprotective parent are high on warmth and restrictiveness, but the overprotective parent again shows more involvement than the organized-effective parent. The argument can be thus carried around the model, showing how the typical concepts for types of parents can be thought of as being defined by various combinations of three dimensions of parent behavior."

**FIGURE 17-1**
**A Model of Parental Behavior**

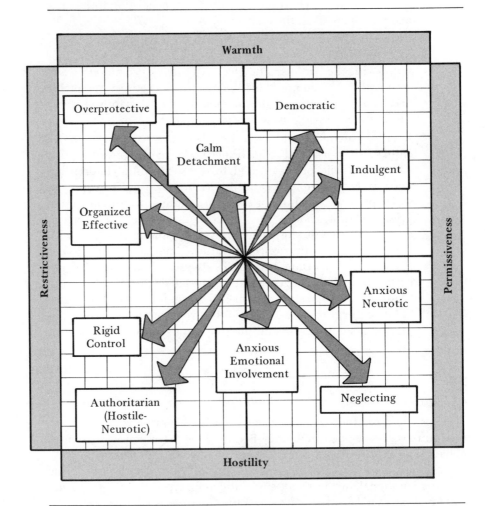

SOURCE: Figure 2 from "Consequences of Different Kinds of Parental Discipline," by Wesley C. Becker, in *Review of Child Development Research*, Volume 1, Martin L. Hoffman and Lois Wladis Hoffman, editors, © 1964 Russell Sage Foundation, New York.

*Summary*

In summary, enactment of the parental role is at best a difficult and complex phenomenon. Many choices and decisions are made by parents with regard to child rearing. A child learns, regardless of whether it is by the operant approach, direct tuition, incidental learning, or through the use of punishment. Socialization occurs whether it is conscious or subconscious, purposive or accidental. There are frequently disagreements between parents as to which is the best or most effective strategy to use in the socialization process. Each child in a family is different, and some child-rearing strategies that work well for one child will fail with another. The forms and content of socialization discussed above will be differentially effective depending on the age of the child. When there are children of widely different ages in a family, the parents may have to use varying strategies and tactics of socialization with each child in order to achieve the desired results. Since there are no hard and fast guidelines for effective socialization, parents must resort to a trial-and-error approach. Fortunately, most if not all children want to respond favorably to their parents and want to learn. Warmth and love seem to be a sure bet for a starting point.

## THE IMPORTANCE OF EARLY CHILDHOOD

Although there is a general consensus that parental role enactment is a difficult and complex phenomenon and that parental warmth and love are generally productive of positive results, no such consensus exists concerning the question of just how crucial early childhood experiences are for subsequent personality development.

### Childhood Experiences and Personality Development

Those who are influenced by psychoanalytic theory, and most of us are, would probably endorse at least the logic inherent in the Freudian scheme of personality development. The following thumbnail sketch includes the outline of the Freudian approach:

1. The influences, experiences, and interactions that occur in the earliest years of infancy and childhood play a ignificant role in the future personal history of the individual. For Freud, the first five or six years were crucial. Any major difficulties with early development could have lasting impacts on the adult's personality.

2. Freudian psychoanalysts conceptualize personality development in terms of relatively fixed stages through which the individual passes. The stages gradually fade one into the next, and there is a considerable amount of overlapping among them. In terms of chronological age there is a certain amount of individual variation with regard to when the various characteristics of a given stage will come into prominence. No stage is completely left behind, but always some of the characteristics of the earlier level are carried forward throughout the later stages of development.

3. All individuals go through the oral-dependency, anal, oedipal-electra, and latency stages of development. In other words, the means used by parents to satisfy childhood oral, anal, and genital needs may seriously affect the child's subsequent personality development up to and through

469

adulthood. Consequently, the dynamics of the interactions between an adult person's id, ego, and superego can be best understood by backtracking to early childhood experiences.

If Freud and his disciples were right, certain child-training practices should be more productive of stable adult personalities than others. For example, breast-fed babies should exhibit greater stability, personality wise, than those fed by the bottle. Those children whose parents induced bowel training early should evidence more personality problems than those whose parents were less anxious about the process. The real question is: Just how important are child-training practices in early childhood relative to their long-range effects on personality development?

WILLIAM H. SEWELL (1952). The most dramatic answer to this question involves research conducted by William H. Sewell on 162 farm children. All the children studied were from intact families, they were all either five or six and had not yet attended school, and all were from old-stock American families. In this way Sewell was assured that any differences he found would not result from social class, age, or ethnic differences. For each child he obtained extensive information from personality tests and equally extensive data on the exact child-training practices used.

The hypothesis tested by Sewell was derived from psychoanalytic theory and posited that there would be significant personality differences between children because of the following opposed child-training practices: (a) bottle fed versus breast fed, (b) nursed on a regular versus a self-demand schedule, (c) weaned abruptly versus gradually, (d) bowel trained early versus late, (e) bladder trained early versus late, (f) punished versus not punished for toilet accidents, and (g) forced to sleep alone versus being allowed to sleep with the mother during the first year of life.

The type of statistical technique used by Sewell is called the "chi-square test." If the child-training practices were productive of major differences in personality the chi-square test would come out statistically significant (that is, the differences observed in personality by the use of different child-training practices would have occurred no more than 5 times out of 100 times by chance alone). His study produced a total of 460 chi-square tests. Of these, only 18 were statistically significant, and seven of that number were in the opposite direction from that predicted. See Table 17–1.

What this means is that personality adjustments and personality traits of children who have undergone varying infant training experiences do not differ significantly. Put another way, the psychoanalytic ideas about early psychosexual experiences of children were not supported.

Sewell's (1952) research does not imply that early childhood is not important, only that the specific infant training practices he studied did not produce significant differences in the personality development of children. Other studies (see Moss and Kagan, 1964) detail the crucial significance of the mother's general treatment of the child. Henry Biller

**TABLE 17–1**

**Relationship of Child-Training Practices to Indicators of Personality Adjustment Among American Farm Children**

| TRAINING PRACTICE AND INDEXES | INDICATORS OF PERSONALITY ADJUSTMENT | CHI-SQUARE | P VALUE |
|---|---|---|---|
| Self-demand feeding schedule | Low feeling of belonging[a] | 3.91 | 0.05 |
| Gradual weaning | High feeling of belonging[a] | 5.83 | 0.02 |
| Gradual weaning | High social standards[a] | 4.61 | 0.05 |
| Late bowel training | Poor school relations[a] | 4.51 | 0.05 |
| Late bowel training | Good temper[b] | 9.26 | 0.01 |
| Late bowel training | Little nail biting[b] | 4.32 | 0.05 |
| Late bladder training | Little nail biting[b] | 9.22 | 0.01 |
| No punishment for toilet accidents | High social adjustment[a] | 8.76 | 0.01 |
|  | High social standards[a] | 8.30 | 0.01 |
|  | Good school relations[a] | 6.74 | 0.01 |
| High sleep security | Low self-adjustment[a] | 4.67 | 0.05 |
| High sleep security | Low personal freedom[a] | 5.87 | 0.02 |
| High sleep security | Poor family relations[a] | 4.12 | 0.05 |
| High sleep security | Sleep disturbances[b] | 3.93 | 0.05 |
| High infantile security | High personal freedom[a] | 4.82 | 0.05 |
| High infantile security | Good temper[b] | 4.03 | 0.05 |
| Favorable toilet training factor | Little nail biting[b] | 6.71 | 0.01 |
| Favorable feeding training factor | Poor family relations[a] | 6.03 | 0.01 |

SOURCE: William H. Sewell, "Infant Training and the Personality of the Child," *American Journal of Sociology* 58(1952):155, Table 3. By permission of the University of Chicago Press. © 1952 the University of Chicago. All rights reserved.

[a] From California Test of Personality.

[b] From interview with the child's mother.

(1969) found that the sex role development of kindergarten boys was strongly influenced by their perceptions of how dominant the father was relative to the father-mother relationship. If the boys perceived their father to be the dominant parent, their own masculinity was likely to be better developed than that of boys who saw their father as less than dominant.

## Children's Games and Play

More recently, Lever (1976) studied the games that children play and how girls and boys differ in their play. She studied 181 ten- and eleven-year-olds for a year. She found that boys and girls spend only 24 percent of their free time (that is, outside school) activities engaged in nonplay (for example, doing chores, homework, and so forth). Another 24 percent of the activities were neither play nor nonplay, but rather consisted of vicarious pastimes. There was virtually no sex difference in the *amount* of time spent watching television—fifteen to twenty hours per week. There was, however, a difference in the *content* of the programs preferred: The girls preferred family-oriented situation comedies, whereas the boys liked adventure stories best. Overall, Lever found six differences that seem to be sex linked:

1. Boys play outdoors far more than girls.
2. When they were involved in social play, boys more often played in larger groups.
3. Boys' play occurs in more age-heterogeneous groups.
4. Girls more often play in predominantly male games than boys play in girls' games.
5. Boys play competitive games more often than girls.
6. Boys' games last longer than girls' games.

Suzanne Arms, Jeroboam Inc.

*Part of growing up is learning how to be grown up.*

The primary significance of these findings is that fifth graders, ten- and eleven-year-old children, rather accurately reflect in their play the distinctions traditionally made between male and female roles. The impact of socialization and its repertoire of roles-positions-norms—prescriptions and proscriptions—do's and don'ts—is seen quite clearly in the games children play and how they play the game. Early childhood socialization and education is crucial if a new order is to emerge. If new generations of children are to become androgynous adults—persons who enact roles that are totally free from scripting based on gender—early childhood socialization must begin ignoring gender in the delivery room and continue doing so in every facet and stage of life.

## Summary

Early childhood is a time of intense learning for children. They observe everything, and virtually everything is a new experience. What they see is internalized into a growing repertoire of words, ideas, values, and attitudes and behaviors. What has become a habitual style of role playing for parents is viewed by the child as something to be imitated and replayed. Parents can learn a great deal about themselves by observing how their children react to stress and frustration, how they play mommy and daddy, how they relate to other adults, and how they express aggression. This process is usually called *identification,* and it is this process that provides the basis for the most widely accepted theory of socialization.

## THE HYPOTHESIS OF IDENTIFICATION

It stands to reason that a very young child does not have the maturity or knowledge to create a self in isolation from adults. As was discussed in Chapter 2 in the section on symbolic interactionism, a self emerges through the process of taking the role of significant others, particular others, and the generalized other or society. This means the child will attempt to put himself or herself in the shoes of the persons whose role is being taken. Then the child will play the role so that that role can be better understood and used by the child to decipher the world in which he or she lives. This in essence is what *positional identification* means. Sociologists have been particularly interested in two questions about identification: (1) How does identification occur? and (2) Why is one role model chosen instead of another?

The latter question is perhaps easier to answer. At least seven reasons, not necessarily mutually exclusive, have been offered to account for the choice of one model over another:

1. *Secondary reinforcement.* A person is chosen as a model because he or she frequently rewards the learner.

473

*Working together teaches a skill and role identification and promotes closeness within a family—all valuable parts of the socialization process.*

2. *Vicarious reinforcement.* A person is chosen as a model because he or she receives rewards that are experienced vicariously by the learner. (This is very similar to number 5 below.)

3. *Withholding of love.* The learner fears that unless the model is chosen, the model will withhold love from the learner. (Number 4 is quite similar to number 3.)

4. *Avoidance of punishment.* A person is chosen as a model because the learner fears that the model may injure him or her.

5. *Status envy.* A person is chosen as a model because he or she is envied as a recipient of rewards from others.

6. *Social power.* A person is chosen as a model because he or she has the power to reward, but does not necessarily reward, the learner.

7. *Similarity to learner.* A person is chosen as a model because the learner perceives that he or she has a trait similar to one of his own.

Although research supports the viability of each of these seven reasons why one model is chosen over another, none of these reasons is indispensable for identification to occur. More likely than not, any child will use most if not all of these tactics in learning how to play roles. The chances are also quite good that no child will ever specialize in one of these tactics, but will use whichever seems appropriate at the moment.

474

## Sex-Role Preference and Identification

The problem inherent in a listing of the reasons for selecting a specific model is that adults play numerous roles daily, with differing degrees of flair and intensity, depending on the situational context. Children are probably quite adept at imitating the role enactments they observe without being able to understand fully the motives behind the model's enactment. This problem has been partially neutralized by David Lynn, who focused his research on the process by which parental and sex role identification occur. The hypotheses[2] listed below are a summary of his views:

1. Males tend to identify with a culturally defined masculine role, whereas females tend to identify with their mothers.
2. Both males and females identify more closely with the mother than with the father.
3. The closer identification of males with their mothers than with their fathers will be revealed most frequently in personality variables that are not clearly sex typed.
4. In learning the sex-typical identification, each sex is thereby acquiring separate methods of learning which are subsequently applied to learning tasks generally.
5. Males tend to have greater difficulty in achieving same-sex identification than females.
6. More males than females fail more or less completely in achieving same-sex identification but rather make an opposite-sex identification.
7. Males are more anxious regarding sex-role identification than females.
8. Males tend to hold stronger feelings of hostility toward females than females toward males.
9. With increasing age, males become relatively more firmly identified with the masculine role.
10. With increasing age, males develop psychological disturbances at a more slowly accelerating rate than females.
11. A larger proportion of females than males show preference for the role of the opposite sex.
12. Where a discrepancy exists between sex-role preference and identification, it will tend to be as follows: Males will tend to show same-sex role preference with underlying opposite-sex

---

[2] Adapted from David B. Lynn, "The Process of Learning Parental and Sex-Role Identification," *Journal of Marriage and the Family 28*(1966):466–70. Reprinted by permission of the National Council on Family Relations.

identification. Females will tend to show opposite-sex role preference with underlying same-sex identification.

13. A higher proportion of females than males adopt aspects of the role of the opposite sex.

Just a brief comment seems relevant here regarding hypotheses 11 through 13 from Lynn's theory. If Lynn is correct in his assumptions, the goal of the women's liberation movement to change the attitudes and values and the hearts of men and women concerning the "immoral" aspects of sex-typed roles may be more easily achieved than the cynics would have us believe. If men really do identify rather easily with the opposite sex, and if women do show a preference for the opposite sex role, a concerted effort by the mothers of society could produce virtual equality in a generation or so. Whether this will come to pass is an empirical question. That it may occur seems to be a question of commitment—I do believe the cultural and sociohistorical context is ripe for just such a change.

## How Does Identification Occur?

Now that we have examined why one model is chosen over another and have briefly examined Lynn's (1966) hypotheses concerning sex role preference and identification, it is time to examine identification from a more sociological perspective. The most thorough theoretical model of the problem of identification available was developed by Robert Winch (1962) (Figure 17–2).

Winch approaches identification from a structure-functionalist perspective. The consequent or dependent variable he is trying to explain is the behavior of the identifier, the child or other person who chooses a model within the family.

It is Winch's contention that the antecedent variables, social structure and social function, provide the basic context and boundaries for role-modeling. *Social structure* consists of the various positions and roles, including the normative prescriptions attached to the roles, from which the identifier can choose a model. Obviously, the larger the social structure of the family, the larger the number of roles available for emulation. The more tightly structured the family (that is, the degree of division of labor within the family by sex), the more limited is the choice of models.

*Social function* consists of the tasks performed by each of the potential role models and those tasks performed by coalitions of members within the family. Thus, the identifier can adopt an individualistic type of model or can emulate the behavior of that model as a team member.

The intervening variables are products of the social structure operating in a normal fashion in the performance of its tasks. A *resource* is

476

merely the outcome produced by the various role-occupants in carrying out their tasks within the family. If there is some degree of probability that the identifier will view a resource as desirable, Winch calls it a reward. He states: "When a person has control over a resource that another person wants, he or she is in a position to influence the latter's behavior. Control over the reward makes a person a model with respect to persons or a class of persons who desire that resource. From the foregoing argument it seems to follow that the model and the reward constitute necessary and sufficient conditions for identification to occur" (Winch, 1962). This process, part of Winch's model, is shown by the diagram on p. 478.

**FIGURE 17–2**
**Identification as an Outcome of Structure and Function**

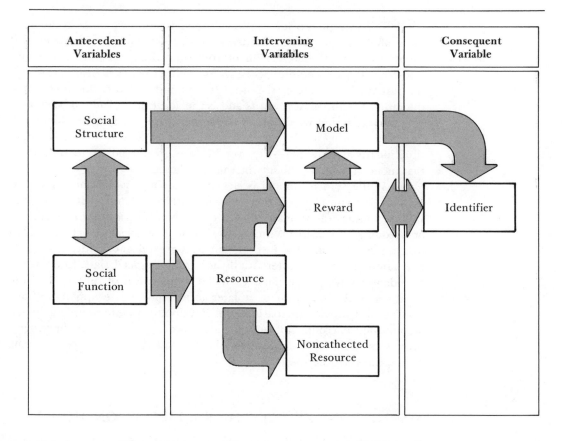

SOURCE: Figure from Robert F. Winch, *Identification and Its Familial Determinants,* copyright © 1962 by the Bobbs-Merrill Co., Inc. Reprinted by permission of the publisher.

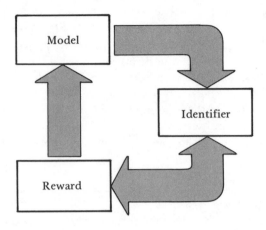

In its minimum form, Winch's model is quite similar to the basic ideas of exchange theory discussed in Chapter 15. The identifier will choose as a model that person or role controlling the valued rewards. Consequently, we would expect a child of either sex to identify most with the parent who has the most power. If the family is father dominant, then the father has the most rewards and is the adult most likely to be chosen. The same criterion would apply in mother-dominant families. Identification with mother or father in an equalitarian family would be more situationally determined—whoever has the greater power to reward, at that moment, would probably be the one chosen.

While Winch's model is elegantly simple, it is deficient in several respects. If Lynn (1966) is correct, male children identify with a generalized masculine role instead of with the father. This cannot be discussed or accounted for with Winch's approach. The social structure Winch discusses is also limited to just the family. A great deal of evidence suggests that families function differentially according to social class. In addition, the identifier is not specified. It makes a great deal of difference if the identifier is the first-born or a later-born child. These apparent shortcomings will provide the basis for my developing a more complete model, attempting to account not only for identification but also for the general process of socialization. However, before getting into my model some assumptions will be specified.

## ASSUMPTIONS ABOUT THE SOCIALIZATION MODEL

Four assumptions may be made about the socialization process. The first two concern the antecedents of this process:

1. Identification is a by-product of the socialization experience. It is best explained as such rather than as a separate and distinct phenomenon.

2. Three levels of social structure provide the contexts within which socialization occurs: (a) the sociocultural milieu or society, (b) the social-class milieu and/or community of residence, and (c) the familial context. The familial context may be defined as the recipient of influences from the social class and sociocultural levels.

THE SOCIOCULTURAL MILIEU. Every society provides for parents a theme of child rearing that is tailored to the historical moment in which the parents and children are located. This is similar to what the anthropologists call "national character"—a societally defined ethos of fatherhood, motherhood, parenthood, and childhood.

The theme of child rearing that is prevalent in a society depends on the complex interfusion of a number of factors and forces. These forces emanate from changes in the institutional structure of society. For example, the economic conditions that pervade a society provide a rationale for certain child-rearing styles. This was certainly evident in our discussion of the rural family in Ireland (see Chapter 7) and the family in Israeli kibbutzim (see Chapter 8). The political system through which a society operates cannot help but affect the forms and content of the socialization process. This is most apparent in the rather totalitarian structure of the Soviet Union. Child-rearing practices there were heavily influenced by the political ideologies of child rearing, which fluctuated dramatically from czarist times through the tumultuous anarchy in postrevolutionary Russia to the present stage of political detente (see Chapter 8). The dramatic influence of religion on child-rearing techniques can be seen in the rather radical practices adopted by the Oneida Community, in the name of religion. The impact of legal institutions on the family and on child rearing in particular is most evident in the ups and downs of the Family Codes in Russia between 1917 and the present. Finally, it is almost axiomatic that changes in the educational realm of society, both in ideology and in practice, can and do have a dramatic impact on the content of socialization in the home.

As discussed in Chapter 4, social change is a ubiquitous phenomenon in society. As the contingencies produced by social change occur, the institutional spheres of society adapt separately and in interaction with the others. The result is a movement toward consistent themes, a congruence of ideology. It is my contention that these changing themes provide a sociocultural context within which parents must socialize their children.

THE SOCIAL-CLASS MILIEU. Parental values about child rearing seem to be systematically influenced by social class, although Bronfenbrenner (1961) says that "the gap between the social classes in their goals and methods of child rearing appears to be narrowing." As Kohn (1959) has shown, parents from the upper lower class are more likely than middle-class parents to value obedience to parents, being able to defend oneself (a father's response), and neatness and cleanliness (mother's responses). Thus, the

479

upper lower-class parents in Kohn's study seem to place a higher premium on how the child physically presents himself or herself to others and on conformity and compliance to adults, particularly parents.

The middle-class parents in Kohn's study expressed child-rearing values that seem to be anchored in the occupational sphere of activity. More so than upper lower-class parents, middle-class parents place a higher value on being considerate of others, being happy and curious (mother's responses), and being dependable and possessing self-control (father's responses).

Miller and Swanson (1958) in *The Changing American Parent* called the middle-class approach to child rearing bureaucratic. They suggested that most middle-class parents still accept the Horatio Alger, Protestant-ethic view of the world: "Work hard, be on time, keep your desk neat, work late, don't be ostentatious, laugh at the boss's jokes, and don't make waves." Nye and Berardo (1973) put it more elegantly: "In short, middle-class socialization is closely tied to the requirements of middle-class occupations, stressing superior performance in the classroom, creativity, and cooperative and congenial interaction with peers and adults."

Research has rather consistently shown social-class differences in the degree of permissiveness associated with child training. Lower-class parents are more likely to use physical punishment while middle-class parents generally adopt the tactics of discussion and the withholding of love and approval (see Bronfenbrenner, 1958). Studies conducted earlier in this century found working-class parents more permissive than their middle-class counterparts. However, Bronfenbrenner's (1958) comprehensive review of sixteen major studies conducted prior to 1945 indicated a shift of permissiveness to the middle-class mothers on the advice of "experts" like Dr. Spock.

In the thirty or so years since World War II this society has witnessed and endured major demographic changes, particularly with regard to fertility, migration, and urbanization; social and legal upheavals that have changed the character of many human and institutional relationships; and a rather pervasive youth rebellion that many social critics attribute to permissiveness in child rearing. The consequences are seen in many areas, but are readily apparent in the narrowing of the gap that once existed between the social classes. Even so, visibly different styles of child rearing persist among the various social strata in our society.

My contention, then, is that the social-class location of parents provides them with a set of values about child rearing. In addition, because social class determines the amount of discretionary income available to a family, families tend to cluster into class-specific and rather homogeneous neighborhoods where the milieu of child rearing reinforces and justifies the child-training practices used by parents. Social class, then, provides another context within which childhood socialization occurs and directly influences the structure and functioning of the family itself.

THE FAMILIAL MILIEU.   No two children are born into the "same" family. The point is that first-born children are different from later born children. For a period of time, the first-born child is an only child, and as such provides the parents with the opportunity to learn parental roles. The second and later children come when the parents are older and more experienced as socializers. Some of the socialization responsibilities are allocated to older siblings. Therefore, birth order is one familial variable that influences socialization, and another is the sex composition of the children. For example, if the sex of the second child is the same as the older sibling, less adjustment is evident within the family than would occur if the second child is of the opposite sex. More adjustment is probably needed when the second child is a male and the first child is a female. This last point is rather clearly shown by Brim (1958), who found that boys who have sisters possess more feminine traits than boys who do not have female siblings. This effect is more marked when the sister is older. By using the concept of role-taking from symbolic interactionism, Brim was able to show that boys with sisters learn to interact more effectively in male-female relationships than boys who have brothers as siblings (see also Sutton-Smith and Rosenberg, 1970).

Suffice it to say that both birth order and sex composition are familial context variables that influence both the form and content of socialization.

Several other familial variables that provide a set of contextual boundaries within which socialization occurs are: (a) the degree to which the nuclear family is embedded in an extended network (classical extended, modified extended, isolated nuclear); (b) the degree and quality of intactness within the nuclear unit (one-parent families for whatever reasons versus families with both parents present, and within intact families the quality of intactness may range from total cohesion to open hostility); and (c) the distribution of power resources within the family (father-dominant, mother-dominant, equalitarian).

I am assuming that all of these familial variables provide the immediate context within which a child is socialized. A failure to consider them ignores the tremendous impact that socioenvironmental factors have on personality development. How these familial variables find expression within a family is determined to some extent by the social-class context and by the overriding sociocultural values operative in the society.

This discussion of assumptions about the antecedents of the socialization process suggests that the family is the "final filter" for social-class and societal values and norms concerning child rearing.

## The Socialization Process in Operation

The third assumption is that the socialization process is composed of two interacting sets of operations. The first set of operations consists of the allocation of (a) types of rewards, controlled initially by the parents as

481

**FIGURE 17–3**
**Antecedents of the Socialization Process**

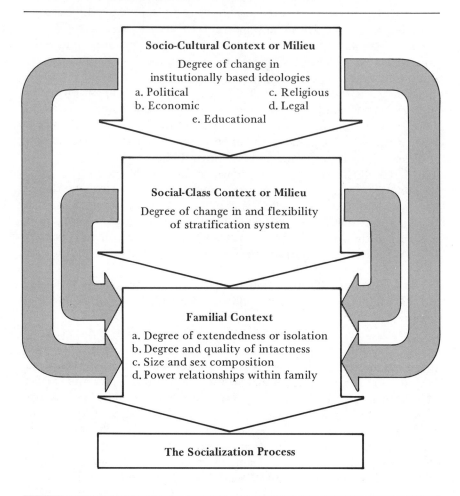

**Socio-Cultural Context or Milieu**

Degree of change in
institutionally based ideologies
a. Political        c. Religious
b. Economic      d. Legal
     e. Educational

**Social-Class Context or Milieu**

Degree of change in and flexibility
of stratification system

**Familial Context**

a. Degree of extendedness or isolation
b. Degree and quality of intactness
c. Size and sex composition
d. Power relationships within family

**The Socialization Process**

authority figures. The second set of operations consists of (b) the behavioral strategies adopted by parents to deal with training their children. The socialization process is depicted in diagram form in Figure 17–3. Blau's (1964) exchange model of power discussed in Chapter 15 may be recognized, and the types of parental behavior from Wesley Becker (1964), which was discussed earlier in this chapter.

TYPES OF REWARDS.   In this section the focus is on how the parent-child relationship changes as the child gets older and as the family goes through the family life cycle. In general, most parent-child exchanges are unilateral with the child receiving from the parent and reacting to parental demands and requests. In the infancy and early childhood stages most socialization attempts by the parents are based in a compliance-power arrangement. The parent tells the child what to do and how to do it. As the child gets older, gains greater autonomy, and begins to establish an identity of his or her own, the socialization efforts of the parents remain unilateral, but are more often based in a respect-prestige type of exchange (Figure 17–4).

**FIGURE 17–4**
**Familial Context of the Socialization Process**

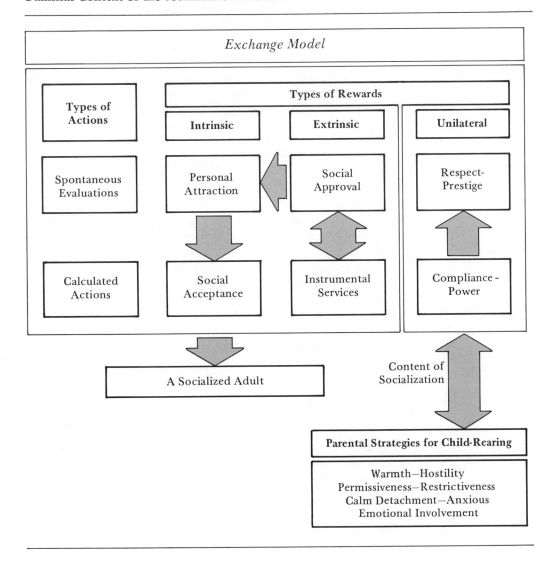

With intrinsic and extrinsic types of rewards, parents use calculated actions and the provision of instrumental services throughout the family life cycle to make their socialization efforts effective and successful. In the earlier stages of the family life cycle parents will dispense or withhold instrumental services to the child in order to obtain the desired behavior. If the child follows the dictums of the parents (that is, conforms to their socialization efforts), the parents will reward the child with social approval (a spontaneous evaluation).

Most children value the approval of their parents and will attempt to gain social approval for their behavior. Children are quick to learn and usually continue to emit a response that will elicit an approving stimulus from the parents. The more often this occurs as the child grows older, the greater will be the personal attraction between parent and child. This is, in essence, an exchange of compliance by the child to the wishes of the parents and their socialization efforts for a continuation of instrumental services and social approval. The end result of a history of these types of exchanges will be the calculated actions of the parents in socially accepting the child as an adult equal. This usually occurs either before the child leaves home or when the child has married and established his or her own family of procreation. By then, the exchange process has evolved to the point of an equalitarian relationship existing among adults. It is not unusual at this stage of development for the children to call their parents by their first names.

PARENTAL STRATEGIES FOR CHILD REARING. The degree to which a child will accept the socialization content offered by the parents is affected by the style of parental behavior used by the parents. As Becker (1964) noted, there are three dimensions of parental behavior: warmth versus hostility, permissiveness versus restrictiveness, and calm detachment versus anxious-emotional control. The crucial task of the parent is to mix these styles of parental behavior with the types of rewards offered the child, both of which are a function of how well the child is progressing in attaining his or her independence, how well the child controls aggressive tendencies, and how well the child has internalized the conventional norms of morality prevalent in the society.

## Success of Parental Socialization

The fourth assumption is that parental socialization is usually successful for most children. They become generally conforming and productive citizens, claiming as their own the values and attitudes of the society and culture in which they were reared. In most cases these children become adults and establish their own families, have their own children, and start the entire socialization process again. The final evaluation of the success or failure of the familial socialization process is out of the hands of the parents. Their efforts to mold their children into productive adults must,

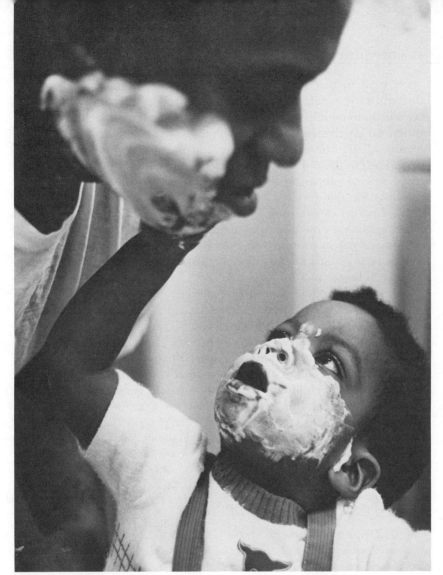

*Sharing a moment and shaving cream creates a memory that will last a lifetime.*

Burk Uzzle from Magnum Photos, Inc.

in the final analysis, be judged by society. If the child becomes deviant, then the parents are blamed for the faulty performance of their duties. If success is the outcome, the parents are congratulated by society and the community for a job well done.

## SUMMARY AND CONCLUSIONS

A great deal of material and numerous diverse topics have been covered in this chapter. The strategy chosen was to develop an abstract kind of model of the parent-child relationship and the socialization process rather than to describe in detail the flesh and blood of real-life interaction.

I have tried to describe some of the many complexities and difficulties inherent in the parental role. It is of little wonder that the marital bond between husband and wife must suffer at the hand of parental responsibilities. To say the least, the social, physical, and psychological impacts of parenthood require major adjustments in the conjugal relationship.

The family in this and other societies has always been allocated the crucial task of preparing the next generation for assuming the reins of leadership in the society. Practically every society exercises stringent informal norms to ensure that the socialization process does not fail. All of the legitimate power sources in society, the legal, political, religious, and educational institutions in particular, carry on a constant campaign to encourage parents not to fail or be derelict in their self-imposed commitment to parenthood.

The socialization process is a complex maze of real and imagined obstacles. Even though most societies provide little formal training in parenthood, the remarkable success of most parents is testimony to the commitment most parents have to their roles. Not unlike the artisan and craftsman, most parents seem to take special pains in molding and polishing the only real products of their job—their children. This commitment is not lost on the children, for generation after generation of children become parents and the process goes on. As Freud (quoting the poet William Wordsworth) sagely remarked, "The child is the father of man." I believe that this comment remains true today, for the family is the source of personhood.

## SOME POSSIBLE IMPLICATIONS

*The civil rights movement of the 1950s and early 1960s is generally acknowledged as the catalytic force that led to significant social changes, particularly in the legal and governmental sectors of society. In the late 1960s and early 1970s the call for sexual equality from a renewed feminist movement was channeled in two directions. First, women were demanding equality of opportunity and treatment in the political-legal and economic-business quarters of society. A second and primary goal of the women's liberation movement has been the obliteration of traditional attitudes about sexual differentiation and the sexist cultural values transmitted through the family and educational institutions.*

*Students of social movements and the social changes they effect say that the next major focus of attention will be on the rights of children, legal and otherwise. It would not be unreasonable to expect the women's liberation movement to join in the battle for children's rights. If these forecasts are even partially correct, what are the implications for parent-child relationships and childhood socialization?*

*From the women's liberation movement there will be continuing pressure to develop and diffuse what the Osofskys (1971) call an androgy-*

*nous marriage structure (that is, the roles within the family are allocated without regard to sex). In such an arrangement, husband-wife and mother-father roles will have to be redefined and reallocated in terms of competence and needs and interests. The children in such family environments will be socialized to think in terms of equality and freedom and that traditional images of the roles assigned by sexual criteria will be anathema. The children's movement will add pressures on parents to be less unilateral and authoritarian in determining what their children may or may not do. Children will have legal sanction to expect more autonomy and a higher quality of parental concern for their well being. In the complex and rapidly changing postindustrial society of the last quarter of this century, the institutions of society and the individuals in them will be required to reassess and redefine the old order of things and to create a new order based on a truly modern world view. Parenthood, childhood, and the adjustments associated with them will be different, to say the least.*

Jean-Claude Lejeune

# 18

# THE FAMILY, WORK, AND LEISURE

*How are the family and work worlds related to each other?*

*If someone advertised for applicants for the job of housewife, who would apply and why?*

*How are marital, job, and parental roles similar yet different?*

*How is it possible for people to mix their family, work, and leisure worlds?*

In all societies, the family system and the occupational system are closely related. The Family prepares the individual for work and it is the immediate beneficiary of his labor. The working group is often coincident with the family circle and even where it is not, the work required by housekeeping engages a large part of the population. Yet occupational institutions are not identical with family institutions even among primitive people, and in the urbanized, secular, middle-class culture of today, the values of the two systems are often in sharp conflict. [Caplow, 1954: 248]

One would think, given the degree to which the occupational world seems to invade the family world and vice versa, that social scientists would have thoroughly investigated how people are able to mix the two worlds without getting them mixed up. Surely no one would question Caplow's contention that the two systems are related. The occupational system obviously recruits its members from family units, usually recognizes the familial commitments of its workers, and certainly realizes its impact on family life through paychecks and other benefits. Just as obvious is the recognition by family members that their lives are daily affected by the occupational worlds in which the family members operate.

Yet, sometimes the obvious is ignored by those whose responsibilities are to "look behind the facades of life." As Rapoport and Rapoport (1965) point out, the explicit interaction between work and family life has seldom been critically examined. "It is as though family structure, organization, and functioning depended entirely on factors associated with the family and the individual personalities within it, while the organization and functioning of work groups could be explained exclusively in terms of the work situation" (Rapoport and Rapoport, 1965:382).

For those few who have attempted to examine the bridge between family life and work, the usual focus has been on the pathological consequences for the family if certain forays are made into the occupational world. For example, there is a plethora of studies dealing with the effects on children and on the family if the mother works. In most cases researchers have gone into the study looking for the negative effects—to hardly anyone's surprise they have generally found what they were looking for. A more recent topic of concern has been the possible consequences of the women's liberation movement and its emphasis on desexualizing occupational roles. Once again the assumption has been that the two worlds are antithetical and separate—a marriage between work and family life seems a priori impossible.

This chapter is intended as a logical continuation of the four preceding chapters, which dealt with marital interaction, power, and adjustment, and the adjustments required of a family and its members by the onset of children. Surely the styles of interaction, distribution of power, and types of adjustments that occur primarily within the family context are affected by and have effects upon the work and leisure activities of family members. Specifically, this chapter is designed to examine the intersections between familial, work, and leisure roles and commitments. My assumption is that all three spheres of activity are integrally connected, yet, to some extent, compartmentalized by individuals.

## BASIC DEFINITIONS AND ASSUMPTIONS

Before examining the overlapping influences of the family, work, and leisure worlds, we will delineate the definitions and assumptions that will guide our discussion in this chapter:

1. Work is generally viewed by sociologists (see Friedmann and Havighurst, 1962) as an activity that can provide one or more of the following benefits to the individual involved: (a) an income, (b) a regulating schedule around which nonwork activities can be arranged, (c) the means by which a person is identified (that is, status-prestige, a location in the community or broader social world), (d) associations with persons who are not integrally a part of one's family network, and (e) the opportunity to define one's primary activities as productive, meaningful, creative, and/or fulfilling.

In other words, we usually think of work as the job a person performs. For practically every job, society determines, either explicitly or implicitly, the qualifications required, the value or prestige of the work involved, and the normative expectations by which an adequate performance of one's work can be evaluated. In my opinion, the definition of work mentioned above is inadequate. It reflects the opposite of wives' sociology or what Jessie Bernard (1973) identified as either "Sociology as a science of male society" or "Sociology as a male science of society." However, we will return to a critical analysis of this definition in the section on the job of housewife.

2. If work is income-producing and so forth, and occupies most of the time and energies of all or most adults, what is leisure and what are its distinguishing characteristics? From an objective standpoint, leisure can be defined as the time we are free from the more obvious and formal duties that a paid job (work role) or other obligatory occupations (family, marital, or parental role; or voluntary associational commitments) impose on us (see Lundberg, Komarovsky, and McInerny, 1934:2–3).

Burdge (1969:262) introduces the distinction between structured and nonstructured leisure: "Structured leisure refers to that activity which is specifically named and has societal recognition to the extent that persons derive status from the social structure for participating in the activity. Structured leisure is the opposite of activity that is nondescript and provides no specific status for the participant."

Veroff and Feld (1970) take a different tack and distinguish leisure activities by whether they are designed for achievement (time spent creating or constructing something) or for affiliation (time spent in the company of other people). Their assumption is that leisure spent in achievement may be used primarily by persons whose need for achievement was not being gratified by the work role. On the other hand, leisure spent in affiliation is assumed to be an alternative way of gratifying a need for affiliation or power.

I would recommend adding one further qualifying condition to the definition of leisure—the degree of intimacy that exists among those with whom the leisure time is enjoyed. It would seem logical to categorize the intimacy/leisure concept into three groups: (a) intrafamily only, (b) close associates (the immediate family and extended family members can also be included), and (c) mere acquaintances or strangers.

Leisure, then, is distinct from the work sphere, but it may be coincident with the family sphere of activity. Leisure may be structured or relatively informal, designed to satisfy a need for achievement or a need for affiliation or power; leisure may occur exclusively within one's family, with close associates, or with mere acquaintances. It is probably safe to assume that some of the time spent at work and perhaps more of the time spent with the family is devoted to planning how leisure time will be spent. The leisure and recreational facets of life in the United States have become increasingly central to family decision making as society becomes more affluent and more urban and as the average work week shrinks from above fifty to below forty hours per week. A consideration of the family, work, and leisure facets of life is important if we are to understand the many sides of married living.

## ASSUMPTIONS ABOUT THE WORK-FAMILY RELATIONSHIP

In one of the few conceptually oriented articles available on the relationship of the work and family systems, the Rapoports (1965:382), who evidently must mutually mix both worlds, suggest that there is consensus on the following theoretical assumptions:

1. "Family and work have become increasingly differentiated." The basis for this assumption is (a) the increasing specialization of work roles (that is, the tendency to split jobs so that the same overall task is accomplished with more people doing smaller parts of the task) and (b) the importance of universalistic norms in contemporary society (that is, the

movement to apply the same standards to all persons regardless of age, sex, creed, or color).

2. "Work and family roles vary in their relative salience." The Rapoports point here to the problem of multiple commitments and how the attention one gives to his or her family and leisure activities may be in direct proportions to the demands made by the work role. Generally speaking, the higher the status-prestige of the occupation, the greater the requirement for commitment to job, and the consequence is that less time and energy are available for family and leisure commitments. As the status of the job declines there is usually a decline in the salience of the job or work role.

The Rapoports fail to emphasize the problem of the working wife-mother, who must, according to cultural norms, split hairs on the problem of the relative salience of what could be, and are for some women, full-time roles in three different areas. This becomes an increasing source of role conflict for society as the proportion of women who have dependent children and work increases.

3. "Work and family modes of interaction are isomorphic." The assumption is that behavior patterns required in one's work role will be similar (isomorphic) to behavior patterns one expresses in the family setting. Thus, the male who endorses the Protestant ethic and who owns

*The family deli—a place where work and family are integrated.*

his own business will seek to encourage individualism in his child-rearing practices. The person whose job requires him or her to be a team member will push the idea of "jointness" in the family.

This assumption is most likely to find support when the work role is salient and not threatening for the incumbent. In occupations in which the work is boring or alienating, in which the worker feels insecure and subordinate, it is quite possible his or her family behavior will reflect an attempt to compensate for needs not satisfied at work.

4. "The life cycle stage affects relations between work and family life." This final assumption offered by the Rapoports (1965:382) suggests that the overall complexity of the roles we play in the family and work areas and the demands made on us by these roles vary with the stage of the life cycle we are in. In addition, whenever a critical transition from one role to another occurs in one area (from married couple without children to parents), the performance in the other area is necessarily affected.

These four theoretical assumptions provide a framework within which the relationship between the work and family spheres of activity can be analyzed. They suggest that several variables may be central to an understanding of how these areas of life (family and work plus leisure) intersect or overlap. The variables are (a) specialization of work roles, (b) universalistic norms, (c) salience of the work role, (d) similarity or dissimilarity of behavior patterns at work and at home, (e) the stage in the family life cycle, (f) social class, (g) age, and (h) sex.

On the surface the four theoretical assumptions suggested by the Rapoports (1965) seem perfectly logical and accurate. No one would question the "facts" that the family and work worlds are becoming increasingly differentiated, that work and family roles vary in their salience, that work and family patterns of behavior tend to be similar, and that the life cycle stage affects the relationship between the family and work. An uncritical acceptance of these assumptions is plausible, if for no other reason than because they are a rejustification of the world as it is and as it has always been.

Thus, although it was probably not intentional, these assumptions are implicitly, almost subconsciously, supportive of the idea that it is the male, husband, breadwinner who must respond to a differentiated set of worlds, who must adapt to problems of varying role salience, who must attempt to be the same person at work and at home, and who must adjust to the pressures brought on by the entrances and exits of children and the effects that will have on his wife, the helpmate. Such is not the case at all. The woman in our society who chooses to work or who is involuntarily forced to do so enters a battle with opponents so formidable, victory is virtually impossible. A critical examination of these assumptions is a necessary precursor to an attempt at understanding how work and the family relate, because the assumptions reveal some of the sources of resistance to women working.

# SOURCES OF RESISTANCE TO WOMEN WORKING

From a macrostructural viewpoint, women are restrained from full and equal participation in the work world because they pose a threat to the assumptions that undergird the entire stratification system. Acker (1973) succinctly outlined the assumptions about the social position of women in our society:

1. The family is the unit in the stratification system.
2. The social position of the family is determined by the status of the male head of the household.
3. Females live in families; therefore, their status is determined by that of the males to whom they are attached.
4. The female's status is equal to that of her man, at least in terms of her position in the class structure, because the family is a unit of equivalent evaluation (Watson and Barth, 1964).
5. Women determine their own social status only when they are not attached to a man.
6. Women are unequal to men in many ways, are differentially evaluated on the basis of sex, but this is irrelevant to the structure of stratification systems.

She continues: "The first assumption that the family is the unit in stratification is basic to the other five. Together, these assumptions neatly dispense with the necessity of considering the position of women in studies of social stratification or considering the salience of sex as a dimension of stratification. To put it another way, the fate of the female in the class system is determined by the fate of the male. Therefore, it is only necessary to study males."[1]

If we would examine the intersection of the family, work, and leisure, we must recognize not only this structural constraint on women but also the transitional state of our society. Women are now involved in rendering inoperative the assumptions that underlie the stratification system in the modern world. The work world is not the exclusive domain of males, and more and more males are recognizing that the family is not a domain in which their responsibility is minimal.

A second structural constraint on women working and one closely tied to the stratification system is the legal one. All women, but particularly married (or divorced) women, frequently encounter social and legal constraints on their activities. These legal limits have their origin in common law. The following legal principles, outlined by Sir William Blackstone in his *Commentaries on the Laws of England* (1765), are still

---

[1] Joan R. Acker, "Women and Social Stratification: A Case of Intellectual Sexism," *American Journal of Sociology* 78(1973):936–45. Used by permission of the University of Chicago Press and the author. © 1973 by the University of Chicago.

influential in defining a woman's "proper place" in our society relative to participation in the work world:

> By marriage, the husband and wife are one person in law: that is, the very being or legal existence of the woman is suspended during the marriage, or at least is incorporated and consolidated into that of the husband; under whose wing, protection, and cover she performs everything. . . .

> Even the disabilities which the wife lies under are for the most part intended for her protection and benefit: so great a favorite is the female sex of the laws of England.

The law has, under the guise of protecting the woman, restricted her participation in the work world, and consequently it has forced the woman to stay in the home. When women have entered the labor force, their participation has been limited to only certain occupations for the same reason: protection. This is also changing as the law is forced to adapt to the contingencies of the modern world and the demands for equality fostered by the feminist movement.

The relationship of the family, work, and leisure spheres of activity must be examined in light of the changing stratification and legal systems in our society. We must therefore detail the extent to which women participate in work outside the home before we can fully understand how these three separate but overlapping worlds interact.

## WOMEN WHO WORK OUTSIDE THE HOME

Over fifty years ago, in 1920, when women gained the right to vote, less than one-fourth of all women 20 to 60 years of age were workers (23 percent). Today, almost half of all women 18 to 64 are in the labor force (49 percent). Most of these women are married, and half are over the age of 39.

The working woman is no longer a "deviant." In fact, participation in the labor force is today a normal and integral part of the life career of most women. A number of forces in society have led to this historically new phenomenon, including (a) changing social values and attitudes, influenced no doubt by the feminist movement, (b) rising levels of education, (c) a decline in the birth rate (see Chapter 19), and (d) federal laws that have increased hiring opportunities for women. However, the most important factor behind the working woman phenomenon has been the impact of inflation. Simply put, the extra money provided by the wife's participation in work outside the home has become a necessity rather than a luxury. However, many women who work are trying not only to maintain the family's standard of living but to improve it. Further, many of the women working do so to provide the *only* income available to them and to their children. The divorce rate has served as a particularly impor-

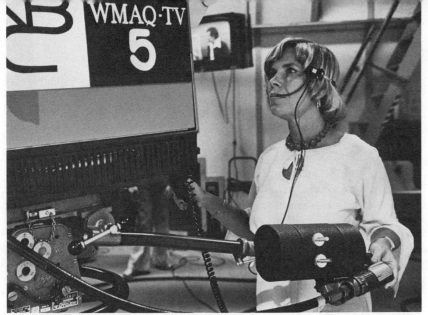

*The eyes behind the electronic eye; a satisfying work role is important to one's well-being.*

Jean-Claude Lejeune

tant impetus for work outside the home for single parents. It should not be ignored that many women, those women included in the reasons cited above, work because they want to—they want to utilize their skills and to participate fully in the marketplace, to find meaning in their lives, and to escape the repressive conditions faced by many women for whom the housewife role is no challenge and is, in fact, degrading and demeaning.

Listed below are some facts about the extent to which women in this society are full-fledged participants in the marketplace:

As of March 1975, 52 percent of married women with children aged six to seventeen were working or looking for work; in 1948 the rate was 26 percent. Moreover, about two-thirds of married mothers who had jobs in March 1975 were working full time.

Thirty-seven percent of all married women with children under six were in the labor force in 1975; this percentage is three times higher than that in 1948.

Almost as many married women with children under three were in the labor force in 1975; about one in three.

All these figures apply only to families in which both parents were present; for the rapidly growing number of single parent families, the proportion of mothers in the labor force is much higher —almost three-quarters (72 percent) for those with children six to seventeen and well over one-half (56 percent) for mothers with children under six. Over 80 percent of these working mothers are employed full time.

A major factor related to mothers' labor-force participation is educational attainment. In 1975, of married working mothers with children under six, 43 percent were college graduates, as compared with 32 percent who did not finish high school.

By 1975, more than one in four parents under 25 who was head of a family was without a spouse.

497

In 1975, two-thirds of all families with incomes under $4,000 in the previous year had only one parent. In families with incomes over $15,000, the proportion of single-parent families has remained consistently below 2 percent since 1968.

It should be apparent that the intersection of work and family and leisure in intact families affects both the husband and wife in many cases. Thus, any clear understanding of how modern families mix work with familial roles must consider the problem of both spouses working. How they trade off their multiple responsibilities and how they mix their roles is of crucial importance.

As the Rapoports (1965) suggested, the life cycle stage does affect the relations between work and family life. However, the pattern of employment throughout the family cycle has changed dramatically since 1920. Suelzle (1973) indicated: "In 1920 female participation in the labor force dropped off at age 25, decreased steadily with age, and by the time they were aged 45 to 54 only 18 percent were working. In contrast, female participation in the labor force today drops off at age 25 but rises again at age 35 to a second peak of 54 percent at age 45 to 54. . . . Today almost half the women at age 35 can expect to work 24 to 31 more years. More than half of today's young women will work full-time for 25 or more years."

These figures refer to women who work outside the home for pay. What about the close to 50 percent of women who work but do not get paid for it—the housewives? They too must engage in the exchanges that take place in marriage, in the vying for power and the attempts to achieve adjustment in all marital and familial tasks. They must also be considered if we are to understand how the family, work, and leisure spheres are mixed.

## THE HOUSEWIFE ROLE

The housewife role poses a dilemma for women in an industrial society like ours because its demands are incongruous with women's experiences prior to assuming the role. Education and achievement are deemed desirable goals for all women. In fact almost all males and females compete for the same scarce rewards in the educational realm from the ages of six to eighteen. For a large percentage of women the competition continues through four or more years of college. On an equal basis women discuss broad philosophical issues, work mathematical formulas, conduct laboratory experiments, and debate political issues as well as, and frequently better than, the men with whom they work and study. For those who marry before they graduate, and for those who marry subsequent to graduation and experience in the labor force, work outside the home can be on fairly equal competitive bases with men. Our society trains women to be anything but housewives. Almost all formal socialization conducted in institutional settings glosses over and plays down the sex factor.

The ideology to which our institutions subscribe and which permeates the socialization process strongly emphasizes (a) equality between the sexes and (b) the idea that work is meaningful and will be rewarded if it is adequately performed. The ideology and the experiences it fosters are almost totally incongruous with the reality of the housewife role. To illustrate, let us examine two jobs that might be performed by a married couple in light of the definition of work discussed previously. Let us make the hypothetical couple college graduates. He is an engineer for a major corporation and she was a buyer for a department store until she married. Now she is a housewife. Table 18–1 presents a comparison of the characteristics of their respective work roles.

Taken to its "logical" conclusion, the illustration implies that the activities associated with the job category "housewife" do not constitute

**TABLE 18–1**
**Comparison of Work-Role Characteristics**

| CHARACTERISTICS OF WORK | ENGINEER | HOUSEWIFE |
|---|---|---|
| A. Income producing | Yes | No. |
| B. Provides a regulating schedule around which nonwork and leisure activities may be organized. | Yes | No. Almost all nonwork activities refer just to the husband's job. She continues to work after he comes home from his job. |
| C. An identification in society's status-prestige system | Yes | No. There is no promotional system and virtually no way that one housewife can get more status or prestige than another. Almost all of the rewards a housewife obtains are, of necessity, primarily intrinsic. |
| D. Associations outside the family network | Yes | No. By societal definition the location of the housewife's job precludes most nonfamilial contacts. The contacts which do occur are usually transitory. |
| E. Meaningful, creative, fulfilling | Yes | Yes, No, Maybe. Our society seems quite willing to view the housewife role as "creative and fulfilling" *if* the housewife thinks it is, and many housewives do. However, society seems equally willing to accept as valid the criticism made by more than a few housewives that the role and work are generally stifling and occasionally dehumanizing. |

499

## *Job Description: Housewife*

QUALIFICATIONS.    Must be female and married. Our society attaches such a stigma to the role that extreme social pressures are applied to the male who forsakes his traditional superior status to take such a job. In the socialization process we inform males they may take the most menial task as an occupation, but they must work outside the home. The female is expected to compete throughout her life to the point of marriage, but it is quite appropriate, in fact her duty, to take a stigmatized role in life as her primary occupation.

TYPE OF WORK.    The housewife will clean house, scrub floors, cook, wash clothes and dishes, shop for food and other commodities, prepare and stick to a budget, serve as chauffeur, and so forth, ad infinitum. In addition she is to serve as hostess; source of ego support for her breadwinning husband; his confidante, mistress, and lover; and mother of "his" children. She must also represent the family at the school, church, and voluntary associations, participate in fund-raising drives and, in general, play a major role in ensuring that the community is a decent place to live.

MAIN BENEFITS.    The financial reward the housewife receives will generally be low, and in a large number of cases, nonexistent. The manner in which she is paid will vary: In some cases she will receive an allowance for expenses on a weekly, biweekly, or monthly basis; generally she is allowed some flexibility in the allocation of these funds, and occasionally she may use excess funds for her own pleasure. In other cases the housewife will receive periodic gifts of money and services as a reward for outstanding performance and productivity. However, in what may be a majority of cases, the primary pay for her work is in terms of "intrinsic satisfaction" that she is doing a "good job." She will receive paid vacations, perhaps every year, and her husband's life insurance, assuming he has some, is a form of "retirement pay" from which she may draw in her old age.

FRINGE BENEFITS.    As her husband progresses in his career she will receive less and less direct help from him, her children will leave home as soon as they are able to make it on their own, the skills she has obtained in school will become obsolete the longer she stays out of the labor force, and she will have ample opportunity to feel lonely and useless.

work, at least not as work is usually defined by sociologists who study work behavior. This ludicrous conclusion deserves further comment. Perhaps the best place to start is with a detailed discussion of the job description for housewife.

## Psychological Effects of the Housewife Role

In other words, the housewife role in our society has a tremendous potential for producing boredom and alienation. The crisis for most housewives is tied to the menial nature of many of the tasks she must perform. She has to do the same menial tasks day in and day out, from sun-up to after the children are in bed, seven days a week, every week of the year, every year of her life. If she happens to hold a job outside the home, she is still responsible by societal definitions for all or most of the onerous and non-"meaningful" (but necessary) tasks that women who "don't work" do during the day. A concomitant and significant source of alienation for many housewives is the lack of sharing by the husband in this responsibility and meniality.

*Dishes in the sink, hair in rollers, baby needs changing—being a housewife is hard work.*

Bill Owens, Magnum Photos, Inc.

One index of the strain produced by the sex-determined occupational role of housewife is the incidence of mental illness. Using a precise definition of mental illness, "functional disorders characterized by anxiety (neurosis) and/or mental disorganization (psychosis)," Gove and Tudor (1973:831) checked information on first admissions to mental hospitals, psychiatric treatment in general hospitals, psychiatric outpatient clinics, private outpatient psychiatric care, the practices of general physicians, and the results of community surveys. They conclude that women are more likely to have these disorders and that the rates are a reflection of the relative positions of men and women. In other words, because the woman's role in modern industrial societies is incongruous with the ideology that informs most of the socialization process and because the jobs that most women must perform are not meaningful or fulfilling, mental illness may be a means of coping with reality.

### The Need for Empathy

I have taken an extreme position on the housewife role. It is certainly true that not all housewives or even most are extremely dissatisfied with their roles or jobs. However, it behooves men to be sensitive to the strain under which their spouses may be operating. These strains are not necessarily imposed by the husband. Many are operative because of structural and ideological forces in existence for centuries. Such conditions should be understood by men and should be subject to change and adaptation. This is not to say that washing the dishes once a week or helping with the chores is an adequate adjustment. A fuller recognition of the housewife-spouse as a human being and the devastating effects such conditions can have on her is a necessary precursor to easing some of the strains. Every man can make an effort to completely empathize. Sympathy will be seen as merely gratuitous.

### Conclusion

We have focused at length on the working woman and the housewife roles for two reasons: First, because work in this society is usually seen from the male's point of view, the woman's role with its special strains is more central to understanding how the family, work, and leisure worlds are mixed in contemporary society. Second, the woman is the catalyst for the adjustment of family members to the varying demands by spheres of activity. Put another way, the housewife role has received special attention because of its importance in facilitating the mixture of the work, leisure, and familial spheres of activity.

With these assumptions in mind, let us examine the work of two major studies that have attempted to examine the intersection of the family, work, and leisure:

## JOHN SCANZONI (1970)

John Scanzoni, a sociologist at Indiana University, conducted one of the most thorough and systematic studies (*Opportunity and the Family*) to date of the relationship between work and family life. His research included a random sample of 497 wives and 419 husbands living in Indianapolis. The respondents represented a cross-section of intact families stretching from the lower working class through the lower upper class.

Scanzoni attempted to combine the most salient and similar characteristics of the structure-functionalist and the symbolic-interactionist frameworks for studying the family. In so doing he articulated an exchange model derived from Heer (1963) and Gouldner (1960) that is very similar to the Blau (1964) model discussed in Chapter 15. The variables he used as indices of the work commitment and rewards obtained from the occupational structure by the male closely resemble what Blood and Wolfe (1960) called "resources." In addition, Scanzoni divided husband and wife roles into the instrumental and expressive categories suggested by Parsons (1951). Scanzoni also accepted, with some reservation, the assumption that universalistic norms are quite applicable in the work world whereas particularistic norms are usually most operative in the family setting.

Perhaps the best way to examine Scanzoni's (1970:19, 21) approach to the interaction between work and the family is to present his theoretical model and his chain of reasoning. Figure 18–1 starts at Wd (the husband's instrumental role, his duty):[2]

1. The more positively the husband performs his economic duties, the more positively the wife defines her economic *rights* (status, prestige, income [Xr]) as being met.
2. The more (1) is true, the more positively she performs her instrumental household duties ([Xd], washing clothes, preparing meals, and so on, either doing them or seeing they are done), and the more positively the husband defines his instrumental household rights (Wr) being met.
3. The more positively the wife defines her economic rights (Xr) as being met, the more positively she performs her expressive duties (primary relations [Xd]).
4. The more (3) is true, the more the husband defines his expressive rights (Yr) as being met, and the more positively he performs his expressive duties (Yd).

---

**FIGURE 18–1**
**A Model of the Interaction Between Work and the Family: Husband-Wife Role Reciprocity**

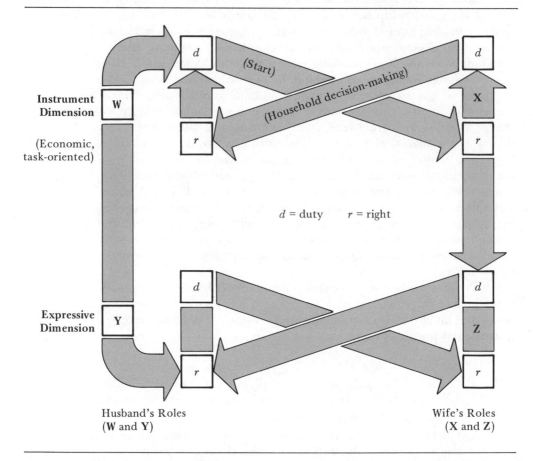

SOURCE: Reprinted with permission of Macmillan Publishing Co., Inc., from *Opportunity and the Family,* by John Scanzoni. Copyright © 1970 by the Free Press, a Division of the Macmillan Company.

5. a. The more (4) is true, the more the wife defines her expressive rights (Zr) being met.

   b. The more (5a) is true, the more motivated the wife is to perform her expressive duties (Zd).

6. The more each spouse defines his expressive and instrumental rights as being met, the more likely each is to experience feelings of gratification "the sentiment of gratitude joins forces with the sentiment of rectitude and adds a safety-margin in the motivation to conformity" (see Gouldner, 1960:176) with each other and with the system or situation in which they find themselves.

7. a. The more (6) is true, the more the husband is motivated to
continue performance of his economic duties (Wd) .

   b. The more (6) is true, the more the shared feelings of solidarity
and cohesion, and the greater the motivation to maintain the
system, and the greater the stability of the system.

## Analysis of Scanzoni's Model

Scanzoni's model is based on two very important considerations: First,
the husband and his integration into the occupational-opportunity structure is crucial. The degree to which he is successful in the work world
gives him control over rewards relative to Blau's (1964) exchange model,
and consequently produces the possibility of providing intrinsic/extrinsic
services to the wife. She, in turn, is obligated to reciprocate by an adequate
performance of her instrumental and expressive duties. Second, the wife
in Scanzoni's model is limited to the traditional reactive role. Her behavioral alternatives are structured by the husband's provision of desirable
rewards. The higher the values of the services he provides, the greater her
obligation to perform duties satisfying to her spouse. The lower the values
of the services, the lower the number of rights she can expect to have.

Put another way, Scanzoni's model relegates the wife role to one of
the two categories described by Blau (1964) as unilateral (that is, she must
give respect-prestige or be subject to the compliance-power arrangement).
In this sense, Scanzoni's discussion of the relationship between the family
and work roles is predicated on an assumption that men are the workers
and that women's proper place is at home, passively waiting for the opportunity to serve their men. Although the model is intrinsically logical, it
seems to be limited to families in which the woman is not liberated and
to a world in which this type of situation may become increasingly rare.

Scanzoni's central assumption was that the interaction between
work and family life results in marital cohesiveness or in discord and
instability. Perhaps his summary, entitled "Toward a Theory of Conjugal
Cohesion" (1970:187), best indicates the results he obtained:[3]

1. Therefore, the greater the degree of material-status rewards provided by the husband, the greater the degree of perceived satisfaction with primary relations (valued goals) and with authority
relations, and thus:

   a. the greater the degree of husband-wife interdependence.

   b. the greater the degree of husband-wife feelings of cohesion and
solidarity.

---

[3] Adapted, and reprinted with permission of, Macmillan Publishing Co., Inc., from
*Opportunity and the Family*, by John Scanzoni. Copyright © 1970 by The Free Press,
a Division of the Macmillan Company.

George Gardner

2. The greater the interdependence, and the greater the feelings of cohesion and solidarity, the greater the probability of system maintenance, stability, and order, and the lesser the likelihood of dissolution.

3. Conversely, the lesser the degree of material-status rewards provided by the husband, the lesser the degree of perceived satisfaction with primary relations and with authority relations. Therefore:

   a. the lesser the degree of husband-wife interdependence.

   b. the lesser the degree of feelings of solidarity and cohesion.

   c. the lesser the probability of system maintenance.

Scanzoni's research seems to reflect a domino theory of the relationship between work and family life. If the man's work experience (the first domino) does not fall down, everything else will be stable and happy. His wife will perform her wifely duties and the family will be cohesive. If, for some reason the husband's work experience is less than satisfactory, his marital and family experiences stand a good chance of exhibiting discord and instability.

Somehow the domino theory seems inadequate as an explanation of marital cohesiveness as it relates to the mix between work and family life. As mentioned previously, there is also some question as to the adequacy of viewing marital roles as either instrumental or expressive and the a priori allocation of the crucial instrumental roles (work and the provision of services/rewards) to the male. Scanzoni only touches on the effect of the working wife on his model of marital cohesiveness. All in all, although Scanzoni's model is interesting and seems to fit the traditional view of family life in America, one cannot help but wonder if it would apply to the contemporary family in which the wife will likely work outside the home at some time.

## VEROFF AND FELD: *Marriage and Work in America*

A second major study attempted to decipher the ways in which people mix their family, work, and leisure worlds. Joseph Veroff and Sheila Feld, two social scientists at the Institute for Social Research at the University of Michigan, analyzed data obtained from a representative sample of the adult American population interviewed in 1957. From the original total sample of 2,460 respondents they selected 1,226 subjects (538 men and 688 women), all of whom were white.

### Defining the Study

Veroff and Feld (1970) were primarily interested in how three types of psychologically based motives (for achievement, affiliation, power) affected the enactment of roles in the marital, parental, and work spheres. To make the discussion of their findings more meaningful, it will be necessary to discuss in some detail what they mean by motives and roles.

MOTIVES. Veroff and Feld assumed that certain general types of motives affect the ways people behave in the various compartments of life. One motive is affiliation. The *affiliative motive* is defined as "the disposition to strive to establish, maintain, and restore positive affective relationships with other people" (Veroff and Feld, 1970:20). The authors indicate that three components of the affiliation motive reflect the notion of intimacy: (a) positive affiliation (that is, the desire to be with someone because of the positive aspects of the relationship), (b) fear of isolation or rejection (that is, the desire to be with someone because the person does not want to be alone or feel rejected), and (c) fear of intimacy (that is, perhaps the seeking of a number of affiliations because he or she fears being intimate with any one person).

507

Another motive, the *achievement motive,* is defined as "a disposition to strive for the sense of pride in accomplishment that accompanies favorable evaluation of performance on a difficult task" (Veroff and Feld, 1970:32). The achievement motive, although it is probably most relevant to participation in the work world, is also applicable to the parental and marital roles. The *power motive* reflects a disposition to strive for control of the means of influencing another person or group of persons (Veroff and Feld, 1970:23). This definition implies that power operates according

**TABLE 18–2**
**Characteristics of the Marital, Job, and Parental Roles**

| CHARACTERISTICS OF THE MARITAL ROLE | |
|---|---|
| ROLE CHARACTERISTIC | DESCRIPTION |
| Marital role demands | *Primary* To provide for the physical and emotional needs of the spouse: this includes financial support by the husband, and care of the home by the wife; sexual gratification of partner; emotional support of partner. To take responsibility for children resulting from legitimized reproduction. *Secondary* To handle decision-making in the prescribed fashion: through dominance of husband and submission of wife in the traditional view of marriage; through an equalitarian orientation in the modern view of marriage. |
| Marital role gratifications | Parental needs satisfied for both husband and wife; recognition of adult status in our society; emotional support for men; physical and emotional support for women; sexual gratification for both. |
| Marital role ambiguities | Conflict about women's role outside and inside the home in certain social groups (based on a lack of consensus); conflict of how many household tasks a man should perform (based on lack of consensus). |

| CHARACTERISTICS OF THE JOB ROLE | |
|---|---|
| ROLE CHARACTERISTIC | DESCRIPTION |
| Job role demands | *Primary* To perform the specific work activity at a minimal level of competence. *Secondary* To engage in social interaction that facilitates the specific work activity. |
| Job role gratifications | Financial security and emotional support of others; status gratification from the occupational position of an employed man; affiliation, achievement, power, independence, mastery, and curiosity in specific jobs depending on the type of activity that is required. |

**TABLE 18–2** (*continued*)

| CHARACTERISTICS OF THE JOB ROLE | |
| --- | --- |
| ROLE CHARACTERISTIC | DESCRIPTION |
| Job role ambiguities | Conflicting role demands coming from role overload, differing expectations from different role senders, and lack of structured expectation about performance. |

| CHARACTERISTICS OF THE PARENTAL ROLE | |
| --- | --- |
| ROLE CHARACTERISTIC | DESCRIPTION |
| Parental role demands | *Primary* To nurture the child: this includes providing shelter and food, and general financial support by the father, and attending to both the psychological and physical health of the child by the mother.<br>*Secondary* To influence the socialization of the child for his adult role in society. |
| Parental role gratifications | Adult status and sexual status of being feminine or masculine through reaching the status of parenthood; affiliative and power gratification in relationship to their children; achievement gratification from performing the appropriate parental role obligations well and from vicarious experiences of achievements of their children. |
| Parental role ambiguities | Conflicting ideologies about socialization of the child (based on a lack of consensus about child-rearing); conflict between attaining socialization through authoritarian conveyance of rules, or through moral generalization from warm acceptance; conflict about age of relinquishing control of child. |

SOURCE: Joseph Veroff and Sheila Feld, *Marriage and Work in America: A Study of Motives and Roles* (New York: D. Van Nostrand Company, 1970), pp. 28, 31, and 34, Tables 1–1, 1–2, 1–3. © 1970 by Litton Educational Publishing, Inc. By permission of D. Van Nostrand Company.

to an exchange process like Blau's (1964) model, which was discussed in Chapter 15 of this text.

ROLES. Veroff and Feld were interested in the influence of the three types of motivational orientations on enactments of roles in the marital, parental, and work areas. For each of these spheres of activity, they examined the relationship of role demands and role gratifications with role ambiguities (see Table 18–2).

509

## The Marital Role

ROLE DEMANDS. The most salient motive in the marital area concerns power. Particularly among highly educated husbands there is the expectation that they will overtly acknowledge the privilege of the wife to make decisions. Less-educated males seem to have more traditionally oriented marriages in which they wield the power, and the wife, if she has any power, obtains it through covert means.

ROLE GRATIFICATIONS. Evidently the wife of a man with a grade-school education achieves her marital role gratification because it is covert. Highly educated women receive their maximal role gratification by the overt exercise of power even though they generally have an egalitarian companionship marriage and in spite of the fact that their exercise of marital power might threaten the needs of their husbands to exercise marital power.

ROLE AMBIGUITY. Marital role ambiguities seem to exist for all three educational levels but for different reasons. For those with a grade-school education the ambiguity or conflict occurs because the norms state that the man is dominant, although in most families the woman has a great deal of power that she obtains voluntarily by covert influence or involuntarily because the male fails to take the lead.

For those persons with a high-school education the work and marital worlds are characterized by a lack of specific prescriptions. They have just enough education to identify with the ideal of husband-wife equalitarianism, but do not have the wherewithal to translate the ideal into workable solutions for structuring the marital arrangement.

The ambiguity for the higher-educated groups seems to result from a lack of isomorphism or similarity between the man's work-related behavior and what occurs at home. The higher-educated male usually provides a large number of rewards/services to his family. He is a leader at work and is compelled by the norms to devote great amounts of energy to his family, yet he must permit his wife to be the more powerful figure at home for her gratification. In other words, marriage interferes with the opportunity of a higher-educated female to achieve in the work world. She compensates by satisfying her need for power at home, to the detriment of her husband, who supposedly gets his need for achievement and power gratified through his job.

## The Parental Role

ROLE DEMANDS. Veroff and Feld (1970:204) tied the idea of the parental role to the family life cycle in emphasizing the functions of (a) nurturing and (b) influencing:

> It is as if the role demands shift from the two parents as their children grow up. The influence function initially starts out as the important

demand for a father, but this diminishes at school age for the least-educated men, at adolescence for those with moderate education, and later for men at the highest educational level.

However, for a father, the nurturing function increases as children mature, possibly as a revised route to influence. For women, the initial role demand of nurturing slowly diminishes and is replaced by the demand for influence and socialization. In passing, it could be pointed out that this pattern reflects an interesting interchange of parental demands which, if properly regulated, can lead to family stability. If there is any disproportionate use of these functions by either the mother or father at the wrong time, perhaps one can predict there would be family difficulties, both for the child and the parents.

ROLE GRATIFICATIONS.    Each motive appears to operate differently for men and women and by education level for each sex. For example, achievement gratification from parental role enactment seems to be primarily the bailiwick of the college-educated female. Men, on the other hand, seem to receive vicarious achievement according to their educational attainment. Whereas college-educated males get the most vicarious achievement when their children are adolescents, the high-school-educated father gets his indirect gratification when the children are of school age. This probably reflects the different values placed by the fathers on the recreational and educational activities of their children. The high-school-educated father probably focuses on the sports activities of his children, whereas the college-educated father tends to focus on the school-related activities.

With regard to affiliative gratification, Veroff and Feld are explicit in stating that there is a basic contradiction in the parent role and the friend role. Parents and children, at least dependent children, are rarely "friends." However, as was discussed in Chapter 5, it is not unusual for a friendship to develop between parents and children after the children have established their own families of procreation.

Power gratification is primarily limited to persons who are much involved with the meaning of parenthood and to mothers who are able to see that a friendship will develop with their children after they are grown. Veroff and Feld note that the lack of power gratification is especially frustrating to fathers when their children are adolescents.

ROLE AMBIGUITY.    Veroff and Feld (1970:205) found virtually no ambiguity in the maternal role for grade-school-educated mothers. The role was very narrowly defined with no room for flexibility. Altogether they identified three general ambiguities about parenthood: (1) "During school age and adolescence, should children be appropriate affiliative objects for a father or mother?" (2) "At what point does the influence a parent has over his child effectively cease?" (3) "How much achievement gratification can there be in the day-to-day necessities for the care of small children?"

Perhaps the preceding discussion sheds some light on the reason why marital satisfaction drops in the stages of the family life cycle when children are present. Children, for all of the joy, happiness, and fulfillment

511

they can bring, can and frequently are the source of much frustration for and discord between parents. It is a shame that legally we fail to enforce the laws against child abuse while socially we fail to develop norms about overdoing the parental role. Excesses of any sort, even physical affection and the expression of love, can be detrimental to a child's development. Perhaps it is amazing that parents seem to do so well because there is virtually no explicit training for the role and few sources of aid and comfort in any form (see Chapter 17).

## The Work Role

ROLE DEMANDS.  Veroff and Feld (1970:294) uncovered what the popular press has been saying for quite a while: work is worshipped in this society.

> A major conclusion from our analysis of men's work and leisure reactions as a function of their achievement motivation, is that the pressure men feel to perform at some kind of job, the pressure men feel to demon-

*A joint effort completed, it is now time for the graduate to move into the work world.*

Jim Harrison

strate that they can achieve at work, is such a potent role demand for all types of job roles that performance in realms other than work—leisure, social roles—cannot compensate for inadequate job performance.

The researchers were somewhat surprised to find that men who were high in achievement motivation were pushing for success, achievement, and the maximum job performance evaluation regardless of the status of their job. Baptist theologian Findley Edge would call these high-achievement persons "workaholics." They think about work all the time—they can never relax or get away from it. They always have five more things going than they can possibly do well, but the "old juice" is pushing them toward the maximum performance in each area. It was the workaholic about whom Sidney Jourard was talking in his discussion of the "lethal aspects of the male role" in American society. We socialize males to achieve and to work hard at achieving, with the possible consequence that they die earlier than women. We push females to achieve until marriage and then to put the lid on their achievement aspirations; then we encourage or coerce them to do menial labor at less than we would normally pay for such labor, and then we wonder about the cause of alcoholism and mental illness among housewives. Our work role demands are not only too high but too costly in terms of human life and mental anguish.

ROLE GRATIFICATIONS.

> One of the most provocative ideas emerging from our analysis of the work and leisure reaction of men with different motives is that the gratifications that are possible and are obtained from work are dramatically different for men at different ages: young men seek the satisfaction attendant to having reached a certain type of occupation; middle aged men seek satisfaction directly from the particular qualities of their job; and older men attempt to find satisfaction from the symbolic significance work has for their broader life goals. [Veroff and Feld, 1970:295]

What they found in essence was the classic situation of men working hard to "make it"; on making it middle-aged men tried to stretch out the gratification obtained from their jobs as long as possible and older men tried to tie the value of the job to other parts of their lives and life goals. Underlying the gratification received in any work role, Veroff and Feld found that personal choice of work style was most important. American men do not like to be required to act and behave a prescribed way. They want the freedom to be their own person, to shape the work role instead of being shaped by it.

ROLE AMBIGUITY.  The work role was found to be ambiguous (a) if it had explicit demands for one type of performance (for example, technical skill), but few guidelines for other performances (for example, affiliation

513

**FIGURE 18–2**
**Model of the Relationship Between Motives and Role Enactment**

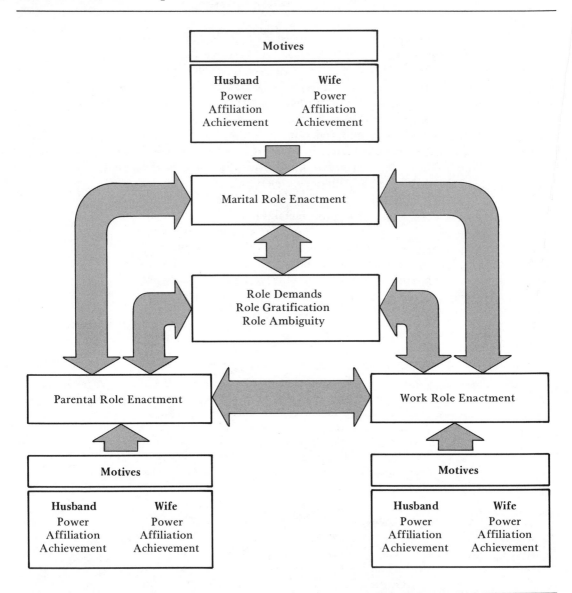

SOURCE: Adapted from textual materials in Joseph Veroff and Sheila Feld, *Marriage and Work in America: A Study of Motives and Roles* (New York: D. Van Nostrand Company, 1970). © 1970 by Litton Educational Publishing, Inc. Reprinted by permission of D. Van Nostrand Company.

norms) and (b) if it did not include means by which the work performance could be adequately and objectively evaluated. A good example of the latter ambiguity would be the college professor who never really knows how adequate his performance is because there are few ways to evaluate teaching success or failure.

## Summary: The Veroff-Feld Study

Veroff and Feld suggest that three primary motives (for power, affiliation, and achievement) affect how a married couple will perform their marital, parental, and work roles. For each of these roles there are various and sometimes conflicting demands made on the members of the family. If the enactment of each role is to produce role gratification, then there must be a minimum of role ambiguity (Figure 18–2).

Perhaps the best way to summarize the implications of the Veroff-Feld study is to illustrate how their model works in a hypothetical situation.

Our hypothetical family consists of the husband, who is a high-school teacher, his wife, a college graduate who formerly worked in a bank, but who is currently employed as a full-time housewife, and three children (a four-year-old son, an eight-year-old daughter, and an eleven-year-old son in the sixth grade).

WORK ROLE ENACTMENT. The primary motive of the work role is achievement. Both spouses want to satisfy their achievement motives in the occupational niche each has carved out. For maximum gratification to be obtained from working, the work role demands on time, energy, and attention have to be within the normal toleration level of both spouses.

For example, if the husband has decided to work on a master's degree at night, a certain amount of role ambiguity is likely to emerge for him at work, in class at night, and at home. The demands on his time and energies will multiply and the strain of playing several roles may appear in his interactions with the family. The same will occur for the wife because she will be required, by necessity, to complete some of the tasks formerly taken care of by the husband. Such a situation can easily produce an overload on both spouses regarding their work and work roles. The consequences of an overload in the work area can produce negative consequences in both the parental and marital role areas.

PARENTAL ROLE ENACTMENT. The primary motive operative in the family area is for affiliation—affiliation of parents with children and of the parents with each other as they jointly participate in the socialization and activities of their children. The opportunities for gratification in the

515

parental role are great. Both parents can receive a primary sense of satisfaction in being creative in a meaningful role and a secondary or vicarious sense of satisfaction in the accomplishments of their children.

However, in our hypothetical family the parental role for the wife may be inundated with affiliative encounters. All day she has the four-year-old, after school and on the weekends she has the other two children as well, and on three nights a week she is left with the children while the husband plays his work/student role. To say the very least, the parental role demands on the wife may be excessive and even beyond her level of toleration. In addition, there is some role ambiguity because she has taken over many parental tasks formerly performed by her husband.

In a relative sense the parental role demands may have also increased for the husband (that is, with the amount of time and energy he has available for playing the parental role, the demands of the three children for their "slice" of daddy may be overwhelming). Without doubt he will experience some role ambiguity because he is aware of the strains present for the wife in her role as a parent. The consequences of these conflicting demands and ambiguities may very well lead to strain in the marital role area.

MARITAL ROLE ENACTMENT.    Although a considerable amount of effort and energy may be expended by each spouse in being parents and in their separate work roles, each spouse has to "work" at being a good husband or wife. The primary motives for the marital role area are affiliation and power.

Gratification from the marital role can be obtained only if both spouses are sensitive to the other's companionship and affectional needs (that is, satisfaction of the affiliative motive). Gratification is also affected by another set of role demands, which concern decision making and the performance of instrumental services for each other, such as repairs and preparation of meals. This is where the power motive enters the scene.

In our hypothetical family the marital role responsibilities and demands are likely to suffer at the hands of overload role demands in the work and parental areas. It is easier to postpone enactment of marital role behaviors than work or parental behaviors. This generally will lead to episodic battles between the spouses over neglect. It can also lead to role ambiguity, since the interactional cues and patterns operative before the husband started back to school no longer work. New patterns of interaction and communication must be developed to fit into the changed schedules and life style of our hypothetical family.

At the very least, the potential for conflict in our hypothetical family is substantial. Veroff and Feld (1970) captured the dynamic quality of the complex relationship between motives and role enactments by focusing on role demands, gratification, and ambiguity. Marriage adjustments and satisfaction, marital happiness and success are tied closely to

Rose Skytta, Jeroboam Inc.

*If everyone "pitches in," a family project can be fun.*

how couples mix their marital, parental, and work roles. Power within the family is very often a function of the give-and-take exchanges between spouses who must continually negotiate the conflicting demands made by each on the other and the demands made on the relationship by conflicting work, parental, and marital roles.

## SUMMARY AND CONCLUSIONS

This chapter outlines some parameters of the question: How do people mix their family (marital and parental), work, and leisure worlds? In the process of developing an answer to this question several points need a concluding emphasis.

517

1. Our society places a great, perhaps too great, an emphasis on the achievement of "success" in the work role, for males in particular. This overriding emphasis probably results in males being generally unable to derive much or enough gratification from their marital interactions and their parental responsibilities. It certainly acts as a constraint on the ability of males to enjoy their leisure activities.

2. Our society places contradictory demands on women for achievement. During their premarital years women are trained to compete in the educational and work spheres on an equal plane with men. At marriage, and particularly at the birth of children, our society places great pressure on women to stifle the achievement motive and to rechannel their focus in an area where few ways are available to evaluate success.

3. Our society places a great burden on the housewife role by demanding too much work and too little recognition. Generally too little attention is given this role and its unreasonable demands by social scientists and by husbands in general.

4. Social scientists who study the family have generally ignored the real dynamics of married life by compartmentalizing the work, family, and leisure activities of family members. A full understanding of the dynamics of marital interaction, power, and adjustment should include an integration of these areas of life, not a segregation of them.

In conclusion, there is a definite need for a theoretical model that will tie commitments to work, family, and leisure roles to problems of marital interaction, family power, and marital adjustment.

## SOME POSSIBLE IMPLICATIONS

*Human beings have been "working" for centuries to build a world in which all people can live with dignity and self-respect. In the preindustrial world work was a vocation, ascribed by the social class and family into which one was born. Work generally involved long hours, little pay, and, for the average member of the working class, a lot of sweat.*

*With the advent of the industrial revolution a new definition of work evolved wherein some persons would "work" with the power harnessed by machines. Other persons, the middle-class, white-collar worker and the managerial class, would "work" by supervising the workers and keeping records of what the workers accomplished. Coincidental with the industrial revolution was what Max Weber called the "Protestant Ethic." This work ethic grew out of the Calvinist doctrine that a person could "work" his or her way into heaven. The workers at all levels of the status hierarchy elevated work to a divine imperative—something to which one should give his or her total commitment.*

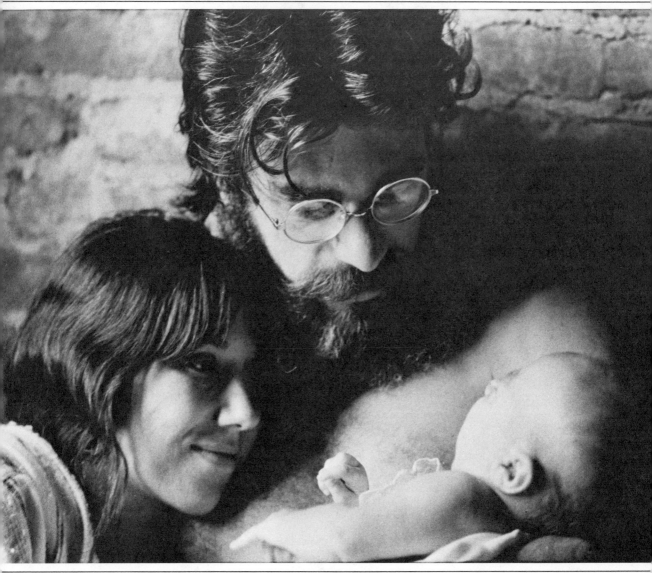

Joel Gordon

# 19

# DEMOGRAPHIC PROCESSES AND THE FAMILY

*Is Zero Population Growth possible or desirable?*

*Why is the proportion of unplanned and/or unwanted births high in our society?*

*What is the effect of moving on the family and particularly on the children?*

*How do people cope with a death in the family?*

Upon ejaculation during sexual intercourse, millions of tiny sperm cells are thrust into the vagina and will perform their biologic function unless adequate contraceptive precautions have been taken. They will swim mightily upstream and into the fallopian tubes. One sperm cell, so small that thousands of sperms could fit on the point of a needle, may penetrate the tough wall of a very tiny egg cell released some time earlier by an ovary—the egg cell released this particular month to make the journey toward the uterus. If conception occurs, cell division begins. A new being is in process, on its way toward birth about nine months later.

This is certainly not an unusual occurrence. In the United States, 3,144,198 births were reported in 1975 alone. After deaths had been subtracted, the net increase in world population was about 78 million persons. In 1650 the world population stood at about one-half billion. By 1900 it was 1½ billion, and 2½ billion by 1950. By 1975 it had surpassed 4 billion. The world population is now doubling about every forty years.

The world today is facing unprecedented food and energy shortages, massive environmental pollution, widespread poverty, and recurring wars; overpopulation compounds these problems. All these so-called social problems extract personal costs. Solutions will require an intrusion in and a curtailment of individual freedoms as well as a shift in cultural values and individual attitudes and behavior. Of these problems, overpopulation may be and probably is the single most important one to be solved, because the other problems are inextricably tied to it.

As Sheldon Segal (1972) notes in a publication of the Population Crisis Committee:

> The world, unless stricken with a great catastrophe, will have to cope with much larger numbers of people. It is not unrealistic to contemplate a world population of 10 billion when today's children are mature adults. Whether the problem be food supply, health care, educational facilities, use of natural resources, pollution of the environment or general improvement of living standards, applied to a population of 10 billion—instead of today's 3.6 billion—it is close to insoluble.

Demography is the field of study that focuses on the interrelationships among phenomena that affect the size, distribution, and change in the population of society. There are three demographic processes: fertility, migration, and mortality, each of which will touch all our lives and will require some adjustment within all our families. Each of these demographic processes will be examined. Let us look first at the fertility process in American society.

## FERTILITY

### *American Fertility Patterns*

Fertility refers to the actual reproductive capacity. There are several ways of measuring fertility. The first, the *crude birth rate,* is the number of live births for a given year per 1,000 population during that year. It is a "crude" rate because obviously not everyone in the population can bear children. The second and more refined measure of fertility, called the *general fertility rate,* involves the number of births in a given year per 1,000 women in the child-bearing ages, 15 to 44. A third way of assessing fertility, the *total fertility rate,* is the number of births that 1,000 women would have in their lifetime if, at each year of age, they experienced the birth rates occurring in the specified year. A total fertility rate of 2,110 represents replacement level fertility for the total population under current mortality conditions.

A cursory examination of the figures from 1960 to 1975 in Table 19–1 may lead to a premature surge of optimism. The number of births

**TABLE 19–1**

**Birth Rates for the United States, 1910–1975**

| YEAR | NO. BIRTHS | CRUDE BIRTH RATE (PER 1,000 POPULATION) | GENERAL FERTILITY RATE (PER 1,000 POPULATION) | TOTAL FERTILITY RATE |
|---|---|---|---|---|
| 1910 | 2,777,000 | 30.1 | 126.8 | no data |
| 1920 | 2,950,000 | 23.7 | 117.9 | " " |
| 1930 | 2,618,000 | 18.9 | 89.2 | " " |
| 1940 | 2,559,000 | 17.9 | 79.9 | " " |
| 1950 | 3,632,000 | 23.6 | 106.2 | " " |
| 1960 | 4,257,850 | 23.7 | 118.0 | " " |
| 1965 | 3,760,358 | 19.5 | 96.6 | 2,928 |
| 1966 | 3,606,274 | 18.4 | 91.3 | 2,736 |
| 1967 | 3,520,959 | 17.8 | 87.6 | 2,573 |
| 1968 | 3,501,564 | 17.5 | 85.7 | 2,477 |
| 1969 | 3,600,206 | 17.8 | 86.5 | 2,465 |
| 1970 | 3,731,386 | 18.4 | 87.9 | 2,480 |
| 1971 | 3,555,970 | 17.2 | 81.8 | 2,275 |
| 1972 | 3,258,411 | 15.6 | 73.4 | 2,022 |
| 1973 | 3,136,965 | 14.9 | 69.2 | 1,896 |
| 1974 | 3,159,958 | 14.9 | 68.4 | 1,857 |
| 1975 | 3,144,198 | 14.8 | 66.7 | 1,799 |

SOURCE: U.S. Department of Commerce, Bureau of the Census, *Population Estimates,* Series P-25, No. 297 (January 1965); U.S. Department of Health, Education and Welfare, *Vital Statistics of the United States,* 1966, Volume 1; *Vital Statistics of the United States—Special Reports,* Vol. 48, No. 17 (November 1958); *Monthly Vital Statistics Report,* Vol. 24, No. 12, 1976.

in that period declined by over one million, the crude birth rate decreased from 23.7 to 14.8, the general fertility rate declined from 118 births per 1,000 women of child-bearing age to 66.7, and the total fertility rate declined, also. In fact, in 1972 the average number of children per completed family was hovering at and a little below the replacement level of 2.1 children per family. To be sure, these are rather positive indications that the population problem in the United States can possibly be controlled.

However, in 1960 there were only 4.7 million women between the ages of 18 and 21 years. In 1965 this had grown to 6 million, and three years later in 1968 the figure was 7 million. Between 1960 and 1980 the number of women who are the richest source of reproductive potential—between the ages of 15 and 34—will increase by two-thirds. Thus, an increase in the actual number of births between 1970 and 1980 appears inevitable. To avoid any increase would require a decline in fertility consistent with a completed fertility rate of 1.8 children per woman by 1985, a figure well below the replacement level, equal to a "net" reproduction rate considerably below 1,000. The likelihood of this occurring is very slim indeed.

What will it take to achieve an "immediate" state of Zero Population Growth? In a fascinating attempt to answer this question, Tomas Frejka, a demographer at the Population Council (1968) indicates that the birth rate would have to be brought down from 17.6 per 1,000 per year to equal the death rate of 9.6 per 1,000, with all immigration stopped. In addition, for the next twenty years or so each family would have to limit its average number of children to about 1.2 children. Thereafter, the mean number of children per family would have to increase gradually to a maximum of 2.8 per family in the period from 2030 to 2035. By the year 2065 the average number of children per family would have to drop back down to about 1.4. As noted in *The Population Bulletin* (February 1971: 28): "In recorded history, no human population has ever had a completed family size as low as 1.2 children as an average family, nor is there evidence that the American people have any thought that conditions require such a drastic change in behavior."

Even if the fertility rate remained at the replacement level of 2.1 children per woman, it would take 65 to 70 years for the population to become stable. Calculating from 1974, this means that the United States would reach a Zero Population Growth in the years between 2039 and 2044. The pressing question is: Can we afford the delay?

## Differential Fertility in the United States

The foregoing discussion has treated fertility as a societal-level phenomenon. Some intrasocietal differences in fertility are by residence, race, socioeconomic status (education and income), and religion. In these differentials the likelihood of stable population growth becomes more apparently problematic.

The data from which we determine the extent of differences in fertility for women with different educational, income, and religious characteristics and how these differences may have changed over time comes from several sources: (1) Some information is available from the national census, which is taken every ten years. (2) The U.S. Bureau of the Census periodically asks questions of a sample of the population in its *Current Population Reports*. (3) There are the national studies (Freedman, Whelpton, Campbell, 1959; Whelpton, Campbell, Patterson, 1966) begun in 1955 and conducted again in 1960 (the Growth of American Families Studies, or GAF). These were followed by the National Fertility Studies (NFS) of 1965 and 1970 (see Ryder and Westoff, 1971) and the *National Survey of Family Growth* in 1975. (4) Studies are always being conducted by scholars who may use smaller and less representative samples, but who are able to focus more intensively on a specific research question. Thus, the data on differential fertility for the United States are especially thorough and reliable. What are the more important fertility differentials and how have they changed in the recent past?

The data in Table 19–2 focus on the General Fertility Rate (children ever born per 1,000 women, aged 15 to 44) and how it has changed from 1960 to 1976 by the following differentials: (a) residence, (b) race, (c) education, and (d) labor force status. These data are from samples of the U.S. population. What has happened?

RESIDENCE. The data in Table 19–2 indicate that the increase, from 1960 to 1976, in the number of children ever born per 1,000 married women was greater for women in metropolitan areas (from 2,431 to 2,951) than for those in nonmetropolitan areas (from 3,000 to 3,300). However, this does not mean that fertility is higher in urban areas. More children were born to women in nonmetropolitan areas (3,300) than were born to women in metropolitan areas (2,951).

RACE. Part of the explanation for the larger increase in the metropolitan figures lies in the differentials in fertility by race. As noted in Chapter 6, blacks today are more urban than whites. The data in Table 19–2 show quite clearly that the number of children ever born per 1,000 black women was higher in 1960 and in 1976; also, the increase for blacks was greater in that time period.

LABOR FORCE STATUS. In 1960 the difference between the fertility of women in the labor force and those who were not was considerably larger (2,191 compared to 2,918 per 1,000 women) than the difference in 1976 (2,888 to 3,270). This reflects the fact that employment is less of a constraining factor on fertility than it once was. More and more women are

525

returning to the labor force shortly after having their children than in earlier years. Perhaps it is because day-care nurseries are more readily available. It could also mean that the norms about mothers sacrificing their work career for the responsibilities of child care are less stringent today than in times past. Regardless of the underlying explanation for this shift, the fact remains that children are less of a hindrance to women who desire an occupational career than they were formerly.

EDUCATION. Table 19–2 shows that the number of children born per 1,000 women aged 15–44 increased for all levels of education between 1960 and 1976. However, the most dramatic increases occurred for those women who either dropped out of high school or who left school after completing the eighth grade. As would be expected, the figures for the college-educated women are considerably lower than those for women who never attended college.

**TABLE 19–2**
**Comparative Birth Figures**

| CHARACTERISTIC | CHILDREN BORN PER 1,000 WOMEN EVER MARRIED | |
|---|---|---|
| | AS OF 1960 | AS OF 1976 |
| *Residence* | | |
| Metropolitan | 2,431 | 2,951 |
| Nonmetropolitan | 3,000 | 3,300 |
| *Race* | | |
| White | 2,572 | 2,979 |
| Black | 3,049 | 3,728 |
| *Labor Force Status* | | |
| In labor force | 2,191 | 2,888 |
| Not in labor force | 2,918 | 3,270 |
| *Education* | | |
| Elementary | | |
| Less than 8 yrs. | 3,478 | 3,908 |
| 8 years | 2,861 | 3,673 |
| High School | | |
| 1–3 years | 2,658 | 3,563 |
| 4 years | 2,373 | 2,944 |
| College | | |
| 1–3 years | 2,361 | 2,768 |
| 4 years or more | 2,233 | 2,431 |

SOURCE: U.S. Bureau of the Census, *U.S. Census of Population: 1950*, Special Report, *Fertility*, part 5; *U.S. Census of Population: 1960, Women by Number of Children Ever Born*, PC(2)-3A; *U.S. Census of Population: 1970*, vol. I, *Characteristics of the Population*, part 1, *U.S. Summary;* and *Current Population Reports*, Series P-20, No. 308.

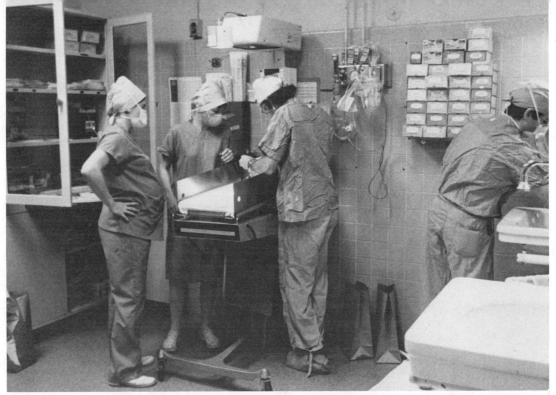

Jim Harrison

INCOME AND OCCUPATIONAL STATUS. The same kind of inverse relationship exists for income and occupation—the higher the family income or occupational status level, the lower the fertility. Such a differential has existed for a very long time and, although a trend toward greater similarity in fertility across social class is evident, the differential still exists.

RELIGION. Religion is a complex phenomenon and one that has been consistently related to fertility. Research has shown that Catholic women desire, expect, and have more children than Protestants, who in turn are more reproductive than Jewish women. The degree of religious commitment, particularly as measured by church attendance and the taking of sacraments, is not very predictive of expected fertility among Protestants, but it is strikingly associated with expected fertility among Catholics. In fact, in the 1965 National Fertility Study (see Ryder and Westoff, 1971:71), the mean number of children expected by Protestant women who scored lowest on religiousness was 2.9. The mean number of children expected for the Protestant women who scored highest in religiousness was only 3.1. The corresponding figures for Catholic women were 3.6 and 4.7, indicating not only the Protestant-Catholic differential but also the tremendous influence of religiousness on the expected fertility patterns of Catholics.

Perhaps the most reliable estimates available of the impact of religion on fertility, expected and actual, is the 1965 National Fertility

527

Study that followed the 1955 and 1960 GAF (Growth of American Families Studies) studies. The 1965 study included the results of personal interviews with 5,617 women randomly selected to represent the continental United States. Altogether it included 4,416 white women and 1,201 nonwhite women (all but 74 of these were blacks) under the age of fifty-four. The summary of the results (see Ryder and Westoff, 1971:91–92) regarding religious differentials is as follows:

*The National Fertility Study (1965)*

1. Catholic women both want and expect more children than either Protestant or Jewish women, a differential that is maintained regardless of the number of children they already have.

2. There is little difference in fertility among women in the various Protestant denominations.

3. Various indices of religiousness among Catholics, including both measures of formal associational involvement and community involvement, reveal the expected direct relationship with fertility.

4. For Protestant women there is a sharp negative relationship between the number of children expected and the wife's educational attainment, whereas among Catholics, a similar relationship prevails only below the college-graduate level.

5. Catholics with four or more years of higher education are a distinctive high-fertility group, and because of this the largest Protestant-Catholic fertility differential is found at the college-graduate level.

6. A similar Protestant-Catholic pattern prevails for occupational status and for income—the higher this level, the more the Catholic exceeds the Protestant expected fertility.

7. The lowest fertility for both Protestants and Catholics is expected by women currently working, and, among working women, the career woman expects the fewest children.

8. Region and size of place of residence do not contribute to any further understanding of the religious differential.

9. Comparison of the Protestant-Catholic differential in expected fertility in 1955, 1960, and 1965 shows no continuation between 1960 and 1965 of the widening that occurred between 1955 and 1960. (Among younger women, moreover, the differential shows some sign of contracting.)

FERTILITY DIFFERENTIALS IN THE FUTURE.    The differentials in fertility discussed above have all shown a undirectional trend over the years—a trend toward convergence. According to Charles Westoff in his 1975 presidential address to the Population Association of America, most of the differences in fertility by race, education, religion, and income education will diminish greatly or completely disappear within the next decade or so.

## Unplanned and Unwanted Pregnancy

Although an examination of differential fertility may be important and informative, it glosses over what may be even more salient to gaining an understanding of the impact of fertility on the family. It would be easy to assume that most children are planned—conceived according to plan— and the object of positive anticipation on the part of the expectant parents. Unfortunately, this is a faulty assumption. Just how faulty it is should give us some clues about the effect the onset of pregnancy, especially accidental pregnancy, has on the family. But first, how extensive is the phenomenon of unwanted births in the United States?

Westoff and Westoff [1] provide an answer based on the 1960 GAF and 1965 NFS data:

> Between 1960 and 1965 in this country it is estimated that some 4.7 million births occurred that were probably unwanted. This is an average estimate between the 5.3 million unwanted by at least one parent and the 4 million reported to have been unwanted by both parents. These are births that, had perfect fertility control been universally available, would presumably never had occurred. These 4.7 million births—about three-quarters of a million a year—constituted nearly 20 percent of all children born during that period.

This quotation chronicles the abysmal record of the American population to control unwanted fertility. In quantity alone, unwanted births are a serious impediment to the achievement of a stable population growth. But the crucial problem may be the effect on the quality of relationships within the family. The potential for strained marital relationships during pregnancy, open marital conflict after birth, and less than effective parent-child relations must be higher for unwanted than wanted births. There is probably no way to estimate accurately the potentially harmful side effects of unwanted fertility on the quality of the intra-familial relationship. The quantitative dimension alone is large enough to justify serious concern.

---

[1] From *From Now to Zero: Fertility, Contraception, and Abortion in America*, pp. 293–94, by permission of Little, Brown and Co., Boston. Copyright © 1968, 1971 by Charles Westoff and Leslie Aldridge Westoff.

Fortunately, something happened between 1960–1965 and 1970 that completely reversed the unwanted birth phenomenon: As Westoff [2] indicates:

> Data from the 1970 National Fertility Study (NFS) reveal a dramatic drop in the rate of unwanted fertility between 1961–1965 period and 1966–1970—a decline of some 36 percent in the number of unwanted births per 1,000 woman years of exposure to the risk of unwanted childbearing. For whites the decline was 35 percent, for blacks, 56 percent. We have estimated that about half of the nationwide fertility decline between the two periods is due to the improvement in the control of unwanted births. Such improvements can result from: earlier or more extensive use of contraception; enlarged or more consistent use of the more effective methods; greater motivation to avoid pregnancy, possibly resulting in more regular contraceptive use or recourse to other means of fertility control, or some combination of such changes.

Westoff's interpretation focuses entirely on social-psychological variables and ignores the impact of macro-level forces, forces like economic "stagflation"—a situation wherein we have high inflation coupled with high unemployment and a sense of dis-ease in the marketplace. It is likely that decisions to prevent or postpone pregnancy are strongly related to the economy in general. How the economy fares can thus intrude even into the marital bed.

Another major demographic variable not referred to by Westoff is the age and sex structure within the population and how it changes. To illustrate: Although the total fertility rate dropped by 50 percent between 1961 and 1975 (from 3,609 to 1,799), the annual number of births dropped by only 26 percent (from 4,268,000 to 3,149,000) because of the substantial increase in the number of women in the prime child-bearing ages. The number of females 18–29 years old increased by 59 percent. If the female population of 1975 had experienced the age-specific birth rates of 1961, there would have been 6.2 million births in 1975. This increase in the number of women entering the prime child-bearing years should begin to moderate, because the baby boom tapered off after 1957—1957 plus 18 years equals 1975.

Gibson (1976:249) states: "Changes in marital fertility have accounted for 83 percent of the decline in total fertility since 1971; changes in marital status accounted for 19 percent, and changes in nonmarital fertility had only a negligible effect. Declines in the level of marital fertility account for a substantial part of the overall decrease; postponement of childbearing did not occur in any significant degree until the 1970s." This conclusion is based on the fact that the average number of lifetime births expected by wives 18–24 years old dropped from 3.1 in 1960 to 2.2 in 1975.

---

[2] Charles F. Westoff, "The Modernization of U.S. Contraceptive Practice," *Family Planning Perspectives* 4 (July, 1972):9.

The corresponding figures for wives in the 25–29 age group were 3.4 and 2.3.

Regardless of which factors are responsible, marital fertility is on the decline, the total fertility rate is below replacement level, and the percentage of all children born who are either unplanned or unwanted has declined markedly. All of this bodes well for the American family system.

# CONTRACEPTION

A solution to the population problem may lie not so much in the technical development and more efficient diffusion of contraceptive devices, although this may help, as in effective contraceptive and sex education. If the population problem is to be solved at the societal level, assuming that this is even possible, it may be necessary to combine socialization about contraceptives with a sex education program that emphasizes rational decision making about recreational sex. A very effective contraceptive, technologically speaking, is of no value if it stays in the dresser drawer or medicine cabinet. And although recreational sex may be most enjoyable, all too often it is also reproductive.

Thus, most young adults, and quite a few older ones as well, married and unmarried, face a recurring set of decisions: What contraceptive(s) should I/we use? Is there any reason why one technique should be better for me/us than another? How serious are the health risks reportedly associated with certain contraceptive techniques? In the sections that immediately follow, some of the contraceptives currently available will be discussed in detail.

## Sterilization

For the individual or couple told by a physician that to have further children would or could be dangerous, for those who either do not want or cannot afford any more children, for the man who should not, for whatever reason, father a child, and for the woman who should not conceive and carry a child, the most effective contraceptive technique available is sterilization. There are three sterilization options, one for men and two for women.

VASECTOMY. For men, this choice involves a minor surgical procedure that can be performed in a physician's office with a local anesthetic. It usually takes only a few minutes. Two small incisions are made and the vasa deferentia, tubes that carry the sperm from the testes, are cut and tied. The operation is accomplished so easily that a man can return to his normal activities the same or at least the next day. It should be noted that a

531

vasectomy does not interfere with hormonal secretions, does not interfere with orgasm, and does not reduce the male sex drive. It merely ensures that no sperm are in the ejaculate. As a matter of fact, many couples in which the male has had a vasectomy note an increase in sexual activity and enjoyment because of the freedom from the fear of pregnancy. A vasectomy is irreversible, so it should not be obtained unless a couple is thoroughly convinced that they do not want any more children.

TUBAL LIGATION.    One sterilization option for women requires an incision in the abdominal wall so that the Fallopian tubes may be tied. Normally this operation takes about fifteen minutes, but it may require four to five days of hospitalization, and some postoperative effects may be evident for three to four weeks.

LAPROSCOPIC STERILIZATION.    In this newer operation the fallopian tubes are sealed off by a tubular instrument inserted through a tiny incision in the abdominal wall. The procedure is generally inexpensive, and like a vasectomy, it may be done under a local anesthetic with only minimal hospitalization necessary. It leaves no scars.

Both tubal ligation and laproscopy are highly effective sterilization techniques. Although they do not prevent ovulation, the released eggs cannot be fertilized, and there are no harmful effects on the woman who has undergone such an operation. Here again, a decision for sterilization should be firm, since the operation is irreversible.

INCREASED USE OF STERILIZATION.    Indications are that contraceptive sterilization is becoming a more prevalent phenomenon in the United States. The proportion of currently married couples with contraceptive sterilizations has risen from 8 percent reported in 1965 to 11 percent in the 1970 National Fertility Study and to 16 percent in the 1973 National Survey on Family Growth (NSFG). The proportion surgically sterilized has grown particularly among couples who have had all the children they want—from 12 percent in 1965 to 18 percent in 1970 and to 29 percent in 1973. The sexual distribution of sterilization varies, however, by race. Westoff (1976:55) notes: "Among whites, male and female procedures are almost equally represented among sterilized couples; but among more than nine out of 10 black sterilized couples, it is the woman who had had the operation."

The sterilization option is being taken by an increasing but still relatively small proportion of the population. Many features of sterilization are attractive: for example, its permanence, the ease with which it can be effected, and the possible salutary effects on sexual activity. With sterilization, the necessity of a decision about recreational versus procreational sex is erased—all sex is recreational and requires no artificial, mechanical, or chemical preparation.

## Oral Contraceptives

According to the 1970 National Fertility Study, 35 percent of the women interviewed were not using any means of contraception. However, only 7 percent were indiscriminately risking getting pregnant. The rest were either pregnant, had recently been pregnant, or were trying to get pregnant (15 percent), or were subfecund (13 percent).

Among all married women 15–44 years old in the 1973 National Survey of Family Growth, 25.1 percent were using the Pill—an increase from 22.3 percent in 1970 and 15.3 percent in 1965. Among contraceptors in 1973, 36 percent were using the Pill, up slightly from 1970. If one compares 1973 with 1970 and 1965 data, the Pill is used by a larger proportion of women in each successive study regardless of age. The younger women are also more likely to use the Pill than older women. In 1973, 65 percent of the 15–24-year-old current contraceptors were using the Pill compared to 35 percent of the 25–34-year-olds and 18 percent of the 35–44 age group. These differences partially reflect the generation gap and a tendency of older women to choose sterilization. Westoff (1976:55) notes that "there is no race differential in the choice of the pill other than the spectacular increase in use among young black married women. Among black contraceptors 15–24, pill use grew from 27.8 percent of all contraceptors in 1965 to 59.3 percent in 1970 and 73.5 percent in 1973."

By 1970, about thirty brands of oral contraceptives in pill form were on the market, all requiring prescriptions. Most of these are called "combination" pills because they contain both synthetic estrogen and synthetic progesterone, the two female hormones. Under normal conditions in the adult female, a small amount of estrogen stimulates the ovaries to produce and release an egg while progesterone prepares the uterus to receive it. If the egg is not fertilized, it, along with the lining of the uterus, is released during menstruation.

The combination pill works by utilizing important properties of the two hormones. A larger amount of estrogen and progestin (the label for the synthetic progesterone) than are naturally secreted prohibit further egg production, and for the twenty days of the cycle when the Pill is taken, the biochemical system is deceived into thinking a state of pregnancy exists. When the Pill is stopped for about ten days, the body automatically responds to the reduction in hormones by producing a menstrual period.

SIDE EFFECTS OF THE PILL. The contraceptive pill does have some side effects—both negative and positive. The disadvantageous side effects have been the subject of much discussion and debate. Perhaps the most serious charge against the Pill is that its usage is associated with higher incidences of cancer of the breast and cervix. Even though at the present time there is no real conclusive evidence that the contraceptive pill causes cancer in women, this charge must be carefully considered by users of this form of contraception, and at the same time manufacturers of the Pill must not cease their efforts to render the charge totally false and have, in fact, done so. There is also evidence that a definite association exists between blood-clotting disorders (thromboembolism) and the use of oral contraceptives. The estimated death rate from blood clotting in women not taking the contraceptive pill is one in 200,000 per year; for users, the death rate is about six in 200,000 each year—another side effect that must be corrected before this type of contraceptive can be considered safe to use. There are other negative side effects of oral contraceptives, but they do not seem to be formidable obstacles for many women. However, physicians do not usually prescribe the contraceptive pill for women with family histories that include circulatory, cancer, liver, or diabetic problems. For women who use the Pill, the threat of a heart attack is heightened considerably if they also smoke. The figures in Table 19–3, taken from Food and Drug Administration data, indicate just how strongly smoking, the Pill, and the risk of a fatal heart attack are interrelated.

Beginning April 3, 1970, manufacturers were required to provide labels warning of the dangers associated with simultaneous use of the Pill and smoking. At a press conference releasing the findings above and the new regulations, the Commissioner of the Food and Drug Administration issued this warning: "If you take the pill, don't smoke; if you must smoke, find another method of contraception" (see Mintz, 1978:A1).

The Westoffs (1971) detailed some of the positive side effects of the oral contraceptive:

> With it doctors are able to treat a number of menstrual problems such as excessive bleeding and painful menstruation, and hormonal problems such as "hot flashes" which afflict women about to enter menopause because their ovaries are no longer working efficiently. The Pill also, as mentioned, is an aid to infertile women in regulating their ovaries, it allows women to have light periods, have them when they want them, or not have them at all. It avoids, for some women, all the symptoms of the approaching natural period—depression, backaches, fatigue, irritability, breast soreness, insomnia. It, of course, prevents the need for abortions which might have taken place because of accidental pregnancies,

**TABLE 19–3**

**Relationship Between the Pill, Smoking, and Fatal Heart Attacks**

| USE PILL | SMOKE | AGE AND RISK OF A FATAL HEART ATTACK | |
|---|---|---|---|
| | | 30–39 YEARS OLD | 40–44 YEARS OLD |
| Yes | Yes | 1 in 10,000 | 1 in 1,700 |
| Yes | No | 1 in 50,000 | 1 in 10,000 |
| No | No | 1 in 100,000 | 1 in 14,000 |

and thus prevents the risks which abortion implies. And for many women, the relief they experience in not having to face the possibility of an unwanted pregnancy which often produced apprehensiveness before, during, and after each act of intercourse, has no doubt created happier and more satisfying sexual enjoyment for them. Finally, and most important, the Pill has allowed millions of women to achieve a higher degree of control over their family planning. Women can now decide not only when and if they want to menstruate, but when and if they want to have children.

## Other Methods

INTRAUTERINE DEVICES.   Another option available to couples who wish to prohibit conception is the IUD—the intrauterine device. These devices are usually made of plastic or metal and are inserted into the uterus through the cervix. Once in place the IUD seems to offer reliable protection against pregnancy.

The IUD was introduced into the United States in 1960 but did not become generally available until about 1964. "By 1973, an estimated 1.8 million married women, nearly 10 percent of all currently married women employing contraceptives, were using the IUD" (Westoff, 1976:55). This approach to contraception has been rather readily adopted by many family-planning agencies because it is inexpensive, can be inserted by a physician in a matter of minutes, may remain in place several years, and if successfully placed, will not be felt by the user.

The IUD does have some disadvantages. Some women expel it (about 10 percent are expelled during the first year after insertion). The estimates are that about 40 percent of women who expel the IUD are able to retain a subsequent insertion. The onset of infection due to the IUD is 3 percent or lower, and accidental perforation of the uterus is rare.

IUDs are now manufactured in a variety of shapes and sizes and types of material. There is no evidence that connects use of an IUD with cancer or other unfavorable health consequences. This is a contraceptive approach that has much to offer. It certainly creates a situation that converts possible procreational sex into recreational sex, and no "messy" preparation is required. It is quite likely that this contraceptive strategy will be more widely used as further technical developments continue to reduce possible discomforting side effects.

FOAMS, JELLIES, AND CREAMS.   A number of contraceptive products are available at the proverbial corner drugstore that, if used properly, can be very effective in preventing conception. A measured amount of the material (a foam, jelly, or cream) is transferred from a container to a tubular applicator and expelled into the vagina, usually immediately prior to intercourse. The material acts in two ways: first to block the cervix and second to kill the sperm that are deposited during intercourse. Contraceptive foams are frequently used by women whose physician will not prescribe the contraceptive pill or insert an IUD until some specified time after a birth.

The major disadvantages of this approach are that it may be somewhat "messy" and it requires either advance preparation or a break in the sexual encounter. It is not effective for an extended period of time; in fact, the effectiveness of contraceptive foam decreases sharply fifteen to thirty minutes after it has been inserted. It also requires a new insertion for each act of intercourse. Even so, contraceptive foams, jellies, and creams are used by millions of couples with satisfactory results, especially when used with another method, such as the diaphragm or condom.

THE CONDOM AND THE DIAPHRAGM.   One contraceptive that is readily available and easy to use is the condom—a thin sheath of rubber that is rolled over the erect penis prior to intercourse. Before the introduction of the Pill, the condom was the most widely used means of contraception. It is still widely used, particularly among the unmarried, who may only irregularly face the possibility of conception. In the 1965 National Fertility Study (see Ryder and Westoff, 1971), among women under 30 years of age use of the condom by their partners was second to the use of the Pill, while among those between 30 and 44 years of age use of the condom by their partners was the leading type of contraceptive device in current use (see Table 19–4). In 1973, 13.5 percent of married women using contraceptives had partners using condoms—down from 14.2 percent in 1970 and 21.9 percent in 1965. Partners of women 35–44 years old in 1973 were more likely to be using condoms than partners of younger women. Among this older group the condom ranked as high as the Pill, 17.4 to 17.7 percent, respectively.

The diaphragm is used more in the older age group than the Pill and is much less prevalent among younger women. The diaphragm is a circular rubber device with a stiff but malleable ring around the outside. It is usually filled with a contraceptive jelly and very precisely inserted into the vagina so that it fits snugly over the cervix. The diaphragm acts as a barrier and the jelly as a lethal agent to the sperm deposited there during intercourse.

Both the condom and the diaphragm are very effective contraceptive devices when used properly. The major disadvantage of both is that they require some advance expectation of and preparation for intercourse. The most prevalent criticism of the condom is that it reduces sensory satisfaction. However, the more expensive lubricated condoms are less frequently criticized.

THE RHYTHM METHOD.   The last contraceptive option to be mentioned here is the so-called rhythm method, which is used almost exclusively by persons affiliated with the Roman Catholic Church. It is the only contraceptive strategy endorsed by that church. The idea behind the rhythm method is that certain days of the month are "safe" for intercourse and other days are not safe for intercourse. Suffice it to say that ovulation is a difficult phenomenon to predict, and most females are less than totally regular in their menstrual cycles.

As Ryder and Westoff (1971:186) note from the 1965 National Fertility Study, "A majority (53 percent) of all Catholic wives 18–39 were not conforming or had at some time not conformed to their Church Magisterium's position on birth control, a significant increase from the 38 percent of 5 years before and the 30 percent estimated in 1955—an increase in reporting if not in fact."

## Some Alternatives for the Future

"When one considers that just 15 years ago, contraceptive sterilization, the pill and the IUD were used by only a trivial proportion of couples or were nonexistent, and that today they completely dominate the picture, one

**TABLE 19–4**

**Current Contraceptive Practice Among Married U.S. Women**

| Contraceptive Practice | AGE 15–44 | | | AGE 15–24 | | | AGE 25–34 | | | AGE 35–44 | | |
|---|---|---|---|---|---|---|---|---|---|---|---|---|
| | 1973 | 1970 | 1965 | 1973 | 1970 | 1965 | 1973 | 1970 | 1965 | 1973 | 1970 | 1965 |
| **All races** | | | | | | | | | | | | |
| U.S. total (in thousands) | 26,646 | 25,577 | 24,710 | 5,977 | 6,212 | 5,324 | 11,311 | 10,484 | 9,316 | 9,358 | 8,881 | 10,070 |
| No. in sample | 7,566 | 5,884 | 4,810 | 1,776 | 1,429 | 1,067 | 3,202 | 2,412 | 1,815 | 2,588 | 2,043 | 1,928 |
| Percentage not using contraception | 30.3 | 34.9 | 36.1 | 31.2 | 36.7 | 40.0 | 27.0 | 31.3 | 31.7 | 33.6 | 38.1 | 38.1 |
| Percentage using contraception | 69.7 | 65.0 | 63.9 | 68.8 | 63.4 | 59.8 | 73.0 | 68.6 | 68.3 | 66.4 | 61.9 | 61.9 |
| Wife sterilized | 8.6 | 5.5 | 4.5 | 2.6 | 0.6 | 0.8 | 8.3 | 5.4 | 4.7 | 12.9 | 9.1 | 6.3 |
| Husband sterilized | 7.8 | 5.1 | 3.3 | 1.5 | 0.8 | 0.9 | 8.2 | 5.0 | 3.7 | 11.3 | 8.1 | 4.1 |
| Pill | 25.1 | 22.3 | 15.3 | 44.9 | 37.1 | 29.2 | 25.7 | 23.8 | 17.2 | 11.8 | 10.0 | 6.1 |
| IUD | 6.7 | 4.8 | 0.7 | 7.2 | 5.6 | 1.1 | 9.0 | 6.6 | 0.9 | 3.5 | 2.2 | 0.4 |
| Diaphragm | 2.4 | 3.7 | 6.3 | 1.1 | 1.6 | 2.6 | 2.3 | 3.8 | 6.0 | 3.4 | 5.0 | 8.6 |
| Condom | 9.4 | 9.2 | 14.0 | 5.7 | 5.7 | 9.4 | 9.7 | 9.2 | 15.9 | 11.5 | 11.7 | 14.7 |
| Withdrawal | 1.5 | 1.4 | 2.6 | 0.8 | 1.0 | 1.4 | 1.3 | 1.4 | 2.2 | 2.1 | 1.6 | 3.5 |
| Foam | 3.5 | 3.9 | 2.1 | 2.7 | 4.8 | 3.0 | 4.4 | 4.8 | 2.8 | 2.9 | 2.4 | 1.0 |
| Rhythm | 2.8 | 4.1 | 6.9 | 1.3 | 2.1 | 4.6 | 2.3 | 3.9 | 6.8 | 4.3 | 5.8 | 8.3 |
| Douche | 0.6 | 2.1 | 3.3 | 0.2 | 1.6 | 3.6 | 0.5 | 1.5 | 2.8 | 0.9 | 3.2 | 3.7 |
| Other | 1.3 | 2.9 | 4.9 | 1.0 | 2.5 | 3.2 | 1.1 | 3.2 | 5.3 | 1.8 | 2.8 | 5.2 |
| Total Percentage | 100.0 | 100.0 | 100.0 | 100.0 | 100.0 | 100.0 | 100.0 | 100.0 | 100.0 | 100.0 | 100.0 | 100.0 |

SOURCE: Charles F. Westoff, "Trends in contraceptive practice: 1965–1973," *Family Planning Perspectives* 8(March/April, 1976):56. Reprinted with permission from *Family Planning Perspectives*, Vol. 8, No. 2, 1976.

must conclude that a veritable revolution in contraceptive practice has indeed occurred." This statement by Charles Westoff (1976:55), the Princeton demographer who has charted these changes since 1955, is a good place to start a discussion of future contraceptive options.

There is little dissent among demographic experts that the future quality of life is tied to our ability to limit the growth and control the distribution of the population. Vast efforts and funds are being expended on the development of new and improved methods of contraception and the diffusion of contraceptive information and techniques to the public. On the horizon are many new possibilities for contraception. The Westoffs[3] offer a partial listing of what future fertility control may offer:

For use by the female:

1. Once-a-month pill—estrogen-progestin
2. Once-a-month injection—estrogen-progestin
3. Long-term injection, lasting 3 to 6 months—estrogen-progestin
4. Continuous low-dose progestin only in the form of:
   a) pill
   b) capsule implant under the skin
   c) removable vaginal insert
   d) long-term injection
   e) skin contact absorption—a highly potent progestin could be absorbed through skin (for example from a ring or cosmetic)
   f) IUD released (from hormone-impregnated intrauterine device)
5. Postcoital estrogen taken orally (morning-after pill)
6. Immunization against sperm
7. Improved methods to detect ovulation
8. Reversible tubal occlusion (fallopian tube would be plugged instead of cut)
9. Sex determination (by choosing the sex fewer children would be required to achieve the desired family of boys and girls)

For use by the male:

1. Implant under skin of male hormone to suppress spermatogenesis
2. Injections to suppress sperm production every 3 to 6 months
3. Implant under skin of progestin to prevent maturation of sperm
4. Pill to act on testes and prevent maturation of sperm
5. Pill to alter chemistry of seminal fluid

---

[3] From *From Now to Zero: Fertility, Contraception, and Abortion in America*, by Charles F. Westoff and Leslie Aldridge Westoff, by permission of Little, Brown and Co., Boston. Copyright © 1968, 1971 by Charles F. Westoff and Leslie Aldridge Westoff.

6. Immunization with substance to counteract sperm production
7. Reversible sterilization (by plugging the vasa deferentia or cutting them in a way that can be reversed

The above listing is only partial, to be sure, but it should give an idea of the alternatives now being considered for the future. However, all this technical progress will be of little or no value unless the "new" and "improved" techniques are adopted by the public. Our culture still has many of the vestiges of a frontier world view. One index of this orientation is the continued positive pronatal approach of many of our institutions, the mass media, and many individuals. A postindustrial substitute for this value orientation may be necessary for population growth to subside.

## Sex and Contraceptive Decisions

Every couple who wish to limit the number of children or to space the children they do want should mutually decide on contraceptive strategies. That decision should be conjoined with an equally strong mutual commitment to religiously practice contraception. But beyond contraception it is important for each couple to reach some decisions regarding sexual behavior.

It should go without saying that sexual activity is an essential ingredient of married life. Such activity too easily becomes ritualistic—Monday, Wednesday, and Friday from 10 to 10:30 P.M.; 20 minutes for foreplay, five minutes for intercourse, five minutes for afterplay; the man on top of the woman 95 percent of the time. But if recreational sexual activity is to be a vibrant and vital part of the marriage experience, it is necessary for some of it to be spontaneous and experimental. Because reproduction often becomes an unwanted result of recreational sexual activity, any educational program dealing with the population problem should include information on sexual behavior. Such a program should include discussions of the frequency with which intercourse occurs, alternatives to intercourse, and techniques of communicating the sexual needs and desires of each partner.

In an interesting spin-off from the National Fertility Studies of 1965 and 1970, Westoff (1974) was able to examine the relationship between type of contraceptive used and frequency of sexual intercourse in marriage. Two of the findings are especially relevant here. First: "On the average, the coital frequency reported by pill users (10.0 in the previous four weeks) was nearly 25 percent higher than the average frequency reported by women using all other methods combined." Second: "There may have been a real increase in coital frequency between 1965 and 1970 among women who are married and living with their husbands. This increase of 21 percent (from an average of 6.8 to 8.2 times in the four weeks

539

prior to the interview in the periods covered by the two nationwide studies) was found in different degrees for all age groups, for women who did not use contraception and for those who did and, among contraceptors, for virtually every type of contraceptive use."

Sexual intercourse and its occasional result, pregnancy, are a central part of the marital experience. Decisions about the practice of sex, contraceptive usage, if and when to have children, how to relate to each other during pregnancy, what to do about childbirth, whether to feed the new child by bottle or breast, sex after birth, whether the woman will go back into the labor force and when—all are part of the tremendous force that fertility exerts on the family. The fact that reproductive decisions and their aftermaths constitute only part of the total configuration of pressures faced by the family makes the demographic process of fertility all the more important for family stability.

## MIGRATION

*Intergenerational relationships among the nonwhite population are frequently closer and more continuing than among the white middle class, partly because most family members remain concentrated in the same geographical area.*

About 40 million Americans change their home addresses at least once in any one year. This fact would seem to be especially salient to an understanding of some strains on the American family concomitant with an industrial and urban environment. In order to understand the effects of migration on the family it is necessary to ask, Just how much migration occurs, and what kinds of migration are most prevalent?

David Austen, Stock, Boston

**TABLE 19–5**
**Mobility of the U.S. Population**

| RACE AND SEX | TOTAL POPULATION IN 1970 [a] | SAME HOUSE IN 1970 AND 1975 (NON-MOVERS) | DIFFERENT HOUSE IN U.S. IN 1975 (MOVERS) | | | | | |
|---|---|---|---|---|---|---|---|---|
| | | | TOTAL | WITHIN SAME SMSA [b] | BETWEEN SMSAs | FROM OUTSIDE SMSAs TO SMSAs | FROM SMSAs TO OUTSIDE SMSAs | OUTSIDE SMSAs IN 1970 AND 1975 |
| Total population | 193,512 | 99,651 | 79,838 | 36,710 | 12,252 | 5,127 | 6,721 | 19,029 |
| Percentage | 100.0 | 51.5 | 41.3 | 19.0 | 6.3 | 2.6 | 3.5 | 9.8 |
| White | 169,147 | 88,248 | 68,910 | 29,911 | 11,187 | 4,615 | 6,349 | 16,848 |
| Percentage | 100.0 | 52.2 | 40.7 | 17.7 | 6.6 | 2.7 | 3.8 | 10.0 |
| Negro | 21,377 | 10,217 | 9,778 | 6,125 | 869 | 463 | 325 | 1,994 |
| Percentage | 100.0 | 47.8 | 45.7 | 28.7 | 4.1 | 2.2 | 1.5 | 9.3 |
| Male | 93,450 | 47,515 | 38,768 | 17,566 | 6,087 | 2,522 | 3,346 | 9,246 |
| Percentage | 100.0 | 50.8 | 41.5 | 18.8 | 6.5 | 2.7 | 3.6 | 9.9 |
| Female | 100,061 | 52,136 | 41,070 | 19,143 | 6,165 | 2,605 | 3,375 | 9,783 |
| Percentage | 100.0 | 52.1 | 41.0 | 19.1 | 6.2 | 2.6 | 3.4 | 9.8 |

SOURCE: U.S. Bureau of the Census, *Current Population Reports*, "Mobility of the Population of the United States, March 1970 to March 1975." Series P-20, No. 285, October, 1975.

NOTE: In thousands of persons 4 years old and over. Based on Current Population Survey; includes members of the Armed Forces living off post or with their families on post, but excludes all other members of the Armed Forces; refers to 243 SMSAs as defined in 1970 census publications.

[a] Includes those abroad on March 1, 1970, and those with no report on residence in 1970, not shown separately.

[b] SMSA stands for Standard Metropolitan Statistical Area.

Information on migration comes from surveys conducted by the Census Bureau. As the data in Table 19–5 indicate, 51.5 percent of the population lived in the same house in 1975 as in 1970. For those who moved, the largest percentage stayed in the same metropolitan area or city.

The real importance of the migration data in Table 19–5 is reflected in a statement by McAllister et al. (1973):

> It is our contention that every change of residence requires some degree of adjustment to new environmental conditions. Since most moves are local, most moves do not require the potentially traumatic readjusting of deeply rooted social conventions. Most of the readjustment faced by such movers "had to do with becoming familiar with a new physical location and with forming new social relationships" (see Gulick, Bowerman, and Back, 1962:357).

McAllister and his colleagues (1973) analyzed data from two interviews with a nationwide sample of 1,476 households, one conducted in 1966 and the other in 1969. What they found is that essentially the amount

541

of interaction increases for women who have previously moved, reflecting the extra effort required to become a bona fide member of the new neighborhood. They also discovered, much like Litwak (1960b), that migration does not appreciably diminish the amount of interaction that occurs between the mover and former neighborhood friends.

One of the greatest anxieties of moving concerns the question of the children experiencing difficulty in making new friends or in adjusting to a new school. Barrett and Noble (1973) found that a rather large percentage (nearly 80 percent) of their mover sample reported that the children had little or no trouble with the problem of either friends or school. To be sure, certain adjustments are required; but most of these adjustments are encountered with a desire for success that is usually forthcoming, more frequently than not, sooner than expected. In actuality, most voluntary moves are begun with an adequate amount of prior anticipatory socialization that defines the move as an adventure and its successful completion producing an even better life than before. Even involuntary moves are usually faced with some optimism, because the result will be a better house and neighborhood, more family income, and more chances for recreation.

Among persons who move from an impoverished area, like white migrants from eastern Kentucky or blacks moving from rural to urban areas, or from South to North, the chances are fairly good that the migration is part of a migratory stream. Schwarzweller, Brown, and Mangalam (1971), in studying white migrants from Appalachia, discovered that these migrants moved into neighborhoods in the city where their former mountain neighbors lived. This same phenomenon has been noted among migratory blacks. This type of move eases the fear of moving to a new environment and adjusting when the destination is reached.

Migration is becoming a way of life in America—something almost everyone experiences, usually a number of times. The real adjustments required by a move are concerned not so much with the destination, but rather with the multitudinous and complex decisions that have to be made prior to and during the move. This is when the family really feels the effects of the move. Everyone gets tired, the household is in a state of massive confusion, things invariably get lost or broken, time schedules are not honored, and everyone gets tense and nervous.

The chances for strained communications and sarcastic remarks must increase at least 500 percent during a move—particularly when the weather is hot. Moves are less demanding on the family when everyone is busy and stays out of the others' ways, when everyone makes an effort not to let frustration show, and when everything is organized but not rigid. Migration is essentially a demographic process that, on an individual and family level, exerts tremendous pressures for conflict. But most families survive because migration is usually voluntary. People generally move in order to get closer to a desired goal. The difficulties involved in moving are costs that most people are willing to make because the profits at the end of the line are worth the effort.

# DEATH

The death of a member of the family, besides having a tremendous emotional impact on one's life, carries with it some extremely important role requirements for those who remain. In the United States at least, the transition from married couple to a widow/widower status is usually accomplished very smoothly, though often painfully. Everybody usually understands his or her role and his or her place in the scheme of things. The spouse who remains is shuffled from one place to another, from one person to another until after the funeral, when the reality that death is final and one is alone hits home. One cannot prepare oneself for the death of a loved one. There is no anticipatory socialization, in America at least, for the bereaved role, and life must go on. Those left must nurse their emotional fibers while the family unit must adapt in both structure and functioning to fill the void left by the member who died.

## Some Factors Affecting the Bereaved Role

Death, like many events in life, must be dealt with cognitively and neutralized or defined so that its impact can be endured and tolerated. How people react to the death of a family member depends on several factors. These factors help define the boundaries of appropriate bereavement:

*Death is never easy to accept, especially for the young. Fortunately, most of those touched by the death of a loved one will be sustained by family and society.*

Ted Polumbaum

RELATIONSHIP OF THE PERSON TO THE DECEASED. Actually two components of relationship should be considered: (a) role in a structural sense and (b) role in a dynamic-interactional sense. A widow is generally allowed much more flexibility than a widower to vent emotional feelings. She is allowed, even encouraged, to openly express the loss she feels. The widower, however, is constrained by the dictum that the male is strong and brave in a crisis. The rules of etiquette for the widower insist that he comfort others at their loss while controlling his own feelings of being left alone. His grief is expected to be private—an experience that must be held back until the public ceremonies are over and the family and friends have returned home.

If the couple had been especially close, a situation in which the husband and wife relationship had been saturated with mutual love and affection, the widower is faced with conflicting bereavement expectations. On the one hand, he is allowed greater flexibility in expressing his grief, while on the other he is expected to show restraint because their relationship was a full and vibrant one. Thus, if the dynamic-interactional relationship between the husband and wife had been rich, the widow/widower bereaved role is more similar than if the relationship had been lacking in quality.

AGE OF THE DECEASED. If the couple had a long life together and the deceased was rather old at death, the widow or widower is allowed and expected to show a more intense reaction to the loss than if the deceased spouse was young. In addition, the length of time in the bereaved role is expected to be greater the longer the couple spent time together. If the spouses were rather young, and the length of marriage relatively short, the widow/widower is expected to have a shorter bereavement. Friends and relatives will, in subtle ways, insist that the younger bereaved person move back into the mainstream of life and to move more quickly toward a "normal" set of activities.

PRESENCE OF DEPENDENT CHILDREN. If the widow/widower must continue the day-to-day process of child rearing, bereavement is almost a luxury that must be curtailed for the sake of the children, who are considered less resilient to the demands of pain and sorrow. For such a situation bereavement necessarily becomes a role that is compartmentalized and private. If dependent children are not present, the person must still bear his or her grief in private, but without the benefit of being forced to compartmentalize that experience. There are fewer daily activities that must be performed and consequently fewer opportunities to abdicate the bereaved role. This can be an excruciating experience for the bereaved person who has no place to go and nothing to do but sit around the home where the dead spouse's absence is painfully obvious. In fact, the most painful aspect of the bereaved role may not be the actual absence of the departed spouse, but rather the manifold evidence of his or her former presence.

CIRCUMSTANCES UNDER WHICH DEATH OCCURRED. When the spouse dies of an illness that is incurable and the last years, months, and weeks of life were exceedingly painful, some comfort is derived from the fact that pain ceases with death. No one wants his or her loved one to endure pain, especially when there was no hope of the pain ever being controlled. By the same token, if death occurred as a result of an accident and the dead spouse never had to contemplate death or endure pain, the bereaved can find some comfort in the speed with which it occurred.

When death occurs as a result of suicide, the bereaved usually suffers guilt, wondering if there was anything that he or she could have done to prevent it. This reaction is especially painful to the bereaved if the supposed reasons for suicide would not have made it imminent. The enactment of the bereaved role when the suicide was seemingly unnecessary and a tragic waste of life is especially difficult, because the bereaved person feels that others will blame him or her for not preventing the act.

The bereaved role is less difficult to enact when the suicide was performed because the deceased had been seriously ill and would probably have died soon anyway. Although it is never easy, the bereaved can at least understand the motive behind the suicide act. Usually less guilt is involved, and the community is much more willing to offer its condolences to the spouse.

## Stages of Bereavement

Although everyone who is left a widow or a widower reacts differently to the death of the spouse and to the bereaved role, there are probably five stages of bereavement that everyone experiences:

1. The first stage is *numbness*. The full force of reality does not occur immediately because of the complex set of activities that must be performed. The funeral arrangements require rational decisions—choice of funeral home, casket, and pall bearers, and letting everyone know that one's spouse died. In addition, arrangements must be made to switch checking accounts from joint to single, to arrange for one's occupational activities to be performed, and to take care of visiting relatives.

2. The numbness begins to become *loneliness* at the funeral and immediately after everyone has returned home. For the first time the remaining spouse is alone—alone with himself or herself and the reality that the spouse is dead and buried. That loneliness is so powerful that the remaining spouse may feel it in every fiber of his or her being. It is perhaps fortunate that the person is usually completely drained, physically and emotionally, from all of the events surrounding the funeral ceremony. As the days go by it becomes necessary for the bereaved person to learn to cope with the facts of death and loneliness. These facts are brought home all too often by seeing old acquaintances, by the painful task of writing thank-you notes for the flowers and other remembrances sent by well-wishing friends, and by the very sobering experience of visiting the gravesite.

3. Loneliness transforms into the experience of *emptiness*—a feeling in the core of one's being that part of him or her is gone. The emptiness is something that is both emotional and physical—something that makes the bereaved person aware that marriage is not just a process of uniting two people. Marriage is a total fusion of two personalities at a deep level of personal involvement.

4. The emptiness subsides slowly, but usually as the bereaved person begins to move back into a *routine of normality,* as he or she begins to take on an identity that is again singular instead of plural. As the bereaved person moves back into the world, he or she begins to accept new responsibilities, to engage in new encounters, and to move toward a more normal life-style, trying to adapt to the only healthy reality available —a new, though perhaps different, life.

5. The last stage in the bereavement process is *adjustment to the new single identity.* For some persons this adjustment involves a resignation to living out one's life alone. For others it entails a consideration of finding a new partner, of starting the marital life anew.

Those who embark on a search for a new marital partner are generally in for quite a shock. They soon discover that instead of being the smooth and suave sophisticates their former spouses claimed them to be, a more apt description would be a bumpkin about 16 years old. Extensive marital experience does not go far in the dating/courting arena—the same mistakes are probably made at 55 or 60 that were made when one was 15 and 16 and just entering the male-female contest.

A young person might ask, "Why do older people get married anyway?" One reason that the youngster might understand is sex. A good friend who is a lawyer in one of the geriatric sections of Florida told me of a little old man and woman, both in their seventies, both using walking canes, who came into his office one morning and asked him to arrange an annulment. They had been married a week. The man said he thought she wanted the same thing he did—companionship. She told my friend, "Honey, he can't do anything for me—I want a real man!"

A misunderstanding of motives is just one of the possible dangers in courting during the late fifties, sixties, seventies, and eighties. But there are some possible advantages. One distinct possibility is that neither of the seekers is necessarily bound by the usual conventions of etiquette that seem to restrain younger people. An older man, whose wife had died about a year previously, received in his mail one day a note saying:

Dear ——,

I understand from —— and —— [mutual friends] that you lost your wife a year ago. My husband passed away 6 months ago, shortly after we moved here from ——. I have had a difficult time meeting people here in ——. I like to drink beer, eat pizza, go to movies, bowl or just sit and talk. I believe the idea that it is the male's prerogative to initiate a relationship is antiquated. If you don't call me by Saturday I plan to call you.

Sincerely,

The next day he called her, they had their first date that Saturday, several weeks later they became engaged, and several months later they did get married. The beauty of the relationship is that they needed companionship and the love each needed to give—they did not want to play adolescent dating games. Courtship in the later years of life, after one's original spouse has died, can be a very exciting and re-creating experience. Unfortunately, in many cases meddling children can prohibit their widowed father or mother from reachieving the type of marital happiness they once had by being too sensitive to what the community might think. Persons who have had a meaningful marital relationship usually need to give their love to someone else—someone who is not a substitute for the departed spouse, but who is a new love object. The death of one's spouse does not mean that the need to love is buried. That a widow or widower desperately needs to express love is usually a compliment to the departed spouse, not an indication that the love for the departed spouse was less than it should have been.

To say that the death of a family member requires a tremendous adjustment in the family is obvious. That adjustment can be generally negative or positive. The most sensible approach to death is to allow the bereaved to fully and sensitively express his or her grief. But grief must subside eventually. Life is too short to require that the widow or widower live out the remaining years in sackcloth and ashes.

Out of the darkness and despair of death can come a new life—a life that is meaningful and vital. Children owe the remaining parent freedom and respect. They owe to the parent the freedom to establish a new life with a new spouse, if that is what is wanted.

## Number of Survivors

The preceding pages have focused on the more dynamic and relatively nonscientific aspects of death and its effects on the individuals and families who remain. Who are the widows and widowers in our society? How many are there? What are some of the forces that regulate their lives?

In 1976 the number of widows in the United States reached 10.7 million, an increase of more than 1 million since 1970. Currently, more than 1 out of every 8 women fourteen years old or older is widowed; among women under thirty-five in 1976 the proportion widowed was less than 1 percent. In the 55–64 age bracket it was 20 percent. Much more than in the past, widowhood comes at older ages. The increase in the number of widows in the 1966–76 decade resulted entirely from increases among women over fifty-five. In 1976, 9 out of every 10 widows were at least fifty-five years old and almost 4 out of 10 were at least seventy-five years old.

Widows now outnumber widowers 5 to 1 compared to a ratio of 4 to 1 in 1970 and 2 to 1 in 1940. There are now 540 widows per 100 widowers in the population.

There are several reasons for this widening gap in the number of widows relative to widowers. The first is that women have a decidedly longer average life span than men. Second, men usually marry women who are two to three years younger. Thus, the age gap at marriage plus the longer life span of women interact to account for the larger number of widows. Third, among the widowed the remarriage rates are considerably higher among men than women. A fourth, though less readily apparent, reason why there are substantially more widows than widowers concerns the age structure of society and the mortality rates. In the twentieth century, advances in medicine have dramatically affected the chances that more persons will survive past the age of sixty-five. Around 1900 about 1 in 25 persons was sixty-five or older. Today the ratio is close to 1 in 10 or 11. By the year 2000 it is estimated that 1 in 5 persons will be classified as aged—as defined in 1970, sixty-five or older. This shift will be accomplished by the reduction in births (that is, a smaller proportion of the population will be "young") and the increasing longevity of life brought about by medical advances and a higher quality of life.

As Paul Jacobson (1966) has shown for the period from 1900 to 1964, the proportion of women losing their spouses at age sixty-five rose from 20 to 32 percent. Women widowed at age thirty-five or earlier in this 64-year-period decreased from 18 to a little over 5 percent. Widowhood is increasingly a phenomenon that occurs in the later years of life in our society.

## Adjustment to Widowhood or Widowerhood

As mentioned earlier, the transition from the married state to survivor status exacts a toll, particularly in terms of role readjustment. There is some disagreement among the experts as to which survivor, the widow or widower, encounters the greater difficulty. Nye and Berardo (1973), drawing upon the work of Berardo (1970), Thompson and Streib (1961), and Bernard Kutner et al. (1956) suggest that the widower is left more socially and instrumentally isolated than the widow. Nye and Berardo (1973:603) state:

> Research evidence suggests that for a variety of reasons survivorship adaptation may be more difficult for the older husband. In comparative terms the role of the wife remains relatively unchanged upon the death of her spouse. That is, she continues to perform her household tasks, such as cleaning and cooking, in much the same manner as when her husband was alive. Indeed, such tasks often may "constitute a very important variety of meaningful activity and ability to maintain certain standards of good housekeeping often represents a challenge and a test of the degree to which the older woman is avoiding "getting old" (see Thompson and Streib, 1961). Consequently, a large proportion of aged widows can maintain separate quarters and are capable of taking

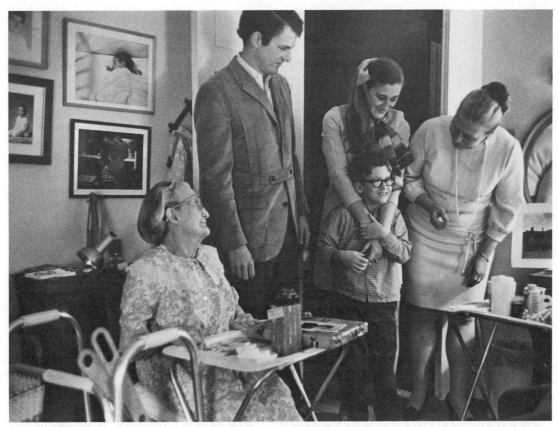

George Gardner

*The family is held together by love, across the generations.*

care of themselves. Moreover, the older widow is more likely than the widower to be welcomed into the home of her married children and to find a useful place there.

Robert Bell (1971:509) reaches a conclusion diametrically opposed to that of Nye and Berardo. He suggests that the widow has the greater role adaptation for five reasons: (a) because marriage is usually more important for the woman, the ending of marriage means the ending of a role more basic to the wife; (b) because there is less personal and social encouragement to remarry, the widow is less apt to do so; (c) because the widow's financial potential is lower, the burdens of responsibility for herself and her children are greater; (d) because culture expects her to be less socially aggressive, the widow's social life will be more restricted; and (e) because of the excess of widows over widowers, the chances of remarriage are much lower.

Although it is probably possible to offer compelling arguments for each side of the debate over who bears the greater burden, the widow or the widower, the fact remains that death creates a necessity for change.

549

The changes that occur are at the individual level (adaptation in one's life style from married to single and from together to alone; adaptation in one's social and personal identity) and at the familial level (interaction with a widowed parent is qualitatively different from the interaction that occurred when the deceased parent was still alive).

As Chevan and Korson (1972:45) have shown, one major problem faced by widows and widowers is location of residence—where to live and with whom. They indicate that proportionately, "more than two and one-half times as many widowed lived alone in 1970 as in 1940, and the percentage increase of widows in this category was slightly higher than that for widowers." In fact, in 1976 more than 87 percent of all widows under age 65 headed households, while 84 percent of those aged 65–74 and 63 percent of those aged 75 and over did so. The fact that our societal and familial norms do not prescribe that married offspring absorb their widowed parents into the family has important policy implications for how the aged will live out the remaining years of the family life cycle.

## SUMMARY AND CONCLUSIONS

This chapter has examined the impacts of three demographic processes (fertility, migration, and mortality) on the family. These processes operate interactively to provide a societal context within which individuals and families make some very personal decisions and adjustments. The most difficult aspect of relating these demographic processes to the family is bridging the gap between macro-level pressures, particularly with regard to fertility, and the reproductive decisions and acts that occur in the intimate environment of the family.

### Fertility

When the fertility behavior of the entire population is examined, certain conclusions seem inescapable. First, the average number of children per family has decreased considerably since colonial days and is now at replacement level. Second, the differences in fertility by social class (education, occupation, income), residence, race, and religion have narrowed markedly in the last 10 to 15 years. Third, a sizable problem in the United States is unwanted and excess fertility. Fourth, although relatively effective means of contraception are now available, its use is far from effective. Last, at the individual level, the problem is not necessarily a reproductive one, but rather a sexual one (that is, how to separate reproductive from recreational sex).

If the problem of overpopulation is to be solved, more is needed than just sound and fury. The public needs education about the potential and real dangers of excessive fertility. Efforts must be made to institute a national population policy, something that is nonexistent now. In addition, efforts must be made to bring about a re-examination of basic cultural values and motives that reflect pronatal ideology. Some social scientists have suggested that we are moving toward an era in which the frontier values about growth and expansion may be irrelevant if not dangerous.

## Migration

Problems related to fertility have received more attention in scientific and popular literature than has migration, although migration is a demographic reality touching the lives of about one in every five American families in any year. Although many of those moving stay within the same city, county, or state, moving requires adjustments by the individuals involved as well as by the agencies, businesses, and institutions in the communities of origin and destination. As noted in this chapter, many common-sense notions about the negative effects of migration have not been supported by research. For example, most children who move do not have major difficulties in making friends or in becoming established in new schools. Even so, the actual process of picking up one's belongings and moving them to a new residence can be a fertile ground for difficulties in a family. Migration is usually voluntary and is generally considered part of the overall goal-achievement strategy of most families. As a demographic process it has not received enough systematic and scientific attention.

## Mortality

The third demographic process examined was mortality—an abstract phenomenon that many people have difficulty coping with at either the cognitive level or the real and personal level. Death is something all of us encounter—of friends and associates or someone in the family. As we get older, the potential reality of our own death, those of parents and spouse become more salient.

Death requires personal adjustment to the loss of a loved one; coping with bereavement and sorrow; altering one's style, pattern, and rhythm of life; adapting one's role enactments to a unilateral from a reciprocal cadence. The entire structural skeleton of a modified extended family reacts to the loss of one of its actors—new role alignments are required and old relationships are reassessed. As our entire population gets older and we approach the twenty-first century, mortality as a societal phenomenon will become a social problem of much the same magnitude that fertility is today.

Fertility, migration, and mortality at the societal level affect the quality of life. At the intersocietal level these forces have serious geopolitical and moral implications, and at the individual and family levels they require serious and sincere concern and attention.

## SOME POSSIBLE IMPLICATIONS

*Every society is significantly affected by the interrelationships among and direct effects of the demographic processes of fertility, migration, and mortality. In our society, serious efforts are being made to develop highly effective contraceptive techniques and new ways to diffuse them to a population thoroughly prepared, ideologically, to adopt contraception as an integral part of married life. The biomedical sciences have been exerting tremendous efforts to control diseases and to extend the average life span while the social sciences and professions have been working on the problems of aging. What are some of the implications of these efforts, assuming they continue to be successful?*

*With regard to fertility, several consequences are possible and plausible. The average size of the American family will probably move closer to four (parents and two children) with a larger proportion of the families having only one child. Excess and unwanted fertility will drop considerably. The incidence of premarital pregnancies will markedly decline and the number of illegitimate children, along with the illegitimacy rate, will begin to decline. One consequence of more effective contraceptive techniques may be a rise in the extensiveness of coital experience prior to marriage. Within marriage, the availability of improved contraceptive techniques should lead to a better quality of marital sex and perhaps to an increase in the frequency of marital coitus.*

*These consequences will in turn have an effect on industries like children's clothing and toys. School enrollments will drop over the long term, thus decreasing the demand for teachers at all levels. Social agencies whose purpose is to aid unwed mothers and to place children for adoption will lose their clientele.*

*The long-range effects of the severe energy crisis that first became apparent in the winter of 1973–74 will be felt relative to migration. Individuals will be required to more seriously consider changing residence, particularly when that entails a long distance move. Seasonal migrations for recreational purposes will markedly decline in order to conserve fuel resources. The expansion of industrial concerns will be affected, to some extent, by the excessive costs of moving employees and by the inability to acquire the necessary energy resources to set up new plant facilities. In effect, the population of the United States will, in the future, be less migratory.*

552

*With regard to the effects of mortality, as time passes larger proportions of the population will be in the retirement stage of the family life cycle. Death and its effect on the family will be a more present experience for young children as the aged population increases. More social service agencies will be dealing with problems of senior citizens. The relationships between families of procreation and families of orientation will become more extensive, intensive, and salient as the average life span continues to expand.*

Frank Siteman

# 20

# MARITAL DISSOLUTION

*Is our divorce rate "too high"?*
*What is the probability that a marriage will end in divorce?*
*What are the effects of divorce on children?*
*Is divorce a "healthy" adjustment to a crisis in life?*

Marriages, at least most of them, are still intended to be for life. We take each other to love and to cherish, in sickness and in health, for better, for worse, until death do us part. Even where this time-honored formula of the Christian marriage ritual is not used, the parties expect, or hope, that their marriages will last. But not all marriages do last. Some marriages collapse; in fact a great many do. And when a marriage collapses, problems arise, for the spouses, their children, and the community. Hopes are dashed, a home is destroyed, and with it the economic basis of a family. Readjustment must be made, children have to be taken care of, wounds should be prevented from festering.

How do we deal with these problems? Not very intelligently. [Rheinstein, 1972:3]

This statement by distinguished law professor Max Rheinstein precisely and lucidly underscores a number of questions with which sociologists have grappled in the study of marital stability and instability. First, what types of marital dissolution exist, and how prevalent is each? Second, how widely does marital dissolution occur where children are directly involved, and what are the effects of this experience on children? Third, from a personal-humanistic perspective, what are the readjustments that must be made to marital dissolution, and how can society facilitate the achievement of stability out of instability? Last, how can our society and we as individuals more intelligently deal with the problem of marital instability?

One thing seems certain at the outset: clear-cut and solid answers to these questions are virtually impossible to obtain. When answers are proposed, consensus, even among the so-called experts, is seldom, if ever, a likely result. The usual consequence is a debate. For example, some experts openly and vehemently abhor the "high" divorce rate in the United States. They see divorce as an indication of weakness in the American family, and if the trend continues, perhaps it is on its way to extinction at worse or at least to a state of atrophy wherein the family will virtually cease to function as a stability-producing institution. Others claim the divorce rate is not only "not too high," but that divorce can be viewed as a positive adjustment to a less than adequate marriage. For them divorce does not signal a danger to the American family system at all. They would argue that the extensiveness of divorce indicates a more honest and healthy reaction to the realities of married life, and that such a propensity for divorce reflects a strength in the American family, not a weakness.

# MAJOR FORMS OF MARITAL DISSOLUTION

All marriages are eventually dissolved—if not voluntarily, then involuntarily, by death. On the surface it would be quite easy to focus on the very real consequence of marital dissolution—absence of a spouse—without distinguishing between the forms of marital dissolution. We shall, however, consider the major forms of dissolution, which are death and divorce.

## Death

Death accounts for the majority of all marriages dissolved within the United States each year. For example, Davis (1973) estimates that in 1970 about 908,200 marriages terminated with the death of a spouse. This is almost 200,000 more than the number of marriages ended by divorce. In fact, in 1970, 19.3 per 1,000 marriages in existence were dissolved by death as compared to 15.2 by divorce. Most of those who decry the massive "divorce problem" in the United States are probably unaware that divorce takes a back seat to mortality. Although the proportion of divorces relative to the total number of marital dissolutions has recently increased, population projections suggest that death will play an even larger role as we move into the twenty-first century. Between 1970 and 1977, the median age of the U.S. population rose 1½ years, to 29.4. By the year 2000 the median age in the U.S. will be 35.5. Since 1972, the average life expectancy at birth has risen by more than a year, to 77 years for women and 69.1 for men. This maturing and "graying" of America will have far-reaching implications, not the least of which may be a greater concern for marital dissolutions caused by death.

## Legal Divorce

Although concern for death as the major cause of dissolutions in the future is important, most of us are more concerned with the present, with what is happening now and what it means. Such concern is merited. The United States has the highest divorce rate in the world and one that has risen dramatically in recent years. If one takes the divorce rate as an index of the health of the family system, prospects for the future are not bright.

As the data in Table 20–1 indicate, it was not until 1967 that the number of divorces reached the half-million mark. Four years later it reached three-quarters of a million, and in 1975, for the first time, more than 1 million divorces were granted in the United States. The total of 1,036,000 divorces represented a 6 percent increase over the 977,000 recorded in 1974. The rate per 1,000 population was 4.9, almost 7 percent higher than the 4.6 per 1,000 observed in 1974—the highest annual rate ever for this country. The record high rate of 20.3 per 1,000 married women in 1975 indicates that more than 2 percent of all married women in the United States divorced during that year. Since 1964, whether one

557

looks at the rate per 1,000 or the rate per 1,000 married women, the results are identical—a doubling. In 1976, there were 1,077,000 divorces for a rate of 5 per 1,000 population—a new high. Graphically (see Figure 20–1), the conclusion is inescapable—divorce is increasing phenomenally.

Although death and divorce are the major types of marital dissolution, they do not constitute all of the possibilities. William Goode (1962b) developed a typology that views marital instability as a result of the failure of one or more individuals to perform role obligations:

**TABLE 20–1**
**Divorce and Annulment Rates in the United States**

| | | RATE PER 1,000 [a] | |
| --- | --- | --- | --- |
| YEAR | DIVORCES AND ANNULMENTS | TOTAL POPULATION | MARRIED WOMEN 15 YEARS AND OVER |
| 1975 | 1,036,000 | 4.9 | 20.3 |
| 1974 | 977,000 | 4.6 | 19.3 |
| 1973 | 915,000 | 4.4 | 18.2 |
| 1972 | 845,000 | 4.1 | 17.0 |
| 1971 | 773,000 | 3.7 | 15.8 |
| 1970 | 708,000 | 3.5 | 14.9 |
| 1969 | 639,000 | 3.2 | 13.4 |
| 1968 | 584,000 | 2.9 | 12.5 |
| 1967 | 523,000 | 2.6 | 11.2 |
| 1966 | 499,000 | 2.5 | 10.9 |
| 1965 | 479,000 | 2.5 | 10.6 |
| 1964 | 450,000 | 2.4 | 10.0 |
| 1963 | 428,000 | 2.3 | 9.6 |
| 1962 | 413,000 | 2.2 | 9.4 |
| 1961 | 414,000 | 2.3 | 9.6 |
| 1960 | 393,000 | 2.2 | 9.2 |
| 1959 | 395,000 | 2.2 | 9.3 |
| 1958 | 368,000 | 2.1 | 8.9 |
| 1957 | 381,000 | 2.2 | 9.2 |
| 1956 | 382,000 | 2.3 | 9.4 |
| 1955 | 377,000 | 2.3 | 9.3 |
| 1954 | 379,000 | 2.4 | 9.5 |
| 1953 | 390,000 | 2.5 | 9.9 |
| 1952 | 392,000 | 2.5 | 10.1 |
| 1951 | 381,000 | 2.5 | 9.9 |
| 1950 | 385,000 | 2.6 | 10.3 |

SOURCE: National Center for Health Statistics, *Advance Report: Final Divorce Statistics, 1975.* Vol. 26, No. 2, Supplement 2, May 19, 1977.

NOTE: Data refer only to events occurring within the United States. Alaska included beginning with 1959 and Hawaii with 1960.

[a] Data are based on population enumerated as of April 1 for 1950, 1960, and 1970, and estimated as of July 1 for all other years.

**FIGURE 20–1**
**Annual Divorce Rate for the United States, 1930–75**

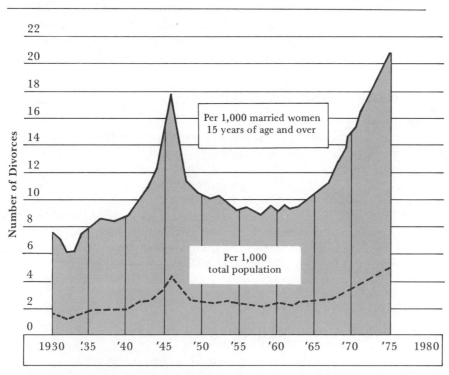

SOURCE: National Center for Health Statistics, *Advance Report: Final Divorce Statistics, 1975,* Vol. 26, No. 2, Supplement 2, May 19, 1977.

1. The uncompleted family unit: illegitimacy. Here the family unit did not come into existence. However, the missing individual obviously fails in his "father-husband" role obligations as defined by society, mother, or child. Moreover, a major indirect cause of the illegitimacy is likely to be the role-failure of both mother and father (see Chapter 6).

2. Instability when one spouse willfully departs: annulment, separation, divorce, and desertion. Instances of job desertion might also be included here, when the individual stays away from home for a long period of time on the excuse of a distant job.

3. The "empty-shell" family: in which individuals interact instrumentally, but fail essentially in the role obligation to give emotional support to one another. Here, of course, there is no public dissolution or instability but the unit is in effect dissolved. The empty-shell family will be discussed later in this chapter.

4. The crisis and strain caused by external events: the temporary or permanent unwilled absence of one spouse because of death,

imprisonment, or some impersonal catastrophe such as flood, war, or depression.

5. Internal crises that create unwilled major role-failures: mental, emotional or physical pathologies; severe mental retardation of a child; psychoses; chronic and incurable physical conditions.

## MARRIAGE AND DIVORCE

Most marital dissolutions result from either death or divorce. Because divorce is increasing in importance, we will examine it further. Two questions will guide our discussion: What is the average length of time between marriage and divorce in the United States? What are the probabilities that a person will get a divorce during his or her lifetime?

Perhaps the best, and certainly the most recent, data on marriage and divorce in the United States come from a nationwide Census Bureau study conducted in June 1975. It covers all adults born since 1900 who were living at the time of the survey. Figure 20–2 shows the fluctuation in the marriage rate between 1925 and 1975.

### Data on Marriage

The number of marriages performed in the United States in 1975 was 2,152,662—down 77,000 or 3.5 percent from 1974—a decline for the second year in a row. This occurred in spite of an increase of about 1.2 million

**FIGURE 20–2**
**Annual Marriage Rate for the United States, 1925–75**

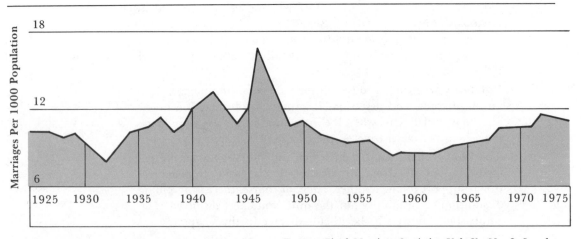

SOURCE: National Center for Health Statistics, *Advance Report: Final Marriage Statistics*, Vol. 2b, No. 2, Supplement, May 9, 1977.

in the number of unmarried women fourteen years old and older. Likewise, the marriage rate per 1,000 population declined from 10.5 in 1974 to 10.1 in 1975—a decline for the third consecutive year. In 1976, provisional figures indicate a further decline to 9.9 per 1,000 population.

The marriage rate per 1,000 unmarried women fifteen years old and older, a more sensitive index because of the age restrictions, showed a more dramatic decline because of the increase in the number of women in these age groups. In 1974 the rate was 72; in 1975 it was 67. This means that less than 7 percent of the women eligible to marry in 1975, did so.

Is marriage an artifact of the past, a custom that is being abandoned for a new status (cohabitation) or an old status now considered legitimate (remaining single)? The answer is *no*. What is happening is a tendency to delay marriage, not to avoid it altogether. As Glick and Norton (1976:8) note:

> During the last 15 years, more and more women under 30 years of age in the United States have been postponing their entrance into marriage. This pattern is apparent from the smaller proportions of women who had married by a given age among those in the youngest group (those born in 1945 to 1949) than among those in the next older group (those born in 1930 to 1934). Thus, only 87 percent of the women who were in the upper twenties in 1975 had entered marriage as compared with 92 percent of those who were in their upper twenties in 1960. When persons in the latter group had reached their early forties 15 years later, in 1975, an additional 4 percent, or a total of 96 percent had married. However, if only 4 more percent of those in their upper twenties in 1975 become married during the next 15 years when they, in turn, will be in their early forties, then a total of 91 percent of them will have ever married. If this should occur, those now in their late twenties would have the smallest proportion who eventually marry of any group in a third of a century. However, there is a reasonable likelihood that enough late marriages will occur among women now in their late twenties to increase to 93 or 94 percent the proportion of them who eventually marry.

Even with the postponement phenomenon, that over 9 out of 10 women marry, is high. Hence, it is evident that marriage is still a popular lifestyle option and will continue to be so in the foreseeable future.

## Duration of Marriage

Perhaps the best data available relative to establishing the average duration of marriage are from a Survey of Economic Opportunity conducted by the Census Bureau in spring 1967. The sample consisted of a random probability sample of 28,000 American households. Because the data for white men are considered somewhat more reliable, we will examine them more closely.

561

As the data in Figure 20–3 show, the median duration of first marriage for divorced white men was 7.6 years. The same figure for white women is 7.7 years. For black men and women the average duration of a first marriage for divorced persons is 8.2 and 8.6 years, respectively, somewhat longer than for whites. As Glick and Norton (1971:311) indicate,

**FIGURE 20–3**
**Median Duration of First Marriages of Divorced White Men, 1960–66**

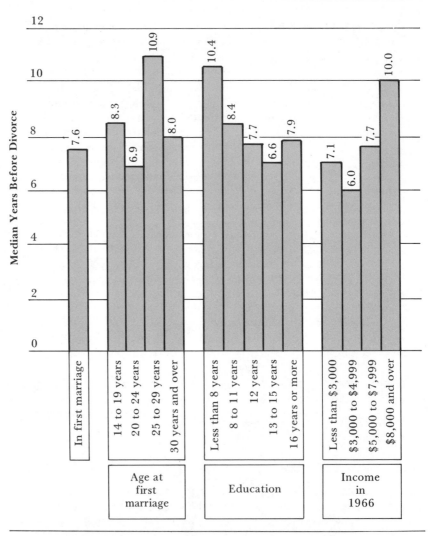

SOURCE: Paul C. Glick and Arthur J. Norton, "Frequency, Duration and Probability of Marriage and Divorce," *Journal of Marriage and the Family* 33(1971):311, Figure 1. Used by permission of the National Council on Family Relations.

"Men who obtained a divorce after the shortest period of marriage were those who married at ages 20 to 24 years, those with an incomplete college education, and those who received incomes of $3,000 to $4,999. Undoubtedly, many of these men had cut short their college training to get married and they had failed to earn as much income as they had hoped to earn, yet they had earned enough to afford the cost of divorce sooner than their peer group who had earned less money." More recent evidence (see Carter and Glick, 1976:430) indicates that the average length of marriage prior to a first divorce is dropping: "In 1973 the median stood at 6.6 years, as compared with 6.9 years in 1969 and 7.2 years in 1965." Use of an average, the median, masks the fact that in 1973 more than one in three of the marriages ending in divorce had lasted 10 years or longer while one in five ended within two years. It should also be noted that Figure 20–3 concerns white *divorced* men. To get an accurate estimate of "risk of divorce" we need to compare persons ever married to those who have obtained a divorce.

## DIVORCE

We know that the divorce rate has been climbing in recent years and that divorce is a subject receiving wide coverage by the mass media. It is also a phenomenon that has personal relevance. Think about your parents and their circle of friends; or think about your own friends and their parents—what proportion is divorced? Your answer may differ from that of other students; however, the chances are good that almost no one would say *zero*. Just how prevalent is divorce in this country?

### Data on Divorce

1. All but 4 percent of the women and 5 percent of the men between 40 and 55 years old in 1975 had married. Of those in their forties who had married, 83 percent had done so only once, 15 percent had married twice, and only 2 percent had married 3 or more times. This means, of course, that more than 8 of 10 persons in your parents' age bracket were or are still in their first marriage.

2. Whites are more likely than blacks to have married only once. Of all persons born between 1900 and 1959, the following percentages have been married only once:

|                |      |
|----------------|------|
| White males    | 64%  |
| Black males    | 53%  |
| White females  | 68%  |
| Black females  | 58%  |

These data do not seem to indicate a divorce epidemic. Most adults seem to marry and stay married to the original mate. However, when one compares younger persons with older ones in the 1975 Census study, the differences and changes are apparent.

3. A greater amount of divorce has occurred among the young, despite the fact that they have been "at risk" of divorce for a much shorter period of time. A total of 22 percent of the women ever married who were 36–40 years old in 1975 (born 1935–39) were divorced, as compared with only 13 percent of those born 1900–1904 (71–75 years old in 1975).

4. More divorces occur at young ages these days than in the past. Only 4.5 percent of the married men who were born 1900–1904 had ended their first marriage by the time they were 25 to 34 years old. For those born 1915–19 the figure is 7.9 percent, whereas it is 10.4 percent for those born in 1930–34 and 13.1 percent for those born 1945–49. As Glick and Norton (1976:4–5) note: "The divorce experience of young adults had already exceeded that of older adults when they were of comparable age."

5. The propensity to divorce earlier is seen most clearly in the median age at which first divorce occurs. Half of the men born 1900–1904 who became divorced after their first marriage did so by age 37. For men born 1930–34, the corresponding age was 31, 6 years earlier. The same kind of decline was evident for women (from 33 to 29 years old). There does not seem to be much difference in median age at first divorce by race.

Over 50 percent of the men and women whose first marriages ended in divorce obtained the divorces during their twenties.

## Probability of Divorce

With the trends outlined above, a plausible question is: *What is the probability that a marriage will end in divorce?* The answer cannot appropriately be given for a particular marriage because each marriage is unique and consists of unique individuals. However, at the macro level it is possible to develop probabilities, which Glick and Norton have done with the 1975 Census data. They say, in reaction to the data presented in Table 20–2:

> The projections imply that about one-third of the married persons between 25 and 35 years old in 1975 may eventually end their first marriage in divorce. This level is between two and three times as high as the estimated 13 percent for persons in their early seventies .... [T]he large difference between these two levels of divorce is one of the measures of the increasing propensity for more young adults to legally terminate their first marriage through a divorce proceeding.

As you can see in the last column of Table 20–2, the projected probabilities of a second marriage ending in divorce are also quite high—between 30 and 45 percent.

These figures are dramatic—one in three for those 25–35 years old and in a first marriage and over 40 percent for those in a second marriage. It is apparent that marriage is a fragile state, sensitive to all kinds of strains and stresses.

Evidence that divorce is becoming democraticized may be inferred from fewer differences in divorce experience by race and socioeconomic status. Although blacks are still more likely than whites to divorce, the differences are not nearly as great as they once were. The same is true for socioeconomic status. In recent years the propensity for divorce among men with high incomes and occupational status has increased, thus narrowing the gap in divorce between lower- and higher-status males. Divorce among women with advanced or professional degrees has always been

**TABLE 20–2**

**Divorce and Redivorce in the United States**

| | PERCENTAGES | | | |
| | FIRST MARRIAGES | | SECOND MARRIAGES | |
| YEAR OF BIRTH | DIVORCED BY 1975 | PROBABILITY OF DIVORCE [a] | REDIVORCED BY 1975 | PROBABILITY OF REDIVORCE [a] |
|---|---|---|---|---|
| *Men* | | | | |
| 1945–49 | 13 | 34 | 5 | 35 |
| 1940–44 | 17 | 31 | 6 | 32 |
| 1935–39 | 20 | 29 | 5 | 28 |
| 1930–34 | 18 | 24 | 8 | 24 |
| 1925–29 | 18 | 22 | 7 | 20 |
| 1920–24 | 18 | 20 | 9 | 18 |
| 1915–19 | 17 | 18 | 9 | 13 |
| 1910–14 | 17 | 17 | 7 | 9 |
| 1905–09 | 15 | 15 | 7 | 8 |
| 1900–04 | 13 | 13 | 6 | 6 |
| *Women* | | | | |
| 1945–49 | 17 | 38 | 8 | 44 |
| 1940–44 | 20 | 34 | 12 | 40 |
| 1935–39 | 21 | 31 | 10 | 31 |
| 1930–34 | 21 | 26 | 11 | 26 |
| 1925–29 | 21 | 24 | 14 | 23 |
| 1920–24 | 18 | 20 | 8 | 15 |
| 1915–19 | 16 | 17 | 11 | 16 |
| 1910–14 | 16 | 16 | 10 | 12 |
| 1905–09 | 15 | 15 | 9 | 9 |
| 1900–04 | 13 | 13 | 5 | 5 |

SOURCE: U.S. Department of Commerce, Bureau of the Census, Series P-20, No. 297, October, 1976.

[a] If their future divorce experience is similar to that of persons in older age groups between 1969 and 1974.

relatively high. However, in recent years the gap between highly educated women and less educated women has narrowed. This trend toward convergence and a greater evenness of the impact of divorce regardless of status does not mean that all differentials will vanish. For men and women now over thirty-five years old, education and income seem to be insulators against marital disruption. The tendency toward convergence is attributable to those under thirty-five—those born since 1940.

Students frequently ask what is the most difficult year of marriage. From the standpoint of adjustments required, the first year stands out. It should be apparent, however, that most divorces do not become final in the legal sense until the second or perhaps the third year, even when the precipitating causes occurred quite early. It is true that the longer a marriage lasts, the less the likelihood it will terminate in a divorce. Over 50 percent of all first divorces occur in the first eight years of marriage; beyond that benchmark the probability of divorce declines considerably. In my estimation, the hardest year of marriage is the current one, since marriage requires a rather constant degree of adjustment. It should not escape attention that if the median duration of first marriages is 7 years, this coincides with the stage in the family life cycle at which one or more preschool children are present in most homes. As discussed in Chapter 16, marital adjustment and satisfaction seem to dip with the onset of children and stay rather low until all offspring have left home.

This leads quite logically into another question of concern about divorce: What are the reasons usually given for the divorce?

## Reasons for Divorce

The reasons used by couples filing for a divorce are usually determined more by what the law will allow rather than by what actually led to the divorce. Some states have what amount to grab-bag categories like "mental cruelty" or "irreconcilable differences." The actual reason for the divorce falling under these headings could vary from psychological torture to picking one's toenails in bed. A more adequate way of assessing the reasons for divorce is to systematically interview persons filing for a divorce.

This was done by George Levinger (1966) for a sample of 600 divorce applicants in the greater Cleveland area. All these couples on the brink of dissolving their marriages had at least one child under the age of fourteen and were required by law to submit to an interview with an experienced marriage counselor.

The complaints raised by the applicants were coded into the twelve general categories listed below:

1. Neglect of home or children: frequent absence, irregular hours, emotional distance.
2. Financial problems: either inadequate support (by husband) or poor handling of family's money.

566

3. Physical abuse: committing overt physical hurt or injury to other partner.

4. Verbal abuse: profanity, name-calling, shouting.

5. Infidelity: attachment to an alternate partner, frequently sexual in nature, which excludes spouse; adultery.

6. Sexual incompatibility: reluctance or refusal of coitus, inconsiderateness and other sources of dissatisfaction.

7. Drinking: drunkenness or excessive drinking.

8. In-law trouble: interference or pressure by in-laws, spouse's excessive loyalty to parental kin.

9. Mental cruelty: suspicion, jealousy, untruthfulness, and vague subjective complaints.

10. Lack of love: insufficient affection, communication, companionship.

11. Excessive demands: impatience, intolerance, strictness, possessiveness.

12. Other: miscellaneous category.

The 600 wives in Levinger's study reported an average of 3.05 separate complaints, while the husbands expressed an average of only 1.64 complaints.

Table 20–3 makes it apparent that men were quite selective in their complaints, registering a higher proportion for only in-law trouble and sexual incompatibility. The highest sources of complaint by women were neglect of home and children (39 percent); physical abuse and financial problems were reported by 36.8 percent of the 600 women. It is interesting to note that about 24 percent of the women and 20 percent of the men claimed infidelity as at least one of the reasons for filing for divorce. American folklore and the daily television soap operas would lead us to believe that infidelity is a leading cause of divorce in our society. Levinger's data do not support this rather pervasive common-sense notion.

The social-class differences for the women are particularly revealing. On only four of the eleven types of complaints did middle-class women come out higher than their lower-class counterparts. These complaints were: (a) neglect of home and children, (b) excessive demands, (c) infidelity, and (d) lack of love. The differences in complaints of husbands by social class are almost at a minimum.

## The Legal System and Divorce

The men and women in Levinger's study gave the reasons in Table 20–3 to marriage counselors in an interview required by the court. However, the grounds for divorce they used in the actual divorce proceedings did not necessarily reflect the actual reasons for divorce.

The blindfolded symbol of justice, weighing the evidence in her unbiased scales, reflects the principles upon which our legal system is

567

**TABLE 20–3**
**Marital Complaints Among Couples Applying for Divorce**

| | PERCENTAGE MAKING COMPLAINT | | | | | |
| | | | SOCIAL POSITION | | | |
| | WIVES | HUSBANDS | WIVES | | HUSBANDS | |
| COMPLAINT | TOTAL [a] | TOTAL [a] | MIDDLE [b] | LOWER [c] | MIDDLE [b] | LOWER [c] |
|---|---|---|---|---|---|---|
| Physical abuse | .368 [d] | .033 | .228 | .401 [c] | .029 | .035 |
| Verbal abuse | .238 [d] | .075 | .200 | .245 | .048 | .082 |
| Financial problems | .368 [d] | .087 | .219 | .402 [c] | .124 | .079 |
| Drinking | .265 [d] | .050 | .143 | .294 [c] | .048 | .051 |
| Neglect of home or children | .390 [c] | .262 | .457 | .374 | .200 | .276 |
| Mental cruelty | .403 [e] | .297 | .372 | .408 | .267 | .306 |
| In-law trouble | .067 | .162 [e] | .038 | .074 | .200 | .153 |
| Excessive demands | .025 | .040 | .057 [f] | .018 | .057 | .035 |
| Infidelity | .240 | .200 | .324 [f] | .223 | .114 | .198 [f] |
| Sexual incompatibility | .138 | .200 [c] | .124 | .141 | .267 | .188 |
| Lack of love | .228 [c] | .135 | .324 [c] | .206 | .200 [f] | .120 |

SOURCE: George Levinger, "Sources of Marital Dissatisfaction Among Applicants for Divorce," *American Journal of Orthopsychiatry, 36*(1966):805, Table 1. Copyright ©, the American Orthopsychiatric Association, Inc. Reproduced by permission.

[a] N = 600; all husbands or wives.

[b] N = 105; "Middle" refers to Class I–III on Hollingshead's Index of Social Position.

[c] N = 490; "Lower" refers to Class IV–V on the Hollingshead Index. Note that five cases could not be categorized for social position, by dint of insufficient information.

[d] $p < .001$, indicating a significant difference in favor of the lettered number in the pair, by $t$ test (two-tailed).

[e] $p < .01$.

[f] $p < .05$.

founded. Those principles are that (1) every person is innocent until proved guilty, (2) the person who initiates a charge (the plaintiff) and the person charged (the defendant) both have a right and responsibility to present all the evidence pertaining to their case, and (3) justice will prevail with the innocent party vindicated and the guilty party receiving his or her just and fair punishment.

On paper these principles seem logically sound and morally defensible. In practice, however, at least with regard to divorce, they do not seem to work. Unlike most criminal and other civil cases, in which it is relatively easy to determine who was harmed by whom and how much, in divorce cases the guilt of each is usually more apparent than the innocence of either. If every divorcing couple could be confronted with the charge Jesus reportedly used for the crowd about to stone the prostitute, "Let the person without guilt cast the first stone," most people would have to "drop their stones." The adversary system of a plaintiff (the person filing the complaint) and a defendant (the person who must show just cause why the suit should not be accepted) is not really applicable in most divorce cases.

Things have changed, however. Everyone knows, and the courts have finally recognized, that blame for the dissolution of a marriage is usually shared by both partners. This recognition has led to no-fault laws. As of 1977, 15 states had no-fault grounds *only*. Three states (Illinois, Pennsylvania, and South Dakota) had fault grounds only. The remaining states had such general no-fault designations as (a) incompatibility, (b) insupportable marriage, (c) irretrievable or irremedial breakdown, and (d) irreconcilable difference, that have been added to the already-extant fault grounds. See Figure 20–4 for a breakdown of the grounds for divorce in the various states.

The human value of no-fault divorce laws is described most clearly by Carter and Glick (1976:458):

> No-fault divorce procedures avoid exploring and assessing blame and concentrate on dissolving the marriage and tidying up the inevitable problems—responsibility for the care of the children (there still are children involved in the majority of divorce cases despite the decline in the birth rate), financial support of children, division of jointly owned property, and spousal support (alimony) if this seems indicated. The moment it is established that the question of blame is irrelevant to settlement of the case, some of the bitterness (but by no means all of it) goes out of the divorce proceedings.

## Children and Divorce

Perhaps the most sensitive part of the divorce problem concerns children. If there are children, the effects of a divorce are primary considerations. Some persons suggest that a divorce should never occur while dependent children are still in the home. From this perspective a divorce requires that the children take part in a bad situation they did not create and cannot participate in as full-fledged and equal actors. As the "bit actors" they are most affected by the play while having the least amount of say about the script. The children involved in a divorce are forced into roles they do not want with lines that exert a tremendous emotional toll on their fragile and sometimes tenuous position with the acting team.

A somewhat different position is advocated by persons who feel, and quite strongly, that children are better off if a marital war is terminated with both sides retreating to neutral ground, so that the children will not be caught in the crossfire. From this perspective comes the idea that the relative quiet of having one parent present is far more conducive to healthy development than the turmoil and noise that accompany a situation in which two parents are rather constantly at each other's throats.

A decision as to which perspective is more valid is not possible. Considerations include questions such as: (1) How old are the children?

569

**FIGURE 20–4**
**Grounds for Divorce**

### A. No-Fault Grounds Only

| States (15) | Effective |
|---|---|
| California | 1-01-70 |
| Iowa | 7-01-70 |
| Florida | 7-01-71 |
| Oregon | 10-01-71 |
| Colorado | 1-01-72 |
| Michigan | 1-01-72 |
| Kentucky | 6-16-72 |
| Hawaii | 7-01-72 |
| Nevada | 4-21-73 |
| Washington | 4-23-73 |
| Arizona | 8-08-73 |
| Missouri | 1-01-74 |
| Minnesota | 3-14-74 |
| Montana | 1-01-76 |

### B. Fault Grounds Only

States (3)

| | |
|---|---|
| Illinois | South Dakota |
| Pennsylvania | |

### C. Mixed Grounds: incompatibility, separation, etc., added to fault grounds

| States (6) | No-Fault Grounds Effective | No-Fault Grounds |
|---|---|---|
| Delaware | 1968 | IC |
| Texas[c] | 1970 | IS |
| Idaho[d] | 1971 | IRD |
| New Hampshire[b] | 1971 | IRD & IRB |
| Connecticut[a] | 1973 | IRB & IC |
| Rhode Island[d] | 1975 | IRD |

### D. Mixed Grounds: incompatibility, etc., added to fault grounds

| States (11) | No-Fault Grounds Effective | No-Fault Grounds |
|---|---|---|
| New Mexico | 1933 | IC |
| Alaska | 1935 | IC |
| Oklahoma | 1953 | IC |
| Kansas | 1969 | IC |
| Alabama | 1971 | IRB & IC |
| North Dakota | 1971 | IRD |
| Georgia | 1973 | IRB |
| Indiana | 1973 | IRB |
| Maine | 1973 | IRD |
| Massachusetts | 1976 | IRB |
| Mississippi | 1976 | IRD |

### E. Mixed Grounds: separation added to fault grounds

| States (15) | Latest Change Effective | Years of Separation Required |
|---|---|---|
| Arkansas | 1937 | 3 |
| Louisiana | 1938 | 2 |
| Wyoming | 1941 | 2 |
| Utah | 1943 | 3 |
| Tennessee | 1963 | 2 |
| North Carolina | 1965 | 1 |
| West Virginia | 1969 new | 2 |
| South Carolina | 1969 new | 3 |
| New Jersey | 1971 new | $1\frac{1}{2}$ |
| New York | 1972 | 1 |
| Wisconsin | 1972 | 1 |
| Maryland | 1973 | 1 |
| Vermont | 1973 | $-\frac{1}{2}$ |
| Ohio | 1974 new | 2 |
| Virginia | 1975 | 1 |

IC = incompatibility
IS = insupportable marriage
IRB = irretrievable or irremedial breakdown
IRD = irreconcilable difference

[a] $1\frac{1}{2}$ years separation
[b] 2 years separation
[c] 3 years separation
[d] 5 years separation

SOURCE: The statutes of the fifty states as of January 1, 1977.

(2) How attached are they to each parent? (3) How important or salient is/are the issue(s) that are in contention, and can these issues be satisfactorily negotiated? and (4) What would the children prefer? No reputable marriage counselor would be willing to adopt a rule of thumb to always follow—what is best for the children depends on a number of factors, all of which should be considered. However, the children are never the "decisive" axis on which a decision to divorce or not rotates. A couple who stay together "just for the children" are ignoring the responsibility each has to the self. The couple who claim that a divorce is necessary "for the children's sake" are creating a myth to hide their own responsibilities.

It is natural to assume that each parent contemplating divorce will consider the effects such action may have on the children—whether they be dependent or out in the world with children of their own. In the latter case the divorce would also have a potential impact on grandchildren, and that impact is a factor entering the decision to divorce. Children are seldom the reason cited for a divorce, and they are likewise seldom the sole reason given for keeping a conflict-saturated marriage intact.

Joel Gordon

*Though faced with difficult pressures and conflicts, the single parent is rewarded by the innocent and uncompromised love of a child.*

How involved are children in the American divorce picture? Have children become less of a restraining force on parents contemplating divorce than in times past? The data in Table 20–4 provide some tentative answers.

In 1955 347,000 children were involved in divorces and annulments; in 1965 the figure was 630,000; and by 1975, 1,123,000 children were involved annually. The average number of children per decree reached a peak of 1.32 in 1965 and declined to 1.08 in 1975. By 1970, 303,-000 more children were affected by divorce than by death of a parent—a dramatic reversal of a long-standing trend and a reflection of the "baby boom" as well as a greater willingness to terminate a difficult situation by divorce. Divorce accounted for close to 60 percent of the children affected by marital dissolutions in 1970 compared to only 41.3 percent twenty years earlier. With later ages at first marriage, an increase in the percentage of all couples who remain childless, and the general movement of the baby boom generation through the life cycle, the chances are good that the percentage of all divorces that include children will decline considerably in the relatively near future.

Therefore, from a macro-level perspective it is safe to say that divorce is nearly as prevalent a factor in the total marital dissolution picture in the United States as death. If recent trends continue, divorce will become the leading form of marital dissolution, a phenomenon that may be possible only in a postindustrial society. The macro-level data also support the conclusion that children are increasingly present in divorce and that the percentage of couples childless at divorce has decreased substantially since World War II.

But what about the impact that divorce has on real children? Although macro-level data are indispensable for gaining an overview of

TABLE 20–4

**Children Involved in Divorces and Annulments, United States**

| YEAR | ESTIMATED NUMBER OF CHILDREN INVOLVED | AVERAGE NUMBER OF CHILDREN PER DECREE |
|---|---|---|
| 1955 | 347,000 | 0.92 |
| 1960 | 463,000 | 1.18 |
| 1965 | 630,000 | 1.32 |
| 1970 | 870,000 | 1.22 |
| 1971 | 946,000 | 1.22 |
| 1972 | 1,021,000 | 1.20 |
| 1973 | 1,079,000 | 1.17 |
| 1974 | 1,099,000 | 1.12 |
| 1975 | 1,123,000 | 1.08 |

SOURCE: National Center for Health Statistics, *Monthly Vital Statistics Report, Advance Report: Final Divorce Statistics, 1975.* Vol. 26, No. 2, Supplement 2, May 19, 1977.

the extensiveness of a societal problem like divorce, only data from the micro level, where individuals and specific family units are studied, can truly gauge what is a highly personal trouble for children whose parents divorce. How does a divorce really affect a child?

Morris Rosenberg (1965:106) examined this question relative to adolescents and their self-esteem:

> If we return to our original question, "Does the broken home have an effect upon the emotional state of the child?" the best answer would seem to be "It depends." First, it depends on religion: if the child is Catholic or Jewish, there appears to be a clear effect; if the child is Protestant, there appears to be little or no effect. Second, it depends on the mother's age at the time of the marital rupture: if the mother was very young, there appears to be a clear effect; if the mother was older, there appears to be little effect. Third, it depends on remarriage: children whose mothers remarried appear to be more disturbed than those whose mothers did not remarry. The negative effect of remarriage is particularly strong among older children.

At an even more basic level, children of divorce face several serious problems. First, there is the difficulty in understanding why two people they love do not love each other any more. Most children, even adolescents, are unable to fully comprehend the complexities of the strains that lead to rupturing the marital bond. In particular they are unaware of the physical-sexual facets of the tie that no longer binds their parents to one another.

Second, children have difficulty in understanding why one parent must leave the home and them and live alone or with someone other than the second parent. Home to them is where "we all live." Divorce requires a new and alien definition of home and family.

Third, it is not unusual for children to bear the brunt of displaced parental aggression in terms of sarcastic remarks and unreasonable demands. All too often splitting parents vie for the affection and support of the child for "their side" in the affair. This frequently leads the children to feel guilty for either taking sides or refusing to take sides in the battle. The effect on an immature child is not infrequently devastating, the result being a sense of aloneness and utter frustration.

Fourth, the children frequently feel they are somehow stigmatized. They must explain to their friends what has happened to their parents, but are not able to fully understand the meaning of divorce or its ramifications for them in the future. They ask questions such as: Will I get to see Dad again? When? Where? Do both of you still love me?

Divorce is an experience that is not healthy for children, emotionally or physically. It is not unusual for children whose parents divorce to show signs of physical and emotional disorders. Suffice it to say that divorce creates a state of disorientation for children that may leave scars that never heal.

573

## ANNULMENT AND SEPARATION

Up to now we have been talking about the major form of willful marital dissolution, divorce. Two other legal actions that are closely related to divorce are (a) annulment and (b) limited divorce. An annulment is a

---

### The Empty-Shell Marriage

The image that usually comes to mind when marital dissolution is mentioned is of a lonely, depressed, and disoriented widow, widower, or divorcee. These people generally elicit from us a sympathetic response. Almost everyone is willing to identify with a person whose life has been affected by the pain of death or the failure of a marriage. We seldom think of marriages that are still legally intact as dissolved. However, as Goode (1962b) describes them, "an empty shell marriage is one in which individuals interact instrumentally, but fail essentially in the role obligation to give emotional support to one another." These are marriages that are unhappy, that exist in name only, that are dead and lifeless. How many marriages are like this? We do not really know, but some data are available that provide a clue.

In a representative sample of 5,373 white and black adults who were married, separated, or divorced, and living in Alameda County, California, Karen Renne found a substantial percentage (shown in Table 20–5) who considered their marriages unhappy.

Renne's (1971:348) conclusions are based on her assessments of the health status, both physical and psychological, of these groups. Her conclusions are important in terms of the effects of an empty-shell marriage:

> Unhappily married people in our sample were for the most part as well off economically as happily married people, and better off than the divorced, yet they registered distress on every health index we examined: disability, chronic illness, neurosis, depression and isolation. . . . the data seem to justify an analogy between unhappy marriage and disability: unhappy marriage is a social disability, analogous in its consequences to physical disability or chronic illness. For this disability, divorce is probably the most effective remedy. A large majority of people in our sample who were ever divorced had remarried, and while the remarried as a group tended to be less healthy than people in stable marriages, those who were satisfied with their current marriages reported better health than those who were still involved in unhappy first marriages. In other words, people who had divorced and remarried successfully were less susceptible to health problems than people who had remarried in an unhappy marriage. If divorce itself were a symptom of illness, signifying

574

judicial declaration that the marriage never occurred, at least in a legal sense. For example, if a second marriage occurred before the first was terminated, then the second one can be declared null and void. Another reason for the use of annulments is "force and duress," which must be proved to the court's satisfaction. If it was used, then the marriage can be

**TABLE 20–5**
**Marital Unhappiness in Alameda County**

| CATEGORY | PERCENTAGE AND NUMBER |
|---|---|
| *Married and Never Divorced* | |
| White men under 45 | 17.5% (174 out of 997) |
| White men over 45 | 12.5% (94 out of 752) |
| White women under 45 | 18.0% (203 out of 1127) |
| White women over 45 | 20.3% (133 out of 655) |
| Black men under 45 | 27.9% (24 out of 86) |
| Black men over 45 | 20.0% (19 out of 95) |
| Black women under 45 | 41.9% (52 out of 124) |
| Black women over 45 | 30.5% (18 out of 59) |
| | |
| *Remarried After Divorce* | |
| White men under 45 | 19.5% (30 out of 154) |
| White men over 45 | 14.1% (26 out of 185) |
| White women under 45 | 24.9% (46 out of 185) |
| White women over 45 | 24.9% (49 out of 197) |
| Black men under 45 | 37.5% (18 out of 48) |
| Black men over 45 | 26.5% (13 out of 49) |
| Black women under 45 | 31.8% (14 out of 44) |
| Black women over 45 | 35.8% (19 out of 53) |

SOURCE: Adapted from Karen Renne, "Health and Marital Experience in an Urban Population," *Journal of Marriage and the Family* 33(1971):349.

physical incapacity, or an inability to sustain close relations with another person, for example, then people who had remarried after divorce would not only have been less satisfied with their marriages, as they were in our sample, but also less healthy in other respects, as they were *not*, to any significant degree.

Far from being a symptom of incapacity, then, divorce seems to indicate relatively good health.[1]

---

[1] Karen S. Renne, "Health and Marital Experience in an Urban Population, *Journal of Marriage and the Family 33*(1971):338–50. Reprinted by permission of the National Council on Family Relations.

declared inoperative and neither spouse will be called a divorcee. Annulment is, in effect, a legal erasure of a marital event that legally should never have occurred.

A second type of willful marital dissolution, but not as final as divorce, is limited divorce or legal separation. In this arrangement neither spouse is allowed to remarry (a crucial part of the divorce process), but both are enjoined to leave the other alone. A limited divorce, then, is a legally sanctioned agreement between spouses to separate but not to divorce.

## REMARRIAGE

The old adage, "Once burned, twice shy," does not apply in the realm of divorce and remarriage. Although the number of partners involved in a divorce each year is quite large, 2,072,000 in 1975 alone (1,036,000 × 2), most of these will remarry. In fact, about three-fourths of all divorced men and three-fifths of all divorced women eventually remarry.

The incidence of remarriage has understandably increased as the divorce rate has climbed in the United States. Using data provided by

*Children from the first marriages watch as they become kin in the second marriage.*

Mike Mazzaschi, Stock, Boston

*The first child of this second marriage becomes the third child in the family.*

Jim Harrison

Paul Glick (1949), Bernard (1956) found that out of every 100 married couples in the United States, one-fifth or 20 percent involve remarriage for one or both partners. The average age at remarriage for divorced men in 1975 was 32.8 and for women, 29.4. When the marriage was dissolved by death, the median age at remarriage was 57.9 for men and 53.2 for women.

The average interval between divorce and remarriage is usually short. Bernard's (1956) study of 2,009 remarriages found that for women it was 4.6 years and for men only 2.5 years. The interval between divorce and remarriage increases as the length of time in the prior marriage increases.

A logical question to ask is: Where does a divorced or widowed person find a second spouse? Bernard's (1956) data on 2,009 remarriages and Bowerman's (1949) data on 13,088 cases in Seattle from 1939 to 1946 indicate that from 20 to 30 percent of all remarriages involved a single man marrying a divorced woman. Some 21 percent of the remarriages in Bernard's—compared to 18 percent in Bowerman's study—consisted of divorced men and single women. Both studies found that from 16 to 23 percent of remarriages involved *both* a divorced man and a divorced woman. More recent data from The Marriage Registration Area in 1969 (see Figure 12–1) indicate that 27.6 percent of all 1969 marriages involved at least one partner who was previously married.

A rather surprising finding of research on the probability of marriage and remarriage is that, at any age, persons who have been married before have higher probabilities of remarrying than single persons have of getting married for the first time. Thus, although some stigma is attached to failure in marriage, that stigma does not preclude, in fact it seems to enhance, the probability of re-entering the marital state. This holds true even when there are children from the first marriage. Widowed persons

577

generally have a lower probability of remarriage than divorced persons of the same age, but both have a higher probability of remarriage than a single person of the same age has of first marriage.

Another question that arises is, What is the probability of divorce after remarriage? The most definitive study relative to this question was conducted by Thomas Monahan (1958) using data from the state of Iowa for the 1953–55 period. During those years there were 70,901 marriages and 15,502 divorces with the ratio of divorces per 100 marriages being 21.9 (Monahan, 1958, 1952).

The data in Figure 20–5 clearly indicate that for the ratio of divorces per 100 marriages by previous marital status, the highest likelihood

**FIGURE 20–5**
**Divorces per 100 Marriages, Iowa, 1953–55**

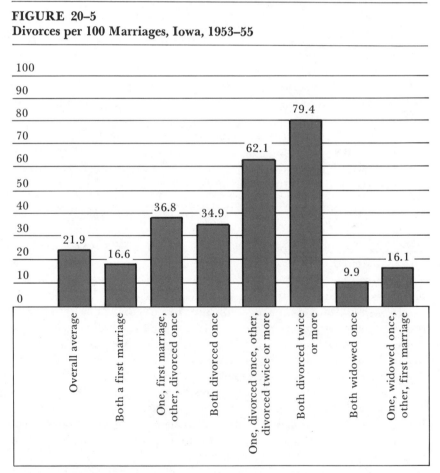

SOURCE: Thomas P. Monahan, "The Changing Nature and Instability of Remarriages," *Eugenics Quarterly* 5(June 1958):82.

of divorce exists if both spouses have been divorced twice or more (79.4). If widowhood was the previous marital state for one or both spouses, the chances of divorce are lower than if the spouses were both previously single. This is probably the result of age at marriage more than anything else. If both spouses were in the second marriage after the first ended in divorce, the probability of divorce is only 34.9.

These data seem to suggest that divorce is not necessarily an indication that a person is unsuited for marriage. Anyone can make a mistake, and evidently a rather sizable proportion of persons make mistakes the first time through the marital merry-go-round. This does not mean they will be making mistakes to remarry. As a matter of proved fact, the second time around may make up for the grinding halt of the first marriage.

## A THEORY OF MARITAL COMMITMENT

Although marital dissolution, and particularly divorce, are inherently interesting topics to study, the purpose of the sociologist is to look behind the obvious camouflage of everyday occurrences and build bridges between phenomena that are usually compartmentalized. The need for this kind of orientation is particularly acute in the study of divorce. Although a number of persons have dealt conceptually with divorce, only one, George Levinger, achieved any notable progress. Levinger (1965) used an inductive approach to develop his hypothesis. He reviewed all the literature available on marital cohesiveness and dissolution and organized variables that had been shown to differentiate between high- and low-cohesion marriages under three categories: (a) sources of attraction, (b) sources of barrier strength, and (c) sources of alternate attraction (Table 20–6). Levinger's (1965:28) final comment indicates his views of the three categories: "A conceptual framework has been outlined for integrating research on marital cohesiveness and dissolution. The concepts are the same as those employed for understanding the cohesiveness of other social groups. The strength of the marital relationship is proposed to be a direct function of hypothetical attraction and barrier forces inside the marriage, and an inverse function of such influences from alternate relationships."

Levinger's analysis is perceptive. He has isolated the crucial and core components of marital cohesiveness. A commitment to the spouse and the marriage, plus the presence of personal, social, structural, and cultural barriers to pressures for dissolution, will reduce the likelihood of a marriage terminating because of alternate sources of attraction. However, several large gaps are in the Levinger coverage. For example, virtually nothing is present in his scheme that relates to the family background and early dating-courtship experiences of married persons. Second—and this refers to the earlier claim that we need to tie together phenomena that are generally treated separately—there is virtually nothing on (a) how the spouses interact with one another, (b) the prevailing power configuration

579

**TABLE 20–6**

Factors Differentiating High- and Low-Cohesion Marriages

| SOURCES OF ATTRACTION | SOURCES OF BARRIER STRENGTH | SOURCES OF ALTERNATE ATTRACTION |
|---|---|---|
| Affectional rewards: Esteem for spouse Desire for companionship Sexual enjoyment | Feelings of obligation: To dependent children To marital bond | Affectional rewards: Preferred alternate sex partner Disjunctive social relations Opposing religious affiliations |
| Socioeconomic rewards: Husband's income Home ownership Husband's education Husband's occupation | Moral proscriptions: Proscriptive religion Joint church attendance | Economic rewards: Wife's opportunity independent income |
| Similarity in social status: Religion Education Age | External pressures: Primary group affiliations Community stigma: rural-urban Legal and economic bars | |

SOURCE: Adapted from George Levinger, "Marital Cohesiveness and Dissolution: An Integrative Review," *Journal of Marriage and the Family,* 27(1965):21, Table 1. By permission of the National Council on Family Relations.

within the family, (c) the level of adjustment and satisfaction achieved in the marriage relative to expectations, and (d) stage in the family life cycle.

To put it another way, Levinger's (1965) integrative review scheme is too inductive (that is, listing variables that seem to fit under broad categories) and not analytical enough. We will fill in those gaps starting with some basic assumptions.

## Basic Assumptions

1. The crucial variable to examine if we are to understand marital dissolution and divorce is not marital cohesiveness, but rather the degree of commitment each spouse has to the other and to the marriage and family—treated both as an abstract object and as a very evident and real group of human beings. In other words, the best way to study divorce is at the individual level.

2. It is highly important to examine the background and experiences of both spouses if one is to understand the dissolution decision. Extensive evidence suggests that certain types of biographies are more divorce prone than others.

3. The crucial elements of a decision to dissolve a marriage are related to how the spouses relate to one another in an interactive, power, and adjustment sense. In other words, every day requires an evaluation—"Is it good or bad, and how good or bad is it?"—and a *decision*—"That's it! I've had it!" or "You know, I think I like married life after all." The daily evaluation and decision are a result of comparing one's recent situation with the past and one's expectations for the future.

4. Factors that compete with the spouse and family for the other spouse's attention and loyalty exist at a demand level and an attraction level. The demands are usually impersonally applied by impersonal forces like a job. The other source of pull away from the spouse is more personal, and the attraction usually results in an alienation of affection for the spouse. If the data available on the extensiveness of extramarital sex are reliable, this latter pull is quite prevalent for both spouses. Add the problem of being married to someone who is totally committed to his or her job—and the probability of such is fairly good—and one might wonder why two people stay together, especially for any length of time.

The diagram we will use to discuss marital commitment (Figure 20–6) was used by Bell and Mau (1971). I have changed the blocks of variables and added some new features. The model assumes that the degree of marital commitment to be studied is in the here and now—not one's marital state some years or months back, but right now. Something may happen tomorrow that may drastically alter one's whole world view. Therefore, it is important that we focus our attention on contemporaneous events and decisions. Most of us are very ritualized and predictable, so previous history and reconstruction of the past is not too much to ask of a researcher or his or her subjects. Commitment to continue or dissolve a marriage is a rational act that can not only be studied but predicted in a probabilistic sense.

PART A: PREDISPOSING BIOGRAPHICAL EVENTS PRIOR TO MARITAL SELECTION. The term *predisposing* is used in the sense that people with certain types of experiences are more likely to dissolve a marriage than are others. The following variables are generally viewed as being more conducive to marital stability:

1. Family Background
    Rural versus highly urbanized residence
    White versus nonwhite
    Educational-occupational income of parents relatively high
    Parental affiliation with and involvement in religious affairs
    Parents happily married
2. Achievement and Identification
    Relatively high educational-occupational-income aspirations, expectations, achievement, and identification
    Involvement in religious affairs

581

## FIGURE 20–6
## A Flowchart Model of Marital Commitment Probabilities: A Decisional Approach

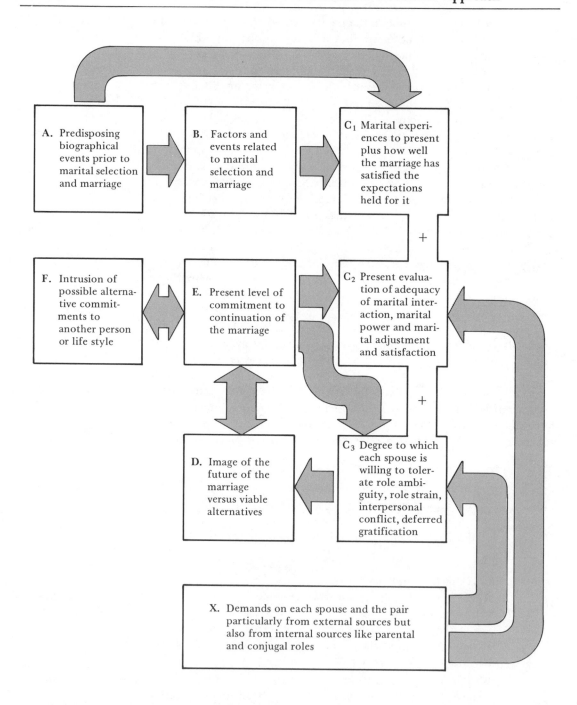

SOURCE: Adapted from Wendell Bell and James A. Mau, "Images of the Future: Theory and Research Strategies," in Bell and Mau (eds.), *The Sociology of the Future: Theory, Cases and Annotated Bibliography* (New York: Russell Sage Foundation, 1971), p. 21, Figure 1. Used by permission of the publisher.

3. Heterosexual Dating Experiences

   Relatively slow involvement with the opposite sex with supervision of adults as an important factor

   Pleasant and enjoyable involvement with the opposite sex with no early pairing

   A variety of dating experiences

PART B: MARITAL SELECTION.   We know that homogamy is more conducive to marital stability than heterogamy, as are marriage at a later age and marriage when the wife is not premaritally pregnant. A relatively long courtship is more conducive to stability than a quick movement from dating to marriage (see Chapters 12 and 13).

PART $C_1$: PRIOR MARRIAGE EXPERIENCES.   Parts A and B of the model have a direct effect on the ease with which adjustment to marriage occurs and on how well the realities of married life fit with the expectations with which it is entered. The early stages of marriage, if they are unpleasant, are conducive to later maladjustment and feelings of being trapped.

PART $C_2$: PRESENT EVALUATION OF MARITAL INTERACTION, POWER, AND ADJUSTMENT AND SATISFACTION.   The crucial determinant of commitment to the marriage and the spouse is how well things are going now. As discussed in Chapters 14 to 19, various pressures exist in marriage that compete for the time, energy, and involvement of the spouses with each other. How the marriage is currently viewed is a result of how well the spouses are able to withstand these pressures and strains while keeping each other satisfied with each other and with married life.

PART $C_3$: TOLERANCE LEVELS.   Each of us has his or her own level of tolerance of role ambiguity and strain, interpersonal conflict, and deferred gratification. Our commitment to a spouse and marriage is directly tied to what we as individuals are willing to take in terms of cost relative to the rewards of married living. For those with low levels of tolerance, the probability of fighting all the various pressures that could easily pull a couple apart are rather slim. Marriage requires a great deal of give and take, most of it take.

PART D: IMAGE OF THE FUTURE VERSUS ALTERNATIVES.   It is not difficult, given the additive effects of $C_1$, $C_2$, and $C_3$ of the model, to project oneself and a marriage into the future. By the same computations, any future alternatives both within and outside the present marital arrangement are rather easy to project. One's commitment to a marriage is essentially a case of asking, "Are any of the viable alternatives more desirable than the future of this current marital arrangement?" Because almost all their efforts are expended in making their marriage work, and at its maximum level of satisfaction, few married people are likely to opt for a future alternative the boundaries and components of which are unknown.

583

PART E: PRESENT LEVEL OF COMMITMENT TO CONTINUATION OF THE MARRIAGE. About the only other thing that, in reality, reduces the commitment to marital stability is the intrusion of an alternative source of commitment that appears more desirable than the present arrangement.

## CONCLUSIONS

Marriage and marital dissolution are activities that have tremendous symbolic import for society and for the individuals involved. They represent moments when the transition for one status-role to another is dramatically apparent. The individuals involved in a marital or dissolution activity are quite aware, as are those who witness the event, that a wholly different set of norms operate on either side of an "I now pronounce you man and wife," and the deafening sound of the judge's gavel and voice when he says, "Divorce granted."

But marriage itself is seldom entered with fear and trembling, although some of both are present in many cases. Marriage is seen by society as a confirmation of normality and a reaffirmation of the legitimacy of the family system. Tears at weddings are the result of happiness, not sadness. This is certainly not true for willful marital dissolution. By the time the divorce is granted most of the tears from hurt have dried up, at least for most people. The response of the primary actors in a divorce play is usually relief. However, society generally responds with a detached but scornful glare. In our society, as in most, divorce is viewed as evidence of failure —individual and collective.

We have tried to show in this chapter that divorce is not the problem. Marriage is. The divorce rate in this society is not unreasonably high relative to other industrialized societies. In addition, ample evidence is that most people in this society desire the marital status—remarriage after divorce is rather common.

Marital dissolution is problematic in this society primarily because we expect too much of married life at the same time that the legal restrictions on who may marry and when are extremely permissive. In other words, the way to solve the divorce problem, is, in my opinion, to change the marriage regulations. We should increase the allowable age at which first marriage may occur. If we, in effect, forced all persons to wait until they are in their twenties to get married, society would be assured that the divorce problem would diminish drastically. Then we could require everyone to become sterilized at puberty. This procedure would be reversible, but only when the person is married and found to be eligible for parenthood. A very positive side effect of this policy would be that premarital pregnancy would cease to exist as a problem and the sexual frustrations of our young people might also diminish considerably.

By now the reader is probably saying—"That's stupid! No one would ever allow that to happen!" And he is correct. Our society is quite willing to accept a moderate to high divorce rate and the rights of persons to divorce and marry as they wish. Perhaps our society is opposed to any radical change in the divorce realm, because divorce is more often viewed as the best remedy to a tired and lifeless, conflict-habituated marital relationship. Regardless, divorce is likely to be endemic in any society that places few restrictions on marital selection and marriage and that encourages unrealistic aspirations and expectations for a situation that is frequently too real for its participants to accept.

## SOME POSSIBLE IMPLICATIONS

*It is not trite to suggest that social change produces social changes that result in more social change, all of which require adjustments in the life-styles of individuals, family units, the family system, and all the institutions of society.*

*Numerous indicators suggest that divorce and marital instability will increase in our society. The laws concerning divorce are becoming more flexible. Many states have* de facto *eliminated alimony because alimony has traditionally been applied only to males. In many states the grounds for divorce have been liberalized so that couples with irreconcilable differences can obtain a divorce with little difficulty. In the early 1970s the concept of no-fault divorce was introduced. One possible consequence of this is that divorce will be more readily sought because it is no longer necessary for one person to accept the role of defendant. It is also possible that the divorce rate will increase because of the no-fault laws. It is too early to know just how great an increase will occur, but some observers believe it will be substantial.*

*Indications also suggest that the divorce rate in the United States has reached a plateau, and will not increase much in the last part of the twentieth century. As the population begins to stabilize, as the median age of the population continues to rise, and as the average age at first marriage goes up, the chances are fairly good that the number of divorces per year will peak and then begin to decline. This may portend an eventual decline in the divorce rate. It is certain that the average number of children annually affected by divorce will decline as the birth rate tapers off and the average number of children per family declines. I believe that these changes and the changes occurring in our society will produce a stronger and more cohesive family unit, thus effecting an increase in marital satisfaction and happiness and a subsequent or consequent reduction in the "divorce problem." In addition, there will be a reduction in the number of empty-shell marriages.*

George Gardner

# 21

# THE FUTURE OF THE FAMILY AND MARRIAGE

*Is marriage an antiquated and soon-to-be-extinct ritual?*

*Is monogamy outdated?*

*Does the family have a future?*

*Will the family and marriage become weaker or stronger by* A.D. *2000?*

"From at least the time of Plato two and a half millenniums ago, wise men have suggested that if human rights are to be guaranteed, if every human being is to be granted an adequate opportunity for the full development of his talents, the family system must be altered" (Goode, 1965). This quotation seems to be an appropriate point of departure for a chapter on the future of marriage and the family. It contains the essence of the "moral" and ideological positions of proponents for alternative life-styles—a focus on the individual and his or her right for self-development or, as Maslow put it, self-actualization. Overzealous critics of the current family system, who are usually equally zealous in their support of an alternative, have frequently failed to distinguish between marriage and the family. Much popular literature that is focused on the individual deals with the mate selection process, with selection and deflection being the crucial axes of interest. The family system is seldom the issue of concern. Thus, the question is not whether the family will survive, but whether it can survive in its present form, given increasing pressure to change the formation of families.

The questions that will serve as guideposts for this chapter are: (1) What is the history of predictions for the family? (2) What are some proposals for the establishment of family-type units and the operation of "families" in the future? (3) What contingency factors may influence the kinds of alternative mate selection and family forms that will be available in the future? (4) What obstacles may impede the realization of these proposals for change?

Several boundaries or delimitations are operative in this chapter. First, by *marriage* we mean the legal binding of two individuals of opposite sexes to each other until that union has been dissolved legally. This is the current minimum meaning of the term. For many the legal features in forming and dissolving the relationship are objectionable. For others, the legal restriction of marriage to two persons at any one time is regarded as an unreasonable invasion of the government into a matter that should be based on individual preferences. For others, the requirement that the partners be of opposite sex creates the bind.

The current meaning of family is not accorded consensus, but generally it includes the following possibilities: (a) husband and wife without children; (b) husband and wife with children; (c) one parent (either husband or wife) and children. Thus, a second delimiting factor in our discussion concerns the fact that the legal system in this country has a rather narrow concept of what constitutes a family.

John Cuber (1970) suggested useful analytic distinctions for viewing marriage and the family in a changing society. The forces that uphold the traditional religious and judicial conceptions of family and marriage he calls *de jure*. These are the oughts, the proper modes of thought and conduct. The *de facto* modes of thought and conduct refer to what is actually practiced—frequently in violation of the de jure strictures. It is the gap between these two that has led many social scientists to suggest that de facto arrangements will become normative in the future as the outmoded de jure ideals become more and more recognized as useless examples of cultural lag.

The third delimitation in this chapter is time. The future will refer to the years remaining in the twentieth century. Because social scientists have been less than successful in their past projections, we shall focus on the immediate future instead of the distant future. Of course, if Alvin Toffler is correct, and he probably is, the next twenty-five years could produce changes so drastic that predictions may be better made if we limited ourselves to Orwell's 1984.

## METHODOLOGIES FOR PREDICTING THE FUTURE

A continuum of approaches for predicting the future can be conceptualized. Some approaches are rational, objective, and "scientific," whereas others are seemingly speculative and analogous to "flying by the seat of one's pants." One thing seems certain: every generation and every culture has developed a role for the prophet, the person whose task it is to read the signs, whether they be stars or statistical charts. The prophet is to come up with "answers" to what life will be like sometime in the future. He might use one of six major methodologies for looking toward that relative unknown, the future.

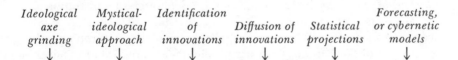

| Ideological axe grinding | Mystical-ideological approach | Identification of innovations | Diffusion of innovations | Statistical projections | Forecasting, or cybernetic models |
|---|---|---|---|---|---|
| ↓ | ↓ | ↓ | ↓ | ↓ | ↓ |

### Ideological Axe Grinding

At the least systematic end of the continuum we are most likely to find the prophets of doom who always offer alternatives to the future. These prophets are found in almost any major city, preaching on the street corners about the sinfulness of modern life and the sure destruction of the world (in the near future, of course) if man does not adopt the only answer—"go back to the ways of the past." These prophets have not been successful in their prophecies, but perhaps they should not be totally discounted by the scientific and educated world.

589

For an ancient example of ideological axe grinding we can turn to Noah. As the story goes, Noah was a devout man who was told by God to build an ark of certain dimensions because a flood was coming to punish those who were sinful. Now a truly reasonable person, a person whose mind works in logical ways, would have seriously rejected the almost impossible task of building such a huge ship. A less committed person would perhaps have started building the ark, but would have stopped because of the ridicule of friends and neighbors. But not Noah. He reportedly spent much time warning the public of imminent doom. Noah was persistent in utilizing what I have chosen to call ideological axe grinding—one methodological strategy for predicting the future.

Current examples of this methodology abound in our society, particularly among ministers of fundamentalist religious sects and others who interpret the Bible literally. These prophets of the end of the world use ideology as a basis for predicting the future and grind out massive amounts of auxiliary information to support their claims.

### Mystical-Ideological Approach

A step up the continuum from these ideologues are the more "established" and modern prophets. It seems each generation has at least one. In the 1960s it was Edgar Cayce, a simple, virtually uneducated man who was anything but spectacular when conscious. However, when he was in a trance Edgar Cayce was able to perform remarkable feats, many of which dealt with predicting future events. The predictions in these cases were almost always focused on individuals. They seldom referred to the future of social institutions or large-scale social systems.

Since the 1960s Mrs. Jeane Dixon, the wife of a prominent businessman in Washington, D.C., has been remarkably successful in "predicting" certain "political" events like the assassinations of John F. Kennedy, Martin Luther King, and Robert F. Kennedy. She also predicted the U-2 incident over the Soviet Union during the Eisenhower administration and the emergence of the People's Republic of China as a nuclear power. Jeane Dixon is a devout Roman Catholic and explains her prophetic ability as a gift of God. In this sense her prophesies are mystical-ideological in form and content. Although she is not an ideologue per se, she is bound to an ideological tradition. Perhaps Mrs. Dixon's prophesies are not scientifically systematic or understandable in any analytic sense, but her results have been uncannily accurate in a number of reasonably well-documented cases.

### Identification of Innovations

This methodology for predicting the future tends to focus on one product or technique or social form that could possibly cause a restructuring of much of society. Who among us today would deny that blacksmiths, feed store owners, and horse lovers everywhere were wrong?—the horseless car-riage did produce amazing changes in our society. Today we find numerous articles written about the computer and its potential for creating a new world. Herman Kahn and Anthony J. Weiner (1967:711–716) listed 100 technical innovations likely before A.D. 2000. Some of these are more reliable and longer-range weather forecasting, major reductions in hereditary and congenital defects, extensive use of cyborg techniques (mechanical aids or substitutes for human organs, senses, limbs), relatively effective appetite and weight control; controlled supereffective relaxation and sleep; three-dimensional photography, illustrations, movies, and television; human hibernation for relatively extensive periods (months to years); simple techniques for extensive and "permanent" cosmetological changes (to features, complexion, skin color, even physique), automated grocery and department stores; programed dreams; and many others that could change life as we know it—and change it drastically. The question for this type of futurist is: What innovation will be the most significant in terms of influence?

## Diffusion of Innovations

The question raised above has special relevance for predicting the future if we choose as our methodology the diffusion process. Many inventions take years to get off the drawing boards, into a prototype testing stage, into the patent books, into mass production, and purchased. Some inventions that have a number of inherently beneficial qualities are not diffused at all because of resistance from the public or because those qualities are largely unrecognized. The specifications of innovations that will be widely diffused is a very difficult process for the futurist.

## Projections

This fifth methodology for predicting the future is more rational, objective, and scientific than those discussed. Quite simply, this tactic involves taking existing data and projecting results for some future time. Assumptions may be varied and projected. This methodology is perhaps better understood when illustrated. The following quotation is from a speech made in October 1970 by Dr. George H. Brown, Director of the Bureau of the Census (see Brown, 1970):

> In 1967 the Bureau of the Census prepared four series of population projections. Underlying these projections was the assumption that completed fertility would range as follows:
>> 3.35 children per woman for Series A (rate of 1950s)
>> 3.10 children for Series B (expectations data)
>> 2.78 children for Series C (rate of early 1960s)
>> 2.45 children for Series D (rate of late 1960s)
> Recently we added a fifth:
>> Series E 2.11 children (in time a zero population growth without immigration. It is assumed that mortality will decline slightly.)

591

Recent fertility trends have caused the Bureau to update its 1967 projections. Series A no longer seems a reasonable possibility for 1985. Between 1940 and 1957, average age at marriage declined; the proportion of women who were married increased; birth intervals became shorter, and fertility rose sharply especially during the postwar years. As a result, population growth between 1947 and 1957 averaged 1.7 percent per year, considered a very high rate for an industrial nation. Since 1957, however, age at marriage and the spacing of births have increased slightly and fertility dropped sharply. The current level of fertility is at Series D, or an average of about 2½ children per woman. We have therefore added Series E.

Brown's remarks underscore the major flaw in using projections as a methodology for predicting the future—they are greatly subject to unexpected inputs. Before World War II many people, including demographic experts, were confident that our population would cease growth altogether and even decline in size. Who in 1941 could have predicted the baby boom? Brown and his experts at the Census Bureau were discarding Series A, formulated in 1967, by the fall of 1970. The addition of Series E was justified by the mid-1970s when the fertility rate dropped to replacement level, 2.1 children. This susceptibility is one reason why projections are sometimes faulty and sometimes absolutely wrong. The same is true of social projections that are not statistically based. Many parents, school authorities, and ministers were seemingly convinced in the late 1950s that the Elvis Presley phenomenon would lead that generation of youth straight to a life of sin and then immediately, if not sooner, to hell. Ten years later these same authority figures were praying for a return to "hell" which had then amazingly become more like "heaven." A new cohort of youth had "turned on" to the Beatles and the Rolling Stones. And another ten years later the trend had gone even further—to Kiss and Alice Cooper.

## Forecasting and/or Cybernetic Models

These are models that are based on statistical and other data that try to "build in" some anticipated or actual feedbacks so as to allow for continual readjustments. As Fred Charles Ikle (1967:733), a political scientist at the Massachusetts Institute of Technology, said: "Our values change. In 1985 we may prefer another alternative for the year 2000 than we did in 1965. This may in part be due to the fact that in 1985 we can see new consequences, say for the year 2010, of the alternative futures in 2000." Put another way, let us assume that we have extensive data that will allow us to project to 1985 from our knowledge in 1979. We can also suggest that five possible reactions to our 1979 projections would occur prior to 1985. On the basis of each of these reactions, we can build into our projections five possible futures for 1990. By feeding back into our model five additional reactions that could possibly occur between 1985 and 1990 we can predict five possible futures for 1995. By this time we have reached

1985 and can evaluate our successes and failures and feed into the model new contingencies. Of course, this is a rather simplistic illustration. The futurist who is using a cybernetic model may be dealing with 100,000 variables and many contingency feedbacks—all on the computer. A more common name for cybernetic models for predicting the future is decision or game theory.

*Summary*

There are certainly more methodologies for predicting the future than the six mentioned here, but these are prototypical. In the last ten years or so social scientists have tried to rely on the last two: projections and cybernetic models. Even with extensive and fairly reliable data, contingency planning and feedback loops, the accuracy is seldom near the desired 100 percent level. Skeptics and critics might suggest that such statistical exercises are relatively useless. They would argue that statistical magic leaves out the individual; and the individual, though his or her actions affect the larger social systems, is seldom if ever concerned with the collective. He or she is existentially concerned with his or her own little slice of life. When over 215 million people in a society, give or take a few of the more altruistic, are either unconcerned or unaware of their impact, projecting, forecasting, or prophesying—call it by any name—may be a fruitless and futile effort.

Most social scientists believe that any information obtainable about possible or probable conditions at future dates is valuable, even if it is not totally accurate. It is perhaps safe to assume that most persons are so involved daily with their own immediate needs and problems that they spend little time and energy plotting even their own futures. Most long-range planning that can and does affect individual futures falls by default, then, to the "experts" employed by various public and private agencies. There is consensus among these experts that we need to exert our efforts toward making those predictions more accurate if science is to have a humanistic impact in society.

## PAST PREDICTIONS

The history of predictions for the future of the family is long. Most major philosophers and social thinkers offered predictions or, if you prefer, prophesies based on ideological-philosophical assumptions. Plato was concerned for the state of Greece if the education and socialization of its most gifted children were left to the family. Rather than risk the collapse of the Grecian world because of a weak family system, he recommended that children with potential be made wards of the state and receive their socialization from scholars.

593

*Behavioral psychologist J. B. Watson predicted that marriage would be nonexistent by 1977. He was wrong.*

Culver Pictures, Inc.

Auguste Comte, the "father" of sociology, feared that the anarchy generated by the French Revolution would creep into and insidiously destroy the basic unit of society, the family. The family must, he said, retain its monogamous and patriarchal structure against anarchic pressures. Comte was not sure that the family could survive those pressures. To bring everything closer to home in time and space, however, let us examine a few of the predictions of twentieth-century scholars.

One early prophet of doom for the American family was John B. Watson, the behavioral psychologist. Writing in 1927, Watson predicted that by 1977 marriage would no longer exist in the United States. Why he chose 1977 as the target date is not known. Nevertheless, he was convinced that family standards were on the way to a complete breakdown and that children would be completely out of control by then. The primary cause in this regression would be the diffusion of the automobile and the factors related to it. Like many other observers of the social scene immediately preceding the 1929 depression, Watson probably reflected the fears of a fatalistic and puritanical segment of society, of which he was a part. What else could be expected from irresponsible youth who had money to spend, the war to end all wars behind them, so much mobility, and so little supervision?

Writing in 1937, about ten years after Watson, the controversial sociologist Pitirim A. Sorokin predicted that divorce and separation would become so pervasive that little or no distinction would be possible between marital and nonmarital sex. He fully expected the home to degenerate into a place to meet for sex and virtually nothing else. "The family as a sacred union of husband and wife, of parents and children will continue to disintegrate—the main sociocultural functions of the family will further decrease until the family becomes a mere overnight parking place mainly for sex relationship" (Sorokin, 1937:109). Sorokin was wise enough not to set a date for the funeral of the American family system.

Culver Pictures, Inc.

*Pitirim Sorokin's gloomy pessimism about the future of the family and marriage has not been borne out.*

Sorokin is an interesting figure whose life and works illustrate an important point about the study of the future. That is, scientists and lay persons alike are affected by the sociocultural environment in which they live and the social and political events they witness. Sorokin received his education in Russia prior to the overthrow of the Czar and was imprisoned several times for his then rather radical views. When the first Russian Revolution occurred, he was secretary to Alexander Kerensky, the leader of the Menshevik faction of the Communist party and provisional leader of Russia. In the infighting that followed the overthrow of the Czarist government, Lenin and his followers ousted Kerensky, and Sorokin went into hiding. He was captured, but escaped, and was recaptured a number of times. The last time he was sentenced to death his sentence was personally commuted by Lenin on the provision that Sorokin leave Russia. These experiences led Sorokin to a very conservative and cynical view of social change and the prospects for the future. Several years after his departure from Russia, Sorokin came to the United States at the invitation of Carle Zimmerman, who was then at the University of Minnesota.

Zimmerman, who was responsible for the developmental theory of social change, discussed in Chapter 4, predicted that urbanization would lead to a completely atomistic family in the United States. This trend, he felt, would signal the end of the family and Western civilization. He was convinced that the similarities between Western civilization and Greek and Roman civilizations, where the atomistic type of family developed, were so great that Western civilization was doomed.

A more recent invitation to the funeral of the American family was issued by political scientist Barrington Moore, Jr. (1958). Moore sees himself continuing the tradition of the great British philosopher, Bertrand Russell, whose suggestion that the family and marriage were obsolete or rapidly becoming so was a shocking pronouncement in 1929. Moore (1958: 160) stated: "I would suggest then that conditions have arisen which, in many cases, prevent the family from performing the social and psychological functions ascribed to it by modern sociologists. The same conditions may also make it possible for the advanced industrial societies of the world to do away with the family and substitute other social arrangements that impose fewer unnecessary and painful restrictions on humanity." The gist of Moore's argument is that the family system as it is now structured cannot withstand the forces of technological change. The family will split asunder because of serious demands on the time and energies of each family member. Moore is not totally pessimistic. His quasi-solution is: "For the home to become again the place where human beings take the first important step toward realizing their creative potentials, parents would have to become willing once more to assert their authority. In turn this authority would have to acquire a rational and objective basis, freed of current attempts to revive religious taboos. Thus there would have to be a philosophical as well as a social revolution whose implications we cannot here pursue" (Moore, 1958:177).

It is fairly obvious that the death knells sounded by Watson, Sorokin, Zimmerman, and Moore were premature and perhaps completely out of tune with factual data. As Vincent (1966:31) aptly pointed out, "Since the earliest writings available, changes occurring in the institution of the family have been used and interpreted to support either an optimistic or a pessimistic premise concerning social change, and the pessimists have consistently outnumbered the optimists."

There are probably two major reasons for the pessimistic point of view of the sociologists discussed above. First, Sorokin and Zimmerman were both specialists in social change, and their interests in possible changes in the family were somewhat peripheral to the major thrust of their work. Second, Sorokin, Zimmerman, Watson, and Moore were more prophets than projectionists in their treatment of the family. In addition, their prophesies were tinged with ideological strains and reflected the culture in which they worked—primarily a conservative one, conservative in the sense that they viewed the family in the United States or industrialized society against the misleading stereotype of "the classical family of western nostalgia" (see Goode, 1963; Chapter 4).

When prophesy fails, projections follow, and sociologists in the middle part of the twentieth century increasingly gravitated to the projection methodology to gain a glimpse of the future. It is to these attempts that we now direct our attention.

## PROJECTIONS FOR THE FUTURE

### Robert Parke and Paul Glick (1967)

In 1967 Robert Parke and Paul Glick, using demographic data from the census, projected probable changes in the patterns of marriage and the family to 1985. Their expectations were as follows:[1]

1. a continued popularity of marriage with almost everyone marrying at some time in their life
2. a further decline and eventual leveling off of teenage marriage
3. a rise in the age at first marriage for women as a result of a relative oversupply of women
4. a further reduction in the relative ages of spouses at marriage
5. a reduction in the frequency of early widowhood and an increase in the proportion of couples who survive jointly to retirement age

---

[1] Robert Parke, Jr. and Paul C. Glick, "Prospective Changes in Marriage and the Family," *Journal of Marriage and the Family* 29(1967):249–56. Reprinted by permission of the National Council on Family Relations.

6. declines in the relative frequency of divorce and separation to the extent that there are reductions in poverty and general improvements in the socioeconomic status of the population

7. the general small size of the American family remaining the same with a further reduction in the number of households with more than two adults present

8. a pervasive tendency for married couples, the aged, and adult individuals to maintain their own households

It should be noted that the Parke-Glick formulations are necessarily tied to changes that occurred up to 1967, and these changes were measured at a level that seems to leave out individual attitudes, values, choices, and exotic actions. The census does not say what will be the premarital consequences of later marriage ages for women or what arrangements will be made for the sexual activity of aged individuals who will maintain separate residences as opposed to going into nursing homes and so forth. More inherently interesting marriage futures will be discussed later in this chapter.

## Meyer F. Nimkoff (1965)

Another sociologist who may be considered a projectionist, though not as statistically based as Parke and Glick, is Meyer Francis Nimkoff, a structural-functionalist who collaborated extensively with William F. Ogburn (see Chapter 4). It is interesting to note some similarities and differences between Nimkoff and Sorokin. Both were émigrés from Russia, but Nimkoff was optimistic about the family in contrast to Sorokin. The reason for this may be that Nimkoff was more interested in change in the family whereas Sorokin was interested, like Ogburn, in social change in general.

Nimkoff (1965) held that all family functions could be viewed as contributing to the maintenance of society as a whole or to that of the members of the family. He identified what he called four maintenance systems that related to certain family functions: (a) biological maintenance —reproduction of the species; (b) economic maintenance—care and feeding of the young; (c) sociocultural maintenance—socialization of the young; (d) social-psychological maintenance—emotional maintenance of interpersonal relationships (husband-wife, parent-child). Nimkoff suggested that there are certain minimal functions of the family, one of which included reproduction. He said, "In no society have the norms over an appreciable period of time ever sanctioned the transfer of the function of reproduction away from the family. If parents continue to have children, and they will, it is reasonable to assume that they will wish to be identified emotionally with them. Parents in the future may delegate more of the care of their children to others, but even so they are likely to want to retain responsibility for the big decisions" (Nimkoff, 1965:360–361). With regard to the care of the very young, Nimkoff pointed out that no society has ever completely relieved parents of the responsibility for nurture during the very early years of life. Of most importance, however, is the social-psychological maintenance (Nimkoff, 1965:361):

> Indeed, in today's impersonal mass society, the need for emotional security, congenial companionship and perfected response between mates is probably greater than it was in earlier folk society. Theoretically it may be possible to find such emotional support in friendships with members of the same sex or with members of the opposite sex in a nonfamily arrangement. But it is difficult to see how either would be an advantage over the marital union, which combines such solid components as division of labor, sexual satisfaction and sentimental companionship, one or another of which is lacking in the other non-familial relationships. As the child usually finds in his parents the best protection against a hostile environment, so happily married couples find it in each other.

### Robert F. Winch (1970)

Another sociologist studying the family who has adopted projection as his methodology and structural-functionalism as his conceptual strategy is Robert Winch (1970). Although Winch's "Some Speculations as to the Family's Future" focused on the functions cited by Nimkoff, the interpretations are somewhat different. Looking first at the replacement function and noting the considerable decline in the crude birth rate from the late 1950s to 1970, Winch speculated that if these data represent a trend toward more childless women and fewer marriages, it would seem to foreshadow an increase in Zimmerman's atomistic family. Winch turned from this rather somber reflection to the impact of the availability of an easy, efficient, inexpensive, and safe contraceptive. He suggested that such would provide a real distinction between procreational and recreational sex and have four major consequences: (a) a disappearance of moral and legal sanctions against extramarital sex; (b) a decline in the marriage rate; (c) a decline in the number of unwanted pregnancies and thus the birth rate; and (d) the creation of a situation where those getting married would be doing so for more exclusively positive reasons (strength of the man-woman relationship and/or the desire to raise children).

The most conspicuous trend in the socialization and education function has been the increasing degree of responsibility assumed by government at all levels. Winch predicted the continued development of public education extending downward to include nursery schools, day-care centers, and kindergartens. Concomitant with the expanding arm of public education it was suggested that educational opportunity will be equalized by state support, thus decreasing the status-conferring function of the family.

The real crux of Winch's view of the family's future is tied, like Nimkoff's, to the emotional gratification function: "But if the importance of the other functions is to continue to decrease, then it seems inescapable that if the nuclear family is to maintain its present strength, the importance of emotional gratification will have to increase, absolutely as well as relatively" (Winch, 1970:10).

If not explicit, then at least implicit in the projections of Nimkoff, Winch, and others about the future of the family are some common assumptions. First, it is assumed that the family has lost and is losing some of its functions, voluntarily and involuntarily. Second, the most likely recipient of these discarded familial functions is the governmental institution. Third, and maybe not intentionally, is an assumption that this transfer is indicative of weaknesses in the family system in the United States.

## Otto Pollak (1967)

One writer who rejects this third assumption is Otto Pollak (1967:193), who says: "The accusation of invasion into the family domain which is repetitively made against the government ignores the change in living conditions which has made governmental intervention and provision of services a necessity rather than an imposition." Pollak sees the family of the future as increasingly stripped of its autonomy to set its own standards in a standardized, bureaucratic, and depersonalized society. However, in the family's bondage can be found new strengths. According to Pollak, an emerging function of the family is to integrate the governmentally provided health, education, and welfare services and to develop expertise in their use. In coping with and mastering these standardized, bureaucratic, and depersonalized services, Pollak sees the sources of greater individualization and human cooperation—a cathartic role the family can play for future men and women.

One thing that seems to emerge from this review of the more scholarly previews of the future family is that while changing, the institution is not bound for extinction. The main focus has been on the shifting functions that most families perform and how they have changed over time. As we will see later in this chapter, much of the focus of more popular views of the family's future has been on alternative marriage forms. But, before we get into this discussion we should examine what kind of environment may be available to humans in the year A.D. 2000.

## SOCIAL CONTEXT, A.D. 2000

One of the more dynamic and interesting phenomena to develop during the 1960s was the increasing ecological awareness of the American public. During that decade pollution became a widely used word, one that was diffused across class, ethnic, and age lines. Underlying the whole ecological crusade is the idea that space is filled with objects, some of which may be dangerous to our health and well being. Thus, a description of the socioenvironmental context that might confront the American family in A.D. 2000 would seem appropriate and even necessary. The social context would include such factors as population size, metropolitanization, the age structure, economic opportunities and labor force participation, and the relative supply of energy resources. A delineation of the projections relative to the socioenvironmental factors should provide a base from which to view specific proposals for alternative marriage and family futures.

## U.S. Population Size, A.D. 2000

As discussed in Chapter 19, population experts study population by focusing on the interrelationships among three demographic processes: fertility, migrations, and mortality. For growth to occur there must be an excess of births over deaths and an excess of immigration over emigration. Even a cursory examination of demographic data for the United States reveals a fantastic increase in overall size.

In 1900 the United States had a population of about 70 million. By 1960 this had increased to 180 million, and by 1977 the population stood at 216 million, an addition of 146 million people in just 77 years. Assuming that in the future, women will be giving birth at an "ultimate" rate averaging 3.1 children per woman over a lifetime, plus the assumptions that reductions in mortality will be slight and that there will be an average addition of about 400,000 persons from net migration, the population by A.D. 2000 could total 322 million. If the average number of children per woman were just above replacement (2.1 children per woman), the population in the year 2000 would be about 271 million. The lower figure, which would be a conservative estimate, would constitute an increase of 200 million in just 100 years (the twentieth century). The more liberal estimate, based on a 3-child average, would constitute an increase of 252 million in the twentieth century. In terms of population size alone, the socioenvironmental context within which the family must operate in the year 2000 is bound to produce some important changes in family functions. In the remaining sections of this chapter we will examine some of the alternative futures of marriage and the family.

## Some Questions About the Future

Is the family institution merely changing, or is it bound for extinction? Will some sociologist in the next 25 to 50 years ask the question, Is the family still universal? and answer with a resounding No? Is the experimentation with alternative intimate life-styles a precursor to the death of marriage as a social and legally sanctioned means of establishing a family unit? The answers to these questions have produced more than a fair share of debate with vociferous proponents on both sides of each question. It is, of course, quite likely that we will not reach consensus in this chapter.

601

However, it is important for us to view critically the various arguments and proposals for change. As pointed out in Chapter 1, a crucial element of the science of society is prediction. Beyond the scientific interests that these questions elicit, personal interests exist. Many reading this chapter will be under 50 years old when the twenty-first century rolls around. Most of them will have their children and grandchildren to observe. What will they be doing relative to marriage and the family?

## THE FUTURE OF MARRIAGE

### The Meanings of Marriage

It is virtually impossible to discuss the future of marriage without specifying just what is meant by the concept of marriage. In everyday usage *marriage* has many different connotations depending on the semantic context in which it is used. Each of the following three meanings of marriage has received some attention in the literature concerning changes that either "need" to be made or may occur by the year 2000:

1. Marriage sometimes refers to a ritual that signals the mutual consent of two persons to claim the rights, privileges, and responsibilities of married life. Our society prescribes that the marriage (ritual) be a legitimated (that is, legal) arrangement, but does not specify the content, location, or form the ritual must take. Some persons object to the legal or de jure binder while others feel that society makes the legal tie too binding.

2. Marriage is also used to refer to the structural character of the relationship between marital partners. In Chapter 2 several forms of marriage in this sense were discussed: group marriage, polyandry, polygyny, and monogamy. At the current time in the United States only one form of marriage, monogamy, is legally sanctioned. Some family specialists claim that in a de facto sense the ease and frequency with which divorce and remarriage occur indicate that the prevailing marriage form in America is actually serial polygamy, one man married to one woman at a time, but with multiple spouses for each over a life-span. Much of the literature on alternative futures of marriage deals with variant marriage forms.

3. A third rather pervasive meaning of marriage refers to the quality of the relationship between marriage partners and the activities associated with marital life. A great deal has been written in recent years about the alternatives available for accomplishing marital activities like sexual adjustment.

Thus, a discussion of the futures of marriage must be approached in terms of these various meanings of the concept *marriage*. In the following pages these distinctions will be utilized to organize the alternative futures of marriage.

## Proposed Marriage Contracts

At least two or three proposals have been offered to replace the traditional marriage ritual, which today is predominantly contracted in a religiolegal and social context and which is defined as "until death us do part." The first, marriage as a nonlegal voluntary association, is designed to take marriage out of the legal sphere. Harold Greenwald (1970), a psychotherapist, would have a couple reach a mutual agreement to voluntarily associate with one another for an agreed upon and specified period of time. The value of such an arrangement is that the duration of the association would not be unlimited. If the arrangement did not work out, little or no stigma and less trauma and legal hassle would be attached to the termination of the "marriage."

The second proposal would institutionalize trial marriage or what Margaret Mead (1966) called "marriage in two steps." The heart of Mead's proposal is the distinction between marriage for just two individuals (individual and relatively nonpermanent marriage) versus parental marriage, which occurs when the couple decides that the relationship should be made more permanent through the introduction of children into the marital-familial arrangement.

The advantage of marriage in two steps is that if a couple decided after a period of experimentation with individual marriage that they did not want to make it permanent, they could terminate the marriage without the difficulties of a divorce. For individual marriages to work there would have to be serious efforts to prevent unwanted conceptions. The real value of individual marriage is that the couple could feel out their mutual views about marital roles with a sense of freedom and flexibility without being trapped on a societally controlled marital track. The advantage of the second step, parental marriage, is that those couples taking this step would be committed to each other and the establishment of a family, thus reducing the possibility of children being affected by divorce.

## Proposed Structures for Marriage

It is important at this point to distinguish between marriage and what may be merely a convenient living, economic, and/or sexual arrangement. The underlying support of a structural marital relationship is the commitment each party makes to the other or others involved. The living, economic, and sexual arrangement is subsidiary to the commitment and mutual identification made in the name of marriage. Thus, the single person does not represent a category of persons with an alternative to the traditional monogamous marriage, whether he or she is: (a) celibate and living with someone with whom certain economic and social agreements are shared; (b) living with someone of the opposite or same sex and engaging in sexual activities as well as sharing the economic and social activities; (c) living with, sharing economic and social resources, and

603

Cary Wolinsky, Stock, Boston

*Some sort of communal family—perhaps a variation of those formed by young people in the sixties and seventies—may be one answer to the economic and social pressures bearing down on the nuclear family.*

having sexual liaisons with several persons (separately or in a group); or (d) "swinging" sexually with whoever comes along for varying lengths of time.

As an alternative life-style, remaining single instead of opting for marriage of any form is a phenomenon that may become more prevalent in this society. At the very least, this life-style may become more common for more people as the age at marriage increases in the United States. In other words, marriage may remain the eventual goal of most people in this society, but a free-wheeling single life may become a more integral part of the premarital experiences of persons in the last part of this century.

A number of proposed alternatives to the traditional monogamous structure of marriage in the United States have received a great deal of attention, particularly in the popular media and in some novels that were built around these variant structures (see, in particular, Rimmer, 1969). What are the alternatives? What are the characteristics that distinguish an "experimental" and a "normative or traditional" marriage structure? (See Cogswell and Sussman, 1972.) The first characteristic is legal-nonlegal. Has society legitimated the marital agreement? The second characteristic is the number of persons involved—any number beyond two alters the structural designation of the "marriage." The third characteristic setting an experimental marriage apart is the sexual accessibility norms operative between members or among members. Each of these should be considered. The following lists possible "marriage" structures:

Legitimated Structures

1. Traditional monogamy, sexual exclusiveness, legally bonded pair of opposite sexes.
2. Corporate families, two or more monogamous couples who enter into a legally sanctioned agreement to share certain resources

and/or to jointly participate in certain activities. This could also include an agreement to forsake previous vows of sexual exclusiveness.

Nonlegitimate Structures

1. Heterosexual cohabitation without legal sanction. Even though the couple has vowed sexual exclusiveness, play the marital roles in an agreed-upon division of labor, have children, and so forth, this is not a legitimated marriage structure.

2. Homosexual cohabitation with mutual perception of marital obligations. Regardless of the de facto arrangement, the de jure status of this structure is "not legal."

3. Multilateral marriage. This structure requires a minimum of three and usually not more than six individuals (see Constantine and Constantine, 1971). Although multilateral marriages may consist of legitimately married couples who have "spiritually" banded together and rejected their "rights" of sexual exclusiveness, the crucial mark of this structure is that each person considers himself or herself married to at least two of the other participants. In some cases this resembles polygyny or polyandry in that the persons added to the original dyad are not maritally attached to anyone else.

4. Communes. There are a number of different types of communal arrangements, many of which require very little of the participants (see Kanter, 1972). For a commune to be viewed as an alternative marriage structure there must be a perception on the part of the members that they are related to one another (that is, married to one or more of the others or to the group). Communes could very easily be subsumed under multilateral or group marriage structures except that the size and possible same sex–opposite sex variations of commitment make it a distinct category.

Because of the cultural, social, and religiomoral traditions that undergird our legal system it is very unlikely that this society will ever become flexible enough to fully legitimate polygamy, multilateral, and/or group marriage. This does not mean they will not exist in a de facto sense.

Although no indisputably reliable data are available on the prevalence of these alternative marriage structures, Cogswell and Sussman (1972) have estimated that about 8 percent of the population may live in nontraditional marriage arrangements. Ellis (1970) contends that a sizable minority (not defined) will live in some form of multilateral or group marriage arrangement in this society, forsaking the confines of traditional monogamy.

One age group for whom multilateral marriage is a viable alternative is the aged. Because men usually die younger than women, there is a relatively large excess of women in the over-60 age group.

605

Victor Kassel (1970), a specialist in geriatrics, outlined several of the advantages offered by polygyny after age 60. They are:

1. the opportunity for the excess of women in this age group to obtain husbands
2. the opportunity to re-establish a meaningful family group
3. a more adequate diet and better eating habits, a health advantage
4. the opportunity to pool funds so that there is enough money for all and the level of living conditions are improved.
5. the likelihood that those who are elderly and ill would receive better health care in familiar surroundings without having to resort to the impersonal and expensive care in nursing homes
6. a reduction in the toll of housework
7. a solution to the problems of sexual frustration and to the guilt that occurs when sex takes place outside the marital bed
8. the likelihood that elderly people will take better care of themselves in a grooming sense if they live corporately
9. a solution to the problem of depression and loneliness
10. the economic advantages derived from a better break in the health insurance field

Although some very real problems are associated with Kassel's suggestions, polygyny or a multilateral marriage after age 60 seems to be a workable solution to what is and will increasingly become a salient and sizable problem—the health and well-being of our senior citizens.

## Proposed Qualities of the Marriage Relationship

The third meaning of the concept of marriage focuses on the quality of the relationship and how marital activities are enacted. This meaning of marriage has generated a substantial effort in detailing the shortcomings of traditional monogamy and in proposing alternative futures of marriage.

The question to which much of the literature on the future of marriage is directed is: Is monogamy outdated? Rustum and Della Roy (1970) suggest that traditional monogamy may have been appropriate and functional a few years ago, but in today's new environment it is dysfunctional. They list what they claim are four causes of the "crisis" with traditional monogamy:

1. The sexual revolution has made it infinitely more difficult to retain monogamy's monopoly on sex.
2. There is a vast increase in the number and variety of man-woman contacts after marriage, and no guidelines are available for behavior in these new situations.

*New forms of decision making are necessary in a larger group that may include adults and children, married and single members.*

3. Traditional monogamy is in trouble because it has not adjusted itself to find a less hurtful way to terminate a marriage.

4. Traditional monogamy does not deal humanely with its have-nots—the adult singles, the widowed, the divorced.

The Roys write from a humanistic perspective that places an optimum value on honesty, freedom, and open options for pluralism in every facet of life, including marriage. They propose several ways that traditional monogamy can and "should" be modified if marriage is to meet human needs in a changing world. Their stratagems for modifying

607

traditional monogamy are (a) institutionalizing premarital sex, (b) expanding the erotic community in the postmarital years, (c) providing a relationship network for the single, (d) legalizing bigamy, especially in the later years of life, and (e) making marital difficulties and divorce less destructive of personalities.

Even a cursory examination of these strategies indicates that the Roys really view the monopolization of sex and the exclusion of the have-nots as the central components of monogamy that need corrective change. What they are really proposing is not the repeal of monogamous principles, but rather the easing of norms concerning premarital, marital, and extramarital sex. Perhaps the available data (see Kinsey, 1948, 1953; Cuber and Harroff, 1965; Johnson, 1970; Neubeck, 1969) on the sexual

---

### Some Predictions for the Future of Marriage

What conclusions can be reached about the future of marriage in the United States to the year 2000? Is the current wave of experimentation with alternative intimate life-styles the wave of the future? Will marriage as we know it be extinct by the year 2000? The answer to the last two questions is No! In the first place, experimentation with marriage and the family in the United States is not at all new. The Oneida Community (see Chapter 8) was only one of the many communal arrangements that flourished in nineteenth-century America (see Kanter, 1972). So the idea that communal or tribal marriages may become rather widespread is not a new fear. It did not happen then, and it will not happen in the last part of this century. The communal movement that flourished in the 1960s is dying in the 1970s. Although communes may always be available as a viable marital style, they will never be very widespread as an experience, and from a total view of the family and marriage experience in society, they will be of minimal influence.

Second, marriage, as we know it, will definitely not be extinct at the close of this century. Although there is little doubt that the proportion of persons entering marriage in the year 2000 as sexual virgins will be relatively small, enter marriage they will, and few will remain single throughout life. In other words, little evidence is available that would lead one to predict a significant reduction in the popularity of married life as the primary life-style option to be adopted. That it may be adopted at a somewhat later average age is probable.

Actually, several predictions may be made about the future of marriage in the United States, given the three meanings of the concept.

activities of Americans are evidence that such a proposal has the de facto support of the majority, although a rather silent majority at that.

While the Roys (1970) claim that monogamy is outdated because of bankrupt sexual constraints, other writers have focused their attention on nonsexual factors that limit the quality of the marriage relationship in traditional monogamy. Howard and Joy Osofsky (1971) would retain the sexual exclusiveness present in monogamous marriage while encouraging role allocation based on sex to be nullified and replaced with nonsex-differentiated allocation norms based on competence and needs. They call this type of marital relationship an "androgynous" one. Nena and George O'Neill (1972) advocate what they call "open marriage," which stresses outside relationships, "expanded monogamy" relative to

The methodology used to obtain these predictions would be a mixture of projections and diffusions of innovations:

1. The popularity of marriage will not diminish substantially. Most persons will get married at some time in their life, although the age at first marriage will tend to go up.

2. Trial marriage, or marriage in two steps, will become institutionalized as a part of the courtship and mate selection systems in the United States. This will almost certainly be true in a de facto sense. It may very well become true in a de jure sense also.

3. Corporate marriages in which two or more couples appear to legally share certain resources and activities will become more prevalent with monogamous sexual exclusiveness retained in almost all cases.

4. Polygyny after a certain age, something beyond seventy, will be not only de facto acceptable, but will receive some positive sanction from governmental and judicial systems. It is quite likely that some of the major religious organizations will also give the practice at least qualified support.

5. Although swinging and multilateral marriages may continue to exist on a de facto basis, the proportion of persons engaging in such life-styles will never be large, and society will not give such practices positive sanction.

6. Androgynous and open marriage arrangements will become more widely accepted as normative in the United States in order for couples to cope with the pressures inherent in the social environment.

609

sex, equal freedom and identity for each partner, individual growth and increased psychic space, and the development of trust.

One other proposal for improving the quality of the marital relationship does not explicitly entail an alternative form of marriage. Rather it is a tactic for eliminating the monogamous monopoly of sex without the clandestine aspect of the more traditional tactic, nonconsensual extramarital coitus. This proposal has been called "swinging." Carolyn Symonds (1968) defined swinging as a husband and wife's "willingness to swap sexual partners with a couple with whom they are not acquainted and/or to go to a swinging party and be willing for both him and his mate to have sexual intercourse with strangers." The actual extent of swinging in the United States is not known, although the Breedloves (1964) have "conservatively" estimated that about two and one-half million couples exchange partners on a somewhat regular basis (three or more times a year). James and Lynn Smith (1970) described the "usual swinger" as having a rather high educational attainment, disproportionately professional and white collar in occupation, and conservative and straight in most respects. The reasons couples engage in swinging are, of course, quite varied. The effects of swinging on marriage also vary, but Denfeld and Gordon (1970) are convinced that "swinging may support rather than disrupt monogamous marriage as it exists in this society." I can see how swinging might enliven a dull monogamous marriage. It can be viewed as a joint leisure activity, like bridge or bowling, requiring the husband and wife to agree on something. But I suspect that the actual significance of swinging as an alternative sexual outlet is probably minimal since it touches such a small proportion of all married couples.

## REPRODUCTION IN THE FUTURE

Technological advances are likely to have the greatest impact on the reproductive function of the family. A real likelihood is that by the year 2000 or even before, it will be possible to preset the sex of one's child and to "program" its IQ, looks, and personality. Congenital birth defects will almost certainly be one specter that parents of the future will not face. Alvin Toffler (1970) predicted an even more amazing and, in some sense, frightening possibility with regard to reproduction. It may be possible by the year 2000 to take an embryo from two different pregnant women, place both of them in a suitable environment and nurture them until they form a single growing mass, and then emplant them in the womb of a third "carrier" female. The baby born would thus share the genetic characteristics of both sets of donors. As Toffler points out, this multiperson would create problems such as: What or who is a parent? When a woman carries in her uterus an embryo conceived in another woman's womb, who is the mother and who is the father?

These ideas sound like something straight out of science fiction—and in a way they are. To many people such prospects are immoral at best and certainly unthinkable at worst. Yet the possibility remains that such things may very well be technologically feasible. The chances that they will ever become acceptable practices are probably slim to none, given the traditional value system of our culture.

I believe quite strongly that the reproductive function of the family will remain the prerogative of married couples. It is quite likely that premarital pregnancy will become virtually nonexistent by the year 2000 as the effectiveness of our contraceptive technology increases. Let me go one step further though, and I expect this will evoke a very negative reaction. I believe that the "decision to reproduce" will be taken out of the hands of married couples before the end of the twentieth century. It is quite possible that eventually the opportunity and privilege of reproduction will be on a quota basis only. By this I mean that every married couple will be allowed to have one child. It will be illegal for a couple to conceive a child without permission to do so by some agency. Any illegal conception will be terminated within the first trimester, at the orders of the controlling agency. After a couple has had one child and after a certain period of time, say two or three years, they may reapply for permission to have another. However, only a certain proportion of parents (a quota) will be allowed the opportunity to bear two children. No couple will be allowed to have more than two.

Although such a proposal sounds drastic and certainly implies not only a curtailment of freedom but also an intrusion into what has been a totally private decision, this policy may become necessary because of limited resources and the pressures of overpopulation. Remember, a great deal can happen in the next twenty or so years that can change how we view children and the reproductive function of the family. Necessity may be the mother of invention. With regard to reproduction, necessity may have to change drastically our entire conception of motherhood.

## CHILD REARING IN THE FUTURE

Now that we have discussed, albeit briefly, the future of the reproductive function of the family, let us examine some of the possible changes that can occur relative to child rearing. Let Toffler (1970) set the stage for the discussion:

> Raising children, after all, requires skills that are by no means universal. We don't let "just anyone" perform brain surgery or, for that matter, sell stocks and bonds. Even the lowest ranking civil servant is required to pass tests proving competence. Yet we allow virtually anyone, almost without regard for mental or moral qualification, to try his or her hand at raising young human beings, so long as these humans are biological

offspring. Despite the increasing complexity of the task, parenthood remains the greatest single preserve of the amateur.

Toffler's concern is with the quality of the socialization experience for children and the allocation of this crucial task to persons who are ill equipped to adequately perform in the parental role. What then are some of the possible futures in child rearing?

Along with predictions of more single-parent families and adoptions by single persons, Toffler also foresees families based on homosexual marriages with children present. Although I am willing to concede that these predictions may become reality someday, I am skeptical. For exam-

Peter Vandermark

*The day-care center is an aid, not a substitute, for the mother who works outside the home.*

ple, there may be more single-parent families, but these will probably result almost entirely from divorce and marital dissolution. Adoptions by single persons may also exist, but such will be fairly rare—not because of societal resistance, but rather because the supply of children available for adoption will decrease significantly by the year 2000. Although homosexual marriages may become a legal alternative before we enter the twenty-first century, it is not likely that society will allow children to be raised in such an arrangement. Human beings are generally committed to heterosexuality as a norm even though the tolerance of homosexuality has increased substantially. I am confident that the next great social movement in our society will focus its attention on the rights of children. This being so, society will make every effort to ensure that children are not exposed to a life and sexual style that is not practiced by the majority. Homosexual daddies and mommies will not be allowed, even in the year 2000.

Both Toffler and psychologist Carl Levett (1970) predict the development of professional parents. These pro-parents will live as active family units, taking children on consignment from biological parents. Such a family-type unit would include other professionals who would serve in the grandparent and uncle-aunt roles. The children accepted into these pro-families would be of varying ages and both sexes, so that the children involved in such an arrangement would encounter the optimum number and variety of familial experiences. The children would, in addition, receive a variety of services including educational instruction and cultural enrichment. The biological parents would have visiting privileges. Such pro-families would have life spans that would range from a summer to as long as five or more years.

One other proposal offered by Toffler also seems to have some potential merit. It would consist of persons who opt for child rearing as an avocation after retirement. Because it is quite likely that the average age at retirement will drop to 55 and the average life span will increase to about 85 years, postretirement child rearing may be one way the extended family could re-emerge as a family type.

Young married couples with children would leave the major parental-role responsibilities to their parents or to pro-parents while they pursue their occupational and other activities. The real advantage of such an arrangement is that it would free the younger members of society to be creative and productive without the normal constraints of child rearing and provide retired persons inclined to it with a purpose in life after their occupational careers have terminated.

Duberman's (1977:22, 39) view of the future focuses on projected changes in the structure of the family resulting from widespread divorce and remarriage:

> The family of the future will be a reconstituted family. People will practice serial monogamy, and children will take the presence of stepkin for

granted. The family unit will continue to perform most of the older functions, but in a greatly attenuated form. It will continue to be a consuming unit and a dispenser of nonsexual love.... In short, the family is likely to become more existential. That is, its members are likely to be less dependent on each other and more concerned with themselves. It follows that parents will minimize their function of socialization, which will be taken over by peers and siblings. The result will be a decline in sex-specific socialization.

Although some of these proposals for alternative child-rearing futures seem logical and workable, I do not think any of them will emerge to any substantial extent. In fact, child rearing in the year 2000 will probably remain the primary responsibility of biological parents. Given the prospect of a population in which virtually all adults will be "educated," a shorter work week (an average of thirty-one hours per week), the likelihood that many jobs will be performed at home due to technological breakthroughs in communications, and extremely flexible work schedules, parents in the latter years of this century will be better prepared and will have more time available to be parents to their children. Besides, little

Ken Heyman

*An increasing life span, earlier retirement, and more working mothers form a post-retirement parental role for grandparents.*

evidence justifies t                         s are better as parents
than their nonpro                            jor difference in child
rearing that will                            y will be an increased
quality in parent-                           gical parents and their
children.

## THE FUTURE OF THE FAMILY

What, then, is the future of the family? Will it be substantially different
as we enter the next century? Will it be stronger or weaker? Will it perform the same functions then that it does now? Will its structure change
very much between now and the year 2000? These questions are, in my
opinion, not very hard to answer.

The nuclear family will not only survive, it will be substantially the
same structure as we have today. The real difference will be in the quality
of the relationships within the family. I foresee the emergence of a truly
equalitarian husband-wife arrangement in which each relates to the other
as a person. The caste-like distinctions between male and female roles will,
for all intents and purposes, cease to exist. Husband and wife will be
coequal partners whose major goal will be to assist the other and themselves as a conjugal pair in achieving true personhood.

Because there will be more opportunities available to understand
the responsibilities of marital living before marriage begins, the extent of
divorce will not be much greater than the levels achieved in the 1970s.
Perhaps it will even be smaller. Married life in the year 2000 will have a
better chance of producing both happiness and satisfaction because the
expectations about marriage will be more realistically appraised by those
who choose to enter it. The prevailing ideology and norms about married
life will be designed to maximize joint satisfaction and to minimize
conflict.

The family of the future will be a modified extended one with even
closer ties across generations. The grandparent roles will become an even
more integral part of the family network, and the quality of the relationships between parents and their offspring and their grandchildren will
take on an expanded significance as we approach the twenty-first century.
There will be especially an increase in the degree to which the extended
family will share leisure time and activities.

Children of the future will experience a level of quality in their
relationships to their parents that has never before occurred. Generally
speaking, living in a family will be an exciting and stimulating experience
for both parents and children. There will be a multitude of joint learning
and leisure activities, shared on a relatively equal basis between parents
and children. Parents in the future will relate to their children with the
aid of more readily accessible child-rearing experts whose function will be
to spot potential difficulties before they occur.

All in all, the family of the future will be a healthy unit promoting strength and self-actualization anchored in a familial context that emphasizes manhood, womanhood, childhood, and personhood as ultimate goals.

## SOME POSSIBLE IMPLICATIONS

*The future of the family and the future of marriage are unknowns about which more is known each day. Social scientists are investing more effective energies into the study of the future as their predictive capabilities increase along with the utilization of more sophisticated research techniques and theoretical models. What are some implications of this scientific development for the future of the family and marriage?*

*One possible answer is that the future will be influenced by our attempts to understand and predict it. For example, multidisciplinary teams of architects and urban planners, anthropologists and sociologists, medical personnel and psychologists may be able to develop new communities that will be structured around "projected future contingencies." These model cities would be essentially self-contained and self-sustaining with the participant community members chosen according to their ages, skills, ideological diversity, and commitment to making the future work in the present. As ongoing social laboratories they would be regularly monitored and altered in accordance with cybernetic methodologies for the study of the future.*

*The future has traditionally been something feared by people who had little information available for determining what it would be like. The future of society may be determined, or at least structured, by the present and a knowledge of what mistakes occurred in planning in the past.*

*Will the family as we know it become an extinct and dysfunctional organization, or will the family be a more integral basic unit of society? Will marriage as we know it fade into the history books as an artifact of earlier, less progressive, and more primitive times, or will marriage take on added significance as a central event of life in a world not overcome by "future shock"?*

# BIBLIOGRAPHY

Acker, Joan. 1973. "Women and Social Stratification: A Case of Intellectual Sexism." *American Journal of Sociology* 78:936–45.

Ackerman, Charles. 1963. "Affiliations: Structural Determinants of Differential Divorce Rates." *American Journal of Sociology* 69:12–20.

Adams, Bert N. 1967. "Interaction Theory and the Social Network." *Sociometry* 30:64–78.

———. 1968. *Kinship in an Urban Setting*. Chicago: Markham.

———. 1971. *The American Family*. Chicago: Markham.

Akers, Donald S. 1967. "On Measuring the Marriage Squeeze." *Demography* 4:907–24.

Axelrod, Morris. 1956. "Urban Structure and Social Participation." *American Sociological Review* 21:13–18.

Bachofen, J. J. 1948. *Das Mutterrecht*. Basel: Benno Schwabe (originally published in 1861).

Bales, Robert F. 1950. *Interaction Process Analysis*. Reading, Mass.: Addison-Wesley.

Bane, Mary Jo. 1976. "Marital Disruption and the Lives of Children." *Journal of Social Issues* 32:103–18.

Barrett, Curtis L., and Helen Noble. 1973. "Mothers' Anxieties Versus the Effects of Long Distance Move on Children." *Journal of Marriage and the Family* 35:181–88.

Bayer, Alan E. 1968. "Early Dating and Early Marriage." *Journal of Marriage and the Family* 30:628–32.

Bealer, Robert Charles, Fern K. Willits, and Gerald W. Bender. 1963. "Religious Exogamy: A Study of Social Distance." *Sociology and Social Research* 48:69–79.

Becker, Wesley C. 1964. "Consequences of Different Kinds of Parental Discipline." In Martin L. Hoffman and Lois Hoffman (eds.), *Review of Child Development Research*. New York: Russell Sage Foundation, vol. 1, pp. 169–208.

Bell, Robert R. 1966. *Premarital Sex in a Changing Society*. Englewood Cliffs, N.J.: Prentice-Hall.

———. 1971. *Marriage and Family Interaction*. Homewood, Ill.: Dorsey Press, 3rd ed.

———, and Leonard Blumberg. 1959. "Courtship Intimacy and Religious Background." *Marriage and Family Living* 21:356–60.

———, and Jay B. Chaskes. 1970. "Premarital Sexual Experience Among Coeds: 1958–1968." *Journal of Marriage and the Family* 32:81–84.

———, Stanley Turner, and Lawrence Rosen. 1975. "A Multivariate Analysis of Female Extramarital Coitus." *Journal of Marriage and the Family* 37:375–84.

617

Bell, Wendell, and Marion D. Boat. 1957. "Urban Neighborhoods and Informal Social Relations." *American Journal of Sociology* 62:391–98.

———, and James A. Mau, eds. 1971. *The Sociology of the Future.* New York: Russell Sage.

Bennett, Lerone, Jr. 1969. *Before the Mayflower: A History of Black America.* New York: Johnson.

Benson, Leonard. 1968. *Fatherhood: A Sociological Perspective.* New York: Random House.

Berardo, Felix M. 1970. "Survivorship and Social Isolation: The Case of the Aged Widower." *The Family Coordinator* 19:11–25.

Berger, Peter L. 1963. *An Invitation to Sociology: A Humanistic Perspective.* New York: Doubleday.

Bernard, Jessie. 1934. "Factors in the Distribution of Success in Marriage." *American Journal of Sociology* 40:49–60.

———. 1956. *Remarriage: A Study of Marriage.* New York: Dryden.

———. 1966a. "Note on Educational Homogamy in Negro-White and White-Negro Marriages, 1960." *Journal of Marriage and the Family* 28:274–76.

———. 1966b. *Marriage and Family Among Negroes.* Englewood Cliffs, N.J.: Prentice-Hall.

———. 1973. "My Four Revolutions: An Autobiographical History of the ASA." *American Journal of Sociology* 78:773–91.

———. 1975. "Note on Changing Life Styles, 1970–1974." *Journal of Marriage and the Family* 37:582–93.

Berschild, Ellen, and Elaine Walster. 1969. *Interpersonal Attraction.* Reading, Mass.: Addison-Wesley.

Biegel, Hugo G. 1951. "Romantic Love." *American Sociological Review* 16:326–34.

Biller, Henry B. 1969. "Father Dominance and Sex-Role Development in Kindergarten-Age Boys." *Developmental Psychology* 1:87–94.

Billingsley, Andrew. 1968. *Black Families in White America.* Englewood Cliffs, N.J.: Prentice-Hall.

Blau, Peter. 1964. *Exchange and Power in Social Life.* New York: Wiley.

Blood, Robert O., Jr. 1955. "A Retest of Waller's Rating Complex." *Marriage and Family Living* 17:41–47.

———. 1962. *Marriage.* Glencoe, Ill.: Free Press of Glencoe.

———, and Donad M. Wolfe. 1960. *Husbands and Wives.* Glencoe, Ill.: Free Press of Glencoe.

Blumberg, Leonard, and Robert R. Bell. 1959. "Urban Migration and Kinship Ties." *Social Problems* 7:328–33.

Bolton, Charles D. 1961. "Mate Selection as the Development of a Relationship." *Marriage and Family Living* 23:234–40.

Bossard, J. H. S., and H. C. Letts. 1956. "Mixed Marriages Involving Lutherans —A Research Report." *Marriage and Family Living* 18:308–10.

Bouma, Donald H. 1963. "Religiously Mixed Marriages: Denominational Consequences in the Christian Reformed Church." *Marriage and Family Living* 25:428–32.

Bowerman, Charles E. 1953. "Assortative Mating by Previous Marital Status, Seattle, 1939–1946." *American Sociological Review* 18:163–77.

———, and Barbara R. Day. 1956. "A Test of the Theory of Complementary

Needs as Applied to Couples During Courtship." *American Sociological Review* 21:602–5.

———, Donald P. Irish, and Hallowell Pope. 1963. *Unwed Motherhood: Personal and Social Consequences.* Chapel Hill: Institute for Research in Social Science.

Bradburn, N. M., and D. Caplovitz. 1965. *Reports on Happiness.* Chicago: Aldine.

Breedlove, William, and Jerrye Breedlove. 1964. *Swap Clubs.* Los Angeles: Sherbourne.

Briffault, Robert. 1931. *The Mothers.* 3 vols. New York: Macmillan.

Brim, Orville G., Jr. 1958. *Education for Child Rearing.* New York: Russell Sage.

Bromley, Dorothy, and Florence Britten. 1938. *Youth and Sex.* New York: Harper.

Bronfenbrenner, Urie. 1958. "Socialization and Social Class Through Time and Space." In *Readings in Social Psychology,* Eleanor Maccoby et al., eds. New York: Holt, pp. 400–425.

———. 1961. *Two Worlds of Childhood: U.S. and U.S.S.R.* New York: Russell Sage.

Brown, George H. 1970. "1985." Population Reference Bureau Selection No. 34.

Burdge, Rabel. 1969. "Levels of Occupational Prestige and Leisure Activity." *Journal of Leisure Research* 1:262–74.

Burgess, Ernest W., and Leonard S. Cottrell, Jr. 1939. *Predicting Success or Failure in Marriage.* Englewood Cliffs, N.J.: Prentice-Hall.

———, and Paul Wallin. 1953. *Engagement and Marriage.* Philadelphia: Lippincott.

Burma, John C. 1963. "Interethnic Marriage in Los Angeles, 1948–1959." *Social Forces* 42:156–65.

Burr, Wesley. 1973. *Theory Construction and the Sociology of the Family.* New York: Wiley.


Campbell, Donald T. 1963. "Social Attitudes and Other Acquired Behavioral Dispositions." In *Psychology: A Study of Science,* Sigmund Koch, ed., vol. 6. New York: McGraw-Hill.

Caplow, Theodore. 1954. *The Sociology of Work.* New York: McGraw-Hill.

Carden, Maren Lockwood. 1969. *Oneida: Utopian Community to Modern Corporation.* Baltimore: Johns Hopkins University Press.

Carter, Hugh, and Paul Glick. 1976. *Marriage and Divorce: A Social and Economic Study,* 2d ed. Cambridge: Harvard University Press.

———, and Alexander Plateris. 1963. "Trends in Divorce and Family Disruption." *HEW Indicators,* September, pp. v–xiv.

Catton, William R., Jr., and R. J. Smircich. 1964. "A Comparison of Mathematical Models for the Effect of Residential Propinquity on Mate Selection." *American Sociological Review* 29:522–29.

Cavan, Ruth S. 1970. "Concepts and Terminology in Interreligious Marriage." *Journal for the Scientific Study of Religion* 9:311–20.

Centers, Richard. 1949. "Marital Selection and Occupational Strata." *American Journal of Sociology* 54:530–35.

———. 1975. "Attitude Similarity-Dissimilarity as a Correlate of Heterosexual Attraction and Love." *Journal of Marriage and the Family* 37:305–14.

619

———, Bertram H. Raven, and Aroldo Rodrigues. 1971. "Conjugal Power Structure: A Re-Examination." *American Sociological Review* 36:264–78.

Chancellor, Loren E., and Thomas Monahan. 1955. "Religious Preferences and Interreligious Mixtures in Marriages and Divorces in Iowa." *American Journal of Sociology* 61:233–39.

Chesser, Eustace. 1957. *The Sexual, Marital, and Family Relationships of the English Woman*. New York: Roy.

Chevan, Albert, and J. Henry Korson. 1972. "The Widowed Who Live Alone: An Examination of Social Demographic Factors." *Social Forces* 51:45–52.

Chilman, Catherine S. 1966. "Dating, Courtship, and Engagement of Marrieds Compared to Single Undergraduates, with an Analysis of Early Marrying and Late Marrying Students." *Family Life Coordinator* 25:112–18.

Christensen, Harold T. 1958. *Marriage Analysis: Foundations for Successful Family Life*. New York: The Ronald Press.

———. 1960. "Cultural Relativism and Premarital Sex Norms." *American Sociological Review* 25:31–39.

———. 1966. "Scandinavian and American Sex Norms: Some Comparisons with Sociological Implications." *Journal of Social Issues* 22:60–75.

———, and Christina Gregg. 1970. "Changing Sex Norms in America and Scandinavia." *Journal of Marriage and the Family* 32:616–27.

Clark, Robert A., F. Ivan Nye, and Viktor Gecas. 1978. "Work Involvement and Marital Role Performance." *Journal of Marriage and the Family* 40:9–22.

Clarke, Alfred C. 1952. "An Examination of the Operation of Residential Propinquity as a Factor in Mate Selection." *American Sociological Review* 27:17–22.

Clausen, John. 1968. "Perspectives on Childhood Socialization." In *Socialization and Society*, John Clausen, ed. Boston: Little, Brown, pp. 139–81.

Clayton, Richard R. 1968. "Religiosity in 5-D: A Southern Test." *Social Forces* 47:80–83.

———. 1969. "Religiosity and Premarital Sex." *Social Forces* 47:469–74.

———. 1971. "Religiosity and Premarital Sexual Permissiveness: Elaboration of the Relationship and Debate." *Sociological Analysis* 32:81–96.

———. 1972. "Premarital Sexual Intercourse: A Substantive Test of the Contingent-Consistency Model." *Journal of Marriage and the Family* 34:273–81.

———, and Harwin L. Voss. 1977. "Shacking Up: Cohabitation in the 1970s." *Journal of Marriage and the Family* 39:272–84.

Cogswell, Betty E., and Marvin B. Sussman. 1972. "Changing Family and Marriage Forms: Complications for Human Service Systems." *The Family Coordinator* 21:505–16.

Constantine, Larry L., and Joan M. Constantine. 1971. "Group and Multilateral Marriage: Definitional Notes, Glossary, and Annotated Bibliography." *Family Process* 10:157–76.

Coombs, Robert H. 1962. "Reinforcement of Values in the Parental Home as a Factor in Mate Selection." *Marriage and Family Living* 24:155–57.

———. 1966. "Value Consensus and Partner Satisfaction Among Dating Couples." *Journal of Marriage and the Family* 28:166–73.

Cuber, John F. 1970. "Alternate Models from the Perspective of Sociology." In *The Family in Search of a Future*, Herbert A. Otto, ed. New York: Appleton-Century-Crofts, pp. 11–24.

————, and Peggy B. Harroff. 1963. "The More Total View: Relationships Among Men and Women of the Upper Middle Class." *Marriage and Family Living* 25:140–45.

————, and Peggy Harroff. 1965. *Sex and the Significant Americans.* Baltimore: Penguin.

Cutright, Phillips. 1970. "Income and Family Events: Getting Married." *Journal of Marriage and the Family* 32:628–37.

Davidson, J. Kenneth, and Gerald R. Leslie. 1977. "Premarital Sexual Intercourse: An Application of Axiomatic Theory Construction." *Journal of Marriage and the Family* 39:15–28.

Davis, K. B. 1929. *Factors in the Sex Life of Twenty-Two Hundred Women.* New York: Harper.

Davis, Kingsley. 1960. "Legitimacy and the Incest Taboo." In *A Modern Introduction to the Family,* Norman W. Bell and Ezra F. Vogel, eds. Glencoe, Ill.: The Free Press of Glencoe.

————. 1973. "The American Family in Relation to Demographic Change." International Population and Urban Research Institute of International Studies, University of California, Berkeley, Rpt. No. 425.

Dedman, Jean. 1959. "The Relationship Between Religious Attitude and Attitude Toward Premarital Sex Relations." *Marriage and Family Living* 21:171–76.

DeFleur, Melvin, and Frank Westie. 1958. "Verbal Attitudes and Overt Acts." *American Sociological Review* 23:667–73.

DeLora, Jack. 1963. "Social Systems of Dating on a College Campus." *Marriage and Family Living* 25:81–84.

Denfield, Duane, and Michael Gordon. 1970. "The Sociology of Mate Swapping: Or the Family That Swings Together Clings Together." *Journal of Sex Research* 6:85–100.

Deutscher, Irwin. 1966. "Words and Deeds: Social Science and Social Policy." *Social Problems* 13:235–54.

Diamond, Stanley. 1957. "Kibbutz and Shtetl: The History of an Idea." *Social Problems* 5:71–99.

Dietrich, Katheryn Thomas. 1975. "An Examination of the Myth of Black Matriarchy." *Journal of Marriage and the Family* 37:367–76.

Dizard, Jan. 1968. *Social Change and the Family.* Chicago: Community and Family Study Center.

Donald, Henderson H. 1952. *The Negro Freedman.* New York: Schuman.

Drake, St. Clair, and Horace Cayton. 1945. *Black Metropolis.* Chicago: University of Chicago Press.

Duncan, O. D. 1959. "Human Ecology and Population Studies." In *The Study of Population,* P. Hauser and O. D. Duncan, eds. Chicago: University of Chicago Press, pp. 678–716.

Dunn, Marie S. 1960. "Marriage Role Expectations Among Adolescents." *Marriage and Family Living* 22:99–111.

Duvall, Evelyn M. 1957, 1962, 1967, 1971. *Family Development.* 4 editions. Philadelphia: Lippincott.

Dyer, E. D. 1963. "Parenthood as Crisis: A Re-Study." *Marriage and Family Living* 25:196–201.

Eckland, Bruce K. 1968. "Theories of Mate Selection." *Eugenics Quarterly* 15:71–84.

Edmonds, Vernon. 1967. "Marital Conventionalization: Definition and Measurement." *Journal of Marriage and the Family* 29:681–88.

———, Glen Withers, and Beverly Dibatista. 1972. "Adjustment, Conservatism, and Marital Conventionalization." *Journal of Marriage and the Family* 34:96–103.

Edwards, John N. 1969. "Introduction to Industrialization, Urbanization, and the Family." In *The Family and Change,* John N. Edwards, ed. New York: Knopf, pp. 13–18.

———, and Alan Booth. 1976. "Sexual Behavior In and Out of Marriage: An Assessment of Correlates." *Journal of Marriage and the Family* 38:73–82.

Ehrlich, Howard. 1969. "Attitudes, Behavior, and the Intervening Variables." *American Sociologist* 5:29–34.

Ehrmann, Winston. 1959. *Premarital Dating Behavior.* New York: Holt.

———. 1964. "Marital and Nonmarital Sexual Behavior." In *Handbook of Marriage and the Family,* Harold T. Christensen, ed. Chicago: Rand McNally.

Elder, Glen H., Jr. 1969. "Appearance and Education in Marriage Mobility." *American Sociological Review* 34:519–33.

Elkins, Stanley. 1964. *Slavery.* Chicago: University of Chicago Press.

Ellis, Albert. 1970. "Group Marriage: A Possible Alternative?" In *The Family in Search of a Future,* Herbert A. Otto, ed. New York: Appleton-Century-Crofts, pp. 85–97.

Elnett, Elaine. 1926. *Historic Origin and Social Development of Family Life in Russia.* New York: Columbia University Press.

Emerson, Richard. 1962. "Power-Dependence Relations." *American Sociological Review* 27:31–41.

Engels, Friedrich. 1884; English translation, 1902. *The Origin of the Family, Private Property, and the State.* Chicago: Kerr.

Exner, R. V. 1915. *Problems and Principles of Sex Education: A Study of 948 College Men.* New York: Association.


Fairchild, Henry P. 1964. *Dictionary of Sociology and Related Sciences.* Patterson, N.J.: Littlefield, Adams.

Farber, Bernard. 1977. "Social Context, Kinship Mapping, and Family Norms." *Journal of Marriage and the Family* 39:227–42.

Farley, Reynolds, and Albert I. Hermalin. 1971. "Family Stability: A Comparison of Trends Between Blacks and Whites." *American Sociological Review* 36:1–17.

Faulkner, Joseph, and Gordon DeJong. 1966. "Religiosity in 5-D: An Empirical Analysis." *Social Forces* 45:246–54.

Feldman, Arnold S., and Christopher Hurd. 1966. "The Experience of Modernization." *Sociometry* 29:378–95.

Feldman, Harold, and Margaret Feldman. 1975. "The Family Life Cycle: Some Suggestions for Recycling." *Journal of Marriage and the Family* 37:277–86.

Fendrich, James M. 1967. "A Study of the Association Among Verbal Attitudes, Commitment, and Overt Behavior in Different Experimental Situations." *Social Forces* 45:347–55.

Ferrell, Mary Z., William L. Tolone, and Robert Walsh. 1977. "Maturational and Societal Changes in the Sexual Double Standard: A Panel Analysis (1969–1971; 1970–1974)." *Journal of Marriage and the Family* 39:255–72.

Firth, Raymond. 1964. "Family and Kinship in Industrial Society." *Sociological Review Monograph* 8:65–87.

Fishbein, M. 1966. "The Relationship Between Beliefs, Attitudes and Behavior." In *Cognitive Consistency*, S. Feldman, ed. New York: Academic.

Fishman, J. 1961. "Some Social and Psychological Determinants of Inter-Group Relations in Changing Neighborhoods: An Introduction to the Bridgeview Study." *Social Forces* 40:42–51.

Fogel, Robert W., and Stanley L. Engerman. 1974. *Time on the Cross: The Economics of American Negro Slavery*. Boston: Little, Brown.

Fortes, Meyer. 1936. "Ritual Festivals and Social Cohesion in the Hinterland of the Gold Coast." *American Anthropologist* 38:590–604.

Fox, Robin. 1967. *Kinship and Marriage*. Baltimore: Penguin.

Frazier, E. Franklin. 1932. *The Negro Family in Chicago*. Chicago: University of Chicago Press.

———. 1939. *The Negro Family in the United States*. Chicago: University of Chicago Press.

Freedman, Ronald, P. K. Whelpton, and A. A. Campbell. 1959. *Family Planning, Sterility and Population Growth*. New York: McGraw-Hill.

Frejka, Tomas. 1968. "Reflections on the Demographic Conditions Needed to Establish a United States Stationary Population Growth." *Population Studies* 22:379–97.

French, John R. P., Jr., and Bertram H. Raven. 1959. "The Bases of Social Power." In *Studies in Social Power*, D. Cartwright, ed. Ann Arbor: University of Michigan Press, pp. 150–67.

Friedan, Betty. 1963. *The Feminine Mystique*. New York: Norton.

Friedmann, E. A., and Robert J. Havighurst et al. 1962. "The Meaning of Work and Retirement." In *Man, Work, and Society*, S. Nosow and W. Form, eds. New York: Basic Books, pp. 41–55.

Fromm, Erich. 1956. *The Art of Loving*. New York: Harper.

Fukuyama, Yoshio. 1961. "The Major Dimensions of Church Membership." *Review of Religious Research* 2:154–61.


Gagnon, John H., and William Simon. 1970. "Prospects for Change in American Sexual Patterns." *Medical Aspects of Human Sexuality* 4:100–117.

Gallaher, Art. 1973. Personal correspondence about field work done in Ireland, the parish of Corofin.

Geiger, Kent. 1965. "The Soviet Family." In *Comparative Family Systems*, M. F. Nimkoff, ed. Boston: Houghton Mifflin, pp. 301–8.

Gibson, Campbell. 1976. "The U.S. Fertility Decline, 1961–1975: The Contribution of Changes in Marital Status and Marital Fertility." *Family Planning Perspectives* 8:249–52.

———. 1977. "Updating the Life Cycle of the Family." *Journal of Marriage and the Family* 39:5–14.

Glenn, Norval D. 1975. "The Contribution of Marriage to the Psychological Well-Being of Males and Females." *Journal of Marriage and the Family* 37:594–99.

Glick, Paul C. 1949. "First Marriages and Remarriages." *American Sociological Review* 14:726–34.

———. 1957. *American Families.* New York: Wiley.

———, and Robert Parke, Jr. 1965. "New Approaches in Studying the Life Cycle of the Family." *Demography* 2:187–202.

———, and Arthur J. Norton. 1971. "Frequency, Duration and Probability of Marriage and Divorce." *Journal of Marriage and the Family* 33:307–17.

———, and Arthur J. Norton. 1976. "Number, Timing, and Duration of Marriages and Divorces in the United States: June 1975." *Current Population Reports,* Series P-20, No. 297.

Glock, Charles Y., and Rodney Stark. 1965. *Religion and Society in Tension.* Chicago: Rand McNally.

Goffman, Erving. 1959. *The Presentation of Self in Everyday Life.* Garden City: Doubleday Anchor.

———. 1967. *Interaction Ritual.* Garden City: Doubleday Anchor.

Goode, William J. 1959. "The Theoretical Importance of Love." *American Sociological Review* 24:39–47.

———. 1961. "Illegitimacy, Anomie, and Cultural Penetration." *American Sociological Review* 26:910–25.

———. 1962a. "Family Patterns and Human Rights." *International Social Science Journal* 23:41–54.

———. 1962b. "Marital Satisfaction and Instability: A Cross-Cultural Class Analysis of Divorce Rates." *International Social Science Journal* 14:507–26.

———. 1963. *World Revolution and Family Patterns.* New York: The Free Press.

———. 1964. "The Process of Role Bargaining in the Impact of Urbanization and Industrialization on Family Systems." *Current Sociology* 12:1–12.

———. 1965. *After Divorce.* New York: The Free Press.

Goslin, David A. 1969. *Handbook of Socialization Theory and Research.* Chicago: Rand McNally.

Gouldner, Alvin. 1960. "The Norm of Reciprocity: A Preliminary Statement." *American Sociological Review* 25:161–77.

Gove, Walter R., and Jeannette F. Tudor. 1973. "Adult Sex Roles and Mental Illness." *American Journal of Sociology* 78:812–35.

Green, Bert F. 1954. "Attitude Measurement." In *Handbook of Social Psychology,* Gardner Lindzey, ed. Reading, Mass.: Addison-Wesley.

Greenwald, Harold. 1970. "Marriage as a Non-Legal Voluntary Association." In *The Family in Search of a Future,* Herbert A. Otto, ed. New York: Appleton-Century-Crofts, pp. 51–56.

Greer, Scott. 1956. "Urbanism Reconsidered: A Comparative Study of Local Areas in a Metropolis." *American Sociological Review* 21:22–25.

Gross, Edward, and Gregory P. Stone. 1964. "Embarrassment and the Analysis of Role Requirements." *American Journal of Sociology* 70:1–15.

Gsovski, Vladimir. 1947. "Family and Inheritance in Soviet Law." *Russian Review* 7:71–87.

Gulick, John, Charles E. Bowerman, and Kurt W. Back. 1962. "Newcomer Enculturation in the City: Attitudes and Participation." In *Urban Growth Dynamics,* F. Stuart Chapin, Jr., and Shirley F. Weiss, eds. New York: Wiley, pp. 315–58.

Gurin, G., J. Veroff, and S. Feld. 1960. *Americans View their Mental Health.* New York: Basic Books.

624

Gutman Herbert G. 1976. *The Black Family in Slavery and Freedom, 1750–1925.* New York: Pantheon.

Hallenbeck, Phyllis N. 1966. "An Analysis of Power Dynamics in Marriage." *Journal of Marriage and the Family* 28:200–203.

Hamilton, G. V. 1929. *A Research in Marriage.* New York: Medical Research Press.

Haney, C. Allen, Robert Michielutte, Carl M. Cochrane, and Clark E. Vincent. 1975. "Some Consequences of Illegitimacy in a Sample of Black Women." *Journal of Marriage and the Family* 37:339–66.

Harmsworth, Harry C., and Mhyra S. Minnis. 1955. "Nonstatutory Causes of Divorce: The Lawyer's Point of View." *Marriage and Family Living* 17:316–21.

Hartland, Edwin S. 1921. *Primitive Society.* New York: Dutton.

Heer, David M. 1962. "Husband and Wife Perceptions of Family Power Structure." *Marriage and Family Living* 24:65–67.

———. 1963. "The Measurement and Bases of Family Power: An Overview." *Marriage and Family Living* 25:133–39.

———. 1966. "Negro-White Marriage in the United States." *Journal of Marriage and the Family* 28:262–73.

Heise, David R. 1972. *Personality and Socialization.* Chicago: Rand McNally.

Heiss, Jerold S., and M. Gordon. 1964. "Need Patterns and the Mutual Satisfaction of Dating and Engaged Couples." *Journal of Marriage and the Family* 26:337–39.

Heltsley, Mary E., and Carlfred Broderick. 1969. "Religiosity and Premarital Sexual Permissiveness: Reexamination of Reiss's Traditionalism Proposition." *Journal of Marriage and the Family* 31:173–90.

Herskovits, Melville J. 1941. *The Myth of the Negro Past.* New York: Harper.

Hill, Reuben, and Donald A. Hansen. 1960. "The Identification of Conceptual Frameworks Utilized in Family Study." *Marriage and Family Living* 22:299–311.

Hinkle, Dennis, and Michael Sporakowski. 1975. "Attitudes Toward Love: A Reexamination." *Journal of Marriage and the Family* 37:764–68.

Hobbs, D. F., Jr. 1965. "Parenthood as Crisis: A Third Study." *Journal of Marriage and the Family* 27:367–72.

———. 1968. "Transition to Parenthood: A Replication and an Extension." *Journal of Marriage and the Family* 30:413–17.

Hollingshead, August B. 1950. "Cultural Factors in the Selection of Marriage Mates." *American Sociological Review* 15:619–27.

Huang, Lucy Jen. 1962a. "Some Changing Patterns in the Communist Chinese Family." *Marriage and Family Living* 23:137–46.

———. 1962b. "Attitudes of the Communist Chinese Toward Interclass Marriage." *Marriage and Family Living* 24:389–92.

Hudson, John W., and Lura F. Henze. 1969. "Campus Values in Mate Selection: A Replication." *Journal of Marriage and the Family* 31:772–78.

Hunt, Morton. 1973a. "Sexual Behavior in the 1970s." *Playboy,* October, pp. 84 ff.

———. 1973b. "Sexual Behavior in the 1970s. Part II: Premarital Sex." *Playboy,* November, pp. 74–75.

Hyman, Herbert H., and John Sheldon Reed. 1969. " 'Black Matriarchy' Recon-

625

sidered: Evidence from Secondary Analysis of Sample Surveys." *Public Opinion Quarterly* 33:346–54.

Ikle, Fred Charles. 1967. "Can Social Predictions Be Evaluated?" *Daedalus* 96:733–58.

Inkeles, Alex. 1969. "Making Men Modern: On the Causes and Consequences of Individual Change in Six Developing Countries." *American Journal of Sociology* 75:208–25.

Inselberg, Rachel M. 1964. "The Sentence Completion Technique in the Measurement of Marital Satisfaction." *Journal of Marriage and the Family* 26:339–41.

Israeli Ministry for Foreign Affairs. 1972. "Facts about Israel, 1972." Tel Aviv.

Jacobson, Paul H. 1950. "Differentials in Divorce by Duration of Marriage and Size of Family." *American Sociological Review* 15:235–244.

———. 1959. *American Marriage and Divorce.* New York: Rinehart.

———. 1966. "The Changing Role of Mortality in American Family Life." *Lex et Scientia* 3:117–24.

Janowitz, Barbara S. 1976. "The Impact of AFDC on Illegitimate Birth Rates." *Journal of Marriage and the Family* 38:485–94.

Jeffrey, Arthur. 1959. "The Family in Islam." In *The Family: Its Function and Destiny,* Ruth Nanda Anshen, ed. New York: Harper.

Johnson, Ralph E. 1970. "Extramarital Sexual Intercourse: A Methodological Note." *Journal of Marriage and the Family* 32:279–83.

Kahl, Joseph. 1968. *The Measurement of Modernism.* Austin: University of Texas Press.

Kahn, Herman, and Anthony J. Weiner. 1967. "The Next Thirty-Three Years: A Framework for Speculation." *Daedalus* 96:705–32.

Kanin, Eugene, and David Howard. 1958. "Postmarital Consequences of Premarital Sex Adjustments." *American Sociological Review* 23:556–61.

Kanter, Rosabeth M. 1972. *Commitment and Community: Communes and Utopias in Sociological Perspective.* Cambridge, Mass.: Harvard University Press.

Kassel, Victor. 1970. "Polygyny After Sixty." In *The Family in Search of a Future,* Herbert A. Otto, ed. New York: Appleton-Century-Crofts, pp. 137–44.

Katz, Alvin M., and Reuben Hill. 1958. "Residential Propinquity and Marital Selection: A Review of Theory, Method, and Fact." *Marriage and Family Living* 20:27–34.

Kelley, E. Lowell. 1941. "Marital Compatibility as Related to Personality Traits of Husbands and Wives as Rated by Self and Spouse." *Journal of Social Psychology* 13:193–98.

———. 1955. "Consistency of the Adult Personality." *American Psychologist* 10:659–81.

Kemper, Theodore. 1968. "Reference Groups, Socialization and Achievement." *American Sociological Review* 33:31–45.

Kenkel, William F. 1957. "Influence Differentiation in Family Decision-Making." *Sociology and Social Research* 42:18–25.

———. 1977. *The Family in Perspective.* 4th ed. Santa Monica: Goodyear.

————, and Dean K. Hoffman. 1956. "Real and Conceived Roles in Family Decision-Making." *Marriage and Family Living* 18:311–16.

Kephart, William M. 1954. "Some Variables in Cases of Reported Sexual Maladjustment." *Marriage and Family Living* 16:241–43.

————. 1955. "Occupational Level and Marital Disruption." *American Sociological Review* 20:456–65.

————. 1961, 1966, 1972. *The Family, Society, and the Individual.* 3 editions. Boston: Houghton Mifflin.

Kerckhoff, A. C., and K. E. Davis. 1962. "Value Consensus and Need Complementarity in Mate Selection." *American Sociological Review* 27:295–303.

Kernodle, Wayne. 1959. "Some Implications of the Homogamy-Complementary Needs Theories of Mate Selection for Sociological Research." *Social Forces* 38:145–52.

King, Karl, Jack O. Balswick, and Ira E. Robinson. 1977. "The Continuing Premarital Sexual Revolution Among College Females." *Journal of Marriage and the Family* 39:455–60.

King, Morton. 1967. "Nine Factorially Derived Dimensions: Measuring the Religious Variable." *Journal for the Scientific Study of Religion* 6:173–90.

Kinsey, Alfred C., Wardell Pomeroy, and Clyde Martin. 1948. *Sexual Behavior in the Human Male.* Philadelphia: Saunders.

————, and Paul Gebhard. 1953. *Sexual Behavior in the Human Female.* Philadelphia: Saunders.

Kirkpatrick, Clifford. 1937. "Community of Interest and the Measurement of Adjustment in Marriage." *The Family* 18:133–37.

————, and Charles Hobart. 1954. "Disagreement, Disagreement Estimate, and Non-Empathetic Imputations for Intimate Groups Varying from Favorite Date to Married." *American Sociological Review* 19:10–19.

Kirkpatrick, E. L., et al. 1934. "The Life Cycle of the Farm Family." University of Wisconsin, Experiment Station Bulletin, No. 121.

Kohn, Melvin L. 1959. "Social Class and Parental Values." *American Journal of Sociology* 64:337–51.

Korson, J. Henry. 1965. "Age and Social Status at Marriage: Karachi." *Pakistan Development Review* 5:586–600.

————. 1968. "The Roles of Dower and Dowry as Indicators of Social Change in Pakistan." *Journal of Marriage and the Family* 30:696–707.

————. 1969. "Student Attitudes Toward Mate Selection in a Muslim Society: Pakistan." *Journal of Marriage and the Family* 31:153–65.

————. 1970. "Career Constraints Among Women Graduate Students in a Developing Society." *Journal of Comparative Family Studies* 1:82–100.

————. 1971. "Endogamous Marriage in a Traditional Muslim Society: West Pakistan." *Journal of Comparative Family Studies* 3:145–55.

Krain, Mark, Drew Cannon, and Jeffrey Bagford. 1977. "Rating-Dating or Simply Prestige Homogamy? Data on Dating in the Greek System on a Midwestern Campus." *Journal of Marriage and the Family* 39:664–76.

Kutner, Bernard, David Fanshel, Alice M. Togo, and Thomas S. Langer. 1956. *Five Hundred Over Sixty.* New York: Russell Sage.

Landis, Carney. 1940. *Sex in Development.* New York: Harper.

Landis, Judson T. 1949. "Marriages of Mixed and Non-Mixed Religious Faith." *American Sociological Review* 14:401–6.

627

———, and Mary G. Landis. 1953. *Building a Successful Marriage.* New York: Prentice-Hall.

Lang, Richard O. 1932. "A Study of the Degree of Happiness or Unhappiness in Marriages as Rated by Acquaintances of the Married Couples." Master's thesis, University of Chicago.

Larson, Lyle E. 1974. "System and Subsystem Perception of Family Roles." *Journal of Marriage and the Family* 36:123–38.

LeMasters, E. E. 1957. "Parenthood as Crisis." *Marriage and Family Living* 19:352–55.

———. 1970. *Parents in Modern America.* Homewood, Ill.: Dorsey.

Lenski, Gerhard. 1963. *The Religious Factor.* New York: Doubleday.

Lerner, Daniel. 1958. *The Passing of Traditional Society.* Glencoe, Ill.: The Free Press of Glencoe.

Leslie, Gerald. 1976. *The Family in Social Context.* 3rd Edition. New York: Oxford University Press.

Lever, Janet. 1976. "Sex Differences in the Games Children Play." *Social Problems* 23:478–87.

Levett, Carl. 1970. "A Parental Presence in Future Family Models." In *The Family in Search of a Future,* Herbert A. Otto, ed. New York: Appleton-Century-Crofts, pp. 161–70.

Levin, Robert J., and Amy Levin. 1975. "Sexual Pleasure: The Surprising Preferences of 100,000 Women." *Redbook* 145 (September): 51–58.

Levinger, George. 1964. "Note on Need Complementarity in Marriage." *Psychological Bulletin* 61:153–57.

———. 1965. "Marital Cohesiveness and Dissolution: An Integrative Review." *Journal of Marriage and the Family* 27:19–28.

———. 1966. "Sources of Marital Dissatisfaction Among Applicants for Divorce." *American Journal of Orthopsychiatry* 36:803–7.

Levy, Marion J., Jr. 1952. *The Structure of Society.* Princeton: Princeton University Press.

Lewis, Robert A. 1973. "A Longitudinal Test of a Developmental Framework for Premarital Dyadic Formation." *Journal of Marriage and the Family* 35:16–25.

Lichtenberger, J. P. 1931. *Divorce.* New York: McGraw-Hill.

Liebow, Eliot. 1967. *Tally's Corner.* Boston: Little, Brown.

Lindenfeld, Frank. 1960. "A Note on Social Mobility, Religiosity, and Students' Attitudes Towards Premarital Sexual Relations." *American Sociological Review* 25:81–84.

Linn, Lawrence. 1965. "Verbal Attitudes and Overt Behavior: A Study of Racial Discrimination." *Social Forces* 43:353–64.

Linton, Ralph. 1936. *The Study of Man.* New York: Appleton-Century-Crofts.

———. 1949. "The Natural History of the Family." In *The Family: Its Function and Destiny,* Ruth Nanda Anshen, ed. New York: Harper, pp. 18–38.

Litwak, Eugene. 1960a. "Occupational Mobility and Extended Family Cohesion." *American Sociological Review* 25:9–21.

———. 1960b. "Geographic Mobility and Extended Family Cohesion." *American Sociological Review* 25:385–94.

Locke, Harvey J. 1951. *Predicting Adjustment in Marriage: A Comparison of a Divorced and a Happily Married Group.* New York: Holt.

———, and Karl M. Wallace. 1959. "Short Marital Adjustment and Prediction

Tests: Their Reliability and Validity." *Marriage and Family Living* 21:251–55.

————, and Robert C. Williamson, 1955. "Marital Adjustment: A Factor Analysis Study." *American Sociological Review* 23:562–69.

Lovejoy, Debi. 1961. "College Student Conceptions of the Roles of Husband and Wife in Decision Making." *Family Life Coordinator* 9:43–46.

Lowrie, Robert H. 1940. *An Introduction to Cultural Anthropology.* New York: Holt.

Lowrie, Samuel H. 1965. "Early Marriage: Premarital Pregnancy and Associated Factors." *Journal of Marriage and the Family* 27:48–56.

Luckey, Eleanor B. 1960. "Marital Satisfaction and Its Association with Congruence of Perception." *Marriage and Family Living* 22:49–54.

Lundberg, F., Mirra Komarovsky, and E. McInerny. 1934. *Leisure: A Suburban Study.* New York: Columbia University Press.

Lynn, David B. 1961. "Sex Differences in Identification Development." *Sociometry* 24:372–83.

————. 1966. "The Process of Learning Parental and Sex-Role Identification." *Journal of Marriage and the Family* 28:466–70.

McAllister, Ronald, Edgar W. Butler, and Edward J. Kaiser. 1973. "The Adaptation of Women to Residential Mobility." *Journal of Marriage and the Family* 35:197–204.

McCary, James. 1967. *Human Sexuality.* New York: Van Nostrand.

McGinnis, Robert. 1958. "Campus Values in Mate Selection: A Repeat Study." *Social Forces* 37:368–73.

McGuire, William J. 1969. "The Nature of Attitudes and Attitude Change." In *The Handbook of Social Psychology,* Gardner Lindzey and Elliot Aronson, eds. Reading, Mass.: Addison-Wesley.

McIntyre, Jennie. 1966. "The Structure-Functional Approach to Family Study." In *Emerging Conceptual Frameworks in Family Analysis,* F. Ivan Nye and Felix M. Berardo, eds. New York: Macmillan, pp. 52–77.

McLennan, J. F. 1896. *Studies in Ancient History.* New York: MacMillan.

Macklin, Eleanor D. 1972. "Heterosexual Cohabitation Among Unmarried College Students." *The Family Coordinator* 21:463–72.

Maranell, Gary M., Richard A. Dodder, and David F. Mitchell. 1970. "Social Class and Premarital Sexual Permissiveness: A Subsequent Test." *Journal of Marriage and the Family* 32:85–88.

Maslow, Abraham. 1970. *Motivation and Personality.* 2nd ed. New York: Harper and Row.

Masters, William H., and Virginia Johnson. 1966. *Human Sexual Response.* Boston: Little, Brown.

Mead, Frank. 1970. *Handbook of Denominations in the United States.* 5th ed. Nashville: Abingdon Press.

Mead, Margaret. 1966. "Marriage in Two Steps." *Redbook* 127 (July): 48–49.

Merton, Robert K. 1949. "Discrimination and the American Creed." In *Discrimination and National Welfare,* Robert MacIver, ed. New York: Institute for Religious and Social Studies.

————. 1957. *Social Theory and Social Structure.* Rev. and Enlarged Ed. New York: The Free Press.

Meyerowitz, J. H., and H. Feldman. 1966. "Transition to Parenthood." *Psychiatric Research Report* 20:78–84.

Middleton, Russell. 1962. "Brother-Sister and Father-Daughter Marriage in Ancient Egypt." *American Sociological Review* 27:603–11.

Miller, Brent. 1975. "Child Density, Marital Satisfaction, and Conventionalization: A Research Note." *Journal of Marriage and the Family* 37:345–47.

———. 1976. "A Multivariate Developmental Model of Marital Satisfaction." *Journal of Marriage and the Family* 38:643–58.

Miller, Daniel R., and Guy E. Swanson. 1958. *The Changing American Parent.* New York: Wiley.

Mills, C. W. 1959. *The Sociological Imagination.* New York: Oxford University Press.

Mintz, Morton. 1978. "Warning Ordered for Users of Pill Who Also Smoke." *The Washington Post,* January 25, Section A.

Momeni, Diamchild A. 1975. "Polygyny in Iran." *Journal of Marriage and the Family* 37:453–56.

Monahan, Thomas P. 1952. "How Stable Are Remarriages?" *American Journal of Sociology* 58:280–88.

———. 1955a. "Divorce by Occupational Level." *Marriage and Family Living* 17:322–24.

———. 1955b. "Is Childlessness Related to Family Stability?" *American Sociological Review* 20:446–56.

———. 1958. "The Changing Nature and Instability of Remarriages." *Eugenics Quarterly* 5:73–85.

———. 1961. "Educational Achievement and Family Stability." *Journal of Social Psychology* 55:253–63.

———. 1966. "Interracial Marriage and Divorce in the State of Hawaii." *Eugenics Quarterly* 13:40–47.

———. 1971. "The Extent of Interdenomination Marriage in the United States." *Journal for the Scientific Study of Religion* 10:85–92.

———. 1976. "An Overview of Statistics on Interracial Marriage in the United States, with Data on Its Extent from 1963–1970." *Journal of Marriage and the Family* 38:223–32.

———, and Loren E. Chancellor. 1955. "Statistical Aspects of Marriage and Divorce by Religious Denomination in Iowa." *Eugenics Quarterly* 2:162–73.

———, and William M. Kephart, 1954. "Divorce and Desertion by Religious and Mixed-Religious Groups." *American Journal of Sociology* 59:454–65.

*Monthly Vital Statistics Review,* various issues.

Moore, Barrington, Jr. 1958. *Political Power and Social Theory.* Cambridge, Mass.: Harvard University Press.

Moore, Wilbert. 1965. *Impact of Industry.* Englewood Cliffs, N.J.: Prentice-Hall.

Morgan, Lewis Henry. 1877. *Ancient Society.* New York: Holt.

Moss, Howard A., and Jerome Kagan. 1964. "Report on Personality Consistency and Change from the Fels Longitudinal Study." *Vita Humana* 7:127–38.

Motz, Annabelle B. 1950. "Conceptions of Marital Roles by Status Groups." *Marriage and Family Living* 12:136–72.

Moynihan, Daniel Patrick. 1965. *The Negro Family: The Case for National*

*Action*. Washington, D.C.: Office of Policy Planning and Research, United States Department of Labor.

Mueller, Charles W., and Hallowell Pope. 1977. "Marital Instability: A Study of Its Transmission Between Generations." *Journal of Marriage and the Family* 39:83–94.

Murdock, George P. 1949. *Social Structure*. New York: Macmillan.

———. 1945, 1958, 1961, 1963. *Human Relations Area Files: Outline of Materials*. 4 editions. New Haven: Yale University Press.

———. 1957. "World Ethnographic Sample." *American Anthropologist* 59:664–87.

———. 1967. *Ethnographic Atlas*. Pittsburgh: University of Pittsburgh Press.

Murray, Henry A., et al. 1938. *Explorations in Personality*. New York: Oxford University Press.

Murstein, Bernard I. 1961. "The Complementary Need Hypothesis in Newlyweds and Middle Aged Married Couples." *Journal of Abnormal and Social Psychology* 43:194–97.

———. 1967a. "The Relationship of Mental Health to Marital Choice and Courtship Progress." *Journal of Marriage and the Family* 29:447–51.

———. 1967b. "Empirical Tests of Role, Complementary Needs, and Homogamy Theories of Marital Choice." *Journal of Marriage and the Family* 29:689–96.

———. 1970. "Stimulus-Value-Role: A Theory of Marital Choice." *Journal of Marriage and the Family* 29:689–96; 32:481.


National Center for Health Statistics. 1977. "Advance Report: Final Marriage Statistics, 1975." Vol. 26, No. 2, Supplement, May 9.

———. 1977. "Advance Report: Final Divorce Statistics, 1975." Vol. 26, No. 2, Supplement 2, May 19.

Nettleford, Rex M. 1972. *Identity, Race and Protest in Jamaica*. New York: Morrow.

Nettler, G., and E. H. Golding. 1946. "The Measurement of Attitudes Toward the Japanese in America." *American Journal of Sociology* 52:31–39.

Neubeck, Gerhard, ed. 1969. *Extra-Marital Relations*. Englewood Cliffs, N.J.: Prentice-Hall.

Nimkoff, Meyer F. 1965. *Comparative Family Systems*. Boston: Houghton Mifflin.

———, and Russell Middleton. 1960. "Types of Family and Types of Economy." *American Journal of Sociology* 66:215–25.

Norton, Arthur J., and Paul C. Glick. 1976. "Marital Instability: Past, Present, and Future." *Journal of Social Issues* 32:5–19.

Nye, F. Ivan. 1976. *Role Structure and Analysis of the Family*. Beverly Hills: Sage.

———, and Felix M. Berardo. 1966. *Emerging Conceptual Frameworks in Family Analysis*. New York: Macmillan.

———. 1973. *The Family: Its Structure and Interaction*. New York: Macmillan.


Ogburn, William F. 1938. "The Changing Family." *The Family* 19:139–43; adapted by Robert F. Winch and Louis Wolf Goodman, eds. *Selected Studies in Marriage and the Family*. New York: Holt, pp. 55–63.

631

————, and Meyer F. Nimkoff. 1965. *Technology and the Changing Family*. Boston: Houghton Mifflin.

O'Neill, Nena, and George O'Neill. 1972. "Open Marriage: A Synergic Model." *Family Coordinator* 21:403–409.

Orden, Susan R., and Norman M. Bradburn. 1968. "Dimensions of Marriage Happiness." *American Journal of Sociology* 73:715–31.

Osmond, Marie Withers. 1978. "Reciprocity: A Dynamic Model and a Method to Study Family Power." *Journal of Marriage and the Family* 40:49–70.

Osofsky, Howard, and Joy Osofsky. 1971. "Androgyny as a Life Style." Paper presented at the 1971 Groves Conference, San Juan, Puerto Rico.

Ovid. 1957. *The Art of Love*. Trans. by Rolfe Humphries. Bloomington, Indiana: Indiana University Press.

Parke, Robert, Jr., and Paul C. Glick. 1967. "Prospective Change in Marriage and the Family." *Journal of Marriage and the Family* 29:249–56.

Parsons, Talcott. 1943. "The Kinship System of the Contemporary United States." *American Anthropologist* 45:23–38.

————. 1949. "The Social Structure of the Family." In *The Family: Its Function and Destiny*, Ruth Nanda Anshen, ed. New York: Harper, pp. 173–201.

————. 1951. *The Social System*. New York: The Free Press.

————. 1965. "The Normal American Family." In *Man and Civilization: The Family's Search for Survival*, Seymour M. Farber et al., eds. New York: McGraw-Hill, pp. 31–50.

————, and Robert F. Bales. 1955. *Family, Socialization, and Interaction Process*. Glencoe, Ill.: The Free Press of Glencoe.

Patai, Raphael. 1955. "Cousin-Right in Middle-Eastern Marriage." *Southwestern Journal of Anthropology* 11:371–90.

————. 1958. *The Kingdom of Jordan*. Princeton: Princeton University Press.

Peterman, Dan J., Carl A. Ridley, and Scott M. Anderson. 1974. "A Comparison of Cohabiting and Noncohabiting College Students." *Journal of Marriage and the Family* 36:344–54.

Peters, E. L. 1965. "Aspects of the Family Among the Bedouin of Cyrenaica." In *Comparative Family Systems*, M. F. Nimkoff, ed. Boston: Houghton Mifflin, pp. 121–46.

Phillips, Bernard. 1972. *Social Research: Strategies and Tactics*. 2nd ed. Boston: Houghton Mifflin.

Phillips, J. B. 1960. *The New Testament in Modern English*. London: Geoffrey Bles.

Pineo, Peter. 1961. "Disenchantment in the Later Years of Marriage." *Marriage and Family Living* 23:3–11.

Plato. 1956. *Symposium*. Trans. by Benjamin Jowett. Indianapolis: Bobbs-Merrill.

Pollak, Otto. 1967. "The Outlook for the American Family." *Journal of Marriage and the Family* 29:193–205.

Pomeroy, Wardell B. 1972. "Alfred C. Kinsey, Man and Method." *Psychology Today* 5:33ff.

Poppleton, Pamela, and G. W. Pilkinton. 1964. "A Comparison of Four Methods of Scoring an Attitude Scale in Relation to Its Reliability and Validity." *British Journal of Social and Clinical Psychology* 3:36–39.

*The Population Bulletin*, February, 1971.

Potter, Charles F. 1954. *The Faiths Men Live By*. Englewood Cliffs, N.J.: Prentice-Hall.

Presser, Harriet B., and Larry L. Bumpass. 1972. "Demographic and Social Aspects of Contraceptive Sterilization in the United States: 1965–1970." In *Demographic and Social Aspects of Population Growth*, Charles F. Westoff and Robert Parke, Jr., eds. Washington, D.C.: Government Printing Office, vol. 1, pp. 508–68.

Putney, Snell, and Russell Middleton. 1961. "Dimensions and Correlates of Religious Ideologies." *Social Forces* 39:285–90.

Queen, Stuart A., and Robert Habenstein. 1967. *The Family in Various Cultures*. 3rd ed. Philadelphia: Lippincott.

Radcliffe-Brown, A. R. 1965. "Introduction." In *African Systems of Kinship and Marriage*, A. R. Radcliffe-Brown and Daryll Forde, eds. New York: Oxford University Press, pp. 1–85.

Rapoport, Robert, and Rhona Rapoport. 1965. "Work and Family in Contemporary Society." *American Sociological Review* 30:381–94.

Reed, Ritchie H., and Susan McIntosh. 1972. "Cost of Children." In *Research Reports, Volume II, Economic Aspects of Population Growth*, Elliott R. Morss and Ritchie H. Reed, eds. The Commission on Population Growth and the American Future. Washington, D.C.: Government Printing Office, pp. 333–50.

Reiss, Ira L. 1960a. "Toward a Sociology of the Heterosexual Love Relationship." *Marriage and Family Living* 22:139–45.

———. 1960b. *Premarital Sexual Standards in America*. New York: The Free Press.

———. 1964. "The Scaling of Premarital Sexual Permissiveness." *Journal of Marriage and the Family* 26:188–98.

———. 1965a. "Social Class and Campus Dating." *Social Problems* 13:193–205.

———. 1965b. "The Universality of the Family: A Conceptual Analysis." *Journal of Marriage and the Family* 27:443–53.

———. 1967. *The Social Context of Premarital Sexual Permissiveness*. New York: Holt.

———. 1970. "Premarital Sex as Deviant Behavior: An Application of Current Approaches to Deviance." *American Sociological Review* 35:78–87.

———. 1971. *The Family System in America*. New York: Holt.

———. 1972. "Premarital Sexuality: Past, Present and Future." *Readings on the Family System*, Ira L. Reiss, ed. New York: Holt, pp. 167–89.

———, Albert Banwart, and Harry Foreman. 1975. "Premarital Contraceptive Usage: A Study and Some Theoretical Explorations." *Journal of Marriage and the Family* 37:619–32.

Reiss, Paul J. 1962. "The Extended Kinship System: Correlates of and Attitudes on Frequency of Interaction." *Marriage and Family Living* 22:263–64.

Rele, J. R. 1965. "Trends and Differentials in the American Age at Marriage." *Milbank Memorial Fund Quarterly* 43:219–34.

Renne, Karen S. 1971. "Health and Marital Experience in an Urban Population." *Journal of Marriage and the Family* 33:338–50.

Rheinstein, Max. 1972. *Marriage Stability, Divorce, and the Law*. Chicago: University of Chicago Press.

633

Richards, A. I. 1965. "Some Types of Family Structure Amongst the Central Bantu." In *African Systems of Kinship and Marriage*, A. R. Radcliffe-Brown and Daryll Forde, eds. New York: Oxford University Press, pp. 207–51.

Richmond, Marie LaLibertie. 1976. "Beyond Resource Theory: Another Look at Factors Enabling Women to Affect Family Interaction." *Journal of Marriage and the Family* 38:257–66.

Riesman, David. 1964. "The New College Atmosphere." In *Sex in America*, Henry A. Gruenwald, ed. New York: Bantam Books.

Rimmer, Robert. 1966. *The Harrad Experiment*. Los Angeles: Sherbourne.

Robertson, Constance Noyes. 1972. *Oneida Community: The Breakup, 1876–1881*. Syracuse, New York: Syracuse University Press.

Robinson, Ira E., Karl King, and Jack Balswick. 1972. "The Premarital Sexual Revolution Among College Students." *The Family Coordinator* 21:189–94.

Rodgers, Roy. 1962. *Improvements in the Construction and Analysis of Family Life Cycle Categories*. Kalamazoo: Western Michigan University Press.

Rogers, Everett. 1969. *Modernization Among Peasants*. New York: Holt.

Rokeach, Milton. 1967. "Attitude Change and Behavioral Change." *Public Opinion Quarterly* 30:520–50.

Rollin, Betty. 1970. "The Motherhood Myth." *Look*, September 22, pp. 15–17.

Rollins, Boyd C., and Harold Feldman. 1970. "Marital Satisfaction over the Family Life Cycle." *Journal of Marriage and the Family* 32:20–28.

———, and Stephen J. Bahr. 1976. "A Theory of Power Relationships in Marriage." *Journal of Marriage and the Family* 38:619–28.

Rosenberg, Morris. 1965. *Society and the Adolescent Self-Image*. Princeton: Princeton University Press.

Rosow, Irving. 1957. "Issues in the Concept of Need Complementarity." *Sociometry* 20:216–33.

———. 1965. "Intergenerational Relationships: Problems and Proposals." In *Social Structure and the Family: Generational Relations*, Ethel Shanas and Gordon F. Streib, eds. Englewood Cliffs: Prentice-Hall, pp. 341–78.

Ross, Heather L., and Isabel Sawhill. 1975. *Time of Transition: The Growth of Families Headed by Women*. Washington: The Urban Institute.

Rossi, Alice S. 1968. "Transition to Parenthood." *Journal of Marriage and the Family* 30:26–39.

Roy, Rustum, and Della Roy. 1970. "Is Monogamy Outdated?" *Humanist*, March/April:19–26.

Rubin, Isadore. 1965. "Transition in Sex Values—Implications for the Education of Adolescents." *Journal of Marriage and the Family* 27:185–89.

Rubin, Zick. 1968. "Do American Women Marry Up?" *American Sociological Review* 33:750–60.

———. 1969. "Reply to Scott." *American Sociological Review* 34:727–28.

Ruppel, Howard J., Jr. 1970. "Religiosity and Premarital Sexual Permissiveness: A Response to the Reiss-Heltsley and Broderick Debate." *Journal of Marriage and the Family* 32:647–55.

Russell, Candyce S. 1974. "Transition to Parenthood: Problems and Gratifications." *Journal of Marriage and the Family* 36:294–302.

Ryan, William. 1965. "Savage Discovery: The Moynihan Report." *The Nation* 201:380–84.

Ryder, Norman B., and Charles F. Westoff. 1971. *Reproduction in the United States 1965*. Princeton: Princeton University Press.

Sacks, Michael Paul. 1977. "Unchanging Times: A Comparison of the Everyday Life of Soviet Working Men and Women Between 1923 and 1966." *Journal of Marriage and the Family* 39:793–806.

Safilios-Rothschild, Constantina. 1969a. "Patterns of Familial Power and Influence." *Sociological Focus* 2:7–19.

———. 1969b. "Family Sociology or Wives' Family Sociology? A Cross-Cultural Examination of Decision-Making." *Journal of Marriage and the Family* 31:290–301.

———. 1970. "The Study of Family Power Structure: A Review 1960–1969." *Journal of Marriage and the Family* 32:539–52.

———. 1976. "A Macro- and Micro-Examination of Family Power and Love: An Exchange Model." *Journal of Marriage and the Family* 38:355–62.

Scanzoni, John. 1970. *Opportunity and the Family*. New York: The Free Press.

———. 1976. "Gender Roles and the Process of Fertility Control." *Journal of Marriage and the Family* 38:677–92.

Schacht, Joseph. 1964. *An Introduction to Islamic Law*. Oxford: Clarendon Press.

Schellenberg, J. A., and L. S. Bee. 1960. "A Re-Examination of the Theory of Complementary Needs in Mate Selection." *Marriage and Family Living* 22:227–32.

Schlesinger, Yaffa. 1977. "Sex Roles and Social Change in the Kibbutz." *Journal of Marriage and the Family* 39:771–80.

Schneider, David. 1968. *American Kinship: A Cultural Account*. Englewood Cliffs, N.J.: Prentice-Hall.

Schoen, Robert. 1975. "California Divorce Rates by Age at First Marriage and Duration of First Marriage." *Journal of Marriage and the Family* 37:548–54.

Schroeder, Clarence B. 1939. *Divorce in a City of 100,000 Population*. Peoria, Ill.: Bradley Polytechnic Institute Library.

Schulz, David A. 1972. *The Changing Family*. Englewood Cliffs, N.J.: Prentice-Hall.

Schutz, William. 1958. *FIRO: A Three-Dimensional Theory of Interpersonal Behavior*. New York: Holt.

Schwarzweller, Harry K., James S. Brown, and J. J. Mangalam. 1971. *Mountain Families in Transition*. University Park: Pennsylvania State University Press.

Scott, John Finley. 1969. "A Comment on 'Do American Women Marry Up?' " *American Sociological Review* 34:725–27.

Scott, Marvin B., and Stanford Lyman. 1968. "Accounts." *American Sociological Review* 33:45–62.

Sears, Robert, Eleanor E. Maccoby, and Harry Levin. 1957. *Patterns of Child Rearing*. Evanston, Ill.: Row, Peterson.

Segal, Sheldon. 1972. "Introduction." In *Mankind's Great Need: Population Research*. Washington, D.C.: Population Crisis Committee.

Sewell, William H. 1952. "Infant Training and the Personality of the Child." *American Journal of Sociology* 58:150–59.

635

Shah, Khalida. 1960. "Attitudes of Pakistani Students Toward Family Life." *Marriage and Family Living* 22:156–61.

Sharp, Harry, and Morris Axelrod. 1956. "Mutual Aid Among Relatives in an Urban Population." In *Principles of Sociology,* Ronald Freedman et al., eds. New York: Holt, pp. 433–39.

Skinner, B. F. 1953. *Science and Human Behavior.* New York: Macmillan.

———. 1957. *Verbal Behavior.* New York: Appleton-Century-Crofts.

Smigel, Erwin O., and Rita Seiden. 1968. "The Decline and Fall of the Double Standard." *The Annals* 376:6–17.

Smith, James, and Lynn Smith. 1970. "Co-Marital Sex and the Sexual Freedom Movement." *Journal of Sex Research* 6:131–42.

Smith, William J., Jr. 1952. "Rating and Dating: A Restudy." *Marriage and Family Living* 14:312–17.

Sorokin, P. A. 1937. *Social and Cultural Dynamics.* Vol. 5. New York: Dutton.

———, et al. 1931. *A Systematic Sourcebook in Rural Sociology.* Vol. 2. Minneapolis: The University of Minnesota Press.

Spanier, Graham. 1976. "Measuring Dyadic Adjustment: New Scales for Assessing the Quality of Marriage and Similar Dyads." *Journal of Marriage and the Family* 38:15–30.

———, Robert A. Lewis, and Charles L. Cole. 1975. "Marital Adjustment Over the Family Life Cycle: The Issue of Curvilinearity." *Journal of Marriage and the Family* 37:263–75.

Spiro, M. E. 1954. "Is the Family Universal?" *American Anthropologist* 56:839–46.

Stampp, Kenneth. 1959. *The Peculiar Institution.* New York: Knopf.

Staples, Robert. 1970. "The Myth of the Black Matriarchy." *The Black Scholar* 1:8–16.

———. 1971. *The Black Family: Essays and Studies.* Belmont, Calif.: Wadsworth.

Stephens, William N. 1969. *The Family in Cross Cultural Perspective.* New York: Holt.

Stetson, Dorothy M., and Gerald C. Wright, Jr. 1975. "The Effects of Laws on Divorce in American States." *Journal of Marriage and the Family* 37:537–47.

Strauss, Anselm. 1946. "The Ideal and the Chosen Mate." *American Journal of Sociology* 51:204–8.

Strecher, Edward A. 1946. *Their Mothers' Sons.* New York: Lippincott.

Stryker, Sheldon. 1972. "Symbolic Interaction Theory: A Review and Some Suggestions for Comparative Family Research." *Journal of Comparative Family Studies* 3:17–32.

Stuckert, Robert P. 1963. "Role Perception and Marital Satisfaction—A Configurational Approach." *Marriage and Family Living* 25:415–19.

Suelzle, Marijean. 1973. "Women in Labor." In *Marriages and Families.* Helena Z. Lopata, ed. New York: Van Nostrand, pp. 325–34.

Sullivan, Harry Stack. 1947. *Conceptions of Modern Psychiatry.* Washington, D.C.: William Alanson White Psychiatric Foundation.

Sussman, Marvin B. 1953. "The Help Pattern in the Middle Class Family." *American Sociological Review* 18:22–28.

———. 1954. "Family Continuity: Selective Factors Which Affect Relationships Between Families at Generational Levels." *Marriage and Family Living* 16:112–20.

———. 1959. "The Isolated Nuclear Family: Fact or Fiction?" *Social Problems* 6:333–40.

———. 1965. "Relationships of Adult Children With Their Parents." In *Social Structure and the Family: Generational Relations*, Ethel Shanas and Gordon F. Streib, eds. Englewood Cliffs: Prentice-Hall, pp. 62–92.

———, and Lee Burchinal. 1962*a*. "Kin Family Network: Unheralded Structure in Current Conceptualizations of Family Functioning." *Marriage and Family Living* 24:231–40.

———. 1962*b*. "Parental Aid to Married Children: Implications for Family Functioning." *Marriage and Family Living* 24:320–32.

———, and R. Clyde White. 1959. *Hough, Cleveland, Ohio: A Study of Social Life and Change*. Cleveland: Western Reserve University Press.

Suttles, Gerald. 1968. *The Social Order of the Slum*. Chicago: University of Chicago Press.

Sutton-Smith, Brian, and B. G. Rosenberg. 1970. *The Sibling*. New York: Holt.

Sykes, Gresham, and David Matza. 1957. "Techniques of Neutralization: A Theory of Delinquency." *American Sociological Review* 22:664–70.

Symonds, Carolyn. 1968. "Pilot Study of the Peripheral Behavior of Sexual Mate Swappers." Unpublished Master's thesis, University of California, Riverside.


Talmon, Yonina. 1972. *Family and Community in the Kibbutz*. Cambridge, Mass.: Harvard University Press.

Ten Houten, Warren D. 1970. "The Black Family: Myth and Reality." *Psychiatry* 27:145–73.

Terman, Lewis M. 1938. *Psychological Factors in Marital Happiness*. New York: McGraw-Hill.

Thompson, Wayne E., and Gordon F. Streib. 1961. "Meaningful Activity in a Family Context." In *Aging and Leisure: A Perspective Into the Meaningful Use of Time*, Robert W. Kleemier, ed. New York: Oxford University Press, pp. 177–211.

Tittle, Charles R., and Richard J. Hill. 1967. "Attitude Measurement and Prediction of Behavior: An Evaluation of Conditions and Measurement Techniques." *Sociometry* 30:199–213.

Toffler, Alvin. 1970. *Future Shock*. New York: Bantam Books.

Trost, Jan. 1967*a*. "Some Data on Mate Selection: Complementarity." *Journal of Marriage and the Family* 29:730–38.

———. 1967*b*. "Some Data on Mate Selection: Homogamy and Perceived Homogamy." *Journal of Marriage and the Family* 29:739–55.

Turk, James L., and Norman W. Bell. 1972. "Measuring Power in Families." *Journal of Marriage and the Family* 34:215–23.

Turner, Ralph. 1970. *Family Interaction*. New York: Wiley.


Udry, J. Richard. 1963. "Complementarity in Mate Selection: A Perceptual Approach." *Journal of Marriage and the Family* 25:281–89.

———. 1965. "The Influence of the Ideal Mate Image on Mate Perception and Mate Selection." *Journal of Marriage and the Family* 27:477–82.

———. 1971. *The Social Context of Marriage*. 2nd ed. Philadelphia: Lippincott.

637

———, Karl E. Bauman, and Charles Chase. 1971. "Skin Color, Status, and Mate Selection." *American Journal of Sociology* 76:722–33.

———, Harold A. Nelson, and Ruth Nelson. 1961. "An Empirical Investigation of Some Widely Held Beliefs about Marital Interaction." *Marriage and Family Living* 23:388–90.

Uhr, Leonard M. 1957. "Personality Changes in Marriage." Ph.D. dissertation, University of Michigan.

U.S. Department of Commerce, Bureau of the Census. 1908. *Marriage and Divorce, 1887–1906.* Washington, D.C.: Government Printing Office, Bulletin 96.

———. 1957. *Current Population Survey* (March).

———. 1965. *Population Estimates.* Series P-25, No. 297 (January 19).

———. 1967. *Historical Statistics of the United States, Colonial Times to 1957.*

———. Various dates. *Current Population Reports.*

———. Various dates. *Statistical Abstract of the United States.*

———. Various dates. *U.S. Census of Population.*

———. 1977. "Marital Status and Living Arrangements: March 1976." Series P-20, No. 306 (January).

U.S. Department of Health, Education, and Welfare, National Center for Health Statistics. 1968. *Trends in Illegitimacy: United States 1940–1965.* Series 21, No. 15 (February). Washington, D.C.: Government Printing Office.

———. Various dates. NCHS *Monthly Statistics Report.*

———. Various dates. *Vital Statistics of the United States.*

Vener, Arthur M., and Cyrus S. Stewart. 1974. "Adolescent Sexual Behavior in Middle America Revisited." *Journal of Marriage and the Family* 36:728–35.

Veroff, Joseph, and Sheila Feld. 1970. *Marriage and Work in America: A Study of Motives and Roles.* New York: Van Nostrand.

Vincent, Clark. 1961. *Unmarried Mothers.* New York: The Free Press.

———. 1966. "Family Spongia: The Adaptive Function." *Journal of Marriage and the Family* 28:29–36.

Waller, Willard. 1937. "The Rating and Dating Complex." *American Sociological Review* 2:727–34.

Walsh, Brendan M. 1972. "Trends in Age at Marriage in Postwar Ireland." *Demography* 9:187–202

Walsh, Robert, Mary Z. Ferrell, and William L. Tolone. 1976. "Selection of Reference Group, Perceived Reference Group Permissiveness and Personal Permissiveness Attitudes and Behavior: A Study of Two Consecutive Panels (1967–1971; 1970–1974)." *Journal of Marriage and the Family* 38:495–508.

Walster, Elaine, Vera Aronson, Darcy Abrahams, and Leon Rottman. 1969. "Importance of Physical Attractiveness in Dating Behavior." *Journal of Personality and Social Psychology* 4:508–16.

Warner, Lyle, and Melvin DeFleur. 1969. "Attitude as an Interacting Concept: Social Constraint and Social Distance as Intervening Variables Between Attitudes and Action." *American Sociological Review* 34:153–69.

Watson, John B. 1928. *Psychological Care of Infant and Child.* New York: Norton.

————. 1930. *Behaviorism*. New York: Norton.

————. 1938. *The Ways of Behaviorism*. New York: Harper and Brothers.

Watson, Walter B., and Ernest A. Barth. 1964. "Questionable Assumptions in the Theory of Social Stratification." *Pacific Sociological Review* 7:10–16.

Weeks, H. Ashley. 1943. "Differential Divorce Rates by Occupations." *Social Forces* 21:334–37.

Weinberg, Ian. 1969. "The Problem of Convergence of Industrial Societies: A Critical Look at the State of a Theory." *Comparative Studies in Society and History* 11:1–15.

Westoff, Charles F. 1974. "Coital Frequency and Contraception." *Family Planning Perspectives* 6 (March/April): 54–57.

————. 1976. "Trends in Contraceptive Practices: 1965–1973." *Family Planning Perspectives* 8 (March/April):54–57.

Westoff, Leslie Aldridge, and Charles F. Westoff. 1971. *From Now to Zero: Fertility, Contraception and Abortion in America*. Boston: Little, Brown.

Whelpton, P. K., A. A. Campbell, and J. E. Patterson. 1966. *Fertility and Family Planning in the United States*. Princeton: Princeton University Press.

Williams, Edith W. 1938. "Factors Associated with Adjustment in Rural Marriage." Ph.D. dissertation, Cornell University.

Willits, Fern K., Robert C. Bealer, and Gerald W. Bender. 1963. "Interreligious Marriage Among Pennsylvania Rural Youth." *Marriage and Family Living* 25:433–38.

Winch, Robert. 1955. "The Theory of Complementary Needs in Mate Selection: Final Results on the Test of the General Hypothesis." *American Sociological Review* 20:552–55.

————. 1958. *Mate-Selection: A Study of Complementary Needs*. New York: Harper.

————. 1962. *Identification and Its Familial Determinants*. Indianapolis: Bobbs-Merrill.

————. 1952, 1963, 1966. *The Modern Family*. New York: Holt, rev. ed., 3 eds.

————. 1967. "Another Look at the Theory of Complementary Needs in Mate-Selection." *Journal of Marriage and the Family* 29:756–62.

————. 1970. "Some Speculations as to the Family's Future." *Journal of Marriage and the Family* 32:133–43.

————, and Rae Lesser Blumberg. 1968. "Societal Complexity and Familial Organization." In *Selected Studies in Marriage and the Family*, Robert F. Winch and Louis Wolf Goodman, eds. 3rd ed. New York: Holt.

————, and Rae Lesser Blumberg. 1972. "Societal Complexity and Familial Complexity: Evidence for the Curvilinear Hypothesis." *American Journal of Sociology* 77:898–920.

————, and Louis Wolf Goodman, eds. 1968. *Selected Studies in Marriage and the Family*. 3rd ed. New York: Holt.

————, Thomas Ktsanes, and Virginia Ktsanes. 1954. "The Theory of Complementary Needs in Mate Selection: An Analytic and Descriptive Study." *American Sociological Review* 19:241–49.

Wirth, Louis. 1938. "Urbanism as a Way of Life." *American Journal of Sociology* 44:1–24.

————, and Herbert Goldhamer. 1944. "Negro-White Marriage in Recent Times." In *Characteristics of the American Negro*, Otto Kleinberg, ed. New York: Harper.

Wolfe, Donald M. 1959. "Power and Authority in the Family." In *Studies in Social Power*, D. Cartwright, ed. Ann Arbor: University of Michigan Press, pp. 99–117.

Wylie, Philip. 1942. *A Generation of Vipers*. New York: Rinehart.

Yinger, J. Milton. 1965. *Toward a Field Theory of Behavior*. New York: McGraw-Hill.

———. 1968a. "A Research Note on Interfaith Marriage Statistics." *Journal for the Scientific Study of Religion* 7:97–103.

———. 1968b. "On the Definition of Interfaith Marriage." *Journal for the Scientific Study of Religion* 7:104–7.

Zelnik, Melvin, and John F. Kantner. 1972. "Sexuality, Contraception and Pregnancy among Young Unwed Females in the United States." In Commission on Population Growth and the American Future, Research Reports, Vol. I, *Demographic and Social Aspects of Population Growth*, Charles F. Westoff and Robert Parke, Jr., eds. Washington, D.C.: Government Printing Office, pp. 355–74.

———. 1977. "Sexual and Contraceptive Experience of Young Unmarried Women in the United States, 1976 and 1971." *Family Planning Perspectives* 9 (March/April):55–71.

Zimmerman, Carle C. 1947. *Family and Civilization*. New York: Harper.

———. 1949. *The Family of Tomorrow: The Cultural Crisis and the Way Out*. New York: Harper.

# INDEX

2　3　4　5　6　7　8　9　10